JEWS ACROSS THE AMERICAS

THE GOLDSTEIN-GOREN SERIES IN AMERICAN JEWISH HISTORY

General editor: Hasia R. Diner

Is Diss a System? A Milt Gross Comic Reader
Edited by Ari Y. Kelman

We Remember with Reverence and Love: American Jews and the Myth of Silence after the Holocaust, 1945–1962
Hasia R. Diner

Jewish Radicals: A Documentary Reader
Edited by Tony Michels

An Unusual Relationship: Evangelical Christians and Jews
Yaakov Ariel

All Together Different: Yiddish Socialists, Garment Workers, and the Labor Roots of Multiculturalism
Daniel Katz

1929: Mapping the Jewish World
Edited by Hasia R. Diner and Gennady Estraikh

Hanukkah in America: A History
Dianne Ashton

Unclean Lips: Obscenity, Jews, and American Culture
Josh Lambert

Jews and Booze: Becoming American in the Age of Prohibition
Marni Davis

The Rag Race: How Jews Sewed Their Way to Success in America and the British Empire
Adam D. Mendelsohn

Hollywood's Spies: The Undercover Surveillance of Nazis in Los Angeles
Laura B. Rosenzweig

Cotton Capitalists: American Jewish Entrepreneurship in the Reconstruction Era
Michael R. Cohen

Making Judaism Safe for America: World War I and the Origins of Religious Pluralism
Jessica Cooperman

A Rosenberg by Any Other Name: A History of Jewish Name Changing in America
Kirsten Fermaglich

A Mortuary of Books: The Rescue of Jewish Culture after the Holocaust
Elisabeth Gallas

Dust to Dust: A History of Jewish Death and Burial in New York
Allan Amanik

Jewish Radical Feminism: Voices from the Women's Liberation Movement
Joyce Antler

Jews Across the Americas: A Sourcebook, 1492–Present
Edited by Adriana M. Brodsky and Laura Arnold Leibman

Jews Across the Americas

A SOURCEBOOK
1492–PRESENT

Edited by
ADRIANA M. BRODSKY *and* LAURA ARNOLD LEIBMAN

NEW YORK UNIVERSITY PRESS
NEW YORK

NEW YORK UNIVERSITY PRESS
New York
www.nyupress.org

Library of Congress Cataloging-in-Publication Data
Names: Brodsky, Adriana Mariel, 1967– editor. | Leibman, Laura Arnold, editor.
Title: Jews across the Americas : a sourcebook, 1492-present / edited by Adriana M. Brodsky and Laura Arnold Leibman.
Description: New York, New York : New York University Press, [2023] | Series: Goldstein-Goren Series in American Jewish History ; 1 | Includes bibliographical references and index.
Identifiers: LCCN 2022050025 | ISBN 9781479819317 (hardback) | ISBN 9781479819324 (paperback) | ISBN 9781479819331 (ebook other) | ISBN 9781479819348 (ebook)
Subjects: LCSH: Jews—America—History—Sources.
Classification: LCC E29.J5 J49 2023 | DDC 970.004/924—dc23/eng/20230105
LC record available at https://lccn.loc.gov/2022050025

New York University Press books are printed on acid-free paper, and their binding materials are chosen for strength and durability. We strive to use environmentally responsible suppliers and materials to the greatest extent possible in publishing our books.

Manufactured in the United States of America

10 9 8 7 6 5 4 3 2 1

Also available as an ebook

CONTENTS

ABBREVIATIONS

ADCJA	Alex Dworkin Canadian Jewish Archives, Montreal, Quebec
AGN	Archivo General de la Nación (National Archive), Mexico City, Mexico
AHN	Archivo Histórico Nacional (National Historical Archive), Madrid, Spain
AJA	American Jewish Archives, Cincinnati, OH
AJHS	American Jewish Historical Society, New York, NY
AMIA	Jewish Argentine Mutual Aid Society
ANTT	Arquivo Nacional da Torre do Tombo [National Archive of Torre do Tombo], Lisbon, Portugal
BARMJHS	Beck Archives, Rocky Mountain Jewish Historical Society, University of Denver, Denver, CO
BDS	Boycott, Divestment, Sanctions movement
BINA	Bene Israel North America
HABS	Historic American Buildings Survey
IACHR	Inter-American Commission for Human Rights
IAPIG	Inventaris van het Archief van de Portugees-Israëlietische Gemeente, Stadsarchief Amsterdam, Amsterdam, Netherlands
JAWDB	Jewish Atlantic World Database, Reed College, Portland, OR
JCBL	John Carter Brown Library, Brown University, Providence, RI
JHM	Jewish Historical Museum, Amsterdam, Netherlands
JJL	Papers of Jacques Judah Lyons, P-15, AJHS
JMNY	The Jewish Museum, New York, NY
JOFA	Jewish Orthodox Feminist Alliance
JTS	Jewish Theological Seminary, New York, NY
KKK	Ku Klux Klan
LCPPD	Library of Congress Prints and Photographs Division, Washington, DC
LMA	London Metropolitan Archives, London, UK
LOC	Library of Congress, Washington, DC
MBMNI	Minute Books of the Mahamad of Nidhe Israel, 1790–1826, Nidhe Israel Synagogue Records, 4521/D/01/01/002, 4521/D/01/01/003, 4521/D/01/01/004, 4521/D/01/01/008, London Metropolitan Archives, London, UK

MDAH Mississippi Department of Archives and History, Jackson, MS
MNV Museo Nacional del Virreinato, Tepotzotlán, Mexico
NA Nationaal Archief (National Archive), Den Haag, Netherlands
NARA National Archives and Records Administration, National Archives Building, Washington, DC
NJH National Jewish Hospital (now National Jewish Health), Denver, CO
NPIGS Inventaris van het digitaal duplicaat van het archief van de Nederlandse Portugees-Israëlitische Gemeente in Suriname, 1678–1909, Nationaal Archief (National Archive), Den Haag, Netherlands
PAJHS *Publications of the American Jewish Historical Society*, Johns Hopkins University Press
RM Rijksmuseum, Museumstraat 1, 1071 XX Amsterdam, Netherlands, www.rijksmuseum.nl
RT Noam Sienna, ed., *A Rainbow Thread: An Anthology of Queer Jewish Texts from the First Century to 1969* (Philadelphia: Print-O-Craft Press, 2019)
SCCCL Special Collections, College of Charleston Library, Charleston, SC
SCLC Southern Christian Leadership Conference
TNA The National Archives, Kew, UK
UNIA Universal Negro Improvement Association
VS P. J. Benoit, *Voyage à Surinam* (Brussels: Société des Beaux-Arts, 1839)
WC Wikimedia Commons, http://commons.wikimedia.org
YUAG Yale University Art Gallery, Yale University, New Haven, CT
YUM Yeshiva University Museum, New York, NY

GENERAL INTRODUCTION

Weinberger?? Is that a Jewish last name?

—overheard in a Shabbat elevator in Panama City, Panama

Stories matter. Many stories matter. Stories have been used to dispossess and to malign. But stories can also be used to empower, and to humanize. Stories can break the dignity of a people. But stories can also repair that broken dignity.

—Chimamanda Adichie, "The Danger of a Single Story"

Olaudah Equiano, in his 1789 slave narrative, suggested the Igbo as one origin for Jews in the Americas. Having grown up surrounded by Jewish rituals on the western coast of Africa, Equiano made sense of his abduction by white enslavers by drawing parallels to the Jews' subjugation in Egypt. Likewise for Equiano, his manumission corresponded to the Israelites' redemption. His narrative is a Jewish story, but one in which the "promised land" is not America but Africa. While Equiano's story resonated with other enslaved Africans, his telling differs from the vast majority of narratives about how Jews came to the Americas. Jewish American history is often told as a migration story, but one that emphasizes European Jews' arrivals to what would become the United States. Like Equiano's narrative, *Jews Across the Americas* reveals that the story of European Jewish migration is only one part of the story of Jewish American history.

The contributors to this volume are not the first to notice that one story of the Jewish people is not enough to explain the current diversity of Jews in the Americas. Equiano's claim would be echoed nearly a century and a half later by Rabbi Arnold Josiah Ford in his short history of the Congregation Beth B'nai Abraham in New York (see chapter 76). "We do not believe," he noted, "as some people do, that it is necessary to be a Caucasian before you can lay claim to the Jewish faith."[1] Rather, members of his Harlem synagogue came to the United States from Africa, the West Indies, and South America, particularly Suriname. Ford was not wrong: recent historians have suggested that by 1800, the majority of Surinamese Jews had at least one African ancestor.[2] The years 1900–1920 were a period of great migration from the Caribbean northward, and by the 1920s, there were at least four African American Jewish congregations in Harlem.[3] Even before the Great Migration of the 1880s–1920s, however, Caribbean Jews had been traveling northward, bolstering congregations throughout the United States.

Equiano's and Ford's versions of Jewish American history are typically not included in Jewish history textbooks today. In the United States, textbooks of "American" Jewish history tend to begin with a single, apocryphal story: the arrival of Jewish refugees from Recife

Frontispiece of *The Interesting Narrative of the Life of Olaudah Equiano, or Gustavus Vassa, the African* (London, 1789)

(located in what is now Brazil) to New Amsterdam (later New York) in September 1654. Forced to leave Brazil when their colony fell into Portuguese hands, twenty-four men, women, and children became the first Jewish community in what would become part of the United States. Migration in this story happens in one direction: northward. Most commonly, this opening is the last that readers hear of Jews living in what is now Brazil, as histories of American Judaism typically focus solely on Jews in the United States.

In contrast, *Jews Across the Americas* takes a hemispheric approach. This approach acknowledges a range of origin stories and investigates the interplay between Jewish communities in North America, South America, and the Caribbean. *Jews Across the Americas* reveals how Jews created thriving communities in the Americas long before the fall of Recife, and Jews continued to flourish across the Americas, settling in Latin America, the Caribbean, and Canada as well as what would become the United States. Moreover, as we will see, Jews often refused to obey national boundaries: the histories of communities across the continents are intertwined. Today, the largest Jewish communities in North America are in the United States and Canada; Argentina has the fifth-largest community in the world, Brazil the ninth largest, and Mexico the thirteenth. Chile and Uruguay are in the top twenty.[4] Reading Jewish American history hemispherically reveals a story composed of many strands. Some of the most important strands underscore the histories of (1) a moving center, (2) antisemitism, (3) Jewish diversity, (4) the rise of a transregional Jewish community and identity, (5) the Americanization of Jewish practice, (6) shifting stories of Jewish gender and sexuality, and (7) the problems of national belonging.

First, a hemispheric history of Jews across the Americas reveals how the geographic center of American Judaism has shifted with time. Looking at the migration of Jews across the Americas helps us understand the changing demographics of where Jews lived in the Americas and why certain cities emerged as major Jewish centers. In the early part of the colonial era, most Jews lived in the Spanish and Portuguese colonies, where they could not practice Judaism openly. By the late eighteenth century, the largest communities were in the Caribbean. Migration during the nineteenth century made the United States the home of the largest population of American Jews. However, during the period between the world wars, immigration to the United States was often restricted, and other Jewish American communities flourished; yet as late as 1933, 60 percent of all the world's approximately 15.3 million Jews still lived in Europe. Moreover, Jewish communities in the Americas were often concentrated on the coasts and in major cities: in the United States, for example, 80 percent of Jews lived in Chicago or on the East Coast between Baltimore and Boston. The Holocaust would radically change these demographics. Today there are roughly thirteen million Jews around the world, but the Jewish communities of the Americas far outweigh those in both Europe and even Israel. This shift in demographics spawned new responsibilities and a pan-American identity. Within the Americas, Jewish communities have become more geographically diverse. In the United States, for example, new centers of Jewish life have emerged on the West Coast and in the South. These shifts have helped highlight the regional flavor of Jewish American culture.[5]

Second, telling the stories of Jews *across* the Americas allows us to understand better the struggles Jews have faced. Before the recent rise of antisemitism and anti-Jewish violence, Jewish history often focused on the United States as an exception to the strife that Jews encountered elsewhere. This "exceptionalist paradigm held that the American [US] experience was unique in that Jews secured equal citizenship from the start, without having to go through a long and uncertain process of emancipation. Moreover, in the exceptionalist view, America was different in that it lacked a strong tradition of outspoken, and especially of overtly political, antisemitism."[6]

Redefining what we mean by "American" shows how this exceptionalist paradigm has always been flawed both across the Americas and within the United States. Before the Dutch occupation of Recife in 1630, most—but not all—Jews who lived in the Americas resided in Spanish and Portuguese colonies. They lived as "crypto" (secret) Jews not only because openly practicing Judaism was explicitly forbidden but also because "New Christians"—that is, anyone who was a practicing Catholic but who had ancestors who had once been Jews—were forbidden to live in the Spanish and Portuguese colonies. Those who wanted to migrate to the Americas had to circumvent this law. Over time, secret Jewish communities formed in Mexico City, Veracruz, Puebla, Guadalajara, Lima (Peru), Cartagena de Indias (Colombia), Potosi (Bolivia), and Brazil and on the west coast of Africa.[7] Yet in each of these places, Jews struggled against the Inquisition and anti-Jewish bias. As we will see, the experience of those Jews living in other colonial settings differed from those under Spanish and Portuguese control, but Jews' rights and restrictions were defined by their usefulness to the imperial projects, which made Jews' position tenuous and unstable.

A hemispheric history underscores that antisemitism is not new. By beginning the history of Jews in American colonies that were under the sway of the Inquisition, this volume counters the commonly told story of US exceptionalism and the United States as a place of refuge for Jews. Putting aside the fact that US exceptionalism has fostered attitudes that some people associate with racism and warmongering, the myth of US exceptionalism has left Jews in the United States confused and surprised by recent surges of antisemitism, whether in Charlottesville, in synagogue shootings, or in response to the COVID pandemic. Recognizing the long history of overt antisemitism *across* the Americas helps us understand which parts of recent events constitute a pattern in, rather than exception to, American history.

To be sure, Jews in the Americas experienced a different degree of persecution and intolerance than those in Europe and in other areas of the world, especially during the twentieth century. Our intention with this volume is to *complicate* the narrative of exceptionalism, to suggest that the Americas, even when they provided Jews with opportunities and options not available to them elsewhere, did not exempt Jews from discrimination, persecution, and even death. Many of our sources precisely show this apparent contradiction: Jews themselves were thankful and praised the American continents for the freedom they provided, while Jews also openly defended their right to a life free from antisemitic discrimination and a life containing equality in line with the equality that American political systems sometimes promised. The danger in the "exceptionalism" story is that it obscures and silences a part of the Jewish experience.

Third, telling the story of Jews across the Americas helps acknowledge how diversity has always been part of the American Jewish story. "Counting Inconsistencies," a recent survey by the Stanford Graduate School of Education, suggests that between 12 and 15 percent of Jews in the United States identify as Jews of color.[8] While some of this 12–15 percent (like all Jews) comprise recent converts or products of intermarriage, early Jewish American communities were multiracial as well. Their descendants make up part of the multiracial profile of American Judaism today. For example, descendants of crypto-Jews in the Spanish colonies intermarried with Indigenous peoples and enslaved Africans. Their descendants comprise an important part of the *converso* revival in the southwestern United States, Brazil, and other locations.[9] Today's diverse Jewish American communities owe at least as high a debt to the intersection of American Jewish history with slavery and settler colonialism as they do to intermarriage and conversion.

Understanding Jewish diversity likewise means acknowledging the long history of Sephardic and Mizrachi Jews in American Jewish history. In the United States, the field of American Jewish history was largely founded by Ashkenazi Jews—that is, Jews from Germany and eastern Europe. This has led to a tendency toward "Ashkenormativity" (the assumption that Jews are not only white but Ashkenazi).[10] *Jews Across the Americas*, however, emphasizes the important contributions of Sephardic and Mizrachi Jews throughout American history. Although in Latin American, the terms "Sephardic" and "Mizrachi" are often used interchangeably, since 1948, there has been a tendency in US society to use the term "Sephardic Jews" to mean Jews who trace their ancestry back to Iberia and "Mizrachi Jews" to refer to Jews whose ancestors settled directly in the Middle East and North Africa. (This distinction is complicated somewhat by the fact that the Ottoman Empire, which controlled much of this region between the fourteenth and early twentieth centuries, not only was the homeland of Mizrachi Jews since antiquity but also, after the Middle Ages, became a place of refuge for Sephardic Jews fleeing Iberia.)

Those who tend to distinguish between the two groups note that Mizrachi Jews and Sephardic Jews had different migration patterns to the Americas. Sephardic Jews played a crucial role in the early settlement of the Americas, but Middle Eastern Jews first began to migrate to the Americas en masse during the nineteenth century, when conflicts within the Ottoman Empire and the need for better economic prospects led to the establishment of Middle Eastern and North African synagogues in Argentina, Mexico, Brazil, and the United States. This migration continued throughout the period between the wars but intensified after 1948. In each era, *Jews Across the Americas* pays attention to the diversity of Jewish experiences, highlighting the importance of thinking about where Jews came from as well as where they landed.

Fourth, the broad scope of the history covered in this volume reveals how Jews' religious life went from being hidden within the home to their envisioning themselves as part of a transnational community. Under the Inquisition, Jews worshiped secretly (see chapter 5). While they had ties to other members of their own ethnic group, they often did not identify with Jews more generally. During the eighteenth century, there was typically only one synagogue per city in a synagogue complex (see chapter 15), with the original synagogue often fiercely defending its authority (see chapters 18 and 33). As new waves of arrivals came to the Americas during the nineteenth century from Germany, eastern Europe, and the Ottoman Empire and as Caribbean Jews relocated northward, a plurality of synagogues emerged within cities. A growing sense of obligation to help Jews across one's city or region followed.

Yet between World War I and World War II, Jewish identity once again shifted, increasingly focused on pan-Americanism and internationalism, rather than being centered around the synagogues within one's home city or country. The rise of cultural centers across the Americas provided Jews with a means to congregate and form a secular Jewish identity. Some American Jews expressed the internationalism of the postwar era by emphasizing ties to Israel, while others, like the founders of the Chicago Loop Synagogue (1957–1958), manifested their international bent vis-à-vis their claim to being a "world synagogue" that served not merely local congregants but also travelers and businesspeople.

A fifth strand in a hemispheric American Jewish history is the constant dialogue between traditional and innovative forms of Judaism. *Jews Across the Americas* reveals how American culture and the Enlightenment reshaped all forms of Judaism. Rather than experiencing one period of revival, American Judaism has repeatedly reenergized itself, and Jewish values have continued to inspire people. Following the Holocaust, for example, some Jews took the need to repair the world (*tikkun olam*) in secular terms as a call to fight for the rights of disenfranchised others, particularly those who are oppressed due to race, class, gender, sexuality, or the history of colonization. During the same years, other segments of American Judaism focused the spirit of renewal on religious revitalization. This revitalization gave rise not only to New American Jewish movements including the Baal Teshuva movement, the Renewal Movement, and Reconstructionism but also movements that deliberately interwove Judaism with other traditions. For some communities, renewal meant bringing back to light communities that had previously been hidden, such as crypto-Jews and Black Israelites.

A sixth strand in this hemispheric history is the changing nature of gender and sex roles within Jewish American culture. Rather than seeing men as the center of Jewish life, this collection reveals the long history of nonbinary Jews and Jewish women. To be sure, this role has changed over time, with women moving from the home into Jewish businesses and taking on a more public role in Jewish organizations. For example, chapters on ritual baths show changes in where and how Jewish sexuality is regulated (chapters 15, 48, 59, and

The Chicago Loop Synagogue, A World Congregation. (Photograph by Laura Arnold Leibman, 2021)

108). Likewise, love letters and songs show how desire was forced underground but not erased entirely.

A seventh and final strand is about the complexity of national belonging. Belonging is often understood as the "good twin" to antisemitism. The earliest Jews in the Americas typically self-identified (or were identified by the Inquisition) as part of the *Nação*—Hebrews of the Portuguese nation. They were a nation apart from both Ashkenazi Jews and Old Christians. While antisemitism often posits Jews as inherently foreign, belonging reveals how Jews became part of American countries. Belonging was key to the acquisition of Jewish rights. Such inclusion, however, is complex. While stories of the American "melting pot," suggest that Jews had to lose their unique flavor if they wanted to become part of the American stew, Jews more often helped create something more like a "mixed salad," in which aspects of their cultures' original textures were retained even as they mingled. From the colonial period to the present, we see a wide range of Jewish groups insisting on the value of their particularity. This volume pays homage to that particularity by emphasizing the range of Jewish experiences.

Yet emphasizing particularity simultaneously highlights why writing a hemispheric history is such a challenge. Most Jewish studies scholars have been trained within one national tradition. We hope this book will be a starting point for comparative studies, one that suggests the great amount of work that remains to be done. Readers will notice that we have not divided the chapters equally between either regions or countries. To a certain extent, the representation of countries in this volume is proportional to the influence of specific Jewish communities during any particular time period. Thus, sometimes countries that have small Jewish communities today (such as Suriname) but had a large influence on Jewish diversity may have an unexpected number of entries. At the same time, the generosity or poverty of entries from countries reflects the experiences of historians today: some countries have longer scholarly traditions of Jewish historiography and have placed more resources toward the writing of those histories. One result of this disparity is that readers will notice that Canadian and US entries are marked by province or state, while other places are marked by country alone. Regionalism has been important to the way certain Jewish histories have been written but not others. Students should question what resources make it possible (or necessary) to write regionally specific histories.

The evidence that constitutes each of these hemispheric strands is complex, arising from a range of new methods. In addition to providing access to a hemispheric history, this volume further aims to help readers see how methodologically diverse the field of American Jewish history is. Foremost, this collection is deliberately a polyphony of voices of scholars who come from a range of countries and backgrounds. Not surprisingly, then, they do not always agree. Jewishness is interpreted in some chapters culturally, and in others religiously. Likewise, some scholars bring their training as historians to bear on the sources they use, while others borrow their strategies from the fields of art, literature, material culture, music, and anthropology. The goal of this diversity is to allow you to gather as many tools as possible in your historical tool box. Although we were limited in what we could include in print, more sources are available on the accompanying website, including many of the original-language versions of sources translated in this edition.

This book's structure bridges these diverse voices and approaches. Each chapter consists of a primary source translated into English and a brief introduction to that source that answers the following questions: What is the original context of this work? What does the source contribute to local Jewish history or history of the era? What does it add to the story of American Jewish history more broadly? Chapters conclude with discussion questions that are aimed to help you start interpreting and connecting sources. Each chapter is accompanied by a map that indicates where the action is happening. However, the maps, which show modern political divisions, may not accurately represent past historical boundaries. For example, New Spain comprised a very large region from what is currently the southwestern US down to the northern part of South America, but maps for this colony show the current country where events took place. Taken all together, the goal of this format is to help you, the student, not just read history but *do* history.

Doing history means thinking critically about how you use evidence to construct stories about the past. The English word "history" comes from the Latin word *istoria*, meaning not just "story" but also an account, inquiry, research, or recorded knowledge of past events. History is composed of details strung together like beads on a necklace. Which beads you choose will determine what history you tell. Yet in each instance, the validity of each bead should be tested. Who collected the bead? What was their agenda? What beads did they overlook and why? We have provided a variety of bead collectors as well as styles and types of beads in this collection so that you can begin to think about the range of ways one might string them together and the implications of whose voices you highlight.

Polyphony helps us in understanding Jews as people. Speaking 220 years after Equiano's narrative was published, the Nigerian author Chimamanda Adichie (the fifth child in an Igbo family) noted that if you want to create a single story about a people, "show a people as one thing, as only one thing, over and over again, and that is what they become."[11] Single stories flatten out the complexities in ways that rob people of their power. As Adichie points out, "The single story creates stereotypes. And the problem with stereotypes is not that they are untrue, but that they are incomplete. They make one story become the only story."[12] *Jews Across the Americas* offers a multitude of scholarly voices and approaches in American Jewish history to help you understand the competing ideas about who Jews are, what is history, and what it means to be American.

NOTES

1. Dorman, *Chosen People*, 189.
2. Ben-Ur, *Jewish Autonomy in a Slave Society*, 155.
3. Haynes, *Soul of Judaism*, 78–80, 100–103.
4. Sheskin and Dashefsky, *American Jewish Year Book 2019*, 265.
5. Sherwin, "World Jewish Community."
6. "Editor's Introduction," xii.
7. Israel, "Jews and Crypto-Jews in the Atlantic World Systems," 8, 10.
8. Jews of Color Initiative, "Counting Inconsistencies," 7.
9. Fogel and Fogel, *Conversos of the Americas*.
10. Carment and Sadjed, *Diaspora as Cultures of Cooperation*, 75.
11. Adichie, "Danger of a Single Story."
12. Adichie.

PART I

Early Colonial Era (1492–1762)

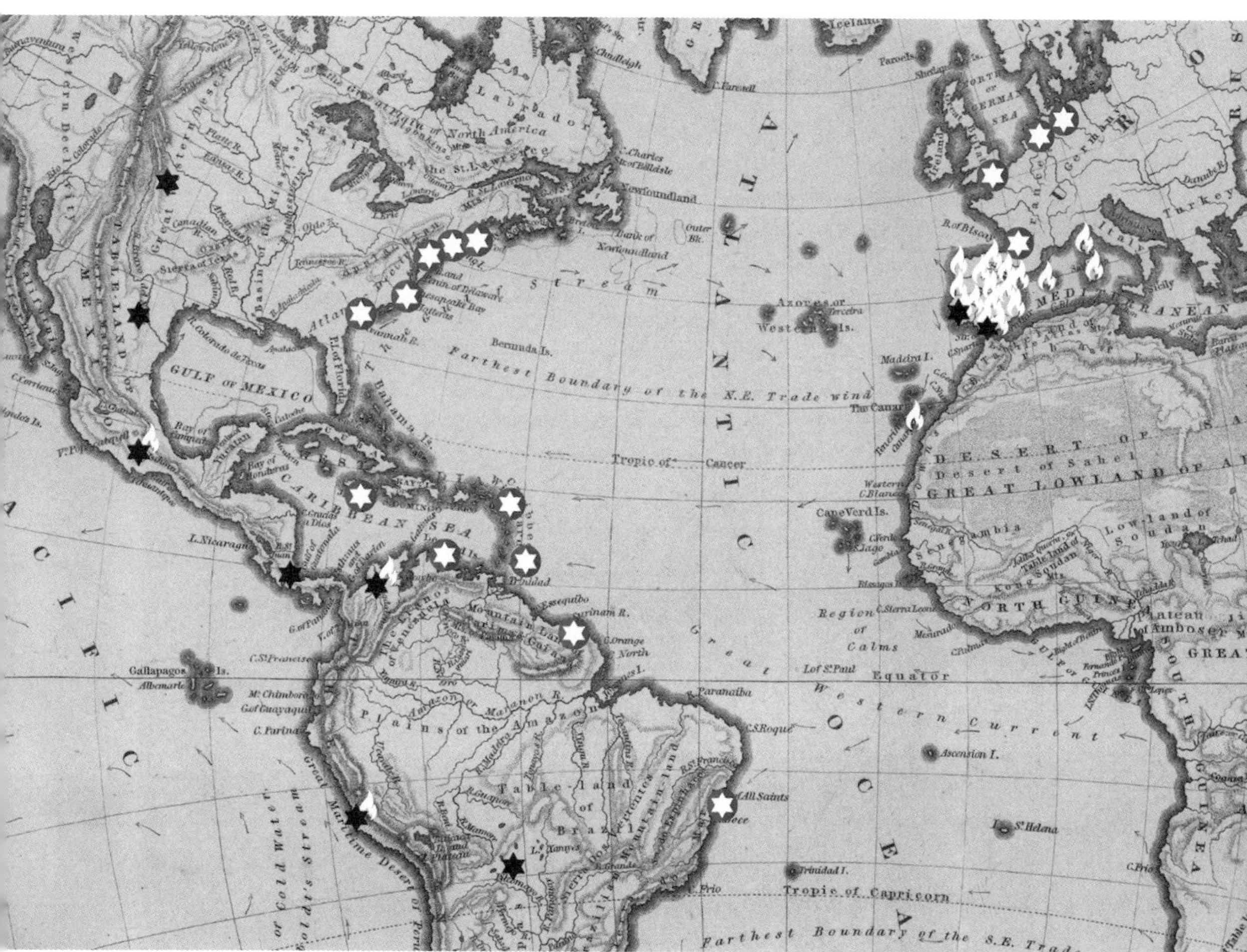

Map of major Jewish feeder communities, 1492–1760. Circled stars are open Jewish communities. Black stars are crypto-Jewish communities. Fires are centers of the Inquisitional tribunals. (Map by Laura Arnold Leibman; European tribunal locations based on Parker and Starr-LeBeau, *Judging Faith*, xvii)

"The Spanish noon is a blaze of azure fire, and the dusty pilgrims crawl like an endless serpent along treeless plains and bleached highroads, through the rock-split ravines and castellated cathedral-shadowed towns." So begins Emma Lazarus's prose-poem "The Exodus (August 3, 1492)," published in *The Century Illustrated Monthly* in November 1886. Under Lazarus's gaze, Spanish Jews, both "noble and abject, learned and simple, illustrious and obscure, plod side by side." Their journey retells the biblical story of how Jews went from slavery to freedom, reimaging Iberian Catholicism as an Egyptian captivity. Although today Lazarus is best known for her 1883 poem engraved below the Statue of Liberty that welcomes "the wretched refuse" of Europe, throughout her poetry, Lazarus emphasized the dual forces of 1492 as the starting point of American Jewish history: Jews' expulsion from Spain and Columbus's journey West. This starting point emphasizes how across the American colonies, Jews shared a common entwined thread: they were, as the historian Jonathan Israel puts it, "both agents and victims of empire."[1] Early American Jews often found themselves at the mercy of colonial powers. At the same time, Jews often took part in empire building and at times had power over other people, such as enslaved Africans.

Perhaps the dual roles of agents and victims is clearest in the Spanish and Portuguese colonies. Much of what we know about Jews in these colonies is based on documents created by the Inquisition. First sent to the West Indies in 1520, the Inquisition set up permanent tribunals in Mexico City (1569–1820), Lima (1569–1820), and Cartagena (1610–1834), whose purpose was to ensure that only approved Christian doctrine was practiced in the colonial world. In addition, the Inquisition sent visiting inquisitors to other parts of the Spanish and Portuguese colonies, such as Brazil. Inquisitional documents raise questions about who and what was a Jew and who decides. Often New Christians were denounced for Judaizing (practicing Judaism secretly) for economic motives: if convicted, the church split the accused's possessions with the accuser. Inquisitional testimony seems unreliable by modern standards. Once imprisoned, the accused often realized that denouncing oneself or others was the only way to end torture. Because the Inquisition never revealed precisely what "crime" the accused had committed, people confessed to what they thought might be the reason they were arrested. This strategy explains why these confessions are usually so full of crimes. While some of those convicted (such as Luis de Carvajal) clearly practiced crypto-Judaism, others (such as Manuel Bautista Perez) always insisted they were good Catholics. Whose testimony should we believe: the Inquisition's or the accused's?

In the colonies, the Inquisition became increasingly racialized, underscoring Jews' complex history with race. Inquisitors had long believed that New Christians contained the "taint" of Jewishness in their blood, but in the Americas, Jewish "impurity" was complicated by the rise of race-based slavery. In Mexico City, for example, half of those accused by the Inquisition had African ancestry, even though they only made up about 10 percent of the city's population. People with Jewish ancestry in the Spanish and Portuguese colonies who passed as Catholic could also be agents of oppression: Manuel Bautista Perez enslaved people, and other New Christians made their money working slaves in silver mines.[2] Even among those accused of being secret Jews, not all fared equally: men accused of sodomy as well as Judaizing were three times as likely to be executed as those accused of only one of these "crimes."

Iberian *conversos* were not the only people in the Spanish and Portuguese colonies who connected their ancestors back to the ancient Israelites. Both European travelers and Indigenous peoples wrote of the connections between Native Americans and Israelites. One common theory during the early colonial era was that Indigenous Americans were one of the Lost Tribes of Jews who had been exiled from the Kingdom of Israel prior to the destruction of the First Temple (see chapter 6). The Lost Tribes was often included in origin stories in the postconquest histories of a wide range of Indigenous peoples in the Spanish, and later British and French, colonies, as well as many of the African peoples who were forcibly brought to the Americas (see chapter 32). For both Indigenous Americans and enslaved Africans, Israelite identity provide an important way to contest European narratives of the conquest: rather than a people to be pitied, the conquered were God's chosen people. Their trials became a temporary test rather than signaling God's abandonment. This motif of eventual redemption would similarly be echoed in the writings of Iberian *conversos* tortured by the American Inquisition.

While descendants of European Jews were officially banned from the Spanish and Portuguese colonies, other empires courted Jews and allowed Jews to practice. Although the "Low Countries" (The Netherlands and Belgium) were once part of the Spanish Empire, they declared their independence in 1581. The new government granted protection to Jewish merchants of the Portuguese nation (*Nação*).[3] Although Jews were initially forbidden to worship in public, by the 1630s, synagogues were built in Dutch cities.[4] These same years were crucial for Dutch expansion into the Americas, with colonies established in Guyana/Cayenne (1590s), New Netherland (1624–1667, 1673–1674), Recife (1630), St. Eustatius (1636), Curaçao (1634), and Suriname (1667). Most of these early congregations were founded by the *Nação* and used their prayer books and customs. As in Amsterdam and London, Ashkenazi Jews were often considered second-class Jews within these congregations.

Response to Jews in the Dutch colonies was mixed. Although the governor of New Netherland (later New York) was openly antisemitic, Jews' knowledge of sugar production and their trade networks made them welcome in Recife, Curaçao, and Suriname. Hence,

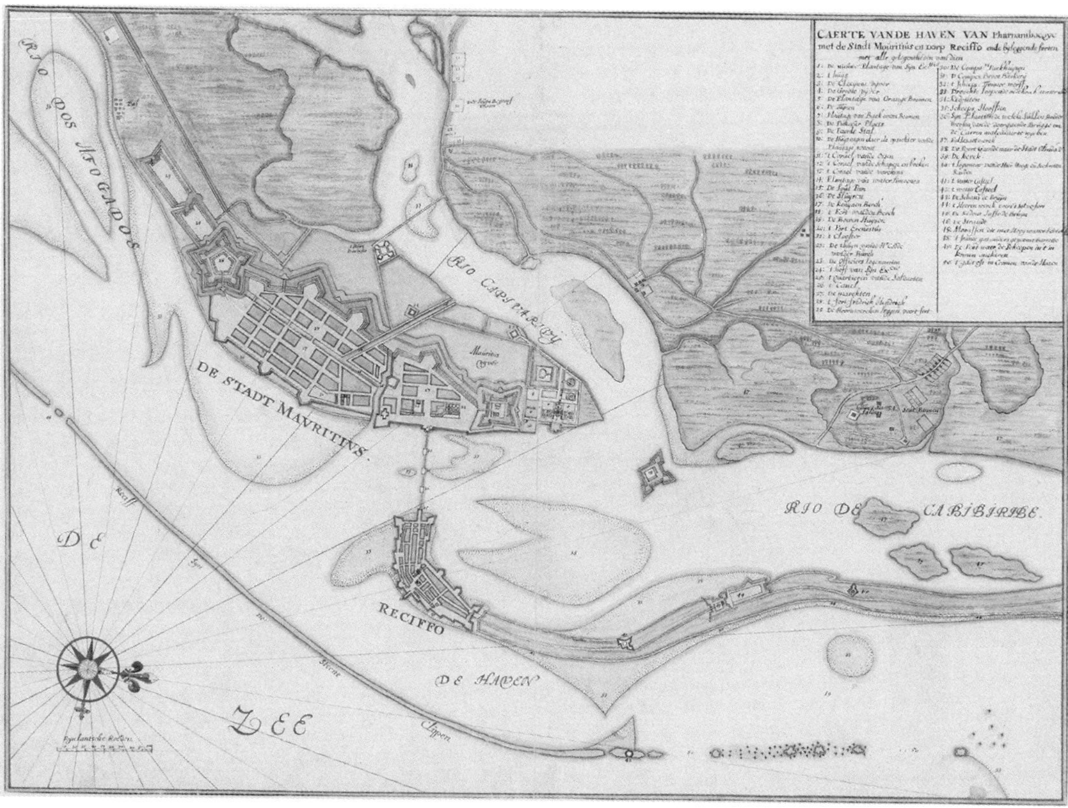

Map of Recife, Brazil. There were synagogues both in Recife and Mauritarius. (Johannes Vigboones, watercolor chart of the city of Recife (Brazil) in the 17th century, 1665; Kaartcollectie Buitenland Leupe van het Nationaal Archief)

the Jewish communities in these locales were quite large, sometimes making up one-third to one-half of the white inhabitants.[5] This population was complemented by Jews of color, who in colonies such as Suriname made up about 10 percent of the Jewish community.[6] Soon synagogues were established in Dutch colonies in Recife (1640), Mauricia (1648), Cayenne (1661), Jodensavanne, Suriname (1685), Curaçao (1692), Venezuela (1710s), Paramaribo, Suriname (1719), and St. Eustatius (1739).[7] Because Jews were allowed to worship openly, the types of sources from these colonies are quite different from the Spanish and Portuguese colonies: there were colonial and Jewish communal records, as well as poetry, gravestones, and architecture. Dutch Jews began to develop a Jewish culture and religion that adapted to local pressures, including racism.

In the British Empire, Jewish communities in the sugar colonies in Jamaica and Barbados were much larger than those in early New York, Newport, Charleston, Savannah, and Philadelphia. Jews thrived in the British colonies because, as in the Dutch colonies, Jews were generally allowed to worship Judaism openly. Hence, many early British colonial synagogues date from this era: Nidhe Israel (Barbados, 1654), Semah David (Barbados, 1660s–1670s), Cassipora Creek, Suriname (1671), Nevis (1684), Neve Shalom (Jamaica, 1703), Shaar Ha Shamaim (Jamaica, c. 1704), Neve Tzedek (Jamaica, c. 1719), and Shearith

Fragment of a gravestone of a girl named Esther, Hunts Bay Cemetery, Jamaica. (Photograph by Laura Arnold Leibman, 2010)

Israel (New York, 1730).[8] Even as the number of Ashkenazi immigrants to the colonies grew, most synagogues continued to use Sephardic rites. Moreover, as the Petition to the Jamaican Assembly demonstrates (chapter 17), Jews in these colonies quickly found that religious freedom did not always lead to civil liberties. Although the Plantation Act of 1740 allowed Jews to become naturalized citizens in the British colonies, their political rights remained uneven. In New York, for example, Jews lost the right to vote between 1737 and 1747.[9] For Jews in the British colonies, being "Jewish" often meant being affiliated in some way with a Jewish community but struggling to receive the same rights their white Christian neighbors received by default.

Although there were never as many Jews in the French colonies as in the Dutch or British Empire, France began its colonial expansion into the Americas quite early. As a Catholic country, France did not officially allow Jews into its colonies. Still several people of Jewish descent arrived in its colonies surreptitiously, most notably Esther Brandeau / Jacques La Fargue whose story appears in this collection (chapter 16). The earliest successful French settlements were in Quebec (1608), La Baye des Puants (Green Bay, Wisconsin; 1634), and Trois-Rivières (1634). It was only with the end of New France in 1760, however, that the first Jewish families began to settle in the region. The Hart, Hays, Solomons, Mayers, Lyon, and Abraham families settled in Quebec City, Montreal, Trois-Rivières, and other cities.[10]

More crucial to early French Jewish settlement was the Caribbean. The most significant French colony in the Caribbean was Saint-Domingue (now Haiti) on the island of Hispaniola. When Recife fell in 1654 again to Portuguese hands, some Jews brought their sugar know-how to Haiti.[11] Even though the Code Noir (Black Code) of 1685 officially expelled Jews from French islands in the Caribbean, some stayed. More Jews arrived, primarily from the French cities of Bayonne and Bordeaux, both of which had long-standing Portuguese Jewish communities.[12] Members of the Gradis family, for example, were able to reside in Haiti due to a special patent they received from the French King.[13] In addition, there were smaller early Jewish communities in Martinique, Guadeloupe, Cayenne (now French Guiana), and Tobago.[14] Once again, Jewish expertise in sugar and chocolate production proved useful. Yet while Jewish expertise benefited local economies, Jewish residents often provoked ire from French Catholic neighbors.[15]

Jews fared somewhat better to the north in New Orleans. Theoretically the 1665 Code Noir prohibited Jewish settlement in Louisiana, but the law was not strictly enforced. Here early Sephardic merchants like Isaac Monsanto were commercially successful, in part because of the trade networks they maintained with coreligionists in Saint-Domingue, Jamaica, Curaçao, and Newport, Rhode Island.[16] Colonial American Jews often arranged marriages with Jews in different ports: individual Jewish communities were small, and marriages could ensure better trading partners. Evidence of early Jewish experiences in French colonies typically come in two forms: (1) restrictions against Jews and ire when these restrictions were violated and (2) evidence of Jews' mercantile activities.

The sources in part 1 reveal how what it meant to be Jewish or American may have been understood differently by colonial Jews than by people today. Most Jews understood America as including North and South America and the Caribbean. Across the colonies, Jewishness was sometimes defined by outsiders. In the Spanish, Portuguese, and French colonies, whether one believed oneself to be Jewish did not always matter, as the Inquisition had the final call regarding whether one was Christian or a heretic. Genealogy, actions, and faith impacted the tribunals' decision-making. In the Dutch and British colonies, synagogues had a much larger say in deciding who was Jewish. Yet, having made that decision, Jews found themselves deemed "resident outsiders," denied full participation in local governance. Moreover, both Jews of color and queer Jews were subject to the Mahamad (synagogue board), which often regulated and stigmatized their bodies much as the Inquisition had.

While certainly some colonial American Jews lived alone among their gentile neighbors, most lived in port towns that were part of a vast network across the Atlantic world. Many lived in multiple ports during their lifetimes, moving to take advantage of new opportunities or because they were forced to flee from persecution. Yet even those who stayed put found themselves both part and not part of the colonies in which they lived. Jews who were not indigenous to the colonies often identified as much with their European and African homelands as they did with where they currently lived. Jews also had ties that bound them to Jews in other ports. Using objects and secular records and works written by Jews themselves expands our sense of the Jewish American past.

NOTES

1. Israel, *Diasporas within a Diaspora*, 1.
2. Gitlitz, *Living in Silverado*, 63–64, 144–147.
3. Huussen, "Legal Position of the Jews in the Dutch Republic," 30–31.
4. Huussen, 31, 34.
5. Rupert, "Trading Globally, Speaking Locally," 110.
6. Ben-Ur and Roitman, "Adultery Here and There," 205.
7. Stiefel, *Jewish Sanctuary in the Atlantic World*, 221–225, 231, 239, 250.
8. Stiefel, 223–224, 230, 236–243, 252–253.
9. Gurock, *American Jewish History*, 13–14; Leibman, *Art of the Jewish Family*, 62.
10. Rome and Langlais, *Jews and French Quebecers*, 4.
11. Arbell, *Jewish Nation of the Caribbean*, 288.
12. Arbell, 288; Ben-Ur, "Jewish Savannah in Atlantic Perspective," 189.
13. Arbell, *Jewish Nation of the Caribbean*, 288–289.
14. Arbell, 36, 45, 58.
15. Arbell, 40–41.
16. Ford and Stiefel, *Jews of New Orleans and the Mississippi Delta*, 17.

1

Edict of Expulsion

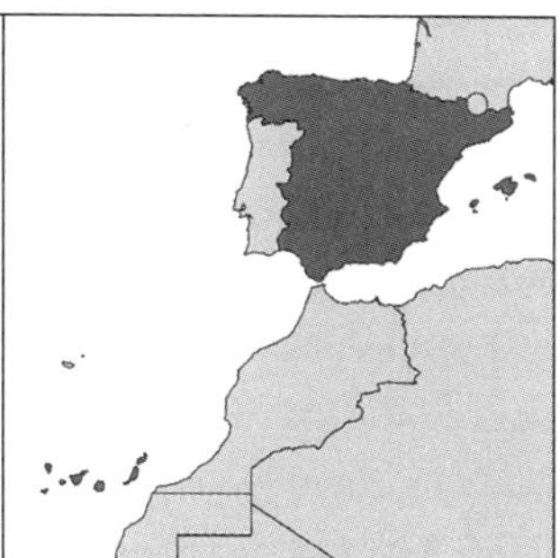

SPAIN, 1492

Jonathan Ray

A major impetus for Jewish migration to the Americas came on March 31, 1492, when King Ferdinand and Queen Isabella summarily expelled all professing Jews from Spain and its territories. Although the motives behind the Edict of Expulsion were complex, the decision to expel the Jews was closely tied to their perceived influence on recent converts to Christianity. Most of these *conversos* (converts) had left Judaism under duress during mass rioting that took place in 1391 or because of the social and religious pressures that followed. While many *conversos* sought to live as faithful Catholics, others continued to practice a form of crypto-Judaism in secret, a heretical crime referred to as "Judaizing" in the Edict. Some Jews converted rather than be expelled. Others left, only to return when life in exile became untenable. Those seeking safe haven in neighboring Portugal were forcibly converted with the rest of that kingdom's Jews in 1497. The decree of 1492 led to the last and largest expulsion of the Jews in medieval Europe, effectively ending centuries of Jewish life in the Spanish kingdoms.

The Edict of Expulsion illuminates the complex relationship between professing Jews and *conversos*. Even after 1492, members of Sephardic families that were split between Judaism and Christianity maintained close contact. Western Sephardic Jews who settled in the Netherlands, France, and England retained linguistic and cultural ties to their Iberian heritage. Other Jews who left Iberia rather than convert settled in the Ottoman Empire and would later become known as Eastern Sephardic Jews (see chapter 2).

The Edict of Expulsion reveals the pressures that Jewish converts faced in Iberia and the Americas. Columbus set sail on August 3, 1492, the day after the last Jews were to have left Spain. Thus, the end to open Jewish life in medieval Spain coincided with the Spanish expansion into the Americas. As the colonies opened up to migration, *conversos* made their way westward. Some *conversos* initially came to the Americas to escape the harassment of the Inquisition. Unfortunately, the Inquisition followed them westward. Undeterred, Sephardic Jews developed important trading networks throughout the Americas, binding families in Iberia to the Spanish, Dutch, and British colonies.

PRIMARY SOURCE

Whereas, having been informed that in these our kingdoms, there were some bad Christians who Judaized and apostatized from our holy Catholic faith, the chief cause of which was the communication between the Jews and [New] Christians; at the *Cortes* (legislature) we held in the city of Toledo [Spain] in the past year of 1480, we ordered the said Jews in all the cities, towns and places of our kingdoms and dominions to separate into Jewish quarters and places apart, where they should live and reside, hoping by their separation alone to remedy the evil. Furthermore, we have sought and given orders that Inquisition should be made in our said kingdoms, which is known, for upwards of twelve years has been, and is done, whereby many guilty persons have been discovered, and made known. And as we are informed by the inquisitors, and many other religious, ecclesiastical and secular persons, that great injury has resulted, and does result, as it is stated, and appears to be, from the participation, society, and communication they [the Christians] held and do hold with Jews, who it appears always endeavor in every way they can to subvert our holy Catholic faith, and to make faithful Christians withdraw and separate themselves therefrom, and attract and pervert them to their injurious opinions and belief, instructing them in the ceremonies and observances of their religion, holding meetings at which they read and teach what they are to believe and observe according to their religion; seeking to circumcise them and their children; giving them books from which they may read their prayers; and explaining to them the fasts they are to observe; assembling with them to read and to teach them the histories of their law; indicating to them the festivals previous to their occurring, and instructing them what they are to do and observe thereon; giving and carrying to them from their houses unleavened bread and meat ritually slaughtered; instructing them what they are to refrain from, as well in food as in other matters, for the due observance of their religion, and persuading them to profess and keep the law of Moses; giving them to understand, that except that, there is no other law or truth. . . .

Notwithstanding we were informed of this before, and we knew the certain remedy for all these injuries and inconveniences was to separate the said Jews from all communication with Christians, and banish them from all our kingdoms, as we were desirous to content ourselves by ordering them to quit all cities, towns, and places of Andalusia, where, it appears, they have done the greatest mischief, considering that would suffice, and that those of other cities, towns, and places [of our kingdoms] would cease to do and commit the same.

But as we are informed that neither that [step], nor the execution of some of the said Jews, who have been most guilty of the said crimes and offenses against our holy Catholic faith, has been sufficient for a complete remedy to obviate and arrest so great an opprobrium and offense to the Catholic faith and religion.

And as it is found and appears, that they, the said Jews, wherever they live and congregate, daily increase in continuing their wicked and injurious purposes; to afford them no further opportunity for insulting our holy Catholic faith, and those whom until now God has been pleased to preserve, as well as those who had fallen, but amended and are brought back to our Holy Mother Church, which, according to the weakness of our human nature and the diabolical suggestion that continually wages war with us, may easily occur, unless the principal cause of it be removed, which is to banish the said Jews from our kingdoms.

And when any serious and detestable crime is committed by some persons of a college or university, it is right that such college or university should be dissolved and annihilated, and the lesser suffer for the greater, and one be punished for the other; and those that disturb the welfare and proper living of cities and towns, that by contagion may injure others, should be expelled therefrom, and even for lighter causes that might be injurious to the state, how much more then for the greatest, and most dangerous, and contagious of crimes like this.

Therefore we, by and with the counsel and advice of some prelates and high noblemen of our kingdoms, and other learned persons of our council, having maturely deliberated thereon, resolve to order all the said Jews and Jewesses to quit our kingdoms, and never to return or come back to them, or any of them. Therefore, we command this our edict to be issued, whereby we command all Jews and Jewesses, of whatever age they may be, that live, reside, and dwell in our said kingdoms and lordships . . . by the end of the month of July next, of the present year 1492, they depart from all our said kingdoms and dominions, . . . and they shall not presume to return to, nor reside therein, or in any part of them, either as residents, travelers, or in any other manner. . . .

Adapted from Elias Haim Lindo, *The History of the Jews of Spain and Portugal* (London: Longman, Brown, Green and Longmans, 1848), 277–280.

QUESTIONS

1. What steps did the Crown take to eliminate Judaizing prior to issuing this decree?
2. What did Spanish Jews do to help New Christians continue to observe Judaism?
3. What reason is given for expelling all Jews when only some may be guilty of Judaizing?

2

Confession of Sodomy and Judaizing

BRAZIL, 1593

Noam Sienna

After the Portuguese Inquisition began in 1546, some New Christians sought refuge in Brazil, where there was not a permanent branch of the Holy Office. Starting in 1591, however, visiting inquisitors began to hear cases against suspected heretics.[1] Joam Bautista, a thirty-three-year-old New Christian merchant in colonial Brazil, was brought before one of these visiting inspectors for sodomy and Judaizing. This is the dossier (*processo*) created by the Inquisition, during the trial of Bautista. *Processos* illuminate the lives and practices of Jewish converts and their descendants in early America but are also problematic, as they tended to be collected under duress. Thus, while inquisitor Senhor Furtado de Mendoça makes it sound as if Bautista just approached him and willingly asked to confess, this is unlikely to have been the case, since Bautista, as David Gitlitz notes, referred to the inquisitors as "devils."[2]

Batista's life trajectory exemplifies the networks of Iberian ex-*conversos* who established Diaspora communities throughout western Europe, the Ottoman Empire, and the New World. The description of his sexual history demonstrates how concerns about sexuality, religion, and race were linked. In this way, Bautista's narrative reflects general trends in the Inquisition as it was performed in the Americas. In the Spanish colony of New Spain, for example, sex crimes were the second most common "deviance" brought before the inquisitors.[3] Bautista's narrative is a good reminder of the ways that Jewishness has often intersected with questions of race and masculinity.

Bautista's experiences with the Inquisition in colonial Brazil illuminates why Jewish settlers in the Dutch colony of Recife (Brazil) were terrified about how they would fare if the Portuguese recaptured the colony, which they eventually did (see chapter 9). Many of Recife's Jewish residents had been born and baptized in Portugal. From the Inquisition's perspective, their baptism made them lapsed Catholics, not Jews. Residents born in Iberia included Isaac Aboab da Fonseca, the main rabbi of Recife. Thus, regardless of their sexual practices, in the eyes of the Inquisition, many of Recife's Jews were heretics who could be arrested, punished, and potentially executed. Confessing and repenting, as Bautista did, was often done to save one's life.

PRIMARY SOURCE

On August 12, 1593, in this city of Salvador Bahia of all Saints, in the place of residence of the Senhor Visitador [Visiting Inspector] from the Holy Office, Senhor Furtado de Mendoça, a man appeared before him named Joam Bautista [João Batista]. Wanting to confess his sins, he received a sentence from the Holy Officers who instructed him to put his right hand under oath, promising to say the truth. He said he was a New Christian, son of Francisco Roiz Montemor and his wife, Felipa Carlos, deceased, [who were] New Christians, Jews in Salonica, the *juderia* [Jewish quarter] of Turkey. From there the confessant, being a Jew, fled for Rome, and from Rome fled for Lisbon where he was reconciled with the Holy Inquisition [that is, he was baptized]. [He is] a native of Lisbon, a bachelor merchant, about 33 years old, more or less.

Being in this city [of Bahia] and confessing, this Jew said that in Turkey, [when he] was about 18 years old, he committed the nefarious sin of sodomy three or four or five times, either as active or as passive with Turks and Syrian Jews, whose names have not been remembered. He had his dishonest virile member in their back vessels, having pollution in them, and himself consenting for them to do it to him in the above-mentioned way. Then he was in Venice for ten or twelve years, spending the nights in his bed with a young lad whose name he does not remember, who was also a Jew who had become a Christian; he did the above-mentioned sin two or three times with him completely, the confessant being always passive. The young lad remained in Venice and he does not know more of his encounters.

After these ten or so years he was [traveling] through Rome; going to his bath he came across a young Italian lad whose name and encounters he does not know, and he also did the above-mentioned sin with him, having completed pollution in his backside. After this the confessant was on the island of São Tomé, and in this city he did and completed the mentioned nefarious sin of sodomy with some Black women, not knowing how many, doing it with them and penetrating their backsides with his dishonest member as if they were doing it in the front, as is natural. With these Black women he did it at least fifteen times more or less.

He confessed further that for [the past] sixteen years, more or less, he had stayed in Lisbon in the house of his uncle Manuel Drago, a merchant, and this uncle had in his house a shop assistant named Pero de Leam [Leão], a young lad that was then bearded under his chin and on his legs or arms, married to a strong woman, the only daughter of a goldsmith. Both being in the above-mentioned house of his uncle, they both slept together in the same bed of Pero de Leam some nights. It is not affirmed how many nights the confessant did and completed the nefarious sin with the mentioned Pero de Leam, [and] it is not affirmed how many times the confessant was always the active one, penetrating with his virile member the back vessel of the mentioned Pero de Leam and finishing in him and doing it with him from behind like one does with a woman from the front.

He confessed further that for the last five years, more or less, while he has been in this city, [that] coming to his house [was] Gonçalo Pires, a young lad who had just begun to show signs of spotty facial hair that [illegible] stayed a night in his house, and both laid down in the bed of the confessant and with the confessant the mentioned Gonçalo Pires did and completed the mentioned nefarious sin, being active in the above-mentioned manner, and the confessant being passive. And this sin completed as described, the two did it just once and the confessant wanted to do the same with him being active, [but] he did not consent to it, so it did not happen more than what has been said.

And for all these sins, he said that he is very repentant, and he asked forgiveness from God our Lord with signs of repentance, and said that he already confessed them to his spiritual parents and he completed the penitence that they gave him. Later the Senhor Visitador showed him much compassion, [instructing him] that from today forward he would not do such horrible and nefarious sins, and if he [illegible] the conversion of the mentioned persons and with all the others that he could have [had] the chance of such dirtiness, because doing the opposite will be gravely punished. He was ordered to confess to the College of Jesus and bring a written confession [of] that [which] he confessed at this table, and he promised to complete it, and questioned about the custom with the different accomplices, he said nothing, and he promised secrecy.

Signed with the Senhor Visitador here: Manoel Francisco, honorary of the Holy Office in this visit, the scribe, [and] Heitor Furtado de Mendoça, [and] Joam Bautista. About which confession I, Manoel Francisco, notary of the Holy Office on this visit, translated well and faithfully on my own and with certainty, the Senhor Visitador agreeing with good word, we both sign here: [signed] Manoel Francisco, notary of the Holy Office on this visit and the scribe; [signed] Mendoça.

Processo 4307, August 20, 1593, Inquisição de Lisboa, ANTT. Transcribed and translated by Michael Waas and Matthew Barrile. Published in RT, 104–106.

QUESTIONS

1. How did Jewishness shape Batista's life choices?
2. Did Bautista articulate his sexual encounters as a distinct identity (e.g., "sodomite")?
3. What is the legacy of the Inquisition's intertwining of Jewishness and sodomy?

NOTES

1. Andrien, *Human Tradition in Colonial Latin America*, 56, 62.
2. Gitlitz, *Secrecy and Deceit*, 599.
3. Behar, "Sex and Sin," 35–36.

3

Jewish Calendar by Luis de Carvajal the Younger

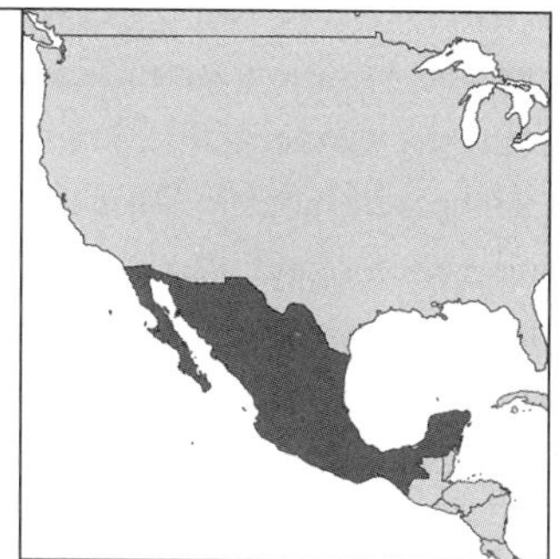

NEW SPAIN, 1590S

Ronnie Perelis

Some of the earliest Jewish communities in the Americas were created by New Christians who formed small groups with similar genealogies and interests. The Spanish colony of New Spain was home to several such groups, the most famous of which rose up around the Carvajal family. Luis de Carvajal the younger was a *converso* who came to New Spain from his native Benavente, Spain, with his extended family in 1580. His uncle Luis de Carvajal y de la Cueva was appointed governor of the northeastern territory of the Nuevo Reino de León, and the younger Luis served as his assistant in administering this sprawling territory made up of swamps, deserts, and silver mines.

From a young age, Luis committed himself to secretly keeping Judaism. He found ingenious ways to obtain Jewish knowledge while living under inquisitorial surveillance. In addition to receiving instruction from crypto-Jewish family members, Luis sought out textual sources for his religious quest. He illicitly bought a Latin Bible to read the Old Testament. In 1589, Carvajal was arrested. As part of his penance, he relocated to Mexico City, where he worked in the monastery of Santiago de Tlatelolco in the northern part of the city. Yet, rather than repenting, Carvajal used his access to the monastery's rich library to poach rabbinic sources that were cited as part of Catholic scholarly works.

Luis took these scattered rabbinic sources, translated them into Spanish, and organized them into anthologies for his tight-knit crypto-Jewish circuit. He bound these texts along with poetic prayers and his stirring autobiography in a leather notebook. The autobiography begins, "Saved from terrible dangers by the Lord, I, Joseph Lumbroso [Joseph the Enlightened] of the Hebrew nation and of the pilgrims to the West Indies in appreciation of the mercies received from the hands of the Highest, address myself to all, who believe in the Holy of Holies and who hope for great mercies."[1] The calendar shown here was part of this collection: it includes a list of biblical and rabbinic Jewish holidays.[2] This manuscript was confiscated as evidence of Judaizing after Carvajal's second arrest in 1595.

American Jewish history, to a great extent, is about Jews leaving Europe, Africa, Asia, and the Middle East and creating new identities and possibilities. But in that move away from the former lands, Jews sometimes sought to anchor themselves in the fundamental elements of Judaism. This calendar reveals how people who were dedicated to maintaining Judaism in secret were able to observe the Holy Days and learn Hebrew. *Conversos* were far from Iberia, where they lived as Catholics for two to three generations; yet they maintained connections with other *conversos* throughout the Sephardic Diaspora, including Jews from Italy. Carvajal's transliteration follows Italian practice, as does the use of numbers from one to seven to denote the day of the week.[3] Access to a calendar allowed American Jews, wherever they were—in the mining region of Taxco or the Port of Curaçao or the wide-open plains of the North American West—to celebrate the Holy Days. Thereby, they connected with the God and People of Israel around the globe.

PRIMARY SOURCE

Hanukkah	Thursday. 22 December	Tysri	September
Esther	Wednesday. 22 February	Hesban	October
Passover	Saturday. 25 March	Quislev	November
Shavuot	Sunday. 14 May	Tebeth	December
[Fast of] Tamuz	Sunday. 5 June	Sebath	January
[Fast of] Ninth of Av	Sunday. 16 July	Adar	February
Rosh Hashanah	Monday. 4 September	Baadar	Only in a leap year
[Fast of] Gedaliah	Wednesday. 6 September	Nisan	March
Yom Kippur	Wednesday. 14 September	Yar	April
Sukkot	Monday. 18 September	Siban	May
Hanukkah	Tuesday. 12 Wednesday	Tamuz	June
Esther	March. 14 December	Ab	July
Passover	Saturday. 13 April	Elul	August
Shavuot	Sunday. 2 May		
Fast of Tamuz	Sunday. 24 July		
Fast of 9th of Av	Sunday. 4 August		
Rosh Hashanah	Monday. 23 September		
Fast of Gedaliah	Wednesday. 25 September		
Yom Kippur	Wednesday. 2 October		
Hanukkah	Tuesday. 31 December		

Luis de Carvajal, "Psalter; Translation of the Hebrew Calendar into Spanish" (1596), 170, Luis de Carvajal Manuscripts, Princeton University Library, Princeton, NJ.

QUESTIONS

1. Locate a contemporary Jewish calendar. How does it compare with Luis's calendar?
2. If you were a Jew living in New Spain in the 1590s, what objects other than a calendar would be important for your Jewish life?
3. Why do you think Carvajal renamed himself Joseph Lumbroso?

NOTES

1. Penyak and Petry, *Religion in Latin America*, 133.
2. Unless otherwise indicated, all transcriptions and translations are by the author of the entry.
3. I thank Bernard Cooperman for this insight.

4

Mencía de Luna: A Woman in Front of the Lima Inquisition

PERU, 1630S

Ana E. Schaposchnik

In 1570, the same year the Inquisition established a permanent tribunal in Mexico City, it set up a tribunal in Lima. The following fragments are from a Trial of Faith conducted by the Lima tribunal involving Mencía de Luna, a woman born in Seville, Spain, who in 1629 followed her husband, Henrique Núñez de Espinosa, to Peru. The trial began in 1635, when the Inquisition incarcerated Mencía de Luna for being a crypto-Jewish heretic. The trial was interrupted in 1638 when she died while being tortured. Mencía de Luna's Trial of Faith was declared unfinished and paused until 1664, when the Lima Tribunal issued its final sentence: Mencía de Luna was condemned as a heretic. As she was already dead, an effigy representing her was burned in 1664 in an auto-da-fé, the public ceremony and procession of the accused.

Mencía de Luna's Trial of Faith is part of a set of one hundred trials conducted by the Lima Tribunal of the Inquisition for the alleged heresy of crypto-Judaism, called *la complicidad grande*—the Great Conspiracy. The imprisoned included Manuel Bautista Perez (see chapter 5) and Mencía de Luna's husband. Like Manuel Bautista Perez, Mencía de Luna and her husband were wealthy and envied by other colonists. Only three women were imprisoned in Peru during the Great Conspiracy: Mencía de Luna; her sister Mayor de Luna; and Isabel Antonia, Mayor's daughter. All three belonged to the same extended family. Of the three trials, Mencía de Luna's is the only one preserved in the archival catalog. As such, her trial transcript uncovers women's experience with the Inquisition, particularly how women in the Hebrew Bible, such as Esther, served as spiritual models for crypto-Jewish women.

Beyond the contribution of Mencía de Luna's trial transcript to women's history, it opens a window into the experiences of alleged crypto-Jews in the Spanish American colonies. A lot of scholarly attention has been paid to the history of alleged crypto-Jews in

Spain and in Portugal, but the Lima Tribunal in particular is often ignored, as the archival collections are not complete. As part of the standard proceedings, this transcript explains the Inquisition's logic about why someone raised Catholic could not legitimately "return" to Judaism but rather should be understood as a Christian heretic.

PRIMARY SOURCE

Mencía de Luna, Her Life Story (folios 36v–37r)

She said that she was born in the said city of Seville and her mother raised her until the age of twelve, [and] that she never met her father and that once her mother died [illegible] in her home and afterwards she remained behind with the said Doña Mayor her sister and at the age of fifteen. . . . She married the said Enrique Núñez de Espinosa, and eight months after being married, he the said [Núñez de Espinosa] embarked to obtain blacks [from] Angola and he was robbed and returned to Seville and embarked towards this kingdom [of Peru]. She [Mencía de Luna] remained in the house of her said sister, and her said sister having come to the Indies she took up residence [illegible] and with the Army in which the Señor Virrey Conde de Chinchón came to Peru in search of the said her husband with whom she has been until she was apprehended and brought to this Inquisition.

Accusation (folios 38r–39r)

Very Illustrious Sirs, the Licentiate Don León Alçayaga y Lartaún, prosecutor of this Holy Office, in the best manner of the said place [Lima], I appear before You and criminally accuse Doña Mencía de Luna born in the city of Seville in the Kingdoms of Spain who is present. I say that the aforementioned Christian was baptized and confirmed, and having as such enjoyed the grace and privilege that loyal Catholics usually have and ought to enjoy with little fear of our lord [but] in great harm to her conscience and condemnation of her soul she has hereticated and apostatized from our holy Catholic faith and evangelical law that preaches and teaches our holy Mother Church of Rome. Switching to and acknowledging belief in the fatal law of Moses, she has guarded its rites and ceremonies and believed it was the good one, and that in that law she would be redeemed especially as a person that had and has been, hears and believes in the said dead law with fondness and love for it [the Mosaic law] and its rites and ceremonies. And in this City of Kings [Lima] in Peru for a long time until today [Mencía de Luna] has continued to attend many meetings with people who profess the said law [of Moses] and in the presence of certain peoples very close to her and others of her caste [New Christian] and descent has said many times and on different occasions that she believed she would save her soul. And she guarded the Saturday as a holiday wearing on the day a clean shirt and clothes in reverence of the holiday, and she made the fast of Queen Esther during the month of September fasting three continuous days, not eating on any of these days until sundown and until the star was out and then only dining on fish eggs and fruit and fish with scales because it was prohibited to eat without scales in the said law. And she fasted on Tuesdays and Thursdays and Fridays per fasting of the said law

so God would give her good success and would forgive her sins. And she did not eat bacon because it was forbidden in the said law and the night of the days she had fasted she did not eat meat in observance of the said law.

Processo de Mencía de Luna, Sección Inquisición, Legajo 1643, Expediente 10, AHN.

QUESTIONS

1. What aspects of Mencía de Luna's early life interest the Inquisition? How does her biography set the stage for her sister's and niece's trials?
2. What aspects of crypto-Judaism is Mencía de Luna accused of?
3. In Rabbinical Judaism, the fast of Esther is considered a minor fast. The figure of Esther and her fast, however, took on greater significance for crypto-Jews. Why do you think the story of Esther resonated with crypto-Jews?
4. How does Mencía de Luna's life before coming to Peru compare to either that of Joam Bautista (chapter 2) or Luis Méndez Chávez (chapter 7)?
5. What role does food play in crypto-Jewish identity and religion?

5

Merchant House of a Convicted Judaizer

PERU, 1639

Laura Arnold Leibman

Like Mencía de Luna (chapter 4), the Portuguese merchant Manuel Bautista Perez was arrested for his supposed role in *la complicidad grande* of secret Jews in Peru. Unlike Mencía de Luna, he survived torture and was executed along with ten other Judaizers in an auto-da-fé in 1639. At the center of Bautista's arrest was his home, which some believed contained a secret synagogue in which crypto-Jews worshiped. One of the features of the house that bothered Bautista's inquisitors was its elaborate, enclosed, second-story, lattice-work balconies and windows. An architectural inheritance from Moorish Spain, the balconies were thought by the Inquisition to enable people inside the house to spy on good Christians below while remaining hidden. Thus, the balcony became a symbol of the crypto-Jews' ability to veil their true beliefs from the Inquisition's peering gaze. This interpretation was somewhat suspect, however, as these balconies were common in both New and Old Christian houses in the colony. Although today the house's wooden balconies have been replaced with glass and metal, they can still be seen in early photographs.

For Jewish merchants in the Americas, houses contained domestic spaces for extended family, storage areas, offices, rooms for receiving guests, and sleeping quarters for the enslaved. The opulent clothing, furniture, table settings, tapestries, paintings, and library attested to Bautista's cosmopolitan identity and his great success. In the end, this success contributed to his downfall. Jealous competitors often accused successful New Christian merchants of Judaizing because if they were convicted, half of their property would go to the accuser and half to the church. The Inquisition described and inventoried Bautista's house to document the property the Inquisition stood to gain and because Bautista's prosecutors, like others in colonial America, believed that the house—its structure, contents, and practices—best reflected the *true* state of Bautista's soul. Local histories have sometimes suggested that after his execution Bautista was nicknamed "Pilate" for Pontius Pilate, the Roman who ordered Jesus executed. Hence, his house became known as "Casa de Pilatos," or Pilate's House. It is more likely, however, that Bautista's house was named for a sixteenth-century Andalusian palace in Seville constructed in a similar style.

Although the Inquisition focused on the way that the latticed balconies provided the family with a private view of the streets below, what may strike us most about the floor plan several hundred years later is the utter lack of privacy that people had, once individuals made it past the front hallway. This was typical of elite early-Renaissance houses, which emphasized connectivity; hence, rooms led from one into another. Even bedrooms were used as passageways to other rooms. Everybody within the house was seen as interdependent, a value that the Inquisition often used to its advantage. Notably, the alleged synagogue was supposedly on the second floor, where guests would be less likely to wander. Even so, it would have been nearly impossible to hold services without the servants knowing.

Conversos like Bautista, Mencía de Luna, and Carvajal raise important questions for Jewish studies about the way we define Jewish identity. As Irene Silverblatt notes, Manuel Bautista Perez was a visibly devout Catholic who tried to erase his identity as a New Christian.[1] Bautista's house was located in central Lima opposite the Church of San Francisco, where he undoubtedly attended services. Yet the Inquisition's emphasis on the house's "secret synagogue" and balconies echoes an important motif in early American Jewish life: secrecy. Revealing that one still practiced Jewish traditions could cost *conversos* their lives; hence, parents often did not tell children about keeping Jewish rituals until they became adults. Secrecy could save lives, but it also impacted the religious traditions of early American Jews.

PRIMARY SOURCES

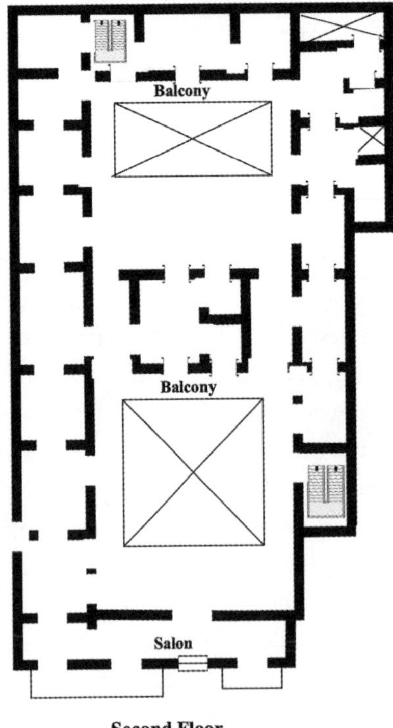

Second Floor

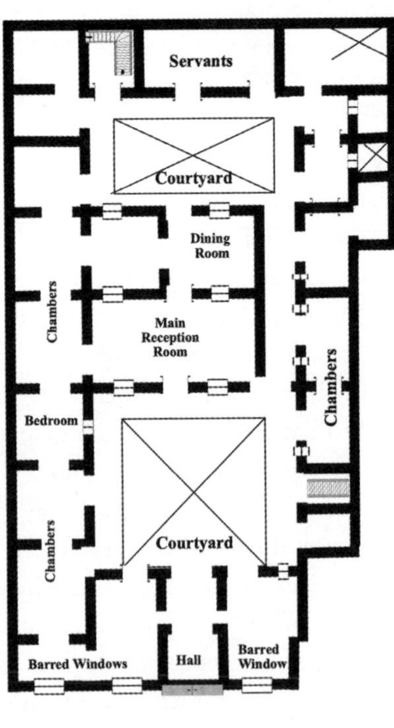

First Floor

Above: Casa de Pilatos, de facto headquarters of the Constitutional Court of Peru in Lima, 2001. (WC)

Facing page: Floorplan of building with possible use of rooms when it was a house. (Redrawn by Laura Arnold Leibman)

QUESTIONS

1. What in your opinion makes a house "Jewish"?
2. Given that Manuel Bautista Perez consistently denied that he was a secret Judaizer, should we accept the Inquisition's categorization of him as a Jew? Why or why not?
3. Draw a floorplan of the house or apartment in which you grew up. Compare it to the floorplan of Manuel Bautista Perez's home. Does your home's structure emphasize connectivity or individuality?

NOTE

1. Silverblatt, "New Christians and New World Fears," 538.

6

The Lost Tribes and Indigenous Judaism

NEW SPAIN, 1644–1652

Laura Arnold Leibman

Both conquistadors and missionaries often identified Indigenous Americans as a lost tribe of Israel. That is, they thought of Indigenous Americans as one of the tribes exiled from the Kingdom of Israel (eighth century BCE), whose return was correlated with the messiah's arrival. In New Spain, the lost tribe theory ran counter to Indigenous enslavement and supported claims that American Indians were vassals, rather than captives in a "just" religious war. In 1542, American Indian slavery was abolished in the Spanish Empire. While the end of Indigenous slavery did not stem the tide of genocide, it did expedite centuries of terror for African peoples, whom European empires enslaved in order to fill the need for labor in their colonies.

The legend of the lost tribes similarly supported the Catholic Church's proselytizing to Indigenous Americans, as the church considered the transition from Jew to Catholic to be both a logical step in an individual's spiritual journey and a sign of Christ's return. Jewish mystics similarly associated the lost tribes' return with the Jewish messiah. Hence, kabbalistic Rabbi Menasseh ben Israel of Amsterdam, a contemporary of Isaac Aboab da Fonseca (see chapter 9), eagerly published the account of a crypto-Jew named Antonio de Montezinos (Aharon haLevi) in his messianic treatise *Mikveh Israel* (The hope of Israel). Published in Spanish in 1650 and English in 1652, *Mikveh Israel* prophesied that the establishment of synagogues in the four quarters of the world would help bring about the messiah. Influenced by this work and vision, several early synagogues in the Americas named themselves Mikve(h) Israel, including in Curaçao, Philadelphia, and Savannah.

Antonio de Montezinos claimed to have found a lost tribe of Israelites (the tribe of Reuben) in the northern Andes in what today is Colombia. Although his account was written around 1644, it was not published until 1650. Little is known about Montezinos's early history other than that he was born in Portugal to *conversos* and that he was arrested by the Inquisition in Cartagena in 1639 on suspicion of Judaizing. Miraculously, however, he was freed, and he made his way to Amsterdam, where he met Menasseh ben Israel. Six months later, he returned to the Americas, but this time he settled in Dutch Brazil, where he could practice Judaism openly. He only survived another two years.[1]

Importantly, Europeans were not alone in treasuring the history of the lost tribes. Several early Indigenous and *mestizo* (multiracial) authors, including Garcilaso de la Vega (Inca, Peru) and Guaman Poma (Quechua, Peru) used the history of Indigenous Americans as a lost tribe to emphasize that American Indian peoples were better Christians than the European colonists were. Similarly, early postconquest Indigenous literature often presents the Nahuas (Aztecs) as Israelites. Here, too, the claiming of Israelite identity reinforced the injustice that Nahuas faced and argued for their higher spirituality, for example, in the lamentation written by the Nahua composer Don Juan de Lienas (1620–1650). Professional singers were an important part of the temple services in preconquest Tenochtitlan (later called Mexico City), and missionary schools typically included musical education that emphasized "singing, dancing, and playing instruments."[2]

Lienas was a chapel master for Convent Encarnación in Mexico City. His hymn was sung on Thursday of Holy Week as part of citywide processions. The lyrics come from the book of Lamentations, a part of the Hebrew Bible mourning Jerusalem's destruction in the sixth century BCE. The author presents the Babylonians as agents of God, who destroyed the city to punish the Israelites. During the seventeenth century (like today), the book of Lamentations was read publicly on Tisha B'Av, a fast day in Jewish tradition commemorating the destruction of Jerusalem's First and Second Temples and the Spanish Expulsion (see chapter 1). In Mexico City's Catholic pageantry, the lyrics provided guidance for the way Nahuas should understand the fairly recent destruction of Tenochtitlan, which was often referred to as the "Jerusalem of the Americas."

PRIMARY SOURCES

Excerpt from "The Relation of Antonio de Montezinos"

After this Conference, Montezinos went to Cartagena, a City of the Indians, where he being examined, was put in Prison [by the Inquisition]; and while he prayed to God, such words fell from him; Blessed be the name of the Lord, that hath not made me an Idolator, a Barbarian, a Black-a-Moore, or an Indian; but as he named Indian, he was angry with himself, and said, The Hebrews are Indians; then he coming to himself again, confessed that he doted [spoke foolishly], and added, can the Hebrews be Indians? Which he also repeated a second, and a third time; and he thought that it was not by chance that he had so much mistaken himself.

He thinking farther, of what he had heard from the Indian, and hoping that he should find out the whole truth; therefore as soon as he was let out of Prison, he sought out Francisco believing that he would repeat to him again what he had spoken; he therefore being set at liberty, through God's mercy went to the Port of Honda, and according to his desire, found him, who said; He remembered all that he had spoken, when he was upon the Mountain;

whom Montezinos asked, that he would take a journey with him, offering him all courtesies, giving him three pieces of Eight, that he might buy himself necessaries.

Now when they were got out of the City, Montezinos confessed himself to be a Hebrew, of the Tribe of Levi, and that the Lord was his God; and he told the Indian, that all other gods were but mockeries; the Indian being amazed, asked him the name of his Parents; who answered Abraham, Isaac, and Jacob; but said he, have you no other Father? who answered, yes, his Father's name was Ludovico Montezinos; but he not being yet satisfied, I am glad (saith he) to hear you tell this, for I was in doubt to believe you, while you seemed ignorant of your Parents: Montezinos swearing, that he spoke the truth, the Indian asked him, if he were not the Son of Israel, and thereupon began a long discourse; who when he knew that he was so, he desired him to prosecute what he had begun, and added, that he should more fully explain himself, for that formerly he had left things so doubtful, that he did not seem at all assured of anything. After that both had sat down together, and refreshed themselves, the Indian thus began: If you have a mind to follow me your Leader, you shall know whatever you desire to know, only let me tell you this, whatsoever the journey is, you must foot it, and you must eat nothing but parched Maize, and you must omit nothing that I tell you; Montezinos answered that he would do all.

The next day being Monday, the Cacique came again, and bid him throw away what he had in his Knapsack to put on shoes made of linen packthread, and to follow him, with his staff; . . . [they] traveled the whole week, into the Sabbath Day; on which day they resting, the day after they went on, till Tuesday, on which day about eight o'clock in the morning, they came to a River as big as the Douro; then the Indian said, Here you shall see your Brethren, and making a sign with the fine linen of Xylus, which they had about them instead of a Girdle; thereupon on the other side of the River they saw a great smoke, and immediately after, such another sign made as they had made before; a little after that, three men, with a woman, in a little Boat came to them. . . . They embraced him courteously, and talked a good while with him. After that, the Indian bid Montezinos to be of good courage, and not to look that they should come a second time to him, till he had fully learned the things which were told him at the first time.

Then those two men coming on each side of Montezinos, they spoke in Hebrew; the 4th verse of Deuteronomy 6. *Shema Israel, Adonai Elohenu Adonai Ehad*; that is, Hear O Israel, the Lord our God is one God.

Then the Indian Interpreter being asked, how it was in Spanish, they spoke what follows to Montezinos, making a short prayer between every particular.

1. Our Fathers are Abraham, Isaac, Jacob, and Israel, and they signified these four by the three fingers lifted up; then they joined Reuben, adding another finger to the former three.
2. We will bestow several places on them who have a mind to live with us.
3. Joseph dwells in the midst of the Sea, they making a sign by two fingers put together, and then parted them.
4. They said (speaking fast) shortly some of us will go forth to see, and to tread under foot; at which word they winked, and stamped with their feet.

5. **One day we shall all of us talk together, they saying, Ba, ba, ba; and we shall come forth as issuing out of our Mother the earth.**
6. **A certain Messenger shall go forth.**
7. **Francisco shall tell you somewhat more of these things, they making a sign with their finger, that much must not be spoken.**
8. **Suffer us that we may prepare ourselves; and they turning their hands and faces every way, thus prayed to God, DO NOT STAY LONG.**
9. **Send twelve men, they making a sign, that they would have men that had beards, and who are skillful in writing.**

Lamentation

Here begin the Lamentation of Jeremiah the Prophet
Aleph. How doth the city sit solitary, that was full of people!
How is she become as a widow!
She that was great among the nations, and princess among the provinces,
how is she become tributary!
Beth. She weepeth sore in the night, and her tears are on her cheeks:
among all her lovers she hath none to comfort her:
All her friends have dealt treacherously with her, and they have become her enemies.
Jerusalem, Jerusalem, return unto the Lord your God.

Excerpt from Menasseh ben Israel, "The Relation of Antonio Montezinos," in *The Hope of Israel* (London: Moses Wall, 1652), 12–14; translation of lyrics of the Don Juan de Lienas Lamentatio (Lamentations of Jeremiah, 1.1–1.2).

QUESTIONS

1. What evidence does Montezinos's account provide that the Indigenous peoples he met were Israelites?
2. The morning blessings said by Jewish men typically bless God for not having made them a woman, a gentile, and a slave. How did Montezinos adapt this prayer while in prison, and what is the significance of the changes he made?
3. What do the cities of Jerusalem and Tenochtitlan have in common? How does thinking about Tenochtitlan as Jerusalem change the story of European invasion of the Americas?
4. In Aztec cosmology, each "century" was composed of a fifty-two-year cycle, at the end of which the world could possibly be destroyed. A "Binding of the Years" (*xiuhmolpilli*) ceremony was performed at each cycle's end to start the new cycle. The main event was the "New Fire Ceremony," which took place at the Templo Mayor in Tenochtitlan, three blocks from Don Lienas's convent. How do rituals like those of Tisha B'Av, *xiuhmolpilli*, and Holy Week help make sense of tragedy and connect past and present?

NOTES

1. Perelis, *Narratives from the Sephardic Atlantic*, 1, 9, 99.
2. Mendoza de Arce, *Music in Ibero-America*, 35.

7

A Jewish Proselytizer in the New World

NEW SPAIN, 1649

Brian Hamm

After establishing tribunals in Mexico City and Lima in 1569, the Spanish Inquisition established a third New World tribunal in 1610 in Cartagena de Indias on the northern coast of South America. The jurisdiction of this third tribunal covered portions of both the Viceroyalty of Peru (New Granada) and the Viceroyalty of New Spain (the Caribbean and Venezuela). One of the *conversos* put on trial by the Cartagena Inquisition was Luis Méndez Chávez, a merchant from Portugal. His journey to the Americas was circuitous. According to his account, he was kidnapped by the Dutch at sea sometime in the mid-1640s and taken to Holland. Accepting circumcision, he soon became an open member of Amsterdam's Jewish community. After a couple of years, he joined a slave-trading voyage that sailed to Guinea, then to Barbados, before landing in Nueva Barcelona in the province of Venezuela in November 1648. During the sixteenth and seventeenth centuries, the province of Venezuela was much smaller than the modern-day country of the same name. Authorities in Nueva Barcelona quickly arrested Méndez Chávez as a contrabandist. Spanish officials soon discovered, however, that Méndez Chávez was smuggling not just slaves but a chest of forbidden Jewish books and liturgical instruments.

Upon this discovery, he was brought before the nearby Cartagena Inquisition, accused of being both a practitioner and proselytizer of "the Law of Moses." In his defense, Méndez Chávez claimed that he became a Jew in Amsterdam only out of economic necessity. The books and instruments, he claimed, belonged to other Jews who had died in Guinea. These protestations failed to persuade the inquisitors, who found Méndez Chávez guilty, sentencing him to three years in prison, two hundred lashes, and exile from the Spanish Indies.

The trial of Méndez Chávez sheds important light on the early days of Sephardic presence in the Americas. Judging from Méndez Chávez's testimony, we can see that soon after the devastating shock of the 1645 rebellion of Portuguese planters in Dutch Brazil, which resulted in Portugal regaining control of the colony, many prominent members of the Sephardic community in Amsterdam began to search for new economic and spiritual markets in the Americas. To this end, several wealthy Jewish merchants, including Abraham Pereyra and Joseph Bueno, financed Méndez Chávez's voyage. Méndez Chávez testified that the Jewish books in his possession were donated by Menasseh ben Israel. This certainly seems plausible, as it is known that Amsterdam's famed rabbi had previously boasted about sending chests of Jewish books to Spain and Brazil.[1] In this way, Méndez Chávez's chest of books was part of a larger transatlantic Jewish project of proselytizing *conversos* to bring them in line with rabbinic norms.

The case of Méndez Chávez underscores how the Jewish history of the Americas comprises locales where Jews were allowed to worship openly, as well as regions in Spanish America that contained significant *converso* populations. Furthermore, despite the absence of openly practicing Jewish communities in Spanish America until the nineteenth century, the voyage of Méndez Chávez suggests that some *conversos* in the Spanish Indies may not have been as ignorant of rabbinic Judaism as is often assumed.

PRIMARY SOURCE

In the city of New Barcelona on the eleventh of April 1649, . . . the following books and items were placed before me, the present notary, in a wooden box:

1) **Firstly, a bound book of half-folio size, written in block letters, 293 folios in length, according to the number of the last folio, and on the first folio, the title is as follows: *The Bible in the Spanish tongue, translated word for word from the authentic Hebrew by very excellent scholars, seen and examined by the Office of the Inquisition with privilege from the Most Illustrious Lord Duke of ~~Fab~~ Ferrara.***
2) **Another book of half-folio size, much shorter than the previous one, in Hebrew or Greek letters, with two copper handles, and with red coloring to the outside edges of the pages.**
3) **Another book of quarto size, bound in white parchment, written in block letters, 379 folios in length, according to the number of the last page, and afterwards, it is followed by an index and all the folios that contain the said index are without numeration—and on the first folio is the title page which is as follows: Menasseh ben Israel, *This is the Conciliator, or the congruence of the places of Scripture that appear to be opposed to one another, drawing on ancient as well as modern sages with great expertise and faith. . . .***
4) **Another book of quarto size with 195 numbered folios, not including an index, and the title page on the first folio reads as follows: *Second Part of the Conciliator. . . .* Authored by Menasseh ben Israel, Hebrew theologian and philosopher, and [published] in Amsterdam in the house of Nicolás de Rabestein in the year 5401 [1640/41].**
5) **Another much smaller book, bound in white parchment, 240 numbered folios in length, including all indices. It is entitled as follows: *Second Part of the Siddur,***

containing Passover, Shavuot, Sukkot, and Yom Kippur. . . . Printed with diligence and expense by Isaac Franco in Amsterdam, 4 Adar Veadar 5372 [February 7, 1612].

6) Another book of octavo size, 223 folios in length, including all indices. It is titled as follows: *The First Part of the Siddur, containing the prayers for each day, each Sabbath, and each month, those for private and congregational fasts, and those for the festivals of Hanukkah and Purim. . . .* Printed with diligence and expense by Isaac Franco in Amsterdam, 4 Adar 5372.
7) Another book of octavo size, bound with black sheepskin boards, 477 numbered folios in length, not counting those of the cover. The title page reads as follows: *Order of prayers of the month . . . and the order of Hanukkah, Purim, and Passover, Shavuot, Sukkot, Yom Kippur, and Hoshana [Rabbah]. . . . Kahal Kadosh Talmud Torah of Amsterdam.* Printed with diligence and expense by Jonah Abarbanel and Ephraim ~~Franco~~ Bueno in the house of Nicolás de Rabestein in the year 5401.
8) Another book of octavo size, bound in white parchment, 222 numbered folios in length. The title reads as follows: *Order of the Five Ta'aniyot* [fast days] *of the year. . . .* Printed by the order of the gentlemen, Ephraim Bueno and Jonah Abarbanel, in the house of Menasseh ben Israel, Amsterdam, in the year 5390 [1630].
9) Another book of quarto size with 625 numbered folios, bound in white parchment and entitled as follows: *A Treasury of Laws that the People of Israel are obligated to know and observe with two very copious tables.* Dedicated to the very noble, magnificent, and prudent gentlemen of the Parnassim of this venerable Kahal Kadosh, and written by Menasseh ben Israel. Printed in the house of Eliahu Aboab in the year 5405 [1645].
10) Another book of octavo size, bound in white parchment with 222 numbered folios and titled as follows: *Order of the Five Ta'aniyot of the year.* Printed by the order of the gentlemen, Ephraim Bueno and Jonah Abarbanel, in the house of Menasseh ben Israel, Amsterdam, in the year 5390 [1630].
11) Another book of octavo size with boards bound in sheepskin, 327 numbered folios in length, and titled as follows: *Order of Rosh Hashanah and Yom Kippur, translated in Spanish, and with the Selichot . . . Talmud Torah Beth Jacob.* Printed with diligence and expense by David Abenatar Melo, 1 Sivan 5377 [June 4, 1617], in Amsterdam.
12) Another small little book, bound in white parchment and in poor condition, the folios numbered until 547 and subsequently another set of folios follows that are numbered to 23. It is entitled: *Order of the prayers of the month, with the most necessary and mandatory of the three festivals of the year, as well as what concerns the fasts, Hanukkah, and Purim . . .* [Printed with] diligence and expense by Menasseh ben Israel, in Amsterdam, 1 Cheshvan 5397 [October 30, 1636].
13) A confession manual entitled: *Order of Selichot, Harbit, and confession of the malqut* in 7 folios.

- A scroll that they say [is] the Talmud as included in the proceedings
- A scapular as included in the proceedings
- A knife without a point as included in the proceedings

- **Straps of sheepskin as included in the proceedings**
- **Slices of wood as included in the proceedings.**

"Proceso de fe de Luis Méndez Chaves," Inquisition, 1620, Exp. 9, ff. 18v–21r—imágenes #92–97 en PARES, AHN.

QUESTIONS

1. What types of books did Méndez Chávez bring with him to Spanish America? What functions might they have served?
2. The inquisitors believed that Méndez Chávez had come to Spanish America as a Jewish proselytizer. What might *conversos* in this region have learned about Judaism from these books, if they had not been confiscated?
3. How did these items connect the *conversos* in Spanish America to the Sephardic Diaspora in western Europe?

NOTE

1. Nadler, *Menasseh ben Israel*, 80.

8

Criminal Case against María de Zárate for Judaizing

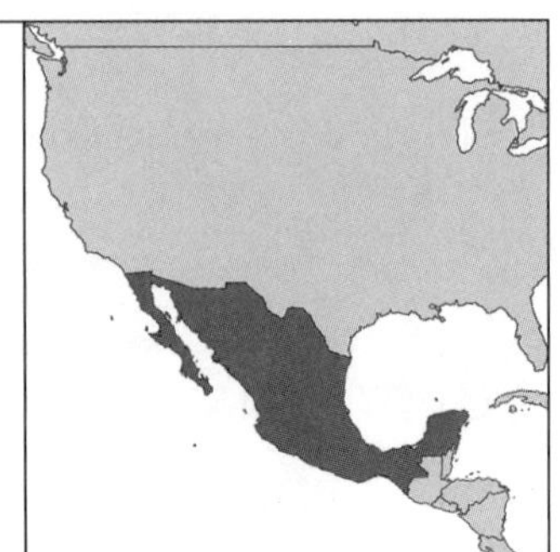

NEW SPAIN, 1656

Matthew D. Warshawsky

In 1656, María de Zárate faced the tribunal in Mexico City that convicted Luis de Carvajal the Younger in the 1590s. Although the tribunal did not close until 1820, it mainly investigated New Christians between the 1590s and mid-1600s. Unlike most people accused of Judaizing, María de Zárate was Old Christian, that is, without Jewish or Muslim ancestry; in fact, her great-great-uncle had authored discriminatory purity-of-blood statutes against Spanish *conversos*. But in Mexico, she married a secret Jew, Francisco Botello, and apparently adopted his forbidden religious practices. The section of trial testimony included here consists of Zárate's account of the conflictive family life that precipitated her arrest. Here she exercises the right of *tacha*, by which she attempts to discredit her principal accuser, her adoptive son José Sánchez (alternately called Jusepe or Joseph), by showing how bitterness, rather than her heretical behavior, motivated his allegation. Zárate further discredits Sánchez by emphasizing that he is a *mestizo*, that is, someone with mixed Spanish and Indigenous heritage.

Unlike the trials of Mencía de Luna (chapter 4) and Manuel Bautista Perez (chapter 5), which grew out of fears of a *converso*-led "Great Conspiracy," the trial of María de Zárate shows the Inquisition exploiting racial tensions and intrafamilial dysfunction. The willingness of José Sánchez to expose his family, including himself, to an Inquisition trial confirms that some individuals used this tribunal to express grievances whose roots were not religious but could be conflated with crypto-Judaism.

These words are not directly those of María de Zárate but rather those of the scribe who recorded them, but they are as close to her voice as inquisitorial protocol permitted. Her account shows how the Inquisition helped make racial distinctions, whether between Jews and Christians or between Spaniards and people with Indigenous ancestry. Just as many

Old Christians regarded their *converso* brethren as unassimilable, so too Zárate and her New Christian husband marginalized José Sánchez for his own supposedly impure lineage.

PRIMARY SOURCE

At the end of the aforesaid accusation [of crypto-Judaism], she [María de Zárate] said that everything in it is false, because she is, has been, and will be a faithful Catholic Christian with the favor of God, as a daughter, granddaughter, and descendant of such Christians. She believes firmly in the law of our Lord Jesus Christ, which she confesses is the only true law for the salvation of souls and in which she insists she lives and dies. She does not know nor had notice of anyone who keeps the Law of Moses, because she would have accused them in this Holy Office. Nor has she kept nor knows what it is. If she, insignificant and wretched, had fallen into it, she would have confessed when she entered as prisoner and would have sought mercy, as she requests [now], imprisoned without guilt, having not passed through her mind the crimes of which she is accused. All these accusations are false, which she presumes some mortal enemy has raised against her.

It seems to her that this person [who falsely accused her] can be none other than a youth named Jusepe, whose surname they say is Sánchez, who was born in the house of the mother of this confessant, and is a *mestizo*, son of an unwed *mestiza* woman whom the mother of this confessant raised. This *mestiza*, having given birth to her son, left him at the age of eight or ten months without reappearing anymore. Thus, this confessant took as her charge his upbringing, and she insinuated that he was an orphan, to exempt him from the shame of being the son of a *mestiza*. She took care of him, teaching him Christian doctrine and, paying a teacher, to read, write, and count, and clothing and feeding him as if he were her own child. Along with him, she had four nieces—Catalina, María, Ana, and Clara—daughters of her sister Ana de la Paz, and of Juan de la Serna, now deceased, a public scribe, as well as her sister, all living in her house in this city. About three years ago, Jusepe, who must have been 16, fell in love with her niece [Ana de la Serna], due to their being raised together. Treacherous, he impregnated her without this confessant, nor her sister, the mother of this girl, finding out until the day she gave birth, about which they became so upset that her sister thought she might lose her mind, especially upon discovering the author of this evil deed.

The two sisters always hid this situation from Francisco Botello [husband of María de Zárate], because if he had known, he would have killed Jusepe without hesitation. Nor did she throw out the said *mestizo*, keeping him in the house they had in the city, as in the one in Tacubaya, where they lived, where her sister went to give an account of all this, and to tell her that the *mestizo* through a priest sought to marry the girl. It seemed to her [Ana de la Paz] that the marriage should take place, given that her daughter was ruined, and without hope. And this confessant responded that the marriage should not occur, because she knew that Joseph was a *mestizo*, and as she knew who his mother was, it would be best to throw through a door the child whom Ana de la Serna had borne, and that Ana de la Paz whip her daughter to death for that destructive act, and inflict many blows on Joseph, and give notice to a judge so that they would send him to China [that is, to the Philippines to row galley ships, a common punishment] so that a *mestizo* dog not marry her daughter and insult her lineage.

All this seemed fine to her sister, and she returned to Mexico City very determined to execute this plan. But it did not happen that way because she had a change of heart and married her daughter to the *mestizo*, to whom she told all that this confessant had said against him. It happened that after they had been married without the knowledge of this confessant for about four months, they went to Tacubaya to enjoy themselves. . . . Botello went up there, and surprised to see them together, and the *mestizo* with their daughter in his arms, asked his niece what she was doing with the lad, and what child was that. Ana, surprised, did not satisfy him [with her response], due to which Botello maliciously went after the *mestizo* and could not catch him, and returned in search of the girl, who had hidden herself.

Furious, Botello related the case to this confessant, and she, to calm him, told him how Ana and Jusepe were married, because Jusepe had taken the girl from her mother's home, and without her knowledge they had married. This confessant had not informed Botello, to avoid upsetting him, due to which Botello became so angry that he swore that he ought to kill Jusepe. He asked Ana de la Paz how she could not be ashamed to have married her daughter to a *mestizo* dog and thief, who had robbed him, keeping the money that [Botello] sent him to collect. And although Botello went in search of the *mestizo*, he did not find him because the young man had hidden in the house of Juana la Taborda, a *mestiza* neighbor from Tacubaya. Ana de la Paz with tears and this confessant with entreaties tried but could not calm Francisco Botello. Rather, he said that wherever he might see the said *mestizo*, he would kill him for the evil act of taking away from his house a niece of his wife.

And [this declaration] having been read to her, she said it was well written, and having been reprimanded she was ordered to return to her cell, and she signed it.

Causa criminal de fe contra doña María de Zárate, mujer de Francisco Botello, por judaizante (1656), Inquisición, vol. 25-1500, 159–162, AGN. Courtesy of AJHS, Collection I-3, Mexican Inquisition Collection, 1572–1914.

QUESTIONS

1. What circumstances motivated José Sánchez to denounce to the Inquisition his adoptive mother?
2. How can we reconcile María de Zárate's devotion to her husband with her unkind treatment of their adoptive son?
3. Given that Zárate maintained that she was not a secret Jew just as persistently as Sánchez insisted she was, how should we interpret the validity of their claims?
4. What does this document teach us about the reliability of Inquisition testimony?

9

Aboab da Fonseca and the Dutch Rescue of Recife

BRAZIL, 1656

Laura Arnold Leibman

Even as communities of crypto-Jews began to take hold in the Spanish and Portuguese colonies, Jews from Amsterdam were able to establish the first openly Jewish community in the Americas, in Recife (Brazil). The religious leader of that community was Rabbi Isaac Aboab da Fonseca, who composed the poem "Zekher asiti leniflaot El" (A memorial to the wonders of God) in the 1650s. Born in Portugal in 1606, Aboab and his family escaped to Amsterdam around 1612 to avoid the Inquisition. In Amsterdam, Aboab became a star pupil of Isaac Uziel. When Aboab arrived in the Dutch colony of Recife in 1642, he was already an important kabbalist. Under his leadership, the Jewish community of Recife became the largest Jewish American community, with somewhere between one thousand and fourteen hundred Jews.

Unfortunately, starting in 1645, the Portuguese attempted to recapture Recife with a naval blockade. As a result, the colony suffered terribly, and many people went hungry. The Jewish community, many of whom, like Aboab, were from *converso* families, were terrified of what might happen to them if the Portuguese won. Aboab's poem addresses the Portuguese attack on Recife and calls on Jews to repent and praise God. The town eventually was lost to the Portuguese in 1654, and Recife's Jews fled. Some returned to Amsterdam, but others migrated to other ports in the Americas, building Jewish communities in Suriname, Barbados, Jamaica, New York, and Newport.

"Zekher asiti leniflaot El" reflects Aboab's mastery of Judaism, Hebrew, and poetics. The poem imitates a famous medieval poem by Rabbi Yehuda Halevi called "Mi Khamokha" (Who is like Thee?), which is about Jews' deliverance from Haman in ancient Persia. Aboab's poem has three main sections, and the excerpt included here is from the first section. In lines 1–11, Aboab calls out to and praises God. He then proceeds to give his account of the attack on Recife in 1646 (lines 12–27). He concludes by modeling how he himself is to blame for what he has suffered during the Portuguese assault, calls on his people to repent, and reminds his congregation of God's greatness.[1] Aboab's poem exemplifies Jewish mysticism's impact on early Jewish American literature. As a kabbalist, Aboab believed that this world provided evidence of God's providence; hence, almost every word in his poem is written to draw connections between his present and the Hebrew Bible. Likewise, Aboab uses the story of Purim as a mirror for understanding the sufferings of Recife's Jews. In Aboab's retelling, the multiracial leader of the 1646 rebellion, João Fernandes Vieira, becomes Haman, the Persian court official who tried to destroy the Jews in the book of Esther. Likewise, when racializing Vieira, Aboab uses the biblical category of "Kushite," that is, the Nubian peoples who controlled the Nile Valley between 2450 to 1450 BCE, a period that overlapped with the time when Jews were believed to have been enslaved in Egypt, even though it is more likely that Vieira's ancestors came to the Americas from western Africa via the triangle trade.

Before 1825, most American Jews who wrote poetry lived in the Caribbean. They tended to be influenced by Hebrew, Spanish, and Portuguese literary traditions, not the English canon. Jews adapted tradition to meet challenges they faced. Aboab's poem memorializes the knowledge and artistry that some early American Jews brought to the colonies.

PRIMARY SOURCE

Who is like Thee? There is none like Thee! Who can be compared to Thee? None can be compared with Thee!
Almighty God *Ha-shem* High above all high Dweller of my sanctuary
His name I mention in the congregation of my faithful, with song we shall call out to Him
For my sins I have been cast to the distant land, the words of His Prophets He fulfilled in me
Though I have fallen from the heavens on high to the depths, fortunate is the man who has strength
Waves of the sea have passed over my head, and yet my soul yearns [for God]
And I have not been false to my Holy One, and I am faithful to His covenant
My soul clings after Him, my footsteps have not strayed from His footsteps
My soul laughs [Yitzchak, the poet's name] (in joy) with His words, therefore I shall set my hope upon Him
Mention that His name is Powerful, He did not awaken all His anger
He raised the crown for His nation, the nation He chose as His portion
And it was, in the [year] five thousand, and four hundred and six [1645–1646]
I feared His strong sword, for we sinned against Him
Remember, O *Ha-shem*, the king of Portugal, whose anger rolled upon us
Make them, their nobles, like chaff (before fire [Psalms 83:14]), the military leaders of the king [of Portugal]

He [the king] plotted in his heart to destroy my [fellow] survivors, to send his fire against my precious ones
He sent legions to pursue my legions, his heart gathered evil to itself
He set his trap against me in his address with a lawless man [João Fernandes Vieira]
From the dung heap he elevated him [João Fernandes Vieira] to protect and strengthen him
Haughty, malicious sinner, a reputed villain, his mother is of the Kushite families.
As for his father, he did not know if he [João Fernandes Vieira] was his son, hence he deemed it a curse on himself.
He [João Fernandes Vieira] gathered large amounts of silver and gold to rebel against me and to stand against me with trickery
And my leaders did not believe the trickery, [but] one who makes light of the matter gets hurt by it
[Those that spoused His cause] were dark people [Ethiopians] . . .
He [João Fernandes Vieira] ran to hide in the forests, clouds hid him
All kinds were mobilized in pursuit, [but] until the arrival of his pale soldiers
Whom the king had commissioned to rendezvous, he was like a wild ass all by himself.
Lament with a doleful lamentations, it was for Jacob (Israel) a day of wrath.
Who will fast as a help, to pacify Him?
My flesh trembles from fear of my enemies, for in my days of plenty, I forgot my Creator
The serpent and the evil inclination led me astray, I [did not] understand him
In his eyes, my heritage was as a speckled bird of prey [Jeremiah 12:9], his counsel consuming my flesh
But he did not remember that *Ha-shem* is with me, [I am] a desired dwelling place for Him.
Fear and trembling came upon me; pangs have taken hold of me as the pangs of a woman in labor,
For the oppressor lies in wait to take my soul, a toiling soul he toils for himself
The oppressor hunted my steps and my soul is painfully bitter, the day my enemy conquered the sea
He thought he would slay my children in my midst with thirst, God will not wish to forgive him
The redeeming angel will diligently listen, he will cry out "woe" upon the exile of Ariel [Lion of the Divine]
Alone from his God, Oh Israel, he cried and He was gracious to him
Oh, Shepherd of Israel, Awesome Almighty, to Your nation send redemption
To his cities and [from] his adversaries, destruction, for they cannot overcome us
The One Who dwells forever, Mighty of mighty ones, turn again to Your nation, who are being sold for a small gain,
Place over their [the enemy's] heads the cursed waters, would You hold back from helping them?

Prepare their hearts and make your ears listen, we will be joyous and happy in the glory of Your exultation
Your own right hand can save you, and the poor who have no helper.

Three works by Isaac Aboab (1605–1693), copied by David Franco Mendes, Amsterdam, 1728, Ets Haim Library, Amsterdam, EH 47 C12. Translation by Tzvi Fischer and Shlomo Truzman, edited by Laura Arnold Leibman.

QUESTIONS

1. Leading up to the 1645 revolt, Dutch Calvinists increasingly blamed the Jewish community for Recife's problems. Whom does Aboab blame for the problems that Jews in Recife face?
2. The book of Esther links Haman's cruelty to his descent from Amalek. What role does lineage play in Aboab's attack on João Fernandes Vieira (lines 19–27)?
3. How can poetry help us understand history? What are its limits as a historical source?
4. Why do you think Aboab keeps embedding snippets from biblical texts into his poems?
5. How does Aboab's description of Vieira as someone whose "mother is of the Kushite families" racialize him differently than merely saying the leader is part African? How does Aboab's racialization reframe the power dynamic between Vieira and the Jews of Recife?

NOTE

1. Leibman, "Poetics of the Apocalypse," 41.

10

The Purchase of Slaves and a Sefer Torah

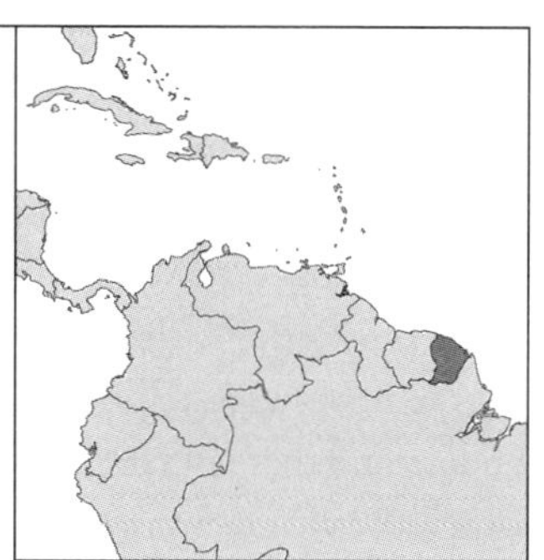

CAYENNE, 1658, 1663

Michael Waas

In 1654, when the Portuguese recaptured Recife, one portion of the refugees returned to Amsterdam. They did not stay there long. Jacob Jessurun Pinto (alias Paulo Jacomo Pinto) began negotiating with the Dutch West Indies Company to resettle poor and destitute Jewish refugees in a new colony called Cayenne near the colony of Essequibo (Nova Zeelandia) on the so-called Wild Coast of South America. For other Jews in Amsterdam, like Abraham Vaez, the proposed colony represented both a religious and business opportunity. In 1658, with the assistance of Pinto and the Mahamad of Amsterdam, Vaez purchased the rights to three African slaves through the Dutch West Indies Company, and in 1663, the Mahamad tasked Abraham, along with Ishac Bravo and Ishac da Costa, with bringing a Sefer Torah, in all of its dress and accoutrements, to Cayenne. This donation reveals the religious importance of Amsterdam's Jewish community for the Portuguese Jews in the Americas. Throughout the early colonial era, Amsterdam served as a spiritual mother and patron to congregations in the Dutch and British colonies.

These two documents shed light on an otherwise forgotten individual whose story was rather emblematic of the movement of the Portuguese Jews in the seventeenth century. Born in Portugal under the Christian name Francisco, Abraham Vaez (alias Vaz Lopes) had much in common with the refugees from Recife. Like Rabbi Aboab and many other members of the *Nação* in the seventeenth century, Vaez had been born to a Judaizing New Christian family. When he was a young child, his family left Portugal for Spain, where they soon ran afoul of the Inquisition in Madrid. After his grandmother was punished and released, the Vaez family escaped northeastward to France in the early 1630s and the Netherlands in the early 1640s, where they began to practice Judaism openly. Sadly, Cayenne does not appear to have been the opportunity Vaez hoped for. The settlement of Jews in the colony only survived a few years before the French expelled them in 1666. Some refugees from Cayenne ended up establishing early Jewish plantation towns in Suriname, but the

Vaez family went back to Europe. By 1675, Vaez's widow, Ester Delgada, and two orphaned young children, Jacob and Ribca, were once again living in Amsterdam and had to get by with *tzedakah* (charity) from the community.

These sources complicate the story of how a man, who was himself a refugee, was a small-scale participant in the African slave trade for a colony settled mainly by Portuguese Jewish refugees from Dutch Brazil. Jewish involvement and participation in the African slave trade has often been either ignored by the Jewish community or amplified to antisemitic proportions.[1] Jewish participation in the slave trade was neither as large as some people have suggested nor as minimal as others have wished; however, it is important to understand that Jews in the Americas were not divorced from the world and the context in which they lived. Sources in later chapters will continue to underscore the importance of slavery and race in the early story of American Judaism.

PRIMARY SOURCES

Purchase of Slaves

[In Dutch] The Director over the Wild Coast, Nova Zeelandia, is ordered to deliver by lottery, to Abraham Vaaz, three slaves, as specified by sex and age in the receipt below, deed signed in the Assembly of Commissioners over Nova Zeelandia, 25 June 1658.

I, Abraham Vaaz, undersigned, declares he received from the Director of the Wild Coast, five slaves, to wit, two men, one wife and zero youngsters and he asks Paulo Jacomo Pinto or my [illegible] on the merit of this declaration to pay for these slaves to the Commission members mentioned above. Signed, Wild Coast, 2 September 1658

Signature: Abraham Vaez

Received by me, the undersigned, 450 pounds Flemish, 3 January 1659

Signature: Abraham Colyn

[In Portuguese] Draw attention to that for the three Africans above delivered to Mr. Abraham Vaez with one on the account of the gentlemen of the Mahamad of the Holy Community of Amsterdam, on the account of Mr. Abraham Pereira, the [other] two, on the account of Mr. Isaac Vaz Lopes [brother of Abraham] on his own account.

Signature: Paulo Jacomo Pinto

Transport of Torah and Torah Ornaments

The term of a Sefer Torah with its ornaments, that was given to the gentlemen, Ishac Bravo, Ishac da Costa, and Abraham Vas, to take to Cayenne.

We say to Ishac Bravo, Ishac da Costa, and Abraham Vas, that have received from the Gentleman of the Mahamad of the Holy Community of Amsterdam, a Sefer Torah and parchment with its green silk, a banner of white Damasco [a pattern] and a cape of the same white Damasco, with its *Rimonim* of metal, to take to Cayenne at whichever time that the

same gentlemen of the Mahamad [say], that we serve to satisfy the above . . . [and] we agree to the task and indeed we sign this in Amsterdam on the 20th of Sivan 5423 [June 25, 1663]. Signed by Ishac Bravo, Ishac da Costa, and Abraham Vaez.

Receipt for the Purchase of Slaves, unknown, 1658, SAA 334, Inventory 1350, scan 6, IAPIG; Escamoth A, Mahamad of PIC Amsterdam, 1663, SAA 334, Inventory 19, p. 519, IAPIG. Translations by Michael Waas (Portuguese) and Ton Tielen (Dutch).

QUESTIONS

1. In the sixteenth through eighteenth centuries, Portuguese Jews were persecuted by the Inquisition in Europe and the Americas. Yet Jews also participated in slavery. What can being simultaneously persecuted and oppressors tell us about Portuguese Jews' lives?
2. Notice the Amsterdam Mahamad's connection to the purchase of the slaves and the transportation of a Torah to Cayenne. What does this say about the importance of Amsterdam for American Jews?

NOTE

1. Nation of Islam, *Secret Relationship between Blacks and Jews.*

11

Doña Teresa Confronts the Spanish Inquisition in New Mexico

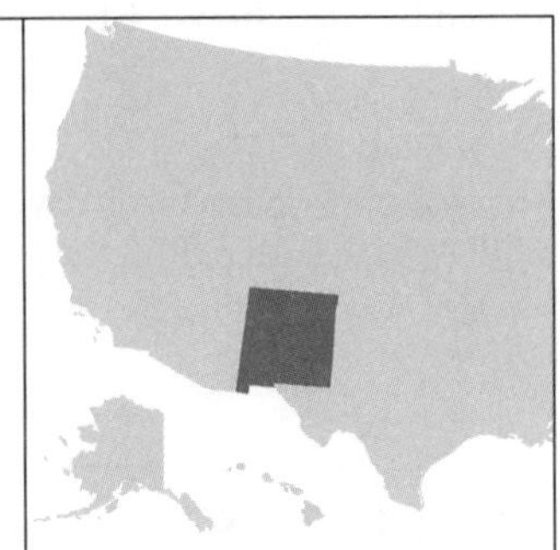

NEW SPAIN, 1662

Frances Levine

While the main tribunals of the Inquisition were in Mexico City, Lima, and Cartagena, large portions of the southwestern United States were originally part of the colony of New Spain; hence, people living in these territories were subject to the laws of Inquisition. In what is now New Mexico, local Franciscan friars (who, along with Dominicans, had been appointed by the pope as inquisitors) at first appeared unconcerned about Judaizing. As a consequence, families of *conversos* strategically settled in this region. The church's disinterest ended abruptly in the summer of 1662, however, when New Mexican Governor Bernardo López de Mendizábal and his wife, Doña Teresa Aguilera y Roche, found themselves among a small group of citizens arrested by local officials of the Holy Office of the Inquisition on charges of practicing Jewish rituals in secret. But were they guilty?

The evidence against the group was supplied by clergy and neighbors as well as their household staff living in the small, isolated Spanish colony in Santa Fe, New Mexico. Don Bernardo's administration (1659–1661) was a contentious one, and from the time he left Mexico City to assume office in Santa Fe, his style and actions heightened tensions between civil and ecclesiastical authorities. More to the point, these tensions stemmed from struggles over power and economics that pitted Franciscan friars—the teachers and enforcers of Catholicism—and New Mexico's governors against each other for control of the limited resources of the province of New Mexico. Tensions intensified in the summer of 1662 when officers of the governor's own staff and local members of the Inquisition clergy seized the governor and his wife. Doña Teresa met several times with her inquisitors before she even learned of the charges against her. On October 26, 1663, fourteen months after her arrest in the palace, the inquisitors presented the forty-one articles containing the accusations against her. The accusations were based on the testimony of twenty-six persons who were not identified to her.

The story of Doña Teresa and her husband illuminates how tricky it is to interpret Inquisition documents and identify who was "really" a Jew. Historians differ on whether the evidence presented is enough to argue persuasively that Governor Bernardo López de Mendizábal and his wife, Teresa de Aguilera y Roche, were secretly practicing rites and rituals of Judaism. Some believe the governor and his wife's social networks included families having documented crypto-Jewish connections. Alternatively, the case may show instead how the Inquisition was used as much to punish political enemies and social deviance as to enforce religious adherence.

The excerpt also reveals how inquisitors located "Jewishness" in daily practice and the home as well as churches or synagogues. Allegations against Doña Teresa, for example, included that she bathed and changed clothes and linens on Friday nights—possible signs of Jewish practices—and that she read books in other languages and laughed over their contents. Neighbors and servants condemned her for her education, her worldly manner, and her personal hygiene. Eventually Doña Teresa sued the Inquisition office in Mexico City to recover her confiscated goods and pleaded with them to clear her name. But the Inquisition left her in limbo, neither proving that she was guilty of practicing Jewish rites nor clearing her of the charges.

PRIMARY SOURCE

Summary of the Charges Against Doña Teresa de Aguilera y Roche Presented on October 26, 1663 Before the Inquisitor Inspector, Holy Office of the Inquisition, Mexico City

I, Dr. Rodrigo Ruíz de Cepeda Martínez y Portillo, who hold the office of prosecutor, do appear before Your Honor in keeping with the full solemnity of the law and lodge a criminal complaint against Doña Teresa de Aguilera y Roche, here present, who declares herself to be a native of the city of Alessandria beyond the Po [River], the wife of Don Bernardo López de Mendizábal, and a prisoner in the secret prison. And I declare that although the aforesaid is a baptized and confirmed Christian and as such has enjoyed the privileges and prerogatives that good and true Christians ought to and do enjoy, she has apostatized from our holy Catholic faith and the law of the Gospel, wickedly and perfidiously contravening the declaration, she made at her holy baptism and turning to observance of the defunct and obsolete law of Moses, observing the rites and ceremonies of Judaism and believing that she would be saved thereby, and committing other offenses indicative of her impudence and apostasy . . . and punishing a member of her household because she observed her performing acts of piety, of which I accuse her in general, as well as of impenitently and perjuriously denying her guilt. . . . I accuse her forthwith, both of observing the rites and ceremonies of Judaism, and . . . believing that the prohibition of meat on Fridays and fast days is not binding, and as a practitioner of witchcraft, . . . condemning the said Doña Teresa to the greatest and most severe penalties imposed on such offenders by the common law . . . and declaring that her property has incurred confiscation from the day on which she committed the said

crimes of Judaism, and applying the said property to His Majesty's treasury, as punishment of this accused and as an example to others. Furthermore, should my intent not be considered adequately proven, and not otherwise, I ask and beseech Your Honors to order that the said Doña Teresa de Aguilera y Roche be put to the question with torture, to be continually and repeatedly applied to her person until she may fully declare and confess the truth. I ask that justice be done, and I swear as prescribed by law that this my accusation does not spring from malice, and if I should do so more formally, I submit it as so done, and in all things necessary, etc.

> **Signed,**
> **Dr. Rodrigo Ruíz de Cepeda Martínez y Portillo [followed by his *rúbrica*, a symbol unique to the author of the document that is incorporated into his signature and signifies that he was the official author of the document]**

Ramo Inquisición, vol. 596, AGN. Translation by María Magdalena Coll, Heather Bamford, Heather McMichael, and John H. R. Polt.

QUESTIONS

1. What evidence does the Inquisition use to support its claim that Doña Teresa is a heretic?
2. What, according to the Inquisition, are the characteristics or attributes of Jewish religion, culture, and identity?
3. After closely reading the summary of the charges, can you identify other reasons why Doña Teresa was suspected by powerful people in the colony?
4. Compare the charges against Doña Teresa, Mencía de Luna (chapter 4), and María de Zárate (chapter 8). Where does each tribunal locate the core of Jewish belief?

12

Biblical Scenes on Gravestones

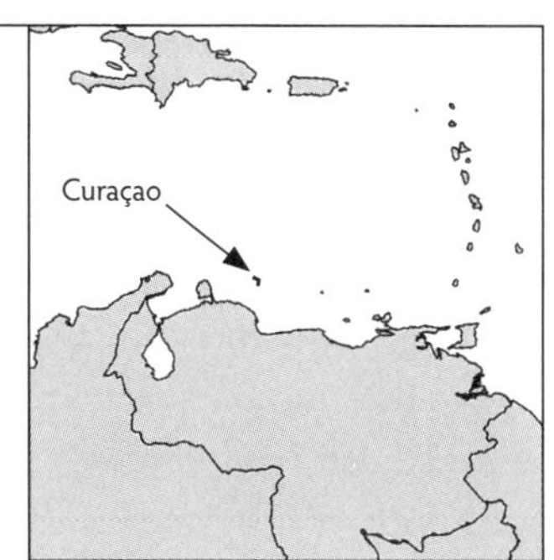

CURAÇAO, 1717, 1726

Laura Arnold Leibman

One Jewish community that benefited from the arrival of refugees from Recife was the community located on the small, arid island of Curaçao, off the coast of modern-day Venezuela. The refugees joined a group of about seventy Sephardic men, women, and children from Amsterdam who came to Curaçao in 1656 when the West Indian Company granted a charter to settle on the island. Curaçao's early economy was built on intercolonial commerce and smuggling, unlike Recife, Suriname, Barbados, and Jamaica, which were sugar colonies. The island served as an entrepôt between the Americas, Africa, and Europe: that is, goods were stored there before being exported to other locales. The island played a crucial role in the Dutch West India Company's importation of enslaved people from Africa and their exportation to the Spanish Americas. While most Jews had a house in the main port of Willemstad near the Mikve Israel (Hope of Israel) synagogue, wealthier members of the congregation owned *landhuizen* (country estates) spread around the island. Prior to emancipation, enslaved people were the primary workers on these estates. The island's oldest Jewish cemetery was built at the edge of three such estates, Blenheim, De Hoop, and Rozendaal, located across the bay from Willemstad.

Curaçao's Jewish community prospered between the 1670s and 1820, such that the island began to replace Amsterdam as the main patron and authority for other Jewish American communities. The size of Curaçao's community is reflected in the Old Jewish Cemetery, which has between fifty-two hundred and fifty-five hundred burials. The gravestones provide important insights into the lives and deaths of American Jews. As the art historian Rochelle Weinstein has noted, "The Jewish tombstone is a stone of memory: a metaphor for immortality. It is an extension of life and identity beyond the personal and into the future; a monument to be encountered by friends, colleagues, and descendants."[1] Gravestones do more than just mark burials: the style and shape of the stone reflect the mourner's hopes for what the dead will experience in the world to come (*olam ha-ba*). The word in Hebrew for a cemetery reflects the traditional Jewish belief in the resurrection of the dead: it is a *beit haim*—a house of life.

The Jewish community of Curaçao and its gravestone art influenced every other early American Jewish settlement. Curaçao's cemetery is famous for its elaborate stones with biblical scenes, angels, and the hand of God cutting down the tree of life. The images found on these tombstones should be compared to later examples found in this volume, by considering the types of images each Jewish community included on its stones, as well as how the languages American Jews have used changed over time.

While cemeteries contain memorials to both rich and poor, the two men whose stones are included here, Elijah Namias de Crasto (d. 1717) and Isaac Haim Senior (d. 1726), were both wealthy leaders of Curaçao's early Jewish community. Isaac and his wife, Rachel, donated the *tebah* (reader's platform) when the fifth synagogue was built in 1703. The Senior and Namias de Crasto families lived in Willemstad near the Mikve Israel synagogue. In addition, Isaac owned a famous *landhuis* named Habaai.

PRIMARY SOURCES

Grave
of the Cut short
Virtuous Man Elijah
Raphael Namias
de Crasto was collected
to his people on the
21 of Nisan of the year
5477
that corresponds to 2
of April of year 1717
May his soul enjoy
Glory

Gravestone of Elijah Raphael Namias de Castro, Beit Haim Blenheim, Curaçao, 1717. (Photograph by Laura Arnold Leibman)

"Look now to heaven" [Genesis 15:5]
"a crown of glory shall she deliver to you" [Proverbs 4:9]
"to David for a remembrance" [Psalms 38:1; 70:1]
Grave
of the Cut short, Virtuous
and very capable man Isaac
Haim Senior who in the flower of his
age passed to a better life on the second day
Of Passover, 16th of Nissan
In the year 5486 having
Suffered infinite
Martyrdoms of illness
"May his soul be bound up in the bond of eternal life"
[1 Samuel 25:29]
"Mine eyes are ever toward the Lord; for He shall pluck
my feet out of the net" [Psalms 25:15]

Gravestone of Isaac Haim Senior, Beit Haim Blenheim, Curaçao, 1726. (Photograph by Laura Arnold Leibman, 2008)

QUESTIONS

1. What languages do these gravestones use, and what is the significance of the language chosen?
2. The gravestone of Elijah Namias de Crasto depicts a scene from the Hebrew Bible in which the prophet "Elijah went up by a whirlwind into heaven" (2 Kings 2:11). Why do you think Elijah Namias de Crasto's family included this scene on his tombstone?
3. At the top of Isaac Haim Senior's gravestone are three men: King David with a harp (Isaac's father's name was David), Rabbi Aboab da Fonseca of Recife (see chapter 9), and the patriarch Abraham "looking to heaven" (Genesis 15:5). What inspiration might mourners looking at the stone have drawn from these three men?
4. At the bottom of Isaac Haim Senior's tombstone, a family mourns at his deathbed, including an enslaved boy who stands in the doorway. Why do you think this boy was included?
5. What do these gravestones tell us about death in the Jewish community of Curaçao?

NOTE

1. Weinstein, "Sepulchral Monuments of the Jews of Amsterdam," 72.

13

Poems of Love and Longing

NEW YORK, C. 1720

Laura Arnold Leibman

While some refugees from Recife returned to Amsterdam and others settled in the Caribbean, twenty-three men, women, and children were captured by mercenaries and ransomed north in the colony of New Amsterdam. Ten years after their arrival, the English took control of the colony and renamed it New York. Early Jewish records from New York are rare, but nearly one thousand pages of records survive related to one early New York Jew: Nathan Simson. Simson lived in New York between 1706 and 1722. Discrimination impacted what jobs were open to Jews, so Simson, like many of the community's early leaders, was a merchant. Most early Jewish immigrants were Sephardic, and hence when the community rented a house on Mill Street in which to hold services, they used the Sephardic rite. Despite Simson's Ashkenazi origins, he served as the president of Shearith Israel from 1720 to 1721, overseeing a congregation of nearly two hundred people.[1] Simson had already returned to England when the congregation built its first synagogue in 1730 with the help of 272 ounces of silver from congregation Mikve Israel in Curaçao.

Simson's account books provide insights into everyday Jewish life. Around 1709, Simson shared rooms with Jacob Franks in a kosher boarding house run by his niece Meriam Levy and her husband, Moses Hart.[2] Later Simson set up his own house, and his household included at least two women: Ester, the servant maid; and Risha, his cook. Most likely it also included unpaid labor, as in 1709 Simson owned an enslaved child, and later he was involved in the slave trade. After Nathan's death in London in 1725, his wife, Dyfie, sold another enslaved child to the Crown.[3]

Simson's manuscripts help us understand Jewish ideas about sex and sexuality in the eighteenth century. While most of Simson's papers deal with business, the poems included here are an exception and provide an intriguing counterpart to what is generally known about Simson. The poems appear in a notebook with Jewish religious verse on the right side in one handwriting and bawdy love poems on the left side written in another script. Even the religious poems, however, are quite erotic, and they include the Song of Songs (*Shir ha-shirim*). The left-hand poems are signed by Solomon Jechiel Levy, while the right pages are unsigned, albeit possibly in the handwriting of Nathan Simson.

There seems to have been both business and friendship among Simson, his roommate Franks, and Levy. Franks, for example, agreed to pay Levy sixty-five pounds and eight shillings when Abigail Levy promised to marry him and another sixty-five pounds when the marriage ceremony was completed. If Franks did not go through with the marriage, the note was void. Perhaps Levy was a matchmaker? The poems, however, suggest other possible relationships between the men. The scholar Anne Lombard notes that male friendships were a crucial part of early American life. Among Christians in the northeastern colonies, understandings of male-male friendships were often based on Protestant values.[4] Might the Song of Songs, which is often read today as depicting an erotic relationship between the soul and God, have similarly influenced how colonial American Jews understood male-male friendships? Moreover, why did Simson use the version of the poem found in the Anglican King James Bible, rather than a Jewish translation?

Scholars have emphasized that queer identities have changed over time and that men have felt freer in the past to have homosocial relationships, even while being wed to women. Moreover, the homoerotic poetry collected by Nathan Simson is ambiguous. The ballad he includes is not original but is nearly identical to the anonymous ballad "The Unfortunate Lovers." Since ballads were an oral tradition, minor variations were common. Simson's collection of poems poses questions of interpretation for queer Jewish history about what should count as evidence of male-male love in the eighteenth century. Spelling, capitalization, and punctuation are maintained from the original.

PRIMARY SOURCE

[On the left side, in the hand of Solomon Jechiel Levy]
When my bonny Jockey left me, Sighing for him weel weight Man, & that surly Mars bereft Me: of my sprightly Companion: oh How Muckle [many] where my Sorrows, to Me Ere before Remained My Grief: on my cheeks the tears made furrows: Since he would not give my heart Relief. who is me Since Cruel fortune, has bereaved me of my Dear: I shall never have Joy for Certain, since to Me they are so severe: Jockey has My heart in keeping: let him go by land or sea: for his Absence I lay weeping, Yet can never happy be: When first bonny Jockey viewed me: he did strive My heart to gain: Muckle times still pursued me: begging love for to obtain; Jockey seemed so charming to me: that I could not him deny: but alas, it does undo me: that so soon I did comply. For as soon As I Consented, Jockey he was forced Away: I for sorrow Am tormented, Cause he Could no longer Stay; oh the grief that I lay under: In this world Can find no Ease: After Jockey I will wander, seek him out by land or seas; blithely I rose when the Cock Crew: putting on my hose & shoon [shoes]: & trudged along the way I knew: was the path Dear Jockey Run: when I saw the foaming billows: of Enraged neptune's wave: to my head the Sands made pillows, for I knew there was My Grave.

[On the opposite page in a different hand, presumably Simson's]
I rose up to open to my beloved and my hands dropped with myrrh and my fingers with sweet smelling myrrh upon the handles of the lock I opened to my beloved but my beloved had withdrawn himself and was gone my soul failed when he spake I sought him, but I could not finde him I called him but he gave me no answer The watchmen that went About the citie found me they smote me they wounded me the keepers of the walls took away my veil from me I charge you o daughters of Jerusalem if ye finde my beloved that ye tell him that I am sick of love what is thy beloved more than another beloved o thou fairest among women what is thy beloved more than another beloved that thou dost so charge us my beloved is wite and ruddy the chiefest among ten thousand his head is as the most fine gold his locks are bushy and black as A raven his Eyes are as the eyes of doves by the rivers of waters washed with milk and fitly set his cheeks are as A bed of spices as sweet flowers his lips like lilies dropping sweet smelling myrrhe his hands are as gold rings set with the beryll his belly is as bright ivory over laid with sapphires his legs are as pillars of marble set upon sockets of fine gold his Countenance is as Lebanon Excellent as the Cedars his mouth is most sweet yea he is all together lovely this is my beloved and this is my friend o daughters of Jerusalem wither is thy beloved gone o thou fairest among women wither is thy beloved turned aside that we may seek him with thee my beloved is gone down into his garden to the beds of spices to feed in the gardens and to gather lilies I am my beloved's, and . . . [continues on next right-hand page]

Invoices, receipts, journals, and freight books relating to the shipping business of Nathan Simson (1700–1720), Papers in Yiddish: London and New York, C104/13-14, TNA.

QUESTIONS

1. Why do you think Nathan Simson used a translation from the King James Bible (1611)?
2. Do you think this manuscript reveals how Simpson or Levy felt about other men? Why or why not?
3. What might the Song of Songs reveal about Jewish understandings of desire during this era?

NOTES

1. Ben-Jacob, "Nathan Simson," 31.
2. Ben-Jacob, 15.
3. Ben-Jacob, 18, 27–29; Oppenheim, "Will of Nathan Simson."
4. Lombard, *Making Manhood*, 46–47.

14

Marriage Contracts

SURINAME, 1720, 1729

Laura Arnold Leibman

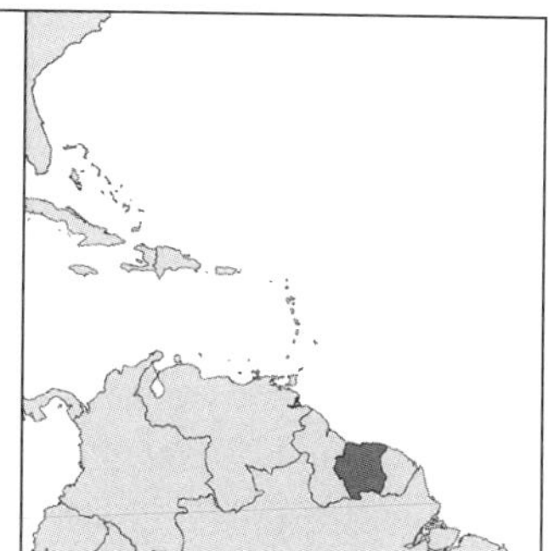

Another colony that benefited from the arrival of refugees from Recife was Suriname. These refugees, led by David Cohen Nassy (b. 1612), not only bolstered the colony's already existing Jewish population but brought with them knowledge and technologies for raising and processing sugar, which would become one of the colony's main crops. Jewish sugar production likewise played a key role in the formation of Jodensavanne (Jews' savannah), a semiautonomous Jewish plantation that was founded while Suriname was under English control (1650–1667). In addition to extending other privileges to Jews, the English gave them the right to practice Judaism openly, and construction was begun on the Beracha ve Shalom synagogue (1665–1671), followed by synagogues in the main port of Paramaribo. When the Dutch took control of the colony following the Second Anglo-Dutch War, Jewish rights and privileges expanded.

These rights along with the colony's demographics made Suriname's Jewish community exceptional. Between 1700 and 1820, Suriname along with Curaçao had one of the largest Jewish communities in the Americas. An initial impediment to the community's growth, however, was the lack of European Jewish women in the colony. The historian Aviva Ben-Ur notes that this gender imbalance made legitimate Jewish offspring scarce and encouraged Jewish men to convert children born to them by enslaved women. These conversions were regulated by Jewish religious leaders, and over time Suriname developed the largest multiracial Jewish community in all of the Americas. Ben-Ur suggests that by 1700, most Surinamese Jews would have had at least one African ancestor, even though racial laws classified many of these people as white.[1] One reason that people with African ancestors might be considered white was that marriage could change one's race: Jews who had only one African great-grandparent were considered white if their parents were legally married and a person of color if they were not. These laws mattered, as Jews of color had a second-class status of *congregante* in the colony's synagogues, while the category of *yahid* (full member of the congregation) was reserved for Jews who were deemed white.

Marriages, and marriage contracts, played a crucial role in defining race and regulating social status in Suriname's early Jewish community.

While both Suriname's High German (Ashkenazi) and Portuguese (Sephardic) synagogues were racially diverse, the documents included in this chapter appear in the congregational register books for the Portuguese Jewish synagogue. These books contain signed, unornamented versions of *ketubot* (marriage contracts) for all marriages in the community. The presence of these *ketubah* registers speaks to seventeenth- and eighteenth-century American Jews' incredible mobility. Most early American Jews lived in multiple ports during their lives, and men often cemented trade ties by marrying extended kin or trading partners' daughters from other ports. Even if their personal copy of a *ketubah* was lost in a fire, war, earthquake, or hurricane, early American Jews could still prove they were married by petitioning the synagogue where the ceremony was performed. Equally crucially, the *ketubah* registers proved that couples and hence their children were halachically (legally) Jewish. Marriage contracts helped define who belonged inside Jewish communities.

In Suriname, however, marriage contracts also defined levels of belonging. Suriname's marriage contracts did this by including racial information about couples. While registers from three other Jewish communities in the Caribbean (Barbados, Curaçao, Jamaica) similarly survived, only the Surinamese *ketubot* cryptically allude to the racial status of Jews of color by indicating that they are "emancipated" (that is free people of color). As the numbers of "emancipated" Jews grew, the synagogues instituted regulations that discouraged their full inclusion in communal life. Between the late eighteenth century and the 1830s, the Surinamese community demoted European Jews who married "emancipated Jews," assigning these European Jews the "same status as a mulatto."[2] Race was not self-evident or uncontested: some European Jewish men protested when they felt their wives' race was assigned improperly.

PRIMARY SOURCES

Ketubah of Gabriel Cardozo and Rebecca DaCosta

In a favorable sign. On the second of the week, the 10th of the month of Nissan, in the year 5481 since the creation of the world, according to the reckoning which we are accustomed to employ here in Paramaribo, located along the Suriname River, how the bachelor Gabriel, son of the master, David Cardozo of blessed memory, said to Miss Rebecca, a virgin, daughter of the master Baruch DaCosta may he rest in Eden, "Be my wife according to the law of Moses and Israel. I will cherish, honor, support and maintain you in accordance with the custom of Jewish husbands, who honestly cherish, honor, support and maintain their wives. I hereby set aside for you the settlement of the virgins, two hundred silver zuzim, which accrues to you according to the law of Moses and Israel, together with your food, clothing and necessities, and I undertake to live with you as husband and wife according to universal custom." And Miss Rebecca, this virgin consented to become the wife of the bachelor Gabriel Cardozo. Her belongings that she brought unto him from her family's home, such as land property, slaves, maid servants, cattle, houses, and house furniture, brought in

a total worth of 20,000 guilders in local currency. All this the said bridegroom accepted, and consented to add from his own property the sum of 10,000 guilders. Thus, the nuptial contract that both parties agreed upon that was written and attested to by two kosher witnesses became effective on April 26th in the year 1720 according to the Gregorian Calendar. And thus, said the aforementioned groom, "The responsibility of this marriage contract, this wedding dowry, and this additional sum, I take upon myself and my heirs after me, so that they shall be paid from the best part of my property and possessions that I have under heaven, that which I now possess or may hereafter acquire. All my property, real and personal, even the mantle of my shoulders, shall be mortgaged to secure the payment of this marriage contract, the wedding dowry, and the addition, during my lifetime and after my lifetime, from the present day forever." Gabriel the bridegroom has taken upon himself the responsibility of this marriage contract, of the wedding dowry and the addition made there to, according to the restrictive usages of all marriage contracts for the daughters of Israel, in accordance with the institution of our sages of blessed memory. It is not to be regarded as an indecisive contractual obligation or as a stereotyped form. We have effected the legal formality of a binding agreement between the bachelor Gabriel, the bridegroom, and his bride Rebecca this virgin, and we have used a garment legally fit for the purpose, to strengthen all that is stated above. And everything is valid and confirmed.

Attested Ab. R. Atias Gabriel Cardozo Baeza [groom]
Attested Ishak Pinto

This is the wedding agreement accorded between the bachelor Gabriel mentioned above and the bride Rebecca mentioned above duly written and contracted between the two marrying parties written by a local scribe and legally completed, and considered legally binding, and everything is valid and confirmed, according to the customs of Israel. If G-d forbid, the groom dies before his bride, whether he left offspring or not, the bride shall receive the full sum as indicated in the *ketubah*, namely 30,000 guilders in local currency as stated above. However, should the bride mentioned above predecease her groom mentioned above, leaving behind no offspring, the said groom shall return the bride's heirs half of her dowry's contribution, namely 10,000 guilders in local currency. If she dies leaving behind offspring, her husband inherits all in conformance with our law, that the husband inherits all that is his wife's. This instrument is legally appropriate for establishing a transaction, and everything is valid and confirmed.

Gabriel Cardozo Baeza Ab. R. Atias Ishak Pinto

Ketubah of Ismael Judeu and Hannah de Mattos

B'siman tov (in a good sign)

On the fourth day of the week, eleventh day in the month of Sivan in the year five thousand four hundred and eighty-nine from the creation of the world according to the count which we account here in Suriname. How Yishmael Yehudi, the emancipated, said to Chana, the emancipated, daughter of Gabriel de Mattos, "Be to me a wife according to the Law of Moses and Israel. I, with the help of heaven, will work, honor, feed, support and clothe you, in accordance with the ways of Jewish husbands, who work, honor, feed, support and clothe

their wives honestly. And I will give to you the settlement of one hundred silver zuzim that is due to you by Rabbinic Law, and your food, clothing, and other needs. And I undertake to live with you as husband and wife according to universal custom." And Chana this bride consented to become the wife of the Yishmael Yehudi, the above-mentioned groom. This is the dowry that she brought to him either in slaves, cattle, and jewelry: one thousand eight hundred florins, coins of the above-mentioned locale. The above-mentioned groom accepted and added of his own another nine hundred florins, thus she will have her *ketubah* of two thousand seven hundred florins, coins of the above-mentioned locale. And thus, said to us the above-mentioned groom: "The security and severity of this *ketubah* document do I take upon myself, and upon my heirs after me, to be collected from the totality of the best assets and acquisitions that I have beneath all the heavens, that I have acquired and that I will acquire in the future, secured assets (real property) and nonsecured property. All these shall be security and bound to collect this *ketubah* document. I accept this upon myself and upon my heirs after me, like the security and severity of all *ketubah* documents that are in accordance with the custom of Jewish women, that are made according to the enactment of our S[ages, of] b[lessed] m[emory]. It is not to be regarded as an indecisive contract nor as a blank document form." And we have acquired from Yishmael Yehudi our above-mentioned bridegroom to bequeath to his bride, the above-mentioned Chana de Mattos, for all the conditions that are written and expressed above, with a vessel that is appropriate to acquire with it a complete and final acquisition. And everything is valid, clear and established.

[witnesses' signatures] [groom's signature]
Manuel de Solis Ismael Judeu
Jos. De Meza

These are the conditions that were made between themselves, the above-mentioned bridegroom and bride with all the power of the commitments that are customary among the Jewish people. That if the above-mentioned bridegroom shall pass away s[ilence] and [peace] (heaven forbid) in the life of the above-mentioned bride, whether she has living children from him, or if she does not have living children from him, she shall take all the sum of her *ketubah* in a payment. This is two thousand seven hundred florins, coins of the above-mentioned locale. If the above-mentioned bride shall pass away before the above-mentioned bridegroom without living children, then the above-mentioned bridegroom will return to the heirs of the bride half [of the dowry] that she brought in to him, which is nine hundred florins. If she [should] pass away and leave living children, her husband will inherit her [portion]. As is the law of our Holy Torah that a husband inherits his wife's portion. And we have acquired from them. And everything is valid, clear and established.

[witnesses' signatures] [groom's signature]
Manuel de Solis Ismael Judeu
Jos. De Meza

Ketubah of Gabriel Cardozo and Rebecca DaCosta, Nissan 10, 5481 [April 7, 1721], 1.05.11.18, no. 408, NPIGS, translation by Shlomo Truzman; Ketubah of Ismael Judeu and Hannah (daughter of Gabriel) de Mattos, Sivan 11, 5489 [June 8, 1729], 1.05.11.18, no. 408, NPIGS, translation by Tzvi Fischer.

QUESTIONS

1. What similarities do you notice between the two *ketubot*?
2. Although both *ketubot* include slaves in the dowry, this was unusual. What do you think their inclusion here tells us?
3. Marriage contracts also include an initial pledge by the groom of either two hundred zuzim if the bride is a virgin or one hundred zuzim if she is a widow, convert, divorced, or otherwise known not to be a virgin. How much is the pledge in each contract? What do you think we learn about the couples and their marriages from each of these amounts?
4. Why do you think that the second *ketubah* refers to the bride and groom as "emancipated Jews"? What is the difference between the way the *ketubah* racializes the couple and the way Aboab racializes Vieira, in chapter 9?
5. What rights does the marriage contract give to women?

NOTES

1. Ben-Ur, *Jewish Autonomy in a Slave Society*, 155.
2. Vink, *Creole Jews*, 285–286.

15

Nidhe Israel Synagogue Complex and *Mikveh*

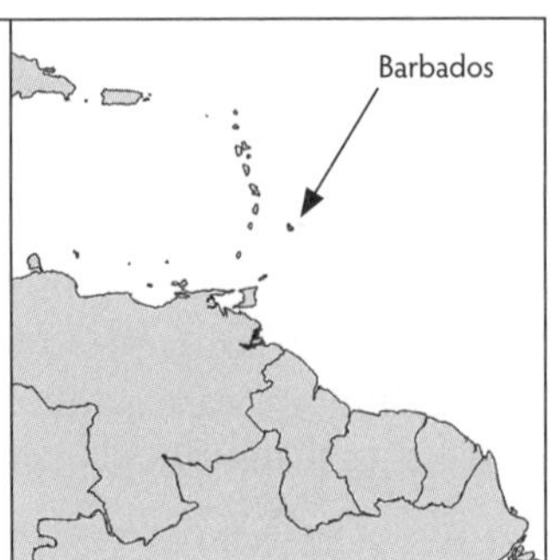

BARBADOS, 1654–1806

Laura Arnold Leibman

A third Caribbean community that was founded in part by the refugees from Recife was the Jewish community of Barbados. Although in early years there was a second synagogue up the west coast in Speightstown, most Jews settled in the main port of Bridgetown near the Nidhe Israel synagogue. Like most early synagogues in the Atlantic world, the Nidhe Israel synagogue was part of a synagogue complex that consisted of the synagogue itself, housing for synagogue staff members, a school, and the ritual bath. In the Barbados instance, there were four houses for staff members: one for the rabbi or hazan, one for the ritual bath attendant (*banadeira*), the kosher slaughterer (*shochet*), and the guardian of the complex (the *shamash*).

One of the unique features of this complex is that similar to Anglican churches on the island, it included the community's cemetery. This was extremely unusual for Jewish communities, largely because members of the priestly caste (Kohenim) are not supposed to step in cemeteries due to death impurities. Walkways and walls around the cemeteries made it possible for Kohenim to attend the synagogue, school, and ritual bath, despite the proximity of the graves. In 1806, Abraham Brandon, the president of Nidhe Israel, asked that a plat (map) be made of the synagogue complex in response to disputes with neighbors who felt some of the property actually belonged to the neighboring Quaker cemetery.

Although the synagogue complex survives today, most of the main buildings have had to be rebuilt several times due to hurricane damage, particularly from the Great Hurricane of 1780 and the 1831 hurricane. Despite these rebuilds, the 1806 plat included here clarifies that the present synagogue has the same proportions as the pre-1831 building. This diagram also indicates where precisely the dwelling houses of the *shamash*, rabbi, bath attendant, and ritual slaughterer were located. In 2007, an archaeological team discovered the remains of the island's ritual bath below one of these houses. The stones used in the bath suggest that it dates to the 1650s, when the synagogue complex was first established. After the house above the bath collapsed in the 1831 hurricane, knowledge of the bath's location was lost. One item not indicated on the plat is the Nook, where disgraced members of the community were buried. This section is mentioned in the community's record books, but it was not known where it was located. Scholars originally thought it was the cemetery section on the plat to the left of the Quakers Burial Ground, as shops were later built on top of it, contrary to Jewish law. Later excavations revealed, however, that many important members of the congregation were buried here, so it is unclear why the congregation allowed shops to be built above their graves.

The map and the photo of the excavated ritual bath help us understand the importance of women's rituals in early America and the continuity between European and American traditions. Although ritual baths can be fed either by rain water or by underwater sources, like most colonial ritual baths, this *mikveh* (ritual bath) is fed from an underground stream. After being excavated, the bath immediately refilled with clean, fresh water. This bath would have been primarily used by married women in the community in order to spiritually cleanse themselves following menstruation and childbirth, as well as by men and women following a conversion. The synagogue minutes indicate that in certain instances, unmarried women of color who had relationships with Jewish men immersed in the bath with the help of the *banadeira*, who lived in the house above the bath. When the Mahamad found out about this practice, they censured the men and fired the female bath attendant. Other than the ritual bath discovered in Recife, the Barbados ritual bath is the oldest *mikveh* in the Americas. It is an important reminder of the importance that early American Jews placed on following Jewish laws and rituals.

PRIMARY SOURCES

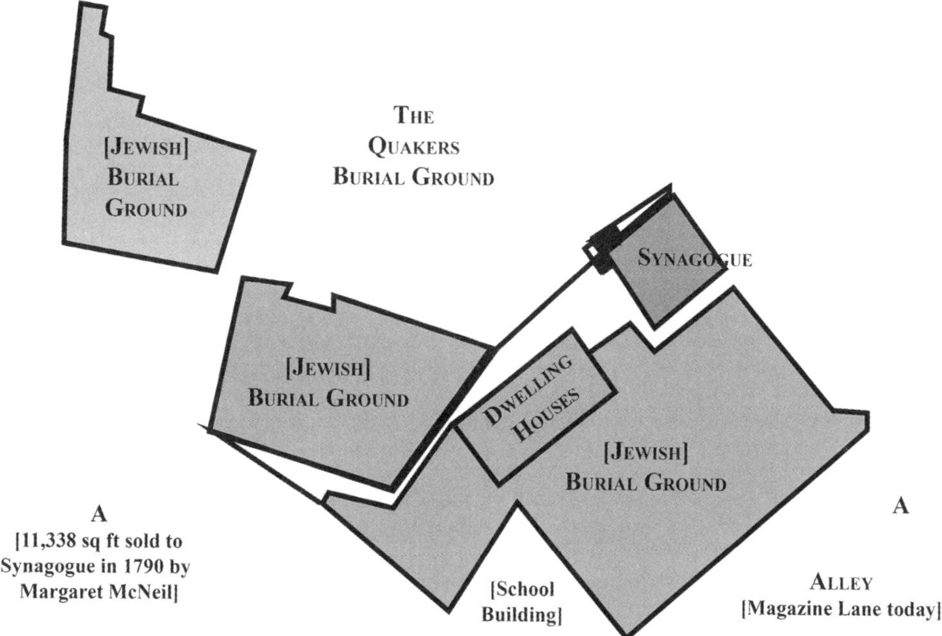

Plat courtesy of Nidhe Israel Synagogue Complex, 1806. (Redrawn by Laura Arnold Leibman)

Interior of the Nidhe Israel ritual bath, c. 1650s. (Photograph by Stevan J. Arnold, 2010, JAWDB)

QUESTIONS

1. What do you think might have been placed in the *mikveh*'s wall niche and why?
2. What are the advantages and disadvantages of placing a bath that gets rid of spiritual impurities next to the cemetery, which is itself a major source of impurity in Jewish tradition?
3. How were notions of purity in life and death used to create community boundaries in Barbados?
4. What is the benefit of having all major Jewish buildings in a central complex?

16

A Gender-Bending Jewish Runaway

NEW FRANCE, 1738

Noam Sienna

In 1627, when Armand Jean du Plessis (Cardinal de Richelieu) founded la Compagnie de la Nouvelle-France (Company of New France), he ensured that non-Catholics could not immigrate to French colonies. Consequently, there were no synagogues or openly Jewish communities in French colonial Canada. Yet Jews and people with Jewish ancestry still managed to travel to New France. One of the earliest known Jewish arrivals was a sailor named Jacques La Fargue. La Fargue's stay was short but notorious, and his *procès-verbal* (detailed certified report written by a magistrate or police officer) is translated here. This report describes the interrogation of a Sephardic runaway, born as Esther Brandeau (Brandon/Brandão) and living under the name Jacques La Fargue. Brandeau was born in Bayonne near the French border with Spain. Bayonne was one of the main Portuguese Jewish communities in western Europe and had strong ties to both Amsterdam and London. Even though prior to 1723 the Bayonne community was not able to worship Judaism openly, it had a congregation and cemetery dating to the mid-1600s. Jewish immigrants from Bayonne settled in other French colonies such as Martinique and Saint-Domingue as well as British and Dutch ports.

Although "gender-bending" narratives are common in literature of this era, it is rare to find one with a Jewish protagonist. The unusual circumstances under which this was recorded—the presence of a Jew in New France requiring official intervention—hint that many similar stories probably have gone undocumented and unrecognized.

Narratives such as the story of Esther/Jacques used to be understood simply as women "cross-dressing" as men purely for economic or professional reasons and thus were not valued as sources for thinking about Jewish approaches to gender diversity. With today's emphasis on nonbinary genders, however, we can now see how in some cases, for individuals assigned the gender identity of female at birth, life as a man may have seemed more authentic, as well as opened new social opportunities or allowed the person to pursue marriage or partnership with women. In certain cases, these individuals understood themselves to be men in every way. Whether we understand stories like this one as analogous to transgender, nonbinary, butch, or some other identity, they are important testimonies to how Jews navigated the changing expectations around gender roles as they moved between social, religious, and political communities.

PRIMARY SOURCE

15th September, 1738.

This day, before the undersigned, Commissaire de Marine, in charge of Quebec's seafaring police, appeared Esther Brandeau, aged about twenty years, who embarked at LaRochelle as a passenger, dressed in boy's clothes, under the name of Jacques La Fargue, on the vessel "St. Michel," Sieur de Salaberry, commander, and declared her name to be Esther Brandeau, daughter of David Brandeau, a Jew, trader, of Saint Esprit, diocese of Daxe, near Bayonne, and that she is of the Jewish religion; that five years ago her father and mother placed her on a Dutch vessel [under] Captain Geoffroy, in order to send her to Amsterdam to one of her aunts and to her brother; that the vessel having been lost on the bar of Bayonne, in the moon of April or May, 1733, she was happily brought safe to shore with one of the crew, that she was received by Catherine Churiau, a widow living at Biaris; that two weeks thereafter she started to dress as a man for Bordeaux, where she shipped as a boy, under the name of Pierre Mansiette, on a vessel commanded by Captain Bernard, destined for Nantes; that she returned on the same vessel to Bordeaux and there shipped again in the same capacity on a Spanish vessel [under] Captain Antonio for Nantes; that on reaching Nantes she deserted and went to Rennes where she took service as a boy at the house of one Augustin, a tailor, where she remained six months; that from Rennes she went to Clissoy where she took service with the Recollets as a servant and to run messages; that she remained three months in the convent and left without warning for St. Malo, where she found shelter at the house of a baker named Seruanne; that she next went to Vitré to get a place there and entered the service of Sr. de la Chapelle, an ex-captain of infantry; that she left the situation because her health rendered her unable to watch the said Sr. la Chapelle who was always sick; that when returning to Nantes, and when one league from Noisel, she was taken for a thief and confined in the prison of Noisel aforesaid; that she was set free, after twenty-four hours, because it was found that a mistake had been made; that she then went to La Rochelle, where assuming the name of Jacques La Fargue, she took shipping as a passenger on the said vessel, "St. Michel."

Upon which declaration we called upon the said Esther Brandeau to state for what reason she had so concealed her sex during five years. Whereupon she said: That when she escaped from shipwreck and reached Bayonne she entered the house of Catharine Churiau, as above stated, that the latter made her eat pork and other meats the use whereof is forbidden among the Jews, and that she thereupon resolved not to return any more to her father and mother in order that she might enjoy the same liberty as the Christians.

Whereof we have drawn up this present as our *procès-verbal.* And the said Esther Brandeau hath signed with us, on the day and in the year aforesaid.

Collated,

(Signed) Varin

Procès verbal de l'interrogatoire d'Esther Brandeau, September 15, 1738; translation by Joseph Marmette, "Report on French Archives," in *Report on Canadian Archives*, ed. Douglas Brymner (Ottawa: Maclean, Roger, 1887), xxxi–xxxviii, republished in RT, 124–125.

QUESTIONS

1. Why did Esther/Jacques choose to live as a man?
2. Is this best understood as a story about gender, a story about movement, a story about religious freedom, or something else?
3. How did Jewishness shape Esther/Jacques's life and choices?
4. How does the Commissaire de Marine understand Esther/Jacques's gender? What methods does he use to assert that understanding? Is he a trustworthy source?
5. What pronouns should we use to discuss Esther/Jacques? What are the advantages or disadvantages of the different possibilities?

17

Petition Solicited by the Jamaican Assembly

JAMAICA, 1750

Dana Rabin

Individual Jewish settlers in British-controlled Jamaica matured into an organized Jewish community during the 1670s. In Port Royal, they benefited from the town's ethnic and religious diversity along with an official colonial policy of religious tolerance. Still, they contended with popular anti-Jewish sentiments along with a local policy of discriminatory taxation. By the eighteenth century, Jamaica had one of the largest Anglo-Jewish communities outside of London. Euro-American Jews made up 5 percent of the white population of Jamaica in 1680, rising to 9.5 percent in 1720 and 7.5 percent in 1740.[1] That same year, Britain's Parliament passed the Plantation Act, allowing the naturalization of colonial subjects who had lived in any American colony for at least seven years. The act exempted Jews and Quakers from the requirement of both the oath testifying to their profession of Christianity and the certificate of communion. Yet Christian planters and merchants in Kingston objected to granting Jewish colonists the vote. They petitioned the Jamaican Assembly, enumerating their fears and anxieties about Jewish suffrage. The island's white, Christian petitioners feared they would be outvoted by the Jews and stripped of all their rights and decision-making power. They warned that the Jews would imperil their religion and property. Thus, in 1750, when Abraham Sanches (naturalized in 1742) tried to vote in a Jamaican election, he was turned away.

When Sanches was turned away from the polls, he petitioned the Jamaica Assembly. The Assembly then sought petitions on the subject from three different parishes on the island. Petitions were used on both sides of such political debates to air grievances and seek redress from Jamaica's representative body. These legal documents provide insight about definitions of subjecthood in this eighteenth-century slave society, about the relationship between London and its colony, and about Jews' knowledge of the law. They allow us to listen in on debates about whiteness. In the eighteenth century, whiteness on the island was defined in the context of a thriving transatlantic slave trade and stood at the intersection of discourses of class, gender, sexuality, ethnicity, and religion. Whiteness signaled the extent to which people were thought to be eligible for the rights and privileges of subjecthood. Over the course of the second half of the eighteenth century, a legal category of whiteness emerged, with male Anglicans of English heritage and middling status as its normative, "core," subjects. Those who did not fit the profile as core subjects used the courts and law to try to secure rights for themselves. These petitions record a debate at the intersection of religious and racial difference.

Defining whiteness as both a cultural concept and a legal category was essential to the process of making difference, setting the limits of equality, and, ultimately, creating empire. This source provides insight into how issues of race, citizenship, and freedom in eighteenth-century Jamaica pertained to Jews. In a slave society where the number of enslaved Blacks far outnumbered free whites, and attempts to recruit new white immigrants were ongoing and generally unsuccessful, the petition asserts that Jews were not white and that granting Jews the full rights of citizens would dissuade white immigrants from settling in Jamaica. The petition is useful for the study of American Jewish history because it illustrates how age-old antisemitic tropes associated with European history were reinvented in the eighteenth-century Caribbean and used to inscribe racial and religious hierarchies. At the same time, Jews and others who were excluded from rights holding used the law to claim rights.

PRIMARY SOURCE

Friday 12 October, 1750

A petition of the Christians, freeholders, and other inhabitants, of the town of Kingston . . .

. . . A petition presented by one Abraham Sanches setting forth, that he . . . had been rejected as a freeholder, at the poll . . . and, he . . . being duly naturalized, and having a considerable freehold, was entitled to vote . . . as any of his majesty's liege subjects. . . .

. . . The petitioners humbly apprehend, that the said Sanches is a Jew . . . and could neither take the freeholder's oath, nor give a vote . . . unless he first became a Christian. . . .

That the people called Jews are a transient people, so widely differing . . . and so repugnant in their principles of government . . . and so abhorred for their behavior, that they have not been able to obtain a share in the legislature of any country upon earth, since they renounced their right of government to the governor Pontius Pilate . . . in order to destroy, and put to the most cruel and ignominious death, Jesus Christ, the lord and savior of mankind: . . . though a mulatto of the fourth descent may vote at elections, yet the Jews (many of whom are mulattoes of that degree) are . . . absolutely excluded from that privilege, it being expressly enacted, that they, the said mulattoes, shall enjoy all the privileges and immunities of his majesty's white subjects of this island, provided that they are brought up in the Christian religion. . . .

That the people called Jews, from the time of William the Conqueror to Edward I, were . . . as absolutely the slaves and property of the king, as the African negro slaves are of their masters the planters in this island; . . . the petitioners . . . apprehend, if the Jews are admitted into the legislature of this island . . . , they [the island's Christians] must inevitably

be ruined in those things they hold most dear and sacred; *viz.* their religion, liberty, lives, and property; . . . that the Jews, in all countries, look on themselves as under the power of the chief magistrates, rather than under the laws and government; . . . so that, admitting the Jews to vote at elections would . . . throw such a weight into the scale of power in the hands of a chief magistrate, . . . so that they [Christians] would be reduced to the most abject slavish state, of being obliged to sit like insignificant cyphers, and see themselves out-voted by the Jews:

. . . If the people called Jews are admitted to vote at elections, every election will be obstinately contested . . . seeing the Jews have, in all countries, been so addicted to creating broils, affrays, quarrels, and even massacres. . . . That admitting the Jews in this island . . . to vote at elections, will . . . defeat the measures the legislature hath taken, or shall take, to people this island with whites, and not only prevent white Christians to come and settle in this island, but also prove the destruction of those already settled in it; . . . even Christianity itself may be brought into contempt, and Christian people forced from this island, to seek shelter elsewhere. . . . And therefore praying that they may be heard . . . against the prayer of the said Sanches's petition.

"Veneris, 12° Die Octobris; Anno 24° Georgii II (di) Regis, 1750," *Journals of the Assembly of Jamaica* 4 (1745–1756): 246–247.

QUESTIONS

1. How many times is slavery mentioned in the petition? How is slavery defined in each instance?
2. According to the petitioners, what are the reasons that Jews should not be able to vote?
3. According to the petitioners, what is the relationship of Jews to the government and governing?
4. On the basis of the petition, how was whiteness defined in Jamaica in 1750?

NOTE

1. Fortune, *Merchants and Jews*, 47–49.

18

Sermon by Samuel Mendes de Sola

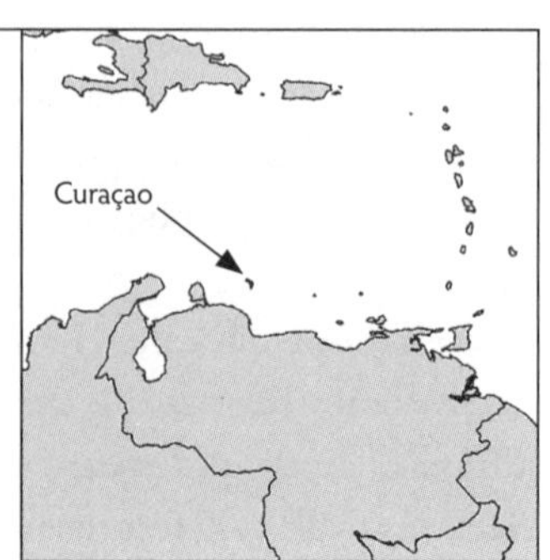

CURAÇAO, 1750

Julia R. Lieberman

In 1745, Hakham Samuel Mendes de Sola arrived in Curaçao to lead congregation Mikve Israel, in its beautiful, sixth synagogue. The Jewish community was near its peak of two thousand Jews, or about half the island's white population.[1] Sadly they were completely divided due to conflicts between members of wealthy families, disputes over inheritances, and the building of the Neve Shalom synagogue by a second congregation, across the bay in Otrobanda. While the conflicts preceded Hakham Mendes de Sola's arrival, they were exacerbated by his confrontational character and his habit of taking sides on disputes and publicly shaming those who opposed him. The sermon printed here, however, was delivered to celebrate the historical moment when the community had found a way to stop the bitter arguments between factions.[2]

Unlike the lay leader of Neve Shalom, Mendes de Sola represented rabbinical authority that the other congregation lacked. Typically, men who led early American synagogues were given the Hebrew title "hazan" or "hakham." Of the two, hakhams were better trained and had more knowledge of the Talmud. Mendes de Sola gained this training despite being born in Lisbon, Portugal, around 1699 to a New Christian family. His father, Luis Mendes de Sola, a tobacco merchant originally from the Portuguese city of Trancoso, was imprisoned by the Portuguese Inquisition of Coimbra between 1703 and 1706 after being accused of practicing Judaism in secret. Consequently, around 1709, Luis and Samuel fled to Amsterdam and were later joined by Samuel's mother, Brites Mendes, and his five brothers. There, they all returned to the Judaism of their forefathers. Samuel was educated at Amsterdam's famous Ets Haim Yeshiva and completed his rabbinic studies in 1724. A year after, he married Lea de Josua Israel. His acclaimed oratorical skills led the Amsterdam Sephardic community to send Mendes de Sola to Curaçao in 1745. He died on the island in 1761.

This sermon provides a rare window into the largest Jewish community in early America as well as insights into Sephardic preaching practice. Most seventeenth- and eighteenth-century records of congregation Mikve Israel have disappeared. Mendes de Sola's sermon reveals the congregation's delicate balancing of local secular authorities, rabbinical jurisdiction, and the power of the Mahamad. This can be seen in the sermon's dedication to Prince William of Orange-Nassau, who interfered and issued a decree to help resolve the conflict. Thus, unlike the sermon given in Newport, Rhode Island, in 1773 by Hakham Isaac Karigal (chapter 27) for the holiday of Shavuot, Mendes de Sola's sermon addresses community problems as much as religious ideals despite being in front of an audience that included non-Jews. Mendes de Sola's sermon also relies just as heavily on the Greek philosophy of Aristotle as it does on the Torah. His use of philosophy is a good reminder that Sephardic education in Amsterdam and Curaçao required students to learn poetry and philosophy as well as the Torah and Talmud.

Mendes de Sola's sermon helps us understand how religious ideas and practices were transferred to and around the Americas. Initially, the Amsterdam Sephardic community and its institutions served as a model and sent rabbis and other religious personnel to Curaçao. By the 1700s, however, Mikve Israel had become the most important of the Jewish congregations in the Americas, a transition signaled by the arrival of the hakham.

PRIMARY SOURCE

A dedication to the Stadtholder . . . Prince of Orange and of Nassau Stadtholder, Hereditary, Governor, Captain, and Admiral, General of the United Provinces. . . . With the submission of a humble son, and with the consideration of a faithful patriot, I come to your feet, your serene highness, not to offer but to pay, not to dedicate but to return. . . .
With profound respect
[I am] your most humble servant
Semuel Mendes Solla

Curaçao January 1, year 1751

[The Sermon's theme (Isa. 63:7–10]:]

G-d's kindness will I proclaim as the praises of G-d, in accordance with all that G-d has bestowed upon us and the abundant goodness to the House of Israel that he has bestowed upon them in his compassion and in His abundant kindness. . . .

An exordium addressed to the audience: Consisting among others of members of the "National Church of the Island" Wigboldus Rasvelt, preacher of the National Church of this island, and the illustrious men, Philip Schonenboom and Pieter de May Lourensz, dignified regents of the said Church. [He also thanks a long list of people, including the members of the Amsterdam Mahamad.]

What a happy day [is today] when . . . we are all triumphant over the most important of our soul's enemy, . . . the disagreement that for so long was among us, . . . the law of honor that under the sight of such a supreme G-d asks us to reconcile with our neighbors. . . . My effort today will be to show the ways we should find so that this peace will last forever and

this reconciliation will be long lasting. To this end, I will divide my discourse [sermon] into two parts. In the first part I will demonstrate that we have to stop the hatred that we [until now] had for one another. In the second part we will see that in order to stop the hatred we must forget the grievances that our next-to-us inflict upon us. G-d help us all with his divine help and [G-d help] me prove such an important point, and [you] my audience be persuaded of such an important matter.

[The sermon proper:]

Point I

Today, my first endeavor is to show that we have to stop our hatred and transform hatred into love and affection. I know too well that this commandment [to love] has against it not only our natural repulsiveness but also the strength of special reasoning [which is that] the object of love, said the philosopher [Aristotle], has to be good, [and as] the enemy is not good; therefore, the enemy cannot be the object of our love. Let reason and truth reply. Or, instead of them, I will respond and reply.

I agree that the object of our love has to be good, however, not only do I disagree [with the second part] that those we call enemies are not good, but I will prove that they are good. The enemy even at his most hostile is good in relation to ourselves because he purifies our virtues and our vices; our enemy's censorship uncovers our faults, makes obvious our defects, makes public our vices and the fear of this censorship, the knowledge of these faults corrects more vices than the love of virtue. If gold in the cupel purifies its carats, virtue purifies itself from the persecution, injuries, insults, offenses and injustices that the enemy does to us, hence because of our enemies we get to correct many vices and practice many virtues.

Now, supposing that abandoning hatred and loving our enemies is in itself or for itself right, I will propose today two reasons that will persuade us that our enemies are worthy of love. G-d willing, the reasons will be effective, but to make them so I will base the reasons on two excellences that will prove to us the necessity that we have to love our enemies. . . .

[De Sola discusses the virtues of *honra* (honor) and *valentia* (bravery). He then discusses the dilemma of wanting to avenge grievances.]

I have concluded the first part of my discourse and have demonstrated that we have to let go of grievances because by forgiving [them] we carve for our nobility the best crowns, and we prepare for our bravery the most glorious trophies.

Point II

Let us now [discuss point 2] where we will see how important it is to forget grievances in order to let go of hatred.

Let us take as an example two aggrieved and offended brothers [in the Bible], the first Esau, aggrieved by his brother Jacob. We are all familiar with the reasons for their grievances and I do not need to go over them here. What I will point out is that Rebecca, their mother, asked her son Jacob to flee and told him these words (Gen. 27:43–45) "*So now, my son, heed my voice and arise; flee to my brother Laban [to Charan], and remain*

***with him a short while until your brother's wrath subsides . . . and he forgets what you have done to him.*"**

If Rebecca's only intention was that Jacob would flee until his brother was placated, only the first clause of the verse would be needed: *until your brother's anger subsides*, but why does she try to send Jacob to live far away until his brother forgets? For the one who forgets, would it not be enough to be placated? [My response is] no, because Rebecca was considering (and rightly so) that while Esau could be placated, one could not be certain about the punishment Jacob would receive, as long as Esau did not forget the aggravation. Let us consider the same [situation] with another offended brother [the story of Joseph and his brothers].

[In Hebrew] Although offended and aggravated, Joseph still loved his brothers, and with so much intensity, that on listening to them telling of their miseries, he could not stop his tears (Gen 45:1–2). [He goes on to explain this example and then concludes.]

Semuel Mendes de Solla, *Triunfo da Uniao contra of pernicioso vicio da discordia. Sermao que em quarta feira 17 de Menahem anno 5510 pregou of H. H. Semuel Mendes de Solla* (Amsterdam: Gerred and Joan de Broen, 1751).

QUESTIONS

1. Like many Western Sephardic sermons from this era, Mendes de Sola's sermon was delivered in Portuguese. What are the ramifications of his choice of language?
2. Mendes de Sola begins with a dedication to Prince William of Orange-Nassau (William IV). How does Mendes de Sola position himself and his congregation vis-à-vis the Stadtholder and why include him?
3. In the second part of the sermon, Mendes de Sola discusses two biblical stories of brothers' rivalry. How do these biblical narratives comment on what happened between him and other members of the congregation?
4. The sermon was delivered in the synagogue in the presence of the local Christian authorities. How might the selected stories have been meaningful to both Christians and Jews?
5. In the first part of the sermon, Mendes de Sola presents a syllogism that he attributes to the philosopher Aristotle. Like all syllogisms, it consists of (a) a major and (b) a minor premise and (c) a conclusion. In this case, these were (a) the object of our love has to be good; (b) our enemy is not good; (c) the enemy cannot be the object of our love. Do you think Mendes de Sola's objection to the minor premise is a valid one?

NOTES

1. Arbell, *Jewish Nation of the Caribbean*, 165.
2. Emmanuel, *Precious Stones*, 309, 341–343.

19

The Charity Petition of Hannah Louzada

NEW JERSEY, 1761

Laura Arnold Leibman

While most early American Jews lived in port towns within walking distance of the synagogue, others remained itinerant or settled inland or in less populated areas. The Louzadas were once such family. Born in London, brothers Aaron and Moses Louzada immigrated to New York, where they joined congregation Shearith Israel. Later they bought property and opened a store across the bay in Bound Brook, New Jersey. Although Aaron prospered, Moses was less successful, and he died intestate (without a will) in 1750. Unfortunately for his wife, Hannah, this meant that their oldest son, Jacob, inherited the entire estate, leaving her impoverished. Regardless of whether Jacob wanted to help his mother, he could not, as he was declared insane and his inheritance went to the town to help support him. The document here is a petition she sent on November 9, 1761, to Congregation Shearith Israel in New York requesting financial assistance to buy basic necessities like wood and food.

In one sense, Hannah's request was not unusual. Other than the almshouse, there was not a government welfare system in the colony. Instead, each religious community was expected to care for its own. Louzada was one of several Jewish widows who relied on Shearith Israel—the only synagogue in New York at the time—for help with food, rent, and fuel. According to colonial laws, married women did not own their own property, and likewise, in certain colonies, women were not guaranteed a portion of their husband's estate if he died without a will. The result is that many women had to rely on charity to cover basic needs. Yet, in another sense, Louzada's petition is striking, as very few requests for charity were saved. Louzada is unique in that three of her petitions survive: the other two are addressed not to the congregation but to Aaron Lopez, one of the wealthiest Jews in the colony. One of her letters to Lopez is written in English, the other in Spanish.

Louzada's letters provide a unique opportunity to learn more about the daily lives and challenges of poor members of early Jewish communities. For many years, histories of colonial American Jews focused primarily on "merchant princes": wealthy Jewish men who got rich because of capitalism. Louzada's story is a good reminder that the majority of Jews in early America were poor and struggled to get by. Her nonstandard English most likely results from English not having been her first language: thus, she renders the proverb "out of sight, out of mind" as "not aut a sigt aut of mind." In contrast, her handwriting is actually very good, and a second letter she wrote to Aaron Lopez in Spanish is elegant. Many women during this era were not educated in the language of the colonies, and when their husbands or fathers died, this made it harder for them to earn a living. We know, for example, that Hannah Louzada owned a store but was not able to make it succeed.

Jews have often been lauded as a model minority: smart, law-abiding, hardworking immigrants who "pulled themselves up by their bootstraps." The problem with this myth is that it suggests that people who do not achieve the "American dream" only have themselves to blame, rather than that they may be facing structural inequalities that make achievement more difficult.

PRIMARY SOURCE

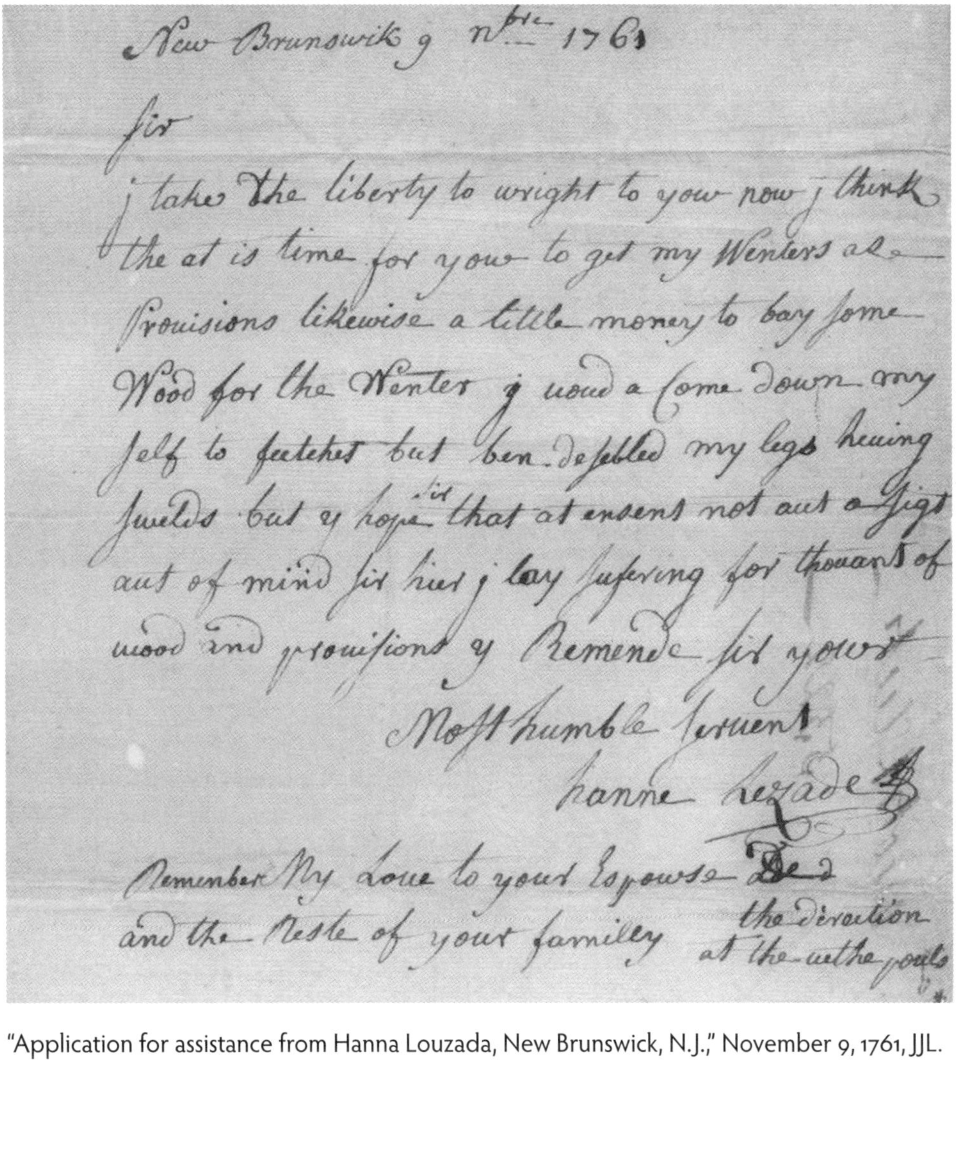

New Brunswick 9 nbre 1761

Sir

j take the liberty to wright to you now j think
the at is time for you to get my Wenters al
Provisions likewise a litle money to bay some
Wood for the Wenter j woud a come down my
self to fetchet but ben desebled my legs heuing
sweleds but y hope sir that at ensent not aut a sigt
aut of mind sir hier j lay sufering for thoant of
wood and provisions y Remende sir your

Most humble servent

hanne Lezade

Remember My Loue to your Espouse and
and the Reste of your familley the diraction
at the wethe poals

"Application for assistance from Hanna Louzada, New Brunswick, N.J.," November 9, 1761, JJL.

j [I] take the liberty to wright to yow now[.] j [I] think the at [that it] is time for yow to get my Wenters [winter's] ase Provisions[,] likewise a little money to bay some Wood for the Wenter[.] j [I] would a Come down my self to feetchet [fetch it], but ben desebled[,] my legs heving swelds [swellings.] but j [I] hope [sir] that at ensent [ancient proverb] not aut a sigt aut of mind [will apply to me.] sir[,] hier j [I] lay suffering for the want of wood and provisions[.] j [I] Remende sir your

Most humble servent

hanne Lezade

Remember My Love to your Espouse and the Reste of your familey

QUESTIONS

1. Some of this text's qualities that seem unique today, such as using the letters "j" and "I" interchangeably, were actually typical of Louzada's era. How does her use of English differ from most printed works published in English today?
2. How does the way Louzada's letter is written shape your perception of her? Does your view of her change at all once you know that she was fluent in Spanish and could write her name in Hebrew?
3. What strategies does Louzada use to gain the sympathy of her readers?
4. Look at Louzada's handwriting. What might we speculate about her education on the basis of her writing style?

20

Hanukkiah

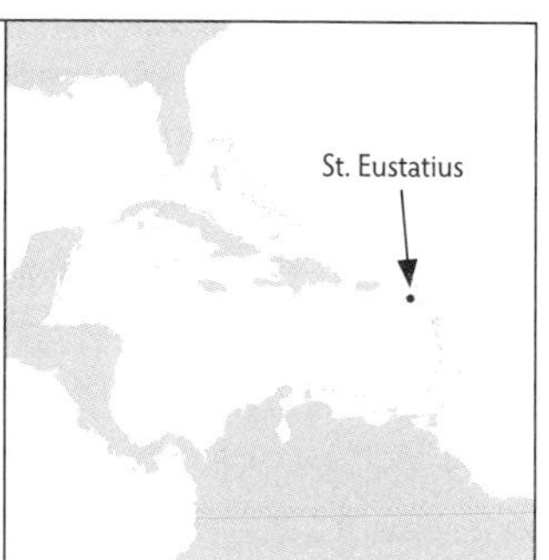

ST. EUSTATIUS, 1761

Judah M. Cohen

While never the size of the Jewish communities of Curaçao and Suriname, St. Eustatius (or "Statia," for short) had a small but thriving Jewish population in the eighteenth century. As on other Caribbean islands, trade drew Jews to Statia, and by 1738–1739, the congregation was large enough to warrant a synagogue, Honen Dalim (Charitable to the Poor). By 1781, at least four hundred Jews lived on the island.[1] Like other congregations around the globe, Honen Dalim benefited from an ongoing relationship with its mother congregation in Amsterdam (the Esnoga), as symbolized by the Hanukkah lamp shown here.

The Hebrew inscription in the frame of this *hanukkiah* (Hanukkah lamp) reads in translation, "Honen Dalim, year 5522," referring to the Gregorian year 1761–1762. On the basis of this inscription and the shape of the *hanukkiah*, it was probably created in Amsterdam and sent to St. Eustatius's congregation around 1761 as a sign of friendship and solidarity. The *hanukkiah* did not stay on the island for long, however. In 1781, toward the end of the Revolutionary War, British Admiral George Rodney sacked St. Eustatius, believing it to be a key port for supplying munitions to the rebelling colonies. Rodney placed particular blame on the Jews and imprisoned the island's Jewish male population for a few days. While the siege lasted only some months, and the island was back in Dutch hands by 1784, St. Eustatius never fully recovered. When Denmark announced its own West Indian colonies (especially St. Thomas) as a free-trade zone in the 1790s, merchants from St. Eustatius migrated there, joining migrants from Curaçao and Saint-Domingue (now Haiti and the Dominican Republic). In 1796, St. Thomas's Jewish population had enough people to start a congregation. As St. Eustatius's remaining Jewish population aged and dwindled, the *hanukkiah* probably came over to St. Thomas for safe keeping.

The *hanukkiah* provides a rather unique glimpse into the material-culture distribution networks of eighteenth-century Jewish life. Amsterdam's Jewish community appears to have sent exact copies of this *hanukkiah* to other congregations around the world, each with a different inscription: currently New York's Jewish Museum has at least two (one of which comes from Jamaica); Amsterdam's Jewish Historical Quarter has at least one on display; and the Musée d'Art et d'Histoire du Judaïsme in Paris has one in its collection (associated with nineteenth-century North Africa). This distribution suggests that the Jewish community of Amsterdam saw this object as a means of communicating with Jewish populations around the world. The inscriptions memorialized those relationships.

The *hanukkiah*'s design reflects the mass production of Judaica from seventeenth- or eighteenth-century Amsterdam. The *hanukkiah* includes a number of generic parts that are relatively easily assembled and disassembled and (judging from other examples) could fit a variety of designs: (1) an outer tray and backing made of a thin sheet of cut and folded brass; (2) a smaller drip tray, made from another thin sheet of brass; (3) eight oil wells (designed to hold oil and wicks) molded as a single piece; and (4) a single, molded oil well that served as the *shamash*, or helper light (it is missing here but would go in the small rectangular hole a few inches up from the eight wells). The thick brass piece that held the *hanukkiah* lamps, by contrast, could be personalized for different recipients: in this case, with elegantly shaped vertical piece with fleurs-de-lis (stylized lilies) on either side and space for an inscription. This one object's design and construction, then, offers insight into broader efforts of parent congregations at the time to connect with their colonial offshoots.

The story of this brass *hanukkiah* provides insights into the complex movements of Jews across the Atlantic over more than two centuries and illuminates how ritual objects become part of museum collections. Over a century after its arrival in St. Thomas, the *hanukkiah* passed into the hands of the lay religious leader David Cardoze. Cardoze, in turn, handed it to his successor, Moses De Castro Sasso. Sasso, witnessing the island's shrinking Sephardic population, subsequently donated the *hanukkiah* to the local history museum at Fort Christian, and the object soon faded from communal memory. In 1995, during a search for artifacts to honor the St. Thomas Hebrew Congregation's bicentennial, the *hanukkiah* was rediscovered. The *hanukkiah*, now on long-term loan from the Fort Christian museum, holds a central place in the synagogue's museum as an evocative symbol of the congregation's own past ties to the Jewish Atlantic.

PRIMARY SOURCE

Facing page: *Hanukkiah*, 1761. (Johnny Weibel Museum of St. Thomas Jewish History, St. Thomas Hebrew Congregation, St. Thomas, US Virgin Islands; photograph by Agnes H. Rampino)

QUESTIONS

1. Hanukkah commemorates the rededication of the Second Temple after the Maccabean Revolt against the Greeks. Why do you think that the Jewish community of Amsterdam would want to send a ritual object associated with this holiday to communities around the world?
2. As Marcel Mauss notes in *The Gift*, "Each gift is part of a system of reciprocity in which the honor of the giver and recipient are engaged. . . . The system is quite simple; just the rule that every gift has to be returned in some specified way sets up a perpetual cycle of

exchanges within and between generations."[2] What do you think Amsterdam expected to be "returned" in exchange for the gifts of *hanukkiahs* and other objects?

3. How does our understanding of objects change when they cease to be used in rituals and instead live in museums?
4. If you were to design a placard for the *hanukkiah* in its exhibit in the St. Thomas Hebrew Congregation, what information would you want to include about it?

NOTES

1. Arbell, *Jewish Nation of the Caribbean*, 174; J. Cohen, *Through the Sands of Time*, 5–6.
2. Mauss, *Gift*, xi.

PART II

Age of Revolutions and Emancipation (1763–1835)

The semiautonomous Jewish plantation town Jodensavanne. ("Vue de la Savane des Juifs sur la rivière de Surinam," VS, Pl. XXI, JCBL)

Between 1763 and 1835, radical political change spread across the Americas, as colonial regimes toppled and new republics rose. Jews living in these colonies responded to these changes, but with a Jewish twist. "I deem myself a patriot," wrote the Surinamese Jew David Cohen Nassy in 1798. "But a patriot in a sense widely different from that in which it is generally understood as such; I love my native country, *despite* its injustices to me."[1] Nassy rejected the idea that "birth, religion, wealth, and rank" should play a role in a person's fate. Rather, he proposed that "all men must have equal rights, equal privileges."[2] Strong words for a slave owner! Yet Nassy was not alone in making this claim or in inconsistently believing in both equality and hereditary enslavement. While some Jews gained civil rights, others found that their lives continued to be limited by racism, antisemitism, and sexism.

Wars as well as cultural shifts impacted Jews' experiences in the colonies. The same Enlightenment ideas that fed Nassy's proclamations led to colonial subjects turning on their imperial masters. Thus, politically, the era's starting point comes from twin events that signaled a shift from wars *between* empires to wars *within* empires. First, the Treaty of Paris (1763) marked the end of decade-long wars between Britain, France, and Spain, and as part of the treaty, Florida and Canada became part of the British Empire. Yet for the British, the treaty only exacerbated problems with their colonies, as colonists refocused their discontent on the English motherland. The second trigger of change was British King George III's Proclamation Act of 1763, which attempted to end disputes with Indigenous peoples in his northern colonies by banning British settlement west of the Appalachian Divide. Like the treaty, this act backfired, sparking the War of Independence (1763–1783). While people in the United States tend to think of this war as *the* American revolution, it was only one of many successful rebellions across the hemisphere between 1763 and 1835. Like Nassy's 1798 *Lettre*, these revolts were as much ideological as political, and they sought to redefine social hierarchies by shifting governments from monarchies to republics. Overall, a republican form of government benefited Jews, but the push for civil rights simultaneously divided communities. Just as Jews had been both agents and victims of empire in the early colonial era, during the age of revolutions, some Jews were more equal than others.

As for other colonists, one of the driving forces in American Jews' changing sense of their rights was the ideology of the Enlightenment. The Enlightenment valued reason and individualism, rather than adherence to tradition. Key Enlightenment principles are freedom, liberty, and autonomy, all of which provided a rationale for the revolutions that spread across the Americas. The Enlightenment augmented Jews' legal status. Although not enslaved for being Jews, Jews were legally discriminated against, as they were seen as unable to be full members of society because of their religion. The Enlightenment, however, began to separate church and state. This separation benefited Jews such as Nassy, who had previously found themselves unable to vote or participate in government unless they converted to Christianity. The recognition of Jews' rights to equality and citizenship is referred to as "Jewish Emancipation." Interestingly, many European countries were willing to emancipate Jews in their colonies before they made Jews fully free at home. Yet these changes had an insidious undercurrent. The scientific thought that promised to "modernize" European and Euro-American culture codified understandings of race. This, in turn, solidified systems of oppression that American communities still bear the mark of today. Even though religion no longer consistently held Jews back, scientific theories about race and gender were used to keep Jews, women, and "nonwhite" peoples in their place. In Nassy's language, now it was people's inherent "vices and inabilities" that kept them from participating in government, not "birth, religion, wealth and rank" (see chapter 42).[3]

While today attaining civil rights may seem a natural good, not all Jews wanted to be emancipated. First, not everyone supported republics. Although later historians would tend to focus almost exclusively on Jews who aided the rebels during the US War of Independence, colonial Jews actually felt quite mixed about the revolt, often dividing equally between British loyalists and those siding with the rebels. Second, the changes disadvantaged certain Jews. The new science that came out of the Enlightenment helped create more aggressive binaries between women and men.[4] Thus, while Jewish women began to perform a new, more public role in society, they still lacked the civil rights earned by elite Jewish men. These generalizations aside, European monarchs responded individually to emancipation requests within their colonies, and hence, Jews in different colonial regimes had divergent experiences.

Throughout Latin America, Enlightenment ideas instigated reforms, and Jews found themselves caught in the uneasy mix. The Bourbon monarchy took the Spanish throne in 1700 and sought to modernize the colonies and limit the church's power. One result was a further codifying of the racial castes in Spanish America (see chapter 21). While in Spain and the early colonies, *limpieza de sangre* (purity of blood) was defined as not having Jewish or Muslim ancestors, by the eighteenth century, the emphasis had shifted toward not having African or Indigenous ancestry.[5] To a certain extent, Jews benefited from this change, since both *conversos* and *moriscos* (descendants of those who had been forced to convert to Christianity) disappeared as stigmatized genealogical categories, even though the term *morisco* was recycled.[6] This racial legacy would have significant ramifications for Jews following the emancipation era, as their Iberian roots increasingly cast them in the category of Spaniards. *Conversos* and crypto-Jews in Brazil had a similar experience, as in

1773 the Marquis de Pombal had nullified regulations regarding *limpieza de sangre*, declaring all Portuguese citizens equal, except people with African ancestry.[7]

The Enlightenment also assisted Jews in Spanish and Portuguese America by helping end the Inquisition. The Liberal constitution, which was adopted in Spain in 1812, undermined the church's power and suppressed the Inquisition in Spain and its colonies.[8] Although the Liberal constitution was soon overthrown and the Inquisition reestablished, by 1820 the Inquisition had ended for good in both Peru and Mexico City, by 1821 in Brazil, and by 1834 in Cartagena. Enlightenment ideals, as well as the backlash against the Bourbon reforms, fed colonial desires to overthrow the monarchy.[9] In Brazil, backlash against the monarchy was even more immediate after Napoleon's invasion of Portugal, as King João VI began to reign from Rio de Janeiro (1808).[10] Although there were no openly Jewish communities in Latin America between 1765 and 1820, the Inquisition's end and the rise of new nations that privileged equality paved the way for later Jewish settlement.

One of the earliest openly Jewish communities to thrive in this new context was in the city of Coro, Venezuela. This community started around 1824 as an offshoot of the Jewish community of nearby Curaçao, but by 1832, Coro's Jews were allowed to establish their own cemetery. At its peak, Coro had around 130 to 160 Jewish residents.[11] The community owed its acceptance in part to the role Jews had played in the region's revolution. In 1812, when Simón Bolívar was on the run from Spanish officials, he took refuge in Curaçao as the guest of the Sephardic Jew Mordechai Ricardo, while his sisters stayed at an octagonal Jewish house by the sea. Bolívar—sometimes called the "George Washington of South America"—had actively courted Jewish support by emphasizing Spain as a common enemy because of the Inquisition.[12] After Bolívar came to power, he supported increasing Jews' rights, including allowing them to settle in the land he now governed.

In the British and Dutch Caribbean, the Enlightenment similarly brought about reforms, rebellion, and a divided legacy for local Jews. Theologically, Dutch and British Jews responded differently to the Enlightenment than did their Christian colonial neighbors or coreligionists in eastern Europe, the latter of whom would compose the bulk of Jewish American immigrants in the late nineteenth century. Starting in the 1780s, Jews in central and eastern Europe had responded to the Enlightenment primarily in two different ways: (1) by engaging in a new mystical, exuberant Judaism that emphasized emotional connections with the divine called Hasidism or (2) by partaking in a Jewish intellectual movement called the *Haskalah*. Both of these traditions emerged out of political and social experiences quite different from what was experienced by Jews of the Portuguese Diaspora or of the Americas.[13] Socially, eastern European Jews often saw a greater tension between Jewish and secular traditions than Western Sephardic Jews: Hasidic Jews eliminated this tension by emphasizing the spiritual interfused with the mundane, while the *Haskalah* emphasized that the secular could be used to interpret the spiritual.

Differing political milieus similarly impacted Jews' response to the Enlightenment. Jewish communities in eastern Europe had their power guaranteed by church and royal powers.[14] Thus, for eastern European Jews, paradoxically, "a lesser degree of Civil freedom . . . [was believed to] create the room for spiritual freedom."[15] In contrast, British and Dutch Jews both in Europe and in the colonies were voluntarily members of their congregations, and synagogues' governing boards often had to negotiate with the state in order to assert their authority. For them, gaining civic freedoms was a crucial part of their experience of the Enlightenment.

Jewish education in early America reflects this different experience of the Enlightenment. Eastern European Jews who partook in the *Haskalah* hoped to achieve their spiritual freedom vis-à-vis a type of secular education that was typically already available to Jews in the British and Dutch colonies. Whereas eastern European Jews traditionally protected the Talmud and Torah from non-Jewish ways of knowing, Sephardic luminaries had long emphasized the compatibility of Jewish thought and Greco-Roman philosophy. Western Sephardic Jews controlled most early American Jewish schools, and hence Jews in the British and Dutch colonies tended not to see a harsh divide between religious and secular knowledge. We see this early blend of secular and sacred in early American Jews like David Cohen Nassy, who had an incredible secular library and was elected a member of the American Philosophical Society but was an important participant in several American congregations that embraced Jewish law and the oral Torah.

In Europe, the *Haskalah* laid the groundwork for the creation of Reform Judaism. While in general this movement did not take off in the Americas until the 1840s, in the 1820s, forty-seven petitioners of congregation Beth Elohim in Charleston, South Carolina, requested reforms, including prayers and a weekly sermon in English (see chapter 41). Eventually the congregation split in two over these requests, but it would not be until the 1840s that the Reformed Society of Charleston had its own building or that other Reform congregations emerged.[16] The 1820s similarly marked a rift in the Jewish community of New York, this time with the breakaway congregation urging "renewed arduor [*sic*] to promote the more strict keeping of their faith."[17] Like the Hasidim in Europe, the breakaway congregation in New York was more mystical. Recent yellow fever epidemics had created a theological rift in the city's original congregation, Shearith Israel, and those who sought mystical guidance on how to survive the dreaded disease broke ranks to form B'nai Jeshurun. Years later, this congregation would itself turn to the Reform movement, but initially its congregants wanted more religion, not less.[18]

Race impacted Jews' experience of the Enlightenment. As seen in the example of the casta paintings (chapter 21), the Enlightenment often intensified racial distinctions. The abolition of the slave trade in the British Empire in 1807 did not end discrimination but rather spawned a backlash in which European intellectuals reaffirmed inequities based on perceived "innate" differences between races. The Enlightenment fascination with subdividing humanity impacted Jewish life. In Suriname, key ceremonies for making people a part of the Jewish nation, such as circumcision, were extended to people with African ancestry (see chapter 24). In addition, some enslaved Africans brought Jewish traditions with them to the Americas (see chapter 32).

Despite the inclusion of Jews of African descent into organized Jewish life, Suriname was a slave society. European Jews both owned and oversaw plantations (see chapter 37) and hence were complicit in race-based discrimination. Moreover, "white" Jews restricted the religious rights of Eurafrican Jews. Surinamese synagogue boards invented a second-class category of *congregante* for Jews with partial African ancestry and thereby denied Jews of color full synagogue membership and honors.[19] This discrimination fed rebellion. By 1759, Surinamese Jews of color had established Darhe Jesarim (Path of the Righteous), and in the late 1780s, they requested the right to have their own space, where they could "'meditate and recite the mourner's prayer [kadiz]' in their own space."[20] White Jews did not tolerate this rebellion (see chapter 33). Likewise, Isaac Lopez Brandon found that his involvement in the Barbadian Vestry Bill led to his losing his membership in the island's synagogue (see chapter 39).

Slavery impacted how Jews understood kinship, as secular law categorized children born by nonwhite women as not full kin by default, by limiting their ability to inherit from white relations (see chapter 34).[21] Jewish fathers who wanted their children recognized in the British West Indies found that they needed to pay for a will to be made, to lobby the Assembly for immunity from the caps, and to explicitly violate the norms of the larger society.[22] Moreover, many of the traditional ways that parents could legally recognize multiracial children at birth were not available to Jews. With the exception of Suriname, where people of color were regularly admitted into the Jewish congregations, Jews who wanted a legal record of their paternity had to baptize their multiracial children or acknowledge them in a will.

Enlightenment-fed revolutions impacted trade across the colonies. Even for people in Dutch, French, and Spanish colonies, conflict between Britain and its "thirteen colonies" had a disastrous impact on the hemisphere's economy, particularly in the wealthy sugar islands that depended on trade for income, food, and basic needs. A revolution that began in Haiti in 1791 and ended in 1804 further rocked the Americas, as African people in other islands rose up to throw off their enslavers. In Brazil, for example, the Haitian Revolution inspired a 1798 revolt in Bahia, where the Black population was so strong that one visitor remarked that the city could be mistaken for "an Africa capital."[23] Taken together, slave revolts helped bring about the official end of the slave trade, which in turn further undercut the economy of American slave societies, that is, communities for which slavery was the primary source of income for elites and in which all lives became entangled with human enslavement.[24]

The Seven Years' War and US War of Independence destabilized the economies of the sugar colonies, and while colonies in the North benefited from their more diverse array of products, they also struggled. At the start of the conflict between George III and the rebels, Newport's Jewish community seemed poised to become a forerunner of northern Jewry, having built a beautiful new synagogue (see chapter 25) and printed the first colonial Jewish sermon in English (see chapter 27). After the war, the community declined. Split loyalties to the Crown and rebels had divided several colonial Jewish communities, and after the British lost, many loyalists fled to Canada, including Samuel Hart of Philadelphia and Jacob Louzada (the son of Hannah Louzada; see chapter 19).[25] The strong ties between Canada's early Jewish community and New York can be seen in the name of Montreal's first synagogue: Shearith Israel (1768). Religious and business ties were so strong that New York's congregation often provided financial support in the early years.[26]

This support was possible in part because after the War of Independence ended, New York, Philadelphia, and Charleston had grown rapidly, as did their Jewish communities. In addition to older merchant families like the Gratzes (see chapter 26), new Jewish refugees from Barbados, Jamaica, Suriname, and other West Indian colonies pushed the cities' growth. While the most established synagogues in each city used the Sephardic rite, the communities were now largely Ashkenazi. Consequently, new immigrants founded

Ashkenazi synagogues in Philadelphia (1795), Cincinnati (1824), New York (1825), and even New Orleans (1828). However, older Ashkenazi Jews often still identified with the Western Sephardic rite, which maintained a certain cachet: most of the original Jewish settlers in Canada were technically Ashkenazi, but they and their descendants identified as Sephardic by choice.[27] As Jonathan Sarna puts it, communities that had once grown up around a single synagogue found themselves revolving around a "community of synagogues."[28]

As these communities grew between 1763 and 1835, women began to take a more public space in Jewish life in the United States and Canada. Several of the documents in this part (chapters 28, 30, and 31) reveal women working in stores and other businesses. Widowhood often opened doors for women to take a more public role. Throughout the British colonies, women did not control any money they earned while working beside their husbands,

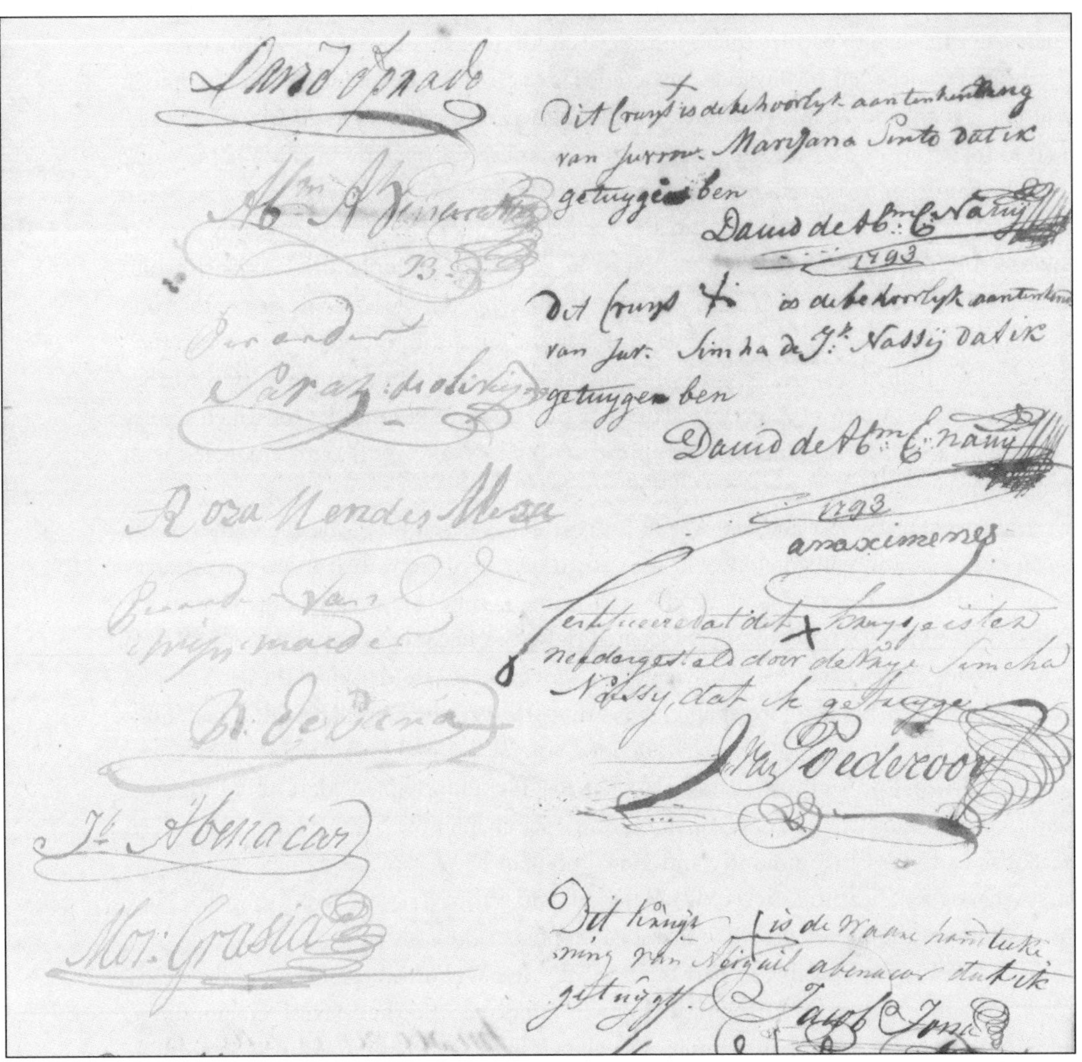

Signatures and marks of six women (Sarah de Oliveyra, Roza Mendes Meza, Abigail Abenacar, Maryana Pinto, Simha de Ysaak Nassy, Simcha Nassy), among others, on the "Memorandum of the Coloured Jews to Governor De Frederici" (1793). (1.05.10.01:528, no. 414, NA)

nor did they have rights over money they brought into marriage. Yet when women were fortunate enough to live in locations that guaranteed them a widow's third or had husbands who wrote wills leaving them a larger portion of their estates, they often had substantially more freedom than before their husbands died. Abigail Minis (chapter 31), Rebecca Gomez (chapter 30), and Hetty Hays (chapter 28) all fell into this category. Yet, as Hetty Hays (chapter 28), Sara Pardo (chapter 29), and Rebecca Valverde Gomes (chapter 38) discovered, money did not mean that women were not still susceptible to the ruling of the local synagogue board, which had the power to govern both the food that Jewish women prepared and women's sex lives.

Even though women were subordinate to the all-male governance boards, Jewish women were implicated in the oppression of others. As the historian Stephanie Jones-Rogers notes, white women "not only witnessed the most brutal features of slavery, they took part in them, profited from them, and defended them."[29] We can see this trend in the biographies of Abigail Minis (chapter 31), Sarah Moses Levy (chapter 34), and Sara Pardo (chapter 29). Jewish women of color did not take gendered oppression lightly. As the petition by the Jews of color (chapter 33) reveals, women were involved in speaking out against fellow Jews who did not treat them as equals.

The overturning of society in the Enlightenment era reshaped the intimate space and structure of American Jewish families. In the United States, intermarriage rates doubled following the Revolutionary War, with men intermarrying more frequently than women.[30] Likewise, marriages began to shift away from the "yoke mates" understanding of kinship toward a "soul mates" model in which marriage and love were seen as essential companions.[31] In states where slavery was still legal, subjugation continued to impact the way Jews understood kinship, limiting the inclusion of multiracial Jewish family members in wills (see chapter 23).

In conclusion, Jews often benefited from the revolutions that spawned new American nations. Throughout Latin America, revolutions toppled Spanish authority and the centrality of the church, thereby ending the Inquisition. In the Caribbean, Jews' attainment of civil rights intertwined with that of people of color. Yet both groups found that emancipation's promise rang hollow: whereas once religion or slavery was used to discredit Jews and people with African or Indigenous ancestry, once these groups were emancipated, they found that white Christians instituted a new system that used "scientific racism" to censure and tear down Jews and people of color, often pitting them against each other. These conflicts were palpable even in northern colonies after slavery was abolished and set the stage for understandings of Jews, race, and rights in the eras that followed.

NOTES

1. Seeligmann, "David Nassy of Surinam," 31 (emphasis added).
2. Seeligmann, 32.
3. Seeligmann, 32.
4. Laqueur, *Making Sex.*
5. Olson, "Casta Painting and the Rhetorical Body," 319.
6. We are indebted to Maxwell Greenberg for this point.

7. Andrews, "Race and the State in Colonial Brazil," 206.
8. Janvier, *Mexican Guide*, 28.
9. Fowler, *Mexico in the Age of Proposals*, 13; Masterson, *History of Peru*, 61.
10. Higgins, *Licentious Liberty*, 7.
11. Cohen and Peck, *Sephardim in the Americas*, 237.
12. Arbell, *Jewish Nation of the Caribbean*, 158–159.
13. Litvak, *Haskalah*, 9, 12.
14. Litvak, 10, 17.
15. Litvak, 20.
16. Meyer, *Response to Modernity*, 228.
17. Sarna, *American Judaism*, 56.
18. Leibman, "Virus as Hyperobject."
19. Ben-Ur, "Peripheral Inclusion," 190–192.
20. Ben-Ur, 192; Ben-Ur, *Jewish Autonomy in a Slave Society*, 176.
21. Vasconcellos, *Slavery*, 56.
22. Vasconcellos, 56.
23. Kraay, "Introduction," 3–4. This population difference would continue to impact race in Brazil moving forward. In 1800, the majority of people in Brazil were either Black or of partial African ancestry. In contrast, this same community made up less than 5 percent of the population in Mexico, Peru, and Argentina. Andrews, *Afro-Latin America*, 5.
24. Parent, *Foul Means*, 55; Ben-Ur, *Jewish Autonomy in a Slave Society*, 5.
25. Tulchinsky, *Canada's Jews*, 15; Leibman, *Art of the Jewish Family*, 52–53.
26. Tulchinsky, *Canada's Jews*, 16–17.
27. Tulchinsky, 16.
28. Sarna, *American Judaism*, 60.
29. Jones-Rogers, *They Were Her Property*, ix.
30. Sarna, *American Judaism*, 27, 45.
31. Cootz, *Marriage, a History*, 145–146.

21

Limpieza de Sangre and Casta Paintings

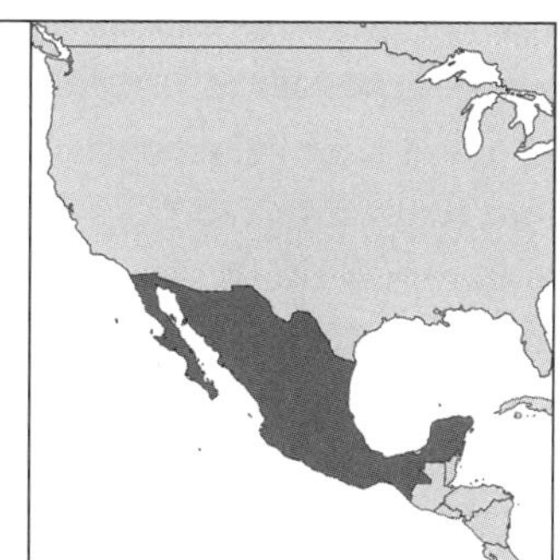

NEW SPAIN,
EIGHTEENTH CENTURY

Laura Arnold Leibman

Jews' relationship to race changed between the early colonial era and the age of revolutions. Originally, people with Jewish ancestry were forbidden to settle in the Spanish and Portuguese colonies, though some circumvented this law. This law had its origins in a medieval Spanish concept called *limpieza de sangre* (purity of blood): that is, the belief that descendants of Jews and Muslims carried a taint of their ancestors' heresy in their bloodlines. In the colonies, understandings of blood "impurity" were complicated by the rise of race-based slavery. New racial categories emerged to justify slavery. People of Indigenous, African, and initially Asian descent had limited opportunities, based on supposedly inherent differences, and the Inquisition in the Americas increasingly regulated their lives. Although possessing heretical blood, Jews were not considered enslavable, and over time, they benefited from the shift in the Inquisitors' gaze.

Casta paintings reveal how race was changing in the Americas and where Jews fit into those changes. Casta paintings were a short-lived genre that began around 1700 and ceased to be made after 1821, when racial castes were abolished in Mexico. They were largely intended for European audiences to help them understand race in the colonies. Their origin dates to the change in imperial power. When Charles II died in 1700, the Hapsburg dynasty ended in Spain and its colonies. His successor, Philip of Anjou (grandson of Louis XIV of France and Charles's half sister), started a new dynasty: the Bourbons. Phillip V instigated a series of reforms intended to increase the Crown's power by creating clearer hierarchies. Some of these laws were sumptuary laws, which regulated what type of clothing and jewelry could be worn by people of different races and classes. Other laws regulated the displays of deference that people of "lower" races had to show Spaniards. Some casta paintings depict scenes of violence that were believed to occur when people of high and low castes chose to create families together. Overall, casta paintings do not reflect the reality of how race worked in New Spain but rather demonstrate the ruling Europeans' attempts to codify and understand race.

The genealogical reasoning of casta paintings can be traced to Enlightenment thought. In Europe, Enlightenment thinkers used ancestry and physical traits to divide people into newly invented races. Jews played an ambiguous role in these new racial categories, as European thinkers sometimes classified Jews with whites and other times placed them in the newly invented category of "Semites." One of the most interesting aspects of the casta paintings is the absence of Jews as a caste. In contrast, the term for descendants of people forced to convert from Islam (*morisco*) was recycled to mean someone with three-quarters Spanish and one-quarter African ancestry. Similarly, the term originally used for someone from Asia (*chino*) was restyled as someone with seven-eighths Spanish and one-eighth African ancestry. The use of *morisco* and *chino* in the new castes may reflect the fact that Muslims and people from Asia had originally been enslavable in the colonies, even though by 1700 they could not be enslaved. Indeed the "chinos" in casta paintings sometimes make textiles, a labor previously associated with enslaved Asians. *Conversos* had never been enslavable, however. Casta paintings created an imaginary order for the population of the colonies. In this imaginary, Jews were specters. They were not codifiable, because they were not meant to be present. Hence, Jews, once a locus of blood impurity, dropped out of the colony's racial system.

PRIMARY SOURCE

Facing page: Casta painting showing sixteen racial groupings. Anonymous, *Las castas*, eighteenth century, oil on canvas, 148 × 104 cm. (MNV, WC)

QUESTIONS

1. In the eighteenth century, clothing, occupations, and religion were often understood as reflecting or creating one's race. Pick two people in the casta painting and describe how their clothing encodes messages about their race.
2. The ability to look at people while remaining invisible oneself was an important part of colonial power structures. Who gazes at whom in the casta painting?
3. What do you think it means that Jews (or Semites) were not considered a caste in New Spain?
4. Although the Inquisition was supposed to root out religious heresy, it assumed that heretical inclinations could be inherited in family lines through one's blood. This suggests a certain blurring of the divide between religious and racial persecution. Consider an instance of antisemitism today and discuss whether the bias against Jews is racial, religious, both, or something different altogether.

Español con India.
Mestizo.
Mestizo con Española
Castizo.
Castizo con Española
Español.
Español con Mora
Mulato.
5
Mulato con Española.
Morisco.
6
Morisco con Española
Chino.
7
Chino con India.
Salta atras.
Salta atras con Mulata.
Lobo.
9
Lobo con China
Gibaro.
10
Gibaro con Mulata
Albarazado
11
Albarazado con Negra
Canbujo.
12
Canbujo con India.
Sanbaigo.
13
Sanbaigo con Loba
Calpamulato.
14
Calpamulato con Canbuja
Tente en el Aire.
15
Tente en el Aire. con Mulata
Noteentiendo.
16
Noteentiendo con India
Tornaatras.

22

The Binding of Isaac

SURINAME, 1763

Hilit Surowitz-Israel

During the eighteenth century, many members of Suriname's Jewish community moved north from Jodensavanne to the main port of Paramaribo, where they established not one but three congregations, including the oldest Ashkenazi synagogue in the Americas and the first Afro-Surinamese brotherhood. Although born in Spain to *converso* parents, Samuel Robles de Medina (1724–1797) served as the hazan of the "High German" congregation Neveh Shalom in Paramaribo, where he played an integral role in the colony's Jewish life. Upon leaving Iberia, the Robles de Medina family emigrated first to Amsterdam and later to Suriname, arriving there in 1729. When the family joined the community, the imposing synagogue was fairly new, with the land being bought by Sephardic Jews in 1716 to build the synagogue (1723). During Robles de Medina's childhood, the congregation split: the Portuguese Jews sold the original building to the growing population of Ashkenazi Jews and built a new synagogue, Tzedek ve-Shalom, a couple of blocks away. However, even after Neveh Shalom became the High German congregation, it utilized Sephardic liturgy and rite. A case in point is Samuel Robles de Medina's small manuscript book, which contains formulas for various Jewish legal documents such as marriage and divorce contracts, instructions for ritual slaughter, and specification for a *mikveh*, ritual bath.

The frontispiece to Robles de Medina's book is an image of the *akedah*, the biblical story of the binding of Isaac (Genesis 22:1–19). The *akedah* tells the story of God's command to Abraham to sacrifice Isaac, one of his sons. Abraham takes Isaac to a place for sacrifice and binds him on an altar. Just as Isaac is about to be sacrificed, an angel of God halts Abraham's hand and commands him to sacrifice a ram instead, thus sparing Isaac. Throughout Jewish history, the narrative of the *akedah* has generally been understood through a prism of self-sacrifice, martyrdom, and obedience to God.

This image and the small manual help us understand both communal life and the presence of Jewish ritual in eighteenth-century Suriname and the role of a hazan during the period. More specifically, this image as the frontispiece for Samuel Robles de Medina's book reflects obedience to God and tropes of martyrdom and salvation found throughout the early-modern Portuguese Jewish world. Tropes of sacrifice and rebirth are common in *converso* imagery, rhetoric, and theology, because *conversos* confronted death and martyrdom as they continued to lead Jewish lives in the face of the Inquisition. Their salvation, understood as the return to public and communal Jewish life, came from God's hand, just as Isaac's did.

This source adds several interesting points for consideration to the story of American Jewish history. Robles de Medina's book raises awareness of the presence of Jewish ritual life in the Americas in the colonial period and the dominance of the Sephardic rite into the nineteenth century. The illustration more specifically illuminates the role that biblical narratives and imagery can play in the construction of collective memory and religious identity. The biblical narrative of the *akedah* has been used, and continues to be used, by Jews to signify martyrdom, covenant, and salvation by God. A few examples of this ubiquitous symbol are Amir Gilboa's post-Holocaust poem *Isaac* (1953), Marc Chagall's painting *The Sacrifice of Isaac* (1966), Leonard Cohen's song "The Story of Isaac" (1969), and the Israeli contemporary photographer Adi Nes's image "Abraham and Isaac" in his series *Biblical Stories* (2007).

PRIMARY SOURCE

"You shall carry out the verdict that is announced to you . . ." (Deuteronomy 17:10).

Frontispiece of Shmuel Robles de Medina's formula and contracts (1763). (Shmuel Robles de Medina c. 1723–1796, P-113, Box P-3, Folder P-113, AJHS)

QUESTIONS

1. What is Samuel Robles de Medina trying to communicate by including this image in his Jewish ritual and legal manuscript?
2. The *akedah* is an emotional story, in which a father is asked to sacrifice his son as a testament of his faith in God. Why do you think that the artist chose to depict the moment when God intervened?
3. How is Abraham depicted in this image? Describe his clothing, body language, and emotion.

23

Wills, Families, and Race

JAMAICA, 1765

Stanley Mirvis

By the middle of the eighteenth century, Jews had become an essential part of Jamaica's trade and plantation economy. In the 1760s, when Moses Levy Alvares composed his last will and testament, Jamaica had three separate Portuguese Jewish communities in Port Royal, Kingston, and St. Jago de la Vega (Spanish Town)—each with its own synagogue—along with smaller, less formal, communities on the west coast in Black River, Lucea, Montego Bay, and Savanna-la-Mar.

The 1760s began in Jamaica with Tacky's Revolt, the largest and bloodiest slave uprising in the Caribbean to that point. After brutally subduing the revolt, the Jamaican colonial government acted to limit the rights of people of color, including their ability to inherit financial assets from their European-descendant parents. Despite the extreme violence of Jamaica's slave regime, the 1760s was a time of general prosperity, significant Jewish population growth, expansion of synagogue structures, and Jewish hope for fuller integration into Jamaican civil society (see chapter 17). Yet, in the shadow of the Seven Years' War (1756–1763), a global conflict between the British and French Empires, Jews—many of whom had come from or maintained familial contacts with France—fought against colonial British suspicions about their disloyalty to Jamaica and to the British Empire in general.

Jamaica was a slave society, and Jews were slave owners. Some Jews, especially in towns, owned only a few domestic enslaved people, whereas others, especially rural planters, owned hundreds. As in all slave societies, single men frequently cohabitated with disenfranchised women of color, both free and enslaved, and raised their children together in non-legally-recognized families. Some legally married Jewish men took free and enslaved women of color as concubines or as surrogate mothers. Thus, by the 1760s, a significant percentage of people in Jamaica who associated with the Jewish community were people of color. In Kingston, Jews and free people of color lived close together in the same neighborhoods, with many of the same occupational profiles. Likewise, Jews and free people of color shared nearly identical civil disabilities in Jamaica and adopted many of the same strategies to lobby against those disabilities.

The last will and testament of the Portuguese Jew Moses Levy Alvares touches on many of the general themes of 1760s Jamaica. His strong commitment to Jewish communal life, through his charitable bequests to the synagogue in Spanish Town along with his ritual bequest of an ornate Bible and prayer book, is characteristic of robust Jewish communal life at the time. The presence of his brother and beneficiary, Mordechai, who was living in France, speaks to a common type of transatlantic and transimperial Jewish family network. His brutal slave ownership further reflects 1760s Jamaica. Moses Levy Alvares, although married to the Portuguese Jewish woman Esther, had a child with an enslaved "mulatto" woman called Elsey. Their child Sally, called a "quadroon" to symbolize her high degree of white parentage, inherited a Black slave of her own called "Nanny." Nanny bore a brand on her right shoulder of the letters "MA," standing for the initials of her owner, Moses Alvares. Branding was a common form of punishment used by slave owners throughout the Atlantic world and speaks to the full extent of Jewish assimilation to broader patterns of slave ownership in the Caribbean.

PRIMARY SOURCE

Liber of Wills 36 Folio 9. Jamaica S.S. In the Name of God Amen.

Entered 25th July, 1765.

I Moses Levy Alvares of the parish of St. Catherine in the County of Middlesex and Island of Jamaica, Shopkeeper, being sick and weak in body but of sound and disposing mind memory and understanding do make and publish this my last Will and Testament in manner and form following, First I will and desire that all my just Debts and funeral expenses be first fully paid and satisfied to the payment of which I subject and make liable all my Estate both real and personal. Item: I give and bequeath unto the Synagogue of the town of St. Jago de la Vega in the parish of St. Catherine the sum of five pounds current money of Jamaica for the use of said synagogue. Item: I give and bequeath unto my Nephew Moses Levy Alvares the sum of five pounds of current money of Jamaica in full lieu and barr of any right which he can or may hereafter have or claim to any part of my Estate whatsoever either real or personal. Item: I give devise and bequeath unto my sister in law Rachel Abenatar the sum of ten pounds of current money of Jamaica to be paid to her as soon after my decease as conveniently can be and my will and desire is that the said Rachel Abenatar do live and reside with my wife Esther Levy Alvares as long as she shall think proper free from all expenses whatsoever. Item: I give devise and bequeath unto my friend Abraham Correa my two Hebrew Books with silver locks to wit one the five books of Moses and the other a Common Prayer Book. Item: I give devise and bequeath unto Judith Correa an infant the daughter of my said friend Abraham Correa my Gold Ring with a red stone. Item: my will and desire is that my Executrix and Executors hereinafter named do immediately after my decease permit and suffer my quadroon child named Sally begotten of the body of a mulatto slave named Elsey belonging to Lewis Fortune to have the free use and service of my negro woman slave named Nanny marked on the right shoulder MA for and during the term of two years next after my decease and no longer and I do also give and bequeath unto the said Quadroon child named Sally the sum of five pounds of current money of Jamaica to be paid to her as soon

after my decease as conveniently may be. Item: I do hereby give unto my said Executrix and Executors hereinafter named full power to sell and dispose of my negro woman slave named Presence and the moneys arising from the sale thereof. I do hereby desire my said Executrix and Executors to apply towards the discharge of my just debts and legacys. Item: all the rest residue and remainder of my estate real and personal whatsoever and wheresoever I give devise and bequeath unto my loving wife the said Esther Levy Alvares for and during the term of her natural life she remitting unto my loving brother Mordecai Levy Alvares now resident in France the sum of ten pounds of current money of Jamaica per annum during his natural life. . . . And Lastly I do hereby nominate and appoint my said wife Esther Levy Alvares my Nephew Moses Levy Alvares and my said friend Abraham Correa Executrix and Executors of this my last Will and Testament hereby revoking and making void all other wills by me at any time heretofore made declaring and publishing this to be my last Will and Testament. In Witness whereof I the said Moses Levy Alvares hath hereunto set my hand and affixed my Seal this third day of June in the year of our Lord one thousand Seven hundred and sixty five.

Moses Levy Alvares. Ls.

Signed Sealed published and declared by the said Testator as and for his last Will and Testament in the presence of us who in his presence and in the presence of each other and at his request have subscribed our names as witnesses to the same.

Thos. McQuistin, Geo. French, Edwd. Elliss.

Will of Moses Levy Alvares (1765), Alvares family wills, 1693–1767, SC-234, AJA.

QUESTIONS

1. How was Moses Levy Alvares connected to Jamaica's Jewish community?
2. What evidence of physical abuse toward slaves is found in the will?
3. What kind of relationship do you think Moses Levy Alvares had with the enslaved woman Elsey?
4. How does Moses Levy Alvares's will compare to Abigail Minis's (chapter 31)?

24

Sefer Berit Yitzhak

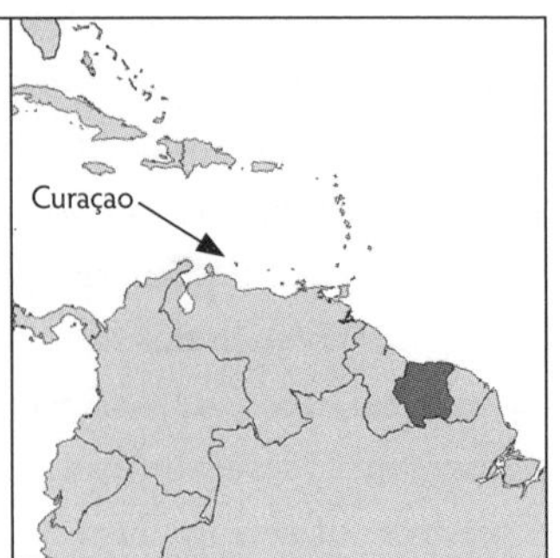

SURINAME AND CURAÇAO, 1767–1768

Hilit Surowitz-Israel

While some descendants of forced converts arrived in the Americas in the sixteenth and seventeenth centuries, New Christians continued to leave Iberia in the eighteenth and nineteenth centuries. While some pursued economic opportunities, others additionally sought places where they could live openly as Jews or at least escape the Inquisition. Amsterdam, London, and Hamburg became important stopping points before this second type of refugee continued on to colonies, and Jewish communities in these cities helped *conversos* return to the Judaism of their ancestors. Jewish printing presses, particularly in Amsterdam, produced literature that helped orient *conversos* to Jewish life. Circumcision and immersion in ritual baths played an important role in Judaizing the former converts. *Sefer Berit Yitzhak*, printed in Amsterdam in 1767 or 1768 (5528), is a circumcision manual that covers a wide range of procedures and the circumstances for bringing Spanish and Portuguese Jews back into the fold. Likewise, the list that concludes the book identifies circumcisers in major cities in the Western Portuguese Jewish Diaspora, such as Hamburg, Amsterdam, London, as well as in Curaçao and Suriname, where there were eight and seven circumcisers, respectively.

Sefer Berit Yitzhak demonstrates the relationship between European Jewish centers, such as Amsterdam, and the burgeoning American communities. Moreover, the text's list of *mohelim* (ritual circumcisers) throughout the Western Sephardic Diaspora, illustrates the Diaspora consciousness of *A Nação*: that is, the way in which Portuguese Jews continued to feel connected to their Iberian homeland and to other members of their ethnoreligious group, regardless of where they currently lived.[1] The list of *mohelim* reveals the intimate knowledge and connections that this community had throughout the Western Sephardic Diaspora. This text insists on the importance of circumcision for the process of re-Judaization for *conversos*, an idea echoed in Portuguese Jewish communal bylaws (*ascamot*), which demand that community members be circumcised in order to enjoy full privileges in the religious community or to be considered full members. Finally, and most importantly, this source points to the question of slavery within Jewish communal life in the Americas. There has been much controversy on whether the biblical practice of Jewish slaveholders circumcising their slaves persisted into the early-modern period. *Sefer Berit Yitzhak* contains an entire section on the circumcision of a slave, a strong indication that the practice existed into the eighteenth century.[2]

This source demonstrates the importance of circumcision in the construction of religious identity, the process of conversion, and the difficult question of slavery. Moreover, it points to religion's role in dictating perspectives toward slavery, enslavement, and manumission and complicates the story of Jews and slavery in the American colonies.

PRIMARY SOURCE

The Ritual Order When One Circumcises an Adult

If he circumcises one of the *conversos* (*anusim*) who come from Spain or Portugal or another adult, the *mohel* shall say the benediction for circumcision and keep the man's genitals covered during the benediction, since he is an adult. And the court or the godfather recite the remaining benedictions, namely, "to introduce him [into the covenant of Abraham our Forefather]" and "who has sustained us"; and the *mohel* shall take a glass of wine and recite the benediction on the wine and the benediction "who sanctified the beloved from the womb"; he then recites the following:

Oh God and God of our fathers, sustain this man by virtue of this commandment, and let his name in Israel be (so and so), maintain him in health and in life and deliver to him healing and life like the healing of King Hezekiah and Miriam the Prophetess who was healed from her skin affliction [leprosy] . . . and it is written: "He remembers his covenant forever, the promise he made for a thousand generations; the covenant he made with Abraham, the oath he swore to Isaac; He confirmed it to Jacob as a decree, to Israel as an everlasting covenant" (Psalm 105:8–10); "Give thanks to the Lord, for he is good, for his steadfast love endures forever" (Psalm 136:1).

This man (so and so), let God heal him; just as he entered the covenant (of circumcision) so too will he enter into Torah and commandments and good deeds, and may (God) show him success in all his endeavors, and give him a long year.

The Order of the Circumcision and Ritual Immersion of Converts

A convert who comes to you for the sake of conversion, three wise men (*hakhamim*) will approach him and inform him of some of the commandments, both the light and the severe, and the punishment for these commandments; and they ask him: "What do you see in us, as we are the most denigrated and despised nation of all?" If he says "Despite all this, I wish to convert," they reply "Know that our Torah instructs that anyone who eats animal fats is to be excommunicated (*karet*) and anyone who desecrates the Sabbath is to be stoned," and so too with the other commandments. And if despite this he says that he wishes (to

be converted), they circumcise him then and there and inform him of the reward for the commandments that God has stored away for the righteous. After he heals from the circumcision, they inform him as they did previously, and if he accepts, they go down to the river with him, or to an immersion pool whose volume is at least forty *seah* [about three hundred liters] of water and they immerse him. And when he emerges from the pool, he covers himself and recites the benediction "On immersion"; (If it is a woman, women set her in water up to her neck and the judges stand outside and inform her of some of the commandments, and afterwards she immerses herself in their presence, and they depart immediately)

One who circumcises the convert recites:

Blessed are you oh Lord our God, king of the universe, who has sanctified us with his commandments and commanded us to circumcise the converts.

And he must cover the man's genitals during the benediction as he is an adult; then he takes a cup of wine and recites [the blessing over the wine]. . . .

Blessed are you oh Lord our God, king of the universe, who sanctified us with his commandments and commanded us to circumcise the converts, and to drip from them the blood of the covenant, for were it not for the blood of the covenant the heavens and the earth would not endure, as it is written: "Were it not for my covenant day and night, I have not established the laws of heaven and earth" (Jeremiah 33:25). Blessed are you Lord, who remembers the covenant.

Our God and God of our fathers, sustain this convert for us who has come to take refuge under the wings of your Torah and your commandments, and let his name in Israel be (so and so). . . . And it is written . . . "So you also must love the foreigner [convert], since you yourselves were foreigners in the land of Egypt" (Deuteronomy 10:17–18). "Give thanks to the Lord, for he is good, for his steadfast love endures forever" (Psalm 136:1).

And they recite the "Song of Ascent: Blessed are all who fear the Lord" (Psalm 128:1); and Kaddish; and they vow to give alms to the poor.

The Order for the Circumcision of Slaves and Their Immersion at the Time When the Temple Was Still Standing

A Jew who purchased a slave had to say a benediction for him, saying:

Merciful one, have mercy and remember the master of this slave, to gladden him with his deeds and to be enslaved to him and to his sons following, as it is written: "You may bequeath them to your children after you as inherited property and make them slaves for life." Blessed are you Lord, who is good and beneficent Blessed are you oh Lord our God, king of the universe, who has sanctified us in His commandments and commanded us to circumcise the slaves.

He takes a cup of wine and says [the blessing over the wine]. . . .

Blessed are you oh Lord our God, king of the universe, who established a covenant with the father of many nations, and who commanded us to circumcise the slaves and to drip from them the blood of the covenant, as it is written: "He who is born in your house and he who is bought with your money, they must be circumcised, and My covenant shall be in your flesh for an everlasting covenant" (Genesis 17:13); Blessed are you Lord, who established his covenant with Abraham and with his descendants.

After he is circumcised and immersed in front of three witnesses, he says:

Blessed are you oh Lord our God, king of the universe, who sanctified us with his commandments and commanded us to immerse.

Selomoh Levy Maduro, *Sefer Berit Yitzhak* (Amsterdam: Gerard Johan, 1768), 15–17.

QUESTIONS

1. What can we learn about the importance of circumcision from this source?
2. What does this source tell us about women's role in Jewish ritual life?
3. What do we learn from this source about the relationship that Jews may have had with people they enslaved?

NOTES

1. Safran, "Diasporas in Modern Societies," 83–84.
2. Schorsch, "Transformations in the Manumission of Slaves," 83.

25

Touro Synagogue

RHODE ISLAND, 1763

Laura Arnold Leibman

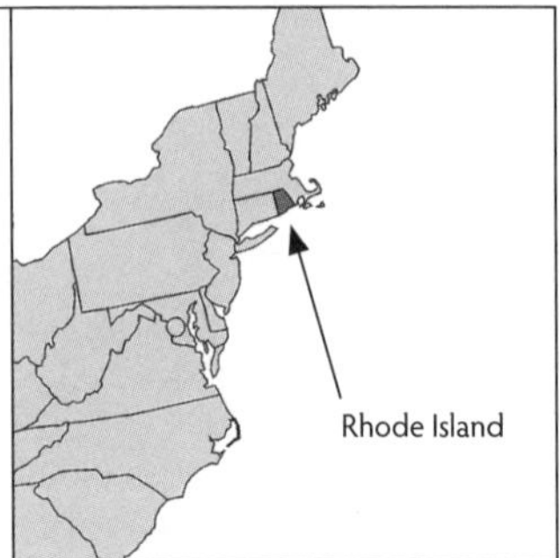

An early Jewish community in North America that benefited from immigration from the Caribbean was the fledgling community of Newport, Rhode Island. In 1677, a group of Sephardic Jews from Barbados (see chapter 15) arrived in Newport and helped establish a long-lasting trade relationship between the two communities. Barbados supplied sugar and molasses, which Newport merchants transformed into rum and other products. Newport's Jews, in return, supplied many essentials of everyday life that were not otherwise available on the island. The community really began to flourish, however, in the 1740s, in large part due to the arrival of refugees from Iberia. The Touro Synagogue was built in 1763, slightly before the early Jewish population of the city peaked at about two hundred people.[1] Like the synagogues in Barbados, Curaçao, Suriname, and New York, it was structurally influenced by the Portuguese synagogues in Amsterdam and London, even as it retained local touches such as a Georgian decorative style.

Designed by the architect Peter Harrison, the Touro Synagogue was dedicated on the second day of Hanukkah. When the synagogue was built, the congregation called itself Nephuse Israel (the Scattered of Israel). Soon afterward, however, it changed the name to Jeshuat Israel (Salvation of Israel), the name the congregation uses today. There was no Jewish ghetto in Newport, and the synagogue is centrally located in the town. The synagogue is two stories tall. Women sat upstairs in the balcony, which is above twelve Ionic columns, while men sat downstairs. The railing on this balcony served as a mechitza, the division required in Orthodox law between men and women. The small attached structure off to the left was a school. Like most American synagogues of the era, Jeshuat Israel followed the Portuguese Jewish rites.

Although not as large as the synagogues in London, Amsterdam, or Suriname, the Touro Synagogue reflects the community's success. One of the members, Aaron Lopez, was the wealthiest Jew in the colonies that would become the United States. It was here in this synagogue that Rabbi Isaac Karigal, whose painting is included in this volume (chapter 27), delivered his sermon for the holiday of Shavuot. These triumphs were short-lived.

The Revolutionary War devastated the town's economy, and when Lopez drowned in an accident on the way back to Newport, the Jewish community floundered. The synagogue fell into disuse until arrivals from eastern Europe revived the congregation. In the 1930s, the building was surveyed and plans were made as part of the Historic American Buildings Survey (HABS).

Many early American synagogues share certain features: a rectangular basilica floor plan, a women's balcony along three sides held up by twelve pillars with a moderate railing, a central *tebah* (reader's platform), and the same proportions used in Solomon's Temple, after which they were all patterned.[2] In addition, many of the synagogues in the Caribbean had sand on the floor, as did the Esnoga (Portuguese synagogue) in Amsterdam. This may have been to echo ancient Israelites' travels in the desert, or it was just a strategy for keeping the buildings clean.

The nickname "Touro Synagogue" is in honor of Judah Touro. Judah was the son of Reyna Touro and Hazan Isaac Touro, who came to the synagogue via Amsterdam and Jamaica. Although at the time of his death, Judah Touro had moved to New Orleans, he left a substantial sum in his will for maintaining the Newport synagogue and the nearby Jewish cemetery. He never married, but he did have a family with Nelly Forrester, a free woman of color. Many generations later, one of his descendants through this line returned to Newport and became a member of the board of the foundation that oversees the building that his ancestor helped preserve.

PRIMARY SOURCES

See following pages.

QUESTIONS

1. Georgian style emphasizes balance, symmetry, and proportions. Where do you see these hallmarks at play in the synagogue?
2. Why do you think the members of Newport's congregation wanted to build a synagogue that resembled the synagogue in Amsterdam?
3. What elements does this synagogue share with any other synagogues you have visited or seen? How does it differ?
4. What do you think is the significance of the synagogue's various names?
5. Why do you think the congregation decided to dedicate the synagogue on Hanukkah?

NOTES

1. Smith and Sarna, introduction to *Jews of Rhode Island*, 2.
2. Leibman, *Messianism, Secrecy and Mysticism*, 63.

Above: View of the interior from the west, Touro Synagogue, 1933. (Photo 9, LCPPD, HABS RI, 3-NEWP,29)

Facing page, top: West elevation, Touro Synagogue, 1933. (Sheet 4, LCPPD, HABS RI,3-NEWP,29); ***bottom:*** Plan of first floor, Touro Synagogue, 1933. (Sheet 2, LCPPD, HABS RI,3-NEWP,29)

SLATE ROOF
WOOD CORNICE — 33 MODILLIONS
SLATE ROOF
WOOD CORNICE
BRICK BELT COURSE & SILLS —PLASTERED—
BROWN SANDSTONE SILLS
STONE BELT COURSE
2ND FLOOR
SASH HEAD
WOOD
SASH FOOT
BRICK COMMON BOND 4 COURSES = 10"
WOOD PORTICO PAINTED & SANDED
BRICK FLEMISH BOND 4 COURSES = 10"
GRADE
CELLAR DOORS —NOT ORIGINAL—
BROWN SANDSTONE STEPS
WEST ELEVATION
SCALE 1/4" = 1'-0"
J. NAGLE . J. MEDEIROS. DEL.
UNDER DIRECTION OF UNITED STATES DEPARTMENT OF THE INTERIOR NATIONAL PARK SERVICE, BRANCH OF PLANS AND DESIGN
NAME OF STRUCTURE
TOURO SYNAGOGUE
NEWPORT — R.I.
SURVEY NO. RI 278
HISTORIC AMERICAN BUILDINGS SURVEY
SHEET 4 OF 27 SHEETS

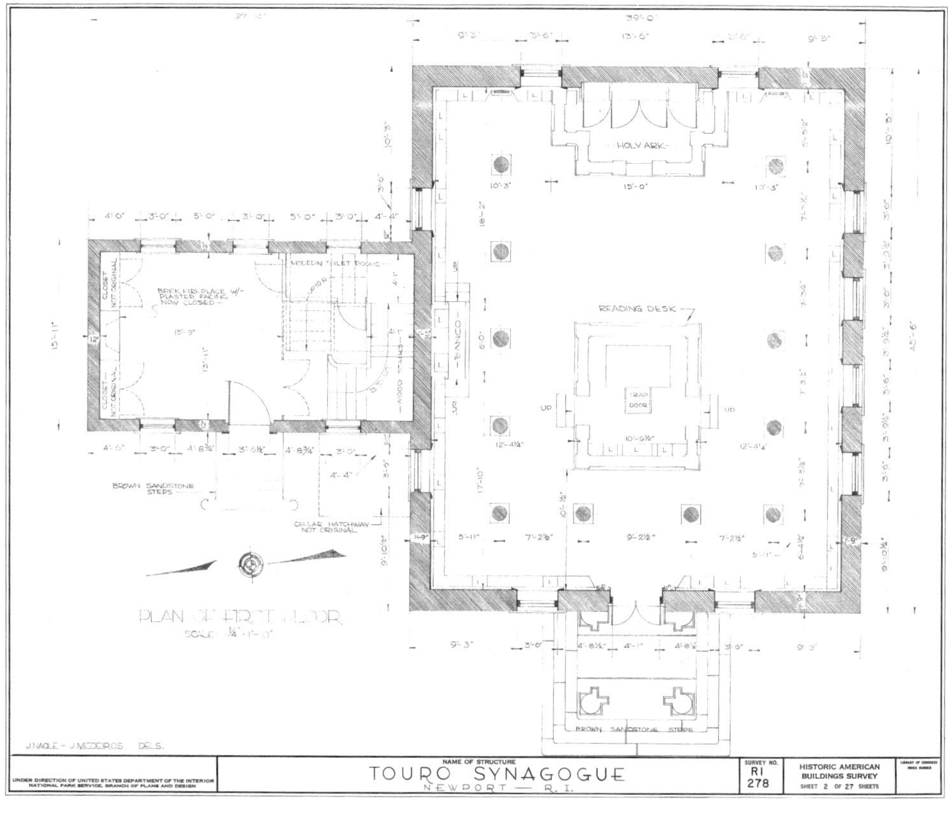
HOLY ARK
READING DESK
TRAP DOOR
UP
BANCO
MODERN TOILET ROOM
BRICK FIREPLACE W/ PLASTER FACING NOW CLOSED
CLOSET NOT ORIGINAL
BROWN SANDSTONE STEPS
CELLAR HATCHWAY NOT ORIGINAL
PLAN OF FIRST FLOOR
SCALE 1/4"=1'-0"
J. NAGLE - J. MEDEIROS DELS.
UNDER DIRECTION OF UNITED STATES DEPARTMENT OF THE INTERIOR NATIONAL PARK SERVICE, BRANCH OF PLANS AND DESIGN
NAME OF STRUCTURE
TOURO SYNAGOGUE
NEWPORT — R.I.
SURVEY NO. RI 278
HISTORIC AMERICAN BUILDINGS SURVEY
SHEET 2 OF 27 SHEETS

26

Merchant Letters from the Gratz Family

PENNSYLVANIA, 1769

Toni Pitock

Like Newport, the Jewish community of Philadelphia took hold in the eighteenth century and owed much of its success to the city's rise as a mercantile center. Many of the original Jewish inhabitants settled along the streets near the Delaware River, whose docks sheltered ships arriving from throughout the Atlantic world. By 1747, a small group of men were holding services in a house near those docks in Sterling Alley. As the congregation grew, it moved to the second floor of Joseph Cauffman's house in Cherry Alley. This space would hold them until the Revolutionary War began and Jewish refugees from New York swelled their numbers such that in 1782, Congregation Mikveh Israel—as it was now called—built its first synagogue on nearby Cherry Street.[1] Throughout these early years, the Gratz family numbered among the most prominent members of this congregation, despite their Ashkenazi origins.

Brothers Barnard Gratz (1737–1801) and Michael Gratz (1739–1811) arrived in Philadelphia from Silesia (a region located in present-day Poland) in the 1750s. They spent their first years working as clerks while they familiarized themselves with the local commercial environment and acquired the necessary skills for trading. By 1769, the year Barnard Gratz traveled to London, they began to invest in their own ventures and had achieved modest success. Gratz's letter typifies the business communications between the brothers. They updated each other about goods that had been ordered and needed to be delivered, outstanding debts, ever-fluctuating prices, and potential new ventures. They discussed their business associates and provided news about friends and family. The brothers hoped to cultivate new relationships with London merchants who could partner in transatlantic trade, a lucrative sector that was closed off to all but the wealthiest and most well-connected merchants. Most of all, Barnard Gratz sought to establish an association with the prosperous and powerful London-based firm of Jacob and Moses Franks, a son and brother, respectively, of the Gratz brothers' former employer and patron David Franks. Unfortunately,

England's Imperial Crisis of the 1760s–1770s interfered with Gratz's aspirations, but in the following decades, the brothers would become prominent Philadelphia merchants.

This letter sheds light on the complexities of trade during the eighteenth century. Jewish merchants had to balance multiple ventures, monitor colleagues, and be on the lookout for new opportunities, all while being alert to the many risks that threatened to undermine their interests. The letter shows Jewish traders' economic and social entanglements. Gratz mentions Jewish colleagues and friends in Philadelphia and far-flung family. He likewise names several non-Jewish colleagues, showing that Jews interacted extensively with non-Jews in business and that commerce gave Jews access to the dominant economic culture.

Scholars often present the arrival of Ashkenazim as occurring during the nineteenth century. However, the Gratzes and almost all of their Jewish colleagues were Ashkenazim. The letters underscore the role of Ashkenazim in Atlantic-world trade during the colonial period. Although the letter was written in English, the Gratzes' comfort with Yiddish is highlighted by their inclusion of names and dates in Hebrew letters, marked in the source below with an asterisk.

PRIMARY SOURCE

London August 10th 1769

My Dear Michael

The fore Going is Copy of my Last to you Via N. York & this Goes per Capt.n Sparks who Goes on monday Next I have now only to acquaint you that since the above have seen Mr Jacob Franks, who promised me & also wrote the same to his father Mr. David Franks that he would Render me any service in his Power & that I should propose anything in what manner he Could be of service, but as he is always busy when in town Desired me at any time when I have any Particular affair to Relate to him I should Come out to his House at Isisford & Promis.d he would Consider & Speake to his uncle Mr. Moses Franks if there Could be anything Done here for me. I have also seen 2 Days ago Miss Richa Franks when she told me she spoke to her brother Moses & he told her that if american business was Brisk or would be settled so as to Export Goods from here he might Employ me as a broker for that purpose. . . . As all the ships for all parts of amarica most are now on sailing it's very Likely I shall be obliged to stay here this vinter, therefore would have you try to Get all the Consignments of skins furrs &c you Can By the Return of this Vessels to Help on the Expenses. . . . There is a young men here says he is a Relation of ours his Name is Liber* a son of Chaim Aftir* his mothers name was Brachah* he wants to Go to America but as I Don't know who he is I told him not Goe as he Could Do nothing there I Gave him a Guinia & told him he must try what he Can Do here for his Living, our Cousin Solomon. Henry had Last week a letter from his brother Yonatan* from Silesia where in he mentions the Death of our aunt Rochel*. Henry & Levy Marks Mother She Died in Sivan* Last & that he Received the money that was sent for her, but will not pay it as she is Dead. . . . Our Fettor Hershel* father to Solo[mon]: Henry is also Dead the Rest of our family there are all well thank God Dr. [Dear] Michael I hope you have Received my several Letters & observed what I wrote you about the Goods of Groaths say Coffee mills wax Cloth &c & Remit the money as also

marks' money for Solo. Henry of the Chest tea I impationally wait for the arrival of the Packett to hear from you &c Especially from my Dearest Little Rachel which hope is well & Healthy & how she Does of which Dr Michael be particular when you write as also about Everything Else as it will Give me a Great Deal of satisfaction I have Nothing more particular to write at Present only that I Remain With my best wishes

Dr. Michael Your Ever Loving & affectionate Brother &c Barnard Gratz

Please to make my Love acceptable to your wife & hope she is Good to my Dear Little Rachel & her Nurse for which I shall make her Retaliation (?) Very Soon if Possible kiss my Dear Rachel for me & Remember me to her nurse Backey I shall send them something very soon My Love to Mr. Joseph Simons & his family hope they are all well, I flatter myself Mr. Simons will assist you in Getting some of the Indian traders to Consign a few Chests skins to me or some of the Iron Masters to send some Good Iron they may Depend on being sold to the best advent. . . . Compliments to Mr. Levy A Levy hope he will Remember his poor mother with something soon as it's uncertain when she will Get anything from Trent whom I have not seen yet My Love to Mr. & Mrs. Bush & Children hope they are all well tho I believe shall write to them by this opportunity (Sparks) Compliments to Mr. & Mrs. Jacobs Miss Sall & Rachel, not for Getting Mr. Benjamin Moses Clava have David his Letter Give my Compliments to Mrs Crathorn & tell her I Could Not Get the things she ordered me Ready to ship by this opportunity but she may Depend shall send them. . . . Dr. Michael if you have any Good old spirit [alcohol] should be Glad you would send me 10 or 15 Gallon keg I spoke to Captain Sparks mate whose Name is Mr. Sutton who promised me he would take Care of it for me

If you send it on board soone . . .

BG My Compliments to Mr. David Sproat / Mr. Milligan Mr. McCay of fort Pitt Give my Compliments to Mr. Foxcraft & tell him David his packets to his Brothers lodging as he was from home Should be Glad to know about Mr M.H bills of Exchange

Letter, Barnard Gratz in London to his brother Michael Gratz in Philadelphia, August 10, 1769, England, Gratz Family Papers 1750–1974 Mss.Ms.Coll.72, American Philosophical Society, Philadelphia.

QUESTIONS

1. Who are some of the people that Barnard Gratz mentions, and what appears to be the nature of their respective relationships?
2. What, if anything, suggests that the letter writer is Jewish?
3. What can we discern about Jews and Jewish life from the letter?
4. How does the tone of this letter compare to Hannah Louzada's (chapter 19)?

NOTE

1. Morais, *Jews of Philadelphia*, 11–12.

27

Portraits of Rabbi Karigal and Ezra Stiles

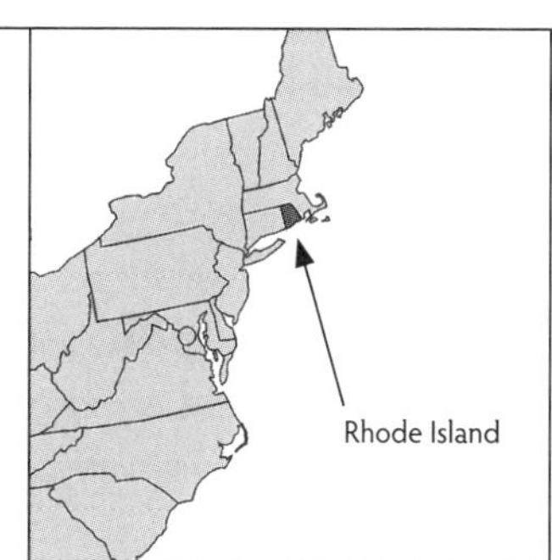

RHODE ISLAND, 1771, 1783

Michael Hoberman

The eighteenth century is often referred to "the age of portraiture," and Jews were by no means immune to paintings' allure.[1] In earlier centuries, portraits in oil and in miniature had been primarily made for "great families," but during the second half of the eighteenth century, the middle classes found portraiture within their reach. As the Earl of Fife noted with a certain disdain, suddenly almost everybody "who can afford twenty pounds has Portraits of himself, Wife and Children painted."[2] Upwardly mobile Jews were among those who embraced the art, and their portraits provide important insights into how Jews dressed, how they wished to be seen, and how others understood them.

Samuel King's 1782 portrait of Haijm Karigal is the product of one of colonial America's most remarkable interreligious encounters. Karigal, a Hebron-born rabbi of Sephardic lineage who traveled the world in order to raise money for his community in the Holy Land (which was then part of the Ottoman Empire), visited Newport, Rhode Island's fledgling Jewish congregation for five months in 1773. The rabbi made a lasting impression on one of Newport's most prominent religious leaders, the Reverend Ezra Stiles, who served as the minister of Newport's Second Congregational Church. Between Karigal's departure from Newport and his death in Barbados in 1777, the two men kept up a prolific correspondence on a range of theological subjects, political concerns, and familial affairs. Stiles became the president of Yale College in 1778, and it was in that capacity that he commissioned the portrait of his Jewish friend. He arranged for the portrait to hang at the library at Yale, where its subject's "comely form and Beautiful countenance" would inspire the college's undergraduates.[3]

King was an experienced New England–based artist who had painted Stiles more than once, most notably in the 1771 version included here. It is worth noting the contrast between King's portrait of Stiles, in which a carefully delineated backdrop absorbs much of the viewer's attention, and his much-less-complex rendering of the rabbi. Since Karigal was no longer living when King made his portrait, the painter had to work with a crayon portrait of the rabbi that had been completed by an unidentified artist during the latter's time in Newport. King may have made use of Stiles's written descriptions of Karigal—"neat and well dressed in the Turkish habit"—from a 1773 diary entry.[4] The money for the portrait was supplied by two of Newport's most prosperous Jewish merchants, Aaron Lopez and his father-in-law, Abraham Rodriguez Rivera.

This work helps us understand Jewish-Protestant relations in early America. Although Jews were only a small percentage of the colonial population, Protestants encountered Jews along the trade routes of the Atlantic world. New England ministers, including Stiles, studied Hebrew and explored kabbalah and other Jewish texts. On occasion, their interest in Jewish subjects inspired them to consult with and develop actual relationships with practicing Jews.

This portrait depicts a Jew who was born in the Ottoman Empire and whose family members had been refugees from the Spanish Inquisition. Karigal spent years of his life shuttling between Jewish communities in Asia Minor, Europe, North Africa, the Caribbean, and North America. His appearance in this Rhode Island portrait represents the global reach of the Sephardic Diaspora. His portrait reveals the degree to which some members of the Sephardic Diaspora managed to influence religious affairs and dialogues, among Christians as well as among Jews, in the period preceding the Revolutionary War.

PRIMARY SOURCES

See following pages.

QUESTIONS

1. Stiles described Karigal in his personal writings as a man of great learning. How does the painting that Stiles commissioned of Karigal seek to convey that view?
2. Compare King's representation of Karigal (a rabbi) with Stiles (a minister). How has King tried to represent his subjects' authority, expertise, and dignity?
3. The writing (now somewhat obscured) on Karigal's portrait reads, "Rabbi Raphael Haijm Karigal, born at Hebron, Educated there & at Jerusalem & died at Barbados Ætat, MDCCLXXII." How do each of the backgrounds of the images compare to one another, and what do they illuminate about the individuals?
4. How does King flag Karigal's Jewishness? How does this help us better understand how Protestants saw Jews in early America?

NOTES

1. Elliott, *Portraiture and British Gothic Fiction*, 79.
2. Duff, *Catalogue of the Portraits*, vi–vii.
3. Stiles, *Literary Diary*, 354.
4. Stiles, 354.

Samuel King, *Rabbi Raphael Haijm Isaac Karigal*, 1782, oil on canvas, 30 × 25 in. (YUAG, 2009.128.1)

Samuel King, *Ezra Stiles*, 1771, oil on canvas, 34 × 28 in. (YUAG, 1953.3.1)

28

Hetty Hays Complains of a Lack of Proper Kosher Supervision

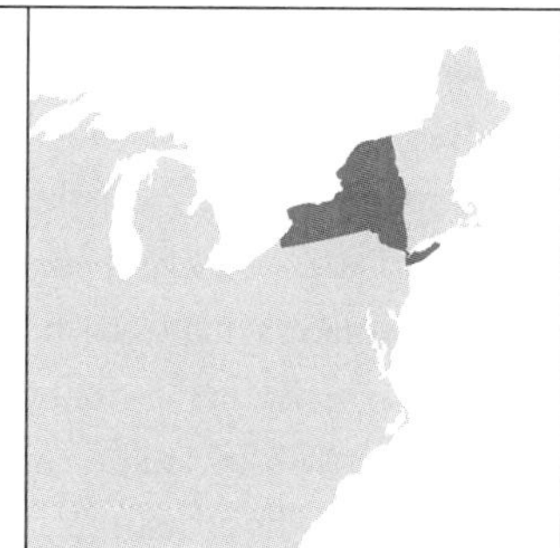

NEW YORK, 1774

Holly Snyder

Many things had changed in New York between 1709, when Nathan Simson rented rooms from his niece Meriam Levy Hart, and 1774, when Hetty Hays ran her boardinghouse only a few blocks away. Perhaps the most extraordinary was that what was once a small town of about 5,000 people had enlarged to nearly 25,000 people. The Jewish community had grown from 20 households to 250 people.[1] The infrastructure to support this community had expanded proportionately: outgrowing its rented rooms, Congregation Shearith Israel built its first synagogue in 1730 on Mill Street near the wharves. Like the Touro Synagogue (chapter 25), the Mill Street synagogue was designed to echo Amsterdam's Esnoga. As in Barbados (chapter 15), the New York synagogue was soon joined by a school, ritual bath, and houses for the hazan and *shamash*. The 1761 regulations specified that qualified men be hired to slaughter and inspect the community's meat.[2] It was these men and their knowledge that Hetty Hays would challenge in her 1774 complaint about kosher supervision.

At the time of her complaint, Hetty Adolphus Hays was the widow of Jacob Hays, who had died in 1760. Although the exact year of their marriage is unknown, she had given birth to six children born, roughly, between 1725 and 1745. She and her husband were both members of large Ashkenazi families that had emigrated to New York from Holland around 1720. Her brother, Isaac Adolphus, and her brother-in-law, Judah Hays, had achieved success in the world of New York commerce and were well-to-do by the time Hetty was widowed. Yet it appears that Hetty's husband, often noted as "Rev." in historical records, chose to serve Congregation Shearith Israel as an adviser on religious functions. Like most of those who devoted themselves to serving religious functions for the synagogue, he had struggled to support his family long before his death and at times had to rely on Shearith Israel's beneficence through its tzedakah fund to provide essentials. So it appears that Hetty's married life, before her husband's death, took place in a home where the head of the household was both observant and religiously knowledgeable.

Hetty, unlike her husband, rarely appears in the records of the early congregation. The lives of Jewish women in this period were circumscribed by the fact that they were considered ineligible to voice their concerns directly within the purview of the synagogue and were expected to rely on the agency of male relations or friends to petition communal leaders on the women's behalf. Within the colonial synagogue, men held all the power. The Mahamad (synagogue board) was made up of one or two Parnassim (presidents) and a group of "assistants"—that is, other members of the board. These men were elected from the membership by (male) members with full voting rights and often included a gabbai, who served as the treasurer.

This governance structure rendered women largely absent from the main body of Jewish communal records, where we might otherwise have expected to hear their voices. When women do appear, they are most often presented either as objects of charity (see chapter 19) or as victims of affronts to the honor of male relations (see chapters 29 and 38). We know nothing of Hetty Hays in her private life as a married woman, and there are no public documents that mention her before her husband's death. Yet this source provides evidence of a self-supporting Jewish widow who challenged communal leaders about kashrut (kosher laws), even though she could not make her complaint in her own voice.

The role of Jewish women as bearers of Jewish culture and inculcators of Jewish ritual observance in the home is often acknowledged superficially but little analyzed. The historian Paula Hyman challenged prior understandings of Jewish American history when she highlighted Jewish women's role in organizing a 1902 boycott in response to the price of kosher meat in New York.[3] Hetty Hays exhibited the same sort of political thinking that informed the kosher meat boycott of 1902: confronting a system that minimized the concerns of women and surmising that her complaint would not be taken seriously by the Parnassim of Congregation Shearith Israel, she invited two of her tenants, both learned men, into her kitchen to examine the suspect piece of lamb at the center of her complaint. Her request indicates that she understood kosher laws well enough to know that proper kosher meat required both being slaughtered a certain way and being inspected (*bedikah*) for internal injuries that could render the meat *tref* (unkosher). She was not alone in her concerns: leaders of the Jewish communities in both Curaçao and Jamaica likewise chastised the New York community for shipping meat that was not properly inspected.

PRIMARY SOURCE

At a Meeting of the Parnasim & Assistants 12th Heshvan 5535 [October 17, 1774]

Present

Messrs Daniel Gomez	**Assistants**	**Mattathias Gomez Parnas Presidente**
Hayman Levy	**Isaac Moses**	**ditto Presidente**
Moses D. Gomez		
Asher Myers		

As Complaint was made to the Parnas President, that the Widow Hetty Hays had bought out of the Market a Quarter of Lamb, that was sealed, but not searched [according to the laws of *bedikah*] & supposed kill'd by Hart Jacobs, our Shoheth [*shochet*], the President, in conjunction with the *Presidente* summon'd the assistants and Rabby Samuel Bar Isaac—a learned man, lately from London via Philadelphia (who has proper Credentials from Haham Moses Cohen de Acevedo, of London & from other Hahamim) to Attend said meeting & to assist us with his advice.

When the Shoheth attending was called in; as also Isaac Marcus (who formerly had been Shoheth in Holland) and now resides at the House of the said Widow Hetty Hays, acquainted us that the quarter of Lamb in dispute was sealed, but from appearance was not Searched, & that Rabby Moses Bar Eleazar had likewise seen said Lamb and was of the same opinion—the Shoheth assured us, on his word, that all the small Creatures & beasts, that he had killed, since he had been Shoheth, was all Searched before he had sealed them.

The Parnassim & Assistants Agreed with the aforesaid Rabby Samuel that there was not sufficient evidence to condemn the said Shoheth and therefore acquitted him of the aforesaid Charge &c. that the said Shoheth Hart Jacobs would attend the aforesaid Rabby Samuel Bar Isaac at his lodgings to be examined by him & if he should be of opinion that the Shoheth should be sufficient to order him to go & kill for the Congregation, which the Shoheth Hart Jacobs agreed to—

It was likewise agreed with the aforesaid Rabby Samuel & by his advice that Mrs. Hetty Hays, be acquainted that as the Quarter of Lamb in question was not Searched, or at least there seems to be a doubt about the same that according to our Holy Law when there's any doubt it's to be looked on as Treffo [*tref*] therefore direct that she do Cassarar [*kasher*] or properly cleanse all her Spoons, plates and all other her Utensil used in her House, otherwise to be look'd on [as] a Treffo house.

Entry for the Meeting of the Parnassim and Assistants on 12th Heshvan 5535, Minute Book of Congregation Shearith Israel 1760–1786, JJL.

QUESTIONS

1. One outcome of Hetty Hays's complaint is that the Parnassim ordered her to kosher her entire house; yet the *shochet* was allowed to continue slaughtering for the congregation. Does this seem like a fair resolution of this dispute? How could this matter have been resolved differently?
2. Why do you think Hetty Hays made a complaint even though it could have significant negative consequences for her?
3. Two witnesses, both learned men, agreed that the meat was not properly koshered. So why do the Parnassim not rule against the *shochet*?
4. In January 1773, Hart Jacobs was authorized to slaughter meat under the direction of another man, then four months later, he was allowed to slaughter on his own. After Hetty Hays's complaint, Jacobs refused to be examined by "Rabby" Samuel Bar Isaac,

as the Parnassim had ordered, and quit his post. After several weeks of drama, Jacobs resumed his post as *shochet* and applied for the synagogue to cover his lost wages. How might this history change your opinion of Jacobs's guilt?

NOTES

1. Rosenwaike, *Population History in New York City*, 8; Rock, *Haven of Liberty*, 71–72; Wolf, "American Jew as Soldier and Patriot," 10.
2. De Sola Pool and de Sola Pool, *Old Faith in the New World*, 45, 259.
3. Hyman, "Immigrant Women and Consumer Protest"; Moore, "Signposts."

29

Desperate Desire in the Dutch Caribbean

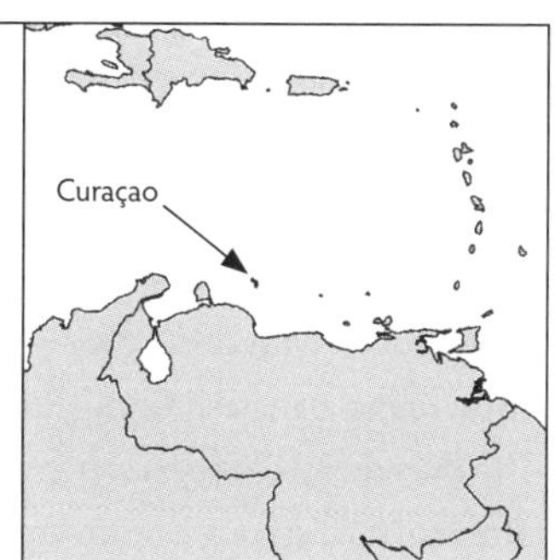

CURAÇAO, 1775

Jessica Vance Roitman

Although Hakham Samuel Mendes de Sola had been able to bring a certain calm to Curaçao's Jewish community in the 1750s (see chapter 18), the Portuguese Jews were once again rocked by a bitter dispute in 1775. Unlike the previous conflict, however, this dispute concerned allegations of sexual misconduct. Sarah de Isaac Pardo was pregnant. Although she was married to her much-older and deathly ill husband, Selomoh Vaz Farro, the closely knit community believed the father to be Abraham de David da Costa Andrade Jr. Sarah and Abraham were frequently seen in each other's company in the narrow streets of the main port of Willemstad, and gossip about their relationship was rife. When a bundle of their love letters was turned over to the heads of the Jewish community by an enslaved woman who had acted as the lovers' courier, Abraham was excommunicated, and Sarah's child was judged to be illegitimate, meaning that he would not receive any inheritance from Sarah's husband upon his death. Moreover, being a *mamzer* (bastard) in traditional Judaism is a grave designation that limits whom that child can marry.

As during the conflicts of the 1750s, the Dutch authorities were entangled in resolving the Jewish community's disputes. After the child was born and Sarah's husband had died, a bitter dispute followed, and Sarah and Abraham went to the Dutch colonial authorities for recourse. The letter included here is based on the Dutch translation of the original Papiamentu documents that had been used as evidence in the court case. This source is the first written evidence of Papiamentu, a creole language spoken in Curaçao (and Aruba and Bonaire). It shows how widespread and deeply ingrained the use of this creole language was.

The letters throw a vivid light on the social dynamics among the island's various population groups. We read of Portuguese Jews interacting with each other, what they were wearing, and how they greeted each other on the High Holidays. We get a view of how enslaved people dealt with each other and with the Portuguese Jewish population, which seems to have been with some degree of intimacy. This source brings to the fore the entanglement of enslaved and manumitted peoples in the daily life of whites, and whites in the lives of enslaved and manumitted people. In the letter, people of color (Malenchy, the unnamed woman with the box, and Little Sian) emerge as major actors. That Jews were tightly interwoven in the fabric of colonial slave-owning societies is well-known, including as plantation owners, traders in enslaved peoples, and employers of manumitted peoples. What is less well-known is how peoples interacted with each other within these deeply divided, yet often quite intimate, spaces.

This letter reveals how Jewish communities in colonial spaces functioned. Most of our knowledge of these communities comes from dry, carefully curated communal records. The overriding concern with how fellow Portuguese Jews were acting toward Abraham gestures toward strong communal bonds and strict social control that this community exerted over its members.

PRIMARY SOURCE

My soul, sweetheart, sweet soulmate, my Aurora. It causes me so much pain that you haven't written me to let me know how you are. I was ecstatic to see you yesterday evening, though I couldn't kiss you. I don't think your father would stand for that.

Darling Angel, yesterday evening a negress came by to try to sell Rachel a sandwich, and Rachel offered her two *patinos* for it and then the negress offered to sell her a box and asked me if the box was pretty and if she should buy it. I told her she shouldn't buy it because I thought it actually belonged to Guy. I found Malenchy and Guy at the warehouse to show them the box and to tell them that the negress had come to try and sell it to me. . . . The negress said that it was a black man in above Petermaaij [location near Willemstad, Curaçao] who had burdened her with selling it. Then Guy said to her to bring the owner to him, and Guy thanked me heartily for bringing the box to him.

My Diamond, I recited my *haftorah* very well, and everyone said that I didn't even speak this well when I climbed the *Sefer* [at the synagogue] and I was so thankful. [I was afraid that] your father, Guy and all your brothers would leave when I began the *haftorah*, and when I read the *haftorah* I only looked at the Torah, and Guy didn't lift his eyes from the book to hear me recite the *haftorah*, and your father and all your brothers stayed in the church [synagogue] yesterday morning.

I went to the warehouse and when I came in, I wished a good [high] holidays to everyone and your father answered back that he wished me good holy days as well and I left and went by Maduro and Guy. I wished Maduro a good passing of the holy days and he wished me the same back, and when I wished Guy a good passing of the holy days, he answered me back and gave me many good wishes: that God should write me in the book of the living and good health in the coming year. I from my side made him many compliments and good wishes, as well. David wished me a good passing of the high holidays and I answered him. It was only Aronchy that didn't wish me a good passing of the high holidays.

Yesterday, Sara Frances saw Rachel and hugged her and gave a hard stare to my mother and my mother pretended not to see her. She greeted my mother and wished her a good passing of the high holidays. She chatted a lot with Rachel and Rica, and this morning she

saw me and greeted me. Yesterday she was dressed in a blue silk cloth. Yesterday Guy was dressed in a white linen camisole and trousers but with a few strips of cotton in bright red. Your brother David bantered a lot with Rachel. Yesterday Guy sat in his place. He has never in all these years come to sit next to me.

My love, I've not dealt with the [Yom Kippur] fasting well, and I had hoped to have seen you pass by.

God wants to inscribe us in the Book of Life and help us past our obstructions. God heard me when I prayed yesterday with tears in my eyes. Amen.

My Angel, I imagine that you will let me know what Rachel Keijzer has said when she saw me pass by her door outside the Gate. God above knows, but please write me, my darling, write me how you are and what the negress said, when it pleases you, and why Joulincy Stroo behaved so. It causes me to tear up. I was at the Petermaaij crossing [ferry crossing near Willemstad] [and] Joulincy came [from the other side the ferry]. I ran into Uncle Lan with Sara Mems. They were coming to the City. My dear, your father brought your brother Aronschy with Tony and Maria and landed in order to waylay that negress Antonia on the way to Petermaaij and they brought her behind the fort and also some unarmed slaves, though I don't know for what reason.

If you know, let me know what Belje was looking for in the city and why so quickly.

My jewel, don't wait to write me and answer everything I've asked of you. I expect an answer tonight.

My Angel, trust God to help you in these difficulties and don't be slow to answer and may your husband that so oppresses you be struck down. My Aurora, was it not prohibited by God I would strike down your husband myself.

"Documents served in the lawsuit of Hubertus Coerman, fiscal, against Abraham da Costa Andrade junior, because of the unwanted pregnancy of Sara Pardo, widow of Salomon vaz Faro," May 28, 1773–February 16, 1779, Tweede West-Indische Compagnie, 1.05.01.02, 223, NA.

QUESTIONS

1. What seems to be the relationship between Abraham and the people of color (Malenchy, the woman with the box) whom he describes?
2. What kind of feeling do you get about Abraham as a person? Why?
3. On the basis of Abraham's letter, describe the Portuguese Jewish community of Curaçao in three sentences.

30

Rebecca Gomez Advertises Chocolate

NEW YORK, 1780

Deborah Prinz

While Hetty Hays was earning her living by running a kosher boardinghouse, another widow in the community kept herself financially afloat as a chocolatier. Rebecca Gomez (1713–1801) advertised her chocolate in New York newspapers in the late 1770s and early 1780s. Her store exemplifies the varied commercial interests of Spanish and Portuguese Jews during this era, of which chocolate was a specialty. Émigrés who left Iberia for the colonies had learned how to source the fermented and dried cocoa beans for trade and import them from regions of origin such as Central America, South America, and the Caribbean. Over time, the dispersion of Western Sephardic Jews mirrored the diffusion of chocolate, as they marketed the American beverage in places such as New Spain (now Mexico), Oxford (England), Martinique, Amsterdam, Bayonne (France), Brabant (Belgium), New York, and Newport (Rhode Island).[1] In so doing, they, along with Catholic clerics and other traders, supplied and extended chocolate and its processing to larger markets.

There were only a few female chocolate retailers and manufacturers in the colonies, and most, like Gomez, were widows. Gomez was unusual in that she was both female and Jewish; she was not the only member of her family, however, in the trade. Five members in two generations of the leading Sephardic Gomez family in New York City, including Rebecca, traded, manufactured, and retailed chocolate. Estate inventories of Gomez family members and other Sephardim included cocoa beans, chocolate grinding equipment, and appurtenances, both for their personal consumption and for business purposes.

Sources like this advertisement highlight the specific contribution of Sephardic Jews, their experiences, and their foods to American and world cuisine. Challenged by repression and persecution, these Sephardic refugees and immigrants sustained themselves through this migrant food. The people and the product traveled new routes and adapted to new cultures.

PRIMARY SOURCE

REBECCA GOMEZ,
Has for ſale at the CHOCOLATE Manufactory
No. 14, upper end Naſſau-ſtreet between
Commiſſary Butler's and the Brick Meeting.
SUPERFINE warranted CHOCOLATE, wholeſale and retail, white wine Vinegar by the caſk or ſingle gallon at 4 ſ.—Spermaceti oil and common Lamp ditto, Fig Blue, ſoap ſtarch, &c. &c. Alſo a few groſs Mogul and Andrew playing Cards, at a low rate and by the dozen.
†

Royal American Gazette, December 2, 1780. (Courtesy American Antiquarian Society, Worcester, MA)

QUESTIONS

1. What does this advertisement indicate about chocolate's importance at the time and to Rebecca Gomez's business?
2. What does the text reveal about chocolate making in Rebecca's day?
3. What do you learn about women in colonial New York from this source?
4. What else does Rebecca Gomez sell? Research where each product is from. How many places contribute to the goods on her shelves? What does this tell us about life and the economy in early New York?

NOTE

1. Prinz, *On the Chocolate Trail*, 7.

31

Abigail Minis's Last Will and Testament

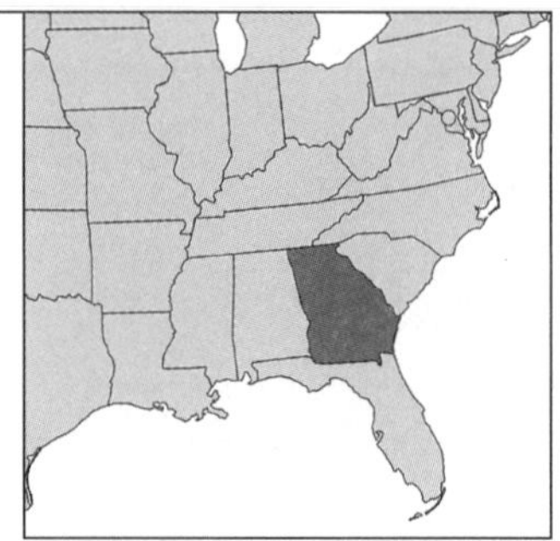

GEORGIA, 1789

Inge Dornan

Between 1763 and 1835, women's economic role in American Jewish communities expanded. In addition to keeping a store, one job women could perform without jeopardizing their reputation was the hospitality trade, such as the kosher boardinghouses kept in New York by Meriam Levy Hart and Hetty Hays (see chapters 13 and 28) or the tavern kept by Abigail Minis in Savannah. Abigail Minis was one of the most successful early Jewish American businesswomen. Though her beginnings were humble, Minis eventually gained a kind of independence that Hart could only have dreamed of. Both Minis's daughters and enslaved labor played a role in her success.

Abigail Minis (c. 1701–1794) and her husband, Abraham Minis (1694–1757), along with their two young daughters, were among forty-two Jewish settlers who arrived in Savannah, Georgia, from London in 1733. A year later, Abigail gave birth to the couple's first son, Philip, famous for being the first white child born in the colony. In 1757, Abraham died, aged sixty-three, and, after dividing his livestock among his three surviving sons and five daughters, he bequeathed the remainder of his estate to Abigail: "the better to enable her to maintain, educate and bring up our children."[1] Abigail swiftly proved herself more than capable of supporting her large family. Over the next four decades, until her death in 1794, at ninety-three years old, she amassed an extraordinary amount of property in both Georgia and South Carolina. This property included a tavern in Savannah, favored by His Majesty's council and Savannah's leading merchants; several town and garden lots in Savannah; at least seven farm lots; plus almost two thousand acres of land in St. Matthew's Parish, St. Mary's Parish, and Sapelo Island. By the time her will and inventory were read, she owned twenty enslaved men, women, and children.

Abigail Minis's will illustrates the recognizable role of Jewish settlers in the development of Georgia during the Trustee period and thereafter. Georgia Trustees were reluctant to welcome Jewish settlers to the colony, lest it deter Christian colonists—an excuse that

Jamaican colonists also used (see chapter 17). Yet Jewish families like the Minises contributed to the development of the colonial economy by purchasing land and enslaved people, established businesses, and became well-known members of Georgia society. Her will further illustrates the extraordinary potential of widows, even in the absence of male kin, to become economically empowered and sustain their family's wealth in the face of religious prejudice, conflict, and war. The Minis family continues to reside in the state of Georgia.

PRIMARY SOURCE

This is the Last Will and Testament of me Abigail Minis of Savannah in the state of Georgia Widow, being of an advanced age, but of sound mind and understanding. After paying any funeral charges, and the full discharge of all my debts, I give devise and bequeath, all my estate real and personal and of what nature soever, and wherever to be found, to my five Daughters, Leah Minis, Esther Minis, Judith Minis, Hannah Minis, and Sarah Minis, who with great affection, have always treated me as their fond mother, and by their Industry, have helped not only to gain what I possess, but by their frugality to keep together my Estate: To have and to hold, all and singular my said Estate real and personal, and of what nature soever, and wherever the same may be found, to my said Daughters Leah Minis, Esther Minis, Judith Minis, Hannah Minis and Sarah Minis and to the survivor of them, and each of them, for and during their natural lives, and the natural life of the survivor of them, fully, freely and in common as they may agree: and after their deaths, and the death of the survivor of my said Daughters, I give devise and bequeath the said Estate, real and personal, and every part thereof, to and among my Grand Children, Abigail Minis, Frances Minis, Abraham Minis, Isaac Minis, Esther Minis and Philippa Minis, Daughters and Sons of my [deceased?] son Philip Minis, to be divided to and among my said Grand Children as they, or the survivor of them, shall respectively marry, or arrive at the age of twenty one years; To hold to them, and each of them, so intitled and to his her or their Heirs, Executors, administrators and assigns forever. And I do nominate my Daughters Leah and Esther Minis Exectrices, and William Stephens, my friend, Executor of this my Last Will and Testament, hereby revoking and making void all former wills, or codicils by me made. In witness whereof I the said Abigail Minis have here unto set my hand and [seal writing my?] name in Hebrew this twenty seventh day of October Five thousand seven hundred and eighty nine.

Abigail [indecipherable script in Yiddish] Minis Her name in Hebrew [*sic*]

Will of Abigail Minis, recorded October 27, 1789, proved December 6, 1794, Minis Family Papers, Abigail Minis Papers (c. 1701–1794), 1505, 2, fo. 1, Breman Museum, Atlanta, GA.

QUESTIONS

1. In colonial America, most colonists did not leave a will. Why do you think Abigail Minis felt it necessary to create one?

2. What evidence does Abigail Minis's will provide about her socioeconomic status?
3. What, if anything, is distinctly Jewish about Abigail Minis's will?

NOTE

1. "Will of Abraham Minis"; Dornan, "Masterful Women," 383.

32

Olaudah Equiano or Gustavus Vassa: An Icon of African Judaism

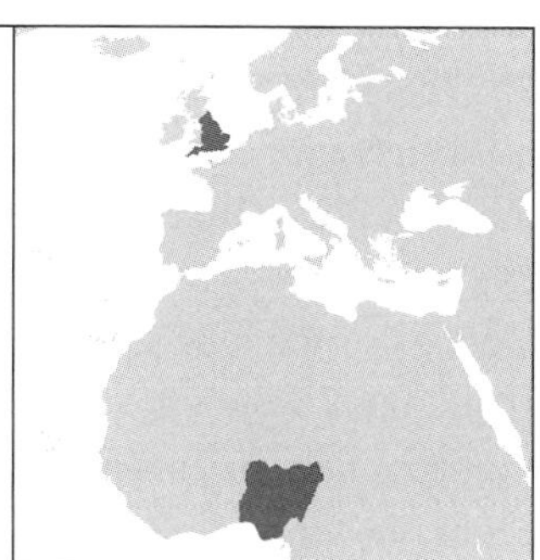

ENGLAND AND NIGERIA, 1789

Edith Bruder

While most histories of Jews in the Americas discuss primarily Jews who came to the Americas from Europe or the Ottoman Empire, Olaudah Equiano provides evidence of enslaved people who brought Jewish traditions with them from Africa.

Olaudah Equiano, also known as Gustavus Vassa, published *The Interesting Narrative of the Life of Olaudah Equiano or Gustavus Vassa, the African* in London in 1789. According to Equiano himself, he was born in 1745 in an Igbo village in the southwest of Nigeria, where his father was a hereditary tribal chief. When Equiano was eleven years old, he was kidnapped, sold to British slave traders, and sent to the West Indies. During his early years enslaved, Equiano learned how to read and write, which enabled him to write down his testimony about the slave trade and the Middle Passage. Over the next thirty years, while passing from master to master, he acquired many skills and traveled widely. Equiano bought his freedom in 1766 and in 1777 settled in London, where he rose to prominence in London's society of free Blacks. His autobiography includes a striking description of religion and culture among the Igbo of West Africa, the nation with which he identified by birth. Drawing parallels between the fate of the enslaved and the Hebrews, he mined a trove of biblical commentary to claim that the Igbo were descended from ancient Jews and that their religion was a modern survival of ancient biblical religion.

Equiano was not alone in sensing a connection between western Africa and the Jewish peoples. During the twentieth century, several self-proclaimed Jewish communities emerged across Nigeria, and their growth is significant. Following the earliest historical hypotheses on the arrival of Jews in Africa, some Igbo communities, in the footsteps of

Equiano, have developed versions of their tribal history that place it as part of the Jewish Diaspora. Nowadays perhaps thirty thousand Igbo, living in the southeastern region of Nigeria, claim that prior to the arrival of British missionaries, they practiced Judaism. They compare their traditional customs—burial rites, circumcision on the eighth day, ritual slaughter of animals, exclusiveness, marriage customs, and agricultural practices—with those of ancient Israelites. They claim that their ancestors came from Israel via the old African trade routes. In the twenty-first century, the belief in the Lost Tribes ancestry of the Igbo, discussed long ago by Equiano, has shown no sign of weakening. The Igbo are not alone: more than a dozen ethnic groups in the African continent have proclaimed their connection to ancient Israel and trace their lineage to the Lost Tribes. Their members number in the hundreds of thousands.

The African origins of American Judaism have been important within American history. As early as the eighteenth century in the United States, African American individuals and groups used the five books of Moses in general, and Exodus in particular, to construct their religious identities. The identification with the Jews of the Hebrew Bible was particularly significant to African Americans who fought for the emancipation of their people. Parallels between Jewish and Black experiences of exile and common histories of oppression, dispersion, and suffering facilitated the adaptation of Judaism within African American religious aspirations and helped Judaism assume particular significance. The first semiautonomous Afro-Jewish community (Darhe Jesarim) appeared in Suriname around 1759 (see chapter 33), but in the United States, the first organized communities of African American Jews appeared later, between the 1920s and 1930s, when several African American synagogues were built in the cities of New York, Washington, DC, Chicago, and Philadelphia. Sources like Equiano's would play an important role in their histories.

PRIMARY SOURCE

We practiced circumcision like the Jews, and made offerings and feasts on that occasion in the same manner as they did. Like them also, our children were named from some event, some circumstance, or fancied foreboding at the time of their birth. I was named *Olaudah*, which, in our language, signifies vicissitude or fortune also, one favored, and having a loud voice and well spoken. I remember we never polluted the name of the object of our adoration; on the contrary, it was always mentioned with the greatest reverence; and we were totally unacquainted with swearing, and all those terms of abuse and reproach which find their way so readily and copiously into the languages of more civilized people. The only expressions of that kind I remember were "May you rot, or may you swell, or may a beast take you."

I have before remarked that the natives of this part of Africa are extremely cleanly. This necessary habit of decency was with us a part of religion, and therefore we had many purifications and washings; indeed almost as many, and used on the same occasions, if my recollection does not fail me, as the Jews. Those that touched the dead at any time were obliged to wash and purify themselves before they could enter a dwelling-house. Every woman too, at certain times, was forbidden to come into a dwelling-house, or touch any person, or

anything we ate. I was so fond of my mother I could not keep from her, or avoid touching her at some of those periods, in consequence of which I was obliged to be kept out with her, in a little house made for that purpose, till offering was made, and then we were purified. . . .

Such is the imperfect sketch my memory has furnished me with of the manners and customs of a people among whom I first drew my breath. And here I cannot forbear suggesting what has long struck me very forcibly, namely, the strong analogy which even by this sketch, imperfect as it is, appears to prevail in the manners and customs of my countrymen and those of the Jews, before they reached the Land of Promise, and particularly the patriarchs while they were yet in that pastoral state which is described in Genesis—an analogy, which alone would induce me to think that the one people had sprung from the other. Indeed this is the opinion of Dr. Gill, who, in his commentary on Genesis, very ably deduces the pedigree of the Africans from Afer and Afra, the descendants of Abraham by Keturah his wife and concubine (for both these titles are applied to her). It is also conformable to the sentiments of Dr. John Clarke, formerly Dean of Sarum, in his *Truth of the Christian Religion*: both these authors concur in ascribing to us this original. The reasonings of these gentlemen are still further confirmed by the scripture chronology; and if any further corroboration were required, this resemblance in so many respects is strong evidence in support of the opinion. Like the Israelites in their primitive state, our government was conducted by our chiefs or judges, our wise men and elders; and the head of a family with us enjoyed a similar authority over his household with that which is ascribed to Abraham and the other patriarchs. . . . We had our circumcision (a rule I believe peculiar to that people): we had also our sacrifices and burnt-offerings, our washings and purifications, on the same occasions as they had.

As to the difference of color between the Eboan Africans and the modern Jews, I shall not presume to account for it. It is a subject which has engaged the pens of men of both genius and learning, and is far above my strength. The most able and Reverend Mr. T. Clarkson, however, in his much admired *Essay on the Slavery and Commerce of the Human Species*, has ascertained the cause, in a manner that at once solves every objection on that account, and, on my mind at least, has produced the fullest conviction. I shall therefore refer to that performance for the theory, contenting myself with extracting a fact as related by Dr. Mitchel. "The Spaniards, who have inhabited America, under the torrid zone, for any time, become as dark colored as our native Indians of Virginia; of which *I myself have been a witness*." There is also another instance of a Portuguese settlement at Mitomba, a river in Sierra Leona; where the inhabitants are bred from a mixture of the first Portuguese discoverers with the natives, and are now become in their complexion, and in the woolly quality of their hair, *perfect negroes*, retaining however a smattering of the Portuguese language.

Excerpt from Olaudah Equiano, *The Interesting Narrative of the Life of Olaudah Equiano, or Gustavus Vassa, the African*, vol. 1 (London, 1789), chapter 1.

QUESTIONS

1. What parallels does Equiano draw between the Igbo and Jews in other locations? Why do you think he makes these comparisons?
2. How does Equiano make sense of the difference in skin color between the Igbo and "modern Jews" in Europe?
3. What does his story add to our understanding of how Judaism came to and developed in the Americas?

33

Petition by the Jews of Color

SURINAME, 1793

Jessica Vance Roitman and
Laura Arnold Leibman

One of the things that set the Jewish community of Suriname apart was the creation of Darhe Jesarim, the first formal African Jewish communal organization in the Americas. Established in 1759, Darhe Jesarim began as a Eurafrican Jewish *siva* (brotherhood / fraternal organization). Yet, by 1790, Darhe Jesarim had begun to organize prayer services, even though officially the communal bylaws of the Portuguese Jewish community forbade Portuguese Jewish minyans to be held outside of Beracha ve-Shalom (in Jodensavanne) and Tzedek ve-Shalom (in Paramaribo). Moreover, when Darhe Jesarim submitted its bylaws to the Portuguese regents in 1791 (as it was required to do), it included regulations that allowed Jews of color (*congreganten*) to have the same ritual status as white Jews (*yahidim*). Suriname was unusual in that being a *yahid* rather than a *congregante* did not just indicate that a person paid taxes and could vote; both were also (contrary to Jewish law) racialized categories. Rather than allow for the change in regulations, the leaders of Darhe Jesarim dug in their heels.[1]

At first, the Dutch governor refused to intervene in the controversy, but in 1793, the regents of the white-led synagogue took legal action against Darhe Jesarim. In response, thirty-one Jews of color signed a twenty-page petition authored by two of their leaders. In addition to requesting that they be allowed to pray independently of the white-led Jewish congregations, the petition outlined the humiliations they had suffered and argued that the exclusion of Jews of color from full religious rights was contrary to Surinamese civil law. An excerpt of the petition is included here. The Portuguese Jews, whose understanding of events differed, responded, as did the leaders of Darhe Jesarim.[2]

Taken as a whole, the exchange of petitions is important on several levels. First and foremost, it shows the racism that Jews of color faced in the early congregations and their resistance to their oppression. Second, it highlights what would continue to be an ongoing struggle in Jewish communities across the Americas: Who has the right to define who is a Jew, and which Jews deserve full privileges? Third, it highlights the diverse means that Jews of color used to gain civil rights and freedom. One of the signatories of the petition was Moses Rodrigues del Prado, who had previously taken part in an armed attack on the Portuguese community of Jodensavanne. Throughout the age of revolutions, legal petitions would provide a second strategy for obtaining equality. Members of Darhe Jesarim were educated well enough in local law to be able to manipulate it to their advantage in petitions. Fourth and finally, of the thirty-five signatories, six were women: Maryana Pinto, Simha de Isaac Nassy, Simcha Nassy, Abigail Abenacar, Sarah de Oliveyra, and Roza Mendes Meza (see the photograph in the introduction to part 2). Their bravery in signing the petition foreshadows the role other Jewish women would take in requesting equality across the Americas.

Despite the brotherhood's tactical brilliance, its request was not approved. The failure of the petition signaled doom for the *siva*, which was forced to pay the cost of the legal expenses of both sides. In 1794, the "prayer house of the mulatto Jews" at the intersection of Dominéstraat and Zwatenhovenbrugstaat in Paramaribo was advertised for sale. Although still standing in 1804, it was demolished soon thereafter, and in 1817, Darhe Jesarim was officially disbanded. Equally painful, the newly revised bylaws of the Portuguese congregation explicitly limited the ritual and economic power of the Jews of color.[3]

PRIMARY SOURCE

The petitioners . . . had sought to what extent they were rightful in the exercising of ceremonies in the church [synagogue] and prayer houses of the Portuguese Nation here [at Darhe Jesarim], seeing as how here [in the synagogues of Suriname] a distinction is made between White and Colored. Specifically, this distinction consists of:

The seats of the mulattos (on what basis the petitioners are trying to determine) "shall be on the bench of the Abilimse"—a name that is given out due to the death of parents, children, and spouses that means "first Days of Grief."

That no mulatto shall be considered nor admitted as members of their Church.

That with no exceptions, their events and ceremonies are held during the daily service and at no other time.

That none of the Jewish nation shall make a *miseberah* [prayers or pleas for blessings that people offer up for others] for a mulatto nor make an *Ascaba* [mass for the soul of people who have died] prayer.

That they are not permitted to buy any *mitzvot* [rights, privileges] relating to the privileges concerning the ceremonies with the Books of Moses [Torah], which on Saturday morning, the normal Sabbath Day, are publicly sold by the gabbai.

That they are not allowed to be called to read from the Books of Moses and are not even allowed by the Regents or Adjuntos to hold them.

That in addition all the white people marrying a mulatto will be considered a source of sorrow and will be relegated to the status of mulattos unto the second generation.

And that the Petitioners are held to be too unknowledgeable and unskilled to take part in the prerogatives of the church to which everyone who professes a religion has had open to them. . . .

The Petitioners . . . wanting to show their commitment, continued meeting with the aforementioned Brotherhood [Darhe Jesarim] after the usual service and prayer times of the Jewish nation, and together they prayed and sang such as a fellowship or *siva* [as] is permitted to do in this settlement without having to be a part of any other Congregation.

These aforementioned recitations of prayers were not only done by themselves, but also with the help of some Portuguese and High German [Ashkenazi] Jews who have supported and helped [the Brotherhood] to take root over the past thirty-four years, not only with the intention of helping found the Brotherhood but also to distribute charity to both the white and the colored Jews.

There had never been any evidence that the Jews within this colony or anyone else had looked upon the practices and observances of the Petitioners as being anything other than as honorable and to be celebrated by their attendance and the Brotherhood as something to be supported.

The Honorable Regents of the Portuguese Jewish nation had approved, announced, and published in their church in the Savannah [Beracha ve-Shalom] and in their Prayer House Tzedek ve-Shalom in Paramaribo whereby it was stated that every mulatto and colored person that was considered a congregant (*congregante*) in their church was invited to meet and come to the house of the Regent D. Nassy and sign their name there [and become part of Darhe Jesarim].

"Memorandum of the Coloured Jews to Governor De Frederici" (1793), 1.05.10.01:528, 396–414, NA.

QUESTIONS

1. What are some of the humiliations Jews of color suffered in Suriname, according to the petition?
2. According to the petition, how did the distinctions that the regents of the synagogue made actually reinforce the right of Darhe Jesarim to exist?
3. Consider this petition alongside the Surinamese marriage contracts in chapter 14 and the photograph of the signatures in the introduction to part 2. Even though the women would not have had full rights in Darhe Jesarim or Tzedek ve-Shalom during this era, what did they have to gain from the petition?
4. Notice that white Jews who marry Jews of color will be demoted to "the status of mulattos unto the second generation." What does this policy tell us about how race was understood in early Suriname?

NOTES

1. Ben-Ur, *Jewish Autonomy in a Slave Society*, 176; Ben-Ur, "Peripheral Inclusion," 192.
2. Ben-Ur, *Jewish Autonomy in a Slave Society*, 178; Vink, *Creole Jews*, 211–212.
3. Ben-Ur, *Jewish Autonomy in a Slave Society*, 180, 189.

34

Portraits of Sarah Moses Levy and Chapman Levy

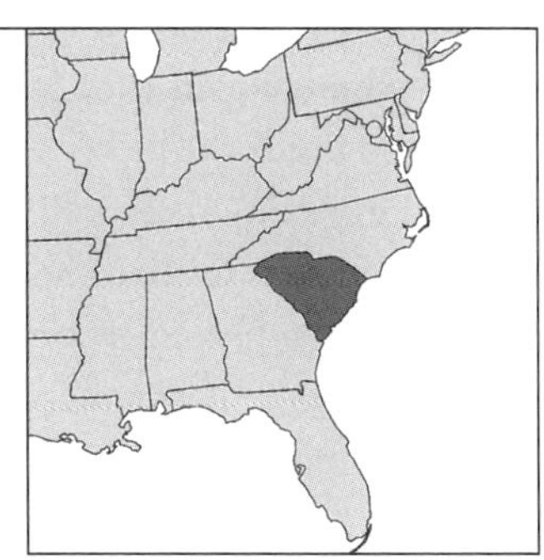

SOUTH CAROLINA, C. 1798

Dale Rosengarten

Both opportunities in trade and Carolina's reputation for religious tolerance drew Jewish settlers to the port city of Charles Town in the early years of the colony.[1] Jews had been welcomed as settlers by the Fundamental Constitutions of Carolina of 1669 and naturalized as citizens as early as 1697. Kahal Kadosh Beth Elohim, one of the first five colonial congregations, was founded in 1749 and dedicated its first synagogue in 1794. Like most Jewish congregations of the era, it followed the Western Sephardic rite. By 1800, Charleston boasted the largest, wealthiest, and most cultured Jewish population in North America—more than five hundred Jewish residents. As we saw in the example of Rabbi Karigal (chapter 27), demands for portraits spread to the mercantile and professional classes, including relative newcomers like Sarah's husband, Samuel Levy, and her father, Henry Moses, who had immigrated to America during the War for Independence. Samuel and Sarah moved to Camden—the second-oldest town in South Carolina—sometime before their son, Chapman, was born on the fourth of July 1787.[2] The portraits were made a little over a decade later, around 1798.

Unlike the portraits of Karigal and Stiles, both painted in oil on a large canvas by a well-known artist, the Levy portraits were painted in watercolor on ivory by an unknown artist. Although small, miniatures—named for minium, or red lead, used by medieval illuminators—cost about the same as full-sized portraits and were extremely popular during this era. Miniature paintings—an ornamental art form brought to America from England—were intimate tokens of love, worn on the bodice or concealed in a pocket or bedside drawer. At the same time, they provided opportunities for affluent families, whether Christian or Jewish, to flaunt their finer feelings along with their wealth and refined taste. Full-size portraits of the period commonly featured women holding or wearing tiny paintings of husbands, children, or President George Washington, but the portrait of Sarah wearing her son Chapman's likeness is a rare instance of a miniature in a miniature. Housed under glass in a well-wrought metal locket, each Levy miniature has a memento on the reverse side. Chapman's memorial depicts a woman at a plinth topped with a dove, painted in sepia watercolor mixed with chopped hair—presumably cut from Chapman's locks but perhaps commingled with his mother's.[3] A square of goldbeater's skin and a thick card, discovered inside the locket in 2001 by the conservator Carol Aiken, ensured a snug fit.[4]

The Levy miniatures testify to the integration of Jews into elite society and the body politic of South Carolina and to their full embrace of southern institutions, including slavery, dueling, and Freemasonry. Chapman studied law and was admitted to the bar in 1806. A militia captain during the War of 1812, he served in both the state house and senate from Kershaw County. In 1820, Chapman owned thirty-one enslaved people, of whom twenty worked at his brickyard near the Columbia Canal, making him the largest Jewish slave owner of his era. Several of his brickyard workers were implicated in the aborted uprising in Camden planned for July 4, 1816, including a man named March, who was tried as a rebel leader and hung with five other men in front of the town jail. Another alleged conspirator, Isaac, had been Chapman's drummer in the War of 1812.[5] Tracing Chapman Levy's career and examining how he and his mother presented themselves to others provides a window into the world of a southern Jewish slaveholder.

PRIMARY SOURCES

See following pages.

QUESTIONS

1. What does the Levys' clothing tell you about their life and times?
2. Whom do you think Sarah's miniature was made for? How could you support your theory?
3. Why do you think artists included chopped hair mixed with watercolors on the back of ivory miniatures? What does this tell us about how the Levy family enshrined memory?

NOTES

1. Rosengarten, introduction to *Portion of the People*, 2.
2. Moore, "Freedom's Fruits," 11.
3. Frank, *Love and Loss*, 10.
4. Aiken, "Conservation Reports."
5. Inabinet, "July Fourth Incident."

Anonymous, *Sarah Moses Levy (Mrs. Samuel Levy)*, c. 1798, watercolor on ivory, 2½ × 2¼ in. (Gift of Lane Dinkins, SCCCL)

Reverse of *Sarah Moses Levy (Mrs. Samuel Levy)*, memento painted on ivory in sepia watercolor mixed with chopped hair. (Gift of Lane Dinkins, SCCCL)

Anonymous, *Chapman Levy as a Youth*, c. 1798, watercolor on ivory, 3 × 2¼ in. (Gift of Lane Dinkins, SCCCL)

Reverse of *Chapman Levy as a Youth*, memento painted on ivory in sepia watercolor mixed with chopped hair. (Gift of Lane Dinkins, SCCCL)

35

Prayer for Jewish Militiamen

SURINAME, C. 1805–1806

Eli Rosenblatt

One reason many members of Suriname's Jewish community moved north from Jodensavanne to the main port of Paramaribo was the ongoing danger of Maroon attacks on the plantation town. Maroons were people of African descent who escaped enslavement on plantations and formed autonomous settlements in the interior. Suriname's plantations were often sites of enslaved resistance from the seventeenth century onward, as Maroons returned to the plantations to attack their former enslavers, gather supplies, and liberate enslaved peoples. While the British had been able to end some of the violence in Jamaica by signing a 1740 treaty with that island's Maroon community that recognized the Maroon's freedom and paid them a yearly tribute, the British takeover of Suriname from 1799 to 1816 did not end violence in Suriname. This handwritten Hebrew supplicatory prayer was composed in Jodensavanne by David Hizkiahu Baruch Louzada (1750–1825) during the British takeover.[1]

Written to be recited on the Sabbath, this prayer formed part of a new liturgy composed specifically to ask God for protection from raids and attacks by Maroons. The circumstances of this prayer are distinct because it was composed upon the revolt of three regiments of "coloured" soldiers serving alongside European mercenaries in a military outpost adjacent to the village of Jodensavanne, rather than in response to a threat from known "Boni" Maroons. These soldiers deserted the colonial militia, raided Jodensavanne, murdered a Jewish watchman, and fled eastward, joining existing Maroon settlements along the banks of the Marowijne River. The "Boni" Maroons whom they joined, known today as the Aluku, are one of the six independent Maroon tribes in Suriname and French Guiana. Some Maroon communities had kin ties to Jodensavanne and Jewish plantations: Paanza, for example, the matriarch of the Kasitu Sramaccan clan, was the daughter of Moses Nunez Henriquez, a Portuguese Jew. She had been captured in a Maroon raid on Joseph Castilho's Kasitu Plantation.[2] Some Maroon communities acknowledged ties to Jews in Suriname or back to Africa; thus, one eighteenth-century explorer described four Djuka villages as "Jewish Maroons."[3] Yet this prayer suggests that the Jodensavanne community perceived both the rebels and multiracial soldiers as ethnically Other.

This source is among the few early examples we have of original Hebrew liturgy produced in the Americas. It gives us a window into the ways that local conditions shaped the religious sensibilities of early American Jews. It is distinguished by its relation to slavery and revolt and for the fact that it does not ask any earthly government or monarch for protection, as was more common for Hebrew supplications during this period. It demonstrates that formerly enslaved people continued to raid and pose a danger to Suriname's declining Jewish plantations well into the nineteenth century, after many of the major revolts had ceased.

By describing the enemy as "rebellious, cruel Kushites who plot against our welfare," Louzada gestures toward the ways in which European Jews understood the delicate balance of Jewish power and powerlessness in a slave society. White Jews were powerful beneficiaries of European identity and origins, while at the same time, they recognized that their cultural autonomy came with a vulnerability quite familiar to Jews in the Diaspora, and so it was to God—rather than an earthly monarch or colonial governor—that they appealed for protection from harm. As Aviva Ben-Ur writes, this prayer shows that "religion is not always about the wolf learning to dwell with the lamb."[4]

Stylistically, the most significant component of this prayer is the two distinct ways that the author refers to Maroons and their allies. In one stanza, the author describes the Maroons as "Kushites" (כושים) and then later as "Blacks" (שחורים). This contrasts with Jews of color in Suriname, who were described in Hebrew/Aramaic as "emancipated" Jews (see chapter 14), rather than as a separate ethnic group. This doubling of rabbinic and Atlantic terms demonstrates that people of African descent who were deemed not Jewish were perceived by the author as members of a biblical "nation" and an inferior racial group defined by its color rather than lineage. Both understandings of what it meant to be Black existed simultaneously, and each contributed to the shifting ways that the Surinamese Jewish community defined itself as both apart from and integrated into the world around it.

PRIMARY SOURCE

Blessed and powerful God, eternal [illegible]
Ruler of all, Lord of Armies; we have come to beg
And pray for the safety of the country,
as You directed us through Your prophet:
"Seek the welfare of the city Where I have sent you into exile,
and pray to the Lord on its behalf, for in its welfare
you will find yours." [Jeremiah 29:7]

God, the great, mighty, and revered King,
Creator of all and savior in times of distress
show mercy to us and pity, save, succor, and protect all those

who, going to war against our enemies,
the cruel and rebellious Blacks,
are fearful of the adversary.

We beseech you, Lord of Armies, lead them in peace,
Guide them to a good life as they desire, and save them
From the hands of the evil-doers and the plunderers,
From evil diseases, from hidden attackers, pillagers and bandits,
And from all wicked, wild beasts, insects and reptiles that thrive
In the forests and deserts, and from all damage
And loss, by day and by night, as it is written:
. . . .
In all your ways acknowledge Him,
And He will make your paths smooth [Proverbs 3:6].
Then you will go your way safely
And not injure your feet [Proverbs 3:23].

We beg you, God, bolster their strength!
Shore up their courage with no sluggishness
Or laxity. Make them nimble, as it is written:
Blessed is the LORD, my rock,
who trains my hands for battle,
my fingers for warfare [Psalms 144:1].
I struck them down,
and they could rise no more;
they lay fallen at my feet [Psalms 18:39].
Instruct and guide them with sound advice
And the spirit of knowledge; be a refuge
And a citadel to them, so that they may
Subjugate, conquer and destroy
Under their feet all enemies; the rebellious, cruel
Kushites who plot against our welfare, as it is written:
When evil men assail me to devour my flesh
it is they, my foes and my enemies,
who stumble and fall [Psalms 27:2].
I pursued my enemies
and wiped them out,
I did not turn back till I destroyed them.
I destroyed them, I struck them down;
They rose no more, they lay at my feet [2 Samuel 22:38–39].
We beg you, Lord, nullify their leaders
And thwart their designs, as it is written:
The LORD frustrates the plans of nations,
brings to naught the designs of peoples [Psalms 33:10].

May their eyes be dimmed,
and make all their loins unsteady [Ezekiel 29:7],
As it is written: Terror and dread descend upon them;
Through the might of Your arm they are still as stone [Exodus 15:16].
They shall be still as a stone,
and terror and dread shall fall upon them.[5]

. . . May our prayer and that of all those who pray for them be as agreeable to you as offerings of oxen in bygone days, for You hear the prayer of every mouth, and so, may it be Your will, and let us say: Amen!

"Prayer at the Time of Revolt of the Negroes, Probably in Surinam," n.d., JJL.

QUESTIONS

1. What is the difference between describing Jews of color as "emancipated" and other people of color in the colony as "Kushites" or "Blacks"?
2. Compare the way this prayer talks about the soldiers who attacked Jodensavanne with the soldiers who supported the Portuguese in Aboab's poem in chapter 9. What strategies do the authors share?
3. Compare the ritual language used here to that in the circumcision manual in chapter 24. How does each use sacred language to define which people of color are insiders and which are not?

NOTES

1. Ben-Ur, *Jewish Autonomy in a Slave Society*, 70, 121.
2. Price, *Alabi's World*, 23.
3. Ben-Ur and Frankel, *Remnant Stones*, 70.
4. Ben-Ur, *Jewish Autonomy in a Slave Society*, 121.
5. From the Prayer for the New Moon.

36

Jews and Epidemics

NEW YORK, 1805–1832

Laura Arnold Leibman

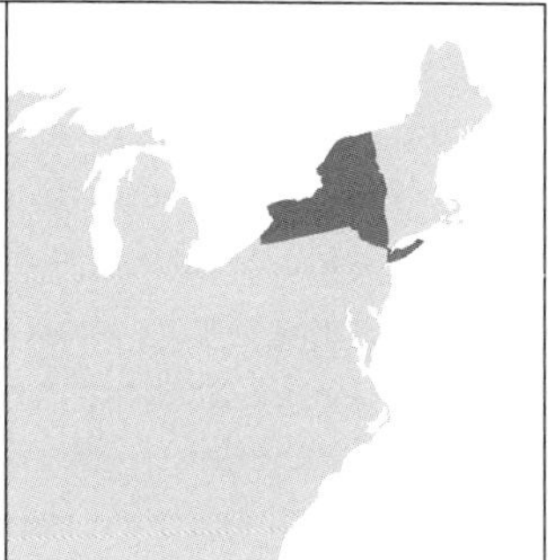

Marriages and trading partners connected Jews across ports in the Americas and the Atlantic world, but so did epidemics. Cemeteries provide some of the best information about Jews' experience of disease, as the stones often record the cause of death and the suffering felt by those who were left behind. Other sources like letters, synagogue records, diaries, sermons, and poetry provide insights into how epidemics influenced Jewish life. During the recent COVID crisis, American Jewish communities innovated their rituals by having Zoom Passover Seders and online services. Death rites were similarly impacted, as burial societies struggled to gather enough protective gear to ensure that the virus did not pass between the dead and the living. Even funerals and memorial services were impacted, as the recitation of the mourner's kaddish requires a minyan, but public-health restrictions often forbade large gatherings. If this were not enough, antisemitic caricatures spread across social media, blaming Jews for the disease or suggesting that vaccines were a Jewish plot. These crises were not new but echoed those faced by Jews generations earlier, as epidemics swept across the Americas. For example, one of the triggers for *la complicidad grande* (see chapters 4 and 5) was a yellow fever epidemic that swept the Spanish-American colonies in the 1640s. Up until the 1930s, when a vaccine was created, yellow fever continued to spread across the Americas, unsettling Jewish lives and disrupting Jews' ability to practice their traditions.

The documents included here are taken from a series of yellow fever epidemics that hit New York City between 1795 and the 1820s. The first is a poem written by Grace Seixas Nathan (1752–1831) in 1805. Nathan and her family lived in the Bowery, at the lower end of Manhattan. Her husband, Simon, a merchant, worked at 27 Water Street, close to the docks where the epidemic started and only a couple of blocks from the Mill Street synagogue. Similar to when COVID began in 2019, when yellow fever struck in 1805, neither city officials nor doctors understood how the disease was spread. The most common theory was that the disease was caused by inhaling miasma—a putrid smell of decaying bodies and vegetative matter. While doctors were wrong about miasma (the virus is carried by mosquitoes), they were correct that residents' best chance lay in evacuating. Yellow fever was incredibly deadly: in 1795, about 10 percent of the city's population (five thousand people) died from the disease in a few short months. When yellow fever hit the city in 1805, most of the city's Jewish community fled along with other inhabitants. In addition, city officials set up a marine hospital off Staten Island to treat the sick. Consequently, many fewer died that year than in earlier epidemics. Nathan's poem, however, shows how stressful evacuations were.

The second document is excerpts from a diary kept by Aaron Levy, another member of congregation Shearith Israel. Levy records how the community responded to various visitations by yellow fever and the prominent members of the community who died from it. Levy and his extended family evacuated the city, including Levy's nephew Joshua Moses, husband of Sarah Rodrigues Brandon (see chapter 39). The couple had vaccinated their children against smallpox, but as there was no inoculation for yellow fever, avoiding crowds was their best bet. The transition from yellow fever to cholera in Levy's diary speaks to the ongoing innovation of diseases: cholera was first documented in India in 1817 and—like yellow fever—spread worldwide thanks to merchant ships that traveled between ports.

PRIMARY SOURCES

Poem by Grace Seixas Nathan

Written on the day that I left the Bowery (1805)

Farewell to the Suns early ray
Which thro' the thin foliage is seen
Farewell, to the Bird on the Spray
And farewell, the now faded green

I go—where Sickness & Death
Have spread their dire influence around
Where Disease was inhaled with the breath
And the victims of both have been found

Where the Parent with sorrowing eye
Has watched o'er her agonized child
And suppressing the heart-rending sigh
Her feelings—so acute made her wild
In madness that rest was procured
Which Reason could never obtain.
And while its bright power was obscured
She felt a relief from her pain
Such scenes fill the Bosom with woe
And caused the unbidden tear

In unrestrained torrents to flow
On the sad and premature bier
Oh God! may my prayer ascend
And be heard in thy Mighty Domain
My city, oh deign to defend
Let millions not lose thee in vain.

Excerpts from the Diary of Aaron Levy

1805, Fever in New York.

September 9. The family moved out of town. Mrs. Sara Levy, wife of Eleazer Levy, Aunt of Aaron Levy, died this day.

1805, Oct. 23, Died at the house of Mr. Aaron Levy—Mr. Abraham Hurtz a native of Germany aged 28. . . .

1807, August, Prevalence of influenza Sickly Season but no yellow fever. . . .

1819, Yellow fever in New York this year and in all the seaports of the United States. . . .

1822, September, A temporary Shule [synagogue] was opened in Oliver Street for the fall holy days by the Congregation, the lower part of the city being deserted on account of the yellow fever. There was also a Minyan at Mount Listen [the Moses family country estate located between Thirty-Second and Thirty-Fifth Streets and Seventh Avenue and Hudson River in New York today]. . . .

1822, July. Early in July 1822 the yellow fever commenced at the foot of Rector St. On the 5th of August Mrs N. Phillips died of the same after 5 days' illness. The infected district was fenced in about the 8th of Aug: and the citizens generally moved to Greenwich [Village] with public offices, Banks &ca., and on the 26th October returned en masse. The 15th November the Custom house, Post Office Banks &ca. returned to their former places and the Houses of Public Worship were reopened after having been so long shut up in the Lower part of the city. The number of cases reported during the pestilence were 401, Deaths 230. Joshua Moses & his family, with my family were at Mount Listen with my mother in law's family during the sickness.

1823, March 29, Mrs. Sarah Esther Brandon, wife of Abm. R. Brandon died. Her funeral had to be deferred to the 31st in consequence of a severe snow storm. She was to have been buried the day before. Buried in Chatham St. . . .

1832, The Cholera raging in the City I did not go to the Lake [George] as usual, nor did I leave the city this year. In consequence of the sickness being so near us we moved a part of our family to M. L. Moses' [his brother-in-law's] house.

Grace Seixas Nathan, "Written on the day that I left the Bowery" (1805), Poetry Manuscript—Grace Seixas Nathan, box 1, folder 10, Nathan Family Papers P-54, AJHS; excerpt from diary of Aaron Levy, from "Items Relating to the Moses and Levy Families, New York," *PAJHS* 27 (1920): 336–343.

QUESTIONS

1. In what ways did epidemics disrupt daily life for Jews in early America?
2. What were the worst aspects of yellow fever, according to Nathan?
3. If 10 percent of New York City had died from COVID in the first year of the epidemic, what impact do you think this would have had on the city?
4. Compare Levy's and Nathan's responses to the epidemics and the role gender plays in their descriptions.

37

Alexander de Lavaux's Map of Suriname

SURINAME, 1806

Eli Rosenblatt

In addition to prayers (see chapter 35), maps like the one made by Alexander de Lavaux were crucial tools for helping colonists win disputes with Maroons and other people living in Suriname. As one historian puts it, "De Lavaux's map fuses a war report with outlines of battle scenes with a detailed layout of the colony's plantations."[1] De Lavaux's map was derived from military intelligence, and the mapmaker de Lavaux suggests that Suriname was a theater for colonial war.

Amid this chaos, de Lavaux recognizes Jewish settlements in his map as agents of empire and stability. The map shows that Jewish settlements were concentrated in certain geographic areas, especially south of Paramaribo on the Suriname River around Jodensavanne. Through the marking of Jewish-owned lands, the map reveals Sephardic Jews' participation in developing a plantation economy, as well as their geographic autonomy. Plantations and adjacent settlements owned by Jews were often named according to Jewish and Hebrew place-names.

The map consists of three sections. On the outer sections in pink are the lists of the plantation owners, divided by regions. In the center section is the map itself. Superimposed on the upper right of the map is the title and the dedication from de Lavaux to the administrators of Amsterdam, the West Indies Company, and the Society of Surinam. On the upper left is a small-scale additional map showing the campaigns against the Maroons. Likewise, across the landscape are Maroon villages, marked in red, often with yellow flames above them and gray clouds of smoke. Below the map is a legend containing a statement that the Roman letters refer to measurements taken by de Lavaux himself. Largely missing from the map are Indigenous villages along rivers and the coast that had been depicted in earlier maps.[2] The absence of such villages stood in contrast to the actual role of Amerindian peoples in the colony, who both traded with the Dutch and Jews and helped fight against the Maroons.[3]

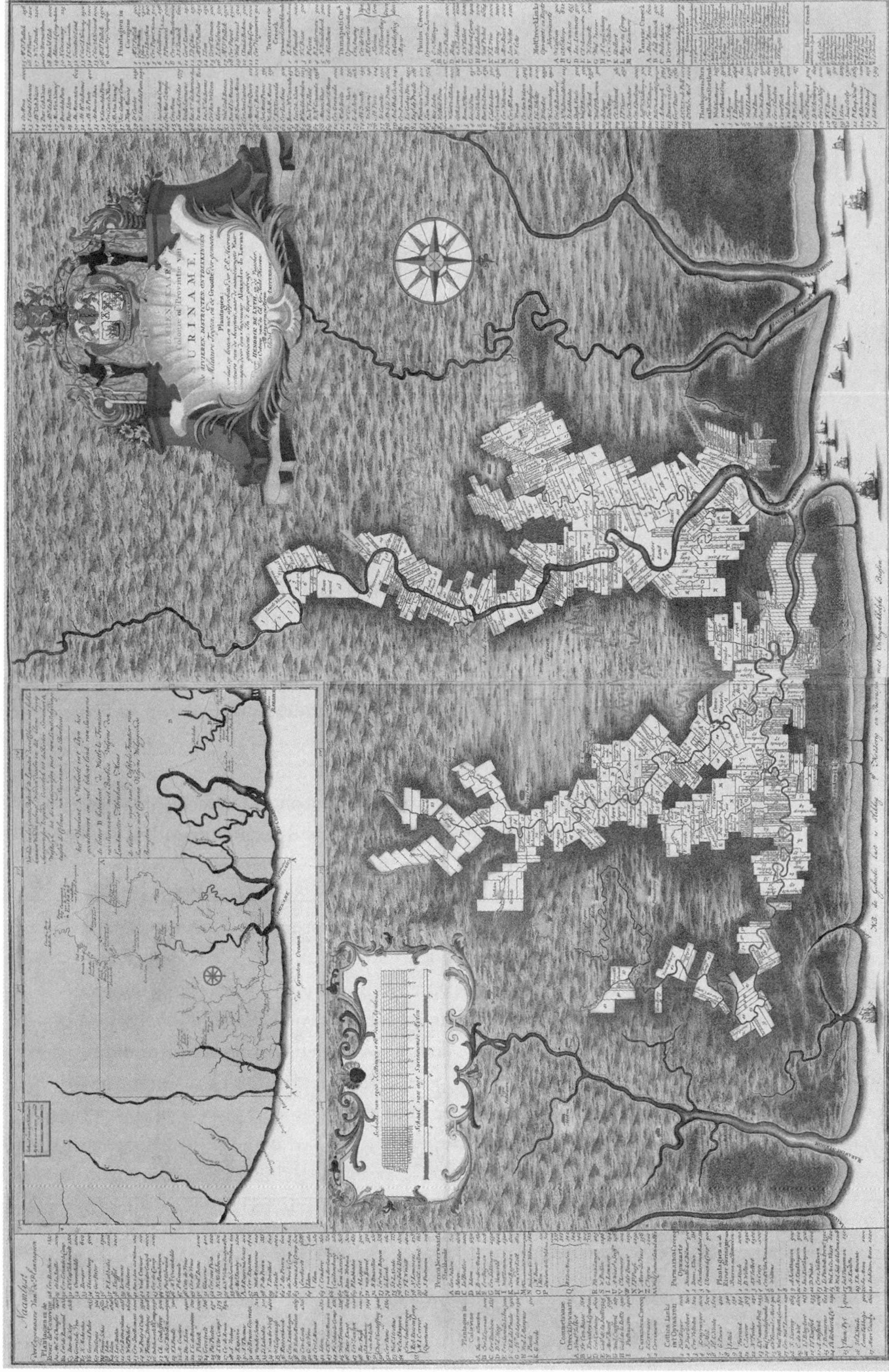

PRIMARY SOURCE

Facing page: Alexander de Lavaux, *Algemene kaart van Suriname*, 1737, watercolor on paper. (Courtesy RM, NG-478)

General map of the Province of Suriname: rivers and districts with all discoveries from the military campaigns, as well as the size of the plantations, which were mapped according to precise observations.

To the Honorable Esteemed Gentlemen,
Egidius Van Den Bempden
Mayor of the city of Amsterdam and Governor of the General Chartered East India Company at the Chamber of Amsterdam, etc. etc.
Cornelis Graafland, Alderman of the City of Amsterdam etc. etc.

[Legend, upper left in inset map:] The square "A" shows the cultivated and known land of Suriname. The letter "B" refers to the western border of Surinam with Barbice, according to the surveyor Abraham Maas. The letter "C" shows the eastern border of Surinam with Cayanne, according to well-founded information.

[Second column on left side of main map:] Plantations in the River Surinam, from top to bottom. [It is a list of owners' names, on the left, with size of the plantation to the right. It continues in the first pink column to the right of the main map. Names of plantations are on the map itself.]

Plantagien in de Rivier Suriname van Booven na Beneeden

No.	Name	Size
1	St. Neale	2000
2	D. Wiltens	1500
3	d'H. Talbot	1500
4	de Crepi	1000
5	Erv. d'H. de Cheusses	1000
6	Wiltens	
7	----------	
8	----------	
9	A. Kinkhuysen	500
10	A. Kinkhuysen	500
11	Sus. Kinkhuysen	500
12	D. Pichot	1000
13	Erv. v. Hallewyn	
14	Is. Pinto de Aron.	3500
15	Wed. Jo. Co. Nassi	800
16	Wed. Sal. de la Para	1208
17	Sal. Turgeman	150
18	Jo. Kastilho	
19	J. R. Monsanto	
20	Sa. Meza	1000
21	Is. de Dav. Meza	1000
22	So. Meza	1000
23	I. Gr. de Fonseca	
24	Abm. Coh. Nassi	
25	Dav. Coh. Nassi	
26	Abm. de Britto	
27	Mo. Nun. Henriq.	
28	Dav. de la Para	
29	Dav. Idem	
30	Ab. Mementon	600
31	Ab. Hz. de Barios	
32	Ab. de Pinto	400
33	Ar. Bueno bibaz	
34	W. Sam. de la Para	
35	Erv. Sam. Co. Nassi	
36	Ab. Nun. Henriq.	
37	Jac. Gabay Crasto	
38	Noph. Messias	
39	Is. Careloo	2250
40	W. Sam. de la Para	1050
41	----------	
42	----------	
43	Jac. Gab. de Crasto	
44	Erv. Mos. Cotinho	
45	Erv. Meza	
46	Sam. d'Avilar	1775
47	Joode Savaane	
48	Jac. Hz. de Barros	800
49	Iz. uz. de Avilar	800
50	Jac. Hz. de Barios	
51	Erv. Ion Witzen	
52	Idem	
53	Wed. Gab. Baeza	
54	Dav. d'Iz. Messias	
55	Ab. Fonseca Meza	
56	Erv. Jan Coutier	
57	Mord. m. Quiro	110
58	Mos. C. Baeza	200
59	Erv. Mess. Penco	550
60	W. Ab. M. Meza	250
61	E. Bn. H. Granada	
62	Erv. Ios. Arias	500
63	Bene Hz. Granada	450
64	Ios. Coh. Nassi	430
65	Dr. Guldesteeden	1223
66	De H. Talbot	1264
67	B. Hz. Granada	1558
68	Moses Naar	
69	Is. de Dav. d'Meza	
70	Erv. Granada	1000
71	Ms. de Britto	100
72	W. Coo Nassi	750
73	Is. de Britto	1081
74	Ab. Dovalle	250
75	Is. Henriq.	140
76	Ab. Pinto	224
77	Is. Carilho	1700
78	Ab. & Is. Pinto	1800
79	Ard. Ab. da Costa	1042
80	Erv. Baeza & da Costa	
81	Ios. Gabay Faro	1452
82	Iaqs. de Prado	288
03	Pardo Gen. Carthago	400
83	Sam. Verhulst	1574
84	Mos. Isidro	
85	W. Ab. de Pina	
8	[illegible]	1000
1	W. Jac. Vz. d'Avilar	1200
2	Esth. Lorenco	200
3	Beni. Hz. Moron	
4	Iac. de Pina	130
5	Iac. Coh. Nassi	130
6	Dav. Vz. d'Avilas	130
7	E. Sal. Ies. Levi	300
87	Erv. Chevalier	2380
88	Erv. Wiltens & Co.	
89	Erv. Abm. Arias	
90	Wriedt	1000

Detail of plantation owners along Suriname River near Jodensavanne, from Alexander de Lavaux, *Algemene kaart van Suriname*, 1737, watercolor on paper. (Courtesy RM, NG-478)

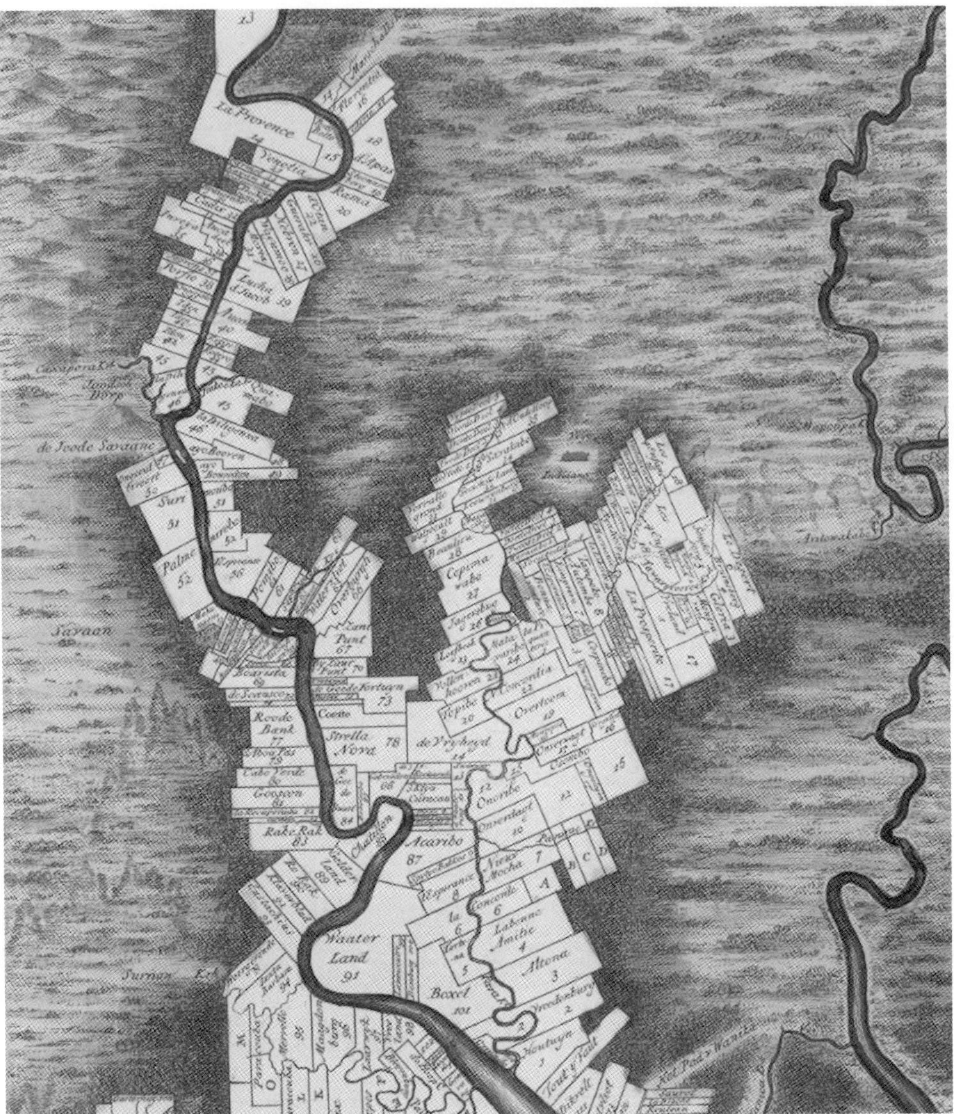

Detail of plantations along Suriname River near Jodensavanne, from Alexander de Lavaux, *Algemene kaart van Suriname*, 1737, watercolor on paper. (Courtesy RM, NG-478)

QUESTIONS

1. The last names Pinto, Nassi, Para, Kastillo, Monsanto, Meza, Fonseca, Britto, Henriquez, Barrios, Bueno, Crasto, Messias, Carreleo, Cotinsio, d'Avilar, Baeza, Quiro, Penco, Granada, Naar, Dovalle, Carilho, da Costa, Gabay, Faro, Prado, Isidro, de Pina, Lorenco, Moron, and Levi are all Jewish. What percentage of the plantations around Jodensavanne were owned by Jews?
2. Match the plantation owners to the plantations in the detail of the area marked by a hill toward the center of the map. What are some of the names of Jewish plantations?

3. In one sense, this map is upside down, as the top of the map is south and the bottom north. Why do you think the mapmaker made it this way?
4. What kinds of evidence can maps provide about Jewish life during this era?
5. What do you think is the significance of the absence of Indigenous communities on the map? What other type of information that is not provided could help us better understand colonial life?

NOTES

1. Fatah-Black, *White Lies and Black Markets*, 71.
2. Fatah-Black, 70.
3. Roitman, "Portuguese Jews," 45.

38

The Rebellion of Rebecca Valverde Gomes

BARBADOS, 1812

Laura Arnold Leibman

The Barbados Jewish community flourished in the first half of the eighteenth century, with high sugar prices bolstering the community's wealth. By 1750, roughly four hundred to five hundred Jews lived on the island, mainly in the main port of Bridgetown.[1] Both the Seven Years' War and the US Revolutionary War, however, signaled a downward turn for the congregation, as these conflicts disrupted trade routes. The end of the slave trade in 1807 further undercut the island's economy, and increasingly congregation Nidhe Israel found itself supporting large numbers of impoverished Jews.

At the start of the nineteenth century, several disputes fractured the struggling community, not the least of which were several scandals that broke out between 1811 and 1814 regarding people engaging in extramarital sex. Most of these incidents involved male members of the congregation and women of color. The example of Mrs. Gomes is unusual among these scandals in that it involved a European Jewish woman. It is not clear who "Mr. Castello"—her partner in crime—was. Possibly it was Abraham Castello, a member of the Nidhe Israel congregation, but there were free men of color with that name in Bridgetown at the time, too, for example, the wealthy and well-connected John Castello Montefiore or Joseph Henry Castello (d. 1820).

More is known about Mrs. Gomes herself. Rebecca Valverde was the young wife of Raphael Gomes. When the couple wed in 1799, Raphael had been a man of substance, who had served on the congregation's Mahamad. By 1811, however, he was on death's door. Fed up for reasons that are unclear, Rebecca left him and began living with Mr. Castello. The synagogue attempted to punish her by refusing to circumcise her son, but instead of bowing to pressure, Rebecca took her infant son, Jacob, north to New York, where they were taken in by the extended Gomes/Gomez clan (the same family of which Rebecca Gomez the chocolate maker was a part of a few generations earlier; see chapter 30). Either the New York branch of the family did not know about the scandal or they did not care.

Typically in Barbados when women misbehaved, they suffered as a consequence, sometimes losing their home or source of income because of the anger of the Mahamad. While the Barbados Mahamad may seem petty, its actions reflect a larger history of restrictions on female sexuality in accordance with Jewish law. Because Rebecca Valverde Gomes did not live with her husband, the Mahamad believed that her child was a *mamzer*, that is, someone born of a married woman and a man other than her husband or a child born of an incestuous union (see also chapter 29). A *mamzer* is forbidden to marry Jews who are not *mamzers*, as are their offspring for ten generations. In all other ways, however, a *mamzer* is obliged to keep the commandments and may be called to the Torah. Indeed, today in some Orthodox communities, the custom is to circumcise the child in the synagogue's courtyard "while announcing that he is a *mamzer* so people should be aware and not intermarry with him or his descendants."[2] The Barbados community may have decided not to circumcise the child, however, to help prevent a marriage to a non*mamzer*. Yet the community's response to Mrs. Gomes's proclamation is questionable: according to the *Shulchan Arukh*—the Code of Jewish Law—even if a woman has been separate from her husband up to twelve months and declares that she was impregnated by someone else, her word is inadmissible, and there is an assumption that the fetus was delayed in the womb (*Shulchan Arukh*, Even Haezer 4:15, 4:29).[3] The rebellion of Rebecca Valverde Gomes helps us understand the history of the way communities responded to and restricted Jewish women's sexuality. Most of the gaps in the text are caused by the way the manuscript was later rebound.

PRIMARY SOURCE

Nidhe Israel At a Meeting of the Mahamad & Ajunta on S[un] 17:th March 1811 Corresponding with the 21st Adar 5571 Present Mr. Isaac Levi Mr. Isaac D Massiah M M DaCosta Phineas Nunes Mr. Abm R Brandon Presidente

The *Presidente* stated the purpose of the present Meeting was to tak[e] consideration the propriety of giving Mrs. Gomes the Honors usually on the Birth of a Son (of which she was then delivered) he having [?] her conduct to be so highly culpable as to bring disgrace on the Comm[unity?].

The Hazan was called in; and stated that on the Night of [deliberate blank space] he was at Mrs. Burgoss's door, that Mr. Castello & others were present, [and] Mrs. Gomes came up and behaved in a most scandalous & indecent mann[er] declared Mr. Castello had kept her nine Months & that if he left [she] would go on the Town & much more to the same effect: That Mrs. Bu[rgoss] had deposed an oath to the same effect in a Court of Indicature, wh[ose] proceedings had since drop'd. The President & Mr. Massiah stated facts to the same effect, when it appearing that no doubt could exc[use?] & that Mrs. Gomes by her conduct had forfeited all claim to co[?] it was directed that no officer or Pensioner do attend to the Circumcision [of] the Child & that no offering be permitted to be made or accepted in Syn[agogue] on the occasion. Nothing further occurring, the meeting was closed.

MBMNI, LMA/4521/D/01/03/003. By permission of the Board of the S&P Sephardic Community of London.

QUESTIONS

1. Rewrite this incident from the perspective of Mrs. Gomes, in the form of a letter, diary entry, or poem.
2. On the basis of the Mahamad's response, how does it expect that women should behave?
3. Even if documents related to women's misbehavior are not the norm, what do they add to our understanding of history?
4. Compare the cases of Sarah de Isaac Pardo (chapter 29) and Rebecca Valverde Gomes. Both were recorded by men, but how does the genre change our understanding of each woman's motives?

NOTES

1. Arbell, *Jewish Nation of the Caribbean*, 199.
2. Halberstadt, "Mamzer in Jewish Cemetery."
3. Brand, "On Suspicion."

39

Multiracial Portraits

ENGLAND, C. 1815–1820

Laura Arnold Leibman

We have heard about the parents of Sarah Rodrigues Brandon (1798–1828) and Isaac Lopez Brandon (1792–1855) in previous entries: their father was Abraham Rodrigues Brandon, the president of the Barbadian Mahamad who oversaw the punishment of Rebecca Valverde Gomes (chapter 38), and their mother was the "wife of Abm. R. Brandon," who Aaron Levy mentioned died in New York in chapter 36. Despite Levy's note, there is no evidence the couple ever married. In fact, Sarah Rodrigues Brandon, Isaac Lopez Brandon, and their mother were all born enslaved in Barbados to the Lopezes, a Sephardic family. Their mother's ability to be accepted as Jewish and buried in Shearith Israel's cemetery speaks to the power of her daughter and son's connections within the New York community. Over the course of their lives, Sarah and Isaac had their race reassigned from people of color to white, and their miniatures played a role in that transformation.

Travel and money were key to the siblings' changing fortunes. After their father, Abraham Rodrigues Brandon, purchased their freedom, the siblings traveled to Suriname. There they converted to Judaism at the Portuguese synagogue in Paramaribo. Rather than staying in Suriname, Isaac Lopez Brandon returned to Barbados, and his sister traveled on to London to attend an elite Sephardic boarding school. When she was eighteen, Sarah married a wealthy Ashkenazi Jew named Joshua Moses in London. Sarah brought prestige to the marriage and a dowry of £10,000. After her wedding, she moved to New York, where Joshua's family lived. Her brother Isaac joined them, first becoming Joshua's business partner and later marrying Joshua's sister Lavinia. When Sarah and Isaac died, they were some of the wealthiest Jews in New York. Family tradition holds that Sarah's portrait was painted just before her 1817 wedding, and clothing styles suggest that Isaac's portrait was made around the same time.

Sarah's and Isaac's portraits help us understand how elite Jews wanted to be seen. The portraits can illuminate how slippery racial categories were during this era, particularly for those who could pay to travel and who were racially ambiguous. Everywhere the siblings lived, race was defined slightly differently. While the earliest records in Barbados and

Suriname identify the siblings as "coloured," when they moved to New York, the siblings were defined as white. These portraits may have contributed to Sarah's and Isaac's racial reassignment. The glowing white of the ivory corresponded to new understandings of skin color as an important marker of race. As all Jews, let alone multiracial Jews, found themselves increasingly designated "nonwhite" by racial scientists, the miniatures attested to the sitters' whiteness. This "whitening" is particularly visible in Isaac's portrait, for which the ivory was left unpainted for large portions of his face.

While their wealth made them unusual, Sarah and Isaac were not the only Jews of mixed African and European ancestry in this era. Their story mirrors the history of other early multiracial Jews, who made up as much as 10 percent of the early Jewish communities in which Sarah and Isaac lived.

PRIMARY SOURCES

See following pages.

QUESTIONS

1. Anyone who has taken a selfie knows that portraits rarely correspond exactly to a person's everyday reality. What aspects of these portraits seem designed to emphasize the sitters' high status?
2. Describe the clothing worn by the sitters. What does the clothing tell us about them as individuals?
3. These portraits are quite small. What are some advantages or disadvantages of their size?
4. What, if anything, is Jewish about these portraits?

Anonymous, *Portrait of Sarah Brandon Moses*, c. 1815–1816, watercolor on ivory, 2¾ × 2¼ in. (Courtesy AJHS)

Anonymous, *Portrait of Isaac Lopez Brandon*, early nineteenth century, watercolor on ivory, 3⅛ × 2½ in. (Courtesy AJHS)

40

Mordecai Manuel Noah on "Africans"

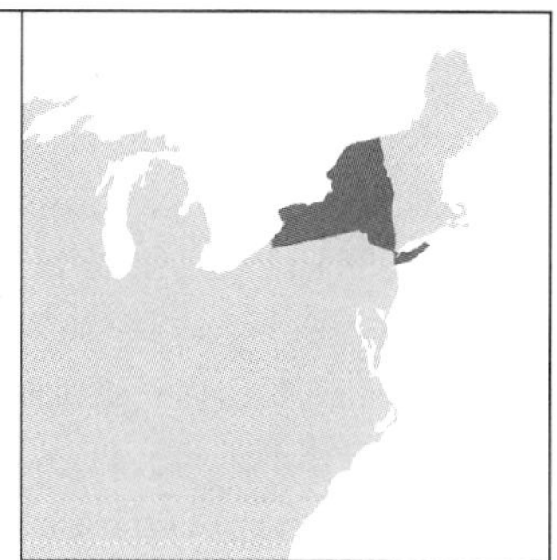

NEW YORK, 1821

Laura Arnold Leibman

One of the Jews who was blamed for the 1822 yellow fever epidemic in New York (chapter 36) was Mordecai Manuel Noah. As the editor of the *National Advocate* newspaper, Noah was an important voice in early New York, and his reluctance to print news about early cases of yellow fever may have contributed to people being caught off guard. Noah is often remembered as the most powerful US Jew of his era: he was a politician, statesman, playwright, printer, and utopian dreamer. Yet Noah also had a racist side, as is extremely apparent in his article on "Africans" included here. His writings about African Americans help us better understand how early American Jews positioned themselves vis-à-vis people they saw as racially other and illuminates the racial climate that multiracial Jews like Sarah Rodrigues Brandon and Isaac Lopez Brandon faced (chapter 39).

Noah was not alone in seeing people with African ancestry as inferior to Jews. Solomon Etting, son-in-law of the merchant Barnard Gratz (chapter 26), was an active member of the State Colonization Society after he moved to Maryland.[1] Founded in 1816, this society tried to end slavery by sending African Americans to Africa. Other Jews in Philadelphia abetted racism, even if they did not author it themselves. Sarah and Abraham Hart, for example, ran the stationery shop "S. Hart & Sons" at 65 South Third Street, where the non-Jewish cartoonist Edward William Clay began his racist series "Life in Philadelphia." Like Noah's complaints a few years earlier, Clay's sketches often focused their ire on dress and cultural "appropriation." The subtext, however, was almost always who was a "good" citizen and deserved the right to vote (what Noah called the "elective franchise"). As other excerpts in this volume show, Jewish emancipation was far from guaranteed in this era (chapter 42). In fact, when Noah visited Newport, Rhode Island, in 1828 to speak about Jewish rights, the cartoonist George Weeden used similar strategies for attacking Noah that Noah had used against African Americans. In Weeden's drawing, Noah imitates the grandiose pose of a Roman orator, yet his thin, slippery hands keep disappearing in his coat's voluminous folds. In Noah's speech, he had proclaimed that Jews could "*raise the world*"—an important assertion given recent legislation regarding Jewish rights in nearby Maryland and other parts of the Americas. Weeden, however, used Noah's clothes to depict him as unmanly, morally suspect, and unworthy of full citizenship.

Although some members of congregations Shearith Israel (New York) and Mikveh Israel (Philadelphia) were abolitionists and explicitly antiracist, Mordecai Manuel Noah's and Abraham Hart's peddling in racist caricatures must have been extremely uncomfortable for Jewish congregants with African ancestry. Noah was certainly loathed by the early African American press in New York, which often quoted Noah's slurs and "bore testimony" against his "illiberal and unjust representations" of Black New Yorkers.[2] Yet, when Isaac Lopez Brandon applied for synagogue membership, either Noah did not speak against him or the synagogue did not record what he said. Brandon went on to be a full member of the congregation with full voting rights both in the synagogue and in the US nation.

Black and Jewish emancipation was often intertwined in this era. Sometimes, as in Jamaica, Jews and people of color united to fight against the white, Christian monopoly on power. In other places, however, Jewish ideas about African Americans and race were quite divided, with some Jews deliberately impeding African Americans' attempts to gain the right to vote and live freely. Jews, like other people, are individuals. Their ideas (positive and negative) are their own.

PRIMARY SOURCES

Africans—People of colour generally are very imitative, quick in their conceptions and rapid in execution; but it is in the lighter pursuits requiring no intensity of thought or depth of reflection. It may be questioned whether they could succeed in the abstruse sciences, though they have, nevertheless, some fancy and humour, and the domestics of respectable families are complete facsimiles of the different branches of it, not only in dress but in habits and manners.

Among the number of ice cream gardens in this city, there was none in which the sable race could find admission and refreshment. Their modicum of pleasure was taken on Sunday evening, when the black dandys and dandizettes, after attending meeting, occupied the sidewalks in Broadway, and slowly lounged towards their different homes. As their number increased, and their consequence strengthened; partly from high wages, high living, and the elective franchise; it was considered necessary to have a place of amusement for them exclusively.—Accordingly, a garden has been opened somewhere back of the hospital called African Grivel not spicy as those of Arabia, (but let that pass) at which the ebony lads and lasses could obtain ice cream, ice punch, and hear music from the big drum and clarinet. The little boxes in this garden were filled with black beauties "making night hideous"; and it was not an uninteresting sight to observe the entree of a happy pair. The gentleman, with his wool nicely combed, and his face shining through a coat of sweet oil, borrowed from the castors; cravat tight to suffocation, having the double faculty of widening the mouth and giving a remarkable protuberance to the eyes; blue coat fashionably cut; red ribbon and a bunch of pinchback seals; wide pantaloons shining boots, gloves, and a tippy ratton.

Edward Williams Clay, *Life in Philadelphia* (Philadelphia: S. Hart, 1829), plate 13. (Courtesy LCPPD, pga 05680)

The lady, with her pink kid slippers; her dine Leghorn, cambric dress, with side work; corsets well fitted; reticule, hanging on her arm. Thus accoutered and caparisoned, these black fashionables saunter up and down the garden, in all the pride and liberty and unconscious of want. In their address; salutations; familiar phrases; and compliments; their imitative faculties are best exhibited. After a vile concerto by the garden band, a company of four in a box commenced conversation, having disposed of a glass of ice cream each.

"You like music, Miss? Can't say I like it much. I once could play Paddy Cary, on the piano; our young ladies learnt me. Did you eber hear Phillips sing, 'Is dare a heart dat neber

lov'd'? I sing xactly like him; Harry tell us some news. De Greeks are gone to war wid de Turks. O! Dat's bery clever; and our gentleman said at dinner yesterday, dat de Greeks had taken Constantinople, and all de wives of de Dey of Algiers. O shocking! Vell, Miss, ven is de happy day; ven vill you enter de matrimony state? Dat's my business; Gentlemen musn't meddle with dese delicate tings. Beg Pardon Miss. O! No offense—Harry, who did you vote for at de election? De fedrilists to be sure; I never wotes for de mob. Miss how you like to go to de springs? I shouldn't like it; to many n—— from de suthard and such crowd of folks, that decent people can get no refrehsments."

Thus they run the rounds of fashions; ape their masters and mistresses in everything; talk of projected matches; rehearse the news of the kitchen, well qualified to move in *haut ton*, as many of the white dandies and butterflies, who flutter in the sun shine. They fear no Missouri plot; care for no political rights; happy in being permitted to dress fashionable, walk the streets, visit African Grove, and talk scandal.

"Africans," *National Advocate*, August 3, 1821.

QUESTIONS

1. Read Noah's article closely. What precisely are his "complaints" about African Americans in New York? What strategies does he use to demean the people he describes?
2. If newspapers create a sense of who belongs in a city or nation, who implicitly in Noah's newspaper article "belongs" in New York City and who does not?
3. Compare the depiction of African Americans in Clay's caricature with the portrait of Isaac Lopez Brandon (chapter 39). What strategies does each artist use to denigrate or elevate the depicted?
4. Compare the strategies used for depicting certain African Americans as outsiders in Noah's article with those used in the Surinamese prayer (chapter 35).
5. What are the advantages or disadvantages of studying the history of Jewish racism alongside antisemitism?

NOTES

1. Wolf and Whiteman, *History of the Jews of Philadelphia*, 192.
2. Bacon, *Freedom's Journal*, 170.

41

Society of Reformed Israelites

SOUTH CAROLINA, 1824

Zev Eleff

On December 23, 1824, a group of young Jews in Charleston petitioned the local congregation to modify its liturgy. One of the largest Jewish communities in the United States at that time, Beth Elohim operated within the Spanish-Portuguese rite. It boasted a very traditional Sabbath service, mainly in Hebrew with a few portions in Spanish. Many of the synagogue's elders did not trace their lineage to that tradition, and the rising generation was even less familiar than their parents with the language in which the prayer was conducted. The forty-seven petitioners, led at the time by Abraham Moise, therefore asked that the ritual be shortened and that English be inserted to help everyone in the pews follow along. In this period of the early republic, the young Jews believed that it was a reasonable request and were not looking for a revolution. As the source that follows shows, they claimed to have in mind the "future welfare and respectability of the nation." By this, the group meant that they could not "place before their children examples which are only calculated to darken the mind and withhold from the rising generation the more rational means of worshipping the true God." English, the petitioners believed, was crucial. They pleaded that it was no longer the case that Jews knew Hebrew. Especially in their generation, very few had "the means, and many ha[d] not the time, to acquire a knowledge of the Hebrew language." Appealing to the congregation's American sensibilities, the petitioners charged that English was the "language of the country."

Beth Elohim's trustees denied the request. Led by this time by the playwright and journalist Isaac Harby, the group left the synagogue and established the Reformed Society of Israelites. In 1825, the group authored a constitution and held a major event on the anniversary of the initial petition. Harby spoke on that anniversary in far more radical terms than the young Jewish Charlestonians had used a year prior. By this time, the Harby-led effort called for American Jews to "throw away Rabbinical interpolations" and embrace the "true legitimate authority of the Bible."[1] By this, Harby meant to strip much of the synagogue customs and rituals and get back to what he deemed the core of his Mosaic faith. The reformers furnished their own prayer book, which did much more than translate the liturgy into English. The Reformed Society lasted a little more than a dozen years. Its briefness had much to do with Charleston's fall as a major center after the War of 1812. Harby's departure to New York hastened the decline. Yet Charleston remained the so-called cradle of Reform Judaism in the United States and set in motion a precedent for reforms against the traditional synagogue structure and the earliest lay-led form of authority in the Americas.

The religious rupture in Charleston indicated the role of young people in transforming the most significant institutions in American religion. It also represented ongoing battles for religious authority within the American synagogue, which at that moment was the major site of Jewish life. By splitting a "synagogue community," as the historian Jonathan Sarna has written, into a "community of synagogues," the reformers empowered themselves and other Jews to make their own choices on how to observe Judaism and how much they needed to abide by the traditions established by earlier generations of Jews.[2]

Beth Elohim did not have an ordained rabbi at that moment. It was led by laypeople, who controlled the congregation as trustees. Therefore, we might view the revolt by Moise and Harby and their efforts to start a type of "Reform Judaism" as a revolution against authority rather than a specific type of religious creed or "orthodoxy." The 1824 episode in Charleston, then, anticipated decades of attempts throughout American Jewish enclaves to reform religious life. Sometimes this was set in motion by laypeople. Sometimes it was started by rabbis. In most cases, Reform Judaism was sparked by a need to upend the established system of authority. No doubt, modifications in rite and abrogation of various customs were theologically charged and reflected a significant affront to a kind of orthodoxy. However, these bouts were usually triggered as an attempt to usurp religious authority—power—more than anything else.

PRIMARY SOURCE

Your memorialists seek no other end than the future welfare and respectability of the nation. As members of the great family of Israel, they cannot consent to place before their children examples which are only calculated to darken the mind and withhold from the rising generation the more rational means of worshipping the true God.

It is to this, therefore, your memorialists would, in the first place, invite the serious attention of your honorable body. By causing the *Hazan*, or reader, to *repeat* in English such part of the Hebrew prayers as may be deemed necessary, it is confidently believed that the congregation generally would be more forcibly impressed with the necessity of Divine worship, and the moral obligations which they owe to themselves and their Creator; while such a course would lead to more decency and decorum during the time they are engaged in the performance of religious duties. It is not every one who has the means, and many have not the time, to acquire a knowledge of the Hebrew language, and consequently to become enlightened in the principles of Judaism. What then is the course pursued in all religious societies for the purpose of disseminating the peculiar tenets of their faith among the poor and uninformed?

The principles of their religion are expounded to them from the pulpit in language that they understand; for instance, in the Catholic, the German, and the French Protestant churches; by this means the ignorant part of mankind attend their places of worship with some profit to their morals and even improvement to their minds; they return from them with hearts turned to piety, and with feelings elevated by their sacred character. In this consists the beauty of religion—when men are invoked by its divine spirit to the practice of virtue and morality.

With regard to such parts of the service as it is desired should undergo this change, your memorialists would strenuously recommend that the most solemn portions be retained, and everything superfluous excluded; and that the principal parts, and if possible all that is read in *Hebrew*, should also be read in *English* (that being the language of the country), so as to enable every member of the congregation fully to understand each part of this service. . . .

Your memorialists would next call the particular attention of your honorable body to the absolute necessity of *abridging* the service generally. They have reflected seriously upon its present length, and are confident that this is one of the principal causes why so much of it is hastily and improperly hurried over.

According to the present mode of reading the *Parasa* [weekly Torah portion] it affords to the hearer neither instruction nor entertainment, unless he be competent to read as well as *comprehend* the Hebrew language. But if, like all other ministers, our reader would make a chapter or verse the subject of an English discourse once a week, at the expiration of the year the people would, at all events, know something of that religion which at present they so little regard.

Barnett Abraham Elzas, *The Jews of South Carolina: From the Earliest Times to the Present Day* (Philadelphia: J. B. Lippincott, 1905), 155–157.

QUESTIONS

1. How do the reformers justify the need for changes?
2. What are the arguments for and against having the service and Torah reading in Hebrew?
3. Why do you think the petitioners call themselves "your memorialists" rather than "reformers"?

NOTES

1. Eleff, *Who Rules the Synagogue?*, 19.
2. Sarna, *American Judaism*, 60.

42

Petition for Civil Rights

LOWER CANADA, 1831

Michael Hoberman

Although Jacques La Fargue / Esther Brandeau's stay in New France was brief (see chapter 16), the 1763 transfer of the province of Quebec from a French to a British colony encouraged Jewish settlement, as Jews were able to practice Judaism openly in British lands. Aaron Hart, a fur trader and purveyor to the British military during its conflict with France, settled in Trois-Rivières, Quebec, in the early 1760s. In 1768, a mixed contingent of Sephardic and Ashkenazi Jews established congregation Shearith Israel of Montreal. Like its New York namesake, this synagogue was also known as the Spanish and Portuguese Synagogue. Quebec was divided into Upper and Lower Canada in 1791, but Jews did not acquire full rights of citizenship until 1832.

Aaron Hart's son Ezekiel was instrumental to early efforts to bring about Jewish enfranchisement in the region. Though Ezekiel Hart briefly sat in the provincial legislature as an elected representative of Trois-Rivières in 1807, he was forced to step down as the result of a popular outcry. Hart's allies insisted that the British Parliament had extended rights of naturalization to Jews throughout the kingdom in the latter part of the eighteenth century. Nonetheless, as one Quebec ("Lower Canadian") newspaper put it in March 1808, "one didn't have to suppose that the Parliament of Great Britain had given to the Jews the right to make laws for Christians."[1] It took more than twenty years for Canadian legislators to clear the way for Jews to become fully enfranchised citizens, as this document from Lower Canada (Quebec) shows. Notably, this 1832 effort on behalf of Ezekiel Hart's candidacy was led by Louis-Joseph Papineau, who had argued against Hart's eligibility for office during the 1807–1808 debates.

Jews across the Americas did not acquire their rights all at once. In Canada, as in the United States, they gained rights of residency, trade, and citizenship in a piecemeal and sometimes intermittent fashion. Often enough, legislation that was passed on a larger scale fell short of effecting changes on a local level. Moreover, reflecting the split in Canada, policies enacted and conducted by English-speaking Protestants and those of French-speaking Catholics were frequently at odds with each other. Enfranchisement in the Americas, however, generally ran a faster course than enfranchisement in Europe. The English Bill of Rights of 1689 had guaranteed that "natural born British subjects" had thirteen liberties including the right to elect members of Parliament, freedom of speech in Parliament, the right to have arms for self-defense, the right to petition the king, and freedom from cruel and unusual punishment. Yet most of these rights applied only to Anglican men of a certain age and property (see chapter 17). Although the Reform Act of 1832 in England expanded the vote to middle-class Christian men who had property (or paid rents) of at least £10, it was not until 1858 that English Jews would be granted the same rights that Canada's Jews had gained in 1832.

While Jews were instrumental players at the earliest stages of the commercial development of the Americas, their ability to participate in civic affairs came about more slowly. By the last decades of the seventeenth century, Jewish merchants were granted rights of naturalization that allowed them to trade freely in accordance with imperial policies. However, it took the political revolutions of the late eighteenth century, as well as the gradual separation of church and state that occurred in those revolutions' aftermath, to bring about Jewish voting rights.

PRIMARY SOURCE

The Provincial Statutes of Lower Canada . . . being the first session of the fourteenth provincial Parliament of Lower-Canada

C A P. LVIII

An Act to Declare persons professing the Jewish Religion entitled to all the rights and privileges of the other subjects of His Majesty in this Province.

31st March, 1831—Presented for His Majesty's Assent and reserved "for the signification of His Majesty's pleasure thereon."
12th April, 1832—Assented to by His Majesty in His Council.
5th June, 1832—The Royal Assent signified by the proclamation of His Excellency the governor in Chief.

Whereas doubts have arisen whether persons professing the Jewish Religion are by law entitled to many of the privileges enjoyed by the other subjects of His Majesty within this Province: Be it therefore declared and enacted by the King's Most Excellent Majesty, by and with the advice and consent of the Legislative Council and Assembly of the Province of Lower Canada, constituted and assembled by virtue of and under the authority of an Act passed in the Parliament of Great Britain, entitled, "An Act to repeal certain parts of an Act passed in the fourteenth year of His Majesty's Reign, '*An Act for making more effectual provision for the Government of the Province of Quebec, in North America*,' and to make further provision for the Government of the said Province of Quebec in North America." And it is hereby declared and enacted by the authority aforesaid, that all persons professing the Jewish Religion being natural born British subjects inhabiting and residing in this Province, are entitled and shall be deemed adjudged and taken to be entitled to the full rights and

privileges of the other subjects of His Majesty, his Heirs or Successors, to all intents, constructions and purposes of whatsoever, and capable of taking, having or enjoying any office of place of trust whatsoever, within this Province.

The Provincial Statutes of Lower-Canada (Quebec: J. C. Fisher and W. Kemble, 1831), 82.

QUESTIONS

1. What does it mean to be a "person professing the Jewish Religion"?
2. Why do you think the British government was willing to let Jews vote and hold office in the colonies before they could do so in England proper?
3. What limits are implied when this bill states that "all persons professing the Jewish Religion being natural born British subjects inhabiting and residing in this Province, are entitled and shall be deemed adjudged and taken to be entitled to the full rights and privileges of the other subjects of His Majesty"?

NOTE

1. *Le Canadien* (Quebec), March 2, 1808. Translation by Michael Hoberman.

PART III

The Era of Mass Migrations and Nationalism (1836–1912)

Crazy quilt made by the Jewish Ladies' Sewing Circle in Canton, Mississippi, c. 1885. (Donated by Isabel Wile Goldman in memory of Bertha Loeb, Museum of the Southern Jewish Experience)

In 1885, Bertha Loeb and the women of the Jewish Ladies' Sewing Circle in Canton, Mississippi, created a crazy quilt to raise money for Temple B'nai Israel, the local synagogue. Yellow fever had swept Mississippi in 1878, and like in early nineteenth-century New York (chapter 36), the result was mass evacuation and economic chaos. Loeb and her family were recent arrivals in Mississippi: their family originally came from German lands to Mexico but migrated north after the US Civil War. The quilt they made was stylish, as was their gathering: the rise of Jewish sewing circles that nurtured women's creativity and charitable impulses were part of the larger reshaping of Jewish American life in the era of mass migrations and nationalism. Jewish immigrants from the Caribbean, Germany, eastern Europe, and the former Ottoman Empire swelled American cities and took part in settler-colonialism in frontier communities. Once American nations had gained their independence, they often found themselves trapped in civil wars over their countries' founding principles. As slavery ended, new immigrants battled for low-wage positions and against a racialized antisemitism. Caught between trying to prove themselves as citizens and as Israelites, the immigrants transformed what it meant to be American Jews.

The journey of Bertha Loeb's family exemplified those during the era. While Jews who came to the Americas during the age of revolutions and emancipation were typically Sephardic and Ashkenazi Jews from western Europe, Jews who came to Canada and the United States during the era of mass migrations primarily came in two waves: Ashkenazi immigrants from German lands (1820s–1870s), followed by Ashkenazi Jews from eastern Europe and Eastern Sephardim from the Ottoman Empire (1880s–1920s). During both waves, Jews from the Caribbean also made their ways north, feeding both traditional Western Sephardic congregations and Black synagogues, including those founded in Tennessee, Philadelphia, and Kansas in the 1890s. By the 1920s, there would be at least four Black Jewish congregations in Harlem alone (see chapter 76).

In Latin America, the arrival of Jewish immigrants was slow until the 1880s. Starting in the 1850s, a handful of Jews from western European countries, usually representing economic firms, arrived, as did a few Moroccan Jews, seeking better economic opportunities. Meanwhile, postindependence struggles between liberals and conservatives continued, with varying intensity, until around the 1880s, when the ideals of Liberalism prevailed. In Latin America, Liberalism came to represent freedom from economic interference by the state, as well as a desire to shape Latin American countries in the image of Europe. And while liberals of the day believed in republican institutions, they were more than ready to change constitutions to remain in power, as Porfirio Díaz did in Mexico. Now in charge, Liberal governments promoted the expansion of railroad lines, the removal of Indigenous groups, and the settlement of "available" land to feed booming export economies.

These changes opened up economic opportunities for immigrants, who were often expressly invited by these young nations. Liberal constitutions came to include religious toleration clauses—even if top leadership positions still required Roman Catholicism. Thus, Jews were no longer barred from settling in these former Spanish and Portuguese colonies. While most Jews eventually would settle in urban centers and begin the process of founding the first Jewish institutions, many found economic opportunities for success in the frontier regions, as Abraham Goldenberg did in Chile (chapter 55).

In the United States and Canada, the numbers of these new immigrants overshadowed the native-born Jews present in already-established Jewish communities.[1] Starting in the late 1820s, Ashkenazi-run synagogues using a variety of Ashkenazi rites emerged. As older congregations moved away from the city center into "better" neighborhoods, new (often Ashkenazi) congregations were built in working-class neighborhoods, typically close to the wharves and factories where the new arrivals worked. Thus, by the 1860s, Ashkenazi congregations flourished in Alabama, Arkansas, British Columbia, California, Connecticut, the District of Columbia, Georgia, Illinois, Indiana, Iowa, Kansas, Kentucky, Maryland, Massachusetts, Mississippi, Missouri, New Jersey, New York, Ohio, Ontario, Oregon, Pennsylvania, Quebec, South Carolina, Texas, Virginia, West Virginia, and Wisconsin. The year 1860 likewise marked the first Jewish wedding in Buenos Aires, and in 1862, wealthy Jewish merchants from France, Germany, and Great Britain came together to pray for the High Holidays, founding the Congregación Israelita in 1868 (now referred to as Templo Libertad).[2] At times, the Ashkenazi immigrants replaced older Portuguese congregations, such as in Newport, Rhode Island, when the Touro Synagogue became the spiritual home of Ashkenazi Jews during the Great Migration of the 1880s–1920s.

Although now the minority rather than the majority of Jews, Sephardic arrivals followed a similar pattern. In the United States, Greek and Turkish synagogues were established in Los Angeles (Avat Shalom Society, 1912), Seattle (Sephardic Bikur Holim, 1913), New York (Berith Shalom, 1914), and Portland (Ahavath Achim, 1916). Even today, these four cities continue to be hubs for Eastern Sephardic Jews in the United States. In Latin America, Moroccan Jews were the first to arrive in the region, founding institutions as early as the 1820s in Brazil and the 1890s in Argentina and Venezuela. Other Sephardim and Syrian Jews followed. In Mexico, the Mount Sinai Alliance Welfare Society was established in 1912, which brought together the Sephardic and Mizrachi Jews (including Syrian Jews) and the few Ashkenazim already settled in that country. It would build a cemetery in 1914 and

Monte Sinai Synagogue in 1923. Other communities of varying size grew in Peru, Panama, and Chile.

New arrivals from the Caribbean, Germany, eastern Europe, and the Ottoman Empire changed the religious landscape of the Americas. The failure of plantation economies following the end of slavery propelled Caribbean Jews north, diversifying long-standing Jewish congregations on the Atlantic seaboard. In addition, some Jews from St. Thomas, Jamaica, and Curaçao migrated west, settling in Panama, where they founded congregation Kahal Kadosh Yangakob (the Holy Congregation of Jacob) in Colón (1890).[3] Leaving behind multiracial communities such as the one in Suriname, Caribbean immigrants sometimes found themselves having to explain to European Jews in the North how someone might be both Black and Jewish.[4] Economic hardship as well as the failed promise of Jewish emancipation in the German Revolution of 1848 similarly pushed Jews out of German lands and into the Americas (see chapter 55). Especially in the United States, many German Jewish congregations began to be influenced by the Reform movement, including several congregations that had originally begun as Orthodox minyans. One new arrival, Isaac Mayer Wise (1819–1900), became one of the most influential proponents of Reform in the early United States, prompting mixed seating and mixed choirs and counting women for minyans in his Albany congregation.

The appeal of "modernizing" reforms spread across the United States and reached the island of Curaçao in 1864, when a liberal faction of the Sephardic congregation Mikve Israel formed the "Dutch Jewish Reform Community," which criticized the "superstition and fanaticism" of traditional Jewish worship on the island.[5] In 1867, this society built Temple Emanu-El. Unlike most US congregations that were Ashkenazi-Reform, this congregation, like the Society of Reformed Israelites in Charleston (see chapters 41 and 44) emerged out of the Sephardic tradition. Early cantors of the congregation tended to combine Reform and Sephardic knowledge, such as Jacob Mendes de Sola, a Portuguese Jew who came to the congregation after serving at congregations Beth Israel (Baltimore) and Beth Jacob (Montego Bay, Jamaica), and Joseph Haim Mendes Chumaceiro, who had presided at Beth Elohim (Charleston) and Nefutsoth Yehuda (New Orleans).[6] In the first decade of the twentieth century, the Reform movement took hold in Canada at Holy Blossom Temple (Toronto) and Temple Emanu-El (Montreal).[7] The movement did not reach Latin America until much later in the twentieth century.

As the Reform movement grew, so did the theology that supported its changes. It was not just that reformers rejected laws related to diet, purity, and dress: they declared that the Oral Torah and Jewish law were no longer binding unless "adapted to the views and habits of modern civilization."[8] This meant that reformers rejected kosher laws and Jewish rituals related to purity, such as immersion in *mikva'ot* and the burial of the dead (see chapters 48, 59, and 61). By the 1885 Pittsburgh conference, the Bible itself ceased to be authoritative. As the rabbis attending the conference proclaimed, the Bible reflected "the primitive ideas of its own age, and at times clothing its conception of divine Providence and Justice dealing with men in miraculous narratives."[9] For reformers like Wise, the authority granted to individuals by the Reform movement was inherently compatible with the cult of individualism of the United States, such that Wise hoped that Reform Judaism "as a

Temple Emanu-El, Curaçao. (Photograph by Laura Arnold Leibman, 2008)

progressive, universal, and non-authoritarian religion, would become the common faith of America."[10] To promote his ideas, Wise used the main community-building platform of his era: the newspaper. *The Israelite* (1854–present) published in Cincinnati, Ohio, became the longest-running Jewish newspaper in the Americas.

Wise was not the first man in the US to turn to the press to build his ideal of a Jewish society. The earliest Jewish newspaper was *The Occident and American Jewish Advocate*, run by one of Wise's great antagonists, Rabbi Isaac Leeser of congregation Mikveh Israel in Philadelphia. While prior to the rise of the Reform movement, it is anachronistic to speak of traditional synagogues as "Orthodox," by the 1840s, we start to see the rise of Orthodox Judaism in the United States in response to the reformers. Thus, while Leeser began his newspaper in part to combat the efforts of Christian missionaries, he soon turned his attention to reformers. While Leeser fought against change, he himself helped modernize traditional practice in the United States, for example, by giving sermons in English. It was in his congregation that Rebecca Gratz helped alter the role of women in traditional Judaism, by expanding women's role in Jewish education and care of orphans and the poor (see chapters 50 and 67). Leeser's newspaper ran articles highlighting women's role in caring for the Jewish family writ large. Leeser's emphasis on women's role in traditional Judaism was echoed in other early Orthodox newspapers, particularly Samuel Meyer Isaacs's *Jewish Messenger* (see chapter 57).

Both Leeser and Isaacs frequently published articles about Orthodox Jews in other cities and countries, deliberately envisioning a diasporic Jewish self. This was not unusual. For new immigrants, Jewish newspapers provided an important bridge to home communities by providing news in Yiddish, Ladino, Hebrew, and other languages. At the same time, columns like the "Bintel Brief" (Bundle of Letters) in the Yiddish newspaper the *Forward* explicitly aimed to help Americanize their followers. During the era of mass migrations and nationalism, Jewish newspapers spread across the United States and began inroads into Latin America with the publication of the Spanish-language *El Sábado* in Mexico City in 1889.

In turning to newspapers to create communities within and across national boundaries, Jews partook in an important part of nineteenth-century culture: nation building. Newspapers allowed Jews to see themselves as both American *and* Jewish. Such imaginings were crucial, as the countries in which Jews landed were often expansive. In the United States, Canada, Argentina, Brazil, and Mexico, new arrivals did not always stay in Atlantic port cities but traveled inland. Some were explorers or peddlers traversing large distances selling wares (see chapters 46, 49, 64, 65, and 66). Wagon trails and settlements followed in the footsteps of the explorers, and here, too, Jews were present. While some were single men working as cowboys on ranches across the plains, most either bought items to resell back east (see chapter 56) or sold goods to other settlers.[11] Communities such as the one in San Francisco grew largely to meet the needs of men trying to strike it rich in the Gold Rush (see chapters 62 and 67). French Jews and Eastern Sephardic Jews played a larger role in the creation of Jewish life along the Pacific coast than they did on the Atlantic seaboard, which was dominated more by German and eastern European communities. Pacific-coast Jews mingled socially, economically, and genealogically with immigrant communities in the region (see chapter 67). Over time, this would give these communities a distinctive feel and would help shape the greater diversity of Pacific-coast communities in the twentieth and twenty-first centuries.[12]

Jewish homesteaders and farming communities helped settle the new nations in both North and South America. Across the plains, new arrivals like the mail-order bride Rachel Calof farmed land with the hope of eventually being able to own it outright. While some, like Calof and her husband, worked individual plots of land, other immigrants joined pre-established Jewish farming communities funded by Baron Maurice de Hirsch. In 1891, Hirsh had founded the Jewish Colonization Association (JCA), which bought more than 1.4 million acres in Argentina, Brazil, Canada, and the United States (see chapter 63).[13] On these lands, the JCA established Jewish Agricultural Colonies, designed to help alleviate the overcrowding, financial suffering, and stigmas that eastern European Jews faced back home in Russia. This legacy of gaining a foothold by taking part in settler colonialism, typically at the expense of Indigenous and racially mixed communities, continues the pattern of Jews as both agents and victims of empire.

Jews found the new American nations immense but fractured. Revolutions and independence had not neatly unified people living within newly formed nations. At times, war offered an opportunity for immigrants and their children to prove their loyalty. The sons of Sarah Brandon Moses (see chapter 39), for example, fought in the Mexican-American War (1846–1848), a dispute that eventually forced Mexico to forfeit nearly a third of its territory. Likewise, women like Rachel Meyer Walker, a Jewish immigrant from Bavaria to Baltimore, stitched themselves into national narratives by including figures of Mexican-American War heroes in their quilts. Yet, by the time of the US Civil War (1861–1865), Jews found that wars—and the ideologies behind them—could just as easily wrench families apart, forcing brothers to fight on opposing sides (see chapter 52). Moreover, despite their attempts to serve the nation, Jews were still subjected to scorn and antisemitism (see chapter 51).

For Jews in Mexico, the end of the era of mass migrations and nationalism marked the beginning of the Mexican Revolution (1910–1920), a conflict that came to present an important challenge to Liberalism's attempts to rid the country of its Indigenous (and Black) past. Gravestones in the earliest section of the Jewish cemetery in Mexico City bear testimony to those who were caught in the crossfire (see chapter 71). In Argentina, by 1910, there were about 68,100 Jews, most of whom lived in the JCA colonies.[14] In fact, they used the celebration of the centennial of independence to write themselves into the nation by highlighting the contributions they had made as Jewish gauchos in the JCA colonies.[15] Mexico's numbers of Jews are somewhat unreliable, listing only 254 Jews by 1910.[16] In Brazil, while official numbers describe a Jewish population of only 300 people by the end of the nineteenth century, it is likely that Jews actually numbered close to 3,000.[17]

While in Latin America, disputes often reflected conflicts between conservatives, who wanted to limit voting, and a powerful church, on the one hand, and liberals, who wanted a separation of church and state and more expansion of voting rights, in the United States and Caribbean, conflicts often centered around questions of race and freedom. In the British West Indies and Canada, slavery was officially abolished in 1834, though many people remained de facto enslaved as "apprentices" to their former owners until 1838. This period marked the beginning of a shift to insisting on inequality as based on inherent and

Racialized depiction of a Jewish retailer vis-à-vis people of other races in Suriname. "On the left, the shop of a *vette-warier* or retailer; on the right, the shop of a *snerie* or tailor." (VS, JCBL)

unchangeable (biological) qualities, rather than a person's religion or status vis-à-vis slavery, both of which were malleable. Jewish and Black emancipation were often entangled in the Caribbean, and hence Jews increasingly found themselves depicted as racial others. As in the portraits made during the age of revolutions and emancipation, clothing and hairstyles played an important role in racializing Jews (see chapters 34 and 39). At the same time, we begin to see profile caricatures emphasizing the Jewish nose. Jews, too, took part in these new "Sketches of Character" and portraits that used body language to enter into debates about ideal citizens (see chapters 43 and 45).

Slavery and its legacy continued to impact the way that Jews were racialized. While slavery ended in the Spanish and British colonies in the 1820s–1830s, slavery was not abolished in Dutch Suriname and Curaçao until 1863, in the United States until 1865, and in Cuba, Puerto Rico, and Brazil until the 1880s. As Eric Goldstein notes, the decade following the end of slavery changed the way that Jews were racialized and the way that Jews understood themselves. As religious divides between Reform and Orthodoxy eroded the sense of social cohesion among Jews, Jews in the Americas increasingly began to self-identify in racial terms. Blood and ancestry now became the basis of shared Jewish experience, rather than religion or culture. Yet, at least in the United States, the place of the Jewish race among other races remained unclear: Were Jews one among the family of white races or something different altogether? In the southern United States, the legacy of slavery pushed Jews further into the category of white (see chapters 52 and 65), but Jews' experience was not always as clear in the northern United States. For some, such as the Harvard dean Nathaniel Shaler, "Jews were not unambiguously white" but could "*become* white through time, training, and most importantly, physical intermixture with the surrounding American population."[18]

The reality of the lived experiences of many Jewish immigrants during the Great Migration of the 1880s–1920s was impacted by the desire to "train" Jews into whiteness, as well as factors that would undermine that education. Social and political upheavals in eastern Europe and the violent collapse of the Ottoman Empire pushed Jews toward the Americas. Between 20 and 25 percent of these arrivals settled in small towns and agricultural communities.[19] Yet, for the vast majority, large port cities became their new home. Living conditions in these urban environments were far from ideal, with overcrowding and poor working conditions being the norm. Tenements—low-rise buildings with multiple apartments—were built to accommodate the new arrivals (see chapter 60). These buildings were largely unregulated, and residents often had no plumbing or sunlight and had to battle with insects and garbage. Diseases like tuberculosis and yellow fever spread rapidly through the cramped conditions (see chapter 64).[20] These substandard living conditions were seen as creating immoral bodies. Thus, Protestant social reformers increasingly associated Jews with crime and prostitution, especially in cities such as Chicago and New York. New York Police Commissioner Theodore Bingham thought that perhaps half of the city's criminals were Jewish, and the reformer Ernest Bell argued that Jews were the "backbone of this loathsome traffic in women" (prostitution).[21] Amid these attacks, ritual baths provided Jewish women with a way of asserting their physical and spiritual cleanliness (see chapter 59). In Buenos Aires, a city that became known as a center for prostitution, Jews were associated with this activity and struggled against this suspicion for many more decades.

Fellow Jews helped Americanize new arrivals. Jews whose families had lived in the Americas for generations gave charity to help new arrivals even as they socially distanced themselves from the squalor of inner cities. In New York, for example, members of congregation Shearith Israel ran a Neighborhood Settlement House on the Lower East Side. Like other settlement houses of the era, it aimed to help immigrants become more American by offering classes, entertainment, and social services. The Settlement House helped bolster a sense of pan-Sephardic community by running a Sephardic minyan and translating American works into Judeo-Spanish (Ladino), the language of Eastern Sephardic Jews.[22]

In Argentina, where the number of western European and Moroccan Jews was not large (around 2,596), they still organized aid for the 824 Jews who had arrived from eastern Europe in 1889, a year that marked the beginning of the mass immigration of Jews to the country.[23] They helped to provide kosher food and to secure basic necessities, and they lobbied the government for land on which arrivals could settle. In addition to the format of aid, the role of women in helping the Jewish poor also changed. In Argentina, the institution imagined to help immigrants become more Argentinean was the public education system, which, in the case of the agricultural colonies, was in the hands of Jews. Whereas a century earlier, Hannah Louzada had to appeal to the all-male Mahamad for financial support (see chapter 19), Jewish women now played a crucial role in charitable organizations aimed at helping the Jewish poor (see chapters 67 and 88). At the same time, Shearith Israel continued to move uptown, thereby physically separating itself from the new arrivals by building new synagogues at Nineteenth Street near Fifth Avenue (1860) and Seventieth

Street at Central Park (1897). The same glorious Louis Comfort Tiffany windows that graced the homes and synagogues of Upper East and West Side Jews shed a brightly colored light on the interiors of their expansive mausoleums (see chapter 61).

Similarly, members of German Jewish congregations in the United States, who had themselves been "greenhorns" a generation or two before, organized charity to the eastern European Ashkenazi immigrants. Earlier in the century, charity work like sewing circles had allowed upper-class Jewish women to give tzedakah from a distance in their elegant homes and congregations on the Upper West and East Sides. Yet, by the end of the era of mass migrations, upper-class women like Rebekah Kohut increasingly made their way into the crowded streets where poor Jews lived.[24]

Jews came to the Americas (or traveled across them) in the era of mass migrations and nationalism to escape violence and antisemitism and in search of economic and social opportunities. While German Jews made up the majority of arrivals to Canada and the United States in the first half of the nineteenth century, only a small number of Jews migrated to Latin America prior to 1880. During this same time, Caribbean Jewish communities, which had once been the largest in the Americas, typically lost members to the emerging communities in the North. In the 1880s–1920s, Jews from eastern Europe and the Ottoman Empire dominated immigration across the Americas. With each wave, the new arrivals shifted the fabric of Jewish American life both culturally and religiously, as Jewish American life became increasingly Ashkenazi and increasingly modern.

NOTES

1. Likewise, in Latin America, where there were almost no preexisting open Jewish communities, Jews from Germany, eastern Europe, and the Middle East quickly outnumbered previous crypto-Jewish enclaves.
2. Mirelman, "Jewish Life in Buenos Aires," 198.
3. Arbell, *Jewish Nation of the Caribbean*, 322.
4. Landing, *Black Judaism*, 199–120.
5. Arbell, *Jewish Nation of the Caribbean*, 156.
6. Arbell, 157–158.
7. Menkis, "Reform Judaism in Canada," 296.
8. D. Kaplan, *American Reform Judaism*, 46.
9. Kosek, *American Religion*, 63–64.
10. Meyer, *Response to Modernity*, 226–227.
11. Schwartz, *Jews in America*, 125; Wolin, *Jews of Wyoming*, 14–15.
12. Jews of Color Initiative, "Counting Inconsistencies," 7–8.
13. Winsberg, "Jewish Agricultural Colonization in Argentina," 487–488.
14. Della Pergola, "Demographic Trends of Latin American Jewry," 92.
15. Gerchunoff and Pereda, *Jewish Gauchos of the Pampas*.
16. Della Pergola and Lerner, "La población judía en México," 28.
17. Lesser, *Welcoming the Undesirables*, 15.
18. Goldstein, *Price of Whiteness*, 47, 11–16, 52, 69.
19. Goldstein, "Great Wave," 73.
20. Goldstein, 74.
21. Ribak, "Jew Usually Left Those Crimes to Esau," 12.
22. Angel, "Sephardim of the United States," 104.
23. Mirelman, "Note on Jewish Settlement in Argentina," 11.
24. Polland and Soyer, *Emerging Metropolis*, 67.

43

Belisario's *Sketches of Character*

JAMAICA, 1837–1838

Jackie Ranston

Like other colonies in the British West Indies, Jamaica underwent drastic changes in the 1830s. Jews were finally given full civil rights in 1831, thanks mainly to the lobbying activities of Moses Delgado. Three years later, the Emancipation Act of 1834 transformed the island's enslaved community into apprentices, who continued working for their former masters without wages until they achieved full freedom in 1838. It was amid this turmoil that the Jamaican-born artist Isaac Mendes Belisario (1794–1849) returned from London to produce his most famous work, *Sketches of Character, in Illustration of the Habits, Occupation, and Costume of the Negro Population, in the Island of Jamaica*. Belisario noted in the preface that one of his motives was "a desire to hand down faithful delineations of people, whose habits, manners, and costume, bear the stamp of originality," and he accomplished this in three folios comprising twelve hand-tinted lithographic prints and twenty-one pages of descriptive text.[1] The most intriguing visuals are those depicting the elaborately costumed characters from the annual Christmas festivities that flourished during the final decades of slavery and known as Jonkonnu—a complex and diverse mix of multiple African cultures and European masquerade, alongside British mumming plays and Shakespearean monologues. Commonly anglicized to "John Canoe," the masquerade had its origins in the early days of slavery, when the Christmas holidays provided the only real recreational opportunities for the enslaved.

Belisario's artistic focus was unusual for his class and time. Although he painted portraits, plantation landscapes, and the renowned interior view of the Bevis Marks synagogue in London, he remains the only artist of the era to preserve the culture of the Jamaicans in bondage in print for posterity. Belisario was fascinated by the way enslaved Africans had succeeded in keeping many of their traditions alive under the guise of Jonkonnu. In this sense, Jonkonnu was the point at which Belisario's Jewish and Jamaican identities intersected. Of *converso* descent, he was only too well aware of how his own people had concealed their identity over the centuries as a condition of survival.

The island's official Jewish population did not grow substantially during the nineteenth century, and as such, Belisario's work represents the end of an era. Financial insecurity and natural disasters pushed key members of the community northward, and their loss was barely offset by the Ashkenazi immigrants who arrived from Germany and eastern Europe. The new arrivals, however, would impact religious life on the island. Shangare Yosher (Kingston, 1787), the second-oldest Ashkenazi synagogue in the Americas, received a new building in 1837, only to be wiped out in the fire of 1882. A second Ashkenazi congregation, Rodephei Zedek (1801–1850), flourished only to merge later with the city's Sephardic congregation. North in Montego Bay, Beth Jacob (1845–1912) was destroyed in a hurricane. When fires prompted the merger of the Kingston congregations, the result was a mixture of the Portuguese rite and the "progressive" reforms experienced by many congregations in the United States.[2] Amid this loss and change, however, Belisario's portraits predict the larger influence of Judaism on the island. While today the island's Jewish community remains small (around five hundred people), according to the World Jewish Congress, "nearly 424,000 Jamaicans are descendants of the Sephardic Jewish immigrants who came to the island throughout its history."[3] Toward the end of the nineteenth century, many multiracial descendants of Jews migrated to the United States and helped found and populate Black synagogues in Harlem and other locations.

PRIMARY SOURCES

See following pages.

QUESTIONS

1. The masking here may have reminded Belisario of Jewish Purim celebrations. How does Purim play with themes of identity?
2. Belisario relied on subscription revenues for this work, and the vast majority of his subscribers were Jewish. What does this tell us about his intended audience?
3. Belisario prefaced each folio with a quote from Shakespeare's *Othello*, "Nothing extenuate, nor set down aught in malice." What is your interpretation of why he included this quote and what it means?
4. Compare the way Belisario uses clothing to construct identity to the images in "Jews and Daguerreotypes" (chapter 45) and "Portraits of Multiracial and Gender Bending Jews" (chapter 75)
5. Compare the representation of people of African descent in Belisario's images with those in chapter 39 or in the introduction to part 3. To what extent are Belisario's images also racial caricatures? Do you think Belisario created his art to support or limit Afro-Jamaican enfranchisement?

I. M. Belisario, "Koo, Koo, or Actor-Boy," from *Sketches of Character, in Illustration of the Habits, Occupation, and Costume of the Negro Population, in the Island of Jamaica. Drawn after Nature, and in Lithography* (Kingston: J. R. DeCordova, 1837–1838), 2. (Courtesy Private Collection: The Hon. Maurice Facey and Mrs. Valerie Facey)

I. M. Belisario, "Koo-Koo or Actor Boy [removes mask]," from *Sketches of Character, in Illustration of the Habits, Occupation, and Costume of the Negro Population, in the Island of Jamaica. Drawn after Nature, and in Lithography* (Kingston: J. R. DeCordova, 1837–1838), 21. (Yale Center for British Art)

I. M. Belisario, "Jaw-bone, or House John-Canoe," from *Sketches of Character, in Illustration of the Habits, Occupation, and Costume of the Negro Population, in the Island of Jamaica. Drawn after Nature, and in Lithography* (Kingston: J. R. DeCordova, 1837–1838), 13. (Yale Center for British Art)

NOTES

1. Belisario, *Sketches of Character*, preface (unpaginated).
2. Arbell, *Jewish Nation of the Caribbean*, 244; Arbell, *Portuguese Jews of Jamaica*, 31–36.
3. World Jewish Congress, "Jamaica"; Chisholm, "Religion and the 2011 Census."

44

Kahal Kadosh Beth Elohim

SOUTH CAROLINA, 1839–1841

Barry L. Stiefel

In 1838, the conflicts that had emerged between the proponents of reform and traditionalists (later called Orthodox) at Kahal Kadosh Beth Elohim (KKBE) in Charleston (see chapter 41) were exacerbated when the original synagogue building burned to the ground. For some members of the congregation, the need to rebuild presented the unforeseen opportunity to include an organ in the synagogue, an instrument that traditionalists understood as contrary to Jewish law but that reformers increasingly interpreted as a sign of Jewish modernity.[1] Although initially the reformers were outvoted, ultimately they prevailed, and the result was that the traditionalists split from the reformers, calling their new congregation Kahal Kadosh Shearit Israel (the Holy Congregation of the Remnant of Israel). Before the split was complete, however, the Sephardic Jew David Lopez Jr. was selected to oversee the construction of the new synagogue for Kahal Kadosh Beth Elohim.

The selection of Lopez was monumental. Lopez is the first known Jewish synagogue contractor in the Americas. Choosing Lopez proved ironic, as he was a self-proclaimed traditionalist. Thus, when the congregation split, Lopez briefly became a member of Shearit Israel. Eventually, however, he had a falling out with this congregation after the passing of his wife, Catherine Lopez, in 1843, due to the congregation's refusal to bury her in its cemetery because she was not Jewish.

The current KKBE building was completed in 1841 on the same location as the former synagogue. As the contractor, Lopez worked alongside both hired and enslaved employees. The Greek Revival–style design was selected because it was at the height of fashion in the antebellum United States, representing the aspired-for democracy of the young republic. Until the nineteenth century, few Jews participated in the construction trades as a means of making their livelihood. Mercantile trade and retail shop keeping were more common professions among Jews. So Lopez's interest in construction was a significant departure from this tradition (his father and uncle had been transatlantic merchants). Besides being architecturally significant within the United States, the KKBE synagogue is considered to be one of the most important early American Greek Revival buildings and is a signifier of new economic mobility for Jews working outside of commerce professions.

In 1846, Shearit Israel had a synagogue built. Its builder was David Lopez Cohen (David Lopez Jr.'s nephew), and it was the second synagogue constructed by a Jewish builder in the Americas. However, Cohen was a member of KKBE. In an ironic twist of circumstances, neither early Jewish builder of synagogues actually used the building that he labored to construct due to personal differences in religious conviction. Therefore, the building of KKBE synagogue exemplifies the story of American Jewish history more broadly by exhibiting how Jews within a single family can belong to different branches of Judaism, such as Reform and Orthodox, and yet maintain relationships with one another outside the synagogue (Cohen had apprenticed under Lopez). KKBE is the first Reform synagogue in the United States, and with the loss of earlier established European Reform congregations during the Holocaust, it has become the oldest surviving Reform synagogue in the world. Unfortunately, the Shearit Israel building was lost during the mid-twentieth century due to redevelopment.

PRIMARY SOURCES

Front façade of KKBE Synagogue. (Photograph by Barry L. Stiefel, 2008)

Interior of KKBE Synagogue. (Photograph by Barry L. Stiefel, 2008)

QUESTIONS

1. What is different about the interior of KKBE and the Touro Synagogue (chapter 25)?
2. Jews did not build their own synagogues prior to the nineteenth century because of laws that limited them to certain professions (such as moneylending). What does it mean to have the ability to choose your own profession?
3. David Lopez Jr. rejected the custom that people work in professions they inherited from their parents. What profession do you aspire to, and how is it different from (or similar to) your parents'?
4. Today is a pluralistic society similar to in the past. David Lopez Jr. identified with Orthodox Judaism, Catherine Lopez was raised a Protestant, and David Lopez Cohen

was Reform Jewish. While we might believe in different things or worship in different ways, how can we still have meaningful relationships that overcome our differences?

NOTE

1. Tarshish, "Charleston Organ Case," 420–423; Rosenstein, "Symbol and Tool of Hybridity," 3–4.

45

Jews and Daguerreotypes

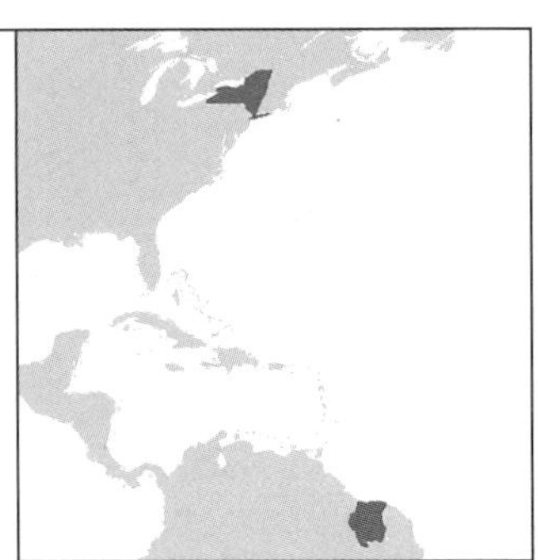

SURINAME, NEW YORK, 1840S

Laura Arnold Leibman

During the age of revolutions and emancipation, Jews used portraits in miniature and on canvas to help bolster their social status as rising elites, to create intimacy, and to memorialize friends and family (see chapters 27, 34, and 39). During the nineteenth century, the tradition of portraiture opened up to the more middling classes, as photographs were cheaper.

Daguerreotypes are an early photographic process developed by Louis-Jacques-Mandé Daguerre and introduced to the public in 1839. The process created a one-off image on a sheet of silver-plated copper. After the image was taken, it was placed behind protective glass. Although the result was fragile and light sensitive, it radically changed portraiture, as it allowed people to purchase fairly inexpensive mirror-like images. By the late 1850s, new techniques replaced the daguerreotype, but for historians of the 1840s–1850s, the photographs provide important insights into how early American Jews saw themselves and the world around them. Carvalho's 1853 portrait of the Cheyenne village is one of the earliest photographs made of the community and is a good reminder of the role Jews played in western expansion.

Solomon Nunes Carvalho (1815–1894) was born in Charleston, though both his family and he had strong ties to Barbados. Solomon's father had been a leader of KKBE's Reform camp (see chapter 41), but Solomon was himself a traditionalist who was married by Isaac Leeser of congregation Mikveh Israel in Philadelphia.[1] In addition to being an accomplished painter, Carvalho was an early master of the daguerreotype. In March 1853, Carvalho accompanied US General John C. Frémont's Fifth Expedition along the thirty-eighth parallel as the group's photographer. Despite bad weather, frostbite, hunger, and near-death conditions, Carvalho managed to take numerous daguerreotypes of the journey with Frémont that survived his return to New York and were used to create engravings for accounts of the expedition. Unfortunately, however, nearly all the originals were lost in a warehouse fire. Only the half-plate view of the Cheyenne village survived.[2] After

Carvalho's return from the West, he struggled financially to make ends meet and briefly ran a photography studio in New York.

Carvalho's landscape daguerreotypes are unusual: most daguerreotypes that survive were made in studios, like the self-portrait Carvalho took around 1850. Indeed, even before Carvalho left on his travels, studios were popping up across the Americas. The art form spread to Suriname in the 1840s, and the first known studio there was opened by the Portuguese Jew Solomon de Castilho in the late 1850s.[3] The earliest known daguerreotype from Suriname, however, came not from de Castilho's studio but from a traveling photographer named John Riker. Riker's sitters were Maria Louisa de Hart and Johannes Ellis. The daguerreotype was taken in 1846, shortly after the couple wed. Unlike Carvalho, the couple was both socially and financially successful. The couple lived in a house on Keizerstraat near the Ashkenazi Neve Shalom synagogue, where Maria Louisa's father, Mozes Meijer de Hart, had been the parnas. Her mother, Carolina Petronella van de Hart, had been enslaved by Hart before he freed her and married her in 1840. Their marriage did more than make their union and children legitimate. By legally marrying Carolina, Hart ensured that the race assigned to his children officially changed from "coloured" to "white." Johannes Ellis also had mixed ancestry: his father was Abraham de Veer, the Dutch governor of Ghana, and his mother was a Ghanaian woman named Fanny Ellis. They never married. Johannes and Maria Louisa's son, Abraham George Ellis, went on to be the minister of the navy in Amsterdam from 1903 to 1905.[4]

Although the photographer of Maria Louisa de Hart and Johannes Ellis was not Jewish, many early photographers in Paramaribo Suriname were of Jewish descent. In addition to Castilho, Augusta Cornelia Paulina Curiel and her sister Anna ran a photography studio in Paramaribo from 1904 to 1937 (see chapter 75). Art historians have noted that Jews in other countries often "took" to the new medium of photography. David Shneer speculates that this is because "unlike many other forms of art, photography did not have an academy or jury. . . . Its relatively low status and lack of officialdom gave aspiring young aesthetically minded Jews an opportunity to create without needing permission from those in power. It was also a new technology and a new medium, one that required entrepreneurialism and risk taking."[5]

PRIMARY SOURCES

See following pages.

Solomon Nunes Carvalho, view of a Cheyenne village at Big Timbers, in present-day Colorado, with four large tipis standing at the edge of a wooded area, 1853–1860, daguerreotype, Mathew Brady's Studio. (LCPPD, ppmsca 39309)

Solomon Nunes Carvalho, half-length portrait, facing slightly left, seated with arm resting on table with tablecloth, c. 1850, daguerreotype. (LCPPD, ppmsca 39308)

John L. Riker, Maria Louisa de Hart and Johannes Ellis, 1846, daguerreotype. (RM, M-RP-F-BR-2009-1-00)

QUESTIONS

1. Compare the clothing and posture of Johannes Ellis and Solomon Nunes Carvalho. What messages do the sitters seem to be sending us about themselves?
2. Scholars of the visual arts often argue that looking at the camera and the photographer rather than away from them transforms one from an object to an agent. To what extent do you think the gaze of the sitters matters in these portraits?
3. What makes a photograph or work of art "Jewish"?
4. David Shneer argues that photography was "a means for Jews to gain access to power without being a part of power."[6] To what extent does this explanation help make sense of why nineteenth-century Jews turned to photography?
5. Compare the portrait of Maria Louisa de Hart to that of Sarah Brandon Moses (chapter 39). How had women's clothing style and hairstyles changed? How did Hart establish her social status?

NOTES

1. Rosengarten and Rosengarten, "First Families," 74.
2. Kailbourn and Palmquist, *Pioneer Photographers*, 152.
3. Groeneveld, *Fotografie in Suriname*, 23.
4. Boom, *First Photograph*, 4, 32.
5. Shneer, *Through Soviet Jewish Eyes*, 15.
6. Shneer, 15.

46

Conversion and Repentance in the Diary of Cora Wilburn

VENEZUELA, 1846

Jonathan D. Sarna

After a tumultuous independence period that had started in 1797, Venezuela finally separated from Spain in 1821. And while the following period was defined by constant strife between conservatives and liberals, the tight control exercised by Spain was gone. Economic opportunities attracted European immigrants, yet these early arrivals were not plentiful. The writer of this diary, Cora Wilburn (1824–1906), arrived in Venezuela in 1844. Born Henrietta Pulfermacher in Europe (most likely Alsace), she traveled the world with her parents—her father, a crooked gem merchant who assumed the name Moritz Jackson, as well as her stepmother—before settling in La Guaira, a port near Caracas. There, under the name Henrietta Jackson, she commenced keeping a diary. The entry included here provides insights into the precarious existence of early Jewish women who immigrated to the Americas.

Wilburn's diary paints a grim picture of her Jewish family, describing her father's alcoholism and the abuse that she and her stepmother suffered at his hands. Upon the death of her stepmother, her father threatened her physically and drove her from the house. Within a few months, he himself lay dead, and whatever of value he owned was stolen. Adrift and impoverished, Wilburn was taken in by sympathetic Catholic neighbors. She succumbed to their pressure and converted to Catholicism on June 24, 1846. But she soon repented of the act, especially when she discovered that her sponsor was a secret adulteress. So, with hopes of returning to her people and her faith, she migrated to the United States, settling in Philadelphia in September 1848.

Once in Philadelphia, Wilburn was denied the welcome she expected from Jews, and she found herself reduced to menial servitude as a seamstress. After four years, she broke free of her hated needle. Aided by Christian friends, she became a professional writer under the nom de plume Cora Wilburn, which subsequently became her legal name. For seventeen years, she aligned herself with the Spiritualist movement, heavily composed of social activist women, which held that the spirits of the departed lived on in a distinct "spirit world" from which they continued to communicate with human beings. During this period, she wrote several serialized autobiographical novels, most significantly, *Cosella Wayne* (1860), based on her diary. In 1869, having become disenchanted with Spiritualism, she announced her return to Judaism and her identification with its "progressive ranks." Thereafter, with support from the Jewish community, she published poetry and essays in Jewish periodicals and promoted women's rights and other liberal causes during a long, bitter, and mostly reclusive retirement.

Cora Wilburn's life, including her conversion and return to Judaism, her attraction to Spiritualism, her spiritual activism, her singleness, and her support for women's rights anticipated themes that would become central to Judaism in the United States, especially within its progressive wing. Like Jews who later participated in such movements as Unitarianism, Ethical Culture, Christian Science, and Buddhism, Wilburn for years espoused religious hybridity. While her traditionalist father had insisted that her Jewish life should properly follow Jewish law and tradition, she rebelled. Her independent spiritual journey finds its parallel in the religious lives of many Jewish people in the United States today.

PRIMARY SOURCE

May 24, 1846. Alas, I have now to note down an event that fills me with reproach and repentance, an event that has called upon me the just anger of a most just God! An event that I long oh how sincerely, how fervently! to atone for, to win the pardon of my offended, my just and Benevolent father! Alas, misled by a fake enthusiasm which I mistook for conviction in a strange country amid stranger[s] my weak and hope forsaken spirit forsook its God!! Forsook the God of Abraham, of Isaac & of Jacob, the Only true God of Israel, for the false one of Nazareth! Bowed these knees in worship to the idols! And since that day of evil memory, a heavy & severe chastisement has fallen upon my guilty head. Had I not forsaken the God who till that day had supported and comforted me in all my troubles, he would not have forsaken me. I forgot what a brother had enjoined me, forgot my God, and as an accusation, a bitter & stern remembrance, do I note down the fatal day & hour now awake to my error repentant and afflicted. I pray for pardon and forgiveness from the only God and curse the Idols I once had the weakness to have faith in. Pardon me my God! Oh pity and pardon thy repentant, thy broken-hearted daughter, thy Marah!

Wednesday 24 June at 6 oclock in the morning [1846] was consummated my sacrifice. I had repented before it began but it was now too late, my word had been given. Mr B became my godfather, Mrs B. my godmother. This evening there was a table laid with refreshments, and the invited danced till 12 oclock.

Nothing particular occurred in July nor in August. I had left off mourning the fatal day I changed my pure and holy religion for a false one. Suffice it to say I suffered day by day unheard of torments: my godmother's icy cruelty, her ironical manner towards me, the over bearing behaviour of her Isabelle were breaking my too sensible heart, I became almost like

an idiot. I would sit on the step of the door that leads to the yard and dream or weep. Strange infatuation! I still prayed to saints that could neither hear nor help me and forgot the God of our ancestors!

"Selections from the Diary of Cora Wilburn (1844–1848)," in *Cosella Wayne*, edited and introduced by Jonathan D. Sarna (Tuscaloosa: University of Alabama Press, 2019), 283–284. Original at AJA.

QUESTIONS

1. Diaries are often reread and rewritten by their authors on the basis of subsequent developments. Do you think that is true here? Why or why not?
2. Why do you think the author converted, and why did she subsequently repent?
3. The author expresses surprise that "she still prayed to saints." Why do you think she did so, and what does it reveal about her?
4. What distinguishes this conversion narrative from others that you may have read, including the stories of New Christians arrested by the Inquisition (chapters 2, 3, 4, 5, 8).
5. Both Wilburn and Brandeau (chapter 16) use travel as an opportunity to change their names, religion, and identities. How do their motivations and strategies compare?

47

A Jewish Statesman and the Peculiar Institution

MISSISSIPPI, 1849–1933

Edward Sanders

So far, we have encountered several individuals born to a white father and an enslaved mother, including Sarah and Isaac Brandon (chapter 39) and Maria Louisa de Hart (chapter 45). Mathew Levy (1849–1933) was born on the plantation of Colonel Chapman Levy (chapter 34) in Attala County, Mississippi, to Sallie, an enslaved woman. Sallie was part of a multigenerational family that had been purchased by Levy from General Reuben H. Grant through a mortgage deal in 1840 in Noxubee County, Mississippi, northeast of Canton.[1] The land on which Sallie had grown up had belonged to the Choctaw Indians, until they were forced to cede their lands to the US government in 1830 and had to travel on the Trail of Tears to Oklahoma. Chapman Levy was one of the lawyers involved in the aftermath of the treaty regarding the Choctaw's removal.[2]

In addition to working as a lawyer and running a plantation, Mathew's father, Chapman Levy, had a remarkable career in public service that extended from his time in South Carolina all the way to the frontier state of Mississippi. A member of the South Carolina House and later a state senator, Chapman Levy was nominated as candidate for governor of Mississippi but declined the nomination.[3] He also enslaved people.[4] There are no records of Levy emancipating any of the hundreds of enslaved persons he bought and sold or any that he personally owned, with one exception: his "mulatto boy," Mathew. Mathew followed in his father's footsteps with regard to civil service: the photograph of Mathew Levy is excerpted from a composite "historic pictorial group," in which Levy appears as one of 119 statewide elected officials, legislators, and state house clerks.

These two items—a provision from an 1849 will and testament and a photograph from the 1882 session of the Mississippi legislature—show the complex relationship between a leading Jewish statesman and one of his enslaved offspring. The will provides a glimpse into the mind-set of a Jewish slave owner in the antebellum South, fulfilling what he probably saw as an act of noblesse oblige toward his mixed-race son. The notable Confederate diarist

Mary Chesnut once observed, "like the patriarchs of old our men live all in one house with their wives and their concubines, and the mulattoes one sees in every family exactly resemble the white children—and every lady tells you who is the father of all the mulatto children in everybody's household, but those in her own she seems to think drop from the clouds, or pretends so to think."[5]

These sources illuminate Chapman Levy's (ineffective) attempt to protect Mathew from the system of slavery and Mathew's eventual success in spite of everything he endured. If Chapman had manumitted Mathew himself, Mathew's freedom would have been secure. Unfortunately, however, Chapman left that task to the children born to him by his first wife, Flora Levy (1803–1823). Before Chapman Levy's will could reach probate, one of those children, Edward, died from a "fit" that caused him to fall into the fireplace.[6] Mathew then became the property of his half sister Flora Eliza Levy Anderson (1823–1851), who died nearly two years later. Mathew and his family then became the heir property of Flora's very young children. Their father, Thomas Salmond Anderson, later married Ellen Mary Davis, a niece of Jefferson Davis. After Anderson died, Mathew was hired out by Mrs. Davis-Anderson to local planters, in direct contradiction to Chapman's will. There is no indication that Mathew was freed until the general emancipation of 1865.

After the war, Mathew attended Alcorn University and was elected in 1881 to the Mississippi House of Representatives as an independent, during which time the photo included here was taken. Mathew died in 1933. His parents were listed on his death certificate as Sallie and Chapman Levy. Although Mathew became an important politician and educator, he has been left out of Jewish genealogies and southern Jewish history. Mathew's story clarifies our understanding of how scholars have defined and limited Jewish American history.

PRIMARY SOURCE

And my mulatto Boy Mathew, child of Sally I desire my Son to take care of till he is grown, and to send him to a country, where he can be free, and give him One hundred Dollars, and if my son dies before that is accomplished, then my Daughter is to have said Mathew, and to dispose of him as above directed. But in no event is he or any share of him to pass to or belong to any person but my Said Son or Daughter or their children.

Mississippi, Wills and Probate Records, 1780–1982, Attala County, Mississippi, Will Book A, 176, under "Chapman Levy."

Facing page, top: Elisaeus von Seutter, *Historic Pictorial Group of the Members of the Legislature, State of Mississippi*, 1882, photograph; ***bottom:*** detail of Mathew Levy (no. 114). (MDAH, PI/STA/L45.5/1882)

HISTORIC PICTORIAL GROUP

OF THE

MEMBERS OF THE LEGISLATURE,

1882 STATE OF MISSISSIPPI, 1882

PHOTOGRAPHED AND COMBINED BY

E. v. SEUTTER,

THE JEWELER AND ARTIST OF JACKSON, MISS.

CENTRE.

ROBERT LOWRY, Gov.

SENATE.

1 SHANDS, G. D. Lieutenant Gov. and Pres.
2 Reynolds, R. O. Pres. *pro tem.*
3 Stewart, James D
4 Noland, T V
5 Brown, L B
6 Cowan, Warren
7 Humphries, W W
8 Henderson, Eliott
9 Walker, J P
10 Brennam, A H
11 Johnson, David
12 Mitchell, C. B
13 Terry, John
14 Eaton, J S
15 Fitzgerald, V H
16 Wilson, S L
17 Roane, W A
18 Dalton, J H.
19 Ratliff, Wm
20 Crigler, J L
21 Liddell, J M
22 Hyer, W F
23 Smith, R C
24 Longino, A H
25 Martin, J McC
26 Cooper, T L
27 Jarnagin, H L
28 Waddell, V B
29 Kyle, J C
30 Roane, S M
31 Boone, F M
32 Hamilton, J G
33 Luse W H
34 Keith, Thos
35 Martin, J McC
36 Jagee, Thos
37 Gayles, G
38 Jones, B F, Seg't-at-Arms

HOUSE.

1 Tison, W H H, Speaker
2 Montgomery, F A
3 Terrall, S H
4 Magruder, T B
5 Foules, Chas D
6 Saunders, T G
7 Howry Chas B
8 Stovall, W T
9 Harrell, Jobe
10 Ayres, Wm
1 Mathison, Neil
12 Smythe, D L
13 McInnis, K
14 Selman B A P
15 Handy, Wm
16 Ervin, A J
17 Buchanan, J W
18 Steven, J A C
19 Stone, W W
20 Jones, W H
21 Marshall, C A
22 Collins, J L
23 Harlow, A M
24 Johnson, M C
25 Nabers, W A
26 Montgomery, J S
27 Buchanan, Wm
28 Mellen, T L
29 Granberry, J M
30 Meyers, A L
31 Provine, R M
32 Wallington, W J
33 Stiles, E H
34 McCool, J F
35 Pope, Henry
36 McAfee, J H
37 Lyle, M
38 Powe, Alexander,
39 Ferguson, P L
40 Downer, J H
41 Armstrong, J W
42 Watts, V B
43 Askew, James. O
44 Rhodes, R E
45 Burdine, J C
46 Cameron, H D
47 Woods, Thos J
48 Harper, W L
49 Rogers, Enos
50 Hurt, W A
51 Griggs, J L
52 Davis, H L
53 Johnso , Peter
54 Ferguson, T C
55 McRae, J B
56 Rees, H
57 Rodman, W D
58 Watson, K A
59 Greaves, J B
60 Byrd, C
61 Rose, Terrell
62 Guyne , A B
63 Williamson, H C
64 Brown, A F
65 Blair, Jno A
66 Simpson, A W
67 Jones, L B
68 Hickman, Sam'l
69 White, F S
70 Chapman, D T
71 Moss, H T
72 McCall, R J
73 Heard, S
74 Boyer, Jesse
75 Gibs-n, Jas M
76 Welbourn, J G
77 Atkinson, Thos
78 McBeath, J C
79 Field, J H
80 Sykes, E O
81 Wise, G W
82 Norrell, A G
83 Farve, T M
84 Blankinship, Jos
85 Gully, Henry J
86 McLain, F A
87 Duckworth, J D W
88 Finley, W W
89 McKie, G W
90 Turnipseed, C B
91 Elmer, F W
92 Dodds, Geo S
93 Montgomery, L F
94 Whitney, J J
95 Knox, N C
96 Crawford, N B
97 Simmons, W F
98 McSwine, Wm
99 Inge, W M
100 Wood, Thos J
101 Terrall, F H
102 Noel, E F
103 Tackett, J P
104 Fredericks, C J
105 Moore, A M
106 McCallum, H M
107 Ivy, F G
108 Berry, N M
109 Granberry, Geo C
110 Poston, A B
111 Shorter, J A
112 Bufford, J H
113 Lynch, W H
114 Levy M
115 Blackwell, S B
116 Wilson, E S, Clerk
117 Wilson, R S, En'l Cl'k
118 N M Myer, J't Cl'k
119 Holland, W T Sg't at arms

QUESTIONS

1. Although it may seem to be a recognition of kinship, the term "my mulatto boy" (or girl) can be used to indicate either kinship or ownership. Why do you think Chapman is not more explicit, despite his desire that Mathew be freed?
2. Malcolm Stern's *First American Jewish Families* (1991) includes only offspring from Chapman Levy's legal wife, Flora, even though the book was updated and revised several times over three decades. What is at stake in the decision regarding who belongs in a genealogical history?
3. How is the excerpt from Chapman Levy's will similar to or different from the will from Jamaica (chapter 23)?

NOTES

1. Noxubee County, Mississippi Mortgage Deeds, 1840.
2. "Message from the President of the United States," 183–186.
3. "Rats Leaving a Falling House," *Vermont Phoenix*, July 31, 1840.
4. Noxubee County, Mississippi Property Tax Rolls, "L" Section, 1840.
5. Chesnut, *Mary Chesnut's Civil War*, 29.
6. "Obituary for Edward Levy," *Kosciusko Chronicle*, January 4, 1850.

48

Coro *Mikveh*

VENEZUELA, C. 1853–1860

Blanca de Lima

As noted in the introduction to part 2, one of the earliest openly Jewish communities to thrive in the post-Inquisition world of Latin America was in the city of Coro, a town on the northwestern coast of Venezuela. This community started as an offshoot of the Jewish community of nearby Curaçao.[1] In 2013, a team from the Universidad Central de Venezuela led by the archaeologist Carlos Alberto Martín discovered evidence about the religious lives of Jews in this city: a *mikveh*. After the ritual bath in Recife, the Coro *mikveh* is one of the oldest in Latin America, and it provides important insights into the ritual life of Jews in the region, particularly women.

The bath was discovered in what was once the house of David de Abraham Senior, a Sephardic merchant from Curaçao. The house, located just two blocks from the main square and cathedral, was bought by Senior in 1852, and the firm of Isaac A. Senior & Son worked from the house between 1852 and the firm's closure in the 1980s. Although Coro never had its own synagogue or rabbi, a prayer room was located in the same house in the lower part of the west wing. We know about the room because David's father, Abraham Senior, wrote in 1853 requesting that his neighbor A. H. Garcia allow him to open windows onto the plot containing Garcia's house for the purpose of "providing freshness and ventilation into the area where he prayed."[2] The *mikveh* is on the same floor as the prayer hall but in the east wing of the house.

Women typically used the baths both on a monthly basis and just before the marriage ceremony, and this bath was possibly built in anticipation of two important weddings shortly after Senior bought the house: that of Exilda Abenatar and David Curiel in 1860 and that of Raquel López Henríquez and Isaac Senior (David's brother) in 1861. The parents of Abenatar and Curiel were influential members of Coro's small Sephardic community. David Curiel's father, Joseph Curiel Suares, was among the first immigrants from Curaçao to Coro and was a *mohel* for his community. Abraham Senior, Isaac's father, was a powerful businessman who for years led Shabbat services for his coreligionists. Six other Jewish weddings took place in Coro in the 1860s, four in the 1870s, and two in the 1880s. All those brides quite possibly used this *mikveh*. The bath was verified to be a halachic ritual bath by Rabbi Samuel Garzón in 2016. It measures 1.70 by 1.70 meters (5.6 by 5.6 feet) and has a capacity of 575 liters of rainwater.

Despite early acceptance, anti-Jewish sentiment broke out in Coro in 1831 and 1855, and the 1855 attacks were particularly violent. Locating the *mikveh*, like the prayer hall, at the back of the house may have been a protective measure on the small community's part. After the incidents, antisemitism remained just below the surface in the town. When Sephardic Jews returned to Coro from Curaçao after things had settled down, they still tended to maintain a low religious profile. Coro remained religiously conservative, and tensions between Catholics and Sephardim only ceased after the oldest Jewish community leaders who provided guidance in religious matters and marriage regulations passed away. Later generations assimilated into Venezuelan Creole society.

The discovery of the *mikveh* radically changed our understanding of Sephardic Jews in Coro. In the absence of a synagogue and rabbi, the community had been thought by scholars to have had a weak religious structure. The *mikveh*, however, speaks of a community that preserved its rites and religion at least into the last quarter of the nineteenth century, after which marriages between Jews and gentiles led to profound cultural change and the disappearance of Coro's historic Sephardic community.

PRIMARY SOURCES

Inside Coro *mikveh*. (Photograph by Blanca De Lima, 2016)

Coro *mikveh* and adjacent reservoir. (Photograph by Blanca De Lima, 2016)

QUESTIONS

1. What attributes does the Coro ritual bath share with the one in the Nidhe Israel synagogue complex (chapter 15)? How are they different?
2. How does the location of the *mikveh* reflect the religious status of Jews in Venezuela?
3. What does the ritual bath tell us about women's role in maintaining Jewish tradition in Coro?

NOTES

1. Cohen and Peck, *Sephardim in the Americas*, 237.
2. Aizenberg, *La comunidad judía de Coro*, 100.

49

Circumcision Deposition

LOUISIANA, 1859

Shari Rabin

The first Jewish immigrants to reach New Orleans were Dutch Sephardim who arrived in the 1720s. Between 1724 and 1803, however, the Louisiana Code Noir officially expelled Jews from the colony. After being acquired in the 1804 Louisiana Purchase, however, New Orleans soon became one of the most significant Jewish settlements in the United States. Jews flocked to the bustling, multicultural port city. Although the first synagogue, Shangarai Chasset (1827), was established by Jacob Solis and used the Western Sephardic rite, by the late 1850s, the city hosted numerous Jewish institutions, including a small congregation of Prussian Jews called Tememe Derech (The Right Path). Established in 1857, Tememe Derech followed the Polish rite and was known as an Orthodox (traditional) congregation. In 1859, Jacob Bernard turned to this congregation to help him establish the Jewishness of his three sons.

Jacob Bernard was one of the many "German" Jewish men, most of them young and single, who migrated to the United States in the decades before the Civil War and settled in the city. Working in many cases as peddlers or merchants, these Jews had moved westward along with the nation. Jacob Bernard was an immigrant from Bohemia who married Mary Young, a Catholic woman, in St. Louis. Intermarriage was in violation of Jewish law but not at all uncommon for Jewish men in the West. After Mary died, her parents took their three sons to a Catholic asylum, but Bernard was able to recover them and flee to New Orleans. In January 1859, the Tememe Derech congregation arranged for the boys to be circumcised by a C. Goldenberg. This case probably elicited the congregation's sympathy because of its parallels to the famed Mortara Affair, which had taken place six months earlier, when the Catholic Church had taken custody of a Jewish child in Italy after he had been secretly baptized by a domestic servant.[1] Since only the children of Jewish mothers were considered Jews, Bernard declared his intent to convert his sons to Judaism in front of a Beit Din (a tribunal of three adult Jewish men, at least one of whom should be a rabbi), although there is no evidence that his sons underwent the ritual immersion required to complete the process.

Bernard's deposition shows how ordinary Jews responded to the challenges of Jewish life in the United States, where religious identity was a choice. There was a shortage of marriageable Jewish women in this period, and religious ritual and practice had to be paid for out of pocket. Congregations were founded to ease these burdens, but their religious authority was not absolute. After all, Bernard could be married by a justice of the peace and assert his children's Jewish identity through a legal deposition.

According to the 2020 Pew Research Center Survey of US Jews, 61 percent of all Jewish marriages since 2010 have been with non-Jews. Research indicates that many of these couples participate in Jewish life and raise their children with Jewish identities.[2] And yet intermarriage, past and present, has usually been seen as an indicator of assimilation away from Judaism. Bernard's case offers an early example of a Jew insisting on the Jewish identity of his children with a Christian. In fact, patrilineal descent, the idea that Jewish identity can be transmitted through the father, came to be embraced officially by the Reform movement over a century later, in 1983.

PRIMARY SOURCE

Sitting as a tribunal of three, we were as one, here in the city of New Orleans, in the fourth day of the week, fifth day of the month of Adar, 5619, as came before us Yaakov son of Avraham and with him three young boys. The first [boy was] seven years of age, the second [boy was] five years of age, and the third [boy was] three years of age. And so said the aforementioned Yaakov—these three boys are my sons, whom my wife bore to me, and she was a gentile women, whom I have taken as a wife according to the law of the state and before a gentile judge in the city of St. Louis. And I hereby come to bring them under the wings of the divine presence and convert them [so that they become] righteous converts according to the laws of Moses and Israel. And also came before us Ze'ev son of David, Shemaiah son of Yitzchak, Dov son of Elazar, and Uriah son of Yehonatan, and they gave testimony on this matter, all according to what they know of the aforementioned man Yaakov and his young sons. And what was done regarding this matter, and the words of the aforementioned Yaakov and what the aforementioned witnesses have testified, all is written as follows in the English language and signed by name.

My name is Jacob Bernard, born in Rakolus, Bohemia of Jewish parents. 29 years of age, arrived in America in 1849, resided in St. Louis about 8 years, married a Christian woman by the name of Mary Young alias Lajeunesse before a justice of the peace on the 17th day of August 1851. I never changed my religion, had born three male children that are now seven, five, and three years respectively. I desire these my children to be educated in the Jewish religion. Had these children circumcised for this object by Mr. C. Goldenberg on the 4th day of January 1859. The elder was named Baruch, the second Shrago (Phillip), the third Joseph.

Jacob Bernard

My name is W.D. Skamper, the above Jacob Bernard came to me and asked me to assist him in getting his sons circumcised was present at the circumcision of the oldest child, heard

the children to be pronounced *Ki dor* [Hebrew: because of the generation, a reference to Deuteronomy 32:20] thought they were Jewish children, and that nothing else but the circumcision was necessary.

W.D. Skamper.

My name is Simon Schwerin, I am President of the Association Tememe Derech. I know Mr. Jacob Bernard and his three male children, was present when those three children were circumcised in the Synagogue of our Association. I think these children were Jewish children. I heard the children named by Mr. C. Goldenberg. I don't recollect the names. I allowed the use of the Synagogue for that purpose in my capacity of President of said Association.

S. Schwerin

My name is B. Oppenheim, am Secretary of the aforenamed Association, I signed and sealed a letter accompanying the communication published in No. 30 of the Israelite, did not write the communication.

[signature missing]

My name is U. Rosenthal, was present at the circumcision of the children of Jacob Bernard, I heard the Mohel name the children [Hebrew: of no mother] I refused to take an active part as Mohel because I was unacquainted with the parties.

U. F. Rosenthal.

[indecipherable signatures]

Circumcision Deposition, 1859, United States, AJA, RD-59. The first two paragraphs were translated by Iddo Haklai.

QUESTIONS

1. Given that Bernard was willing to violate Jewish law by marrying a Christian woman, why do you think he circumcised his sons?
2. There are many ways to define and categorize Jewish identity (genealogy, practice, race, ethnicity, religion). How would you describe Bernard's understanding of Jewish identity?
3. How might this source differ if the incident had been described by Mary Young's parents (Bernard's in-laws)? What does this case tell us about Jewish-Christian relations in the nineteenth century?

NOTES

1. "A Circumcision Story in New Orleans," *Israelite*, January 28, 1859, 237.
2. Pew Research Center, "Portrait of Jewish Americans."

50

Rebecca Gratz's Sunday School Speech

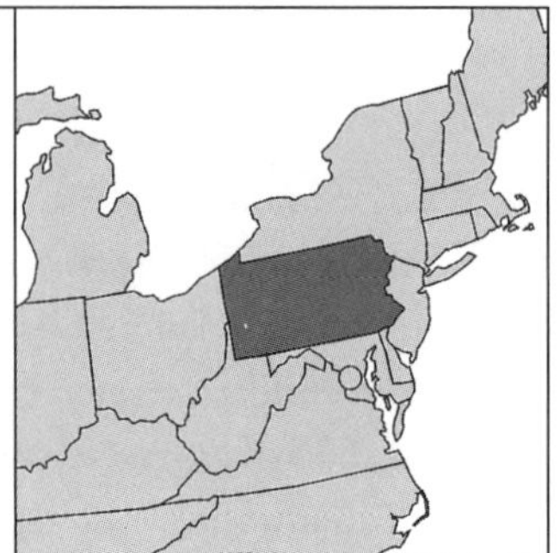

PENNSYLVANIA, 1862

Dianne Ashton

One of the major innovations in nineteenth-century American Judaism was the increased role women played in Jewish schooling in both traditional and Reform congregations. While most early American synagogues had a school, prior to the 1830s, these schools tended to be organized by men and employed men as teachers. Under the leadership of Rebecca Gratz, however, women's role in Jewish communal life began to change. Between 1815 and the 1830s, Gratz founded Philadelphia's Jewish Orphan Society (1815), the Female Hebrew Benevolent Society (1819), and the Hebrew Sunday School (1838), all of which encouraged women to take a more active role in caring for the Jewish children and the poor. Jewish social services modeled on those founded by Gratz spread across the United States. Even Jewish women's sewing circles, like the one in Canton, Mississippi (see the quilt photograph in the introduction to part 3), grew out of the Female Hebrew Benevolent Societies. One of Gratz's most lasting contributions to American Judaism, however, was the creation of "Sunday schools." Gratz's own superb education and speaking abilities helped model the new Jewish woman that her schools sought to create.

In March 1862, Rebecca Gratz, superintendent and founder of Philadelphia's Hebrew Sunday School (HSS), delivered this annual report to the parents, children, and interested individuals assembled to hear the school's students demonstrate knowledge that they had acquired that year. Although the school had begun as a humble gathering of students and teachers in one room in 1838, by 1900, the educational institution offered classes in eighteen different locations around the city. As new immigrants from central and eastern Europe settled in this port city, Philadelphia grew from about 4,000 to approximately 455,000 in 1960. During these years, the school continued to serve the city's Jewish population even as the new arrivals established families and created new religious institutions. In Philadelphia, the HSS continued to serve the city's Jewish children despite the growth of congregational schools, until the late twentieth century. Its influence nationwide shaped American Jewish education far into the future.

Jewish Sunday schools marked a new trend in Jewish education. Boys and girls together learned the fundamentals of Judaism: a belief in a singular God who created the world and provided moral guidance, a few key stories from the Hebrew Bible, and core holiday and worship practices. This curriculum made the school acceptable to the city's Jews despite differences in their place of origin, approach to Judaism, or economic class. While those distinctions divided congregations and ultimately gave rise to various denominations of Judaism in the Americas, the HSS successfully brought together Jewish children from all camps. Indeed, the school succeeded because its curriculum focused on the basics of Judaism that everyone agreed on, because it cost little to nothing, and because it taught in English—the language that nearly all immigrants realized that their children needed to learn. Its all-female faculty donated their time and energy. Their work forced local religious leaders to, in turn, educate the women teachers. In Gratz's 1862 annual report, she takes the opportunity of the public exam to solicit the aid of more women, inviting anyone who could donate her time without neglect of her domestic duties to join the schools' "holy cause." No mention is made of the Civil War that had been roiling the nation for more than a year—a measure of the North's experience of a war that neither consumed its resources nor despoiled its countryside or cities.

The HSS offered women the opportunity to teach Judaism formally for the first time in Jewish history. The HSS educated Jewish children in the basics of the religion, brought diverse Jewish children together, gave Jewish women a public role in religious life for the first time, and increased public support for women's religious education. In addition, it provided a Jewish school in a format that paralleled the many Protestant Sunday schools that were then popular in most sections of the US, including Philadelphia, thus adapting Jewish education to American culture. The format implemented by the HSS proved so successful that it was adopted by many Jewish communities and synagogues around the country, and it is safe to say that most Jewish children who obtained a formal Jewish education in the nineteenth century did so in a school where women taught a similar curriculum.

PRIMARY SOURCE

The 24th Annual Examination of the Hebrew Sunday School was held at the Synagogue 7th Street below Cherry, on Sunday, March 30th 1862. A very large number of Pupils was present & were examined in their several studies. The meeting was opened with a prayer by the Rev. S. Morais followed by singing an English hymn and repeating the weekly prayers after which the following reports were read.

Superintendent Report—

The Superintendent and Teachers of the Hebrew Sunday School Society have again the privilege of introducing into the presence of parents and friends the numerous pupils of the Institution on this 24th Anniversary. They feel thankful for the undiminished confidence

reposed in them, and owe gratitude to a higher Source for permission to learn and teach from the Holy Scriptures, the life-giving principles of the Jewish Faith. They delight to record that in several classes are found the offspring of former pupils—and among the young teachers recognize the daughters of one who studied there in its earlier days, thus beautifully illustrating the wisdom of the Royal Bard who said "train up a child in the way he should go" & we hope may realize his truth also that "when he is old he will not depart from it."

The number receiving instruction vary from 200 to 250, under the care of 25 teachers—which hardly meets the requirements of the School, and therefore every willing minded among the daughters of Israel in the congregations of our people who desire to assist in this most interesting labour, and without sacrifice of their domestic duties—will find a blessed reward in the consciousness of doing good & acquiring while they impart a knowledge of the Laws, Customs, and duties of our Holy Religion as taught by Moses to our forefathers—"the chosen people of God."

"The 24th Annual Examination of the Hebrew Sunday School . . . March 30th, 1862," Hebrew Sunday School Society of Philadelphia (Pa.) Records, 1859–1882, SC-9579, AJA.

QUESTIONS

1. Who is the "Royal Bard," and why do you think Gratz is quoting him?
2. Why do you think that the examination began with a prayer and "English hymn"? What did these add to the ceremony?
3. What are the advantages and disadvantages of holding a Jewish religious school on Sunday?

51

General Grant's Order No. 11

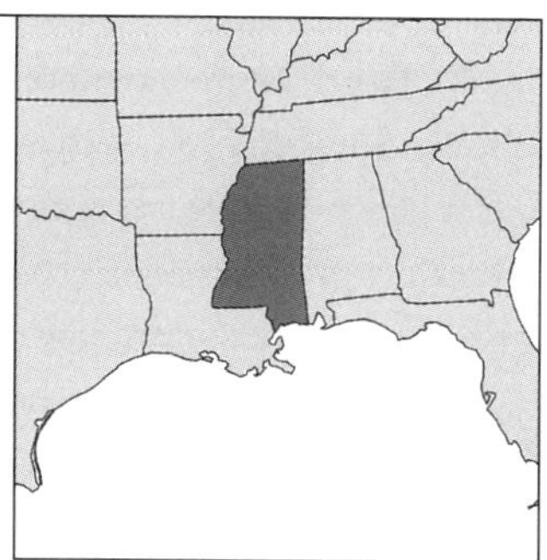

MISSISSIPPI, 1862

Steven Jacobs

This text, issued on December 17, 1862, by Union Major-General U. S. Grant (1822–1885) reminds us that the antisemitism that Jews experienced in earlier eras persisted in the nineteenth century. Yet, whereas earlier complaints were based on issues of religion (see chapters 2–5, 7–8, and 16) or race (see the illustration of the Jewish retailer in the introduction to part 3), Order No. 11 was a response to what was then seen as an illicit market in Southern cotton by unscrupulous traders thought to be mostly Jews. While several of Grant's generals and other high-ranking officers supported the order, Jews, particularly the leadership of the community in Paducah, Kentucky, under Cesar J. Kaskel (1833–?) protested directly to President Abraham Lincoln (1809–1865) via a strongly worded telegram. They regarded the order as "an enormous outrage on all laws and humanity, . . . the grossest violation of the Constitution and [their] rights as good citizens under it," and followed up their telegram with a visit to Washington, DC, on January 3, 1863. Prior to the visit, however, protest rallies were held in St. Louis, Louisville, and Cincinnati. Lincoln additionally received telegrams protesting the order from the B'nai B'rith Lodge of St. Louis, Missouri, and the Board of Delegates of American Israelites, New York, New York.

These strategies worked. Lincoln revoked the order on January 4, 1863, and on January 6, 1863, Lincoln received a delegation led by Rabbi Isaac Mayer Wise (1819–1900) of Cincinnati thanking him for his decision. Grant himself, responding to both supporters and protestors, revoked the order on January 17, 1863. In 1868, when Grant chose to run for president, the issue resurfaced, and he was forced to distance himself from it, telling voters that he harbored no prejudice against Jews. He won the election with Jewish support.

This important and historical document serves to remind us that the story of the US Civil War is, indeed, a complex one. One popular myth that emerged after the conflict is that of the "Lost Cause," which claimed that the conflict itself was mainly about economically related issues (rather than slavery) and that enslaved peoples were, by and large, treated well. Roots of this story can be seen in the diary of Emma Mordecai (chapter 52), and evidence against the myth can be found in chapter 47. Another myth that persists today is that before the Civil War, Jews only lived in the northern US, a fantasy that chapters 31, 34, 41, 44, 47, 49, 51, and 52 all undermine. Jews fought on both sides, and even in the North, some favored abolitionism while others supported slavery. The most well-known Southern Jew was Judah P. Benjamin (1811–1884), who served the Confederacy as secretary of state, secretary of war, and attorney general, having already served as a US senator from Louisiana. While Benjamin claimed that "slavery is against the law of nature," he himself owned more than 140 people who worked on his sugar plantation.[1]

Grant's order began with a conspiracy theory about Jewish traders. He was not alone. Throughout the nineteenth century, conspiracies about Jews spawned anti-Jewish violence. At the time of Grant's order, one of the most recent was the Damascus Affair (1840), in which the Jews of Damascus, Syria, were accused of ritually murdering a priest. Although Grant's order was rescinded, conspiracies continued to haunt Jews in the United States. In 1913, Leo Franks was convicted of murdering thirteen-year-old Mary Phagan in Atlanta, Georgia. When the US Supreme Court overturned the conviction, Frank was lynched by local residents. Even today, the notorious antisemitic nineteenth-century forgery *The Protocols of the Elders of Zion* is still available online.

PRIMARY SOURCE

Head Quarters, 13th Army Corps, Department of the Tennessee, Oxford, Miss., Dec. 17th, 1862. General Orders No. 11

1. The Jews, as a class, violating every regulation of trade established by the Treasury Department, and also Department orders, are hereby expelled from the Department.

2. Within twenty-four hours from the receipt of this order by Post Commanders, they will see that all of this class of people are furnished passes and required to leave, and any one returning after such notification will be arrested and held in confinement until an opportunity occurs of sending them out as prisoners, unless furnished with permit from Head Quarters.

3. No permits will be given these people to visit Head Quarters for the purpose of making personal application for trade permits.

By Order of Maj. Genl. U.S. Grant
Jno. A. Rawlins
Assistant Adjunct General. [signed]

Head Quarters, 13th Army Corps, Department of the Tennessee, Holly Springs, Miss., January 6, 1863. General Orders No. 2

In pursuance of directions from the General-in-Chief of the Army, General Orders No. 11, from these Headquarters, dated Oxford, Miss., December 17th, 1862, is hereby revoked.

"By Order of Maj. Genl. U.S. Grant," January 6, 1863, in *Ulysses S. Grant Papers*, vol. 7, p. 50, LOC.

QUESTIONS

1. Do you think Grant's apology was sincere or just politically expedient?
2. How do historians and "conspiracy theories" use and understand evidence differently?
3. Just because Grant's views were distasteful does not mean that he was wrong. What evidence could we use to support or undermine his claim that Jews had violated "every regulation of trade established by the Treasury Department, and also Department orders"?

NOTE

1. Traub, *Judah Benjamin*, 2, 30.

52

Diary of Emma Mordecai

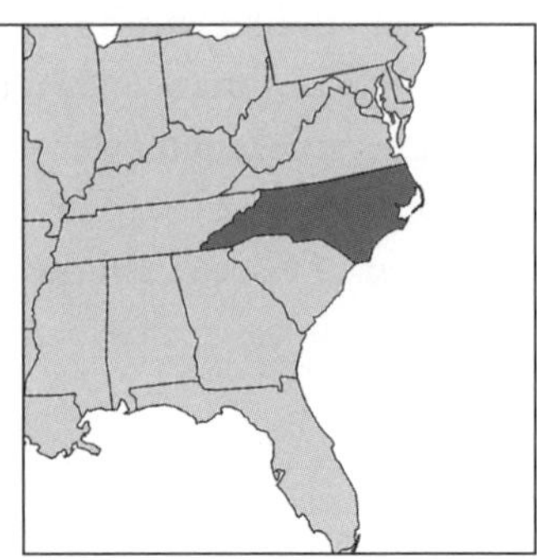

NORTH CAROLINA, 1864–1865

Dianne Ashton

The US Civil War not only disrupted families but forced Jews to choose sides and at times fight against kin. The Mordecai family was one such clan, with most siblings living in the South and others in the North. This diary describes daily events experienced by one of the Southern family members, Emma Mordecai (1812–1906) while she was living with her brother's widow, Rosina Young Mordecai, during the last year of the Civil War. Emma had lived in Richmond together with her widowed mother and a brother and sister, but after her mother's death, and with Union troops advancing on Richmond, the siblings closed the house and scattered to other households. Emma moved to the farm of her sister-in-law Rosina, only a few miles from Richmond and not too far from the Jewish family relations and synagogue in the city she loved. Her older sister, Ellen, relocated to their brother George's large estate in North Carolina. Rosina was a widow and suffered from several ailments that severely limited her. Emma provided emotional support, physical assistance, and companionship. Emma maintained this diary almost daily until several weeks after the Confederacy's defeat. It documents the ways in which she coped with wartime challenges that she shared with other white Southern women. Additionally, Emma faced the challenge of finding a way to maintain her Jewish religious life while living under her Christian sister-in-law's roof.

The diary gives us a rare glimpse into the personal religious attitudes and activities of a Jewish woman during the Civil War. Jews composed only 0.2 percent of the Confederacy. In the decades leading up to the war, Southern society had experienced enthusiastic evangelization by Protestant groups and the dramatic growth of Methodist and Baptist denominations. Emma grew up in North Carolina and later Virginia, where evangelizing neighbors and friends urged members of her family to accept Christianity. Emma's older sister Ellen did so with enthusiasm. Several of her siblings married Christians; after her brother Augustus married Rosina Young, the couple's four children were raised as Christians. Emma never married. Her diary shows us how a southern Jewish woman maintained her faith and found ways to practice it despite those challenges.

Emma's diary reveals how an individual Jewish woman participated in broader American society and Confederate beliefs. Emma echoes the widely shared belief that the South could expect divine support in the war. Southern culture turned to Christian understandings of the Bible—both Old and New Testaments—to justify its particular social order, along with its decision to go to war to defend its slave society. Thus, Christianity was not merely a private decision of the vast majority of Southerners but a broadly shared cultural belief. Because slavery existed in ancient Israel (though with many more restrictions than in the South) and because Jesus did not specifically state that slavery was wrong, Southerners claimed that it was approved by God.

With that religious foundation, ministers, politicians, newspaper editors, and average Southerners alike drew proslavery support from biblical texts. Many Southern Jews like Emma Mordecai joined that broader effort by affirming proslavery meanings in their understandings of their own Bibles. Because almost no Southern Jew could read and understand Hebrew—the original language of their Bible—they read English translations. Emma read either the Old Testament of the King James Bible, because it was widely available, or the English translation of the Hebrew Bible recently completed by Isaac Leeser, an important Jewish religious leader whom she knew. Thus, religion became a vehicle both for amalgamating Jews into Southern society and for defining their differences from it. It reveals the tensions at play for religious minorities in the United States.

PRIMARY SOURCE

On Thursday, April 18th **I left our house on 6th street, for the last time. Sister Ellen & Brother George had departed early that morning. . . . There were still remaining a few articles of furniture to be sent away, after attending to which . . . I came . . . out to Rosewood in the cars. . . . I felt strange without a home anymore, and very still & quiet, tho' not overcome with depression—the reverse, however, of all excitement. Rose [Rosina] had prepared most kindly for my reception, and my room was the picture of neatness & comfort. She received me very kindly, but we made no demonstration or professions to each other. I only know that my inward resolve and humble prayer was & is that I may make my residence with her, for as-long as it may last, a blessing & not a torment or inconvenience to her. There was a time when I should not have doubted this, but the longer we live, the more we doubt ourselves, & now I am not certain—I only hope.**

The following week I went to town to spend the Passover with my kind cousins, returning at the close of the festival, the time having been spent very satisfactorily, attending the services at the Synagogue, and visiting many of our friends whom circumstances had prevented my seeing before we broke up. By all I was most kindly greeted, & I was gratified at the unvarying regret expressed at our family having left Richmond, & at the kind invitations I received from various friends to pass days or nights with them whenever I could. I returned to Rosewood on Friday 30th.

May 14 Saturday Cloudy & showery all day. Firing heard all day, heavy & constant. Apparently directly south of us: probably in Chesterfield near the Danville R.R.—Negroes report firing at Drawry's Bluff. The day was an anxious one as we could learn nothing of what was going on. After reading my services for the day, read aloud to Gusta [her niece Augusta Mordecai (1847–1939)] while she finished her bonnet, which looks as if it had come from a milliner's. Gusta got a note, written this A.M. from Marion Stuart, . . . It is as follows—

"Dear Gusta, Mother asks me to write to you to see if you have heard anything from your brothers. We have made every possible inquiry concerning them but can hear nothing. Please let us know if you know anything, we feel anxious. Oh: Gusta, the Yankees:—but thank God we are safe. They did not do us much damage, as we had warning of their approach, & sent our horses, meal &c. to town: They stayed here from 1 o'clock in the day, until five the next morning. O, such a night!—Eight of their pickets guarding our house to prevent our escape. At least 10,000 camped—[torn] and we heard their [torn out] wagons and artillery [lost] by; they took three hours to pass! just think of it. I hope they did not reach you. . . . We had a severe fight at Yellow Tavern, & then 60 of our men contended against a regiment of Yankees, every inch of ground to our gate, when our men, overwhelmed, retired in good order. I saw a Yankee shot in our yard by the third Linden tree on the left side, by one of the Confederates, in the back. I am very glad I saw it. I can't write all about the Yankees, so much was crowded into that one day & night. Did you know Hutchie Rennie was killed: I feel extremely sorry for his family. I am very much grieved that we lost Genl. J.E.B. Stuart in the fight at the Yellow Tavern, but I expect others will be raised up to take his place. Hoping your mother is in better spirits & that you have good news from your brothers, I remain ever your friend, Marion Stuart."

. . . Mrs. B.P. Peterkin of West Ys. George Peterkin who came down from Lee's Army yesterday, was the bearer of three tidings we have no reason to doubt their truth, & I got provoked with Rose for not crediting them, & made her angry by telling her she hugged Worry with the closet affection, whereupon she had nothing to say to me the rest of the evening, & I went to bed feeling very unhappy. . . . When we met at breakfast this morning, I told her I was very sorry to have made that disagreeable remark to her last night, to which she replied, she had given me as sharp an answer, & that she was very sorry too, & so ended our first quarrel, all unpleasant feelings having left us both, except that I feel a sadness I did not have before. If I do not keep the friends I have I shall indeed be bereaved.

Sunday 15th. Went to Church with Rose. Heard some excellent remarks by good Mr. Walker upon the present state of things & our duty under them. Began to write to Raleigh after our return & was interrupted by a shriek from Lizzy, "Mas Georgey's come." I knew not what to think but feared something terrible had happened to one of the boys. Ran down & saw George [George Washington Mordecai (1844–1920), brother of "Gusta" and son of Rosina] and his Uncle John [Rosina's brother, John Brooke Young] sitting in the buggy at the door, a crutch was there too—but George assured his mother & Gusta who had rushed out full of alarm that he was not hurt, and presently he limped in. He was very slightly wounded in the left thigh.

Excerpt from Diary of Emma Mordecai, Rosewood farm, near Richmond, Virginia, 1864, Subseries 3.1, Diaries and Travel Accounts, 1815–1865, Mordecai Family Papers #847, Southern Historical Collection, Wilson Library, University of North Carolina at Chapel Hill.

QUESTIONS

1. What are some of the challenges that Emma Mordecai and her family face in this excerpt that non-Jewish Southern women did not face?
2. Other passages in Emma's diary reveal that she often spent Saturdays (the Jewish Sabbath) in her room reading her Bible and a Jewish prayer book. Yet during Passover, Emma traveled to Richmond. What did Richmond offer that her sister-in-law's house did not?
3. Other entries in the diary suggest that after Emma and Rosina fought, Emma attended church with Rosina to undo conflict between the two women. How does Emma's experience of church strike you in this excerpt?

53

Antisemitism and Slavery in Cuba

CUBA, 1866

Stephen Silverstein

Even though most of the Spanish colonies became independent countries at the beginning of the nineteenth century, Cuba and Puerto Rico remained under Spanish control until the end of the century. The desire to hold onto these sugar-producing colonies forced Spain to listen to the liberals in an effort to discourage independence movements. In 1866—the same year that Francisco de Armas y Céspedes penned *De la esclavitud en Cuba*—the two colonies sent deputies to Madrid to the Junta de Información de Ultramar (Antillean Reform Commission), where they argued for greater civil liberties and political representation. Liberal-minded creoles had been insisting on these same rights throughout the century, and the continued denial of these rights culminated in Cuban and Puerto Rican independence in 1898. A significant pretext reiterated by the peninsular government in denying colonial liberties, which it apprehended as a threat to the imperial arrangement, was the colossal number of slaves in Cuba. Madrid argued that any easing of its authoritarian administration of the profitable colony would surely result in a slave revolution like that witnessed on the neighboring island of Haiti.

These circumstances—more than humanitarianism—saw slavery and the slave trade take center stage in Cuban liberals' minds, debates, and texts throughout the nineteenth century—it was only in 1873 and 1886 that slavery was abolished in Puerto Rico and Cuba, respectively. The circumstances permitted creoles to deploy the metaphorical Jew as an important discursive element of the abolitionist genre. Francisco de Armas y Céspedes's *De la esclavitud en Cuba* exemplifies this tendency.

The American tribunals of the Inquisition were so efficient that, as Eva Uchmany reports, "by the eighteenth century, Spanish America was almost clean of Jews."[1] Given that Jews were rare in Latin America until the end of the nineteenth century, questions surrounding the intersections of Jewishness and late Spanish colonialism have received scant critical attention. But as texts such as *De la esclavitud en Cuba* and many more make clear, despite the near absence of real, living Jews in Latin America until the twentieth century, the imaginary Jew arrived in the Americas with the conquistadors and remained a constant presence ever since, occupying a position near the core of American self-fashioning.

In 1991, the Nation of Islam published *The Secret Relationship between Blacks and Jews*, which, iterating an age-old antisemitic canard, contends that Jews dominated the transatlantic African slave trade. Harold Brackman has forcefully illustrated that the myth's origins lie not in reality but rather in the Catholic Church's striving to concretize St. Augustine's theological doctrine of *servitus Judaeorum*, or that "the Jew is the slave of the Christian," and not vice versa.[2] This led to a proliferation of codes forbidding Jews from participating in slavery, which ironically led to a proliferation of the trope of "Jewish" enslavers. Anyone looking to halt a slaver's trade, be they competitor or abolitionist, could appeal to these laws by insinuating that a particular slave trader or owner was a Jew. This is exactly what Francisco de Armas y Céspedes does in *De la esclavitud en Cuba*.

PRIMARY SOURCE

To assure tranquility of conscience, and to put an end to the abuses that Jews were committing in the slave commerce, the Third Council of Orleans, in 538 [CE], prohibited returning to Jews slaves that took shelter in the church, either because their owners demanded of them things contrary to religion, or because of bad treatment. The Fourth of Orleans, in 541, did not just order observance of the former, but it punished the Jew that perverted a Christian slave with the loss of all his slaves. The First of Macon, in 581, prohibited Jews from acquiring Christian slaves, and with regard to those that already possessed them, it permitted any Christian to rescue them by paying twelve dollars (*sueldos*) to the Jewish owner. The Third of Toledo, in 589, dictated the same prohibition, giving free liberty to the slave that was induced into Judaism or owned by a Jew. The Fourth of Toledo, in 633, prohibited Jews from having Christian slaves entirely. That of Reims, in 625 or 630, prohibited selling Christian slaves to gentiles or Jews, under the penalty of nullity; a prohibition reiterated in a letter from Pope Gregory III in 731, and in the council of Ciptines in 743. That of Chalons, in 650, prohibited selling Christian slaves beyond the territory comprising the kingdom of Clodoveo. And the Tenth of Toledo, in 656, severely reprimanded clerics that sold their slaves to Jews.

Francisco de Armas y Céspedes, *De la esclavitud en Cuba* (Madrid: T. Fortanet, 1866), 27–28.

QUESTIONS

1. How did slavery function as a sort of proxy war in the debates around Cuban independence?
2. What was the role assigned to the imaginary Jew in some abolitionist texts?

3. How did the codes meant to enforce *servitus Judaeorum* ironically become self-fulfilling prophecies?
4. The civil rights lawyer Anthony Julius defines antisemitic "canards" as "sensational reports, misrepresentations, fabrications, all intended to deceive the public."[3] During the nineteenth century, canards increasingly linked Jews to capitalism and its abuses. How do canards and conspiracies in this source compare to those in Grant's Order No. 11 (chapter 51)?

NOTES

1. Uchmany, "Participation of New Christians and Crypto-Jews," 199.
2. Brackman, *Ministry of Lies*, 41.
3. Julius, *Trials of the Diaspora*, 67.

54

Jewish Sacred Music

NEW YORK, 1869/1875

Judah M. Cohen

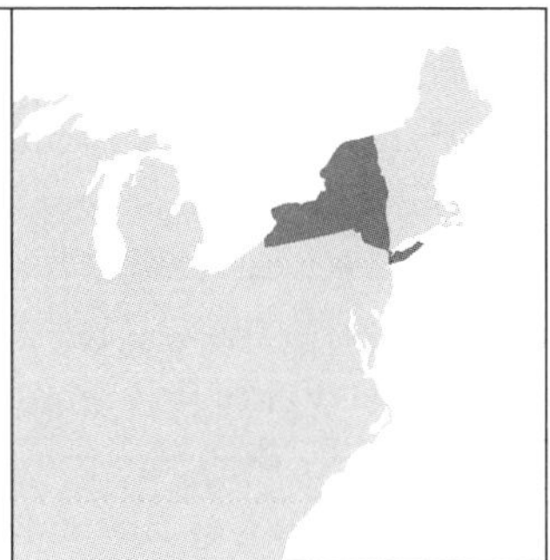

One of the innovations that broke apart Kahal Kadosh Beth Elohim in Charleston in 1839–1841 was the desire by certain congregants to include an organ in the new building (see chapter 44). Like the organ, the choir (particularly the mixed-sex choir) came to be seen as an emblem of modernity and the Reform movement.[1] Unlike organs, however, all-male choirs could also be employed by the new "enlightened Orthodoxy," as technically they did not violate Jewish law. Hence, choir lofts began to be installed in some traditional US synagogues, such as Shearith Israel's Seventieth Street Synagogue in New York (1897). With the advent of the choir came the cantor. Unlike the early US hazan, who had less religious training than a rabbi or hakham, the cantor brought a new skill set to US congregations as a highly trained singer and choir director.

"Der Herr ist König" (Psalm 93: "The Lord Is King") placed cantor Samuel Welsch at the center of the US synagogue music scene. Born in Prague and trained in Vienna, Welsch developed a smooth bel canto voice and skills as a choir director. He worked with Vienna's famed *Oberkantor* Salomon Sulzer, whose choral music collections represented a new standard for progressive synagogues on both sides of the Atlantic. Welsch came to the United States in 1865 and served the New York City congregation Ahawath Chesed (today Central Synagogue) through 1880, forming a partnership with his fellow Prague transplant Rabbi Adolph Hübsch (who arrived in 1866). In the standalone piece "Der Herr ist König," Welsch made a statement about the transformation of the cantor/hazan figure in the United States from a skilled layperson into a respected Jewish music professional. Together with other Sulzer students, including Alois Kaiser and Morris Goldstein, Welsch set a new standard of Jewish musical authority in the synagogue.

"Der Herr ist König" ultimately became a calling card for Welsch's efforts to establish a US style of synagogue music. The piece quickly circulated to several congregations around the country, where rabbis and congregations appeared to like it for its refined style, its major tonality, its upbeat sound, and its contemporary format. Welsch followed up this work with the massive, four-volume compilation *Zimrath Yah* (1871–1886, compiled with Isaac L. Rice, Cantor Morris Goldstein, and Cantor Alois Kaiser), which provided music for choir and organ across the Jewish liturgical year, with variants to accommodate the nation's major Jewish prayer books. "Psalm 93," then, heralded this new era, in which the cantor sought recognition as a composer, conductor, and full member of the clergy. While this movement created a paradigm for the height of synagogue music, only the best-endowed urban congregations could do the work well. Thus, "Psalm 93" highlighted divisions between aesthetic aspirations that represented liturgical progress and the more down-to-earth musical needs of many other congregations—divisions that continue to exist in the twenty-first century.

This source shows how important it is to consider sound and music on their own terms in understanding American Jewish history. Analyzing this piece provides a number of illuminating details. First, liturgically, this piece was sung during the early part of the Friday-evening Sabbath service (Kabbalat Shabbat). Second, regarding necessary musical skills, Welsch created this piece for organ and four-part mixed choir (soprano, alto, tenor, and bass); however, we can see by the high notes that the piece required skilled (and probably paid) singers. Third, regarding the text, the practice of adapting Psalms poetically into other languages for popular singing was common in the eighteenth and nineteenth centuries. Fourth, regarding form, this piece, on its largest level, has three parts: (1) a grand, march-like choral section uses music to illustrate the text sonically; (2) a male solo in a different key and rhythm focuses on the theme of divine truth; and (3) a grand choral finale. Taken together, these qualities suggest the genre of the "sacred chorus," a popular mainstream musical type of the time. It also reflects a (largely central-European-descended) Jewish community that viewed practices such as choral singing as progressive values but engaged with these musical conventions on their own terms. The style and structure of a musical work, in other words, helps us understand how Jewish Americans created a meaningful soundtrack in different eras.

PRIMARY SOURCE

Following pages: Samuel Welsch, "Psalm 93" ("Der Herr ist König") (New York: Schuberth, 1869).

PSALM 93.

Allegro moderato.
S.Welsch.
SOPRAN.
ALT.
TENOR.
BASS.
Allegro moderato.
ORGAN.
Der Herr ist Kö - nig, Ho-heit legt er an, der Herr hat sich in Allmacht an-ge -
The Lord is Ru - ler clad in ma - je - sty The Lord has girt with might his pa-no -
than.
nicht wan-ket sie, hoch thront der Herr, hoch thront der
ply. Da steht die Welt, un - moved, se - cure his heav'n-ly throne will e'er en-
Firm stands the world his hea - ven - ly throne

3
più lento
Herr, hoch thront der Herr, hoch thront der Herr und wan-delt nicht. Es er - he - ben die Strö - me, o
dure will e'er en-dure will e'er en - dure will e'er en - dure. The rivers have up - lif' - ted o
più lento
Herr, es er - he - ben die Ström' ihr Ge - tos, es er - he - ben die Strö - me ihr
Lord o Lord up - lif - ted their voice the rivers have up - lif - ted their
Brausen, doch ü - ber der Strö - me Ge - tö - se rauscht mächtig das branden - de Meer. All -
clamor yet might ier than wild Ocean's cry is all - migh - ty God on high All -

mäch-tig All - mäch-tig im Him-mel ist Gott. All - mäch-tig im Him-mel ist Gott.
migh - ty All - migh - ty in hea-ven is God. All - migh - ty in hea-ven is God.
Andante. Tenor or Baryton Solo
Dein Zeug-niss Herr ist treu be-währt, Dein
Thy law o God is truth di - vine thy
Hei - lig - thum ist still ver - klärt, Dein Zeugniss Herr ist treu be - währt,
Glo - ry filleth thy ho - ly shrine Thy law o God is truth di - vine

Andante religioso.
5
Dein Zeug-niss Herr ist
Dein Hei-lig-thum ist still ver-klärt.
Thy glo-ry fill-eth thy ho-ly shrine.
Thy law o God is
Tempo I.
treu be-währt, Dein Hei-lig-thum ist still ver-klärt. Der
fill-eth thy ho-ly shrine.
truth di-vine, Thy glo-ry filleth thy ho-ly shrine. The
rallentando
Herr ist Gott in E-wig-keit, in E-wig-keit, in E-wig-keit, in E-wig-keit.
Lord is God for e-ver-more, the Lord is God for e-ver-more, for e-ver-more!

QUESTIONS

1. Look closely at the lyrics. How are they split up among the three sections of the piece? Which lyrics are repeated? How does Welsch use music to illustrate the text's different images and ideas?
2. The addition of a professional choir was a major change in the US synagogue experience. What might be some advantages or disadvantages of this innovation?
3. "Psalm 93" appeared in a number of contexts in the late nineteenth century. How might you imagine this piece working in (a) a synagogue service, (b) a concert of sacred music, or (c) a significant Jewish event such as a synagogue dedication?
4. From the twenty-first century, this music might look and sound "classical." But actually, it reflected some popular music practices of the time, similar to the way that Debbie Friedman reflected some popular music practices of the 1970s and Basya Schechter in the 2010s. In this context, what might it have been like to hear Welsch's "Psalm 93" for the first time?

NOTE

1. J. Cohen, *Making of a Reform Jewish Cantor*, 178.

55

Abraham Goldenberg's Letter Home

CHILE, 1870

Judith Riquelme Ríos

Chile declared its independence from Spain in 1818, and as was the case in other former Spanish colonies, a small number of Jews from German lands began to settle there. This document is written by one of those early settlers, Abraham Goldenberg (1850–1900), who arrived in Chile with his brother Manuel in 1870. There he joined his uncle Salomón (1810–1864), who immigrated in 1854, and his two older brothers, Benjamin and Carl, who had arrived in 1859. The family settled specifically in Chillán, a city in central Chile south of Santiago. The name Goldenberg was new for the family, having only been adopted by Abraham's grandfather Calmon Emanuel, a native of Geseke (Westfalia) after 1812, the year of the emancipation of the Jews in Prussia. This particular letter was written by Abraham from Valparaíso on October 25, 1870, to his father, Moses, back in Geseke. Minna (1847–1902) was the boys' sister, their mother, Bella, having died in 1858. Minna, like her father, had stayed behind in Westfalia. The letter gives an account of Abraham's arrival in Chile after a 124-day voyage and as such provides insights into the lives of new arrivals, their travels, and the ties that bound them to family back home. In the letter, for example, Abraham expresses his worries about the Franco-Prussian War, which had broken out during his sea crossing.

As Abraham notes in his letter, he was hardly alone. German Jews founded many of the organizations that later came to bring together German immigrants in Chile. In 1856, Salomón Goldenberg founded the German Club, which the family led. Likewise, in 1879, Salomón's nephew Manuel founded the Club Gimnástico Alemán (German Gymnastic Club). German Jews, together with local non-Jewish partners, were behind the economic development of this region in Chile with the mill they built. The Goldenbergs, for example, aided in the creation of the firefighter brigade in Chillán (where they settled) and built the first mill in the town of Bulnes, which contributed to the economic growth of the region.

The presence of German Jews in the United States has been well documented, but the story of early German Jewish immigrants to the rest of the Americas less so. This source suggests that their experiences were similar. Many, like Salomón and Abraham Goldenberg, traveled to regions far removed from important towns, became involved in the conquest of the "frontier" and contributed to the economic development of the new nations in which they settled. Of these early pioneers, the Goldenberg family left the most complete documentation about German Jews in Chile. Numerous letters, photographs, genealogical notes, religious books, and many other documents, originally found in both Germany and Chile, came together at the Archivo Histórico de Judaísmo Chileno (Historical Archive of Chilean Jews).

PRIMARY SOURCE

Valparaiso, October 25th, 1870

Dear Father and Minna,
We finally arrived yesterday morning at 8:00 a.m. at the port of Valparaiso, after sailing for 124 days. I disembarked immediately with my trip partner, whose parents live here. They welcomed us and you can imagine how happy that made us, because the ship to Chillán leaves on Sunday and I will then be able to stay at the Olguins. Regarding the state of my health, I am, thank God, very well, which is what I also hope for you. I have already looked around Valparaiso, and it is a very pretty city, as you might see from my description. Since we have been apart for 14 weeks, we have just learned that a war has broken out between Germany and France. You can imagine that all that has shaken us a lot, because here, in Valparaiso, people were already saying that our ship had been hit and sunk by the French, and then they saw us come into the port with all flags flying.

I have learned that the Germans have defended themselves very well, however, people say that over there [in Europe? Germany?] there is a lot of misery. Have many [soldiers] joined the war? I am sure that you will let me know the details about [the war], and, in general, about what has been happening all this time, since I am very interested about all that is taking place over there.

I want to finish now; I could write 10 more lines, describing my experiences, but I know this does not interest you. Once in Chillán, I will write a long and detailed letter. Hoping that these lines find you in good health and mood, which is how I feel here, and that [the good health] remains every day, I raise my glass seven times for it to continue like that. I will love and write to you always

Abraham

Many greetings to all the people I know and to the family . . . not forgetting either old neighbors and above all the Gruenbaurn family with all my heart. I will also write to them from Chillán.

d. A.

This letter will reach you in the coldest time. Here it will be very hot, like it is now, as [it is] the beginning of summer.

d. A.

Abraham Goldenberg to Moses and Minna Goldenberg, October 25, 1870, CL AJ ADGB-01-FG-10, Archivo Judío de Chile, Santiago, Chile.

QUESTIONS

1. What are the central themes and ideas of this letter?
2. What does the letter say about the experiences of early Jewish immigrants to Chile?
3. What does the letter say about staying in touch with news about events in the home country?
4. Scholars have found that discussions of "chit-chat" (talk about trivial matters) and how one's day went are an important way that families and couples that are separated are able to maintain personal relationships.[1] How might Abraham's letter fit within this tradition?

NOTE

1. Carter et al., "Something to Talk About," 23.

56

Jews and Native Americans

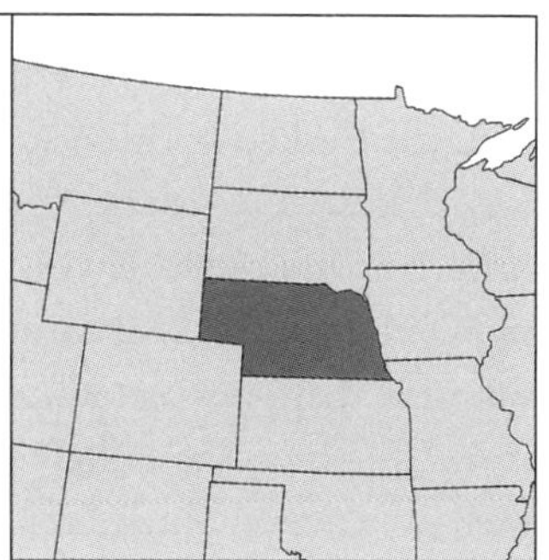

NEBRASKA, C. 1875

David S. Koffman

Just as Jews from German lands, such as Abraham Goldenberg, put down roots in the interior of Chile, so too German Jewish immigrants helped settle states in the Midwest and Great Plains, with Jews among the early settlers of cities like Chicago (1837), Dubuque (1836), and St. Louis (1844). Shortly after Omaha, Nebraska, was founded in 1854, Jews like Julius Meyer began to settle there, seeking opportunities in this "gateway" to the West.[1] As with the Goldenbergs, the early arrivals were typically single men seeking economic opportunities. Synagogues would come later.

Born in the 1830s in Bromberg (Prussia), Julius Meyer emigrated to Omaha, Nebraska, as a young, single man. After serving as an interpreter for General George Cook, Meyer played a significant role in the development of the so-called Indian Curio trade in the Plains in the last decades of the nineteenth century and the early twentieth century. One of many Jewish "Indian trader" merchants in the Midwest, the Southwest, and the Pacific Northwest, Meyer made a living buying artifacts and objects from his Native American suppliers and selling these objects that symbolized Native America to mostly white, mostly middle-class customers via mail orders, in lowbrow souvenir shops that advertised themselves as museums, or to one of the many burgeoning ethnological or natural history museums opening up in North American and European cities. These commercial relationships between Jews and Native Americans in the rural West were but a subset of business relations between these two "tribal" peoples from the eighteenth through the twenty-first centuries. As such, they were part of a still-larger history of Jewish-Indigenous encounters in the United States, Canada, Latin America, Australia and New Zealand, and parts of Africa.

Photos, business ledgers, advertisements, and other ephemeral sources capture something of Jewish social and economic life in small cities, smaller towns, and the rural margins of the United States during the era of mass migration of Jews from central and eastern Europe, in which urban life usually takes center stage. In these settings—from Nebraska to New Mexico and Alaska to Arizona—Jewish life was necessarily full of engagements with non-Jews. These encounters helped shape Jews' sense of their own Jewishness, even as they afforded new opportunities for vastly different experiences of the United States to intersect.

Little has been written about Jews as agents in the long process of "settling" the Americas, that is, of Jewish experiences of and participation in settler colonialism. Professional historians and public Jewish memory tend to frame American Jewish history as an urban immigrant story of successful adaptation to the United States. Sources like these help show not only that Jews had all sorts of dynamic relationship with "other others" all over the rural US—from the earliest of Jewish migrants right through to the present day—but that their presence on Turtle Island (as North America was known to some Indigenous peoples) was necessarily part of a history of colonialism—that immigration history and colonial history describe much the same processes, though with radically different meanings.

PRIMARY SOURCE

Facing page: Julius Meyer and a group of Native Americans posing in front of his store on 163 Farnam Street, Omaha, Nebraska, c. 1875. (Library/Archives, Nebraska State Historical Society, Lincoln, NE, RG2246-06)

QUESTIONS

1. What do you think Julius Meyer hoped to accomplish by having this portrait posed for and taken, and what features of the photo's composition help tell this story?
2. What other sorts of primary sources may exist to illuminate interactions between Jews and Native Americans in this decade?
3. How do you think the Jewish encounter with Native Americans was similar to and different from Jewish encounters with other American minorities, such as Latinxs, African Americans, or Asian Americans?
4. What is similar and different between the representation of Native Americans in this photo and in the daguerreotype by Solomon Nunes Carvalho in chapter 45?

NOTE

1. Gendler, "Pioneer Jews of Omaha," 175–176.

INDIAN WIGWAM
JULIUS MEYER 163
US
6

57

Women and Religion in Jewish Newspapers

NEW YORK, 1877

Zev Eleff

While roughly a fifth to a quarter of the German Jewish immigrants to North America settled in small towns or farming communities, most settled in major metropolitan communities like New York, Philadelphia, Baltimore, Cincinnati, and Toronto, where manufacturing provided entry-level jobs. Like the Goldenbergs (chapter 55) and Julius Meyer (chapter 56), many were single. Most were men, though some women traveled with brothers or with the promise of marriage upon arrival. Newspapers like those run by the traditionalists Isaac Leeser and Samuel Meyer Isaacs helped repair the family structures broken in transit and insisted on the important role that women played in Jewish life.[1] Letters like this one from "Sylvia," which appeared in Isaacs's *Jewish Messenger*, showcased the conflict between the new entertainments that the US offered and traditional services.

Newspapers were the most crucial conduit for America's Jews to debate ideas and share their sentiments on a host of social, religious, and cultural issues. Rabbi Isaacs was the longtime religious leader of congregation Shaaray Tefila, at the time a prominent Orthodox synagogue in New York. In 1857, Isaacs founded the *Jewish Messenger* to serve as a traditional-leaning weekly organ. Isaacs's periodical was one of the first Jewish newspapers in New York and was an important counterbalance to Rabbi Isaac Mayer Wise's *Israelite*, founded in 1854 in Cincinnati as a reform-minded publication. Both newspapers carried a wide audience, well beyond their local communities.

For traditionalists like Leeser and Isaac, Jewish newspapers provided a space to address the problems facing new arrivals and their congregations. In the 1870s, rabbis in the United States encountered an unforeseen paradox. On the one hand, the Civil War had proven a great need, especially in the North, for centralized authority in all realms of US life. Union sympathizers believed that the war might have been avoided had all US residents abided by the decisions of the federal government. Moreover, these champions of centralization sought to redouble their efforts to fortify top-down authority. This was certainly the case in religious spaces, where even Congregationalists (a Protestant denomination that accorded decisions to each local church) formed organizations to unite their previously disjointed efforts. In addition, this trend supported the cause of the US rabbinate and the clergy who had spent decades trying to topple synagogues' lay-led authority. But in response, many of the rank-and-file Jews stopped frequenting Sabbath services and other religious occasions connected to congregational life. Therefore, as Jewish clergy gained traction, the disenfranchised laypeople, particularly the younger ones, underwent a period of religious decline.

Instead, Jewish women and men sought out other institutions to receive doses of culture and enlightenment. For instance, the Ethical Culture Movement founded by Felix Adler (1851–1933) sponsored Sunday lectures that attracted Jews in locales like Chicago, Philadelphia, and, of course, New York. Historians have noted the impact that Adler had on Reform Judaism, the growing religious group that advocated for changes, among others, to worship and introduced mixed pews and an organ to the synagogue. However, Orthodox Jews fell sway to this charismatic intellectual (and son of Samuel Adler, a prominent New York rabbi). This document, drawn from a New York–based Orthodox newspaper, throws light on this aspect of the religious condition among Jewish laypeople and their search for alternative forms of cultural engagement, whether they aligned with Orthodox or Reform groups. It betokens the overall concern of American Judaism to raise the stature and reach of rabbis to attract the interests of their coreligionists. This was an issue that dogged Jewish leaders in later epochs and in newspaper columns. That this document was authored pseudonymously by a Jewish woman is important. Since the early nineteenth century, there existed traditional-leaning Jewish women who were open to attending Sunday church meetings to quench their thirst for intellectually and culturally stimulating discourse. As "Sylvia" in this text demonstrates, this had not changed by the final decades of the century.

PRIMARY SOURCE

Would it be very wrong for our Jewish preachers to take a hint from the ethical professor, and discourse occasionally on themes not directly connected with the weekly *parassah*. I have no personal objection to Bible texts, and feel sure that there is enough mental food in the old Book to last our pulpit just as Mr. Thomas [music director of the New York Philharmonic] is compelled, despite his strenuous protests, to diversify his concerts. I think that once a month we might have our rabbi's ideas of morality, contradistinguished from doctrinal religion, of ethics in fact, and leave Moses, Jezebel and Job for other days. We are an enquiring age—we look for variety, and if any of us drop in on Sundays at Mr. Frothingham's [Rev. Octavius Brooks Frothingham, a Unitarian minister] or Dr. Adler's [Cornell professor Felix Adler], it is not because we have abjured Judaism, but because we like to be instructed on subjects with which we sympathize. We prefer to listen to all sermons on Saturdays; but if our rabbis decline to leave the beaten track and cull flowers for us in the open fields, do not blame us for figuring among the Sunday audiences. Besides, many of us young ladies are not long from school—a foreign accent, and occasional breaches of grammar, grate upon our ears, and not all the Saturday preachers are perfect orators.

I like Vienna coffee, and if I can not get it at my favorite old restaurant after repeated requests, I must perforce cross the street and patronize the new café.

Sylvia

Sylvia, "A Hint to Our Preachers," *Jewish Messenger*, March 28, 1877, 5.

QUESTIONS

1. Presuming that the anonymous letter was in fact authored by a woman, what does it say about women's agency in discussions about the male rabbinate?
2. What are Sylvia's complaints about the rabbi's sermons? What is the "Vienna coffee" that she seeks?
3. Compare Sylvia's willingness to "drop in on Sundays at Mr. Frothingham's or Dr. Adler's" lectures with the diary of Emma Mordecai in this volume (chapter 52). What forces drew women in the Mordecai family to seek out "religion" outside traditional Judaism?

NOTE

1. Leibman, *Art of the Jewish Family*, 175.

58

Praying for British Royalty and Republican Government

QUEBEC, 1877

David S. Koffman

The printing of this *machzor* (High Holiday prayer book) marked not only the hundredth anniversary of Canada's first synagogue, Shearith Israel (the Spanish and Portuguese Synagogue of Montreal), but also the tenth anniversary of the Canadian Confederation in 1867, which united the Province of Canada, Nova Scotia, and New Brunswick into Canada. Thus, the *machzor* includes two separate but nearly identical prayers to be recited on the Jewish New Year: one for the queen and royal family and one for the current "republican government." Edited and revised by the Montreal rabbi Abraham de Sola, the *machzor* was a modified version of an earlier prayer book written by two leading Orthodox figures of the mid-nineteenth century: Rabbi Isaac Leeser of Philadelphia and the author's father, the Amsterdam-born Rabbi David de Aaron de Sola. These prayers, known as *Hanoten Teshua*, are part of a long tradition in Diaspora countries of Jewish prayers for their political overseers, often poetic verse of both supplication and praise. They gave expression to Jewish communities' insecurity and political vulnerability, as well as their wishes for the privileges of the regimes under which they lived. *Hanoten Teshua* blessings have been recited in synagogues for hundreds of years, though probably not in the biblical or rabbinic eras, despite the prophets' call to "seek city . . . and pray to the Lord on its behalf" (Jeremiah 29:7) or to "pray for the welfare of the government" (Avot 3:2). They proliferated widely in modern Western democracies and continue to be recited across the Americas today.

Since prayers tend to get added to prayer books more often than they are removed, looking at new additions can cue us to the concerns that preoccupy Jewish communities at a given moment. In blessing Queen Victoria, Prince Albert, the Princess of Wales, and "all the Royal Family," early Canadian Jews highlighted their political allegiance as Loyalists and their attachments to the monarchy. They were, at the time, still officially subjects of the

Crown (the first citizens were minted with the 1947 Canadian Citizenship Act). In offering a distinct blessing for the "constituted officers of the government," the congregation also reminded itself, and any guest that might have been present, that Jewish political interests were wrapped up in very local power arrangements, even as these Jews professed loyalty to the Crown and championed full political emancipation, having been granted full legal equality in 1832, well before such equality became law in England.

The seamless blending of realpolitik (politics based on current circumstances) with traditional religious language in these blessings highlights the fuzzy boundary between religion, society, and politics at the end of the nineteenth century. Many Jews from Montreal's Shearith Israel regularly crossed other sorts of borders, as they were involved in business, family affairs, and religious practices that took them to the Caribbean, England, Scotland, and the United States. In the lifetimes of some of the people who recited these *Hanoten Teshua* prayers, Jews saw and responded to many political changes, including the cleaving apart of the North American British colonies into two very different countries, the early struggles of the descendants of French colonists as a minority in English Canada after France itself retreated from the Americas, and the rapidly changing conditions of settler-Indigenous relations. The prayers are windows into Jewish communal ideas about belonging, political loyalty, and emancipation articulated in a deeply religious idiom and setting.

PRIMARY SOURCE

Prayer for the Queen and Royal Family

May he who dispenseth salvation unto kings, and dominion unto princes; whose kingdom is an everlasting kingdom; who delivered his servant David from the destructive sword; who maketh a way into the sea, and a path in the mighty waters; bless, preserve, guard, assist, exalt, and raise unto a high eminence, our most gracious Sovereign, Queen Victoria, Albert Edward, Prince of Wales, and the Princess of Wales, and All the Royal Family. May the Supreme King of kings, through his infinite mercy preserve them, and grant them life, and deliver them from all manner of trouble and danger. May the Supreme King of kings exalt and raise her on high, and grant her a long and prosperous reign. May the Supreme King of kings, through his infinite mercy, inspire her and all her counsellors and officers with benevolence towards us and all Israel our brethren. In her days and in ours may Judah be saved, and Israel dwell securely; and may the redeemer come to Zion. May this be the will of God, and let us say, Amen.

A Prayer for a Republican Government

May he who dispenseth assistance unto kings, and dominions unto princes; whose kingdom is an everlasting kingdom; who delivered his servant David from the destructive sword; who maketh a way into the sea, and a path in the mighty waters; bless, preserve, guard, and assist the constituted officers of the government.

May the Supreme King of kings, through his infinite mercy preserve them, and grant them life, and deliver them from all manner of trouble and danger. May the Supreme King of kings exalt and raise them on high, and grant them a long and prosperous rule. May the Supreme King of kings, through his infinite mercy, inspire them and all their counsellors and officers with benevolence towards us and all Israel our brethren. In their days and in ours may Judah be saved, and Israel dwell securely; and may the redeemer come to Zion. May this be the will of God, and let us say, Amen.

"Prayer for the Queen and Royal Family" and "A Prayer for a Republican Government," in *The Form of Prayer According to the Custom of Spanish and Portuguese Jews*, New Year's Service, edited and revised by Abraham De Sola (Philadelphia: Sherman, 5638 [1877]).

QUESTIONS

1. What do these prayers reveal about the way the reciters thought about their government, patriotism, or the society in which they lived?
2. What, according to the text, were the Jews who recited these prayers doing or asking for?
3. What is the relationship between Zion and the blessings for non-Jewish authorities?
4. Do these prayers balance this-worldly political concerns with messianic hope, or does one of these impulses seem more crucial?
5. As a researcher, how might you figure out the extent to which prayers for secular governments recited by Jewish congregations were nervously apologetic versus genuinely patriotic?

59

The Eldridge Street Synagogue's *Mikveh*

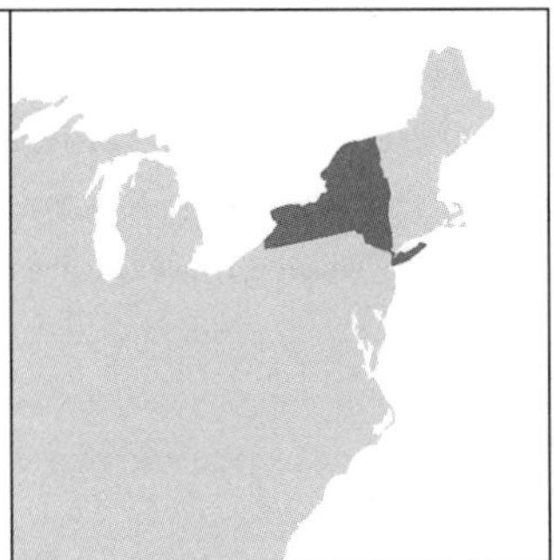

NEW YORK, C. 1887

Celia J. Bergoffen

By 1880, a new wave of immigrants had begun to reach American shores: the Jews of eastern Europe and the Ottoman Empire. German Jewish immigration had swelled the population of Jews in the United States from fewer than 3,000 Jews in 1820 to between 230,000 and 300,000 Jews in 1880. This too paled in comparison to the number of Jews arriving in the next decades: 2 million Jews arrived in the United States from Russia alone between 1880 and 1914, bringing the total Jewish population in the United States to over 3.3 million in 1920. By 1890, 175,000 Jews lived in New York City, the majority of whom were Russian.[1] The *mikveh* pictured here was located in a Russian bathhouse at 5 Allen Street and is but one example of the changes these immigrants brought to New York Jewish life.

The Russian bathhouse on Allen Street was located in New York's Lower East Side, behind and catty-corner to the Orthodox Eldridge Street Synagogue. There was no *mikveh* in the synagogue's basement, as existed in some other synagogues, nor do the synagogue's minutes record any official connection with Yitzhak Natelsohn's Allen Street baths, although he was their *shamash* and had moved his baths near the new synagogue's building the same year that it opened, in 1886. We imagine that many congregants went there, but the baths were privately owned and operated for profit. The bathhouse's elegant *mikveh*, lined with white ceramic tiles rounded along the edges and graced with marble steps and a bronze railing, was built according to the highest standards of kashrut at the time, under the supervision of Rabbi Josef Ash, the foremost authority on *mikveh* construction, and Rabbi Yehoshuah Siegel.

Bathhouses proliferated in the Lower East Side's densely populated neighborhood. Most tenements did not have bathing facilities, and bathhouses were therefore required to meet both secular and religious needs. The other facilities installed in the semibasement included a twenty-foot swimming pool, showers, and a hot room containing a stone-built oven and three tiers of seats. Since bathing is required before ritual immersion, it made sense to install a kosher *mikveh* in a bathhouse, but very few other instances are known. From Morris Kittner, whose father ran the baths in the late 1930s and 1940s, we know that the family lived on the third floor above the baths and that one could buy food there prepared by Morris's mother. In that era, if not already earlier, both Jews and non-Jews frequented the baths, but except for Ladies Day, on Wednesday, the clientele was male.

The sources illustrated here—an advertisement in the *Jewish Gazette*, which recorded that two rabbis certified the *mikveh* as kosher, and the photograph of the *mikveh* itself, recovered through archaeological excavation—provide rare evidence of how the specifications for rendering a *mikveh* kosher, set forth in the *Shulchan Arukh* (the code of Jewish law), were interpreted and executed in brick, mortar, and tile in 1880s New York. The sources reveal that ritual immersion in a kosher pool might take place in the context of an otherwise secular Russian bathhouse.

The primary sources reveal that the interpretation and experience of Orthodox ritual immersion are not monolithic but have varied over time and place. The practice looks quite different today, when facilities housing *mikva'ot* are devoted exclusively to ritual immersion without other entertainments and the clientele is virtually all Jewish and, with the exception of some Hasidic communities in Brooklyn, primarily female.

PRIMARY SOURCES

[In Yiddish] "Moved! Moved! Moved! Kosher ritual bath."

This is what you should tell the house of Jacob: (to the women) you should tell this to the Jewish community; (to the men) Mrs. Gittel Natelsohn the *sheitel* [wig] maker the wife of Reb Yitzak Natelsohn, *shamash* of the Beit Hamidrash Allen Street who had the *mikveh* in the Allen Street shul [synagogue] moved it to 5 Allen Street between Canal and Division where she can accommodate everybody to the highest and finest place [i.e., satisfy to the fullest]. I have two new large [illegible] *mikvehs* installed with 14 bathtubs and everything is completely kosher in the best way as declared by Rabbi Josef Ash and Yehoshuah Siegel. Everything with the most beautiful [illegible] from early in the morning to late evening. This is the only place in New York where it's good and cheaply served. Gittel Natelsohn the wig maker. I. Natelsohn 5 Allen St., NY

[In Hebrew] The *mikveh* at Allen Street that belongs to Rav Yitzak Natelsohn, *shamash* of the beit hamidrash [hall for Torah study] Allen Street was made according to the *Shulchan Arukh* the best of hechshers [kosher certifications].[2]

Advertisement, *Jewish Gazette*, September 24, 1886.

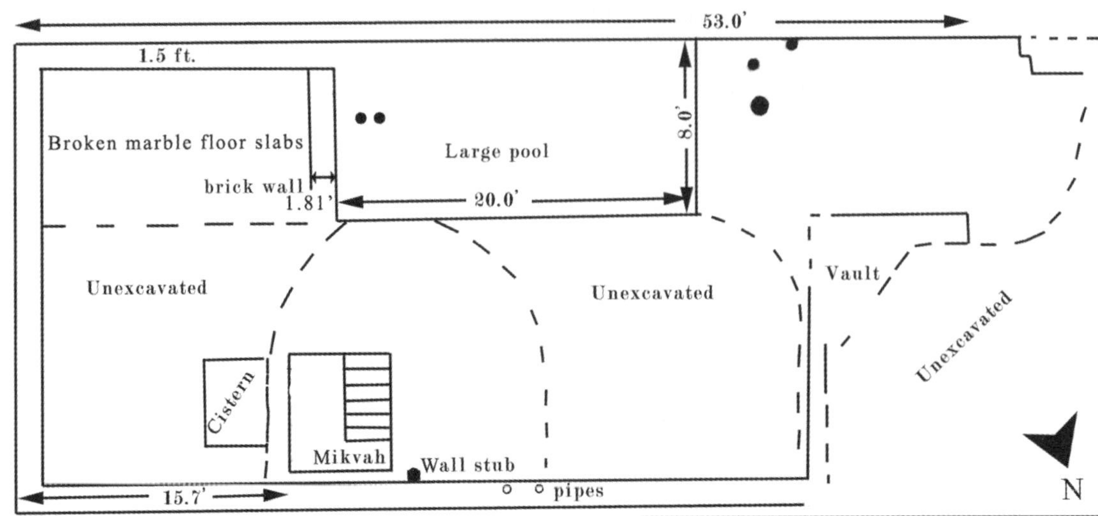

Plan of the ground floor of the 5 Allen Street baths. (By Celia J. Bergoffen)

Excavated *mikveh* at 5 Allen Street. (Photograph by Celia J. Bergoffen)

QUESTIONS

1. Aside from the two sources included here, what other types of sources might be useful to reconstruct Jewish life on the Lower East Side of New York?
2. How did the social context of ritual immersion change between the Barbados *mikveh* (chapter 15), the Coro *mikveh* (chapter 48), and the Allen Street *mikveh*?
3. What strategies did the advertisement use to convince bathers that the ritual bath was religiously acceptable? What does this tell us about the values of the intended users?

NOTES

1. Sarna, *American Judaism*, 5; Gilbert, *Routledge Atlas of Jewish History*, 83; Rosenwaike, *Population History in New York City*, 87.
2. Translated by Shmuel Pultkin.

60

Documenting Tenements

NEW YORK, 1890–1895

Laura Arnold Leibman

While even in the late eighteenth century the working class often had to share housing, by the 1860s the surge of immigrants made tenements a necessary part of US cities. In New York, multifamily dwellings were built on small lots, often twenty-five feet wide and one hundred feet long. Crowding was intense and—as Jacob Riis's floorplan of an 1863 tenement shows—not all rooms typically had access to air or light. Toilets were shared and consisted of outhouses maintained in the backyard, and tenements typically lacked running water. By way of example, the building at 97 Orchard Street, now the Tenement Museum, did not have water and tub sinks installed until 1895, and electricity was not added until 1924.[1] The lack of bathing facilities made bathhouses like the one at 5 Allen Street popular (chapter 59). Weather exacerbated problems in tenements: on hot days, the suffering was intense, as there was not enough to drink and little ventilation. Living quarters often doubled as sweatshops, where garments were sewn by day and people slept by night. Fires, rodents, and insect infestations were common, as was child labor. Poor maintenance complicated the situation. Shared water and toilet facilities meant that disease spread quickly from one apartment to another. To make matters worse, Jewish residents were often blamed for their own abuse: their poverty and lack of sanitation tended to be interpreted by reformers as a moral (and sometimes racial) failing.

Help for people living in the tenements came incrementally. A series of legislative acts was passed to improve living conditions. The Tenement Housing Act of 1867, for example, outlawed cellar apartments, mandated fire escapes, and required one toilet for every twenty residents. Yet the apartments remained dense, with poor access to light and air. The tenement Reform Law of 1879 tried to ameliorate this problem by making minimum requirements for access to air and light, giving rise to buildings built in the shape of an *H*. Overcrowding and filth persisted. The Tenement Act of 1901 finally mandated indoor plumbing and lighting, though the costs for implementing these upgrades were typically passed along to residents who could ill afford them. These changes can be seen in "The Evolution of Tenement Design" included here.

Like the legislation, Jacob Riis's *How the Other Half Lives: Studies among the Tenements of New York* (1890) sought to improve the lives of tenement dwellers, primarily by bringing the horrors experienced there to the attention of the wider US public. Riis was an early photojournalist, and his photos documented the housing crisis. Riis's photos focus on a range of ethnic groups, including Jews. Like many "muckrakers" of the era, Riis sought to provoke controversy. While Riis's images did eventually help promote reform, he was outwardly critical of many of the immigrant groups he documented, including Asians, Italians, and Jews. As one scholar puts it, "the image of the Jews as an alien, exotic, unassimilable race, as a group expressing the destructive spirit of capitalism unchecked, as a people resistant to the promises of Christian universalism was never entirely absent from his writings."[2] Nor did his bias fail to infiltrate the gaze he cast at the tenement dwellers in his photos. Like Liberalism in Latin America, Progressive-era (1896–1916) reformers in the United States sought to improve the lives of Jews and other immigrants, but at a cost: inclusion in the nation was typically predicated on immigrants ridding themselves of their ethnic particularities, which were understood as holding them back. Riis's images are a good reminder that even documentary photography often is infused with bias.

PRIMARY SOURCES

See following pages.

QUESTIONS

1. Look closely at Riis's photograph of a man in a coal cellar. What strategies does Riis use to call attention to the man's Jewishness? What other scenes could Riis have used to highlight the Sabbath? Why do you think he chose this one?
2. What messages does *Talmud School in a Hester Street Tenement* convey about traditional Jewish education?
3. Riis's photos both try to convey the dark interiors of the tenements and yet require light to be taken. How does Riis balance light and darkness in his works?
4. What aspects of the photos manipulate viewers' emotions? Are we meant to feel sympathy or pity for the people depicted? What is the difference?

NOTES

1. Cromley, *Alone Together*, 52; National Park Service, *Lower East Side Tenement*, 9; Epstein, *At the Edge of a Dream*, 46.
2. Fried, "Jacob Riis and the Jews," 14, 8.

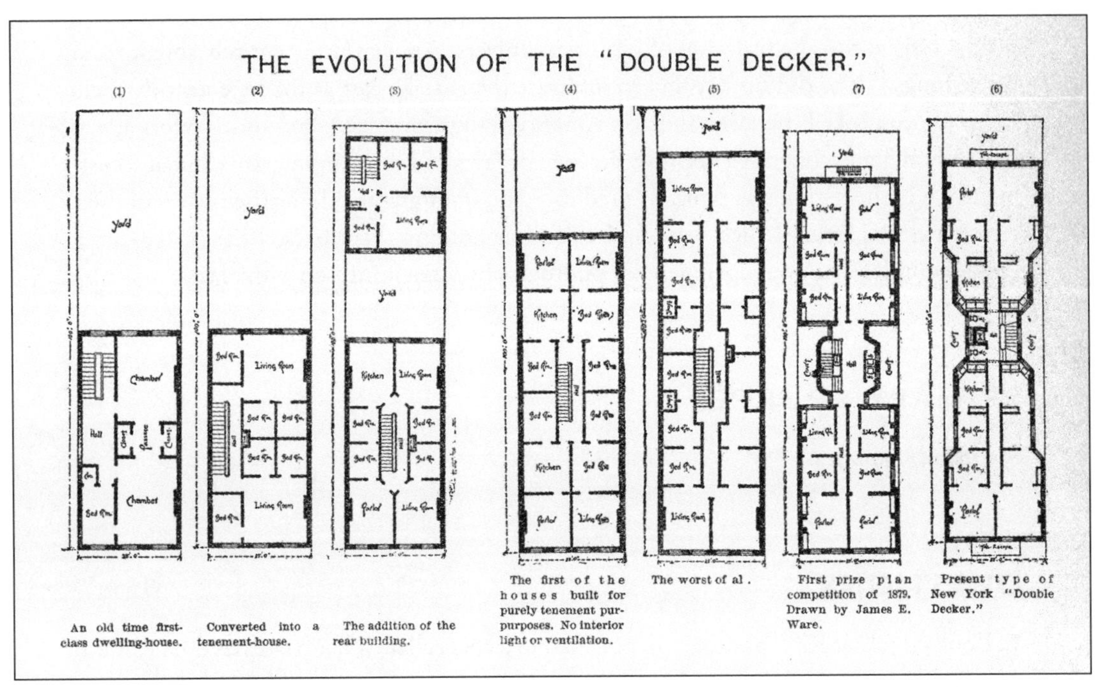

The evolution of tenement design, from pre-law to old law to new law, in *Tenement House Commission Report of 1895* (Albany, NY: J. B. Lyon, State Printer, 1895), 12.

Jacob Riis, *Ready for the Sabbath Eve in a Coal Cellar on Ludlow Avenue.* (WC)

Jacob Riis, *Talmud School in a Hester Street Tenement*, c. 1890. (WC)

Jacob Riis, *Necktie Workshop in a Division Street Tenement*, c. 1890. (LCPPD, 2002710291)

61

Salem Fields Cemetery

NEW YORK, 1890–1945

Sophia Levin

While many of the new Jewish immigrants to New York in the 1880s–1910s practiced Orthodox Judaism, the older generation of synagogues established by German Jews in the 1820s–1860s had increasingly turned to the Reform movement. Established in 1845, Temple Emanu-El was the city's first Reform congregation. Like many synagogues of the era, it began as an Orthodox synagogue, but reforms slowly chipped away at the traditionalism, including an organ that found its way into the service in 1848. By 1868, Emanu-El had become one of the city's most influential synagogues. Unlike the "storefront shuls" of later Russian immigrants, Temple Emanu-El was housed in a large Moorish Revival building on Fifth Avenue and Forty-Third Street. Both the interior and exterior were exquisite. In 1927, Temple Emanu-El moved into its current building at Fifth Avenue and Sixty-Fifth Street, which is in a Romanesque Revival style. As elaborate as the congregation's spiritual homes were, so too were their homes after death. Here, too, the congregation chose an architectural style that emphasized Jews as an ancient, cultured people.

Temple Emanu-El's cemetery, known as Salem Fields, was built across the river in Brooklyn, due to a city law banning burials in Manhattan. Salem Fields Cemetery is home to a wide range of beautiful memorial art, including six hundred family mausoleums. These mausoleums are made of luxurious marble, mosaics, and stained glass and were designed in the refined Art Nouveau and Art Deco aesthetics of the time. Through community members' choices in memorial art, they navigated their identity as Jewish Americans.

The memorials at Salem Fields show us a community balancing a proud Jewish identity with a cultured American taste. Exquisitely crafted mausoleums represented the peak of cultural elegance at this time and were popular with Jews and non-Jews alike. Salem Fields was designed as part of the transcendentalist Garden Cemetery Movement, whose lush garden landscaping associated a peaceful garden cemetery with the peaceful repose of a soul. This restful landscape subtly lays claim to a pastoral, garden afterlife, which suggests that Emanu-El members found resonance with this idea despite the fact that traditional Judaism rejects the notion of a heavenly Garden of Eden. The name Salem Fields links the cemetery to Jerusalem, claiming it as a Jewish space. At the same time, the English name reflects Emanu-El's identity as a culturally liberal US congregation—standing in contrast to nearby Orthodox cemeteries, which have Hebrew names.

The stained-glass windows in the mausoleums at Salem Fields also show how a popular artistic style was adapted to a Jewish context. These windows were made with the textured and swirling art-glass technique popularized by Louis Comfort Tiffany and John La Farge in the late nineteenth century. Many of the windows depict rivers and lakes, which represent the flow of time and the passing of the deceased. These landscapes were popular with Jewish patrons, as *halakha* forbids figural images in sacred spaces. Although many patrons chose designs that were not explicitly Jewish, some mausoleums do display religious motifs. For example, several windows include a seven-branched menorah, a biblical image popular in US Reform synagogue design.

Landscaped like a miniature house, each mausoleum represented a final, deathly home for its inhabitants. Many families even put furniture inside their mausoleums, including tables, chairs, and rugs. Walking through Salem Fields, one has the feeling of a tangible afterlife rooted in the natural world, with family and friends close at hand—each miniature house a site of transition from this world into the world to come.

The American Jewish community has always been theologically and culturally diverse. Classical Reform is a liberal Jewish movement that first flourished in German American communities in the early 1800s. Even the mere existence of these mausoleums shows how this movement broke with Orthodox *halakha*, which favors in-ground burial. In this community's blending of Jewish and modern American identities, members expressed a new way of being Jewish.

PRIMARY SOURCES

See following pages.

QUESTIONS

1. What images do you notice in the stained glass? How do the themes and designs compare to the stained glass at KKBE (chapter 44)?
2. What emotions do you think the artists and architects wanted to evoke through their designs?
3. How did these families express their Jewish identity through their memorial art?
4. What, if anything, is Jewish about these designs?
5. How do these mini houses compare to earlier Jewish cemeteries and gravestones (chapter 12)?

Row of mausoleums, Salem Fields Cemetery, Brooklyn, New York. (Photograph by Sophia Leven, 2013; courtesy Congregation Emanu-El of the City of New York)

Mausoleums, Salem Fields Cemetery, Brooklyn, New York. (Photograph by Warren Klein, 2013; courtesy Congregation Emanu-El of the City of New York)

Stained-glass window, Salem Fields Cemetery, Brooklyn, New York. (Photograph by Sophia Leven, 2013; courtesy Congregation Emanu-El of the City of New York)

Mausoleum interior, Salem Fields Cemetery, Brooklyn, New York. (Photograph by Sophia Leven, 2013; courtesy of Congregation Emanu-El of the City of New York)

62

"The Kitchen"

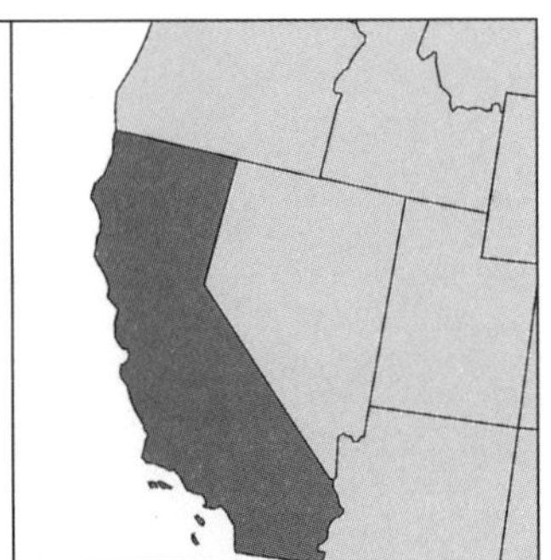

CALIFORNIA, C. 1890S/1947

Lori Harrison-Kahan

Jewish settlement in San Francisco began in 1848 when news of the Gold Rush drew to the city German-speaking Jews from Bavaria and Prussia, French Jews from Alsace, English Jews, and Jews from the East Coast of the United States. To get to California, some crossed the continental United States in covered wagons, while others either sailed around the Horn of South America or cut across Nicaragua or Panama, where the American continents were at their thinnest. Regardless, the trip was dangerous. By 1849, the arrivals led High Holiday services, and by 1854, the cornerstones for two synagogues (Sherith Israel and Emanu-El) were placed on Stockton and Broadway Streets, respectively. Although they both began as traditional synagogues, by the end of the Civil War, Emanu-El had become Reform, like its New York namesake. Sherith Israel held out longer, gradually undergoing reform under the leadership of Rabbi Jacob Nieto, who was hired in 1893. Ten years later, when the congregation began to build a new synagogue on California Street, it aligned itself with the Reform movement.[1] Harriet Lane Levy's memoir provides an insider's view into early Jewish life in the city.

The daughter of immigrants from Prussia, Harriet Lane Levy was born in California in 1867 and grew up at 920 O'Farrell Street in San Francisco. The area was home to Jewish middle-class families, and the Levys belonged to Sherith Israel. Unlike most women of her time, Levy attended college, graduating from the University of California, Berkeley, in 1886. She then published short stories and articles in California periodicals and was considered one of the city's most promising young writers. In the aftermath of the 1906 San Francisco earthquake and fire, which devastated the Jewish neighborhood, Levy and her next-door neighbor Alice B. Toklas traveled to Paris and became part of the circle surrounding the modernist writer and art collector Gertrude Stein. In 1910, Levy returned to San Francisco, bringing artwork by Matisse and Picasso, while Toklas stayed behind to make a life with Stein. In 1947, at age eighty and a few years before her death in 1950, Levy published her only full-length work of prose, *920 O'Farrell Street*, a memoir that describes her experiences growing up in late nineteenth-century San Francisco. "The Kitchen," the memoir's tenth chapter, describes the multiethnic environment surrounding her family's kosher kitchen and exposes the barriers between the Levys and the residents of nearby Chinatown.

Levy's memoir chronicles her upbringing in an affluent San Francisco Jewish family prior to the 1906 earthquake, at a time when the city boasted the second-largest population of US Jews outside New York. Her description of the kitchen offers insight into the family's domestic religious practices, specifically the observance of kosher dietary laws, as well as its relationship with other ethnic minorities and immigrants in a diverse, cosmopolitan environment. The memoir exposes tensions between tradition and modernity and between religion and secularism. Food embodies those tensions in this excerpt, which allows us to consider how a US-born daughter of Jewish immigrants viewed her parents' adherence to kashrut.

Studies of late nineteenth-century Jewish American history tend to focus on the experience of working-class, eastern European immigrant Jews living in East Coast ghettos. Set in a middle-class community on the West Coast, Levy's memoir testifies to the diversity of American Jewish life in urban spaces. Scholars have addressed Jews' interactions with other minorities; for example, the topic of Black-Jewish relations in the context of the twentieth-century civil rights movement has received a good deal of attention. In nineteenth-century San Francisco, Jews' primary cross-ethnic and cross-racial encounters were with individuals of Irish and Chinese descent, as exemplified by Levy's descriptions of the family cook, Maggie Doyle, and the fish and vegetable seller, Chung Lung.

PRIMARY SOURCE

The kitchen was the temple in which Mother was priest and Maggie Doyle, Levite. When Maggie first came to us to do general housework, Mother explained to her the custom regarding diet and the use of kitchen utensils. Not only was there a gulf between animal food, including all that had its origin in flesh, milk, and its derivatives, but the distinction also applied to the utensils with which they came in contact. No butter must touch meat of any kind nor be served at table when meat was a course; no meat pot must know the contact of milk. The distinction held to the least knife and teaspoon. So Moses had decreed, and so Mother explained to the tall, gawky, bobbed-haired Irish girl come to take service.

Maggie Doyle smiled the amused, red-gummed smile that was destined to elude us for more than a decade and said, "I know. I've cooked Jews before."

In the tall dresser that stood between the two large closets were two drawers and two small cupboards. Milk knives, forks, and spoons were kept in the right-hand drawer; in the right cupboard below it were milk pots and pans. The meat cutlery and tins were arranged in the left compartments. Between them lay a gulf as deep as that between ancient Jew and Philistine. The distribution in the closet was more intricate. The lower shelf held the milk dishes, the second shelf the meat dishes. On the two upper shelves, undisturbed for fifty weeks of the year, the Passover dishes waited for the spring observance of the feast of the unleavened bread, in commemoration of the days when Israel, hastening the pursuit of Pharaoh, dared not wait for the dough to rise. As the Bavarian Jew and the Polish Jew became Jew under a common persecution, so the meat and milk dishes, individualized during the

ordinary flow of circumstances, united as leaven under the taboo of the Passover, and were thrust into the shadow of the upper shelves during the week of holiday celebration. The lower shelves were dusted, washed, purged of dishes and of any leaven that they may have contained, even in memory, and they were as if they had never been.

All through the year, like a searchlight, the eye of Mother ranged over the kitchen. Woe to the lovelorn cook who stirred the mutton broth with a milk spoon, or to the brazen one who basted the turkey with a lump of butter. Woe, woe to the waitress who, breaking the plate, hoped to fill the gap with another purloined from the upper Passover shelf. Triple her guilt if she dared to return it after the contamination. A Passover vessel, once deflowered, though passed through flame could never recover its native purity.

Temptation to delinquency lay ambushed in cupboard drawer and closet bin. To possess one's self of a slice of bread and butter without committing a Mosaic offense was a feat. No movement was too slight to stir a sense of danger, as feet felt for safe ground between the taboos; and always present was the zest of an unpremeditated transgression undetected. If a sudden contraction of my heart gave warning that I had cut into the butter with a meat knife, I turned toward Mother, bent under the effort to cut stars into the cookie dough, and over her back I intercepted in Maggie Doyle's eyes the gleam of amused complicity. Nowhere was my fear of Mother so great as in the kitchen, where her native capacity for anger was reinforced by her priestly office. Awe of His agent, rather than dread of the displeasure of the Lord, secured my faithful obedience. When I heard the tablets crack, I fled beneath her wrath.

As a little girl, and when I grew older, I loved the kitchen. . . . There was exotic food that never appeared except upon holidays—beet soup, hard-boiled eggs eaten with salt water, home-brewed raisin wine, epicurean dishes made of Matzoth meal and the soaked Matzoth. So many people were about—God, Moses, Mother, tradespeople, and Maggie Doyle. . . .

Many nations and races united to furnish us with our supplies. The baker was German; the fish man, Italian; the grocer, a Jew; the butcher, Irish; the steam laundryman, a New Englander. The vegetable vendor and the regular laundryman who came to the house were Chinese. The Chinamen were the high note of color and piquancy in the kitchen traffic of the day. Chung Lung was fruit and fishman. He carried the combined stock, suspended in two huge wicker baskets balanced upon a long pole, across his shoulders. He did not come to the kitchen door, but remained outside in the alley. We heard the back doorbell and hurried down, Mother, Maggie, and I. The uncertainty of the contents of the baskets—today only apples and cauliflower; tomorrow, cherries and corn; today, shiny silver smelts; tomorrow, red shrimps with beards and black-beaded eyes—made a delight of his coming. Such laughter at the weighing: Mother adding a potato to the scale, Chung, his eyes screwed into slits, removing it; Mother scowling in indignation, Chung showing three black fangs in merry insistence upon his rights—all of us knowing all the while that we were playing a game. . . . Chung talked and talked a language, unintelligible to any of us but himself, his cadences rising high and falling again into murmurs.

"Yes, yes," cried Mother, red in the face with determination.

"No, no," cried Chung, grown suddenly solemn as if in defense of a religious conviction. Anger, indignation, resentment, an impasse; then the concession of a head of lettuce here, the withdrawal of an apple there, laughter, good humor, Maggie carrying the fruits

of victory to the kitchen and I remaining outside so that Chung might teach me how to twist the tail of the shrimp to make the meat pop out, unbroken. I loved Chung Lung, and when, with a straining of muscle, he lifted the bent pole to his shoulders and trotted off, a little bowed under the heavy baskets, I called out to him, "Good-by, Chung, bring me a big peach tomorrow."

"All light, all light," he called back.

Harriet Lane Levy, *920 O'Farrell Street: A Jewish Girlhood in Old San Francisco* (Berkeley, CA: Heyday Books, 1996), 136–138, 140–141.

QUESTIONS

1. How does Levy describe the family's Irish cook and the various tradespeople who supply her home with food? What do these descriptions tell us about middle-class Jews in San Francisco society?
2. During Levy's years in Paris, she was part of a circle of writers and artists who were at the vanguard of the modernist movement, which brought greater experimentalism and abstraction to art and literature. How would you describe her prose style?
3. How does Levy describe the space inside and outside the kitchen and its objects? What do these descriptions tell us about domestic religious practice in the late nineteenth century?
4. How do Levy's reminiscences of Jewish American life in San Francisco differ from autobiographical writings in this volume about Jewish life in other regions?
5. Compare Maggie's and Chung's use of dialect with chapter 40. How do the authors use dialect or unmarked speech to reflect who they believe belongs in the US?

NOTE

1. Rosenbaum, *Cosmopolitans*, 2–4, 13, 16, 45–46, 50, 106; Zerin, *Jewish San Francisco*, 23.

63

Alliance Israélite Universelle School Curricula

ARGENTINA, 1898

Adriana M. Brodsky

In 1891, the Jewish French philanthropist Baron Maurice de Hirsch created the Jewish Colonization Association (JCA) with the purpose of helping Russian Jews in the wake of terrible pogroms (organized massacres). The JCA purchased lands in Ottoman Palestine and North and South America and founded agricultural colonies where these persecuted Jews could settle and live their lives as farmers. The project, conceived to alleviate the suffering of so many, additionally sought to "regenerate" the image of Jews, similar to the Neighborhood Houses in US cities. Turning them into farmers was, in the eyes of the JCA, a change that would facilitate their "redemption" in the eyes of those communities among which they settled. These agricultural colonies included synagogues and schools for the children, which would allow them to continue with their traditions. In Argentina, the JCA bought the land for the first colony in 1891, and the schools it built came to be led by teachers graduated from the Alliance Israélite Universelle (AIU), another Jewish philanthropic organization, created in Paris in 1860 by Adolf Cremieux.

The purpose of the AIU was to "civilize" the Jews of the Mediterranean, Iran, and the Ottoman Empire through education. Young men and women from these communities would be selected to attend the school in Paris and then return to teach the students from the Sephardic and Mizrahi communities of the Mediterranean. Because many of these "Oriental" Jewish teachers spoke Ladino, a language that was close to fifteenth-century Spanish, they became useful for this project in Argentina, where they had to teach not only "Jewish" subjects but the Argentine curriculum as well.

In the JCA colonies, many teachers were Ashkenazim and hired in Argentina. They served as vehicles of Jewish culture and education and of the Argentine government too. In the late nineteenth century, the educational system was in its infancy, and there was neither labor power nor infrastructure to educate many people in the countryside and even less in the agricultural communities founded by distinct ethnic groups. The JCA and AIU partnership, thus, was useful to both the Jewish community and to the Argentine government, which could impart its curriculum to Jewish children. Starting in 1916, the Argentine state took over the control of the schools in the agricultural colonies, and while in many cases the same teachers remained and the buildings were "handed over" to the state for their continued use, it was now the state that controlled the buildings and the teachers. The work done by the AIU teachers until then was, in the words of federal and provincial inspectors, quite good. They played a central role in educating Jewish Argentines who had arrived with no knowledge of the national language, symbols, and history.

Jewish education has tended to be associated with ethnic (or religious) goals. The JCA-AIU schools in Argentina were viewed by the Argentine state as official partners in the shaping of Argentine citizens. As well, the American continent became a stage on which the AIU carried out its desire to "educate" Jews who were imagined to be lacking "civilization."

PRIMARY SOURCE

Teaching Description (Third Trimester, 1898)

	2ND GRADE	1ST GRADE
I. National Language		
1. Reading and explanations	6 reading lessons from the first book in the series *El lector americano* (The American Reader)	We have worked on printed characters, and on characters on the chalkboard
2. Reading exercises	The same reading lessons	We have read various sections of the third book in the series *Anagnocia*
3. Writing	We have copied the readings, and other material	We have written out parts of what we read (on individual chalkboards)
4. Spelling	Dictation of words and phrases from the readings done	Students have worked on various words from the "objects taught"
5. Grammar	Nouns, adjectives (first introduction), personal pronouns, first and second verb conjugation (regular)	
6. Objects	Human body (activities and properties), and the school	Human body, and School.
II. Arithmetic	The four operations: exercises and problems	Numbers, and the first three operations from 1 to 10.
III. Singing	National Anthem, Morning prayer, Song "El Cordelero" (the ropemaker) and (in Hebrew) two different prayers to be said when entering school (with violin)	Same as 2nd grade
IV. Physical Education	Arm movements, and marching	Same as 2nd grade
V. Jewish education	1. Reading exercises 2. Prayer of the week with translation 3. Pentateuch 4. Yiddish writing and spelling 5. Biblical history from "The Creation" to the "12 tribes"	1. Teaching and reading exercise 2. Hebrew language 3. Yiddish writing and spelling.

Colonia Clara, October 19, 1898; signed: Isaac Hurwitz and L. Vinocur

"Descripción de la Enseñanza," Colonia Clara, October 1898, in Argentine I O 2, Archives de l'Alliance israélite universelle, Paris, France.

QUESTIONS

1. How would you define the education imparted to these students?
2. What constituted the "Jewish" element of their education?
3. The signers of this document were probably Russian Jews (perhaps educated in Russia) who were from among the population of the colonies. What might this detail tell us about the use of Yiddish in the classroom or the knowledge of Spanish by the recently arrived Russian Jews?
4. Compare the education that this school offers to that discussed by Rebecca Gratz (chapter 50). What values are encoded in each?

64

Jews and Tuberculosis

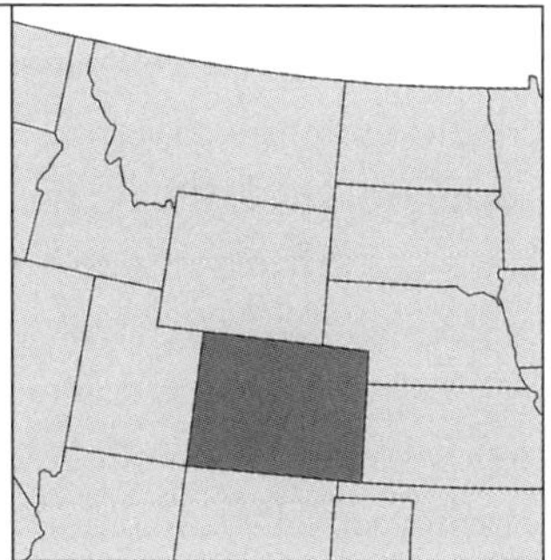

COLORADO, 1904–1930S

Jeanne Abrams

Thanks in no small part to living conditions in tenements as well as poor understanding of how the disease was passed from person to person, tuberculosis (TB) was the leading cause of death in the late nineteenth-century and early twentieth-century United States and had high death rates across the hemisphere. No accepted standard for treatment prevailed in the early years, but by 1880, medical opinion emphasized fresh air for respiratory ailments. Because of Colorado's high altitude and dry and sunny climate, by the 1880s, the state became a mecca for TB victims and earned the nickname of "The World's Sanatorium." Thousands of consumptives flocked to Colorado to "chase the cure." Since no publicly supported institutions for consumptives existed in Colorado at the turn of the nineteenth century, the challenge for adequate care was left to private ethnic and religious institutions. In Denver, two Jewish-based sanatoriums initiated the first concerted effort to deal with the growing plight of destitute or struggling consumptives: the National Jewish Hospital (NJH) and the Jewish Consumptives' Relief Society (JCRS).

The National Jewish Hospital was founded and funded by acculturated, largely affluent German Reform Jews, and it opened in 1899. Because some people believed that the NJH did not adequately address the needs of patients with advanced cases of TB and the religious and cultural preferences of some patients, the Jewish Consumptives' Relief Society was organized by eastern European Jewish working-class immigrants, and it opened in 1904. Both the NJH and the JCRS were founded as *national* institutions, and their funding and patient populations were drawn from cities and towns throughout the United States. Driven by Jewish traditions of philanthropy, they provided all treatment free of charge, and both were formally nonsectarian, although the vast majority of patients through the 1930s were impoverished eastern European immigrants, many of whom had contracted the disease in the sweatshops of New York and other large urban centers. As premier medical institutions, the NJH and the JCRS built national reputations and became leaders in the US tuberculosis crusade and treatment of respiratory illnesses.

These four iconic images, in black and white, reflect the major impact that TB had on Jewish Americans and the key role the Jewish community played in providing innovative treatment for the disease. The treatment of TB patients by the two Denver Jewish sanatoria changed the course of Denver's local Jewish history. Many of the Jewish TB victims whose condition improved settled in Denver and were joined by friends and relatives. Before the opening of the NJH in 1899, Denver's Jewish population was about five hundred. By the late 1920s, it had grown to over seventeen thousand, significantly influenced by the number of Jews who had migrated to the Mile High City to "chase the cure."

US Jewish history has tended to be East Coast–centric. The story of Jews in Denver demonstrates the unique role that what began as a western frontier town played in health care both locally and nationally in the Jewish and general community.

PRIMARY SOURCES

See following pages.

QUESTIONS

1. How do the photographs reflect the types of early tuberculosis treatment available in the late nineteenth- and early twentieth-century United States?
2. In what ways do the NJH and the JCRS mottos displayed in two of the photographs illuminate the traditional roots of and influences on Jewish American philanthropy?
3. How does the presentation of Jewishness in these photos compare with that in photos taken by Jacob Riis (chapter 60).
4. Discuss the role that gender plays in the images.

Early gate at the Jewish Consumptives' Relief Society, 1904–1917. (Photo by Mile High Photo; B0002.04.0216.0001.00001, BARMJHS)

Heliotherapy at the Jewish Consumptives' Relief Society, c. 1930s. (B002.04.0345.0003.00001, BARMJHS)

Nurse taking patient's temperature on the porch of the National Jewish Hospital for Consumptives, 1907. (B063.03.0035.00102, BARMJHS)

Dr. Allan Hurst outside the (NJH) B'nai B'rith Building, c. 1950. (B063.03.0003.00096, BARMJHS)

65

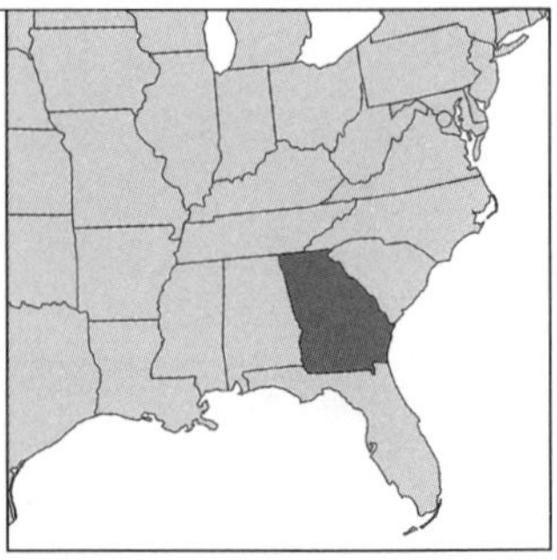

The Pogrom against the Blacks in Atlanta

GEORGIA, 1906/1974

Josh Parshall

While massacres and famines pushed Jews to immigrate to the Americas, the countries in which they arrived were not free from violence. The Yiddish memoir *The Passing Years* documents the experience of a Jewish peddler in early twentieth-century Georgia; demonstrates the spread of Yiddish culture beyond large, coastal cities; and reflects one Jew's response to anti-Black violence in the US South. The chapter reproduced here describes a pogrom against Black Atlantans—an event that is euphemistically known as the "1906 Atlanta Race Riot." This outbreak of anti-Black terrorism, like the more focused mob violence of a lynching, was an organized and ritualized occurrence that targeted the Black community at large and reinforced legal and economic systems of white supremacy. For Jewish newcomers, the performative brutality of such events underscored the subordinate position of Black southerners and suggested the risks of violating racial customs. The author, David Davis (1884–1978), explains in a subsequent chapter that the 1906 attack led him to begin peddling in the countryside, as Black Atlantans now regarded him with suspicion and he lacked the English skills to assure them of his good intentions.

Davis was born in a shtetl called Ternivke (probably Ternivka, Vinnytsia Oblast, Ukraine). He immigrated to the United States in 1905 and moved to Atlanta a year later. Published in 1974, *In gang fun di yorn: Zikhroynes fun beyde zaytn yam* (The passing years: Memories of two worlds) describes Davis's early years in the towns of Ternivke and Nemirov, his journey to the United States, his first impressions of Yiddish culture in the US, and the development of Jewish life in Atlanta. Davis's introduction emphasizes that his primary motivation for writing the memoir was the division between immigrants and subsequent generations.

Davis's memoir is an important reminder that Jewish migrants to the Americas often encountered new systems of racial stratification upon arrival in their new homes. In the US South, Jews entered a society that was defined by divisions between white and Black.

While Davis expresses empathy for African Americans in the passage included here, he and other immigrant Jews generally lacked the power and resources to meaningfully resist systems of segregation and oppression. Additionally, immigrant and native-born Jews in the South and other regions often internalized aspects of white-supremacist ideology, so Davis's account is just one perspective. As seen in chapter 52, other white Jews accepted racist ideas about Black Americans, used anti-Black racism as a means to assert their own white identities, and/or actively promoted practices of segregation, exclusion, and disenfranchisement.

PRIMARY SOURCE

One morning when I set out for the square, as I used to do each day, I passed by the peddler supply store. I ran into many more peddlers than usual, and as soon as I went inside, Jack ran over to me and said, "It's good that you're here! I had planned to send someone to your home to tell you that you shouldn't go out peddling today; it's dangerous in the city. There is a riot, a pogrom by the whites against the Blacks, and frankly it would be dangerous for a white man to show up in a Black neighborhood. Right now it's dangerous just to be out in the streets in general. Nearly all the shops are closed. The blood is flowing like water, and you'd really be risking your life if you went peddling in the Black neighborhoods."

I was stunned by the news, and I noticed that in the street outside the peddler supply, where people usually passed by constantly—white, Black, horse-drawn wagons with Black coachmen, and various ordinary business—at that moment the street was nearly empty. I saw hardly anyone going by, on foot or by wagon.

When the pogrom against the Blacks broke out, it was a few months after my arrival in Atlanta. In that short time, I had already observed the fearful and slave-like situation that the Black population experienced in the South at the time. I saw the injustices that were done to them. They were deprived of their human dignity, looked at and treated like animals. They were contained separately and isolated in ghettos and the most crowded, narrowest, and muddiest streets. Their oppression was worse than the situation of Jews in Tsarist Russia.

One of the peddlers, an acquaintance and a fellow newcomer, asked me, "Would you be interested in going to Five Points [a five-way intersection in downtown Atlanta] to take a look and see what's going on there?" He continued, "We don't have anything to fear. After all, we're 'white'—the 'strong ones,' unfortunately. Come on," he said, "let's go."

As we approached the square, we witnessed drunk, excited, and unruly white hooligans running around with iron pipes, clubs, revolvers, and rifles in their hands. Whenever they spotted a Black person, they dragged them off and beat them. Gunshots rang out. We watched as Black passengers were pulled from the streetcars and shot. It was terrifying to witness the brutality. We quickly returned to the peddler supply store.

This horrible slaughter went on for two or three days, until the large business owners began to complain to the city fathers that the chaos was paralyzing the city, particularly its businesses. Thankfully the city militia and the local police put a stop to it. Afterward, everything looked normal, but it took weeks before Black residents dared to return to work. Also, white people refrained from visiting Black neighborhoods. The newspaper wrote that the

pogrom resulted from a rumor that a Black man had harassed and attacked a white woman. I can remember, even now, that going to and running back from the square, I was unable to speak a word, because I was so shocked. I asked myself, "Where am I? What have I seen? Is this the free America?" These and other sad thoughts raced through my mind.

Understand that peddling was out of the question that day, even in white areas. I went home with my pack. I described what I had seen with my own eyes, and my aunt Sonia and uncle Reuben saw how upset and nervous I was. Uncle Reuben began to tell me about the historical background of the Civil War in America—how the South in general and Atlanta in particular were left shattered, burnt, and destroyed as a result of the war that freed the Black citizens from their enslavement to the white owners. This was still fresh in the memories of the white population in the South, and they unleashed their anger and hatred on innocent Black victims at the slightest opportunity.

David (Yampolsky) Davis, "Pogrom af shvartse in Atlanta in yor 1906" [The pogrom against the Blacks in Atlanta in 1906], *In gang fun di yorn: Zikhroynes fun beyde zaytn yam* [The passing years: Memories of two worlds] (Tel Aviv: Nay lebn, 1974), 160–162.

QUESTIONS

1. How does Davis's acquaintance convince him that they should go to Five Points, and what is the significance of his argument?
2. How does Davis compare Jewish experiences in eastern Europe to the conditions of Black life in the US South? What is the significance of his comparison?
3. This passage was written more than sixty years after the events it describes. How might developments in the intervening years have affected Davis's telling of the story?

66

Types of Immigration

MEXICO, 1908

Devi Mays

In the waning years of the nineteenth century and the first decades of the twentieth, tens of thousands of Ladino-speaking Jews from the Ottoman Empire emigrated beyond its borders. By and large, they were not escaping persecution but were propelled by the desire for economic and social advancement. Ladino periodicals from Istanbul, Salonica, Izmir, and elsewhere published articles about increasing numbers of emigrants, included advertisements and schedules for transatlantic passenger lines and Ladino-speaking travel agents, printed reports on newly established Jewish communities from throughout the Americas, and printed letters from émigrés both extolling and discouraging migration. Here, Moses Ben Ghiat, one of the founders and editors of the Ladino-language periodical *El Meseret* from the Ottoman Aegean port city of Izmir, reported on an interview with a migrant who returned to Izmir from Mexico in 1908.

Just around the turn of the century, Jewish migrants from the Ottoman Empire—speakers of Judeo-Arabic and Ladino alike—began to migrate to Mexico, a country that appeared on its way to stability after decades of civil strife after independence from Spain. As this source notes, Mexico was only one of a number of destinations from across the Mediterranean, Europe, and the Americas that drew Ottoman Jewish migrants; some of the earliest Ladino-speaking migrants to Mexico were from Izmir. Many of these migrants, like their non-Jewish counterparts, became peddlers, known as *aboneros* in Spanish, who sold on the installment system. While some peddlers eventually earned sufficient sums to establish small stands or storefronts, others found this occupation challenging and unrewarding financially.

Histories of Jewish migration to the Americas are often framed as stories of upward financial and social mobility. Jewish rates of return migration are touted as much lower than return migration among Italians, Germans, and others who migrated in large numbers in the nineteenth and twentieth centuries, linked in part to narratives of Jewish persecution that dissuaded return. Often, the migrants themselves contributed to tales of immigrant success by contacting friends and relatives in their natal lands only once they had achieved some level of success, downplaying the financial and personal hardships they experienced, and dressing in expensive and fashionable clothing on return visits. Here, Izak Algranati reveals how the financial challenges of living as a peddler in Mexico City propelled him to return to his native city of Izmir and how the Ladino press of Izmir sought to use his story to dissuade others from migrating to Mexico.

PRIMARY SOURCE

Every season has its inconvenience and every month its devil, many say. This could be true, but what you still have not noticed is that: each year our youth and even our aged are leaving for a new country of immigration.

At one point, it was Paris; then it was London; then Buenos Aires; then New York; then Egypt, and, a little later, immigration to Mexico suddenly took off.

The idea of immigration is a sickness that takes hold of the minds of many, and no matter how dark you paint for them the situation of the place to which they want to immigrate, they do not hear you, nor do they believe you, only later, when they go and they become sick and without *gentizmo* [people, community], or they remain there in captivity because they do not have the means to repatriate. . . .

One day last week, I was seated in a café with one of my acquaintances who had recently gone to Mexico and who had the fortune of returning after three or four months, alive and healthy, but without anything remaining of the significant sum of money that he had brought with him.

"Tell me," I said to him, "what is there in Mexico that all your companions that you left there do? Why did you return and the rest stayed there?"

"You should know," he tells me, "that all natures are not equal, not everyone has the same *tabiyet* [lit. nationality, fig. character]; Mexico is a poor place and to immigrate there with the idea of wanting to make a fortune is a fantasy."

"I will recount to you a little," he continued, "about how I lived and how some of those who stayed there live; I was accustomed to dressing and eating cleanly, and I am among those who never asked for anything from those in front of me. I arrived in Mexico and I became a peddler, like all the rest of the *turkinos* there. Selling takes this form: a client summons you and purchases from you, for example, 20 francs of clothing. She gives you two francs immediately and the rest at two francs per week. In this way, it is necessary to possess a large capital and a large number of clients in order to be able to live. Otherwise, there are no means to be able to meet the necessities of each day.

"I tried to work like this, being that it is the custom of the country, but I could not do it because it requires a large capital that no one would lend me on credit and that I do not have.

"This was the reason that I decided to repatriate before I was left without any money at all, as many are.

"As for the others, you should know," he said, "that all natures are not the same. There are people who are born to beg and to be ashamed of nothing. As for Shalom Segura, with whom I left and who remains there, it does not matter to him to attach a smile in his eyes

and to ask for alms. He is all day asking one person or another for a cigarette, five cents for food, and many other pittances.

"Such types could perhaps be able to lengthen their trip, but they will never be able to return with money, because first: the country is poor and it does not allow the foreigner to earn; second: once accustomed to begging, they can procure for themselves with much struggle the needs of the day and, accustomed to living from it, without caring for their families, prolong their stay there.

"This is the wealth that my colleagues will be able to bring from there, yes, after having escaped begging in Mexico City and descending to Veracruz [port of Mexico, ten thousand inhabitants], they do not extend their time there and earn the only wealth of the place, which has the name 'yellow fever' (a malady that comes from the great heat and dirtiness of the country)." . . .

I write these notes today at the instigation of Mr. Izak Algranati, newly arrived from Mexico, and it is he himself who pleaded that I write all of this, in the hopes of making those who will want to immigrate to this country renounce this idea.

Moses Ben Ghiat

"Types of Immigration," *El Meseret* (Izmir, Ottoman Empire), January 9, 1908, 5.

QUESTIONS

1. Moses Ben Ghiat describes immigration as a "sickness" and destinations as being fads. Why might he frame it this way?
2. How does Izak Algranati describe the types of immigrants who are able to remain in Mexico, and how does he distinguish himself from them?
3. Why might peddling be a profession that drew Jewish migrants and others? What were some of the challenges with this work?
4. Migrants often felt pressure to highlight their success and to downplay personal hardship in new places. What was at stake for them in doing so, and how might this distort the types of history we tell?

67

The Philomath Club

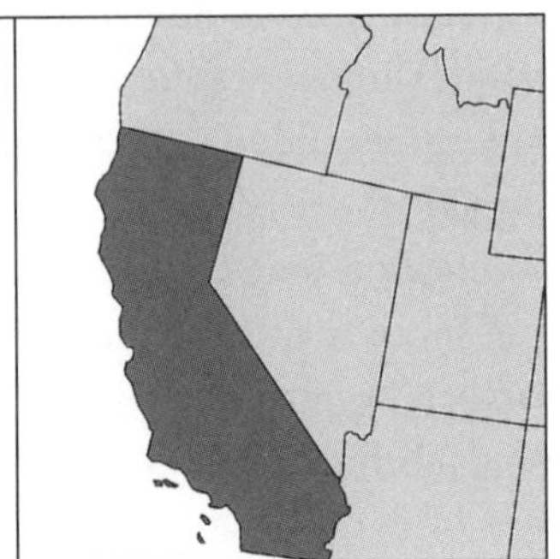

CALIFORNIA, 1909

Lori Harrison-Kahan

In the late nineteenth century, the club movement flourished throughout the United States, as middle-class women formed organizations to discuss literary and intellectual topics and engage in philanthropy. Clubs tended to promote ideals of "proper" womanhood, believing that the woman's sphere of the home could be extended to have a positive moral influence on public affairs. In 1894, the socialite Mrs. Isidor (Bettie) Lowenberg founded San Francisco's first club exclusively for Jewish women, drawing on the sisterhood of Temple Emanu-El, a Reform congregation whose members were wealthy Jews, mostly of German descent. Lowenberg described the Philomath as a "conservative, but progressive" woman's club that "promote[d] the general culture of its members through discussion of educational, moral and social topics."[1] The Philomath Club's activities were covered regularly in the California press. For this article, Harriet Watson Capwell, a non-Jewish columnist for the *San Francisco News Letter*, attended the social worker Sadie American's 1909 speech to the club. A founder of the National Council of Jewish Women, American spent her career working with immigrants in settlement houses in Chicago and New York. Capwell uses the occasion of American's speech to share her impressions of the Philomath women.

This article allows us to consider how affluent Jews were perceived in San Francisco's mainstream press in the early twentieth century. The source raises questions about the ways that perceptions of Jewish women trafficked in gendered stereotypes that scholars such as Riv-Ellen Prell have linked to cultural anxieties about assimilation.[2] Capwell's observations provide opportunities to compare representations of Jewish women from various regions as well as working-class and middle-class Jews. The author's implicit antisemitic biases remind us why the clubwomen chose to downplay Jewish identity in their self-representation and offer further insight into strategies of self-fashioning used by members of the club. We might reflect, for instance, on why the club's name did not draw attention to Jewishness but rather emphasized its members' shared love of learning.

Studies of turn-of-the-twentieth-century American Jewish history often overlook the experience of West Coast Jews, focusing instead on the experiences of eastern European immigrants living in East Coast ghettos. The Philomath Club offers a glimpse into upper-middle-class Jewish life in turn-of-the-twentieth-century San Francisco. Capwell, for example, suggests that the Philomath women are knowledgeable about art history and would be able to differentiate between the painting styles of the Italian Renaissance artist Sandro Botticelli, who was most famous for *The Birth of Venus*, including the detail of Venus's beautiful face and forehead (or brow), and the pre-Raphaelite Italian artist Dante Gabriel Rossetti, who painted several versions of *The Blessed Damozel* to accompany his poem of the same name.

Capwell's depiction serves as a reminder that Jewishness is not a monolithic category. The source encourages us to think about class and regional distinctions that persist today, as well as the ways that gentile attitudes toward Jews and Jewish stereotypes have both shifted and remained static over time.

PRIMARY SOURCE

We went to the Philomath Club the other day to hear Miss Sadie American talk of the work among Jewish emigrants who land at Ellis Island with little baggage save Hope. And Hope is such perishable luggage in the City of Dreadful Days, where the sweat shop soon lays on dull washes of drab over rose-colored dreams. On the way out I conjured up a picture of Miss American, for I know her type—the emancipated product of two or three generations of this soil, but widely differentiated from the sort that, after a generation or two in this land, cannot be identified with the Jewish stock. Miss American is the type illuminated by the desire to help her own race into sweetness and light, and when I looked into her face, which, even when smiling, has something ineffably sad about it, as though the ghost of all the misery she is trying to check, haunted her smiles, I knew that here was another woman divinely appointed for her work. I have met women in all walks of life, . . . and it always brings a glow of satisfaction to find a woman and her work well mated. . . . Whatever the work, if the woman loves it, she gets full measure of happiness out of life. The misfits are the unfortunate and sometimes the humorous examples of unhappily directed energies. For example, a young woman I met out at the Philomath Club, who told me in one breath that she spent an afternoon every week doing settlement work in the Emanuel Sisterhood, and her next sentence, addressed to a friend at my elbow, was jammed full of class distinctions. Here is a young woman who is not appointed to lovingly lead the way for the poor until she herself has seen the light.

Charitable workers give generous praise to the ready response of the Jewish people in any community. Even the funny papers, in the days when the utility joke was the Jewish merchant sending his stock up in smoke, ran parallel stories displaying the generosity of the Jew. While Miss American talked, I watched her audience, for after all, my chief interest was in the Philomath Club, and this young Eastern woman helping to solve the problems of the poor of her race was not my first concern. How volatile and emotional the Jewish women are, and how their faces reflect every shade and nuance of their feelings. . . . I doubt if any other woman's club in San Francisco would give anything but attention stiff as buckram. This facile, pliable, emotional interest is not in the average American make-up. The Philomath is an

organization recruited . . . from the wealthy and prominent Jewish women. They are not the first generation on this soil, and they have been educated in your best schools, have traveled and lived and loved even as their most fortunate neighbors. And yet they have retained that gracious flexibility of feature, the abandon of responsiveness which is a part of the temperament which has given the world so many artists and musicians.

The club is patterned after the ubiquitous women's club. It takes excursions into the land of culture, and knows the Botticelli brow from the blessed Damozel; literature made thoroughly antiseptic and harmless; science by the painless method; every sort of culture . . . is buttered over the tea-cakes, served at a woman's club, and gently assimilated with no harm to the patient. . . . After all, a club that takes itself too seriously intellectually is a dreadful bore. It is the good-fellowship, the weekly intimacy, the pleasantries of the programme that make a club worthwhile.

One often hears that Jewish women err on the margin of overdress. They are sometimes pictured be-ribboned and be-chiffoned and be-plumed and be-jeweled. Diamonds are said to be as necessary to their make-up as a marrow bone to a good soup. Well, if I am to judge by the Philomath, overdress and decoration are more vehemently checked among these women than any other class. At no afternoon gathering in San Francisco have I seen such elegant restraint in apparel. . . . [Th]is is an epoch of overdress; of bizarre jewelry; of confusion and eccentricity in millinery; of "rats" and puffs and curls and every artifice of false hair. . . . So I was particularly impressed with the subdued and sane interpretation of the mode shown by the Philomath members. As I said before, in the matter of dress, nowhere in San Francisco have I seen a pleasanter exhibition of good taste.

Harriet Watson Capwell, "The Philomath Club: An Object of Admiration," *San Francisco News Letter*, August 21, 1909, 3, Bettie Lowenberg Scrapbook, Oversize Box 2, Bancroft Library, University of California, Berkeley.

QUESTIONS

1. Clubs often bring together people with common interests, values, and backgrounds. What does this article tell us about the makeup of the Philomath Club?
2. The Philomath Club usually hosted lectures by non-Jewish speakers on topics unrelated to Jewishness or Judaism. The speech by Sadie American was a rare occasion in that the lecture drew attention to the plight of fellow Jews. What clues does the article offer as to how and why the Philomath members tended to deemphasize their Jewishness?
3. How does Capwell's attitude toward the Philomath women compare to her view of Sadie American? What do these observations reveal about the relationship between Jewishness, class, and femininity?
4. Where does Capwell evoke stereotypes about Jews and Jewish women? In what ways does Capwell's encounter with the Philomath Club challenge stereotypes?

NOTES

1. Lowenberg, "Philomath Club," 57–58.
2. Prell, *Fighting to Become Americans*.

68

The Jewish Gauchos of the Pampas

ARGENTINA, 1910

Adriana M. Brodsky

In May 1910, Argentina celebrated the centennial of its independence from Spain. The date served for the ruling elites to highlight the successes of this (young) country since its liberation, in particular, the economic growth achieved by an aggressive export economy (grain mostly) and the access to lands previously held by Indigenous communities. The celebrations included an International Exposition sponsored by the Rural Society and the Industrial Union and beautification projects to turn Buenos Aires into a modern city (modern transportation upgrades, important new buildings, and monuments to the country's "founding fathers") to show off to the many dignitaries who had been invited. And while Spain had been the enemy back in the 1810s, by 1910, it appeared newly connected to the new country; representatives of the Spanish Crown were received by proud elites in Buenos Aires. Of course, not all was glitter. The main events of the celebration took place under martial law, as anarchists had initiated a strike a few days before and were suppressed violently, and most of the population of the city lived in poor tenements (called *conventillos* in Spanish), far away from the newly built ample boulevards of the center of the city.

Alberto Gerchunoff, the Jewish author of *The Jewish Gauchos*, had left Russia as a young child with his family (perhaps in 1890?) and settled in Moisesville, one of the agricultural colonies of the Jewish Colonization Association in Argentina (chapter 63). Shortly after the family's arrival, Gerchunoff's father was murdered by a local gaucho, and the family moved to another colony to be closer to other family members. It was in this new colony, Rajil, that Gerchunoff learned how to be a gaucho, to work the plot given to the family by the JCA, as well as how to speak and read Spanish. He attended the school in the colony and was taught by Joseph Sabah, a young man from the Ottoman Empire who had been trained in Paris by the AIU and who eventually oversaw many of the schools in the colonies. The centennial of independence, with its focus on the country's booming export production, turned the gaucho into a central symbol of that success.

But Gerchunoff lived most of his life in the city of Buenos Aires, where his family moved in 1895, forced by the failure of the harvest. In Buenos Aires, he worked many menial jobs while preparing for the exam that would allow him to continue his education at the prestigious Colegio Nacional de Buenos Aires. He frequently attended the Centro Socialista (Socialist Center), where he met many of the leading intellectuals and politicians of the day. Eventually, he was able to turn to writing full-time, and he began his successful career as a journalist, publishing in a variety of outlets. Starting in 1906, tales of his experiences in the JCA colonies appeared in the daily *La Nación*; the stories were collected and published in 1910, as part of the celebration of the centennial.[1]

The original twenty-four short tales published in 1910 were organized to highlight Gerchunoff's experiences as a move from suffering and persecution to freedom and work. The collection began with a story titled "Genesis," set in Russia before the family's departure, and ended with "The Anthem," a story about the celebration of the independence of Argentina in the JCA colonies. The overall tone of the 1910 edition was hopeful, even when Gerchunoff included a story about the murder of his father. In the prologue, Gerchunoff likened the centennial celebration of independence to Passover: "Do you remember how," he asked, "back in Russia, you laid the ritual tables for our Passover's glory? *This* is a greater Passover," he concluded.[2] The 1936 edition tempered that hope, as Gerchunoff added two new stories to the original twenty-four that are indicative of the rise of Nazism and Gerchunoff's awareness of the dangers lurking even in Argentina.[3]

The text included here is from the story "The Anthem," in which members of the Rajil JCA colony learn of a celebration, about which they did not know much, being organized in a close-by town that was not part of the colony.

PRIMARY SOURCE

On [an] afternoon, a neighbor brought news of a coming festival in Villaguay. He told of the arches and flags and banners being erected in the streets of the municipality. This news was commented on everywhere and another colonist proposed that they find out the reason for the festival.

The colonists did not know a word of Spanish. The young men had quickly taken up the dress and some of the manners of the gauchos, but they could manage only the most basic Spanish phrases in their talk with the natives. It was decided, nevertheless, that their gaucho herdsmen, Don Gabino, . . . should be consulted about the matter. [He] thought that the preparations might be for some local fiesta, or might be for a coming election, perhaps. . . . Finally, it was the Commissary for the colonies, Don Benito Palas, who cleared up the matter of the preparations for the Jews and explained to the *shochet*, in eloquent yet simple form, the full significance of May 25th, Argentina's Independence Day. . . .

It was Israel Kelner who first offered the idea [to celebrate the anniversary]. . . . He took a trip to Las Moscas [another colony] and learned from Don Estanislao Benítez all the necessary details about the 25th of May.

The commemoration of the day was decided upon, and the Mayor and *shochet* were designated as organizers for the festival. Jacobo, the *shochet*'s helper, who was the most

acclimated of all the young men, put on his best pair of gaucho pantaloons and rode from house to house on his smart little pony to announce the holding of an assembly that very night in the synagogue.

At the meeting, the details of the celebration were discussed and it was decided first not to work on the holiday, of course, to bedeck the doorways of the houses with flags, and to hold a big meeting in the clearing, at which Reb Kelner would deliver an appropriate speech. . . .

During the preparation, a further difficulty arose. It was discovered that no one knew the colors of the Argentine flag. . . .

The dawn found Rajíl bedecked like a ship: the doorways were covered with flags and banners of all colors. The Argentine colors were there, too, though the colonists did not realize it. . . . The Commissary sent his little band, and they swept into the music of the National Anthem as soon as they arrived at the colony. The hearts of the Jews filled with joy at the sound and, though they were still confused about what this date meant, the thought of this patriotic festival they were celebrating in their new homeland filled their spirits with a new happiness.

The service in the synagogue was attended by all the men and women. Their Jerusalem tunics shown white and resplendent in the sunlit room as they listened to the Rabbi bless the Republic in the solemn prayer of *Mischa-beraj*, a special prayer in praise of the Republic.

After the reading from the Sacred Book, the Mayor spoke. He was a less learned man than the Rabbi, but he knew how to keep people enthralled. . . .

"I remember," he said, "that in the city of Kishinev, after that most terrible of pogroms, we closed our synagogues. We did not want to have to bless the Czar. Here, in our new country, nobody forces us to bless anyone. That's why we bless the Republic! That's why we bless the President." Nobody knew who the President was, but that didn't seem to matter. . . .

It was growing late when Don Benito Palas appeared with his escort, carrying the Argentine flag. The ceremony began. The Commissary drank his cup of wine and Reb Israel Kelner stood on the dais to speak. In the simple Yiddish of the people, and in the name of his colony, he saluted this country "in which there are no murders of the Jews," and illustrated his feelings with the parable of the two birds—a story that his neighbors had heard on many occasions.

"There was once a bird imprisoned in a cage of iron. He believed that all birds lived as he did, until a certain day when he saw another bird flying freely through space and flitting from tree to rooftop and back again. The imprisoned bird grew very sad; he rarely sang. He thought so much about his imprisonment that he finally got the idea of breaking out and picked at the bars of his cage until he was free."

Jacobo explained the story to Don Benito, who, being a native, could make little of the involved discourse. In his answer to Reb Kelner, Don Benito recited the stanzas of the Anthem.

The Jews could not understand their meaning, but they recognized the word *libertad* (liberty) and remembering their history of slavery, the persecutions suffered by their brothers and themselves, they felt their hearts beat faster at the word. *Libertad!* It was here. It was theirs. Speaking from their souls, with their truest feelings, they answered the word with one voice. As they did in the synagogue, now they exclaimed together: "Amen!"

Alberto Gerchunoff, *The Jewish Gauchos of the Pampas*, translated by Prudencio de Pereda (Albuquerque: University of New Mexico Press, 1998), 12–15.

QUESTIONS

1. How are colonists depicted here with regard to their assimilation to the new country?
2. Who are the intermediaries between the Jewish colonists and their new country's traditions and practices?
3. What are the comparisons made between the Jewish colonists' lives in Russia and in Argentina?
4. How does the National Anthem function here as a metaphor?
5. Compare the prayer said in Canada (chapter 58) to the mention of the prayer in this short tale.

NOTES

1. Szurmuk, *La vocación desmesurada*, 103–112.
2. Gerchunoff, *Jewish Gauchos of the Pampas*, xxix.
3. Aizenberg, *On the Edge of the Holocaust*, 57–58.

PART IV

The World at War (1913–1945)

Joint Distribution Committee of the American Funds for Jewish War Sufferers and Underwood & Underwood Photographer, *First Shipment of Kosher Meat Sent to Danzig, Poland*, 1919. (World Digital Library, 2021670907)

In 1938, Salvador Tarica, the president of the Chalom synagogue in Buenos Aires and a speaker at a fund-raising event for victims of European antisemitism, underscored the responsibility American Jewry had to aid Jews in Europe.[1] Using beautifully poetic language, he reminded those in attendance of the "complete misadventure in which our brethren in the old continent find themselves in [living] in Western countries that pretend to represent civilization." In the Americas, he continued, "democracy reigns, and [under its shelter] a new civilization grows, one which will, eventually, save decaying Europe."[2] To American Jews, Europe appeared as a crumbling civilization, in stark contrast to the youth and freedom that their continent represented. While European Jewry had, until the turn of the century, symbolized the hope of assimilation and civilization, the rise of Hitler suggested that the future of the Jewish people was on the western side of the Atlantic. Without Americans' support (financial, political, and moral), many more of those who were fighting in Europe and seeking refuge in Palestine would have perished.

This part covers the period between the beginning of World War I and the end of World War II, years during which the liberal ideals that many had believed to be the solution to the "Jewish question" were completely shattered. The rise of fascism and the Holocaust changed European Jews' lives forever, and the conflicts spilled over into the Ottoman Empire and Northern Africa, impacting local Jews. In these last two scenarios, the challenges of the world wars were complicated by internal political changes and European imperialism. Yet, as Salvador Tarica reminded his audience, the lives of the Jews in these areas were closely linked to those in the Americas who had sought a solution to economic troubles and persecution. These international events, together with their local ramifications and the economic collapse that came in the 1930s, had important repercussions for Jews across the Americas.

Tarica's understanding of the importance of American Jews to their suffering brethren was based on the massive growth of Jewish populations in the Americas. The United States, the country that received the largest number of Jewish immigrants during these decades, had grown from around 280,000 in 1880 to slightly over 4 million Jews by 1927.[3] Canada's Jewish population grew from 16,000 in 1900 to 150,000 by 1930.[4] Argentina had gone from 10,000 in 1895 to around 200,000 in 1930.[5] Brazil's Jewish population grew from 300 in 1900 to 55,666 in 1940, and Mexico's Jewish population increased from 134 in 1900 to 18,500 in 1940.[6] Although other countries in the Americas received smaller numbers of Jews, these five countries attracted the largest number of Jews.

While the chaos in Europe, North Africa, and the Ottoman Empire prompted people to search for new shores, these years saw a marked increase in the restriction of movement within Europe. Mass migration out of Europe slowed down significantly due to limitations on immigration to North and South America. The steady influx of Jewish immigrants to the Americas continued in the early years of the new century, as many left Europe and the Ottoman Empire in search of new and better economic opportunities as well as to escape persecution (see chapters 70, 82, and 85). Persecution and political and social changes in the Ottoman Empire that had begun in the nineteenth century made many Sephardic and Mizrachi Jews try their luck in the Americas. In the process, Sephardic Jews built, and took advantage of, important transnational ties that provided them with economic and social networks to adjust to life abroad. These same pressures led Syrian Jews to immigrate and found synagogues in New York (Congregation Magen David Synagogue, 1921) and Panama (Shevet Achim, 1933).

The growth of nativism in the 1920s affected Jews, as in many instances they came to be imagined as others. In Argentina, for example, Jews became targets in what came to be called "The Tragic Week": the first anti-Jewish "pogrom" on American soil. One reason for this pogrom was that, due to Jews' participation in workers' movements, they had come to be equated with communist and socialist ideology (see chapter 73).[7] In the United States, the revived Ku Klux Klan similarly targeted Jews, although the brunt of their violence was reserved for Blacks and Catholics. Many Canadian and US universities placed limitations on the number of Jews accepted. Similarly, restrictions on belonging to clubs and attending resorts and hotels became quite common.[8] During the world wars, Jews defended their right to belong to their (new) nations, even as they were made to feel they did not belong to the countries they fought for.

Xenophobia and economic crises led to restrictions on Jewish immigration and that of other groups such as Asians in the 1920s to 1930s. The United States passed the Immigration Acts of 1921 and 1924, which set immigration quotas based on the population census of 1890. Canada followed suit with restrictions but handed over immigration policy to the railroad companies that had embarked on a westward expansion that required immigrants.[9] Although many immigrants entered the country anyway, all these changes severely affected Jews, who began to consider alternative destinations within the Americas. The Caribbean in particular became an important first point of entry as other options dried up.

The worldwide depression that started in 1929 further affected the ability of people to move freely. With massive unemployment and the halt of economic activities, the Americas no longer appeared as the land of "streets paved with gold." As American nations weathered the depression, they looked for ways to limit the entry of "undesirables," immigrants imagined as potential burdens to the already thinly stretched coffers or, worse, as incompatible with existing racial ideas about the nation. Argentina restricted its open-door policy in the early 1930s.[10] Mexico passed a series of confidential memos that circulated among immigration officials restricting entry of Jewish refugees during this period.[11] Similar policies also existed in Brazil and other Latin American countries.[12] For German Jews, mobility was further restricted during the years of Nazi rule in Germany, with its openly antisemitic ideology. By the beginning of World War II, doors would be shut to those Jews seeking to escape, and those who could leave found themselves with very limited options of where to go. Many resorted to illegal means to get to their desired destinations.

Against this picture of diminishing opportunities—and of courageous action against restrictions and limitations—was the growth of Jewish communal life in the Americas. In the United States, after 1924, growth was internal, while in the rest of Latin America and Canada, migration continued until the 1930s and increased significantly once the United States passed the Johnson-Reed Act in 1924. Jews in the United States and Canada had founded institutions like the Hebrew Immigrant Aid Society (HIAS) to aid newcomers in the second half of the nineteenth century and the Jewish Immigrant Aid Society (JIAS) in the first decade of the twentieth century. However, in Latin America, these communal organizations, including self-aid, medical, social, and sport institutions, were mostly created after the 1910s. In Mexico, after the 1910 Revolution, liberal policies that secured religious freedom provided fertile ground for the creation of Jewish institutions. Similarly in Brazil, the founding of the first synagogues in Rio de Janeiro and São Paulo in the early 1910s was quickly followed by the creation of the Sociedade Beneficente das Damas Israelitas in 1915. Rather than seeing the new communities as a rupture from the past, some synagogues built during this era deliberately imitated ones left behind in war-torn Europe, even as they offered a new sense of hope.

During these tumultuous decades, Jews in Latin America continued to build the institutions that could ensure both their adaptation to their new homes and the maintenance of their religious and ethnic traditions. Throughout this era, the family provided a safe harbor amid economic suffering, even as literature often represented the tensions that arose between immigrant parents and native-born children. In the United States, stories of Jewish family life would make it into popular culture, with *The Rise of the Goldbergs* appearing nightly on the radio throughout the 1930s and 1940s.[13] More than ever, Jews in the Americas came to talk about *America* as a land of freedom and acceptance, as illustrated by Salvador Tarica's speech. They continued to participate actively in the cultural, social, intellectual, and professional arenas of their countries and looked to the future and past. The first Jewish museums in the United States, for example, were founded during this time period in Cincinnati, Boston, and New York (see chapter 88).

The growth of the Jewish communities in the Americas allowed for the rise of diverse religious and ideological positions, which contributed, in many cases, to internal conflict over religious practices and over who would represent Jews to the respective governments (see chapters 79 and 83). International wars such as World Wars I and II and local historical events like the Mexican Revolution of 1910–1920 and the military coups in Latin America of the 1930s dislocated normal life in the Americas. Unlike countries on the mainland, many Caribbean communities were not independent, and hence Jews from the Caribbean were swept into international conflicts. Young Jews from Suriname and Curaçao who were

Ashkenazi Synagogue Nidjei Israel, Mexico City. The Torah ark of this synagogue echoes one in Lithuania where congregants used to pray. (Photograph by Laura Arnold Leibman, 2018)

attending University in the Netherlands, such as George Maduro, got caught up in the resistance to Nazi occupation. Others ended up in the Nazi camps, like Josef Nassy (1904–1976), a multiracial Jewish art student from Paramaribo who famously documented the lives of Blacks imprisoned by the Nazis.[14]

Likewise, about 225,000 and 550,000 Jews enlisted in the US military for World War I and World War II, respectively (see chapters 72 and 89), serving at a higher rate than their percentage in the US population.[15] During moments of crisis, Jews, as well as other migrants, were asked to openly display their loyalty to their new nations, especially as their previous homes were involved in these conflicts. Jewish languages, like Ladino and Yiddish, thrived in the Americas, and many Jews used them as vehicles to describe their experiences and discuss their belonging to the new nations (see chapters 70, 73, 80, and 81).

During these violent decades, Jews in the Americas openly expressed their anguish at the fate of European Jews (see chapter 78). In addition to helping refugees who came to the Americas, aid organizations began to work on more international and transnational fronts. In the United States, the American Joint Distribution Committee (known as the "Joint") in 1914 began distributing aid for Jewish relief in Palestine and the Ottoman Empire and quickly expanded its relief efforts in Russia and eastern Europe. The rise of Hitler and World War II strengthened the resolve of American Jews to find a solution to the "Jewish question" once and for all and to save those who were being persecuted. While the existing restrictions to entry during these years sealed the fate of many Jews in Europe, Jews across the Americas sought to provide havens to refugees. Many officials from Latin American governments, for example, issued passports that allowed Jews to leave Europe and settle in new homes.[16] Institutions helped, too: the Joint, for example, accepted the invitation made by the Dominican government and funded the setup of a colony for German refugees in Sosúa, the Dominican Republic (see chapter 82).[17] Jewish American organizations like the Jewish Labor Committee helped European Jews bypass entry restrictions and secure visas. Acting transnationally and locally, Jews across the Americas pressured, when possible, local government, as well as helped refugees circumvent existing restrictions when that was the only course of action left (see chapters 83 and 85). While the number of refugees, especially those who came in illegally, is hard to calculate, these figures suggest that a significant number Jews personally affected by the Holocaust found their home in the Americas. Around 125,000 German refugees (mostly Jews) arrived in the US between 1933 and 1945; 33,000 to 40,000 went to Argentina; 23,582 settled in Brazil; only 7,400 Jewish refugees went to Canada.[18]

In addition to aid relief, American Jews attempted to help Jews abroad by writing petitions and applying political pressure. Jews attempted to bring attention to the plight of European Jews to their local governments and pushed Great Britain to allow for unlimited entry to Palestine. Campaigns were organized by Jews all over the Americas in order to bring help to European Jews, who were desperately fighting for their survival. Institutions like the World Jewish Congress (WJC), which had been created in Europe but could not function there any longer, found a new home in the United States—and from there, it came to influence all of the Americas. The Joint and WJC fund-raised in order to send help to communities in need. In addition, they supported the work of the Allies and lobbied to get permissions to move people out of Europe. Leaders of all Jewish communities across the Americas attended the Inter-American Conference in Baltimore 1941 and the 1944 War Emergency Conference in Atlantic City, both called by the WJC. These meetings consolidated the birth of a regional identity as American Jews and made evident the resolve to fight for Jews in the Diaspora and for the creation of a Jewish state (see chapter 83). Many people, however, only imagined that future state as a solution for Jews left behind in Europe.

Jewish communities reimagined their responsibilities at home. Within the United States, the rise of Neighborhood House that had appeared during the Great Migration slowly changed American Jews' expectations about what a synagogue would provide. Similar to the colonial era, when synagogues were often created as part of a complex that provided a space for a school, *mikveh*, and kosher butcher, between the wars, American Jews began to expect not just a place to worship but a "synagogue center" with social activities and education. This expectation rose in part in an attempt to compete with new Jewish Community Centers (JCC) that offered themselves as a secular alternative to synagogues. Rather than a study hall, the JCC offered a gym; a swimming pool replaced the *mikveh*; and a café replaced the kiddush room.

Community centers provided a gathering place that was open to all Jews, without requiring that religion be placed at the center of Jewish identity.[19] In Latin America, the founding of cultural secular institutions was also a very visible phenomenon. The absence of the Reform movement (which would not make inroads in Latin America until the 1960s) had made participation in organized religious life a hard sell for the younger generations, which were increasingly educated in state schools. Jewish communities expanded their social and sports clubs in order to provide their members with a Jewish alternative to existing non-Jewish institutions. For Jews who lived in areas where they were actively excluded from country clubs, Hebrew Cultural Centers (like the Centro Israelita de Cuba, 1924), Jewish sports clubs, and Jewish Community Centers provided a place for Jews to gather socially, make business connections, and relax. Yet, whereas JCCs in the United States were often explicitly open to Jews of all ages and social classes, Jews in Latin America tended to congregate for social, cultural, and sporting events with others of similar backgrounds, whether of origin, political orientation, economic class, or shared linguistic culture.

The rise of Jewish sports clubs and cultural centers not only created community but also helped liberal Jews counteract rising stereotypes of Jews as weak and unmanly. During the 1930s–1940s, the Nazi regime's ideology focused on Jews as sexually impure and deviant, and *Mein Kampf* explicitly spread fears of "black-haired Jew-boy[s]" who would sexually defile unsuspecting Aryans with their blood and bodies.[20] Jewishness and homosexuality were likewise seen as correlated.[21] The Americas were no haven from this idea. In the North, US President Teddy Roosevelt had argued that "personal sexual immorality and racial degeneration were connected."[22] Likewise, Jewish participation in prostitution and crime across the Americas was often used by Protestant and Catholic reformers to denigrate Jews more generally (see chapters 69 and 81). Eugenics, a popular mode of thought during this era, created a "scientific model of 'fitness'" that was used to limit the lives of both LGBTQ people and Jews. People who stood at the center of these categories found their fitness doubly suspect.[23]

Swimming pool, Jewish Community Center of San Francisco, c. 1930. (LOC, HABS CAL,38-SANFRA,204-)

For gender-queer and gay Jews, the era between the wars was characterized by both suppression and possibility. On the one hand, gay GIs like Allen Bernstein found that open expression of one's sexuality could cost a person their career (see chapter 89). Yet Bernstein was not the only Jew who railed against the new manhood. Traditional Jewish notions of manhood often found themselves in conflict with American values. The rise of a new "strong, forceful, muscular male as an icon of white heterosexual masculinity" clashed with the studious Talmudic scholar valued by Orthodox Judaism.[24] This conflict between Jewish values and American ones was often staged in the depiction of the four sons in various American editions of the Haggadah, in which the wise son sits at a table reading Jewish books while the *rasha* (evil) son plays sports, drinks, and smokes. Moreover, despite the rise of eugenics, transgender performers proliferated in Jazz Age clubs, films, and vaudeville. If the Jewish family provided a haven from oppression and financial instability, the entertainment industry provided a way to reenvision the nature of Jewish communal life. The Polish Jewish émigré Eva Kotchever, for example, ran a lesbian club first in Chicago (1921–1923) and then in Greenwich Village (1925), where she was known as "the queen of the third sex." After she was discovered to be the author of *Lesbian Love*, she was charged with obscenity and deported back to Europe. There she opened a lesbian club in Paris before being executed by the Nazis.[25] Jews from this era who dressed as both women and men in their private lives and took the risk of being photographed in both modes should be understood in this context of both new opportunities and abuse (see chapter 75).

For Jewish women, the era between the wars held the promise of new rights. Across the Americas, many Jewish women of various backgrounds and classes were involved in the successful fight for female suffrage, as the vote came to women in Canada in 1917 and then the United States in 1919. These triumphs were followed by women gaining suffrage in Uruguay (1932), Brazil and Cuba (1934), Panama (1941), and Jamaica (1944), with women in other Latin American countries and the Caribbean getting the vote after the war. The women who voted and engaged in politics held a large range of views. At one end were women like Emma Goldman (1869–1940), a writer and anarchist who, like Eva Kotchever, was deported, albeit this time to Russia. (Before either was exiled, Kotchever attended an antidraft rally led by Goldman in 1917.)[26] US women likewise became active in "genteel" politics and charity on an international level, particularly with the founding of the International Jewish Women's Organization (1923), which focused on relief in eastern Europe; American Mizrachi Women (1925), a religious Zionist organization; and Hadassah (1912), a Zionist organization that focused on public health.[27] In Latin America, Jewish women were often relegated to "domestic" roles in Jewish organizations, like women's commissions in charge of organizing fund-raising events and social affairs. The founding of WIZO (Women's International Zionist Organization) centers in Latin American countries, however, provided a more visible arena in which they could participate. In many cases, WIZO became the single-largest Zionist institution in the countries, as the male Zionist camp was usually fractured along political and ideological lines. Despite these advances in the public sphere, women throughout this era found themselves disadvantaged by social structures including unequal pay.

The sources that appear in this part illustrate the struggles faced by Jews as they grappled with discrimination both at home and abroad, dealt with the fear of losing their Jewish identity, kept their sense of community across borders and oceans, and continued to demand change when needed. Like the challenges that Jews faced, some of the sources are private (such as autobiographical literary pieces or private letters still held in family archives), while others, such as journalistic accounts and comic books, addressed the challenges of the era publicly. They bring us the voices of people from a range of gender, racial, and economic experiences. The challenges they faced, during these years, were even more poignant because the threats were coming at a time when, they felt, guarantees had been put in place.

NOTES

1. The Chalom congregation was founded by Jews from Rhodes.
2. "Discurso pronunciado por el Sr. Salvador Tarica," *La Luz*, July 8, 1938, 345–346.
3. Jewish Virtual Library, "Total Jewish Population in the United States."
4. Schnoor, "Jews of Canada," 123.
5. Cited in Nouwen, *"Oy, My Buenos Aires,"* 22.
6. Lesser, *Welcoming the Undesirables*, 179; Della Pergola, and Lerner, "La población judía en México," 28.
7. Mirelman, "Semana Trágica of 1919," 62.
8. Dinnerstein, *Antisemitism in America*, 85; Schnoor, "Contours of Canadian Jewish Life," 181.
9. Thompson and Weinfeld, "Entry and Exit," 188.
10. Senkman, *Argentina*, 11.
11. Gleizer, *Unwelcome Exiles*, chap. 4.
12. Lesser, *Welcoming the Undesirables*, 51–52.
13. Prell, *Fighting to Become Americans*, 126, 140, 142.
14. Casteel, "Making History Visible," 28.
15. Moore, "When Jews Were GIs"; Cooperman, *Making Judaism Safe for America*.
16. Zadoff, "Muñoz Borrero," 115.
17. M. Kaplan, *Dominican Haven*, 27.
18. United States Holocaust Memorial Museum, *Americans and the Holocaust*; Senkman, *Argentina*, 421; Lesser, *Welcoming the Undesirables*, 52; Koffman and Anctil, "State of the Field," 403.
19. Kaufman, *Shul with a Pool*, 2–3.
20. Lambert, *Unclean Lips*, 37.
21. Herzog, *Sexuality in Europe*, 73–74.
22. Bronski, *Queer History of the United States*, 134.
23. Bronski, 132–133.
24. Boyarin, *Unheroic Conduct*, 2, 23–29.
25. Chauncey, "Manhattan's Roaring Gay Days."
26. Katz, *Daring Life and Dangerous Times of Eve Adams*.
27. Feingold, *Time for Searching*, 46.

69

Jewish Prostitution

ARGENTINA, 1895 AND 1920S

Mir Yarfitz

As mentioned in chapter 68 the modern Argentine Jewish community took shape during the early years of the twentieth century, as larger numbers of eastern European Jews began to arrive. The maps in this chapter illustrate the large number of legal brothels in which Jewish women worked as prostitutes in the heart of Once (pronounced ON-say), the newly established central Jewish neighborhood in downtown Buenos Aires and the site of the "pogrom" of 1919. The Argentine capital was known around the world in this era as a sin city, with a legally regulated system of prostitution and a huge immigrant population fueling a male-dominated demographic imbalance. Jews were not the only immigrants involved in prostitution, but they were the most infamous and tightly organized.

In part due to a desire to save Jewish women from exploitation and in part due to fear that all Jews in Argentina would be associated with immorality, some community leaders labeled men and women involved in prostitution *tmeim* (impure) and barred them from Ashkenazi burial grounds and mainstream religious and social organizations, which as the maps show, were located in close proximity to the spaces of the "impure." In response, Jewish brothel owners established their own burial and mutual-aid society (originally called Varsovia, for the city of Warsaw, from which several founders came), providing hundreds of members with cemetery plots, health insurance, loans, support for widows and orphans, and space for weddings and parties in a lavish mansion that included a synagogue.

The data in these maps make visible the large amount of prostitution in this Jewish neighborhood during its primary period of development. Between the 1890s and the 1930 court case that broke up the sex workers' burial and mutual-aid society, brothels continued to permeate the Jewish center of Buenos Aires, intermixed with mainstream institutions. Upwardly mobile Jews began to move out of this crowded downtown zone, westward into residential and suburban neighborhoods, but Jewish organizations continued to be headquartered in Once. The conflict between those who styled themselves respectable and those whom they called impure played out in the local Yiddish press and Yiddish theater and extended to the floor of the League of Nations. This battle played a key role in the foundational and long-term development of Argentine Jewish identity and institutional life. Later generations have often been defensive about this story, uncomfortable with the overidentification of Jewish women as prostitutes and the role of Jewish men as pimps and brothel owners.

Traditional avenues into the Latin American elite, including the church, the military, and land ownership, were closed to Jews, and newly emerging professions were not particularly friendly. Mostly excluded from farming in eastern Europe, many Ashkenazim lacked the skills to succeed in agriculture and raising livestock, then the predominant sectors of the Argentine economy. Prostitution and its management thus became a viable option in this period for Jewish men and women, in networks that stretched between eastern and western Europe, the Americas, and the Middle East. While often characterized as involuntary trafficking, migratory prostitution frequently involved individuals making difficult choices for themselves, from among a limited range of options. This can be seen as one of many complicated histories in which Jews, like other people, are neither perfect victims nor heroes.

PRIMARY SOURCES

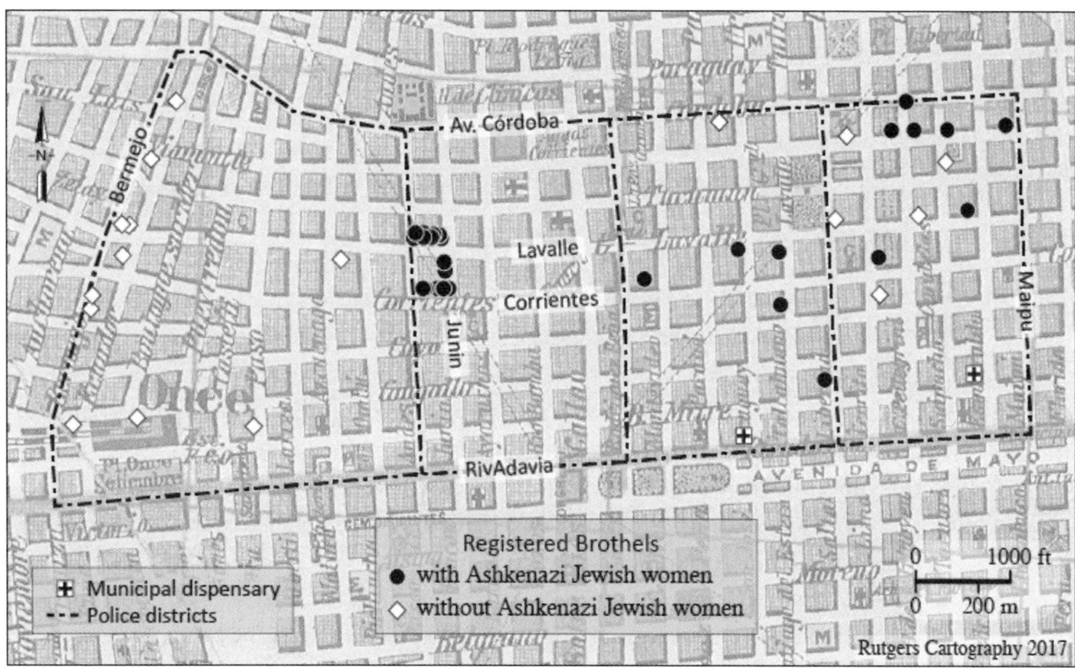

Map of registered brothels in Buenos Aires, 1895. (By Mir Yarfitz and Michael Siegel; for sources used to create this map, see Yarfitz, *Impure Migration*, 106)

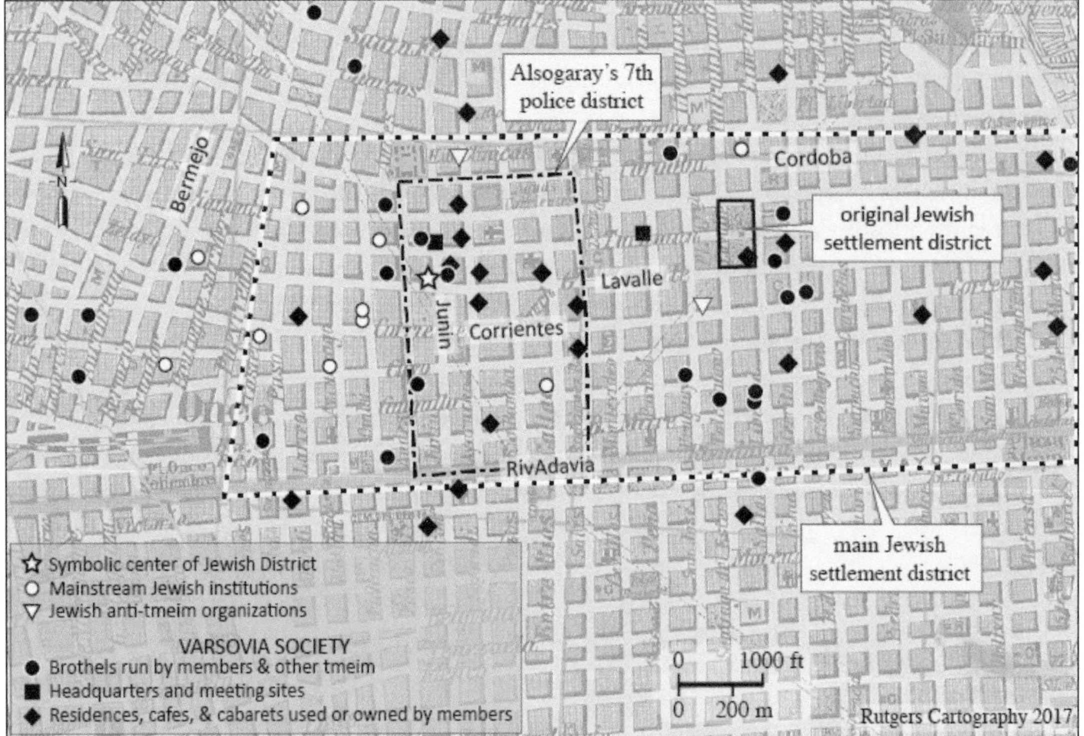

Varsovia Society and Jewish organizations in Buenos Aires in the 1920s. (By Mir Yarfitz and Michael Siegel; for sources used to create this map, see Yarfitz, *Impure Migration*, 111)

QUESTIONS

1. How might the location of these brothels in a Jewish urban neighborhood have shaped how Argentines thought about prostitution and Jewish identity? How might perceptions of Jewish sinfulness have been related to the Tragic Week (see chapter 73)?
2. The concentration of black dots around three sides of one block in 1895 represents over two hundred Jewish women working as prostitutes in a cluster of addresses. How might this concentration have affected their daily experience and that of their neighbors?
3. What changes appear between the maps, and how might they reflect larger patterns of Jewish immigration and assimilation?
4. What kinds of dilemmas do people face when limited access to education and jobs pushes them to consider entering illicit economies? How might being a member of a stigmatized group affect how people grapple with these choices and how others inside and outside that group react to those choices?
5. Whether a particular job or behavior is respectable is often debated in families and communities. Consider arguments about respectability today. What assumptions underlie opposing positions?

70

A Judeo-Spanish Love Letter

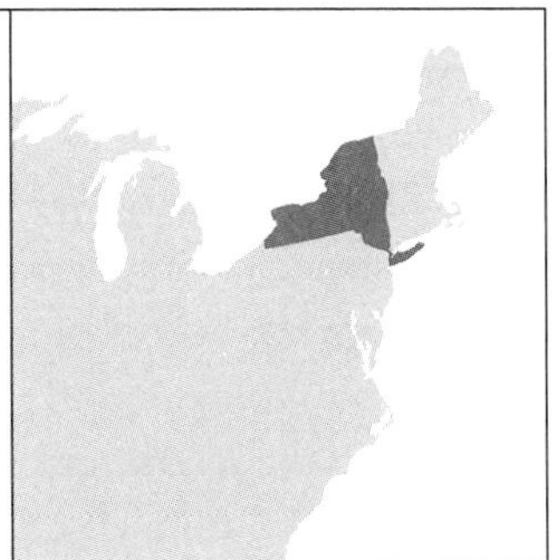

NEW YORK, 1913

Max Modiano Daniel

We have seen in part 3 that the Americas attracted immigrants from the Ottoman Empire as they escaped poverty in search for a better life. Although their adaptation to the new life took place alongside a continued attachment to the land, traditions, and language that they had left behind, their settling on this side of the Atlantic brought elements of their past life into stark contrast with the new environment. Many returned home (see chapter 66). Nissim Saul (1889–1972) and Sarah Rebi (1892–1974), the protagonists in the exchange included here, were born in the large Ottoman port city of Izmir and raised within the city's large Sephardic Jewish community—at one time the city's most populous group after Turkish Muslims and Greek and Armenian Christians.

Nissim and Sarah were engaged to be married sometime around 1910, when Nissim was smuggled out of Ottoman Turkey and made his way to New York City, where he became a stationer selling paper goods. Sarah, meanwhile, remained in Izmir and witnessed the deprivations and rapid changes wrought by the Balkan Wars (1912–1913), eventually arriving in New York City in May 1915 and marrying Nissim a few weeks later. During the Great Depression, their growing family moved westward to Los Angeles, where Nissim and Sarah lived for the rest of their lives. Mostly written in Ladino (Judeo-Spanish), the vernacular language that Sephardic Jews had developed in their postexpulsion Diaspora, the letters sent across the Atlantic by this couple reveal an immigrant's adaptation to the Americas and a future emigrant's frustration with the mores of their homeland alongside the romantic yearnings of a young couple.

This letter in particular helps us to better understand the diverse makeup of Jewish-immigrant New York in the early twentieth century by viewing it through its Ottoman Sephardic dimension. We get a hint of the particular struggles that Ottoman Jews experienced (as they were considered "Oriental"), as well as the potential benefits that accrued from the widespread Western-style education that many Sephardim had obtained at the Alliance Israelite Universelle system of schools that spread throughout the Middle East and North Africa (see chapter 63). The French influence extended into Nissim's language, as seen in this letter's greeting, "très chère adorée." Furthermore, Nissim addresses Sarah's concerns—echoed in many of her letters to him—about the rights and privileges of women in the US vis-à-vis a backward-seeming Ottoman Turkey and sheds light on the specifically gendered aspects of immigration.

Although the history of eastern European immigration to the United States has been told and retold many times and in a variety of ways, few narratives have turned their attention to the unique experiences and worlds of Ottoman Sephardic immigrants. The adjustments and comparisons between Ottoman and American life reveal a new axis of immigrant life that considers broader concerns about Orientalist and patriarchal cultural patterns, helping us contextualize Sephardic life in the United States. We also get to see how Westernization efforts in immigrants' home countries could be thought of as boons to Americanization and a way to separate themselves from negative conceptions of their foreignness.

PRIMARY SOURCE

New York Novelty Co.
134 West 23rd Street

May 5, 1913

Very dear and adored one,
I am confirming my letter of the 26th, and I hope that you will already be responding as soon as you see it, and since I promised to write to you weekly, I hope that you will do the same so that we have news of each other regularly.

As we have not yet important issues to discuss, I will begin to tell you a little about life here in general. In the end, you will know what awaits you here.

Here, my dear adored one, one lives very tranquilly, happily, well, and clearly when one gets the idea to take on American customs.

I want to tell you that, here, families do not live in the same style as in Turkey, always closed off like the Turks are used to. Here women enjoy some of the freest privileges as much as everyone in general. I admit that in the beginning it is a little difficult especially for a daughter of the orient, but there is a difference between the ignorant oriental woman and the educated oriental woman. The latter can very easily adjust all their habits, which are beautiful, and because of this she absolutely understands the need to change her attitude.

Therefore, I do not doubt that you will very easily handle American life and it is certain that it will be to your liking. To summarize, I wanted to write you something about life here that I hope interests you.

I beg of you, dear, write to me everything you are thinking, and if you have some questions, ask me. Ask me whatever you want and I will quickly provide a response, and if you need something write me and I will do whatever you ask.

Thus, I await the good hour when you will read this letter. I remain greeting you from the depths of my heart and I remain embracing you with respect.

Your very sincere fiancé,
NS Saul

Please say hello to papa and mama and everyone from me

I beg of you, dear, if it's not too difficult, give me some details concerning the matter of Rene Rebi, the daughter of Mr. Nissim Rebi, who I heard had left after she wrote to us that their daughter was married on Purim. If true, it would give me great pleasure if a letter congratulating them could be sent. Let me know about everything I'm asking from you—the same.

Nissim Saul to Sarah Reby, May 5, 1913, in Nissim Saul and Sarah Reby Letters 1911–1915, box 39, folder 2, Sephardic Temple Tifereth Israel Records, Collection 2340, UCLA Library Special Collections, Charles E. Young Research Library, University of California, Los Angeles.

QUESTIONS

1. What might we learn about the broader history of a period or region from private letters between a couple?
2. What kinds of subjects does Nissim bring up in his letter? What does he leave out that a long-distance couple might otherwise talk about?
3. What might "Oriental" mean to Nissim? What other meanings might this label have had in the early twentieth-century US?
4. Compare this letter to the ones in chapters 29 and 55. What are some of the similarities and differences? What conclusions can we draw about changes in letter writing between the eighteenth and early twentieth centuries?

71

Gravestones

MEXICO, 1914–1940

Paloma Cung Sulkin

As we have seen in part 3 of this volume, Jews had begun to settle in Mexico once again following its independence. Ladino- and Arabic-speaking Jews from the Ottoman Empire arrived first, followed by a few Yiddish-speaking immigrants from western and central Europe. In the second decade of the twentieth century, when immigration to the United States was limited, large numbers of eastern European Jews arrived in Mexico. Given that Jews can pray anywhere but cannot be buried in any burial ground, these Jews with significant linguistic and cultural differences came together in order to found a Jewish cemetery in 1912. The Mount Sinai Cemetery acted as a glue that bound isolated and diverse groups. Thus, it can be argued that the cemetery's founding marked the beginning of the contemporary Jewish Mexican community. Later on, however, and as numbers of these individual groups grew, Ashkenazim, Ladino-speaking Jews, and Jews from Aleppo separated and founded their own cemeteries. Mount Sinai continued, now as the cemetery for Jews from Damascus.

In the Jewish cemeteries in Mexico, founded by two generations in transition (the immigrants and the first generation born in the new land), we can read the different migratory waves: their countries of origin, languages, types, styles, architectural elements (traditional and those adopted in Mexico), and the use of materials given the time period or fashion. The funerary art and gravestones provide clues about the variety of Jewish experience in Mexico: traditional, secular, or religious symbols, for example, as well as signs that described political ideology or professions. The cemeteries likewise reflect tragic events, like earthquakes, epidemics, and those who died during the Mexican Revolution. In Mexico City, there are five cemeteries, belonging to the Ashkenazim, to the Ladino-speaking community, to the Jews of Aleppo, to those of Damascus, and to the Jewish Conservative movement (founded in 1988).[1] There are four other cemeteries in other parts of México: (1) Pachuca, Hidalgo, founded by crypto-Jews who survived the Inquisition; (2) in Guadalajara, Jalisco; (3) in

Monterrey, Nuevo León; and (4) in San Diego, California, where the Jews from Tijuana built theirs. In these provincial cemeteries, Jews from different origins ended up sharing the space.

Importantly, Jews in Mexico had freedom to bury their dead according to traditional Jewish practices. Jewish Mexicans felt strongly connected to their land, as the gravestones reveal. These immigrants initiated a new life on the American continent, and the cemeteries allow us to see how Jews on this side of the Atlantic viewed events like the Holocaust and the creation of the state of Israel, among others.

PRIMARY SOURCES

Gravestone of Moises Rosenberg, founder of the newspapers *El Camino* and *La Verdad* and editor of the Spanish edition of Graetz's *History of the Jewish People*, Ashkenazi Cemetery, Mexico City, 1942. (Photograph by Laura Arnold Leibman, 2017)

"Dear Little Son, You Haven't Died, You Live in Us," gravestone of Eduardo Zaltzman, Ashkenazi Cemetery, Mexico City. Evocative and nostalgic photographs such as this are currently a controversial topic in Mexico City's Jewish cemeteries. (Photograph by Laura Arnold Leibman, 2017)

Communist gravestones at the Ashkenazi Cemetery, Mexico City. Esther Komarofski vaguely remembers that at the funeral of her father, the socialists sang "The Internationale" (the socialist anthem). (Photograph by Laura Arnold Leibman, 2017)

Gravestone of Rosa Sidahui de Cohen, who died in a bus accident, Mount Sinai Cemetery, 1930. (Photo by Laura Arnold Leibman, 2019)

QUESTIONS

1. Have you visited a (Jewish) cemetery? If so, list the similarities and differences with the Mexican Jewish cemeteries and gravestones.
2. Photos on gravestones are seen by some Jews as violating the commandment against having images of humans where one prays. Why do you think they were included on these gravestones anyway?
3. How do the gravestones in this cemetery compare to those in Curaçao (chapter 12)?
4. Frida Kahlo was famously injured when a bus she was riding hit a trolley car in Mexico City in 1925, a moment she memorialized in a tin votive painting that gives thanks to the "Virgin of Sorrows" for having saved "her daughter Frida." How does Rosa Sidahui de Cohen's family use religion or art to make sense of Cohen's accident and the pain of losing her?

NOTE

1. Cung Sulkin, *Tierra para echar raíces*, 227, 229.

72

American Judaism and World War I

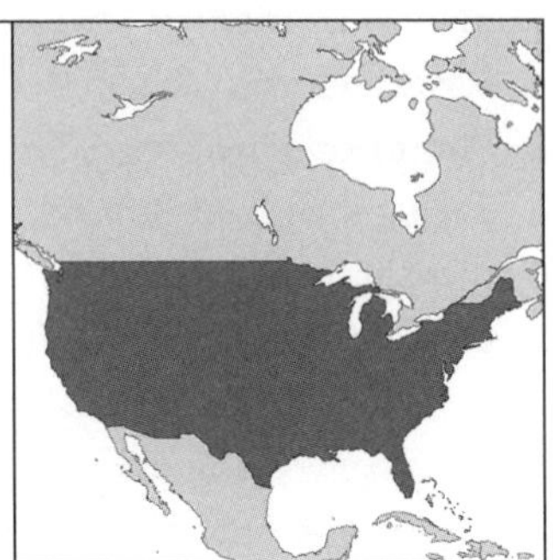

UNITED STATES, 1918

Jessica Cooperman

In the United States, World War I afforded Jews the chance to make visible their loyalty to their "new" nation. The posters shown in this entry were produced by the Jewish Welfare Board (JWB) to encourage Jewish civilian participation in the government's United War Work Campaign, held in November 1918. The campaign was a fund-raising drive to support the provision of "welfare" services for the nearly five million Americans who served in World War I. These welfare services included everything from sports and sing-alongs to classes on US history and government to pastoral counseling and religious services. The funds raised were divided between seven officially recognized "soldiers' welfare" agencies: the Young Men's and Young Women's Christian Associations (YMCA and YWCA), the Knights of Columbus, the War Camp Community Service, the American Library Association, the Salvation Army, and the Jewish Welfare Board.

The YMCA had lobbied for two separate funding drives, placing itself and other agencies in the first tier and relegating the Catholic Knights of Columbus, the Salvation Army, and the Jewish Welfare Board to the second one. Catholic and Jewish leaders strongly protested this division, arguing that it would put their agencies at a financial disadvantage and that it would reinforce a sense that Jews and Catholics were not equal to Protestants in the military or in US society. After the United States entered World War I, in April 1917, JWB leaders had worked hard to ensure that the nearly 250,000 Jewish men in the wartime military had access to Jewish religious and social services and that the public knew that American Jews were "doing their bit" through military service and support of the country's war efforts. They hoped that by doing so, they would be able to disprove suspicions that Jews were less than "100 percent American" or that they had loyalties to countries and homelands other than the United States. The JWB and its Catholic partner were successful in their protests against the divided funding drive. President Woodrow Wilson and Secretary of War Newton Baker announced that there would be only one, united, funding drive to support soldiers' welfare work and that Protestants, Catholics, and Jews would all be equally represented.

The posters shown here underscore some challenges that Jews faced during the World War I era. The language of the posters—Yiddish—reminds us that many of them were new immigrants to the United States and may not have read English comfortably. Like other immigrants, they faced accusations of "dual loyalties" and skepticism about their ability to make positive contributions to US society. The posters, however, represent a significant victory over some of these challenges. The fact that this was a United War Work Campaign offered an indication that the leaders of the JWB were influential enough to move the government toward policies of greater religious inclusion. Even as calls for restrictions on immigration grew louder during the war, the War Department and the military increasingly represented Judaism as a fully American religious tradition.

Today, we often talk about "Judeo-Christian culture" in the United States as if it is something that has always existed and enjoyed widespread acceptance, but this is clearly not the case. Ideas about American religions have shifted a great deal over time and continue to do so today. The acceptance of Judaism as an American religion resulted from focused advocacy by Jewish organizations, like the JWB, but it was also the unforeseen result of shifts in government and military policies. These sources remind us to pay attention to structures of state power as we think about Jewish history and to remember that the position of Jews within US society has always been tied to broader social goals and political debates.

PRIMARY SOURCES

See following pages.

QUESTIONS

1. How is Jewish identity represented in these images? What marks the people in these images as Jewish? What can that tell us about how the JWB wanted Jews and other Americans to think about Jewishness?
2. These posters were all part of a fund-raising campaign. What messages are they trying to send to potential donors? What worries are they trying to allay?
3. What can we learn about Jews' experience of the US in 1918 by studying the people and activities portrayed in these posters?

Joseph Foshko, *He Has Taken Care of Everything*, the Jewish Welfare Board United War Work campaign poster. (New York: Hegeman Print, 1918; SCCCL)

Joseph Foshko, *Don't Worry, He Is Alright*, the Jewish Welfare Board United War Work campaign poster. (New York: Hegeman Print, 1918; courtesy YUM, gift of the Jesselson Family)

We Have Built a Home for Them, the Jewish Welfare Board United War Work campaign poster. (New York: Hegeman Print, 1918; courtesy YUM, gift of the Jesselson Family)

73

Koshmar— The Nightmare of the Tragic Week

ARGENTINA, 1919

Perla Sneh

After the civil wars between liberals and conservatives that plagued state formation in the mid-nineteenth century, the Argentine nation embarked on a policy to encourage European immigration. With a population of 1.7 million inhabitants in 1867, Argentina grew to 20 million by 1959.[1] Jews had trickled into Argentina from the middle of the nineteenth century, many settling in the agricultural colonies set up by the JCA, but they began arriving in larger numbers in the early decades of the twentieth century alongside other immigrants. While their numbers were meager compared to those of Spaniards and Italians, their visibility in particular neighborhoods of the city of Buenos Aires, as well as their activity as politicized workers, made them the object of antisemitic attacks and accusations of dual loyalty. *Koshmar* (Nightmare), written in Yiddish in 1929 by the journalist Pinie Wald (1886–1966), is the first comprehensive chronicle of the attack of vigilante forces, with the support of the police, that took place during the week of January 7–14, 1919, in Buenos Aires. The cruel repression of the striking workers of a steel factory, called Vasena, paved the way to a full-scale pogrom in the Jewish neighborhood called Once.

The outbreak, which came to be called "The Tragic Week," took place amid the development of Argentine trade unionism, during the first presidency of Hipólito Yrigoyen (1916–1922). While the reaction to the strike can be explained by the fear and anxiety of the middle and upper classes in the face of events in Europe (for example, the rise of communism), the anti-Jewish element was so strong that the violence spilled into the Jewish quarter, where there was looting, burning of books and objects, killings, beatings, and rapes. The exact number of casualties is still unknown, though according to different sources, they range from seven hundred to fifteen hundred. Wald recounts in *Koshmar* how he was arrested and tortured, accused of being the future "president of the Soviet" that "the Maximalist revolution" was supposed to establish in Argentina.[2]

This text constitutes not only the first detailed chronicle written in Yiddish of one of the bloodiest pogroms in Jewish Argentine history but also a fundamental contribution to the history of the Jewish Argentine labor movement, which was very active at that time. In fact, Jewish activist workers were so common that people tended to identify the Jews with the revolutionaries, calling both of them *rusos* (Russians). This chronicle remained completely unknown to Argentine culture until 1987, when it was translated into Spanish by the Yiddish-Spanish writer Simja Sneh and published as a part of the book *Crónicas judeo-argentinas / Los pioneros del ídish 1890–1944* (Judeo-Argentinian chronicles / Yiddish pioneers 1890–1944). The same translation was reissued in 1998 by the writer Pedro Orgambide. In 2019, a new annotated and corrected version with a preliminary study and other related articles was issued to mark the one hundredth anniversary of the events. Written from an Yiddishist left-wing perspective, *Koshmar* sheds new light on present-day debates about antisemitism, as well as on the multiplicity of ideological currents and postures that always pierces through—and even divides—the Jewish Argentine community.

PRIMARY SOURCE

January 8th

The city remains silent. The factories [are] closed. Businesses are locked, closed and with low blinds. Cars and trucks, as well as carts and cars, must have hidden somewhere. Trams rush back to their stations. Here and there a noise is heard: it comes from shattered windows that had generated envy and exacerbated the mob, primitive as the elements. Here and there you can see a tram upside down, with broken windows and split beams; in some places you can see the burning cars of those who—it seems—tried to cross the dense and tangled rows of this primitive force; here and there goes through as if floating in thin air, an improvised street demonstration with red scarves tied to hand canes or branches freshly plucked from the trees on the street. In the air hang isolated stanzas of revolutionary songs, of slogans shouted out loud.

January 9th

Even wilder were the manifestations of the "niños bien" [lit. good children, but connotes upper-class, spoiled children]. They shouted: "Death to the Jews! Death to the maximalist foreigners!" and celebrated bloody orgies and tortured passersby in refined and sadistic manners. Behold, they stop a Jew and, after the first blows, blood flows from his mouth. Then they order him to sing the National Anthem. He cannot do it. They kill him right on the spot.

• • •

At the entrance of a building stands a boy who, surely, stepped out from home a little while ago to watch the "parade" pass; his gaze shows curiosity. A "niño" suddenly says to another:

—A "little maximalist" . . . !

Another one points his revolver and shoots in the direction of the boy, who falls and stays there lying, motionless, on the sidewalk.

—"Bravo, bullseye!"

January 10th

The cell was getting darker and darker. Dusk was setting in.

The day had been long and painful, but—nonetheless—it was still daylight. In our cement chamber we only had half a meter of an opaque reflection of daylight; through the bars, above the tall black gate. But, even so, it was a sign that the day existed.

Now we were sitting in the dark. There, the night began before it did outside. Only when the darkness became very dense in the courtyard a lamp was lit, whose pale reflection reached the interior of the cell through the bars, stopping at the top of the left wall.

January 15th

The light of the white sun rays was withdrawing from the cell, which became increasingly dark; that darkness also invaded my soul and the black wall, . . . and in my mind thoughts intermingled. . . . But, suddenly I heard the clink of keys. The pin moved. The heavy gate opened slowly, creaking with all its weight. Two policemen appeared; in the hand of one of them I could see the whiteness of a sheet of paper.

—Let's go!

As soon as I crossed the threshold, the second policeman took my right wrist and, with a strong pull, handcuffed it to his. The blood flooded my head. A terrible idea—ending all that comedy—passed through my mind like a lightning bolt. I felt that I could not cope with new offenses, like that of taking me like a dog tied to a chain; but somehow I managed to control myself, refreshing myself with my own perspiration.

Pinie Wald, *Koshmar—Pesadilla*, translated into Spanish by Simja Sneh (Buenos Aires: Astier Libros, 2019), 42, 47–48, 56, 115.

QUESTIONS

1. Why do you think the history of the pogrom of 1919 did not become part of Argentine history until *Koshmar* was translated in 1987? What does this case say about historical narratives, the topics that get included, and those that remain in the dark?
2. What examples of class antagonism or open antisemitism can you identify in the text?
3. What characteristics of this antisemitic attack have you seen in earlier chapters?
4. What do the accusations about the author's desire to become the "president of the Soviet" say about the fears of Jews' dual loyalty?

NOTES

1. Germani, *Política y sociedad*, 198.
2. Wald, *Koshmar—Pesadilla*, 65.

74

Adelia's Wedding

BRAZIL, C. 1920/1967

Regina Igel and Merrie Blocker

The first Jews—Moroccan—to arrive in the newly founded country of Brazil came in the early 1820s, after the newly independent country had passed a constitution guaranteeing freedom of religion. They settled in the northeast and participated in the rubber boom of the late nineteenth century as merchants (see chapter 105). Later, after the abolition of slavery in 1888 and of the monarchy in 1889, Brazil embarked on a policy of encouraging European immigration to particular regions that required workers and where the government wanted to "whiten" the population. The JCA, as mentioned in chapter 68, had been founded in Europe to alleviate the suffering of eastern European and Balkan Jewry and by the early 1890s had bought land to create Moisesville, its first colony in Argentina. In 1901, the JCA began studying the possibility of expanding its presence into Rio Grande do Sul, a state in southern Brazil, one of the regions interested in welcoming European immigrants. Starting in 1904, the JCA founded two Jewish agricultural colonies there. This chapter focuses on Filipson, one of these colonies in Brazil. Like the colonists who settled in the JCA colonies in Argentina, the Jews in Filipson arrived with little to no farming knowledge, lived in rustic conditions, and endured sparse harvests. Yet, given the conditions they left behind, Brazil became their home of choice. They were in Brazil to stay—even if not in the colonies.

The JCA colonies in Brazil were highlighted in English brochures printed by the government of Rio Grande do Sul at the St. Louis International Exhibition of 1904 in order to attract immigrants to the country.[1] In fact, Brazilian politicians as well as landowners were happy to accept any immigrant who was willing to live in these "frontier" regions, and they would even support the arrival of those of other religions.[2] But this initial acceptance of Jews was short-lived. Once the number of Jews coming into the country increased in the next decades, as a result of the restrictions passed in the United States and Canada, and many of the colonists left the colonies for nearby towns, nativists soon began to complain about the visibility of Jews. Between 1920 and 1930, close to thirty thousand Jews migrated to Brazil, making the country one of the top four in number of Jews received. The "Jewish question" became a topic of discussion among contemporary scholars and intellectuals, but while Jews were denied visas starting in 1935, Jewish influx into the country was only slightly impacted.[3]

Overall, the JCA colonies in Brazil ended up welcoming only a few thousand immigrants, and they eventually failed. Many colonists, as mentioned earlier, left for nearby towns and cities that provided more opportunities and in which they formed thriving urban communities. This era in Jewish agricultural experiments slowly came to an end in the early twentieth century.

"Adelia's Wedding" is a chapter from *Filipson*, a short story cycle about growing up in one such Jewish agricultural colony in Brazil, written by Frida Alexandr. The collection of stories was published in 1967, but they describe events that took place around 1920. By this time, the majority of the Jewish settlers in Filipson had left for nearby cities. Brazilian non-Jews were replacing some of the original colonists or working in Filipson for wages. The selection provides a window into these very changes, the allure and danger of the outside world in a community that had remained somewhat insular until then. Several memoirs, novels, and short stories, like Alexandr's, give firsthand accounts of these settlements and of the lives of the Jewish colonists. Alexandr's, written in the 1960s, was the first by a woman. While written post facto, these narratives still contributed to revealing the role these immigrants had in the construction of the nation, discussing, as well, the challenges many endured.

PRIMARY SOURCE

It is the eve of Adelia's wedding. With the help of neighbors and the friends of the bride, preparations are finishing up.

Papa takes the sweets in the ox cart to the home of the *mechutem*, the groom's father, where the ceremony will take place, since our shed fell apart and lies on a heap of lumber and thatch, a real kingdom of rats and snakes.

The civil marriage, something unprecedented in the Colony, will take place in the afternoon. The justice of the peace came from Santa Maria to perform it. And since, among the guests and relatives, there are some couples who were only married in religious ceremonies, they will take advantage of this opportunity to be legally married as well. On their birth certificates, brother Jacob's first children and others in the same condition are registered as natural children.

On the morning of the wedding day, our teacher, Mr. Frankenthal, gave me a speech in honor of the bride and groom. I was supposed to memorize it before that evening. If he hadn't stayed by my side, the speech would have resulted in a disaster.

After the meal, dessert was served, and soon after, the bride and groom started the dancing with a Viennese waltz, followed by contra-dances and polkas. Leaning against a door, observing the party's unfolding, there was a young man wearing shining boots, *bombachas*—silky wide gaucho pants—and around his neck a white silk scarf, fastened by a gold ring. A little further down, a group of girls were dancing, doing pirouettes and other fancy steps. I was also among them. The young man approached our group and invited me to dance. At

first, I thought that I had misunderstood, but in the next flicker of a moment, I was dancing with him.

I was so overwhelmed by the unexpected invitation that I lost the rhythm and, ashamed by my failure, confessed to the young man that it was the first time that I was dancing with someone I didn't know and that, really, I didn't know how to dance. We stopped for a few seconds. Immediately we were surrounded by my girl friends who appealed to the youth:—Dance with me! Dance with me! Once again, we spun around the room. Finally, I caught on to the steps and I surrendered to the fascination of the dance, guided by the hands of a real master.

I don't know for how long we danced together. As soon as the music stopped, it started up again. I only awoke from my enchanted spell when I realized that I was the target of everyone's eyes, especially the *mechutem*, whose glaring stares pierced me with lightning speed. However, I hardly had time to breathe when I felt myself again being dragged into a whirlwind polka. My mother's eyes followed me, worried. It was difficult to ignore them. But I didn't want to spoil the joy I was feeling for the first time in my life. I closed my eyes and decided: "I will suffer afterwards."

Once the polka finished and I returned to my parents, I found the *mechutem* talking with them. Mother, with a voice that hardly restrained her anger, asked who was the *schleper*—the bum—with whom I had been dancing and how could I have behaved so horribly, just at my sister's wedding. "Didn't you feel ashamed hanging onto the arm of a stranger, and never letting go? We have a score to settle at home." (When mother promised to settle scores, she did just that.)

I tried to explain: "I didn't hang from his arm . . ." But the *mechutem* cut me short, addressing himself to my mother: "Didn't I tell you, a long time ago, that you should keep your eyes on this girl? If you don't watch out for her, nothing good will come of it." Without even looking, I sensed that the young man was close by. Right away, I saw him dancing with Luisa Averbach who, as always, was the prettiest of all. Together, they were the most beautiful couple in the party. Then, for the first time in my life, I felt hatred. I hated the *mechutem* for his spite. I hated the low-heeled shoes that squeezed my feet. And I hated myself for having created that situation, even though I couldn't have known that I was doing something wrong.

At dawn, the ox carts, the two wheeled carriages and the horses scattered around the yard were getting ready to return to their destinations. Startled faces emerged from the tops of hay piles or from mounds of straw, asking if the party had ended. Children who were sleeping on top of benches or all over the floor inside the house, cried when awakened. It was a mess. Everyone was confused. They all seemed lost.

In the afternoon of that same day, we accompanied the new couple to the station. The good-byes couldn't have been more dramatic. It was as if Adelia and her husband were departing for the end of the world.

Frida Alexandr, "Adelia's Wedding," in *Filipson, Memórias da primeira colônia judaica no Rio Grande do Sul* (São Paulo: Editora Fulgor, 1967), 65. Translation by Regina Igel and Merrie Blocker.

QUESTIONS

1. What details does the narrator include that might explain why so many people left the colony?
2. Which interactions show how the young lady became aware of her attractiveness as a woman toward a man?
3. Which details show the young woman's being critical of her family environment?

NOTES

1. Lesser, *Welcoming the Undesirables*, 17.
2. Lesser, 16.
3. Lesser, 20–21.

75

Portraits of Multiracial and Gender-Bending Jews

SURINAME, 1920S–1930S

Laura Arnold Leibman

As we have seen in previous chapters, the Jewish community of Suriname was racially diverse. Family photos such as the 1908 one of Isaac Fernandes and Klasina Elisabeth Vroom and their eight children help provide a visual record of how matriarchs of Jewish families balanced Jewish and African identities by proudly wearing the *kotomisi* and *angisa*, the traditional dress and headgear of Afro-Surinamese women. Early photographs of Purim spiels (skits) reveal that white men sometimes wore *kotomisi* in jest.

While commonly associated with slavery, the *kotomisi* and *angisa* began to flourish immediately following general emancipation in Suriname (1863). By the late nineteenth century, the Afro-Surinamese ("Creole") middle class had begun to use European-style clothing to elevate their social status, while the *kotomisi* became associated with the lower classes. Yet the *kotomisi* also became a symbol of women's resistance and their pride in their African ancestry. *Kotomisi* were typically made from imported cotton fabric that recalled the materials used on the western coast of Africa. The dress sent messages to other Afro-Surinamese people. The way a *kotomisi*'s ribbons were folded and the shoulder wrap was placed, for example, communicated if the woman was married, engaged, or free. The style of headwrap (*angisa*) conveyed messages and moods. Even the pattern on the fabric had specific names that added unspoken lessons about the wearer.[1] Klasina Elisabeth Vroom's *kotomisi* fabric suggests that the photograph was intended to commemorate one of her "crown year" birthdays, most likely her fiftieth.

The festive family context of Vroom's outfit contrasts with the portrait that Philip ("Phili") Samson had taken at a portrait studio in Paramaribo around 1935 while wearing a *kotomisi* and *angisa*. At the time, Samson was the *hulpchazan* (assistant hazan) at the Ashkenazi Neve Shalom Synagogue on Keizerstraat. Born in 1902, Philip was married to

Hanna Samuels in 1928. While the couple never had any biological children, they adopted their nephew Salomon Alfred Bruijning, son of Hanna's sister. Most of the surviving photos of Philip show him either in or near the synagogue or his law office. Sometimes he appears with family members. The 1935 photo of Philip in a *kotomisi* is the only photo of him in women's dress and the only one in which he is smiling.

The photos of Phili Samson raise important questions about how we understand gender and race across time and space. Is the photograph of Samson wearing *kotomisi* and *angisa* an instance of a sort of racial and gendered "blackface," in which Samson—a white, male, cis, heterosexual Jew—appropriated the cultural garb of the less enfranchised part of the Jewish community in the colony? Or—given that Samson's family had branches that reached back to Africa—was it an instance of a multiracial Jew dressing in the garb of the parts of his family that were often pushed aside? Or, perhaps even more radically—given that it is the only instance in which he is smiling—was this Samson's true self as he (?) wished to be a seen? What evidence would we need to support any of these claims? What does it mean that we may desire evidence that is unlikely to have been preserved?

While we do not know who took the first three photographs, the last photograph, taken by Augusta Curiel, is a good reminder how much it matters who is taking a photo. Augusta Cornelia Paulina Curiel (1873–1937) and her sister Anna ran a photography studio in Paramaribo. The sisters came from a multiracial, middle-class Creole family, whose ancestors included Jews, Africans, and Europeans. While many early photographs of Surinamese women wearing *kotomisi* often depict women in a joyless mood or women who seem to be avoiding the photographer's gaze, Curiel's lens often elicits more positive responses from her subjects, or at least they hold their gaze with hers.[2] For centuries, Creole women were subjected to what Frantz Fanon has called the "psychological splitting of the black consciousness under a white gaze," in which the sitter felt, "I am being dissected under white eyes, the only real eyes, I am fixed."[3] Curiel's images suggest that through the right lens, "the viewer can also be directed to look and see differently."[4]

PRIMARY SOURCES

See following pages.

Isaac Daniel Fernandes and Klasina Elisabeth Vroom (*middle, seated*) with their eight children and a daughter-in-law, c. 1908, photograph. (Courtesy JHM, Private collection)

Portrait photo of Phili Samson in a *kotomisi* in Suriname, c. 1935, photograph. (Courtesy JHM, F011967)

Phili Samson with prayer shawl standing on the bimah in the High German (Ashkenazi) synagogue in Paramaribo, c. 1939, photograph. (Courtesy JHM, F011933)

Augusta Curiel, Dominéstraat in Paramaribo after heavy rainfall, 1924, glass-plate photograph. (Tropenmuseum, Amsterdam, TM-10020476)

QUESTIONS

1. What is your interpretation of the Phili Samson photographs vis-à-vis gender and race? What evidence can you imagine that might change your understanding of the photo? Do you think we are likely to ever find that evidence? Why or why not?
2. How does the way Samson uses clothing frame our understanding of who Samson is and what it means to be a Jew in Suriname?
3. What are the advantages and disadvantages of applying categories like "trans" and "non-binary" to the way people were gendered in the past?
4. We have used male pronouns to refer to Samson in this chapter. What criteria should we use for deciding what pronouns to use for people in the past?
5. The ability to compel a smile is a function of power.[5] Who smiles in which of these photos, and what might their smiles (or refusals to smile) tell us? What do you think is the significance of Samson's smile? Try to come up with more than one interpretation.

NOTES

1. De Jonge, *Kotomisi*, 27, 30, 36, 41, 47, 56; Cristidou, "Representation of Suriname and Surinamese People," 156–157.
2. Van Russel-Henar, *Angisa tori*, 27, 28, 33–34.
3. Smith, *Photography on the Color Line*, 33.
4. Smith, 31.
5. Smith, 11.

76

Black Congregations of Harlem

NEW YORK, 1924–1930

Jacob S. Dorman

Just as the Jewish Great Migration brought millions of European and Ottoman Jews to the Americas between the 1880s and 1920s, so too between 1916 and 1970, another Great Migration brought six million African Americans from the Caribbean and rural South into industrialized cities in the North, Midwest, and West. The result was that between 1919 and 1930, at least eight different Black Jewish organizations set down roots in the North, with four of those congregations emerging in Harlem alone.[1] The 1920s were particularly prolific, with the Commandments Keepers (1921), Moorish Zionist Temple (1921), and Beth B'nai Abraham (1923) all emerging in that decade. The origins of these congregations (and their congregants) were diverse, as Rabbi Arnold Josiah Ford, leader of Beth B'nai Abraham, explains in his short history of his congregation, an excerpt of which is included here.

Rabbi Arnold Josiah Ford has justifiably been called the father of Black Judaism. While Black Hebrew congregations in the US from the 1890s often called themselves churches, Ford's generation, in the 1920s, consciously practiced Judaism. Rabbi Arnold Josiah Ford was one of the most extraordinary and influential figures in the creation of Black-directed Jewish communities in North America and the West Indies. Born in Bridgetown, Barbados, on April 23, 1877, Ford joined the British navy as a musician before migrating to New York City in 1912.

Like many West Indians in interwar New York, Ford was very active in political causes and was involved in the socialist African Blood Brotherhood as well as Marcus Garvey's Universal Negro Improvement Association (UNIA). When the UNIA held its first large convention, in Harlem in 1920, Ford was an official representative and one of the signers of the "Declaration of Rights of Negro Peoples of the World." Ford became a close friend of Garvey's and was the music director and composed hymns for the Garvey Movement, including cowriting its "Universal Ethiopian Anthem."

Ford met Garveyites and fellow Freemasons who were interested in exploring Judaism as a religion uniquely suited to Black people and advocated for Judaism as the "Future Religion of the Negro" at the 1922 UNIA convention. Likewise, he included Judaic references in several Garveyite hymns. Along with other Garveyites, he founded synagogue Beth B'nai Abraham in 1924. By 1929, the congregation had amassed two Torahs, eighty-five adult members, and seventy-five Hebrew school students between the ages of five and fifteen. Ford and his congregants discussed Black nationalist politics so prominently that one observer claimed that Garveyism was "the essential matrix of the B.B.A."[2]

Ford was a spellbinding speaker, who used humor, biblical exegesis, historical knowledge, and appeals to racial solidarity to argue that the original Israelites were Black and that contemporary Black people were their descendants. Paralleling the testimony of Olaudah Equiano so many years earlier (see chapter 32), Rabbi Matthew claimed that "all genuine Jews are black men."[3] African Jews, he argued, traced their lineage back to Abraham via King Solomon and Queen Sheba, who had produced a line of kings that ruled Ethiopia for three thousand years.[4]

Ford was not content to limit his activism to the Americas and founded a pioneer's club with hundreds of members, with the aim of settling in Ethiopia. In June 1931, Ford sent a certificate of ordination to his Harlem associate Rabbi Wentworth Arthur Matthew, who would go on to call his synagogue the Ethiopian Hebrew Commandment Keepers Congregation. Ford became a leading figure in the American expatriate community in Ethiopia and reportedly perished during the Italian invasion in 1935. Through the efforts of Rabbi Ford's student Rabbi Matthew, this Judaic form of Black Israelism would attain even greater prominence.

PRIMARY SOURCE

Our Aims

The Congregation Beth B'nai Abraham is a number of Black Jews (Hebrews, we call ourselves) who have resolved to found a Synagogue or temples among their racial brethren in Harlem for the purpose of congregating and worshipping the One Supreme Being pursuant to the Laws and Customs of Ancient Israel.

To observe, as nearly as our deplorable economic condition will allow us, Sabbath, Holidays, Fast Days and all other ritualistic observances and Laws of Brith, the Laws of the household women and children.

To train our children to observe these laws and customs and to bring them up as Israelites.

To teach respect for Law and Order in the various communities in which we may be domiciled, to disseminate Love, good will and Peace to all mankind.

Our Origin

We are Africans. We do not believe as some people do, that it is necessary to be a Caucasian before you can lay claim to the Jewish faith; our belief is that the Jewish race is one of culture

and human virtues evolved through generations of obedience to certain Laws, Statutes, and traditions, and not one to be determined by the color of the skin or modern geographical classification and restrictions.

Here is a very significant fact, that those of us here never even had a Caucasian teacher to instruct us into the principles of our faith up to the present, this alone is evidence that as regards our faith as original.

However, we ourselves do not hasten to take advantage of the forgoing as a proof of our Jewish originality, because although our teaching came through our parents, our parents might have had theirs from our Caucasian brethren with whom they suffered side by side during the horrible years of the Christian Inquisition and the Christian slave-trade in Africa, the West Indies and South America. This is a fact that can be proven by us.

It is not customary for Caucasian (is that a nice name?) Hebrew brethren to admit that behind the African mind there are originally roots of Hebrew culture; but this is our contention; and although in ritualism we may differ and perhaps be found wanting; in heart and in custom we are Hebraic and nothing else.

Our History

Added to this is the contact, through family life with free Africans in the West Indies and dispersed Jews from Spain during the Inquisition who had settled in the West Indies and South America. In one instance a shipload of Sephardim [*sic*] Jewish youths over 600 of them exiled from Spain were shipwrecked on St. Thomas and the Virgin Islands, now owned by the United States. They never left there. They grew up, intermarried with the Africans, propagated, and their descendants bear their names, customs and blood to the present day. These are facts.

In Barbados and other ports, deserted synagogues bear silent but unmistakable testimony to that which had been.

In South America the Jewkas of Surinam Guiana tell another Jewish story and may well augment real Jewish history.

In 1863 the Dutch Government finding the natives hostile to the Christian Religion which had enslaved them, gave them the alternative in Paramaribo, Dutch Guiana, of becoming Jews before obtaining their freedom. They were freed thereby.

Christian suppression and proselytism was carried out vigorously, relentlessly even cruelly after these events, but nothing has ever yet destroyed the Jewish faith when rightly founded.

Rabbi Arnold Josiah Ford to Jacques Faitlovitch, "Short History of the Congregation Beth B'nai Abraham, New York, NY," n.d. (c. 1924–1930), Faitlovitch Collection, Sourasky Central Library, Tel-Aviv University.

QUESTIONS

1. What is the distinction that Ford makes between "Judaic" and "Hebraic"? Which label does his community claim and why?
2. What kinds of rituals does congregation Beth B'nai Abraham practice?
3. What is Ford's theory of Jewish ancient history in Africa?
4. How does Ford's history illuminate why he was interested in making Judaism the official religion of the Garvey movement?

NOTES

1. Haynes, *Soul of Judaism*, 78; Gold, "Black Jews of Harlem," 184.
2. Dorman, *Chosen People*, 127.
3. Gold, "Black Jews of Harlem," 186.
4. Gold, 186.

77

The Sephardim— Our "Latin" Brothers

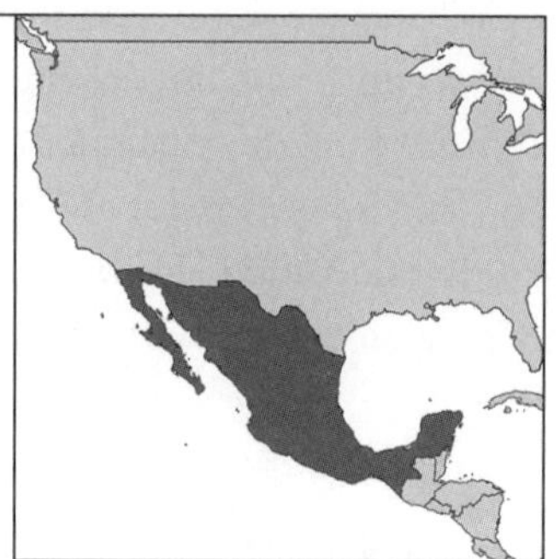

MEXICO, 1925

Gina Malagold

While Ladino-speaking Sephardic Jews settled across the Americas in the 1880s–1920s, many preferred to settle in Spanish-speaking countries. Thus, in Mexico in the early 1920s, Sephardim outnumbered Ashkenazim. Given the Sephardim's understanding of Hispanic social, linguistic, and cultural norms, this group had greater opportunity in Mexico for upward mobility compared to their religious counterparts of Yiddish- and Arabic-speaking origins. The multilingual background cultivated in this group's Ottoman origins allowed them to publicly perform national belongings that did not correspond to their Middle Eastern origins. Anita Brenner's article introduced this group to a wider Jewish audience.

Brenner, an anthropologist, journalist, and art historian, was born in Aguascalientes, Mexico, to Ashkenazi Jewish immigrants from Latvia. During the Mexican Revolution, which started in 1910 and engulfed the country for about ten years, Brenner's family left Mexico for the United States three times, finally settling in San Antonio, Texas, in 1916. The internal tension that Brenner experienced as a Jewish Mexican girl across the border led her at the age of eighteen to take a train from her home in San Antonio to Mexico City, where she eventually became part of the Mexican Renaissance cultural scene. Brenner wrote her observations of the emerging Jewish community in Mexico and sent them to Jewish journals in the United States, transforming herself into an expert insider on the Mexican Jewish community. The article included here was sent as a special contribution for the *Jewish Morning Journal*, a Yiddish-language publication in New York, in December 1925.

Anita Brenner's "The Sephardim—Our 'Latin' Brothers" strategically presented Jews to readers across the border in a way that fit Mexico's revolutionary national project. Brenner described a Sephardic identity that emphasized connections to an Iberian past and shared histories with Mexicans to justify and legitimize the presence of Jews in Mexico. The Sephardim's Iberian backgrounds and their expulsion from Spain the same year that

Columbus sailed for the Caribbean produced an origin myth for Sephardim that was shared by Mexico.

While Brenner acknowledges an Iberian Sephardic presence in Mexico dating back to the sixteenth century, she is somewhat vague on the differences between these early arrivals, who were forced to convert and were not allowed to practice their religion, and later Ottoman Jews. At the same time, her observations open a window into the ways in which Jews interacted with Jews of other origins, with other immigrants, and with Mexican society. The article, not referenced by scholars until now, demonstrates Brenner's intention to support her claim that Mexico was an appropriate place for Jews to settle. Brenner strategically used her writing to claim Jewish belonging to Mexico vis-à-vis Sephardic linguistic similarity and perceived shared Iberian origins.

PRIMARY SOURCE

The Sephardim—Our "Latin" Brothers

Yom-Kippur in the Sephardic Synagogue in Mexico City: rows of swarthy, red-lipped men, and above, women, gorgeously attired. Silks, velvets, metal laces, bare shoulders, heavy chains, large jewels; brilliant colors; nowhere the forbidden black. Oriental [Sephardic] women, seeming to lack the face-veil; languid eyes, and a fritter of brightness in all the assembly. This is a holiday. Where is the woe, the wailing, the passive funeral murmur, which hereto has to me meant Yom Kippur? This is my idea of a Hanukkah, of Rosh Hashanah. The service continues. The women fan themselves with costly ostrich feathers and rustle their Spanish laces. Suddenly—a pause, a stillness, and breaks forth from them one single, piercing wail, concentration of long sorrow into one unbearable, eternal instant—ebbing back into that stillness, and then again, the brightness and the joyous fans.

There are at present at least several thousand Sephardic Jews in Mexico City. Unlike the occidentals [Ashkenazim], who are all comparatively recent immigrants, the Sephardim have been in Mexico for a long time—since the beginning, one might say. For they were Spanish and Portuguese Jews—Sephardim—who accompanied and followed the conquistadores (1500) into the Spanish colonies. Their banishment from Spain practically coincided with the occupation of New Spain. And from that year on, the exiles preferred to go to Spanish colonies, where they could lead the same lives as before, without much transplantation.

The Inquisition in Mexico began to function not more than fifty years later, but this did not stop the immigration, even with its threat of almost certain death for Jews and Judaizers. . . .

The Inquisition brought about forced assimilation, so that many families of illustrious name and unquestionable Catholicism—now—have been founded by some sixteenth or seventeenth century exile. Their names often drop a hint; for the "ladinos" as the Sephardim were called, adopted a certain set of names, just as the German Jews have done. But whereas the Germans chose mountains and waters and metals and flowers, the Spaniards called themselves most frequently after the places from which they came, revealing perhaps even in this deep, amazing love for Spain. A love so intimate that they carried Spain over into the

countries which gave them shelter, making in Turkey, Greece notably, spots of sixteenth century Spain that endure until today. And among the most common of the names adopted we have Lopez, Treviño, Gonzalez, Perez, De la Silva or De la Selva, Castillo, Granada, Toledano....

The Sephardim [who arrived after Mexico's Independence], I found, were not at all like the other Jews I had been accustomed to. Impulsive, passionate, with a love of color and show and gesture. Apt to do business in sweeps, staking much on a risky venture and usually coming out with flying colors, and following with a splurge of spending. Their women dress with what Americans would seem bad taste—would seem over-dressing, but which I find consistent with their luscious charms. The Sephardim do not indulge in intellectual discussion over tea, they are not given to prophesying or analyzing or philosophizing, and there is little that could be called shrewd about them—for where your occidental is shrewd, they supplement cunning.

They do not take themselves seriously, as Jews, in the same sense that the occidentals do. To them, being a Jew is having a certain religion. There is scarcely any Zionistic enthusiasm among them, and nothing of that social self-consciousness which seems almost the most important "Jewish" trait in the occidental. If Judaism is a nationality, then they are far less Jews than we; but if Judaism is a religion, then the Ashkenazim lose in the running.

This fundamental difference in the attitude toward that which is the only bond between us may account for the mutual suspicion, distrust, and dislike and contempt that exists between the two sects here....

The difference, however, remains, and Sephardim and Ashkenazim often speak slightly of each other—as "the Turks" and "The Yiddishkin." There is a difference, also, in their attitudes toward the country both have adopted. To the Sephardim, Mexico is their home, but still consider themselves as "Spaniards," and the only Jewish paper published in Mexico, *El Noticiero*, of Sephardic origin, advocates a return to Spain under the terms of the recent repatriation decree.

Unlike the occidentals, also, who when not Zionists are enthusiastically Mexican nationalists, they accept their country passively, without bothering to delineate possible consequences. They do not worry much over assimilation, retaining the religious prohibition of intermarriage where the others argue from social consequences. Yet it is curious to note that, even though the occidentals are the most recent comers, there is on the whole more intermarriage among them than among the Sephardim, who in appearance and custom can hardly be told apart from the Mexicans. Sephardim have always been in Mexico, have always intermarried, and yet there remains a constant, conscious group. It is to me an illustration of how the much-feared assimilation might work out—according to the laws of progression. An answer that is neither yes or no, in spite of assimilation, there is no obliteration.

Anita Brenner, "The Sephardim—Our 'Latin' Brothers," *Jewish Morning Journal*, December 1925, typescript of an unpublished article, Anita Brenner Archives, Harry Ransom Humanities Research Center, University of Texas at Austin.

QUESTIONS

1. There is a possibility this article was never actually published by the *Jewish Morning Journal* in December 1925, given the fact that no publication or translation to Yiddish has been located to date. Does this change your reading in any way?
2. How does Anita Brenner describe the Sephardim? What is the overall tone of the article? What may have been Brenner's objectives in writing this article?
3. What may this article reveal about the emerging Jewish community in Mexico City, in particular, the Sephardim? How does this article present Sephardic Jews as performing their public "Jewishness"?
4. Why would Jews need to resort to myths to claim their belonging to the nations in which they settle? Why does Brenner insist on Sephardim's love for Spain? To what extent does Brenner assume that "good Jews" will also be Zionists?

78

La Luz Magazine Cover: The Rise of Hitler

ARGENTINA, 1933

Adriana M. Brodsky

By the 1930s, Argentina had close to two hundred thousand Jews.[1] Although mostly Ashkenazim, Sephardim from Turkey and Morocco and Mizrachi Jews from Syria had also chosen to settle in this country.[2] *La Luz* was a Jewish Argentine biweekly publication in Spanish started by David Elnecavé (born in Istanbul) in 1931. Zionist in perspective, the magazine sought to bring this ideology to the Sephardim living in Argentina, who, until then, had mostly thought of *Eretz Israel* in exclusively religious terms. As antisemitism in Germany and in Europe became more open and violent, *La Luz* insisted on the need to fight for a Jewish state that would provide refuge to those who were being persecuted in Europe. The illustration included here, making overt reference to the book burnings that had taken place in Germany in May 1933, appeared on the cover of the magazine on August 25 of that year. In the pages of this issue, *La Luz* included descriptions of the fund-raising campaign being done in Argentina by the Jewish community to help Jews in Germany, of the limits imposed by Great Britain on Jewish immigration to Palestine, and of the pressing issues being discussed by the eighteenth Zionist Congress: how to fund the Yishuv in Palestine.

Just as Brenner thought that there was "scarcely any Zionistic enthusiasm" among the Sephardic Jews in Mexico (see chapter 77), Sephardim in Argentina were accused of not participating very actively in Zionist activities; they were imagined as not interested in the political project of a Jewish nation, as their brethren the Ashkenazim were. Likewise, it was assumed that Sephardim were not directly impacted by the Holocaust and were not active in the efforts to denounce the violence against Jews and to aid the victims. This magazine cover and the content in its pages show quite the opposite.

The illustration suggests that, as early as 1933, Argentine Sephardim imagined a terrible future for European Jews. The concrete depiction of death and overall destruction is surprising. The suggestion that a Jewish state is the only solution to that bleak reality was not new, however. Zionists had made that claim every time there were antisemitic incidents. What is interesting is the argument the illustration is making about antisemitism as an affront to humanity (burning of books, for example) and about the hopes that the new state would bring to *all* humanity as well (as evident in the factories and other signs of progress). There are no visible signs of "Jewishness" in the picture.

PRIMARY SOURCE

"From the ashes of the catastrophe of Hitler's Germany arises the splendor of the rebirth of the Land of Israel," *La Luz*, August 25, 1933, cover page.

QUESTIONS

1. Given what we know *now* about the Holocaust, this illustration may not surprise us. But what did people know in 1933? In that context, what is extraordinary about the illustration?
2. Focus on the top part of the image. How is *Eretz Israel* imagined? What hope does it represent?
3. What does this early depiction of the consequences of antisemitism say about the need to denounce, and act against, injustice? What does it say about the effectiveness of such actions?

NOTES

1. Della Pergola, "Demographic Trends of Latin American Jewry," 92.
2. Brodsky, *Sephardi, Jewish, Argentine*, 17–19.

79

"Are *Tref* Butcher Shops Really *Tref*?"

QUEBEC, 1934

Ira Robinson and
Yosef Dov Robinson

By 1931, the Jewish population in Canada had increased 26 percent from its 1921 numbers, reaching 155,614; yet that growth significantly slowed down during the 1930s.[1] In French-speaking and historically Catholic Quebec, where Montreal is located, the existing Sephardic community was soon outnumbered by the arrival of eastern European Jews, which built a myriad of institutions that supported Jewish life in the city.[2] As in every major Jewish community in North America in the early twentieth century, in Montreal, there was a major communal effort to control kosher meat markets, of which, in 1934, approximately fifty existed in Montreal's Jewish neighborhoods. Regulation of kosher meat in Montreal was one of the primary goals of the Va'ad Ha'ir (Jewish Community Council) and its associated Va'ad Harabbonim (Rabbinical Council), founded in the 1920s. This regulation necessitated the cooperation of rabbis, *shochetim* (ritual slaughterers), abattoirs, wholesale and retail butchers, and consumers, all with different and often conflicting interests. As with nearly every major Jewish community in this era, the Montreal Jewish community's attempt to regulate kashrut (Jewish dietary laws), was beset with strife.

The source here is an abridged English translation of an article in Yiddish published in *Der Keneder Adler* (Canadian Jewish Eagle), a Yiddish-language daily newspaper in Montreal, Quebec, Canada, that was founded in 1907 and ceased publication in 1977. It covered both general and Jewish news and served as a center for Jewish communal and cultural creativity in Montreal. The source attempted to convince Jewish consumers, primarily women, that they should buy meat only from butchers certified by the Va'ad Ha'ir and not from Jewish butchers whose claim to be kosher was not backed up by the community's certification. The source was primarily addressed to women, because, at the time, they were the main customers of kosher butchers. These women were assumed to be essentially loyal to the Jewish tradition but not able to completely appreciate the technicalities of kashrut as stated in the codes of Jewish law, to which they, as women, had little access. Therefore, the article goes into great detail concerning how kosher butchers worked and interfaced with the community's certification agency and why the pleas of *tref* (not kosher) butchers that their meat was really kosher were false. The source thus adds insight to our understanding of how immigrant Jewish communities at the beginning of the twentieth century functioned internally. It also nuances our view of the agency of Jewish women, able to exercise their power as consumers to influence the outcome of the kosher meat controversies that affected the evolution of Jewish communities across North America.

PRIMARY SOURCE

There are women, and some men, who doubt the notices of the Va'ad Ha'ir [Jewish Community Council] and the Va'ad Harabbonim [Rabbinical Council] in the press, or from the *bimah* [synagogue podium], that a butcher shop was declared *tref*.

This lack of trust has several reasons. First, a woman is attached to her butcher and doesn't feel like breaking off the relationship. Secondly, the Va'ad Ha'ir and Va'ad Harabbonim often announce that a butcher shop is *tref*, and then, a few weeks later, declare the shop to be "kosher." Thirdly, the butcher runs to his customers and asks them to have pity, and because the customers don't have faith in the rabbis, or in kashrut, butchers influence them to buy meat from them. The fourth is that the Va'ad Ha'ir, and Va'ad Harabbonim, allegedly demand money from the butcher, and if he does not give, they declare his shop *tref*.

I don't wish to expound *Yoreh De'ah* and *Shulchan Arukh* [Codes of Jewish Law]. I only wish to remind our Jewish women concerning the respect due the *shochet*, who is the embodiment of what an observant Jew should be.

If an animal isn't slaughtered as [Jewish] law mandates, whether it's killed by a hammer or otherwise, the meat is *nevelah* [nonkosher]. All butcher shops not under the supervision of the Va'ad Ha'ir and the Va'ad Harabbonim buy meat killed with a hammer, whether imported from other cities, or from farmers from nearby villages. When I say "all butcher shops," I mean even those that hang a sign with the word "kosher" on their windows. Without exception, they sell *tref* and *nevelah* [meat].

The epidemic of *tref* butcher shops has appeared in our city in the last few years together with the most recent immigrants. I don't intend, God forbid, to cast aspersions on Jewish immigration. It is simply that with each major immigration wave, a bit of debris from the other side of the ocean slips in and we Jews are no exception. . . . In their hometowns, they would never have become butchers. Here in America they reveal their shamefulness.

. . . In the beginning, they kept their businesses kosher, but gradually they began to smuggle in *tref* livers, tongues, and other cuts, and seeing that the customers were not harmed, they continued their disgusting work.

Such butcher shops, however, cannot proceed for long with smuggled goods. The Va'ad Ha'ir and the Va'ad Harabbonim keep a vigilant eye, and news of smuggling is received from the *mashgichim* [kashrut supervisors], and from other butchers. The smuggler will be caught with the *tref* merchandise, if not the first time, then eventually.

What should the Va'ad Ha'ir and Va'ad Harabbonim do with a disgusting soul who consciously deceives customers who put their trust in him? They call for a committee of all the rabbis and the kashrut committee of the Va'ad Ha'ir—altogether, fifteen *balebatim* [laymen] and eight venerable rabbis.

The trial takes into consideration whether the accused butcher is an honest man who committed the crime in a moment of panic, is fundamentally responsible, and could set himself on the right path, or whether he is consciously *tref* and a liar.

Usually, for a first offense, the butcher gets away with a small penalty and must hire, at his own expense, a *mashgiach* [kashrut supervisor] for several weeks to make sure he doesn't bring in any *tref* meat.

I wish to mention here that the Va'ad Ha'ir and Va'ad Harabbonim do not take any money from kosher butcher shops for their service. In contrast to New York and other cities, where butchers pay from five to ten dollars a week for supervision, here it is absolutely free. Therefore the assertion of butchers who became *tref* that the reason the Va'ad Ha'ir declared them *tref* is because they wanted money, is a criminal lie which each Jewish woman should throw back in the faces of the *tref* butchers with scorn.

When a butcher is caught with *tref* meat, . . . several weeks pass for an appeal to be made, and the matter is again deliberated. The butcher comes with his wife and children, and everyone starts to cry. In such a situation, they give the butcher a chance to demonstrate anew that he is honest. However, it may happen that after several months, the butcher takes it upon himself to resume his *tref* business.

Is it the Va'ad Ha'ir's fault that the butcher is declared *tref* again? If he was assigned a *mashgiach* after the first crime, it was for compassion. If, after that, the butcher was assigned a permanent *mashgiach* for a period of several months should the Va'ad Ha'ir let him continue to sell *tref* meat because it earlier treated him with compassion?

Jewish women and the Jewish masses must have the fullest confidence in their own representatives, who are chosen from the Jewish organizations in the city to administer kashrut. . . . Jewish women and the Jewish masses should surround the Va'ad Ha'ir, which they themselves have chosen, with a wall of trust that the Va'ad Ha'ir and the rabbis will do their best to strengthen kashrut in the city.

No lies! No bluffs! What is said by self-interested *tref* people and by ordinary gossips should receive no further consideration.

A. D. Carpas [pseudonym], "Tsi zenen di treyfe butshers virklikh tref?," *Keneder Adler*, April 4, 1934, 5–6.

QUESTIONS

1. Why were butchers' claims to be selling kosher meat subject to doubt and controversy?
2. What is the source of conflict between kosher butchers and Jewish communal agencies?
3. Why was it important that women were addressed primarily in the source?

4. How does the controversy over the definition of kosher illuminate the development of North American Jewish communities in the early twentieth century?
5. How does this controversy compare to Hetty Hays complaint (chapter 28)? What has changed or remained the same? Has the gendering of kashrut changed at all?

NOTES

1. Tulchinsky, *Canada's Jews*, 199.
2. Y. Cohen, "Sephardi Jews in Montreal," 169.

80

Kristobal Kolon: The Yiddish Columbus

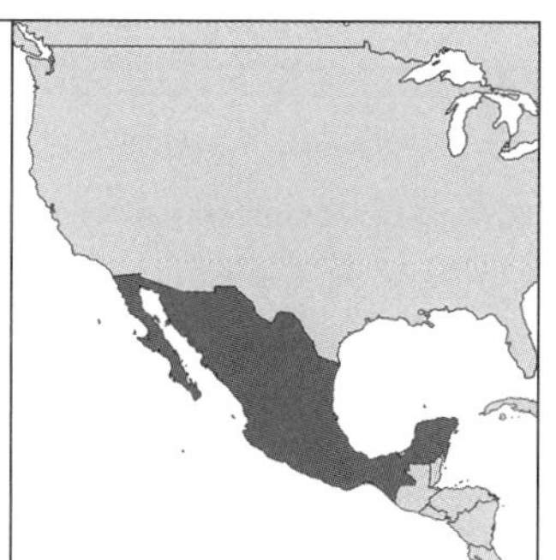

MEXICO, 1938

Rachel Rubinstein

For Spanish readers, Jacobo Glantz may be most familiar as the protagonist of his daughter Margo Glantz's family memoir, *Las genealogías* (1981; translated as *The Family Tree*), in which she describes her parents' experiences of migration and her own coming of age as a Jewish woman in Mexico. But in the world of interwar Yiddish, Glantz was one of the most important poets of his day. Born in 1902 in a small town near Odessa, Glantz and his family were frequently uprooted by the wars of 1905, 1914, and 1918 and the pogroms that followed. In 1924, they finally received visas to the United States, but the Reed-Johnson law had been passed, immigration quotas had been enforced, and they could not enter the United States. Like many others, the Glantzes instead went to Mexico City, which in the 1920s had become a transnational hub of radicals, revolutionaries, and artists attracted to Mexico's postrevolutionary, progressive regime, as well as a growing immigrant community of Jews from eastern Europe and the former Ottoman Empire.

Jacobo Glantz's epic was previously published in sections in Yiddish (in magazines based in New York, Mexico City, and Vilna) and in Spanish, but it was never translated into English until now. *Kristobal Kolon* retells the Americas' most iconic foundational myth using two unlikely guides: Luis de Torres, glancingly mentioned by Columbus as a Jew hired to serve as an interpreter, is at the center of Glantz's retelling, with substantial passages dedicated to the narrative of Guacanagari, a *cacique* (Indigenous leader) briefly described in Columbus's journals. In Glantz's poem, both De Torres and Guacanagari are traumatized survivors of the Inquisition and of conquest, whose imagined experiences of war and enslavement in the New World serve to connect disparate geographies, histories, and peoples in a powerful revisionist narrative.

During the 1930s, Mexico saw a wave of critical and revisionist historiography that sought to reframe narratives of the conquest from a countercolonial perspective. Glantz was keenly aware of these cultural currents. At the same time, like many of his fellow Yiddish

Mexican writers, he embraced a vision of Jewish Mexican hybridity, even as Jews were often excluded from the national narrative. Fascism was on the rise in Mexico, just as it was in Europe. In January 1939, Glantz was beaten in the street by members of the Golden Shirts, Mexico's fascist organization, a trauma that may have informed his reworkings of *Kristobal Kolon*.[1] The Inquisition and the conquest became ways for Yiddish writers to refer to their own experiences of eastern European anti-Jewish violence, their commitment to the Left's fight against fascism in 1930s Spain, and the shared histories of Indigenous, African, Jewish, and Muslim subjects under Spanish terror, conquest, and captivity.

Written in a multilingual Yiddish with Spanish, Taino, Latin, and Hebrew borrowings, Glantz's masterwork offers a transnational vision of the Americas that insists—in Yiddish—on its Jewish, Muslim, Indigenous and African origins. Recentering the story of the Jews in the Americas through the imagined experiences of Luis de Torres, an Arabic-speaking Jew who has been claimed by some people as Columbus's "Moorish" or Arab navigator, suggests a new geography for American Jewish literature that exceeds the boundaries of what we understand America and Jewishness to be and challenges our expectations of what Yiddish literature can contain.[2]

PRIMARY SOURCE

Christopher Columbus: Poem in Three Parts (Section 38)

Colon's great journey, for generations, has been
Consigned to parchment maps
Its beginning and end.
If the sea devoured
Colon's body
His legacy would remain
His name would survive:
Legend.

His name swims on
until today
In casks of gopherwood
Sealed with pitch. . . .
Columbus's name
Is fused with the bloody curses
Of the first peoples
The ocean currents a scourge
Slowly flowing
By the coasts of their islands
For years, centuries
Until they brought
—the conquistadores.

The Slave Ship

1.
When the first slave ship
Cut through the salty sea-foam
All the blind forces that had slumbered
For a thousand years
At the bottom of the sea
Unbound themselves
And sought the way to freedom

The mast
Like a ghastly finger
Points, warning
Of naked bones—
Torn sails
The admiral's terrorized compass
No longer knows the
ship's direction.

In the mute pain of slaves
and howling winds
The ship descends
Through stormy depths
Drawing nearer
To dry land
Where storms rock
In the souls of the men
Doomed to remain abject slaves
Household chattel.

Marom Tenebrasom

1.
The sea, the blue sea, is full of fury
From the deepest depths winds gust
And a ship makes its way, lost from God

On the deck, in the wind, sailors climb, experienced and agile.
The ship cuts quickly through the open sea
Steered by slaves.
Captives.
And Columbus, the white king, is like a stag
Running from the forest with broken horns.

Over the mast, the setting sun hangs
As from a gallows
—a slave.

And in the quiet night
The winds chatter and warn:
Oh, the turbulent sea is wrathful
And the heart of the old admiral will fill several times over with venom
Until he sees his land of dreams again

Now the bitter-black ship sails
Not towards the dreamlands recorded in those brilliant,
Blind *mappamundi*
The wind drives the ship with its captives
And Columbus, the white king
Away from the setting sun
Back to the royal court.

2.
And on the ships deck
In a corner
His heart windowless and dark
Lies De Torres on a plank
Shackled by chains

And the wind, the wind
Frothing with unending lamentation
Carries the Jew back home into exile
To his mother's grey head
To pure childhood dreams
The tattered, tender fringes
Of his first fifteen years
And to the tinder-red tongues of flame
Of his blazing people.

Yaakov Glantz, "Kristobal Kolon: Poeme in dray teyln," in *Zamlbikher* 3, edited by Y. Opatoshu and H. Leyvik (New York: Astoria, 1938), 52–53; Yaakov Glantz, *Kristobal Kolon* (Tel Aviv: Farlag Y. L. Peretz, 1980), 154–155, 241–243.

QUESTIONS

1. In what ways does the poem present a different story of America's "discovery" than the one often told? In what ways does it subvert the foundational myth of the Americas?
2. At the end of the poem, Luis de Torres is being brought in chains back to Spain, where he will be burned at the stake for heresy. How does the poem connect his experience as a *converso* with the experiences of enslaved Africans and Indigenous people?
3. The poem is written in Yiddish but borrows words from other languages. What might this reading experience have been like for Glantz's audience? What is lost in translation?

NOTES

1. *Jewish Telegraphic Agency* 48 (January 29, 1939): 1.
2. Abdullah al-Ahari, "Caribbean and Latin America," 443.

81

A Comedic Yiddish Song on Unemployment

ARGENTINA, 1930S

Patricia G. Nuriel and Alan Astro

By the 1930s, Buenos Aires, like Warsaw, New York, and Mexico City, hosted a vibrant Yiddish cultural scene. The following lyrics were written and performed by Jevel Katz (1902–1940), who was born in Vilna and immigrated to Argentina in 1930, at a highpoint in Buenos Aires Yiddish theater. There is little doubt that he soon became the most popular Yiddish songwriter and singer in the country. His celebrity status reached the ears of promoters of the North American Yiddish stage industry. As he was about to initiate his artistic tour there in 1940, he died unexpectedly of complications following a tonsillectomy. Tens of thousands gathered at his funeral—a massive attendance, considering that Jews in the country numbered approximately 250,000 by the 1940s. His popularity was such that he was branded "el Gardel judío" (the Jewish Gardel), after the tango star Carlos Gardel, who also had died at the apex of his career in 1935.

Much has been written on Jewish immigration to Argentina, including recent research into the Yiddish literature that flowered there. However, "lower" forms of Argentine Jewish culture have rarely been touched on. This stands in contrast to the significant attention paid in the last few decades, for example, to klezmer music in the United States. Specifically, Katz's song "Der arbetslozer ganef" (The unemployed thief) may well reflect—in a jocular, self-mocking, unassuming way—something quite shameful: the existence of criminality among Jews. As we saw in chapter 69, in Argentina, Jewish crime was particularly vexing due to the presence of notorious Jewish prostitution rings—a scourge that the organized community ultimately wiped out. In this way, "Der arbetslozer ganef" recalls another song, "Mucho ojo," in which Jevel Katz combines Yiddish and Spanish as he does in many of his other songs, mirroring the everyday language of Jewish immigrants. "Mucho ojo," meaning "watch out," warns against dangers in the new country; however, for audiences of the time, the lyrics clearly alluded to the perils of frequenting unsavory elements in their midst.

Yiddish popular music often dealt with poverty, whether portraying urban misery, as in the song "Papirosn" (Cigarettes), about a child vendor of tobacco and matches, or proletarian revolt, as in "Motl der operator" (Motl, the sewing-machine operator), about bosses sending in gangsters to break a strike. "Der arbetslozer ganef"—through its treatment of a criminal, petty though his offenses be—adds to the story of the Jewish poor and working class in the Americas. It may be placed alongside the classic song "Avreml der marvikher" (Abie, the pickpocket) by the Polish Yiddish composer Mordechai Gebirtig, who was born in Cracow in 1877 and died in that city's Nazi-imposed ghetto in 1942. Katz's performances reenacted in sharp comic mode aspects of life in Buenos Aires' Jewish neighborhoods, the tenements where immigrants lived, and the agricultural colonies in provincial Argentina. He portrayed the newcomers' economic challenges and slow process of acculturation.

PRIMARY SOURCE

The Unemployed Thief

**Turnin' 'round pointless, might as well go nuts.
Where and what to grab ain't there.
Even the jerks all smartened up.
Might as well go honest, sucker.
The good ol' days are gone for good.
No more rich guys to be found.
All that's left is to rob each other,
And I'm turnin' 'round pointless, nothin' to do.**

**[Refrain:] Roamin' here 'n there. What's the point?
Times are bad, the devil take 'em.
Wherever you turn, nothin's to be had.
Might as well be an honest sucker.**

**Not so long ago, I crawled my way
Into a bank to get a little pay.
'Twas no easy job to break in
'N make it to the big ol' safe.
All that trouble ain't helped me none.
'Cause someone beat me to the till.
Completely empty, zilch, kaput.
Even the teller's learned the trick.**

[Refrain:] Roamin' here 'n there . . .

**Went runnin' into a dark alleyway
Up to a passerby, quick as lightnin'.**

Flashed a knife before his eyes,
And snatched the wallet from his hand.
Took it, looked 'n opened it.
Saw it belonged to a writer.
Found nothin' there but articles
Stolen by the bum himself.

[Refrain:] Roamin' here 'n there . . .

Held a rich lass 'gainst the wall,
'N ripped a diamond from her hand.
The blazes take her! She's fooled me too.
That diamond ain't worth no two cents.
The good ol' days are gone for good.
Now diamonds are fake. So is gold.
All that's left is to rob each other.
Might as well be an honest sucker.

[Refrain:] Roamin' here 'n there . . .

Jevel Katz, "Der arbetslozer ganef," in *Di Yidishe tsaytung* (c. 1939–1940), Fundación IWO, "Jevel Katz" Collection, Buenos Aires, Argentina.

QUESTIONS

1. How does the text represent the economic and social atmosphere of the 1930s in Argentina? How does humor contribute to communicating that socioeconomic reality?
2. Vilna, Buenos Aires, and New York are linked to Katz's life and artistic fame. What do the trajectories of Yiddish speakers and of their cultural products across continents and countries tell us about their lives and the construction of their identities during the first decades of the twentieth century?

82

Miriam's Letter

DOMINICAN REPUBLIC, 1941

Marion Kaplan

The Evian Conference of 1938 was intended to solve the refugee crisis caused by a dangerously expanding Nazi Germany; yet no countries in attendance agreed to welcome more Jewish refugees. Afterward, however, the Dominican government extended an invitation, and the American Jewish Joint Distribution Committee, a philanthropic organization in New York, set up Sosúa, a small refugee agricultural settlement on the northeastern shore of the island. The refugees could only describe this abandoned banana plantation as "paradise," but they faced daunting problems. They were mostly middle-class people who now had to quickly learn to farm, and there were more men than women. Still, the Sosúa refugees could not have survived without the support of the Dominican government, which offered them a shelter, the American Jewish philanthropists who subsidized their escape and settlement, and the Dominican people who came to Sosúa to work with them and for them. Ultimately, Sosúa housed fewer than eight hundred people, because wartime shipping slowed the refugee flow and the United States, fearing that Jews would abandon the settlement and come to the US after the war, put obstacles in the path of refugees aiming for Sosúa.

Miriam Gerber was nineteen when she wrote this letter. A German Jew, she had suffered through incarceration in the Gurs internment camp in southwestern France and had just arrived in Santo Domingo (the capital of the Dominican Republic). She was overwhelmed by its beauty and the kindness of its people. Yet she brought central European prejudices with her, as can be seen in her comments about the local people she encountered. Later, she spent a semester in the capital, learning nursing, and worked as a nurse at Sosúa, where the clinic invited Jews and neighboring Dominicans to use its facilities.

Narratives about the fate of Jewish refugees in the Americas tend to focus on their limitations set by the 1924 Immigration Act in the United States and not on the places where Jews did find refuge. The Dominican Republic developed a policy to attract these Jewish refugees, as other countries failed to welcome them. The story offers a glimpse into Jewish refugee life in the Dominican Republic. It highlights refugees' first impressions of the

Dominican Republic, their stereotypes of Indigenous peoples, and their gratefulness to these same people.

PRIMARY SOURCE

The trip took from June 5 until June 15. The trip was not very pleasant, lots of storms and the resulting sea sickness. The poor, third class sleeping rooms that were very hot were also to blame. . . . [She mentions that relatives provided them with tropical-weight clothing while they waited on Ellis Island for US permission to enter Santo Domingo.] We can't use the things we brought [from Germany]. . . . In this hot climate we naturally need more . . . light clothing. . . . On July 13 we landed in Puerto Plata . . . only 20 kilometers from Sosúa. . . . The population, mostly Black and also of Portuguese and Spanish heritage, is very friendly. The houses, even the simplest ones, are very clean. Also, Black people are well dressed and more intelligent than one generally assumes. . . . When one arrives in Sosúa, which lies directly on the sea, one is spellbound by the beauty of the landscape. There is almost always a cool breeze, which makes the heat bearable. . . . Due to the climate, no one works during the midday lunch hours. . . . Everything grows here: bananas, pineapples, lemons, oranges, squash. . . . And then there are trees I've never heard of. . . . Very little has been built in Sosúa to this point, but . . . there are large communal houses for unmarried people and married couples live in small, very nice houses, two families to a house. . . . After a year, a settler receives two cows, a horse, and a donkey and the necessary feed as well as $500 credit. [The American Jewish Joint Distribution Committee, or JDC, subsidized Sosúa. These were loans to be paid back within three years.] . . . At this point there are 450 people in Sosúa.

"Miriam's Letter, 1941," Jack and Miriam Gerber Family Collection. Courtesy of Leo Baeck Institute, New York.

QUESTIONS

1. What kinds of knowledge and prejudice did the refugees bring with them?
2. What countries and what geographies (urban, rural) did most settlers come from?
3. What did the settlers notice regarding the environment they entered?
4. In what ways is Miriam's description of her new life similar to or different from the other accounts of Jews who settled in agricultural colonies in chapters 68 and 74?

83

Inter-American Jewish Conference

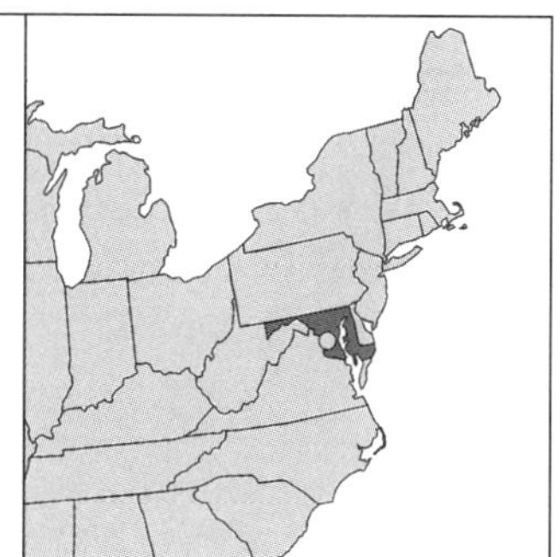

MARYLAND, 1941

Adriana M. Brodsky

After Hitler's rise to power, and in the context of Jewish suffering in Europe, several Jewish leaders began to discuss the need for a transnational organization that would work toward the creation of a Jewish state and defend Jewish people in the Diaspora. In 1936, the World Jewish Congress (WJC) was eventually founded in Switzerland, at the initiative of US Jewish leaders like Reform Rabbi Stephen S. Wise and Nahum Goldmann, among others. It was initially headquartered in Paris but moved to New York in 1940 as the war reached France. Seeking to tackle a number of issues including "Jewish migration, . . . anti-Semitism, . . . and Jews' basic human rights," the WJC believed that the existing transnational philanthropic organizations were not prepared to face the challenge the rise of Nazism posed.[1] In particular, the WJC saw itself as a political arm that could engage with the League of Nations and political leaders to demand assistance and seek solutions during these trying times. Disregarding concerns about how the existence of such a transnational organization would appear to non-Jewish eyes, the founders contended that the realities of the 1930s made it clear that Jews had to act as one to address the harsh realities that Jews were living.

The World Jewish Congress reached out to communities in Latin America. The meeting described in this source, held in Baltimore in 1941, is an example of their wish to enlist Latin American Jewish communities to help address the issue of refugees. While it was clear that the Roosevelt administration would not change the existing immigration laws that made it very difficult for Jews to escape Europe and enter the United States legally, it asked Jews in Latin American nations to lobby *their* governments to open up *their* countries to future refugees. The US administration promised to use its power to put pressure on Latin American governments to make that happen.

The "Good Neighbor Policy" departed from previous administrations' foreign policy doctrines with regard to Latin America and sought to respect the nations to the south and treat them as partners in joint projects. Nahum Goldmann, one of the founders of the

WJC, clearly articulated this idea when he visited Buenos Aires in August 1941, just a few months before the Baltimore meeting. To an enormous crowd gathered at a fund-raising event, Nahum explained that "the policy of the good neighbor and the coming together of democracies depends on the understanding [that the United States would reach] with [Argentina]." And he concluded with, "this applies also to you, its Jewish community."[2] The WJC was acting as a representative of the US administration, and it requested Jewish communities in Latin America to do their part in this hemispheric project of defending democracy from Nazism.

PRIMARY SOURCE

An appeal to Latin-American countries to adopt a more liberal policy toward admitting refugees was voiced by Under-Secretary of State Sumner Welles addressing today's session of the Inter-American Jewish Conference, which opened at the Southern Hotel here in the presence of over forty delegates from every country in Central and South America with the exception of Brazil where the government refused permission to Jews to participate in this conference. Twenty-five Jewish communities and organizations from the United States and Canada are also represented here.

Revealing that Pres. Roosevelt urged the Inter-Governmental Refugee Committee to start "a serious and expanding effort to survey in detailed fashion the geographical and economic problem of resettling several million people in new areas of the earth's surface after the war ends." Secretary Welles stated that the United States government believes that after the war there will be not one million but ten million or more refugees. He praised the Dominican Republic for being generous in permitting a Jewish settlement and declared that this settlement "conclusively demonstrated that European refugees can be resettled in sub-tropical climate and can prosper and thrive." He assured the delegates that the United States government will "participate in every practicable manner, contributing with other governments towards successful realization of that great human enterprise of making it possible for the refugees to find a safe haven."

Rabbi Stephen Wise, addressing today's session, bitterly attacked "the lamentable viewpoint of Lindbergh" and accused the flier of accepting "the spirit of Nazism." Rabbi Wise predicted that the day of the overthrow of Nazism is not far off but warned that when peace comes, Jews on the American continent will have the huge task of formulating demands for post-war restoration of Jewish life including demands for Palestine.

Moses Goldman, leader of the Argentine delegation, addressing the meeting, said: "No people can so sense the greatness of America as the Jew." He called on Jews of the entire American continent to promote pan-Americanism in contradiction to the evil forces who are busily engaged in destroying inter-American unity through racism, antisemitism and other methods of disturbing harmony among the American nations.

The prediction that three to four million Jews in Europe will perish during the war and that six or seven million Jews who may survive, will remain without any means of existence was made at the Conference today by Dr. Nahum Goldman [*sic*], leader of the World Jewish Congress. Goldman urged that "everything should be done to enable world Jewry to come

into closer contact with Russian Jewry." He said that Russia's entry into the war against Nazism changed the Soviet's international position and is bound to break the wall which separated Russian Jewry from World Jewry.

"Inter-American Jewish Conference Opens in Baltimore; Hears Sumner Welles," *Jewish Telegraphic Agency*, November 24, 1941.

QUESTIONS

1. What were some of the objectives of this meeting?
2. What are some of the clues that the WJC and the US administration were working together to achieve their aim to solve the refugee crisis?
3. How was the "Good Neighbor Policy" deployed in order to put pressure on Latin American nations to provide the refuge that Jews needed?
4. What elements of this press release highlight the idea of a pan-American Jewish identity?

NOTES

1. Segev, *World Jewish Congress during the Holocaust*, 3.
2. "En el Luna Park fué proclamada la Campaña Pro-Víctimas de la Guerra," *La Luz*, August 15, 1941.

84

Punching Hitler in World War II Comic Books

NEW YORK, 1941–1944

Laurence Roth and Mark Fertig

Popular culture provides an important way for historians to understand how everyday American Jews made sense of the struggle in Europe. While comic books' solutions were not always realistic, they show that American Jews combated the ideology of Nazism and Hitler using various means. This chapter focuses on the work of Joe Simon (1913–2011) and Jack Kirby (born Jacob Kurtzburg, 1917–1994), among the most famous creative duos in comic book history.

Simon and Kirby met in the late 1930s while trying to make it in New York's fledgling comic book industry. As with other Depression-era Jewish illustrators, publishers, and magazine distributors, they were attracted to the wide-open field of comics, which was overlooked by mainstream publishing and welcomed young, streetwise entrepreneurs like them. As employees of Timely (Marvel) Comics, they worked for the publisher Martin Goodman (1908–1992), the son of Jewish immigrants like themselves, who hoped that his comics could be used to sway the public against Nazism despite the isolationist attitudes of the time. Goodman immediately saw the potential of Captain America—known as Cap—a character created by Simon and Kirby in the fall of 1940. For Simon, Cap offered "a chance to make a mockery of the Nazis and their mad leader."[1] Kirby's legendary cover of Cap throwing a massive roundhouse at Hitler's face and breaking up his "Sabotage Plans for U.S.A." is an iconic work of wish fulfillment. In the guise of a superpatriotic superhero, a trio of US Jews exercised their desire to warn their country of the danger that Hitler posed and to strike back, if only imaginatively, at the man responsible for the loss of their relatives' freedoms, homes, and lives.

The 1941 cover earned Simon and Kirby death threats from Nazi supporters but persuaded others, young and old, to see Hitler as an enemy who opposed their values and needed to be destroyed. It became one of the most enduring wartime images of how to confront evil, reimagined countless times by both Jewish and non-Jewish illustrators alike, as shown by the examples by Al Gabriele, Alex Schomburg, and Alex Kotzky included here. Gabriele's cover portrays Hitler and the Japanese as both alien laughingstocks and barbaric objects of fear. Schomburg's disturbing cover features the Commando Cubs, a "kid gang" that young readers were meant to identify with, including their delight in violence. The heroes, including the racist stereotype Pokey Jones, give Hitler the third degree while Mussolini hides under the bed, his cowardice linked with homosexuality and villainy. Kotzky's Hitler is the embodiment of the illicit marketeering and economic double-dealing that deserve Uncle Sam's wallop. These covers both reflected and helped construct what valor, patriotism, and identity meant in the United States during this era, meanings whose influence lasted long after the war ended.

Kirby's Captain America cover is a landmark of comics history and is an important example of how US Jewish comic book creators imagined an American identity that was both modern and inclusive. Similar to the Jewish Hollywood moguls of the day, Kirby's, Simon's, and Goodman's wartime creations defined a number of enduring American values that reinforced their conception of the American Dream. But Captain America's origins in World War II ground those values in the context of power—what it means to have it and what is at stake in using it to pursue justice. While the question of how to wield political and martial power responsibly is one that troubles the modern history of Jewish national and cultural self-determination, the fantasy of punching Hitler is specifically an American Jewish one. For whether the image is of Cap or Quentin Tarantino's Bear Jew in *Inglourious Bastards*, it embodies a tantalizing belief about power and striking back at evil: that a punch, thrown by the righteous, results in a morally happy outcome, that in the end, justice feels like satisfaction. Given the resurgence of violent antisemitism in the US, this aspect of US Jewish history is still as relevant and perplexing as ever.[2]

PRIMARY SOURCES

See following pages.

QUESTIONS

1. Each of these covers uses humor in its depiction of Hitler. Why do you think humor was important for the illustrators?
2. Look carefully at each cover's details. What do they tell us about the values and attitudes promoted by these comic books?
3. What does it suggest about US wartime culture to see children, such as the Commando Cubs or Captain America's sidekick, Bucky, engaged in such violence?
4. Compare Hitler here with his representation in chapter 78 and Adolf Eichmann in chapter 106. What differences and similarities strike you?

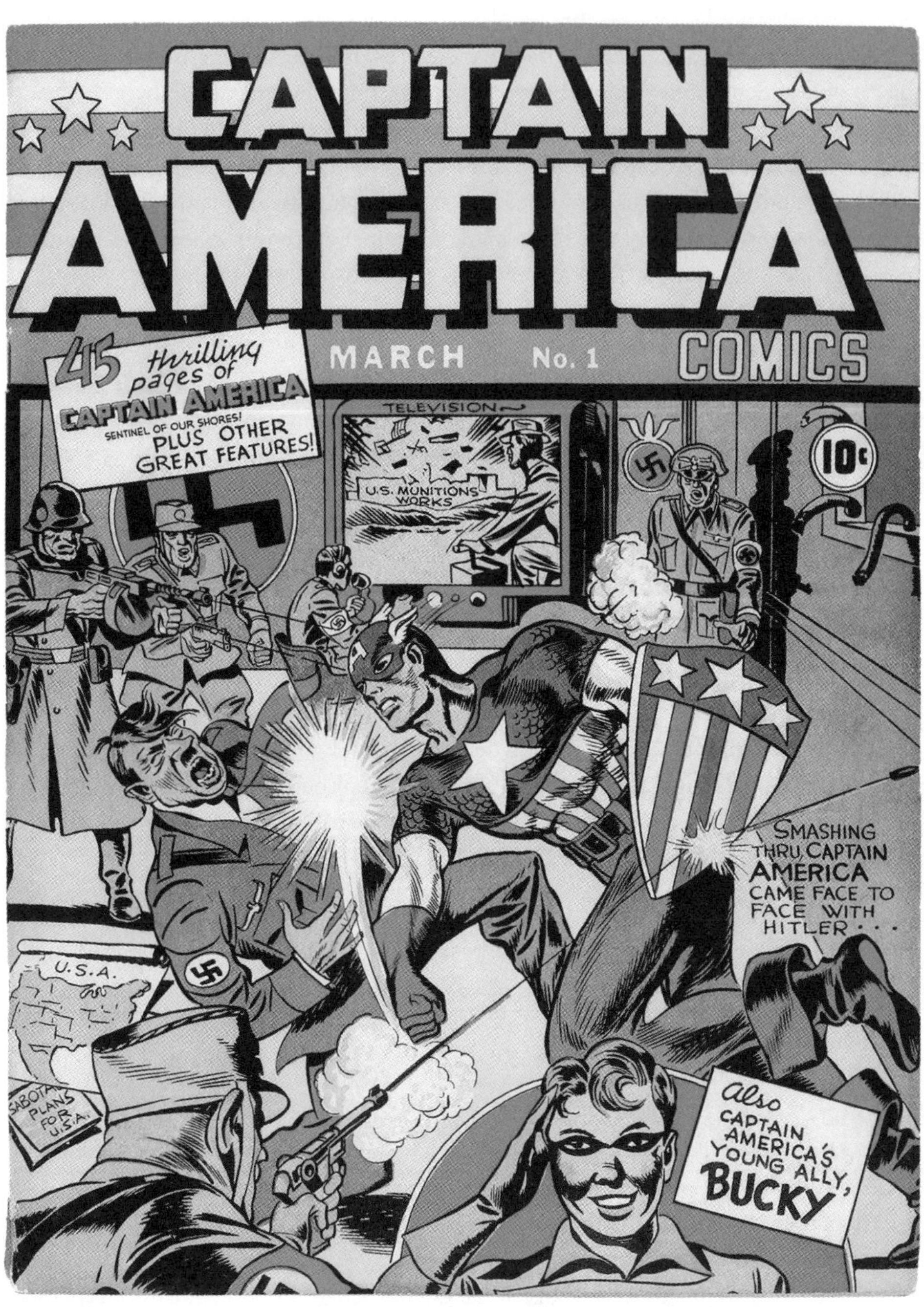

Joe Simon and Jack Kirby, *Captain America Comics* #1 (March 1941), Timely Comics.

Al Gabriele, *Mystic Comics* #9 (May 1942).

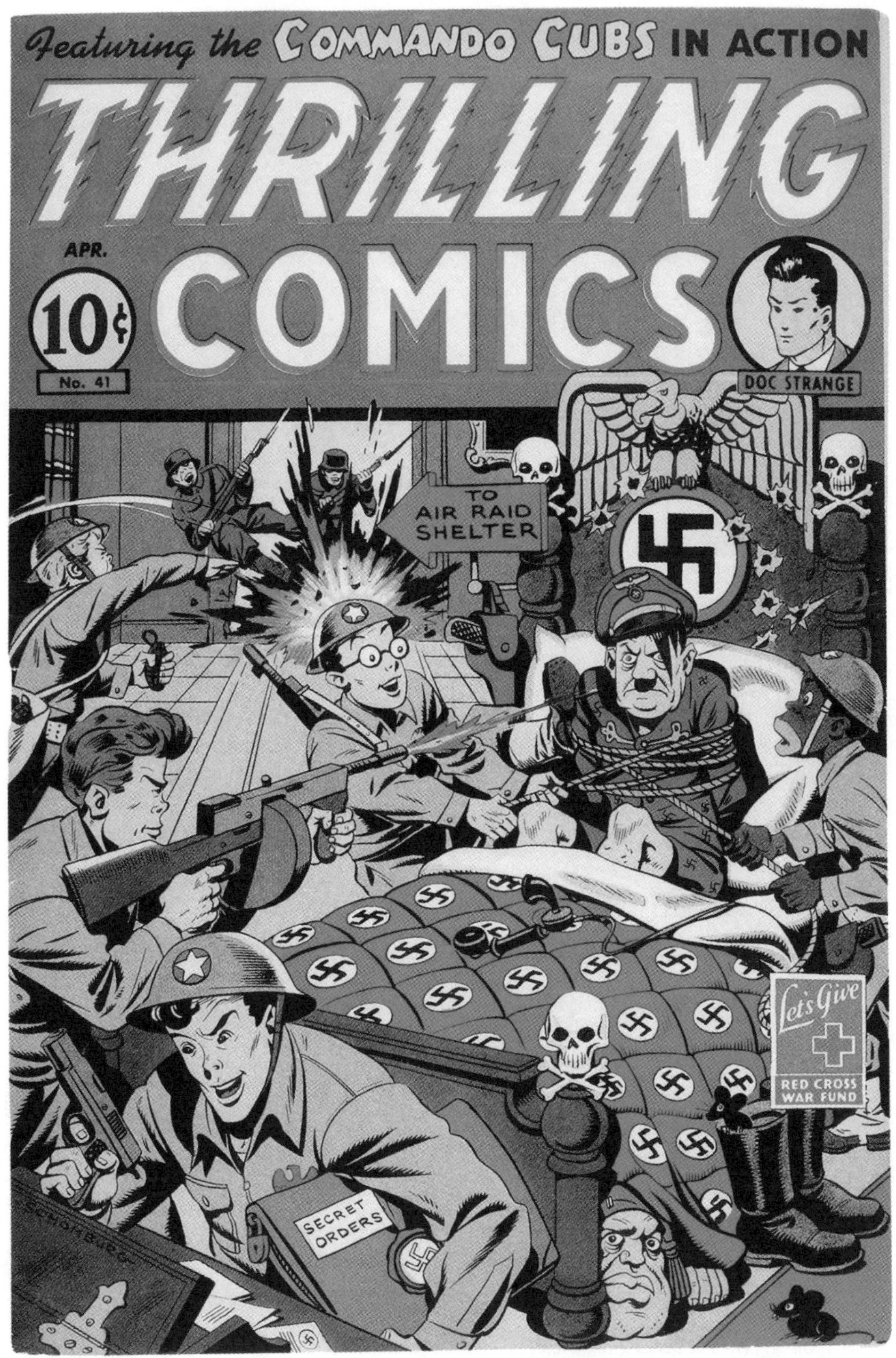

Alex Schomburg, *Thrilling Comics* #41 (April 1944), Nedor.

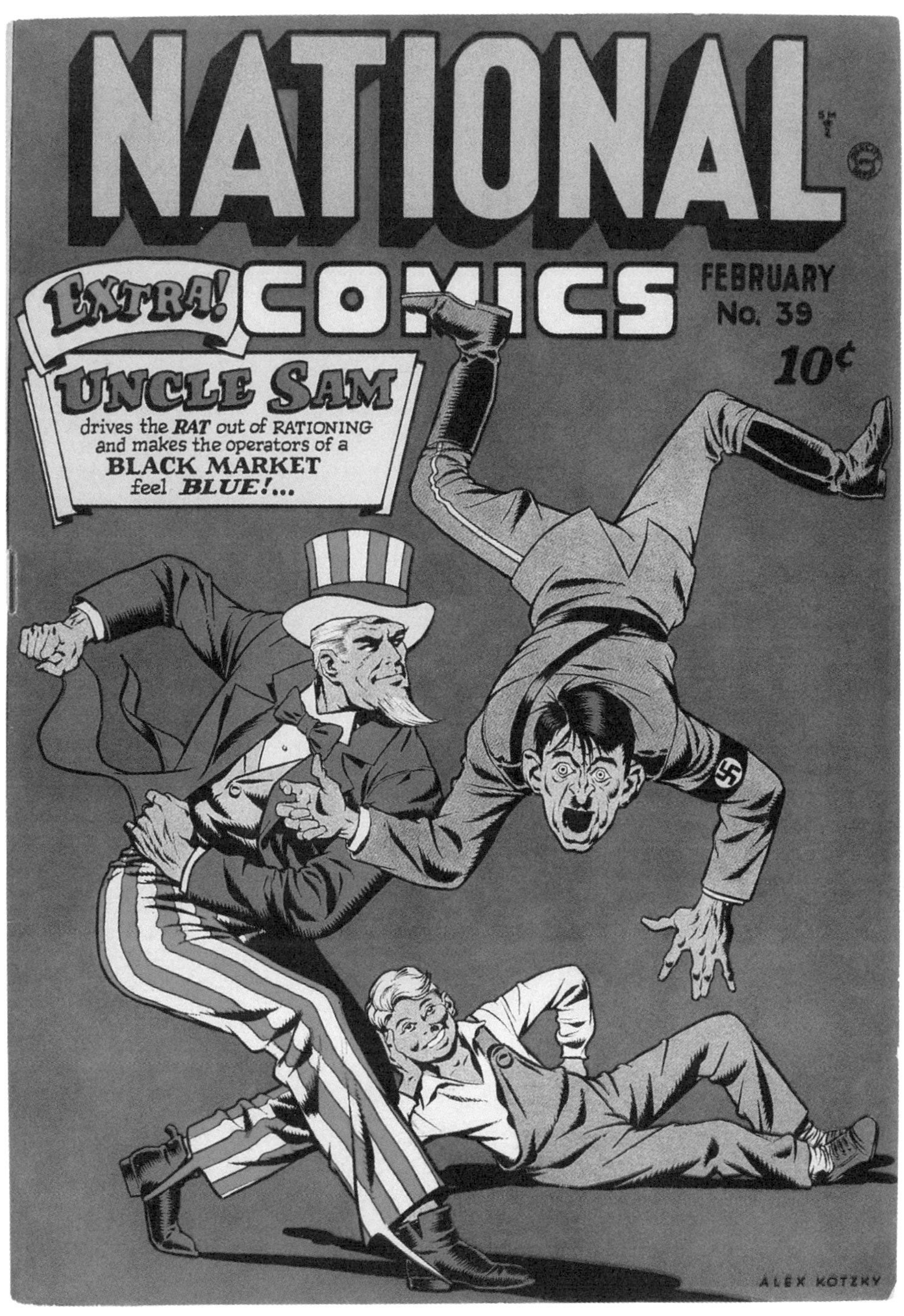

Alex Kotzky, *National Comics* #39 (February 1944), Quality Comics. (Courtesy of Fantagraphics Books)

NOTES

1. Simon and Simon, *Comic Book Makers*, 50.
2. This chapter contains parts of prior work written by the authors: Fertig, *Take That, Adolf!*; and Roth, "Coda."

85

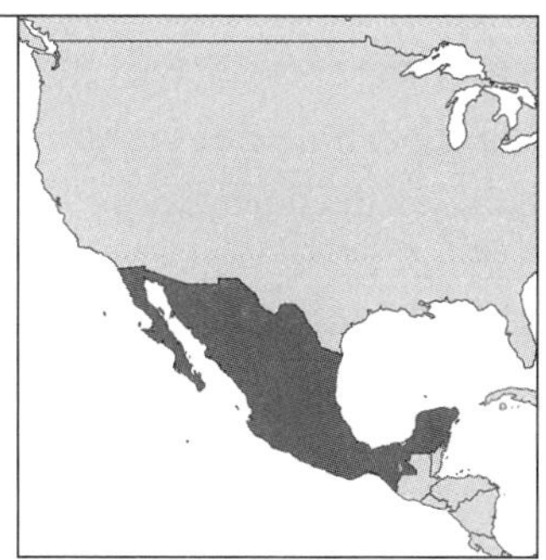

Fighting for Mexican Visas during World War II

MEXICO, 1942

Tamara Gleason Freidberg

As the war spread, a variety of Jewish organizations worked to get entry visas for Jews and political refugees stranded in nonoccupied Europe and Africa. One of these organizations was the Jewish Labor Committee (JLC), founded in New York in 1934, which sought to combat Nazi and fascist activity; in particular, it worked to secure US visas to members of the Bund (the General Union of Jewish Workers in Lithuania, Poland, and Russia) and Social Democrats who were being persecuted back in Europe. Once the JLC was no longer able to get more visas for the US, it tried to get Mexican visas. As we have seen previously, countries south of the Rio Grande became entry points to the Americas.

In Mexico, the organization in charge of securing these visas was the Gezelshaft far Kultur un Hilf (Association for Culture and Aid; GFKH), which was associated with the JLC. The JLC sent the lists of names of the refugees as well as money to cover expenses, while the Mexican organization dealt with the local bureaucracy. The GFKH managed to bring only around fifty refugees to Mexico due to the bureaucratic barriers of the immigration process in that country. While dozens of visas were approved by the Mexican government after much GFKH work, Gilberto Bosques (the Mexican consul in Marseille) refused to actually issue them. As a result, several refugees stranded in Marseille were not able to travel to Mexico and were later killed in extermination camps.

In this letter, written in Yiddish in April 1942, the secretary of the GFKH explains to the JLC the difficulties in obtaining the Mexican government's permission to issue the visas, in the aftermath of Gilberto Bosques's intervention. As well, the letter portrays the resistance of the Mexican government and specific diplomats to issuing visas to Jews and the corruption involved in the process. Bosques, until recently, was perceived, by the general public and academics alike, as an exceptional bureaucrat who challenged the Mexican discretionary anti-Jewish immigration regulations and saved Jewish lives. Although Bosques helped rescue thousands of Spanish Republicans from Franco's regime and a few Jewish communists stranded in Marseille, the JLC archival corpus on Mexican immigration and some documents recently found in the archives of the Secretaría de Relaciones Exteriores (Exterior Ministry) have clearly shown that Bosques refused visas to Jewish refugees by requesting pointless documentation—including proof that they were actually refugees.

Some of the sources regarding American Jewish responses to the Holocaust have been previously overlooked because they were written in Yiddish. This methodological problem resulted in erroneous interpretations about how Jews in the Americas reacted to the Holocaust. Analysis of Yiddish letters like this one and the Yiddish press continue to debunk the myth of silence in Jewish communities during and after the Holocaust. As well, this two-page letter shows how Jewish ideological organizations established transnational networks across the Americas to save refugees during World War II, using Yiddish as the language for communication.

PRIMARY SOURCE

9th of April, 1942

Jewish Labor Committee in New York.
Dear comrade Pat!
I answer hereby to your letters from March. . . . It took me long to reply because I do not have positive news and therefore, I have not written to you. Although there are no concrete achievements to announce I have to answer you. Nevertheless, we have received promises again. We were promised that they will handle around 20 [visa requests]. God willing, if this happens, I will not waste one minute and will send you a telegram immediately. . . .

Now, related to the topic of the visas, it has already been around 3 weeks since this impasse began. I do not know why. There are several hypotheses. It is said that your [US] government may be extremely careful in allowing immigrants in. They likely would want nobody to get in. . . . Others say that there are intrigues among different officers and therefore nobody ends up with anything. I personally think that this is not true. It was simply . . . holidays. Officially Pesakh [Passover], (which coincides with the Catholic Holy Week) is not a holiday and the bureaus are open as usual but in reality, nobody is doing anything. All the officers find excuses and travel out of the city for a couple of days. . . .

. . . We are not sure when exactly we will receive the visas. They have promised us that today or tomorrow they will bring them to us, but we also see other visas being issued, so. . . . If you have other chances to get the visas in another country, do try that. . . .

We have handed back the corrections for the visas of the next group of people, especially, as you announced given the problems encountered in Marseille with the Consul. A petition to the Consul in Marseille by the representative of Friedrich Adler will be sent to request him to give us the visas. . . .

With regards from your comrades,
Sh. Jezior

Shimen Jezior to Yankev Pat of the Jewish Labor Committee, April 9, 1942, in Yiddish, Part I: Holocaust Era Files, Series III: Foreign Countries, box 34, folder 10, microfilm 2102, Tamiment Library and Robert F. Wagner Labor Archive, New York University, New York, NY.

QUESTIONS

1. What does the writer identify as the problems encountered in Mexico for securing the entry visas?
2. What other forms of communication were these organizations using? What seems to have made them decide to write letters? How is this relevant for historians?
3. What does the letter suggest about how taxing, time-consuming, and uncertain this process was?

86

Hadassah and the "Arab Issue" in Palestine

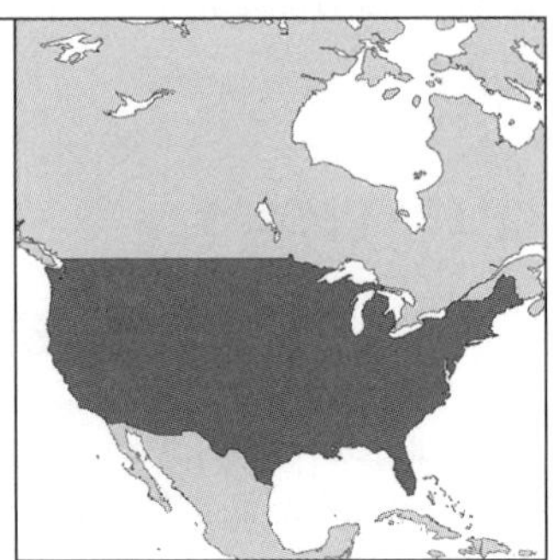

UNITED STATES, 1942

Zohar Segev

Hadassah, the Women's Zionist Organization of America, was established by Henrietta Szold (a German American Jew) in 1912. By the 1930s, it was the largest Zionist organization in the United States. Hadassah's work centered on improving the welfare and health of the Jews living in Palestine long before the establishment of the state, but it also pursued the objective of spreading Zionist ideals in the US among women and youth. Hadassah was instrumental in setting up Youth Aliyah, a project founded by the Zionist movement in 1933 to rescue Jewish children from Europe and bring them to Palestine (and later to the new State of Israel) prior to, during, and following World War II and the Holocaust.

In 1933, Hadassah became officially independent from the Zionist Organization of America, making it possible for Hadassah to enter Zionist politics on its own and to pursue projects of its choosing. Hadassah's president Rose Jacobs (1930–1932, 1934–1937) was elected to the Jewish Agency Executive in 1937. Although she resigned shortly after, given her disappointment at not being assigned any responsibilities, Jacobs fought to make women part of Zionist politics in Palestine. In particular, Hadassah became concerned with the issue of Arab-Jewish relations, which led to the creation of the Committee on Jewish-Arab Relations. Hadassah hoped that understanding the Palestinian Arabs' opposition to Zionism could lead to a peaceful solution of the Palestine problem. Composed of both Hadassah officials and outsiders, the committee's members included Rose Halperin (president, 1932–1934, 1947–1951), Etta Rosensohn (president, 1952–1953), the historian Salo Baron, and the American Zionist leader Emanuel Neumann. Conflict arose between Hadassah leaders and the Zionist establishment in Palestine. At the center of the conflict lay the question of whether American Zionist women had the right to address "the Arab issue," namely, what to do about the Arab peoples living on the land that Zionists wanted to settle.

During the 1930s and 1940s, Rose Jacobs in particular and Hadassah in general made important and unprecedented inroads into the Zionist establishment. The political, international, and economic crises of the 1930s and 1940s enabled Hadassah to expand out of the traditionally female areas to which it had originally been restricted (health and education) and make its voice heard on other issues, among them Jewish-Arab relations. Hadassah broke the limitations under which Jewish women's organizations had theretofore operated and used its newfound influence to offer alternatives to the male Zionist leadership's cultural, social, and political doctrines.

The story of Hadassah leaders' involvement in Zionist politics in the 1940s demonstrates the importance of integrating women's history into general historical research and, in particular, into research on the history of Zionism and the American Jewish community. Hadassah leaders carried on meaningful political activity and participated in broad historical processes within the Zionist movement. Although they were involved in Zionist politics for a relatively short time, their activity took place during the most critical of all modern periods for the Jewish people, a time when the basic elements of Jewish nationality were fashioned. To recognize the uniqueness of what Hadassah leaders did in the 1940s is to reexamine basic issues in Zionist history. A case in point is their involvement in the Arab issue in the source included here. Their position sheds new light on the options that were possibly available to the Zionist movement in this regard. A historical narrative that may appear exclusively female and American thus becomes one that reflects Zionist history as a whole.

PRIMARY SOURCE

Copy of a letter from Henrietta Szold to Mrs. Jacobs. Received April 24, 1942
(Note: Since this is a personal letter, it must be considered *strictly confidential.*)

Jerusalem, March 10, 1942

Dear Rose Jacobs:
Yesterday I wrote you a personal letter, and today I am again writing a personal letter but while putting my thoughts on paper I shall have before my eyes Rose Jacobs, my friend indeed, but more particularly in her capacity as Chairman of the Committee dealing with the subject of the Arab-Jewish relations. We all who are following Zionist development in the United States rejoiced when the information reached us that you were going to head the group that is to go into our outstanding problem with a view to a practical application of the findings. . . .

. . . When I planned to write to you on the Arab question one of the considerations I had in mind to bring up was the method of approaching the second in my trilogy of dealings with the involved question just mentioned—judgment. You, with the help of Dr. Perlmann, your research worker, will amass raw material of mountainous proportions. It cannot be otherwise in studying a problem that goes back to Isaac and Ishmael, to Jacob and Esau, and winds its labyrinthian way through the Middle Ages into our times and penetrates into every cultural cranny, religion, art, science, custom, politics, life in the whole. It seems to me

that with the end we have in view at present—how to shape our action towards our political, material goal—we have to be thinking first and foremost of the character of the goal we want to reach. Simply: Do we want a Jewish state, or do we want Palestine as a home for our people, a home in which our people can develop freely and wholly in accordance with its history, its law, its cultural needs and aspirations? . . .

We may argue until doomsday that the Arabs can afford to give up Palestine since they are the masters of a vast expanse of territory in which Palestine protrudes no more than by a pin's head. The argument is of no avail unless it is accepted by those who are vested by public opinion or public indifference with the power of decision, notably by the Arabs themselves. Argument will not prevail, no matter how clamorously or how brilliantly we demonstrate that for the very sake of the world, the "Jewish question" must be solved and put out of the world. The Arabs and others in the seats of the mighty may assent that the tiresome Jewish problem should be made to disappear, but why in this way, by means of Palestine. True, there exists a political document, the Balfour Declaration, which demonstrates incontrovertibly—it assumes authoritatively—the historical connection of the Jew with Palestine. But we and those others live in a "realistic" world in which wars of conquest are still decisive. In that "realistic" world, possession is nine points in the law, and the Arabs are in possession.

The premises suggest the use of two instrumentalities—force and negotiation. The first instrumentality does not lie in our hands, neither as diplomats nor as fighters. It can be wielded only by those who will sit at the peace table, which thus would be turned into a table of incipient warfare, exactly as the Versailles peace table as it were, authorized renewed wars. The other instrumentality negotiation does lie in our hands—negotiation first and foremost directly with the Arabs themselves, and secondarily with others, for want of a better expression I repeat, "who will sit at the peace table." . . . Our Jewish life problem in its Arab phases will call for a reciprocal attitude between Jew and Arab first of all, and between the "others" on the one side and Jew and Arab together on the other side. . . .

Of one thing I want to assure you, that all of us here who know you and the problem as well are deeply satisfied that you are devoting yourself to the investigation. We are convinced that under your chairmanship the Committee will be made to respond to the solemn responsibility involved in its task.

My fond love to you
Affectionately,
Henrietta Szold

Henrietta Szold to Mrs. Jacobs, March 10, 1942, A123/191, Central Zionist Archives, Yosef Herlits St 2, Jerusalem, Israel.

QUESTIONS

1. In the letter, Szold presents two options for action regarding how the Zionist movement can deal with the Arab question. What are the two options, and which option did Szold prefer?
2. What can we learn from the document about Henrietta Szold and Rose Jacobs's worldview from their desired relationship between Jews and Arabs in Palestine?
3. Hadassah is an American Jewish women's organization. Why do you think the organization's members chose to operate mainly in Palestine? What does this choice tell us about American Jewry between the wars?

87

Ladino Songs

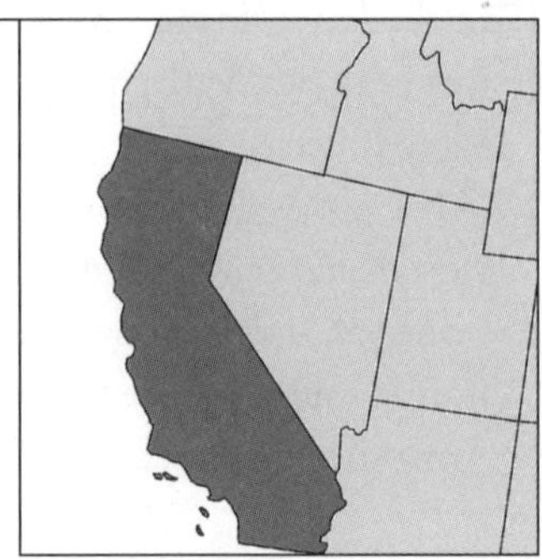

CALIFORNIA, 1942–1979

Simone Salmon

As we have seen in previous chapters, music played an important role in Jewish American life, at times helping immigrants adjust to their new surroundings and at other times helping them maintain connections to the past (chapters 54 and 81). Popular songs, whether in Ladino or in Yiddish, like Jevel Katz's lyrics, can help us better understand the Jewish working class. Emily Sene, a sweatshop seamstress and an amateur archivist from Silivri, Turkey, met her husband, Isaac Sene, in Havana, Cuba, while awaiting admittance into the United States. A carpet layer born in Edirne, Turkey, Isaac Sene was an oudist and singer who performed at Turkish, Greek, Arab, and Hispanophone events. Isaac possessed an encyclopedic knowledge of Judeo-Spanish (Ladino) songs, and Emily collected and transcribed Ladino lyrics in the different cities through which the two of them traveled: Miami, New York, Los Angeles, Tijuana, and other locales. The Senes moved to Los Angeles to overcome poverty. During 1945–1979, there were weekly picnics in Los Angeles and Orange County at which the Ottoman Sephardic community would gather to hear Judeo-Spanish songs played live by Greek, Turkish, Armenian, and Jewish musicians. Isaac had a large following at these performances. The majority of the Sephardim in attendance had left the Ottoman Empire at the time of its transition into the Republic of Turkey, hence the picnic's name, "Turktown." As the Sephardim established themselves in the Americas, they brought with them the stylistic traces of the land and relationships that they left behind.

Like "Der arbetslozer ganef," the songs collected by Emily Senes sometimes talked about taboo subjects. The song "El hermano infame," for example, deals with incest between siblings. In it, a man demands a marriage to his orphaned sister and kills her after she refuses his advances. Its origin is in the Iberian Peninsula, and it was probably commissioned for a group of blind boys in the nineteenth century as part of "la literatura de cordel," a practice in which pamphlets containing songs and poems were strung for sale across city squares. The events in the song happened in the town of Santa Amalia in Iberian versions or in

Santa Elena in Sephardic versions. Emily Sene's version of the song appears to be a combination of two existing versions (one Mediterranean and one from Cuba/Puerto Rico), which makes sense given her stay in Cuba before her immigration to the United States.

Variants of "El hermano infame" have been collected from Colombia, Puerto Rico, Costa Rica, the Dominican Republic, Mexico, Morocco, Turkey, Yugoslavia, Bulgaria, and Rhodes. The lyrics resulting from Emily Sene's migration are a hybrid that share their ending with the Mexican *corrido* (a narrative octosyllabic genre of song). This demonstrates the global lengths to which one popular song, brought to the Ottoman Empire by Sephardim, can travel, encapsulating Hispanophone audiences across time in every hemisphere.

PRIMARY SOURCE

El hermano infame [The Infamous Brother]

In Santa Elena lived a young girl,
As beautiful as jasmine.
She worked alone
Embroidering clothing for Madrid.

At thirteen the young beauty
Was left without a father or mother
Under the protection of a cruel brother,
A rascal who fell in love with her.

"My sister," he told her one day,
"My dearest sister,
Your beauty makes me crazy
And I want to be your husband."

The young beauty was shocked.
Quietly she replied,
"I'd rather die a thousand times
Than have you besmirch my honor."

The evil brother picked up a knife
And thrust himself over his sister.
"Oh, brother, don't kill me.
I only live thanks to your protection."

The young beauty met her doom.
He quietly picked up her body.
There was a small field right in front.
That is where he buried her.

She was found by dogs
Because of the stench;
Three peasants passed by
And realized the crime had taken place.

The killer, in front of her corpse
Was crying out of remorse.
They asked him
If he was the one who killed her:

"I killed her out of love,
because I wanted her as a wife.
My sister, you will go to heaven
I will pay for this in prison."

Sephardic Temple Tifereth Israel Archive, Special Collections, University of California, Los Angeles.

QUESTIONS

1. How and why do you think certain songs have been repurposed over time and across cultures?
2. What does "El hermano infame" say about the male-female power differential?
3. How can music, art, and literature be used as primary sources?
4. How does the discussion of love here compare with that in chapters 13, 29, and 70?

88

Frieda Schiff Warburg's Jewish Museum

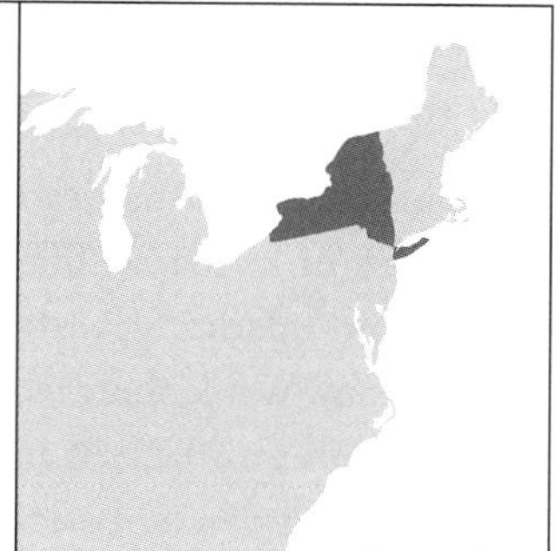

NEW YORK, 1944

Ariel Paige Cohen

This chapter reveals Frieda Schiff Warburg's decision to highlight and make visible Jewish life in the United States in the midst of Jewish destruction in Europe. Frieda Schiff Warburg (1876–1958) was born in New York City's Upper East Side among a cadre of German Jewish elites. Her mother, Therese Loeb, was from a prominent family of German Jewish immigrants. Her parents exposed her, from an early age, to the arts, culture, and philanthropy. Both were exceptionally and widely involved in giving; they ran settlement houses, donated artworks and money to museums, organized literary clubs, financed the library at the Jewish Theological Seminary (JTS), and more. Yet, as a woman living in the early twentieth-century US, Schiff Warburg was limited in her independent philanthropic expression. While she learned to speak then-masculine languages of power and wealth, giving her own objects and money to museums, libraries, JTS, and other Jewish communities, she was not always publicly acknowledged or understood in her power.

After Schiff Warburg's husband died, she still had tremendous wealth and the tools and connections to influence New York City's Jewish community as well as its arts scene. Schiff Warburg became the first and, for most of her tenure, the only woman to serve on the Board of Trustees of the JTS. She donated her mansion to inaugurate a Jewish museum on New York's famous Fifth Avenue. Through cultural philanthropy, she increased the perceptibility of the arts and of Jews in the US, in spite of the ways in which she was socially and societally limited by her gender.

Schiff Warburg's letter included here reveals some of the factors that both cultivated and constrained the power of American and Jewish women. By choosing to donate her own mansion, emphasizing that the donation was not a memorial for her husband, Schiff Warburg expressed her own desires for the future of the space. At the same time, she leaned on references to the men of her upbringing and life to legitimize the expression of her own power. Through her letter and the donation it represented, Schiff Warburg fundamentally shifted the boundaries of acceptability for (Jewish) American women. While her gift housed exhibitions that ultimately helped fashion American Jewish identity within its galleries, Schiff Warburg herself also curated a new kind of American femininity outside the museum's walls and profoundly altered the course of American, Jewish, and curatorial histories. Other women followed her lead by expressing their own cultural philanthropy; the Jewish community ultimately accepted her leadership and allowed space for more women to mold and shape American Jewish culture.

The gift of Frieda Schiff Warburg's home to JTS launched one of the most important episodes in American Jewish history: the birth of the flagship cultural institution, the Jewish Museum. While there were two other Jewish museums in Cincinnati and in Boston at the time, this was the first autonomous space to display Jewish objects that was not physically attached to a rabbinical school or synagogue. The museum housed curatorial questions, conversations, and expressions about how best to self-represent Jews and became a project that reflected back the questions of American Jews about how to fit into an American democracy, how to represent themselves, and how to stake a claim to a Judeo-Christian heritage in a country that built Christians and Jews into its own fabric from the very start.

PRIMARY SOURCES

Jan. 14, 1944

Dear Dr. Finkelstein:

After my conferences with Alan Stroock and with the consent of my children, I am now ready and glad to offer my former home at 1109 Fifth Avenue and the adjoining fifty foot lot, if the latter can be freed from paying taxes, to the Jewish Seminary of America to be used as a Museum and for the further purposes as outlined in your statement of plans to me.

I would like my gift to be entered as under date of January 14th, 1944, my husband's seventy-third birthday. It is not specifically a memorial to him, but rather my affirmation of my faith in the fundamental principles of our Jewish Traditions, which can be helpful and constructive in the problems of our World Today, and also my tribute to the men of my family, my father, my husband and my brother Mortimer, who each in his own way has done so much to build up the Seminary towards its present effective usefulness.

It gives me great happiness to think that the house that my dear husband built thirty-six years ago as his conception of Beauty and Dignity and which for so many years harbored our harmonious family life and was always open to Community interests, should now continue to live on to further the ideals of our family traditions.

With the wish that 1109 Fifth Avenue will fulfill all these hopes and that many new years of usefulness lie ahead for it, in its new transformation,

Believe me,
Sincerely
[signed] Frieda Schiff Warburg

Frieda Schiff Warburg to Louis Finkelstein, January 14, 1944, Felix M. and Frieda Schiff Warburg Scrapbooks, ARC.1000.167, 1937–1951, box 2, JTS Library Archives, New York, NY.

The Warburg mansion, New York, NY. (Photograph, 2020, WC)

QUESTIONS

1. Describe the tone of Frieda Schiff Warburg's letter. Why might she have announced her gift in this way?
2. Frieda Schiff Warburg invokes several men in her letter: her lawyer, Alan Stroock; her son, Edward Warburg; her husband, Felix Warburg; her brother, Mortimer Schiff; and her father, Jacob Schiff. Why might she have included them so prominently in her letter?
3. Frieda Schiff Warburg and her husband belonged to Temple Emanu-El. How does the style and tone of the family's mansion compare to the mausoleums found in chapter 61?
4. Compare the façade of the merchant house of a convicted Judaizer (chapter 5) to that of the Warburg mansion. What message does each send about Jews' relationship to the city in which they lived?

89

A Rabbi Counsels a Gay Jewish GI

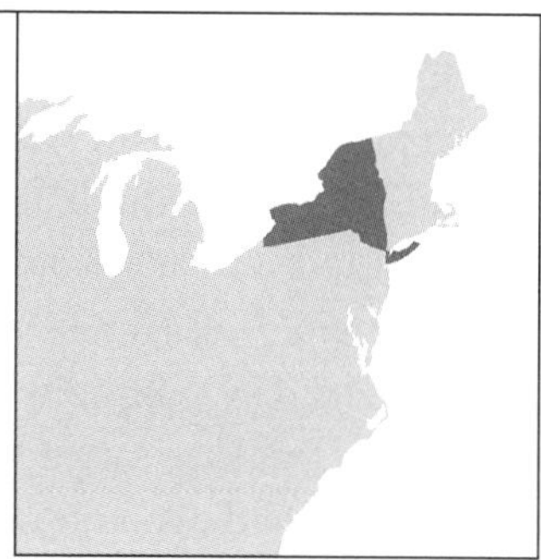

NEW YORK, 1944

Noam Sienna

The years between the world wars spelled both promise and repression for queer Jews. This is a letter by US Reform Rabbi Bernard J. Bamberger (1904–1980) to one of his congregants, Allen (also spelled Alan) Bernstein (1913–2008), a Jewish US soldier who had just been discharged from the army for homosexuality. In January 1944, Bernstein was arrested after picking up a fellow soldier while stationed at Fort Lee, Virginia, and given a "less-than-honorable" discharge. From the letter, it seems that Bernstein had written to Bamberger explaining his situation and perhaps asking for advice; Bamberger's response is an unusually candid reflection on the problems facing an American Jewish homosexual GI in the 1940s.

This letter appears to be part of an ongoing relationship (in the letter, Bamberger alludes to "a letter written a long time ago" and an earlier conversation from 1937), although unfortunately no other correspondence between the two men has survived. Bamberger concludes his letter by saying that he is about to take up a post in New York City. This was congregation Shaaray Tefila in Manhattan, where he served from 1944 to 1971 (and then as rabbi emeritus until his death). President of the Central Conference of American Rabbis (1959–1961) and the World Union for Progressive Judaism (1970–1972) and involved in the Jewish Publication Society's revision of its English Bible, Bamberger is regarded as one of the most influential figures of the American Reform movement of the mid-twentieth century.

Like many who enlisted during World War II, Allen Bernstein was inspired, at least in part, by his Jewish heritage and desire to help aid the war effort in Europe. But while his entrance into the army was typical of US Jewish history—about five hundred thousand Jewish soldiers enlisted—his departure was less so: Allen Bernstein was issued a Section 8 discharge from the US military for homosexuality. Thousands of US soldiers were given so-called blue discharges (named for their blue paper) between 1942 and 1946, although few testimonies from gay Jewish GIs remain. Remarkably, Bernstein was already "out" among his friends and colleagues as early as the late 1930s, and in 1940, he authored a 149-page manifesto, titled *Millions of Queers (Our Homo America)*, which provides rare insight into the experience of a gay Jewish American at a time when the very concept of modern gay identity was just beginning to coalesce. Perhaps Bernstein's unusual openness about his identity contributed to Bamberger's equally remarkable frankness about Bernstein's "problems of social adjustment," while assuring Bernstein that he would always find Bamberger "a sympathetic friend." This letter is the first known document in which a US rabbi addressed homosexuality; the next would be the fictionalized novel of Rabbi Israel J. Gerber, *Man on a Pendulum: A Case History of an Invert* (1955), published a decade later.

In general, US rabbis did not make public statements about homosexuality until the early 1960s. This letter, intended for private readership, is a glimpse into one rabbi's attempt to make sense of the complexities of changing ideas about sexuality and identity in the mid-century US; it shows his early struggle to balance his commitments to his understanding of Jewish law, his concern for respectability, his growing understanding of homosexuality as an immutable facet of identity, and his personal and pastoral relationships.

The mid-twentieth century was a time of great change, as large numbers of US Jews (mostly, like Bernstein, the children of immigrants) increasingly assimilated into mainstream American culture, with attendant values like the emphasis on heteronormative family life. The experience of LGBTQ Jews, for whom that vision was unattainable, adds nuance to our picture of Jewish life in the United States. The fact that Bernstein sought comfort and guidance in the pastoral relationship reminds us that the typical documents that survive of Jewish life—books, newspaper reports, published sermons, and the like—do not always capture the emotions, experiences, and relationships that shaped people's lives.

PRIMARY SOURCE

Congregation Beth Emeth
Albany, N.Y.
Bernard J. Bamberger, D. D., Rabbi
106 Melrose Ave.

February 10, 1944.

Dear Alan:
I needn't say that I am deeply distressed over the news your letter contained. While you know that I shall not indulge in the rhodomontades [i.e., blustering] of your c.o. [commanding officer], nor draw away from you like the chaplains of whom you wrote, I am not at all sure that I am in the mood to give you much spiritual comfort. Indeed, your cheerful admission that you "semi-deliberately" got yourself into this mess, while commendable for honesty, seems to me to make the whole thing worse, and inspires me to offer you a good swift kick in the pants.

In a letter written a long time ago, I expressed my doubts as to how deep-seated and genuine were the homosexual tendencies which you avowed, and suggested that they might represent a short cut solution to some of your problems of social adjustment. Whether there was anything in this theory or not, is something only a competent psychiatrist could determine—and even that may be questioned. However, supposing that you are a classic

sample of the sexual invert, I still find no reasonable explanation of what has happened. An acceptance of the facts as they are—the means by which you feel you have unified a schizoid personality—is not a license to be a damn fool, on the ground that this is *Kismet* [destiny]. Does the recognition that a desire exists necessitate its fulfillment at all costs? I don't put you on a level, mentally or otherwise, with those heterosexual buddies of yours who take it for granted that when they feel the urge they must get a woman at once, regardless of what she is. And even these crude sensualists generally realize that they must refrain from rape, and that they must be a bit cautious as to whom they solicit. There are lots of normal, healthy men who find it possible to restrain their sexual impulses for long periods of time, without serious physical or mental harm to themselves, and without loss of sexual capacity when a proper outlet is afforded them. By the same token, it beats me why a person whose sexual life is less conventional, and who is intelligent enough to know that many people regard his ways as depraved and horrible, should not observe simple prudence in regard to it.

What's done is done. I wouldn't even indulge in what you may regard as reproach, if it weren't of some importance for the rest of your life. At the present time, you will be able to find some sort of job, possibly a remunerative one. But your entire future depends on your making a much more extensive adjustment than the one you made in 1937, and which was apparently an adjustment of your inner life. You have yet to make an adequate vocational adjustment anywhere except in the army—and damn it, that's why I get so mad at the way in which you tossed your career overboard. God knows I don't regard money as the chief end and aim in life; nevertheless everybody ought to find some line of work for himself which he can do with satisfaction to himself and with honor, and which will provide him with a measure of economic security. He also ought to find some sort of social milieu, which cannot be based entirely on similarity of sexual tastes. These two problems remain to be worked out. They cannot ever lead to satisfactory conclusions if you are going to drift about casually, and if you are going to get yourself periodically into police courts.

Can psychiatry help you to advance beyond your present state to one of heterosexuality? And if such a development is possible, would you be willing to attempt such a course of treatment? These are the first questions to be answered. If you can't or won't be other than you are, then I have no doubt that in the larger cities you can find congenial companionship; but you will have to observe such discretion as everybody else in the world has to practice.

You will always find me a sympathetic friend, and it's precisely for that reason that I have spoken my piece as frankly and directly as I have. I'm very glad that you felt free to write to me when you did, and hope you will always call upon me if I can help you. As to the interpretation of the Book of Job, we'll take that up another time.

By this time you may have heard that I am accepting a call to a pulpit in New York—a fact which may in the future make it possible for us to meet more frequently. It is also a call for many adjustments, which I hope we will be able to meet successfully.

Always yours faithfully,
BJB

Bernard J. Bamberger to Allen Bernstein, February 10, 1944, Bernstein Family Collection, published with the permission of the Bernstein family and Randall Sell.

QUESTIONS

1. How does Bamberger respond to the stereotypes and internalized beliefs of his time around homosexuality?
2. To what extent is Bamberger's letter a religious response to homosexuality?
3. What seems to be the greatest problem facing Bernstein, in Bamberger's view?

90

Warsaw Ghetto Uprising Commemoration Meeting

QUEBEC, 1945

Hernan Tesler-Mabé

Canadian Jews, like their coreligionists in the United States, Latin America, and the Caribbean, sought to help Jews in Europe and provide refuge. Founded in 1919, the Canadian Jewish Congress (CJC) assumed a prominent position on the Canadian landscape in the 1930s as it confronted the rising tide of antisemitism. Despite its limited success in lobbying the Canadian government to open Canadian borders to Jewish immigrants from Europe through the 1930s and into the 1940s, the CJC nonetheless played an important role in disseminating news about the Holocaust as it was unfolding, as well as helping Jewish refugees and immigrants come to Canada.

In the 1930s–1940s, the CJC spearheaded critical initiatives aiming to bring Jewish refugees and immigrants to Canada and, in the postwar period, administered the War Orphans Project, which brought eleven hundred child Holocaust survivors to Canada, and the Tailor Project, which opened Canadian borders to twenty-five hundred Jewish tailors and their families. The CJC participated in the Inter-American Jewish Conference, representing the Canadian Jewish community in Baltimore (see chapter 83), and was instrumental in the early negotiation of Holocaust memory. The event documented in the source in this chapter is believed to represent the second Canadian commemoration of the Warsaw Ghetto Uprising, the first having taken place at Toronto's Massey Hall Theatre on April 20, 1944, when two thousand attendees crowded into Toronto's Massey Hall to honor "the 40,000 Jewish heroes who died in the Battle of the Polish Ghetto" and simultaneously mourn at the "mass funeral service for the three million Polish Jews exterminated by Nazi gas chambers, firing squads and imposed starvation."[1]

This handbill serves as an early example of Holocaust commemoration in Canada, one that appeared even before the war officially ended in Canada on May 8, 1945. (The war did not end in the United States until September 2, 1945.) In this type of commemoration, the overarching message of remembrance was very quickly linked to Jewish survival, with the

Warsaw Ghetto Uprising of April–May 1943 standing in for the Holocaust. Employing the Uprising's Jewish "heroic fighters" as surrogates for the hapless victims of the Shoah, the narrative connected the Holocaust to other heroic Jewish battles. As Baruch Zuckerman of the World Jewish Congress proclaimed in front of the capacity crowd at Montreal's Baron Byng High School on April 18, 1945, "the Battle of Warsaw would go down in Jewish history beside the struggle of the Maccabees as expressive of the desperate and courageous struggle of the Jewish people for survival in the face of tyranny and persecution."[2]

Until fairly recently, the prevailing view was that Jews across the Americas possessed little interest in remembering the Holocaust and were ambivalent about the plight of European Jewry and refugees during World War II and in the years that followed. Yet this document demonstrates that discussion of the Holocaust was already occurring toward the end of the war in Canada. As such, it counters the long-held perception that the Holocaust was not confronted by the Jewish community in Canada until after the 1961 Eichmann trial. Given that the document affords equal space to the message in English and Yiddish, it provides us with a window into the continued importance of Yiddish as a language in the local community.

PRIMARY SOURCE

Handbill for Warsaw Ghetto Uprising Commemoration Meeting, Montreal, April 18, 1945, Canadian Jewish Congress organizational records, chronological series ZA, file CJC-ZA1945-8-139. Courtesy of ADCJA.

פֿאַרפֿעלט ניט צו קומען צו דער

מאַסן פֿאַרזאַמלונג

אַראַנזשירט פֿון דעם

קאַנאַדער אידישן קאָנגרעס

כדי אָפּצוגעבן כבוד צו די קדושים פֿון דעם

העלדישן אויפֿשטאַנד אין דער

וואַרשעווער געטאָ

מיטוואָך, 18טן אַפּריל, 8:30 אָוונט

אין זאַל פֿון באַראָן בינג היי סקול

4251 סט. אורבּיין גאַס

Do not fail to attend the

Commemoration Meeting

under the auspices of the

CANADIAN JEWISH CONGRESS

In Honor of the Heroes of the

Warsaw Ghetto Uprising

WEDNESDAY, APRIL 18, 8:30 P.M.

at the Baron Byng High School

4251 St. Urbain Street

1945

QUESTIONS

1. Why do you think Canadian Jews commemorated the Holocaust, given how far they were geographically from the event?
2. Why do you think the Holocaust was represented primarily through the lens of the Warsaw Ghetto Uprising in the first few years of its remembrance?
3. Given that the document appears in both English and Yiddish, who do you think is the intended audience? What does language reveal about the Montreal Jewish community at the time?

NOTES

1. "Ghetto Heroism Rouses Stalwart Faith in Race," *Globe and Mail* (Toronto), April 21, 1944, 4.
2. "Warsaw Dead Paid Homage: Jewish Memorial Rites Held at Baron Byng High," *Montreal Daily Star*, April 19, 1945, clipping found in ADCJA, CJC Series E, box 2, file 10 (1945).

91

Hasidic Architecture

NEW YORK, CALIFORNIA, QUEBEC, BRAZIL, 1940–2005

Laura Arnold Leibman

In 1940, the Lubavitcher Hasidim purchased a red-brick building at 770 Eastern Parkway in Crown Heights, Brooklyn. The building played a crucial role in the transformation of Lubavitch Judaism from a European religion to an American religion after the community's relocation of the Lubavitch dynasty to New York in the 1940s. Today, Hasidism make up about 5 percent of Jews in the world, with Lubavitchers making up 13 percent of Hasids. Also known by the acronym "CHaBaD" (חב"ד), Lubavitcher Hasidism's name references not only the town that the dynasty was originally from in Russia (Lyubavichi) but also the first three *sephirot* (attributes) of the kabbalistic tree of life (Chochmah, Binah, and Da'at), a clear acknowledgment of the group's mystical leanings. 770 Eastern Parkway would eventually become an icon for this branch of Judaism.

As one branch of Hasidic Jews, Chabad traces its origins back to the Polish-Lithuanian Commonwealth. There, in the mid-eighteenth century, groups of pietistic Orthodox Jews responded to the Enlightenment by creating an ecstatic, mystical version of Judaism centered around charismatic leaders called "rebbes" and their court of followers. As David Biale and colleagues note, "From its beginnings, Hasidism was far more than an intellectual movement. It was also a set of bodily practices, including prayer, storytelling, singing, dancing, and eating, all performed within the frame of the reciprocal relationship between rebbe and Hasid."[1] Hasidism was originally a unified movement around the teachings of the Baal Shem Tov and his student Rabbi Dov Ber of Mezeritch, but over time, the descendants of these men founded numerous dynasties, each with its own line of rebbes and typically with distinctive dress and customs.

With the Great Migration of the 1880s–1920s, numerous individual Hasidic Jews migrated to the Americas, but whole dynasties did not relocate en masse to the Americas until the crisis leading up to and following the Holocaust. Two of the most influential rebbes to relocate during the 1940s were the rebbe of the Satmar Hasidim, Rabbi Yoel Teitelbaum (1887–1979), and the rebbe of the Lubavitcher Hasidim, Menachem Mendel

Schneerson (1902–1994). While Teitelbaum settled the Satmar court in the Williamsburg section of Brooklyn, Schneerson's father-in-law, Yosef Yitzach Schneerson (the sixth rebbe), established the Lubavitcher court in Crown Heights. While both Satmars and Lubavitch share ultra-Orthodox practices, Satmar Hasidim have taken a strong stance against Zionism and emphasize isolation from outsiders. In contrast, Lubavitcher Hasidim radically shifted toward outreach, starting in the 1950s, when the seventh rebbe, Menachem Mendel Schneerson, created a network of *shlichim* (emissaries) who focused on spreading observance of mitzvoth (fulfillment of religious commandments) to non-Orthodox Jews (see chapter 102). This outreach was intended to help bring the Jewish messiah (*moshiach*).[2] By the 1980s, some of Schneerson's key followers believed that he might be that messiah, an idea that some of his followers continued to believe in after his death in 1994. Schneerson left no successor, and today Lubavitchers still refer to him as *the* Rebbe (capital *R*).

The building at 770 Eastern Parkway has become one of the most visible symbols of this diasporic network of emissaries and the Rebbe's desire to radically transform the world by enhancing Jewish observance and spirituality. Built in 1920 in a Gothic Revival style and previously used as a doctor's office, the building was purchased by Chabad in 1940 for use as a synagogue, yeshiva, office space, and living quarters for the sixth rebbe. Starting in 1984 with the construction of the UCLA Chabad House in Los Angeles, the (seventh) Rebbe's emissaries began to deliberately evoke 770 Eastern Parkway. This was quickly followed by a 770 look-alike in Kfar Chabad, which was designed at the Rebbe's behest.[3]

Today, Chabad schools, synagogues, outreach centers, and camps around the world imitate the distinctive façade of 770 Eastern Parkway. These replicas can be found in cities and countries around the world, including in Israel, Los Angeles, New Jersey, Montreal, Brazil, Italy, Argentina, Australia, Washington, DC, Chile, Ukraine, Maryland, Florida, the Philippines, and Nigeria. These centers connect the Diaspora of emissaries back to Crown Heights. In some instances, not only does the façade point worshipers back to 770, but the inside has been designed to include a copy of the "Rebbe's Room," the now-empty ground-floor study at 770 that was originally the Rebbe's study but that, after his wife's death in 1988, was the place where the Rebbe lived and held court. The original Rebbe's Room, like his grave, is visited as a holy site where people come to pray and is considered "a beacon of light . . . suffused—with awe."[4]

PRIMARY SOURCES

See following pages.

Original building at 770 Eastern Parkway Brooklyn, New York. (Photograph by Andrea Robbins and Max Becher, 2005)

Gayley Avenue, Los Angeles, CA. (Photograph by Andrea Robbins and Max Becher 2005)

Camp Gan Israel, near Montreal, Canada. (Photograph by Andrea Robbins and Max Becher, 2005)

São Paulo, Brazil. (Photograph by Andrea Robbins and Max Becher, 2005)

QUESTIONS

1. What do you think is the purpose (spiritual and otherwise) of making Chabad houses that imitate or reference 770 Eastern Parkway? How do these references to 770 signal the United States as a spiritual center of the Lubavitcher movement?
2. What makes a building or tomb holy? In what sense can an imitation of a place also have a certain sacredness?
3. How do you see the proliferation of 770s relating to the messianic mission of Chabad Hasidism?
4. The scholar David Biale and colleagues emphasize that Hasidic Judaism is about bodily practices that maintain the reciprocal relationship between rebbe and Hasid. What role does 770's architecture play in maintaining connections between the Rebbe and his extended court? How is architecture an embodied practice?

NOTES

1. Biale et al., *Hasidism*, 1–2; M. Katz, *Visual Culture of Chabad*, 13.
2. Deutsch and Casper, *Fortress in Brooklyn*, 20.
3. M. Katz, *Visual Culture of Chabad*, 145, 152–154.
4. Feuer, "No One There."

PART V

Jews in the Postwar Americas (1946–Present)

Gottscho-Schleisner, *Levittown Houses. Mrs. Robert Berman, residence at 3626 Regent Lane,* 1958. (Gottscho-Schleisner Collection, LCPPD, LC-G613-72798)

On June 21, 1962, in the outskirts of the city of Buenos Aires, Graciela Sirota, a Jewish university student, was kidnapped in broad daylight, tortured, and then thrown from a van, alive but injured. The thugs, members of a right-wing nationalist group called Tacuara, carved a swastika on her chest and burned her body with cigarette butts. This event was one of the most violent in a series of anti-Jewish attacks that had started after Adolf Eichmann's apprehension on May 11, 1960, in the town of Tigre. Some of these events included vandalizing Jewish institutions, throwing Molotov cocktails at Jewish events and individuals, and even armed attacks against Jewish students in state schools. Jews were accused of loyalty to Israel, a country that had violated, in the view of ultranationalist groups, Argentina's sovereignty (see chapter 95).[1]

For some Jews, the persecution and attack on Jewish Argentines in the 1960s came as a surprise, especially since, in the aftermath of World War II, many Jews believed that the Americas were a haven from persecution and death and uncertainty. To be sure, although some entry restrictions continued, US President Harry Truman had nonetheless passed an executive order in 1945 (later referred to as the "Truman Directive") that brought 23,000 Jewish refugees to the United States in 1946 alone. Additionally, in 1948, the US Congress finally passed the Displaced Persons Act (which still included limitations for Jewish survivors with possible "Communist connections"). Likewise, the Hebrew Immigrant Aid Society claimed that about 24,804 Jewish refugees went to Latin American countries between 1946 and 1951, even if many of them had to enter their destinations illegally.[2] Yet the persistence of antisemitism in Argentina was not anachronistic but rather reflected the changes in American Jewish life following World War II.

The loss of European Jewry during the Holocaust shifted American Jews' role in the world: for the first time in world history, there were more Jews in the Americas than on any other continents.[3] American Jews' increased visibility was accompanied by critiques from both the left and the right. Jewish Americans adapted to this new world role in three chronological (but sometimes overlapping) stages: (1) refuge, recovery, and responsibility, (2) renewal and empowerment, and (3) intersectionality and deassimilation.

The first stage of Jewish American postwar transformation occurred largely between 1945 and 1967, a period during which Jewish Americans recovered from the ravages of the Holocaust by reenvisioning the Americas as a refuge. Antisemitism persisted but now often was complicated by Jews' relationship to Israel, which increasingly split Jewish American communities along political lines and added complexity to American Jews' understanding of national belonging. Despite these fractures, one thing that tended to unite American Jews was an increased sense of responsibility, as Jews across the Americas worked together to care for refugees and the Jewish poor. For some segments of American Jewry, this postwar era was accompanied by a moral imperative to prevent similar atrocities from happening to other disenfranchised groups. For others, the desire for safety meant embracing assimilation.

The birth of the State of Israel (1948) both helped and complicated the project of refuge and recovery in the postwar era. Not all American Jews favored the rise of the new state, as some Orthodox groups took the creation of a secular state to be an attempt to "force the messiah." Yet Jewish communities across the Americas often played a central role in the political struggle for the birth of the State of Israel by providing economic support both for the newly created state and for Holocaust victims settling there. The Joint continued to be actively involved in aiding the surviving Jews in Europe, and its representatives worked in many Latin American countries to raise funds and purchase products that were then sent to Europe.[4] The World Jewish Congress continued working to rehabilitate the Jewish communities in Europe, supporting their claims for the restitution of Jewish property, and fighting for the opening immigration to Palestine/Israel.[5] In Latin America, the presence of these two institutions, one clearly seen as a US organization (JDC) and the other representing world Jewry (WJC), brought about conflict as they sought donations from the same people for the same objectives. By the end of the 1940s, these clashes came to an end, and the fund-raising campaigns in Latin America joined together in a United Appeal, modeled after the US example that had started in 1939. This unification made it easier to raise money for refugees, Israel, and local needs.

For many American Jews, the existence of Israel meant a reconfiguration of what it meant to be a Jew in a Diaspora. Although that Diaspora had always been envisioned vis-à-vis an ancestral homeland, that land could now be much more easily returned to. Moreover, according to the Israeli Law of Return (1950), all Jews—regardless of where they were born—could automatically become citizens of Israel upon moving there. In essence, this law encouraged American Jews to consider themselves dual citizens, with one future foot in Israel. This dual allegiance impacted how American Jews interacted with each other and Israel. In 1950, and after a few clashes, Jewish leaders from the US and Israel agreed on what their relationship would look like: US Jews would contribute monetarily, with know-how, and with other types of financial support, but there would be no expectation that US Jews would need to make *aliyah* ("ascent"/return) to Israel. Moving to Israel had been particularly important in the early years as the young new country encouraged the immigration of young Jews to settle in kibbutzim that acted as military defense outposts. In Latin America, many pioneers (members of Zionist youth groups: *ḥalutzim* in Hebrew) answered this call,

LA LUZ

XIX — No. 13 (500)

Viernes, 22 de julio de 1949

Ernst Miller (Chile) | Mordejai Wainerman (Argentine) | Iasha Ginnesim (Chile)

Iaacov Kroch (Argentina) | Devora Epstein (Uruguay) | Abraham Gueler (Uruguay)

נפלו בקרב

JOVENES JUDIOS LATINO-AMERICANOS CAIDOS EN EL FRENTE DEL NEGUEV, DONDE REGARON SU SANGRE EN ARAS DEL FLORECIMIENTO DE ISRAEL.

VISTA ISRAELITA PARA TODA SUDAMERICA"

"Latin American Jewish youth who perished in the Negev front, whose blood now contributes to the flowering of Israel." (*La Luz*, July 22, 1949, cover page)

not only in the aftermath of the declaration of independence but later on, especially during the 1960s.

Compared to the number of US Jews, fewer Latin American Jews moved to Israel, yet they represented a higher percentage of said Latin American Jewish communities.[6] Moreover, Latin American Jews tended to stay in Israel rather than return or travel between the two regions. Ideology was not the only reason for this phenomenon. For many Latin

American Jews, Israel appeared as an option to improve their economic situation, as well as to escape political upheavals (see chapters 103 and 110).

After 1948, some Jews from around the world sought refuge in Israel, while others sought out countries across the Americas where they could escape the processes of decolonization, internal political/religious reconfigurations, and the impact of the Israeli-Palestinian conflict. Especially after the creation of Israel, Jews from many Middle Eastern and North African countries migrated to the United States, Canada, Brazil, Argentina, Mexico, and other American countries. An exception to this trend was the Jews of Iran, who did not start to migrate en masse until after the shah was overthrown in 1979 (see chapter 99).

World politics complicated Jewish identity building and recovery for both new arrivals and native-born American Jews. The rise of the Soviet Union following World War II and the Cold War created further tensions within American Jewish communities about Jewish loyalties and responsibilities. In Latin America, clashes between Zionist and non-Zionist Jews (mostly communists and Bundists) had existed since the beginning of communal life in the early 1920s; but when the Soviet Union adopted a policy against Israel during the Cold War and repressed Zionism and Yiddish culture within its borders, the conflicts escalated, as Jewish communists around the world began to be accused of siding with Moscow. Thus, in Argentina in 1952, Jewish communist institutions were expelled from the DAIA (the umbrella organization that represented Jews to the government). In Brazil, as well as in Mexico, similar clashes existed between the various groups (see chapter 92).

Another source of in-group tension was disagreements about Jewish responsibility toward non-Jews and social justice movements in general. Across the Americas, Jews, especially youth, actively and visibly participated in Jewish as well as in non-Jewish causes.[7] In Latin America, Jews felt attracted to, and participated in, the revolutionary fervor initiated by the Cuban Revolution in 1959. Many of these Jews had grown up in Jewish institutions that had instilled "universalist" ideals that encouraged involvement in non-Jewish organizations.[8] Some Jews joined non-Jewish political parties, sometimes because of family tradition and sometimes as indicative of the lure that revolutionary ideology had on Jews who recognized how Jewish values had opened them up to respond to injustices. Others reacted to the context of the times by joining *Jewish* revolutionary options. In fact, the organized Jewish communities in many Latin American countries felt the need to provide youth with Jewish alternatives that would pursue the same ideals of revolutionary change that their non-Jewish counterparts were engaged in, in an effort to keep these young people within Jewish boundaries. In Argentina, for example, "Jews [ended up] reinvent[ing] the Jewish tradition and Zionism in radical terms and framed the Jewish community as supportive of 'national liberation'" in the country.[9]

In the United States, Reform congregations began to set social action goals. Many Jews in the US marched in the South to help bring an end to discrimination, even though other Jews tried to maintain the Jim Crow system (see chapter 96). Jewish participation also made Jews targets, even when, ironically, the bombs attacked southern congregations whose members were probably not sympathetic with the civil rights struggle.

While some Jews turned to social activism to heal the wounds of the Holocaust, others turned to assimilation. Like Liberalism during the 1920s, assimilation offered the promise that Jews would be accepted if they would just be more like other Americans. In the

United States, the rise of the suburbs played an important role in assimilation. One of the rewards offered for serving in World War II was the GI Bill (1944), which provided low-cost mortgages and low-interest business loans and paid for college tuition to veterans who had served at least ninety days and not been dishonorably discharged (see chapter 89). The sociologist Karen Brodkin has argued that this bill was essential to transforming US Jews from a quasi-white ethnic group into "white folks."[10] Access to education made an entire Jewish American generation upwardly mobile, even as low-interest home and business loans allowed the same Jews to obtain property to pass along to later generations.

Yet, even as these programs helped European American Jews climb the social ladder, Black veterans were denied the same opportunities due to quotas and restrictions in higher educational institutions and "redlining" in real estate. (Redlining is the practice of systematically refusing loans to minorities on the basis of race or neighborhood.) Thus, while the GI Bill helped many white Jewish veterans escape impoverished, inner-city neighborhoods and buy their first house in the suburbs, Black Jews and other African Americans found themselves unable to relocate out of inner cities or even to get loans needed to adequately maintain properties in those areas. Consequently, even when they were able to invest in real estate, there was little inheritable income to pass along to the next generation.

This lifting up of white Jews vis-à-vis the economic disenfranchisement of African Americans has been interpreted as one of the strategies used to gain the cooperation of Jews in systemic racism. In more concrete terms, European American Jews were allowed to take part in the "white flight" to the suburbs, much as they had taken place in settler colonialism across the Americas in the era of mass migrations and nationalism by distancing themselves from other disenfranchised minorities. One of the prices paid for this new "whiter" social status was the sublimation of cultural and ethnic difference. While the racial politics were different in Mexico, during the 1950s–1970s Jews in Mexico City similarly moved from apartments in Roma and Condesa to single-family homes in Polanco and other neighborhoods. In other Latin American cities, many Jews slowly left Jewish neighborhoods behind for new higher-status ones.

The rise of suburbs changed the ways that Jews related to communal organizations. While a generation or two earlier, Jews in the United States might have lived within walking distance of a synagogue, the suburbs now dispersed Jews geographically, leading to an even greater rise in popularity of Jewish Community Centers and non-Orthodox synagogues that allowed congregants to drive to services. Jewish summer camps began to take on the task of helping children develop a sense of Jewish peoplehood.[11] While some camps reached out to specific denominations, community camps focused on children with weak ties to organized Jewish life.[12] This trend started somewhat earlier in Latin America, as Jewish life among non-Orthodox groups had, since the beginning, revolved around Jewish institutions that provided sport, cultural, and other types of activities. Jewish sport clubs, alongside Zionist youth movements, had offered summer camps for decades, and in the 1960s, Jewish schools and other Jewish institutions began running their own. These organizations helped American Jews find ways of identifying with Jewish traditions outside of religious institutions, providing multiple sources for cultural identification.

Yet, even as some Jews assimilated and moved to the suburbs, others set up urban enclaves to separate themselves from the American Jewish majority. Many of the refugees and survivors who had started arriving in the 1930s until the 1950s were Hasidic. They congregated in tightly knit communities, like New York and Montreal, and sought to distance themselves from modern life, dedicating themselves to religious practice. When other Jews left inner-city neighborhoods like Williamsburg, Brooklyn, for the suburbs, Hasidim like the Satmars stayed behind, preferring poor Black and Puerto Rican neighbors to assimilated Jews who "confused the otherwise clear-cut taxonomical distinction that was supposed to exist between 'the people of Israel' and the 'nations of the world.'"[13] Racial divisions were seen as useful in this context, as they could "only help reinforce the more fundamental difference between Jews and non-Jews"—a premise based on the assumption that Jews were inherently white.[14] While Hasidic groups like the Satmars were ultimately able to assert their political influence, their presence in low-income housing projects is an important reminder that not all Jews prospered during the postwar boom economy. Nor was economic prosperity their primary goal: Hasidim often favored building a strong home and foundation in the spiritual world-to-come, rather than accumulating wealth in this world.

Language became a key strategy for isolation. We saw in part 4 (chapters 73, 79, 80, and 81, among others) that Yiddish was central to secular American Jewish culture between the wars. Yet, after an initial revival of Yiddish following World War II, Yiddish slowly became associated with the past. Pressure to stop using Yiddish grew stronger as the century progressed. Over time, Yiddish was only a daily language spoken to communicate in largely insular Orthodox communities (see chapter 112).

One important exception to Hasidic Jews' tendency to isolate themselves is the Lubavitcher Chabad movement, which starting in the 1950s began sending *shlichim* (emissaries) to set up "Chabad Houses" in order to encourage and teach Orthodox practice, particularly the mystical type favored by Hasidim. A religious version of the now ubiquitous Jewish Community Centers, Chabad Houses offered a range of social services. Hasidic groups like the Lubavitchers moved from the United States to Argentina in the mid-1950s and to Mexico in the late 1990s.[15] Thus, it was not until the 1990s that Hasidim as well as ultra-Orthodox groups (Sephardim as well as Mitnagdim) became a visible presence in many Latin American Jewish neighborhoods (see chapter 102). In many small towns in Latin American countries, religious holiday services are run by Chabad *shlichim*, rather than permanent rabbis, as the communities cannot afford to hire rabbis.

Regardless of whether Jews assimilated or separated themselves, antisemitism continued to flourish, as seen in the example of Graciela Sirota. If antisemitism was not new to the postwar era, what was different was the non-Jewish response, as well as Jews' shifting sense of their own national belonging. Following the 1962 attack in Argentina, for example, some of the major Argentine newspapers included headlines such as "Acts of Barbarism," "This Is Not Argentine," "Beasts."[16] Jewish and non-Jewish institutions organized a "strike" as a protest, as well as issuing strong statements in opposition to the actions of the ultranationalists. The "racial discrimination" against Jews by Argentine ultranationalist Catholic groups made Jewish Argentines doubt, once again, their place in the nation, even when most Argentines categorized such acts as barbaric and un-Argentine.[17] Many Jews, however, continued to feel unsafe; thus, in 1963, the largest number of Jewish Argentines moved to Israel since its creation, and a similar amount appears to have settled in other countries (such as the US).[18] Across the Americas, the postwar period has witnessed deadly assaults, some very recent; but, importantly, these intense and violent attacks by a (loud) few have tended to be accompanied by the visible support of the majority.

For many, anti-Jewish violence reopened the wounds suffered during the Holocaust and is an important reminder that for American Jews, recovering from the Holocaust has taken emotional as well as social work. The Holocaust, as Hasia Diner has so eloquently demonstrated, was not a taboo topic among Jews in the United States; the same can be said about the ways in which Jews in Latin America from very early on sought to remember and memorialize those who perished.[19] Even before the end of the war and continuing into the following decades, the uprising of the Warsaw Ghetto had become a rallying point around which Jews celebrated the courage of those who fought the Nazis—even if such commemorations engendered conflict between Jewish communists and Zionists about the lessons to draw from the uprising. Memorials, prayers, and many other types of events of collective action sought to make sure that the Holocaust, and those who perished during it, were not forgotten (see chapter 90).

The tentative optimism following World War II gained a sudden boost in 1967 due to the unexpected success of Israel during the Six-Day War, a conflict that reverberated with a period of renewal across the Americas. Prior to the Six-Day War, Israel often was seen as an underdog by American Jews, who tended to feel that the country's very existence was precarious. However, at the end of the Six-Day War, Israel not only emerged safe but had gained territories in the West Bank of the Jordan River, the Sinai Peninsula, the Gaza Strip, and the Golan Heights. Some American Jews saw the victory as a sign that Jews could, for the first time, "walk with their backs straight."[20] The "miracle" of Israel's success helped religious revivals flourish. This religious enthusiasm was bolstered by the adaptation to American Judaism to meet a wider community, as counterculture movements helped boost the profile of women, LGBTQ, and nonwhite Jews. The number of young Jewish volunteers who joined in Israeli forces during this armed confrontation was significant, as were the donations raised and sent.

The optimism that followed the Six-Day War increased the spirit of religious innovation and change already present in the immediate postwar era. With the flight of US Jews to the suburbs in the 1950s, the Conservative movement experienced an important growth by offering a combination of modernity and observance, educational options for young Jews, and the participation of women in synagogue life. For example, by the 1970s, almost all Conservative congregations in the United States offered Bat Mitzvah ceremonies.[21] A few congregations in Latin America likewise offered this option for young girls. Suburban Jews reshaped rituals and objects to meet modernist aesthetics (see chapter 94).

In Latin America, the split into different religious denominations was imported from abroad. Here, too, the divisions began before 1967 but flourished afterward. The Seminario Rabínico Latinoamericano (SRL), for example, was founded in Buenos Aires by the US rabbi Marshall Meyer in 1962. Affiliated with the Conservative movement (known as Masorti outside the US) and the Jewish Theological Seminary of America, the SRL trained rabbis to work all over Latin America. The Union of Reform Judaism for Latin America was founded only in 2009. Orthodoxy in Latin America was similarly the result of individual rabbis more than the work of transnational institutions. The community of Jews from

Aleppo, Syria, for example, experienced a marked move to Orthodoxy starting in Argentina in 1956 and similarly in Mexico, Panama, and the eastern United States.

Following the Six-Day War, many Jewish American denominations experienced spiritual renewal. To be sure, religious practice was never static and even found expression outside the three main Jewish religious movements. In Latin America, there were fewer open challenges to institutional religious life, although some Jews there called for more "modern" religious services. In 1958, for example, a young Sephardic woman in Argentina wrote to the editors of a Zionist newspaper requesting that services be held in Spanish "for youth to return to the synagogue."[22] What was different following the war, however, was the attempt to make services a more spiritually enriching experience and, for at least some denominations, to bring about the messianic age. Within the US, the *havurah* movement, for example, which began in the late 1960s in the United States, was a reaction to what many Jews perceived to be cold, unwelcoming, and nonegalitarian communities. Jews gathered together for study and prayer, without a rabbi, although later many of these groups came to be part of existing congregations or formed new denominations such as the Renewal movement, which combined Hasidic mysticism with egalitarianism and meditation.

In both liberal and traditional Judaism, women's role in this world and cosmic renewal was often highlighted, and American Jewish women took on new leadership roles in communal and secular life. Orthodox communities increasingly emphasized the importance of female education. After World War II, the center of the Bais Yaakov educational movement had shifted to the United States, and the result was a new generation of well-educated Jewish American women leaders, who with the founding of Stern College in 1954 could even gain an Orthodox college education. In 1997, the Jewish Orthodox Feminist Alliance (JOFA) was created to help promote women's education.

The 1970s likewise marked the rise of gay and lesbian synagogues. The earliest was Beth Chayim Chadashim (House of New Life), founded in 1972 in the Pico Robertson neighborhood of Los Angeles near West Hollywood. Shortly thereafter, Sha'ar Zahav (Golden Gate) was founded near the Mission District in San Francisco. Sisterhood cookbooks had become a staple for community-building and fund-raising following the war, and Sha'ar Zahav was no exception. During the AIDS crisis, the gay Jewish cookbook *Out of Our Kitchen Closets: San Francisco Gay Jewish Cooking* played an important role in supporting congregants.[23] Importantly, both of these congregations were spawned on the West Coast in openly gay neighborhoods. The year 1976 marked the First International Conference of Gay Jews in Washington, DC, and by the mid-1990s, many major American Jewish communities could boast of having a queer synagogue.

For Jews in Latin America, the Israeli success and the new openness of US Jewish life directly conflicted with the political repression they were experiencing. The military dictatorships that took over, especially but not exclusively, in the Southern Cone in the 1970s persecuted left-wing activists, including many Jews, as a way to extinguish revolutionary fervor. In Argentina, for example, the percentage of Jews who became victims of state-sponsored repression was significantly higher than the percentage of Jews within Argentine society (between five and twelve times, depending on the estimations).[24] And while it is important to stress that Jews became victims not necessarily because they were Jewish (as mentioned earlier, many participated in non-Jewish circles), the fact that they were Jews meant that they experienced "special" treatment while tortured, a horror that echoes the experiences of Joam Bautista four hundred years earlier (see chapter 2).[25] In other Latin American countries, like Brazil and Chile, Jews fell victim to dictatorships (see chapters 97 and 109). Their insecurity was further reinforced by the 1994 bombing of the Asociación Mutual Israelita Argentina (Jewish Mutual Aid Association) building in Buenos Aires (see chapter 100). One result of this political climate is that the presence of queer organizations in Latin America only dates to the early 2000s.

Political persecution coupled with economic downturns meant that Jews moved not only to but around the Americas during these decades, with some Latin American Jews migrating to the United States and Canada.[26] Similarly, starting in the 1970s, Jews from the Soviet Union left for the United States and Canada, with various waves arriving even after the fall of the Soviet Union (see chapter 107). The economic uncertainty following India's independence led some of the Bene Israel (Jews of India) to Canada in the 1970s (see chapter 98). The Iranian Revolution in 1979 also prompted the departure of Jews from this country, many of whom settled in the United States and to a lesser extent in Canadian cities like Toronto (see chapter 99). Religion also propelled immigration, as some American Jews made *aliyah* to Israel, while some Israeli Jews moved to the Americas. In many cases, these new immigrants lived transnational lives, moving from one nation to the other, maintaining ties with all, and continuing to shape new forms of Jewish identity that combined national and ethnic transnational borders.

As American Jews entered the twenty-first century, Jews remained divided regarding issues of diversity and inclusion. While the attack on the World Trade Center in 2001 was initially followed by a surge in anti-Islamic sentiment in the United States, over the next two decades, it ultimately led to a push for intersectionality and an embrace of Jewish difference, particularly on the left.

Following the backlash against Islamophobia, there has been a rise of a vocal minority of US Jews who are highly critical of Israel. A 2021 study from the Pew Research Center noted that eight out of ten Jews in the United States still say that "caring about Israel is an essential or important part of what being Jewish means to them." Likewise, "nearly six-in-ten say they personally feel an emotional attachment to Israel."[27] At the same time, more than half of US Jews were critical of Israeli prime minister Benjamin Netanyahu, and 10 percent supported the BDS (Boycott, Divestment, Sanctions movement), with support rising to 13 percent among both Jewish Democrats and Jews between the ages of eighteen and twenty-nine and to 18 percent among unaffiliated Jews.[28] Founded in 2005, the BDS movement is a pro-Palestinian movement that seeks full rights for Arab-Palestinian citizens of Israel. BDS also overturns the way American Jews traditionally interpreted the Six-Day War. While initially Israel's preemptive strike in the war of 1967 was celebrated by many American Jews on both the left and right, BDS reframed the strike as an unjustified attack against Palestinians and uses it as further evidence of Israel being a settler colony. Thus, BDS argues vociferously for Israel's withdrawal from the territories it won during the Six-Day War in 1967. BDS's characterization of Israel as a settler colony—that is, a colonized territory in which the original population has been replaced by settlers—conflicts with many Jews' perception that the land of Israel is their indigenous homeland.

Although 10–18 percent of US Jews supporting BDS may seem minimal, the percentage marks a significant uptick since the movement began in 2005, when most American Jews who knew about the movement associated it with an antisemitic attempt to eliminate the Jewish state. What caused this change? First, some liberal Jews who embrace intersectionality—the notion that discrimination and disadvantage are created through overlapping and interdependent systems—have found it increasingly difficult to reconcile a uniformly pro-Israel stance with the ethical imperative to repair the world following World War II. Second, for others, the embrace of aggressively pro-Israel policies by right-wing leaders like former US president Donald Trump and former Brazilian president Jair Bolsonaro has (rightly or wrongly) led them to associate pro-Israel politics with racism, xenophobia, homophobia, transphobia, and other regressive policies (see chapters 109 and 111). Thus, they view the values of Zionism and social justice as clashing, a trend that exacerbated already-existing fissures among American Jews. Third, the rise of the Black Lives Matter movement (2013), particularly the mass protests of 2020, brought a new sense of urgency to intersectionality and raised the consciousness among white Jews about the need to be allies in struggles that do not center on Jews. Regardless of the source of the shift, differences of opinions on Israel have led to a large number of difficult conversations and divides within American Jewish communities.

On the positive side, within Jewish American communities, intersectionality has often led Jewish communities—particularly those with a liberal bent—to embrace the values of diversity and inclusion, as well as the gradual reshaping of Jewish communal space to be more inclusive toward LGBTQ Jews. While the founding of gay and lesbian synagogues began to decline by the early 2000s, Gregg Drinkwater argues that rather than signaling the exodus of queer people from Judaism, this shift was a result of liberal synagogues becoming better about inclusion and queer belonging.[29] Transgender Judaism has similarly taken a much more public turn from what was seen in chapters 16 and 75. In 2008, Joy Ladin became the first openly transgender professor at an Orthodox institution (see chapter 104), and by 2013, there were at least six transgender ordained rabbis or rabbis-in-training.[30] An important part of rethinking American Judaism has been the adaption or reinvention of Jewish rituals and space to meet queer spiritual needs (see chapter 108).

American congregations also began to reckon with the long-standing racial diversity of their congregations, as Black, Latinx, Asian, Indigenous, and multiracial Jews brought their stories to the forefront of American Jewish history. Similar to the history of LGBTQ Jews, one of the first steps has been to organize nonwhite Jewish spaces run by and for Jews of color. Some of these include the Jews of Color Initiative, the Jewish Multiracial Network, Jews in All Hues, and Be'Chol Lashon. In addition, Lewis Gordon (University of Connecticut) and Rabbi Walter Isaac have created academic centers for the study of Black Judaism.

Intersectionality and attention to the diversity of Jewish cultural experience encouraged the rise of deassimilation among American Jews. For example, Yiddish has been revived both in academia and among a younger generation (see chapter 112). Ladino and Arabic are experiencing similar resurgences within Jewish communities. Young Syrian Jews in Mexico today, for example, use Arabic words when speaking Spanish as a way to signal their belonging not just to the Jewish community but to the Syrian collective.[31] Likewise, an

LGBTQ Jews of color. (Photograph by Josie Fraser, 2019, WC)

overnight Sephardic Adventure Camp run by Seattle congregations integrates acquisition of Ladino into its programming, and crypto-Jews in New Mexico are openly embracing their past (see chapter 101). The embrace of ethnic-specific Jewish cuisines on YouTube and in print media parallels this trend (see chapters 98 and 105). For more radical Jews, however, like Sophia Sobko, who in 2015 founded the Kolektiv Goluboy Vagon ("a virtual collective of queer, trans, and gender-marginalized post-Soviet Jewish immigrant-settlers who live in the U.S. and Canada"), deassimilation means understanding the violence of complicity in American systems of oppression that accompanied assimilation originally, in addition to embracing the particularity of one's ethnic past (see chapter 113).[32]

This volume opened with Jews as both victims and agents of empire, a trend that has continued forward until the present era, though with much of the concern about being agents of empire thrust off onto the Israeli state. By the twenty-first century, American Jews had become the center of world Jewry. Antisemitism, which was once based primarily on religious or racial difference, was increasingly framed in political terms. Jewish practice continued to adapt to the American cultural landscape by taking into account the shifting needs of an increasingly diverse Jewish community. Jewish women, LGBTQ Jews, and Jews of color, who had once been asked to sublimate those aspects of their identity in order to belong, increasingly have taken on leadership roles and modified what it means to be a Jew living across the Americas.

NOTES

1. Rein, "Argentine Jews and the Accusation of 'Dual Loyalty,'" 170.
2. Wischnitzer, *Visas to Freedom*, 229–230.
3. Shapiro, "World Jewish Population," 195.
4. Raber, "Beyond Borders," 42.
5. Segev, *World Jewish Congress during the Holocaust*, 168.
6. Jewish Virtual Library, "Total Jewish Immigration to Israel."
7. Brodsky, Gurwitz, and Kranson, "Editors' Introduction," 2.
8. Rom, "Brazilian Belonging," 248.
9. Gurwitz, *Argentine Jews in the Age of Revolt*, 3.
10. Brodkin, *How the Jews Became White Folks*, 38.
11. Rothenberg, *Serious Fun at a Jewish Community Summer Camp*, 6.
12. Rothenberg, 5.
13. Deutsch and Casper, *Fortress in Brooklyn*, 11.
14. Deutsch and Casper, 11.
15. Seider, "Looking Forward to the Past," 54; Hamui Halabe, *Transformaciones*, 245.
16. "Inaudito salvajismo de los discípulos de Eichmann en la Argentina," *La Luz*, June 29, 1962, 15.
17. The expression "racial discrimination" was used when discussing these attacks.
18. Klor, *Between Exile and Exodus*, 129.
19. Diner, *We Remember with Reverence and Love.*
20. Oren, *Six Days of War*, 309.
21. Sarna, *American Judaism*, 287.
22. Bendjoya, "Los templos y la juventud," 4.
23. Feder, "During the AIDS Crisis."
24. DAIA, "Informe sobre la situación de los detenidos-desaparecidos judíos," 24.
25. The CONADEP, the National Commission on the Disappearance of Persons, included the issue of antisemitism in its final report submitted to the Argentine government in 1984 (CONADEP, *Nunca mas*, section on antisemitism).
26. Limonic, *Kugel and Frijoles.*
27. Pew Research Center, "U.S. Jews' Connections with and Attitudes toward Israel."
28. Pew Research Center.
29. Drinkwater, "LGBTQ Jews on Their Own Terms."
30. Zeveloff, "First Generation of Transgender Rabbis Claims Place at Bima."
31. Dean-Olmsted, "Arabic Words in the Spanish of Syrian Jewish Mexicans," 27.
32. Kolektiv Goluboy Vagon, home page.

92

Border Crossing Cards

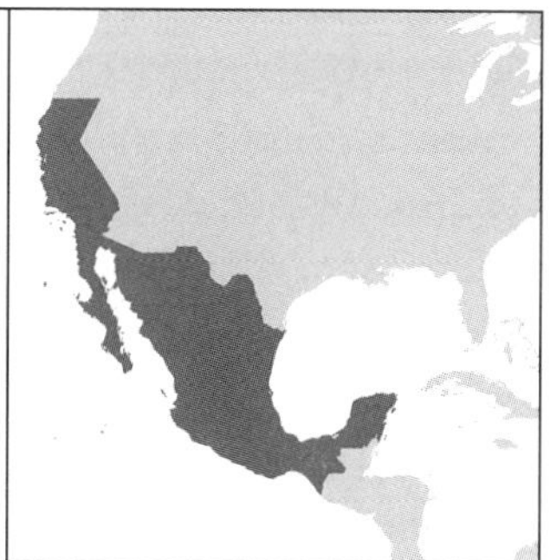

MEXICO/CALIFORNIA, 1947

Maxwell Greenberg

Immediately following World War II, Jews from around the world sought refuge across the Americas. Yet not all border crossing was for the purpose of immigration: some Jews moved between American nations on a daily or weekly basis for work. The Border Crossing Card (BCC, or B1/B2 visas) shown here belonged to Alberto Roció Benguiat, and it was issued September 19, 1947, at the Mexican Immigration Office in the border city of Calexico, California. At the time of issue, Benguiat worked as a merchant and, for business purposes, routinely engaged in cross-border travel between the Mexican states of Baja California, Sonora, and Chihuahua and the US states of California, Arizona, New Mexico, and Texas. Born in Tepatlaxco, Benguiat spent the early years of his working life in Mexico City, before moving to the Baja California border city of Tijuana around 1945 to pursue new economic opportunities in the wake of further industrialization and militarization in the border region. Alongside his commercial life, Benguiat served for many years as the secretary for Centro Social Israelita, one of Tijuana's most important Jewish religious institutions.

The B1/B2 visa in Benguiat's possession is a form of nonimmigrant visa issued by the US government that allowed non-US border residents to enter the US for up to a seventy-two-hour period for the purposes of shopping, visiting relatives, earning employment income, and purchasing goods in the US for resale in Mexico. Benguiat's visa suggests that Jewish entrepreneurs in Mexico were among the border residents with access to legal identification documentation in the mid-twentieth century. Beginning in the 1920s, the question of "illegal immigration" grew to become the central focus of US-Mexican immigration. Restrictive immigration laws, alongside new military strategies to enforce the laws, created new demands for government-mandated identification to surveil border residents and crossers. Requirements for visas and passports transformed a long tradition of fluid, regional mobility into a costly, limited, and hypermonitored process of cross-border travel. Benguiat's possession of a B1/B2 visa sheds light on one of the legal mobility strategies employed by Mexican Jewish entrepreneurs living in the border region and may suggest that these entrepreneurs faced fewer obstacles in accessing transborder and transnational networks and markets.

US essentialist approaches to immigration histories, alongside numerically insignificant Jewish populations, have relegated the US-Mexico border region as both a peripheral and incidental site of Jewish settlement in the Americas. Modern Jewish American immigration histories that do consider Mexico's northern geography have focused on the space as a backdoor to the US yet do not consider how both sides of the border region might have offered entrepreneurial opportunities to Jewish migrants. Benguiat's story emphasizes both Jewish presence and rootedness to the US-Mexico border, as well as how Jewish residents influenced the economic landscape of a region undergoing sociopolitical transformation in the mid-twentieth century. Furthermore, Benguiat's experiences suggest that the Jewish migrant profile, which was multinational by nature, may have marked Jewish border entrepreneurs as uniquely suited to navigate and occupy commercial niches in a time and space wherein categories of national and racial inclusion and exclusion were colliding and in process.

PRIMARY SOURCE

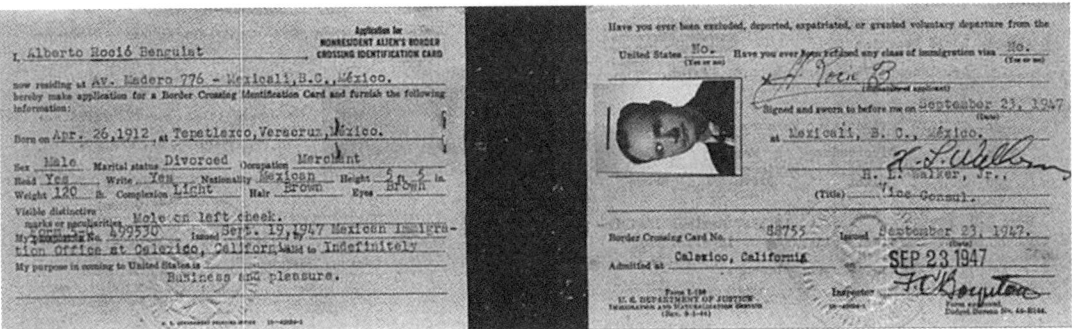

Application for NONRESIDENT ALIEN'S BORDER CROSSING IDENTIFICATION CARD

I, Alberto Rocío Benguiat

now residing at Av. Madero 776 - Mexicali, B.C., México.

hereby make application for a Border Crossing Identification Card and furnish the following information:

Born on Apr. 26, 1912 at Tepatlaxco, Veracruz, México.

Sex Male Marital status Divorced Occupation Merchant

Read Yes Write Yes Nationality Mexican Height 5 ft. 5 in.

Weight 120 lb. Complexion Light Hair Brown Eyes Brown

Visible distinctive marks or peculiarities Mole on left cheek.

My passport No. 499530 Issued Sept. 19, 1947 Mexican Immigration Office at Calexico, California Valid to Indefinitely

My purpose in coming to United States is Business and pleasure.

Have you ever been excluded, deported, expatriated, or granted voluntary departure from the United States No. Have you ever been refused any class of immigration visa No.

Signed and sworn to before me on September 23, 1947

at Mexicali, B. C., México.

H. L. Walker, Jr.

(Title) Vice Consul.

Border Crossing Card No. 88755 Issued September 23, 1947.

Admitted at Calexico, California on SEP 23 1947

Inspector

Arrival manifest of Alberto Roció Benguiat, 1947. (Manifests of Alien Arrivals at Calexico, California, NARA; courtesy Ancestry.com)

[left side]

I *Alberto Roció Benguiat*, now residing at *Av. Madero 776—Mexicali, B.C., México* hereby make application for a Border Crossing Identification Card and furnish the following information.

Born on *Apr. 26, 1912* at *Tepatlaxco, Veracruz, México*
Sex *Male* | Marital Status *Divorced* | Occupation *Merchant*
Read *Yes* | Write *Yes* | Nationality *Mexican* | Height *5* ft. *5* in.
Weight *120* lb. | Complexion *Light* | Hair *Brown* | Eyes *Brown*
Visible distinctive marks or peculiarities *Mole on left cheek.*
My passport No. *499530* | Issued *Sept. 19, 1947* | Valid to *Indefinitely*
My purpose in coming to United States is *Business and pleasure.*

[right side]
Have you ever been excluded, deported, expatriated or granted voluntary departure from the United States ***No.*** **| Have you ever been refused any class of immigration visa** ***No.***
Signature of applicant
Signed and sworn to before me on ***September 29, 1947*** **at** ***Mexicali, B.C., México.***
Signed by ***H. L. Walker, Jr.***
(Title) ***Vice Consul.***
Border Crossing Card No. ***88755*** **| Issued** ***September 23, 1947***
Admitted at ***Calexico, California*** **on** ***Sep 23 1947***

Manifests of Alien Arrivals at Calexico, California, March 1907–December 1952, NAI: 2843448, Records of the Immigration and Naturalization Service, 1787–2004, Record Group 85, Microfilm Roll 22, NARA.

QUESTIONS

1. During World War II, the US Bracero (farmhand) Program allowed US farmers and railways to hire Mexican workers temporarily during the wartime worker shortage. The program, however, was halted at the end of 1947, after which many workers were arrested and deported. During the same years, the US became more open to European refugees, partially due to competition with the Soviet Union. How do these policies, and Benguiat's card, help us better understand who could cross US borders during this era?
2. According to the card, what were the US requirements to access a nonresident alien's border-crossing identification card in 1947?
3. Is Benguiat's Jewish identity visible (directly or indirectly) through the information presented on this identification card?

93

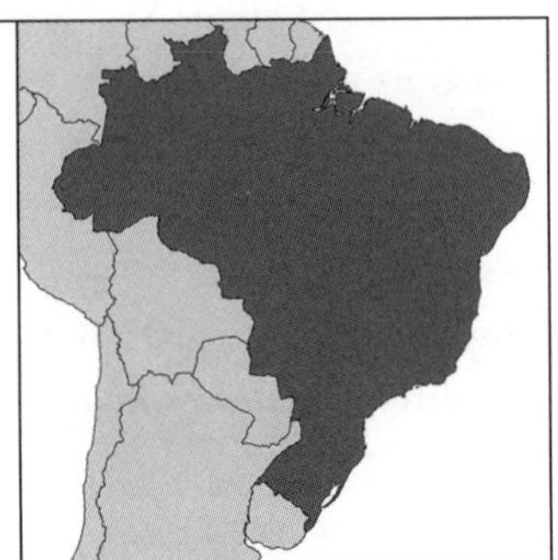

"From Birobidzhan Shall Go Forth the Torah"

BRAZIL, 1951

Michael Rom

The restoration of Brazilian democracy following the end of World War II revitalized Brazilian Jewish cultural and political life, which had been prohibited under Getúlio Vargas's Estado Novo (New State) dictatorship (1937–1945). Freed from restrictions on foreign-language periodicals, *Idishe Prese* (Jewish Press), a Zionist newspaper based in Rio de Janeiro, resumed publication in 1946 after a five-year hiatus, while Jewish communists in São Paulo founded their own Yiddish newspaper, *Unzer Shtime* (Our Voice), the following year. Although Zionists and Jewish communists initially worked together to establish new Jewish communal institutions, such as the Jewish state federations of Rio de Janeiro and São Paulo, the onset of the global Cold War severely strained relations between the two groups, as it did between Zionists and Jewish communists elsewhere in the Americas, turning communal institutions and the Yiddish press into ideological battlegrounds. A particularly acute issue was the repression of Jewish cultural life in the Soviet Union, including the closure of Jewish schools, newspapers, theaters, and publishing houses. Brazilian Zionists condemned the arrests of prominent Soviet Yiddish writers, while Brazilian communists (who called themselves "progressives" and their opponents "reactionaries") stridently denied that they were occurring.

This source illustrates how the cultural Cold War between Zionist and communist journalists in Brazil largely revolved around questions about Jewish life on the other side of the Iron Curtain. Written by a Polish Jewish Holocaust survivor named Konrad Charmatz under the pseudonym Melekh Evyon (King Pauper), this satirical piece lampoons Brazilian Jewish communists' claims of Jewish cultural freedom in the Soviet Union. The piece recounts an alleged conversation between two Jewish communists that Charmatz improbably claims to have overheard in the synagogue. In it, one communist informs another about the thriving religious life of Jews in the Soviet Union, which he has read about in

Unzer Shtime. The Soviet religious renaissance is supposedly centered in the Jewish autonomous district of Birobidzhan, which was established in 1934 in a far-eastern region along the Chinese border and which never became home to more than a small percentage of Soviet Jews. By presenting ludicrously exaggerated claims about Soviet Jewish religious life that would have been anathema to militantly atheistic communists, Charmatz mocked the unreliability of *Unzer Shtime*, ridiculed the naïveté of Jewish American communists regarding the realities of Jewish life in the Soviet Union, and made subtle—but no less polemical—counterclaims about life in the Soviet Union, furthering the marginalization of communists within the Brazilian Jewish community.

This source reveals the intensity of Jewish Cold War political struggles, which determined the ideological direction of Jewish communities in the Americas over the next half century. Thanks to the Soviet Union's defeat of Nazism and initial support for the State of Israel, it enjoyed significant prestige among Jews in the West during the early postwar years. However, the emergence of reports about Soviet antisemitism provoked bitter conflicts between Zionists and Jewish communists. This source demonstrates the important role of Holocaust survivors in these political struggles, contrary to their frequent portrayal as passive victims.

PRIMARY SOURCE

In the synagogue, between the afternoon and evening prayers, I overheard a conversation between two progressives, in which they related to each other the latest news of the world.

In order that you, my readers, are not left in the dark, but also know what is happening in the wide progressive world, I will relate the contents of the conversation—word for word.

***First progressive*: Have you heard what the reactionaries have pulled off? They kept it a secret, and didn't allow the truth about Birobidzhan to come out.**

***Second progressive*: Indeed! How did you find out about it?**

***First*: What do you mean, how? By reading our progressive newspaper *Unzer Shtime*, you can see how the whole swindle was exposed. You'll read about a delegation that came back from the Soviet Union, describing the wonder of wonders about the country. [For example:] the living standard in the Soviet Union is the highest in the world. Every worker has his own house, a recreational vehicle and a vehicle for work. They work for three months and spend the other nine months traveling around to different spas. . . .**

The greatest lie that the reactionaries invented is that there is slave labor in Soviet Russia. The worker goes to work when he feels like it. If he is tired from a party, he stays home for a couple of days to rest up, or he goes to a lakeside resort. Concentration camps do not exist in the Soviet Union. Neither does Siberia, nor the Ural Mountains, which the enemies of the Soviet Union have made up. Siberia is a luxury hotel, where one goes to rest and have a good time. . . .

Strikes do not exist in the country. Why should you strike, when you can't even spend all the money that you earn?

In Soviet Russia they don't know the meaning of the word secret police—there are no police there whatsoever. They don't need them. Since everyone has more than they need,

they have no need to rob or steal from one another. The houses and stores are wide open, and nobody bothers to take anything.

There is complete freedom of speech, press, and radio. Anyone can listen to whatever radio station they want. People tune in to the BBC and the Voice of America, and make fun of the reactionary news.

Second: What about the letters, why don't they arrive?

First: I'm sure that they write, but the Western governments, [US president Harry S.] Truman's agents, don't allow the correspondence in.

The finest of all the reports is about religious freedom. It is not true, as the reactionaries claim, that there are no Jewish schools in the Soviet Union. In every city and town, and even in the villages, there are Jewish schools and even yeshivahs [religious seminaries]. The study houses and Hasidic *shtiblekh* [prayer houses] are open, and young men and even young women devote themselves to Torah and divine service. In Kherson there is a press, which prints only holy books—Talmuds, Chumashes [Pentateuchs], Tanakhs [Hebrew Bibles], and even penitence books. The government pays a stipend to the young men who sit and learn. In Dnipropetrovsk, there is a factory that makes *tsitses* [ritual fringes] and *tallesim* [prayer shawls]. *Gartels* [ritual belts] and *shtreimels* [Hasidic fur hats] are manufactured in the workshops of Kiev. *Tfillin* [phylacteries], *mezuzahs*, and other small items are produced in Berdichev. What is more, everyone must learn a daily page of Talmud, and if they don't, they are punished.

Second: Indeed! Those reactionaries, they hid all this from us. Those fascists, bastards!

First: Yes, but now we know everything. Birobidzhan is a place of Torah. [There are] hundreds of yeshivahs, where they learn the Torah for its own sake. Even *goyim* [gentiles] learn in the yeshivahs, and they are required to know the Yiddish language.

Melekh Evyon, "Ki mi-birobidzhan teytse toyre: An untergeherter geshprekh tsvishn tsvey 'progresive'" [From Birobidzhan shall go forth the Torah: An overheard conversation between two "progressives"], *Idishe Prese*, October 5, 1951, 5.

QUESTIONS

1. What are the Jewish American communists' main claims about the Soviet Union?
2. Why are these claims humorous within the context of their time?
3. How does Charmatz subtly undermine these claims?
4. What polemical counterclaims does Charmatz make about the Soviet Union?
5. Typically, Jews were accused during this era of having ties to Israel that conflicted with the interests of the nations in which they resided. How do Jewish ties to the Soviet Union differ?

94

Hanukkiah

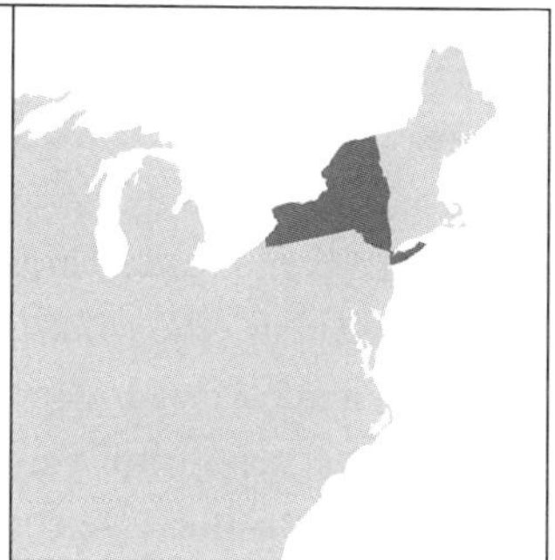

NEW YORK, 1958

Rebecca Sandler Perten

As American Jews moved to the suburbs, midcentury modernism became a way to show that Jews had risen above ethnic particularism. Flourishing between 1945 and 1969, the midcentury modern style favored clean, simple lines and, according to the art critic Kristina Wilson, was "a powerful tool for constructing Whiteness to White consumers," even as it claimed that modernism was racially agnostic. Like white suburbs, modernist design became a way to "maintain rationality and cleanliness . . . and constrain delinquency and mess."[1] Religious objects and rituals, among non-Orthodox groups, were adapted to the times and modern aesthetics. Their audience was women like Mrs. Robert Berman of Levittown (see the photograph of her house in the introduction to part 5).

This Hanukkah lamp was created by the German-born Israeli metalsmith Ludwig Wolpert (1900–1981). It was one of the first ritual objects that Wolpert crafted as director of the Tobe Pascher Workshop (in operation 1957–1989), at the Jewish Museum in New York (see chapter 88). The workshop was founded by the pediatrician and art collector Abram Kanof (1903–1999) with the express purpose of providing the American Jewish community with Judaica in a modernist idiom. Following formative years in Germany, Wolpert established his design principles serving on the faculty of the Bezalel School for twenty years, before moving to the United States, where he expanded his oeuvre over the course of three decades while at the workshop, until his death in 1981. Throughout his long career, Wolpert's aesthetic demonstrated the principles of German modernism of the early 1930s, which prioritized efficiency, practicality, and accessibility. Visually, his interpretation of modernism is evidenced in the spare geometric composition of this lamp. Additionally, this object is made of brass and of easily reproducible components, keeping its price point accessible to the young families who were the consumers targeted by Kanof for the workshop. Its design was meant to complement interiors of American homes and synagogues.

As a design object, this lamp opens a dialogue as to how Jewish religious and cultural identity were conveyed through the arts. Wolpert worked at the museum at a time of great change at the institution. The museum's leaders redirected its exhibition programming toward contemporary art and made a name for itself in the New York City art scene. In doing so, they challenged the parameters of Jewish art as too narrow and reimagined the Jewish Museum as more than a repository for Jewish artifacts. Modernist Judaica was part of an emergent discourse among Jewish artists and institutions questioning the aesthetic ethos of ritual objects to best suit and shape Jewish religious observance in the changing cultural and political landscape of the postwar United States. As an émigré, Wolpert also can be counted among the many European Jewish artists and designers who came to the United States and made definitive contributions to graphic design, industrial design, architecture, and craft. The workshop was a business, and there, Wolpert essentially created the American market for modern Jewish ritual objects.

The global repositioning of the Jewish community in the wake of the decimation of European Jewry shifted Jewry in the Americas now as its foremost constituent. The design of this lamp reveals the concerns and convictions of Jewish religious leaders, specifically a tandem desire to fortify Jewish religious identity as well as to connect with the way Jews moved through the secular space of American society. Created to counter indifference and ignorance among American Jews, the design, production, and intended consumption of this ritual object embody the concern with definitions and expressions of "authentic" Judaism that has emerged consistently among Diaspora Jews.

PRIMARY SOURCE

Facing page: Ludwig Wolpert, Hanukkah lamp, copper alloy, hand worked, Tobe Pascher Workshop, New York, 1958. (Tobe Pascher Foundation, JMNY, JM 51-58)

QUESTIONS

1. Who buys Jewish ritual art? Why might a Hanukkah lamp be among the first objects produced by the workshop?
2. Wolpert's Hanukkah lamp serves a Jewish ritual function. In what other ways can an object be defined as Jewish?
3. Today museum shops provide a way for visitors to take a memory of a museum home with them and to display their acquisition of culture. What does it say about the Jewish Museum that it was selling ritual objects?
4. Compare Wolpert's Hanukkah lamp to the *hanukkiah* in chapter 20. What are the stylistic and physical differences?
5. Do you agree with Kristina Wilson that midcentury modern designs like this Hanukkah lamp are designed to "maintain rationality and cleanliness . . . and constrain delinquency and mess"?

NOTE

1. Wilson, *Mid-century Modernism and the American Body*, 3.

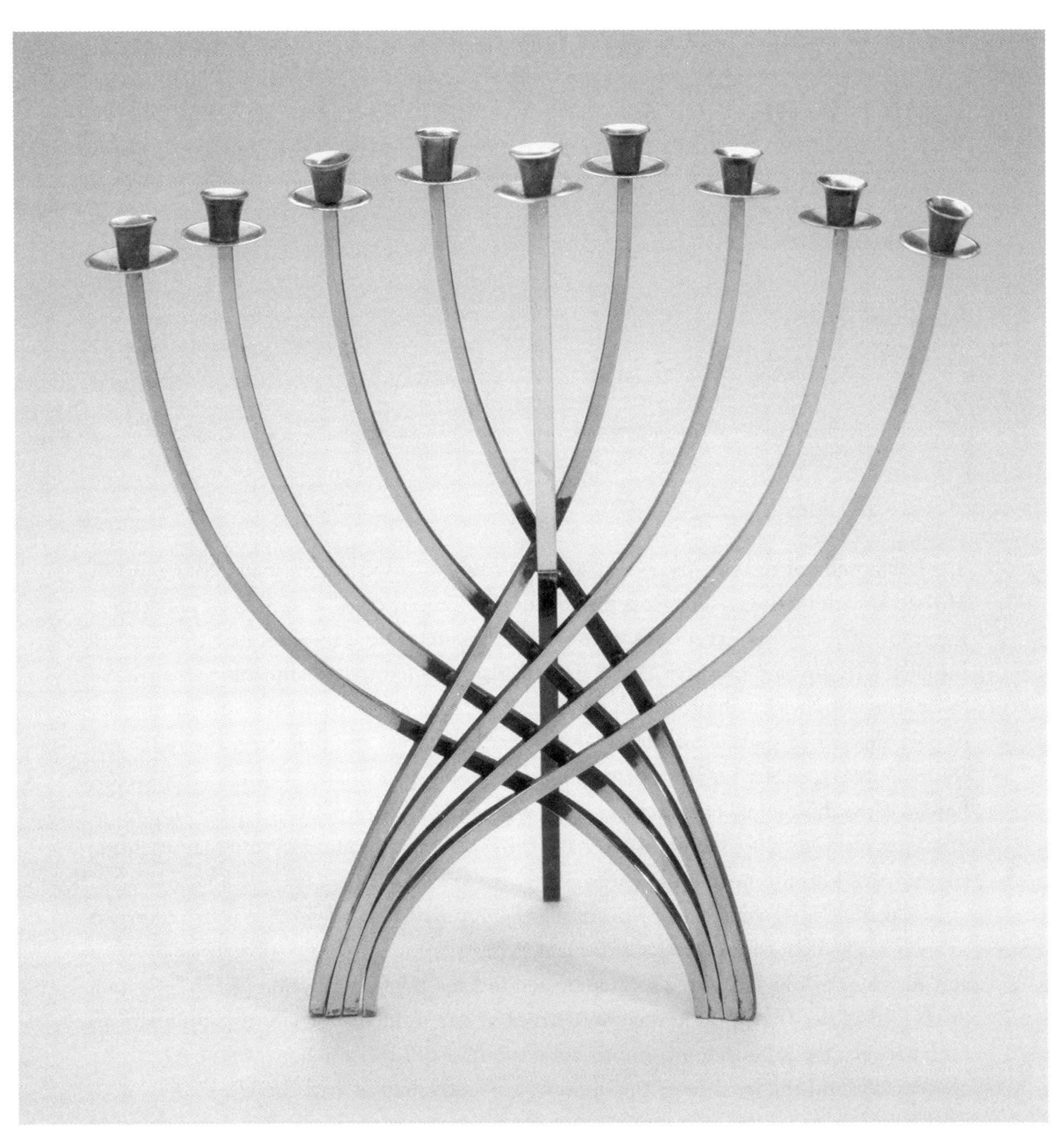

95

The Eichmann Affair in the Shadow of the Cold War

ARGENTINA, 1960

Raanan Rein

The kidnapping of the Nazi war criminal Adolf Eichmann in Argentina in May 1960 by Mossad (Israeli intelligence) agents provoked a diplomatic crisis, as well as an antisemitic wave, in which Jewish Argentines were accused, again, of dual loyalties (see chapter 73). Initially, Israeli prime minister David Ben Gurion claimed that Eichmann was captured by "a group of Jewish volunteers," thus denying direct Israeli participation. Argentina, for its part, demanded that Eichmann be returned to Argentina and that Israel apologize and compensate Argentina for the violation of its national sovereignty. Within a few weeks, however, the diplomatic crisis was resolved with the publication of this brief joint communiqué, elaborated by Shabtai Rosenne of the Israeli foreign ministry and his Argentine counterpart, Luis María de Pablo Pardo.

It was thus foreign-policy considerations that ensured that bilateral relations returned to their normal course. Argentine president Arturo Frondizi was worried about his own and his country's image in the United States and the possible reaction of US Jews to a prolonged crisis. This episode was more proof of the influence of US Jews on relations both between the Argentine government and the State of Israel and between the Argentine government and the local Jewish community. While relations with Israel were repaired, violent manifestations of antisemitism brought substantial deterioration in the position of Argentina's Jews for at least a couple of years. Jewish Argentines found themselves characterized as a "fifth column" in the service of "Zionist imperialism." The joint communiqué gave priority to Israel's state interests, leaving Jewish Argentines in a precarious situation.

The repercussions of Eichmann's kidnapping highlighted the complex relationship between the State of Israel and Diaspora Jews. More than a few Jewish Argentines collaborated in locating the Nazi war criminal and helping Mossad agents in hiding Eichmann until he was smuggled out of the country. Community organizations supported the initiative of their Jewish homeland. At the same time, Argentine nationalists took advantage of the affair to accuse Jews of dual identities and of giving priority to Israeli interests over Argentine sovereignty. The joint communiqué of both governments revealed, however, the priority that both gave to diplomatic and international considerations in their effort to maintain close relations with the United States in the larger context of the Cold War.

The status of Jews across the Americas depended on the relations between local governments and the hegemonic power of the hemisphere. Pro-Jewish and antisemitic political leaders alike tended to exaggerate the importance of the US Jewish community and its influence on policy makers in Washington. Therefore, often, governments would shape their attitudes and policies toward the Jewish community and the State of Israel so as not to antagonize the "Jewish lobby" of the United States. This was precisely the case of the Frondizi government in Argentina. Similar incidents of the conflation of Jews and Israel's national interests occurred in the following decades. Most saliently was the case of the US citizen Jonathan Pollard, who was accused of passing classified information to Israel. His arrest in 1986 gave rise to similar discussions in the United States about the supposed divided loyalties of Jews.

PRIMARY SOURCES

See following page.

QUESTIONS

1. The UN Security Council resolution of June 23, 1960, expressly indicated that Israel had violated Argentina's sovereignty and needed to make reparations. To what extent does Israel appear to have apologized with the statement here?
2. Are Jews unique among ethnic groups in their split loyalties? In what ways do other ethnic groups manifest their ties with their real or imagined homeland?
3. In chapter 83, we saw the United States playing an important role in situations even when it was not directly involved. In your own words, can you explain why the Jewish Argentine community's needs became secondary to political considerations in the United States and Israel?

S

UNITED NATIONS

SECURITY COUNCIL

Distr.
GENERAL

S/4349
24 June 1960
ENGLISH
ORIGINAL: ENGLISH/SPANISH

RESOLUTION ADOPTED BY THE SECURITY COUNCIL AT ITS
868TH MEETING ON 23 JUNE 1960

The Security Council,

Having examined the complaint that the transfer of Adolf Eichmann to the territory of Israel constitutes a violation of the sovereignty of the Argentine Republic,

Considering that the violation of the sovereignty of a Member State is incompatible with the Charter of the United Nations,

Having regard to the fact that reciprocal respect for and the mutual protection of the sovereign rights of States are an essential condition for their harmonious coexistence,

Noting that the repetition of acts such as that giving rise to this situation would involve a breach of the principles upon which international order is founded creating an atmosphere of insecurity and distrust incompatible with the preservation of peace,

Mindful of the universal condemnation of the persecution of the Jews under the Nazis, and of the concern of people in all countries that Eichmann should be brought to appropriate justice for the crimes of which he is accused,

Noting at the same time that this resolution should in no way be interpreted as condoning the odious crimes of which Eichmann is accused,

1. Declares that acts such as that under consideration, which affect the sovereignty of a Member State and therefore cause international friction, may, if repeated, endanger international peace and security;

2. Requests the Government of Israel to make appropriate reparation in accordance with the Charter of the United Nations and the rules of international law;

3. Expresses the hope that the traditionally friendly relations between Argentina and Israel will be advanced.

60-15564

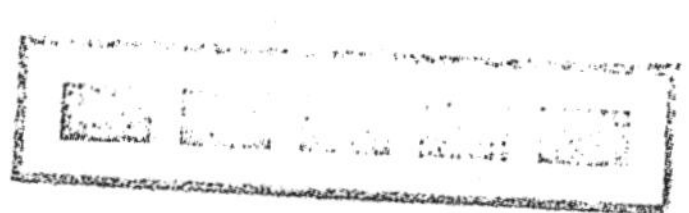

Resolution adopted by the UN Security Council at its 868th meeting on June 23, 1960 (on questions relating to the case of Adolf Eichmann). (© United Nations, 2021; reprinted with the permission of the United Nations)

The governments of the Argentine Republic and Israel, motivated by the purpose of complying with the [United Nations] Security Council resolution of 23 June 1960 with the hope of improving the traditional friendly relations between the two countries, resolve to declare that the incident, originated by an action committed by Israeli nationals against the fundamental rights of the Argentine state, is concluded.

Joint Announcement, August 3, 1960, File A3071/4, Israel State Archives, Jerusalem.

96

The Selma March

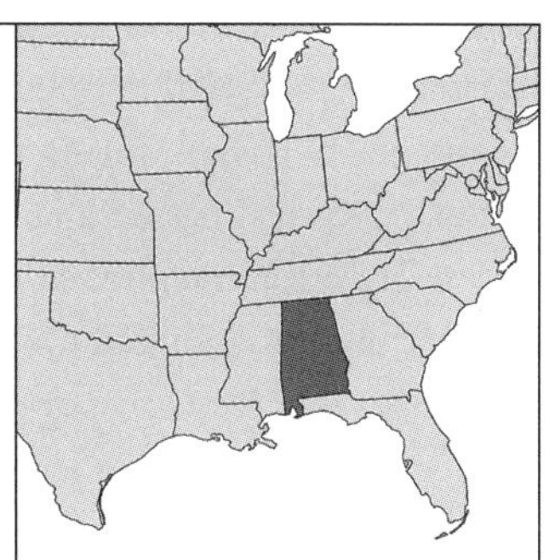

ALABAMA, 1965

Susannah Heschel

"I felt my legs were praying." With those words describing his experience of the march from Selma to Montgomery, Alabama, that took place in March 1965, Rabbi Abraham Joshua Heschel, professor of Jewish ethics and mysticism at the Jewish Theological Seminary, transformed a political march into a moment of profound religiosity. Heschel had long been close to Rev. Martin Luther King Jr. after meeting him in January 1963 at a conference on religion and race held in Chicago. At that meeting, Heschel delivered the sharpest repudiation of racism ever formulated by a Jewish thinker. He and King frequently spoke together to groups of Jews and Christians, emphasizing their shared concern and offering the country a vision of unity between African Americans and Jewish Americans.

Heschel and King's friendship became a symbol that has long been invoked, sometimes with nostalgia, other times with hope for reconciliation, and the photographs of that event continue to inspire pride and hope in Jews. For many US Jews, the civil rights movement came to be intertwined with the Exodus from Egypt as it was celebrated in the Passover Seder. Likewise, photographs from the march seem to affirm that Jews and Blacks stand together. For some Jews, however, the friendship between Heschel and King is a sign of an unrequited relationship: while Jews supported the civil rights movement, some African Americans have not supported Jewish concerns, especially the State of Israel. Moreover, starting in the 1970s, numerous Jewish organizations joined legal challenges to affirmative action, in opposition to civil rights leaders. Other Jews rejected Jewish engagement altogether: the writer Hillel Halkin, in a 1976 book, argued that Jews should work for Jewish concerns, not for those of African Americans—utterly ignoring that some Jews are African American. The rise of neoconservatism in the 1980s further split the Jewish world between those who view social justice as central to Judaism and those who see Jewish ethnicity and Israel as most important.

Heschel was hardly the only Jew or rabbi to participate in the Selma march. On the contrary, Jews flocked to the South to participate as Freedom Riders and in efforts to register Black voters. Andrew Goodman and Michael Schwerner were two Jews murdered by the

KKK along with James Cheney in Philadelphia, Mississippi, during Freedom Summer in 1964. Dozens of rabbis, from Reform to Orthodox, went to march in Selma, many raised funds to support the Southern Christian Leadership Conference (SCLC), and many were arrested for their civil rights protests.

The places passed during the march also show the other side of the coin. During the march, protesters passed a large billboard advertising Tepper's, a department store owned by Sol Tepper, a member of Selma's Jewish community and an outspoken proponent of segregation. A member of the White Citizens Council and a friend of the notorious Sheriff Jim Clark, Tepper's active opposition to the civil rights movement was shared by nearly all members of Selma's small Jewish community.

Yet the march was also a cause for celebration, as the Selma photographs emphasize. The marchers often smile because President Lyndon Johnson and the US Congress were finally on the verge of passing a Voting Rights Act. A previous attempt to march from Selma two weeks earlier, on March 7, 1965, ended in disaster when Alabama state troopers charged the marchers, attacking them with wooden clubs and tear gas; that day came to be known as "Bloody Sunday." The troopers' violence was filmed and shown on television throughout the United States that evening, and many people were appalled. Governor George Wallace of Alabama refused to protect civil rights workers or meet with them. President Johnson, who viewed King as an ally, intervened and sent federal troops to protect the marchers. On March 15, Johnson convened a joint session of Congress to press for passage of the Voting Rights Act, concluding his speech, shown on national television, by dramatically declaring, "We shall overcome." Thus, the march from Selma to Montgomery ultimately took place, starting on March 21, 1965, with the air of celebrating an achievement.

Still, we might question the long-term accomplishment of that march. The Voting Rights Act was passed by Congress and became law in August 1965, but in recent years, state legislatures, especially in southern states, have successfully curbed voting rights for many Americans, particularly African Americans. Voter ID laws and laws permanently prohibiting ex-felons from voting have disenfranchised large numbers of voters in numerous parts of the country. The requirement that the US State Department's Office of Civil Rights monitor voting laws was struck down by the US Supreme Court in 2013, with Chief Justice John Roberts writing for the majority.

Does the Selma march of 1965 continue to mark a moment of celebration? Jews have long been proud of Jewish support for Dr. King and the civil rights movement. Groups of Jews from around the US make pilgrimages to Birmingham, Montgomery, and Selma to view memorials and museums related to the movement, and the photograph of the Selma march serves as a point of pride and inspiration for further Jewish social activism. On the other hand, numerous commentators have argued that relations between Blacks and white Jews deteriorated starting in the late 1960s after the death of Dr. King. From that perspective, the photograph might be viewed not as a celebration but as a moment lost in a relationship that no longer thrives.

As the daughter of Rabbi Heschel, I have long felt that the iconic photographs of Heschel and King at the Selma march should not signal celebration but challenge: Are we as Jews addressing racism? Are we actively forging alliances with the African American community? When will African American and Asian American Jews feel fully at home in

Jewish institutions? Can we put aside our pride in the efforts of Jewish civil rights workers of the 1960s and recognize how much work is left for us to do?

Let us take responsibility for the entire Selma experience: for the warm smiles on the faces of the front row of marchers wearing leis and full of optimism for the future but also remember the horrific violence, physical and verbal, that surrounded the marchers. Photographs of the Selma march can bring inspiration only when we understand them as a challenge. We need to remember that we have both racists and antiracists in our Jewish community. The right to feel pride in these photographs must be earned through our ongoing hard work.

PRIMARY SOURCES

Third Selma march, 1965. (Photo by William Lovelace/Daily Express/Hulton Archive/Getty Images)

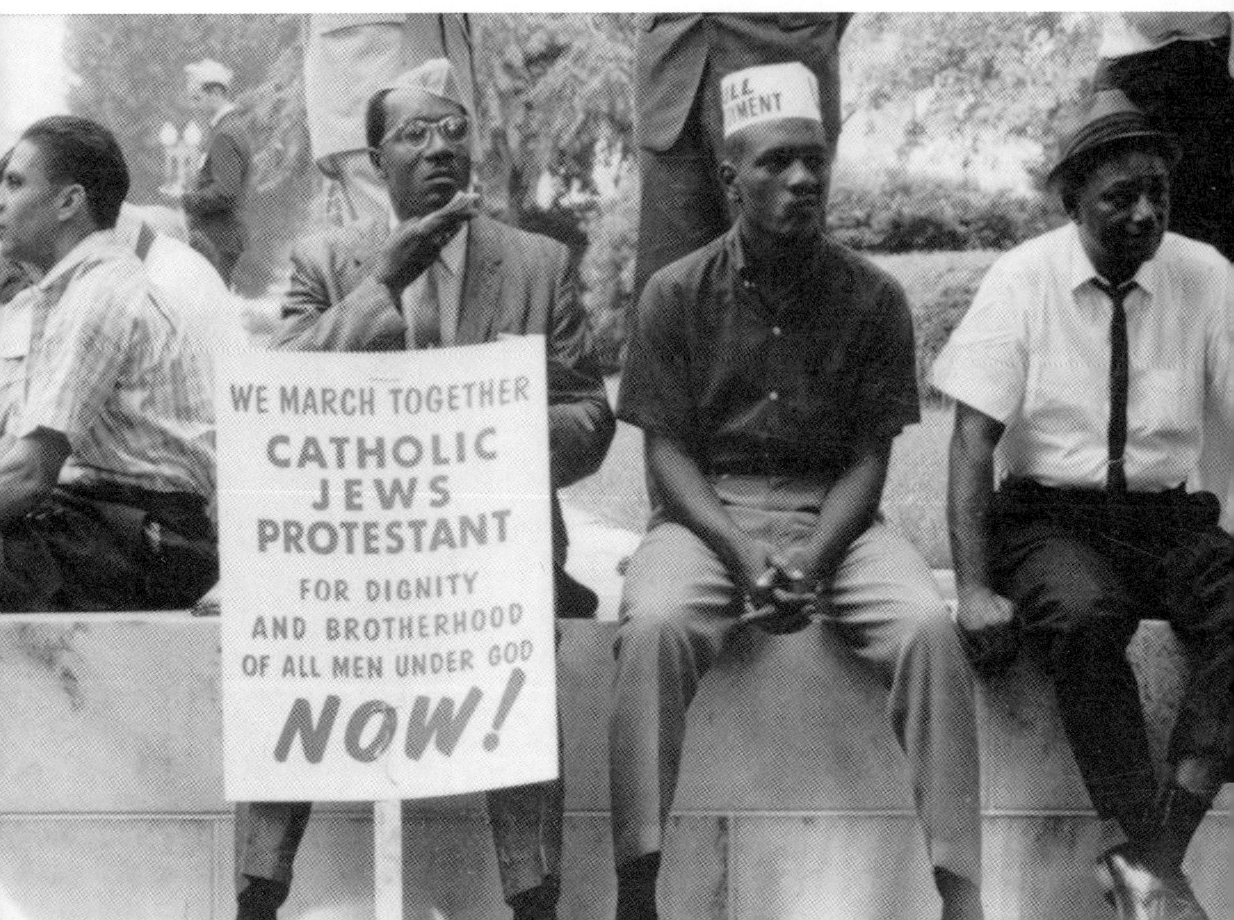

The civil rights march from Selma to Montgomery, Alabama in 1965. (Photograph by Peter Pettus, LCPPD, LC-USZ6-2329)

QUESTIONS

1. Why do you think Jewish participation in the civil rights movement has become so important to Jews?
2. Do you think it matters to African Americans that Jews marched at Selma?
3. What further work needs to be done to make the Selma photographs a point of celebration?
4. Why are Black-Jewish relations important?
5. How might the photographs here challenge the perception that all the Jews participating in the Selma march were white?

97

Jewish Disappeared

CHILE, 1978

Valeria Navarro-Rosenblatt

During the Cold War, military governments in the Southern Cone persecuted leftist activists. Some activists, like the Chilean journalist and lawyer Carlos Berger Guralnik (1943–1973), were Jewish. His family, originally from eastern Europe (Hungary and the Soviet Union), had always been very active in politics. His parents, Dora Guralnik and Julio Berger, militants since the late 1930s, had joined the Chilean Communist Party with their friends, as a way to advance the Jewish cause during World War II. Berger, whose experience of Judaism was cultural rather than religious, also participated as a young intellectual in the Chilean Communist Party, whose main purpose was to improve the quality of life of all Chilean citizens. During Salvador Allende's presidential campaigns (1964 and 1970), Berger worked for the socialist candidate. Later, after Allende's election (1970) and the establishment of the Popular Unity government, Berger worked as a journalist in the young communist magazine *Ramona*, in the Ministry of Economy, and as director of El Loa Radio in Chuquicamata (in the north of Chile). His job at the radio station was to promote the government's agenda at the copper mine Cobres Chuqui. It was in Chuquicamata where Berger and his family were at the moment of the coup d'état that overthrew Salvador Allende in 1973. Berger was arrested and sent to the Calama prison, where he was executed on October 19, 1973. His death was never officially confirmed, and his body was never returned to his family.

Berger's family was shattered. His wife, Carmen Hertz, began a long exile, together with their son, Germán Berger, fearing for their lives. His parents, Julio and Dora, later committed suicide because of the impact that this tragic event had on their lives. Most of their social network, embedded in Jewish and non-Jewish leftist and communist groups, went into exile. After Hertz's return to Chile in 1978, she began to work at Vicaría de la Solidaridad, a Christian human-rights organization founded in 1976 to help victims of political persecution and their families. She was a representative for the Communist Party at the National Congress between 2018 and 2022. The following document was written by Hertz, to claim Berger's remains in order to bury him at the Jewish Cemetery in Santiago.

Communist Jews were a central component of Jewish life in Chile. Their activities and political activism reflect both an early Jewish commitment to local and community issues and integration into local societies. Yet the death of Berger as part of the military repression that followed the 1973 coup d'état shows what Jewish Chileans shared with other Chileans. They lived and died alongside their conationals. The letter exemplifies how the language of human rights was used as part of the struggle against the dictatorship. This was an important change: by highlighting and emphasizing the violations of human rights in the legal cases and the petitions for habeas corpus, a legal mechanism to demand the government produce the "body," human-rights organizations used international law in an effort to help, rescue, or gather information about those who had been imprisoned or kidnapped.

PRIMARY SOURCE

Santiago, October 19, 1978

Mr. President of the Chilean Bar Association,

Today, October 19, 1978, marks the 5th anniversary of my husband's execution. The execution of Carlos Berger, lawyer and journalist, took place in Calama, only 22 days before he was set to be freed after fulfilling the sentence issued by the Calama Military War Trial.

Until September 11, 1973, my husband was the Director of El Loa Radio, in Chuquicamata. He was arrested while broadcasting about the national events. He was taken by Calama military personnel, and later sentenced by the Calama Military War Trial to 60 days at the Calama Jail.

On October 19, 1973, close to 4:30 pm, Carlos was suddenly taken from the jail together with other 25 political prisoners; all of them were executed at 6 pm, as stated in his death certificate. I was with Carlos just moments before he was taken from his cell, as I was his lawyer and was able to visit him daily.

I was told, after long and multiple conversations [with authorities] in my search to find him, that he had "tried to escape." I was not allowed to see his body and was not told about the real circumstances in which the murder of my husband took place. My request to move his remains to the Jewish Cemetery in Santiago was denied.

By the end of October 1973, I had informed both the Journalists' and Bar Associations about this painful event, but received no answers to my plea to recover and bury my husband's remains.

As none of the measures I took to get help worked, I fled the country with my then 11-month-old son.

Today I am back home, five years after the absurd and horrifying death of my husband. I find it crucial to share my thoughts with those who were his colleagues. Carlos's illegal and arbitrary execution, justified [by them] by what they called "the law of escape," which does not exist in our country's jurisprudence, should be understood, together with several other cases, as the beginning of a systematic violation to the most fundamental Human Rights in our country.

I am not driven by vengeance or hate; I strongly believe that clarifying this event is needed for real democracy, and above all, to prevent similar acts as the painful one described above, from ever happening again.

I write to you as President of the Bar Association, so you can ask the Interior Minister to do whatever is in his power to determine the context and responsibilities in Carlos Berger's death. Any help would be highly appreciated; I will also continue with requests of my own. My final objective is to bury Carlos Berger's remains at the Jewish Cemetery in Santiago. A similar request was sent to the President of the Journalists' Association, as he was also a journalist.

Thanks in advance. Looking forward to a positive answer from you.

Best regards,
Carmen Hertz, widow of Carlos Berger.
Lawyer. [ID number]

"Letter to the President of the Chilean Lawyers' Bar Association from Carmen Hertz," JC 5-10-85, Carlos Berger Folder, Fundación de Documentación y Archivo Vicaría de la Solidaridad, Santiago de Chile.

QUESTIONS

1. What, if anything, is Jewish about this letter?
2. If Carlos Berger and his family were not religious, why would his wife, Carmen Hertz, wish to have his remains buried at the Jewish Cemetery?
3. What is the objective of the letter? Does it have any political meaning?
4. By presenting Berger's Jewishness as part of the argument, where does Hertz locate the death of her husband in local Jewish and national histories?

98

Indian Jewish Experiences and the Creation of Congregation BINA

ONTARIO, 1979–2010

Kelly Amanda Train

A 2021 Pew Research Center report noted that about 3 percent of Jews in the US identify as "Asian, American Indian, or Hawaiian/Pacific Island—or with more than one race."[1] While some of these Jews joined Judaism through adoption, conversion, or intermarriage, others' families immigrated already practicing Judaism. Two such groups are the Bene Israel (Sons of Israel) and Cochin Jews from India/Pakistan. Although similar data to that compiled by the Pew Research Center is not available for Canada, between 1964 and 1980, small numbers of Jews immigrated from India to Canada.[2] As they settled, primarily in Toronto, some attended the preexisting synagogues for holiday services and Shabbat. Most of these congregations were Ashkenazi, as the first Sephardic synagogue was not established in Toronto until 1958 and was still quite small in the 1960s. However, many Indian Jews were uncomfortable attending Ashkenazi synagogues, despite the fact that in India they were an English-speaking community.

Almost immediately, Indian Jews had people question their Indian Jewish identities. Ashkenazi Jews demanded that Indian Jews explain how they could be Jewish, on the basis of their "brown" skin color, and how they had become Jewish. Ashkenazim were further confused by the fact that Indian Jews claimed to be Jewish and yet were unfamiliar with Ashkenazi foods and Yiddish phrases. Indian Jews found the persistence and tone of these questions to be marginalizing, exclusionary, and racist.

By 1978, as more Indian Jews arrived, several families organized community "Socials" for Indian Jewish families to gather, socialize, and feel a sense of belonging and community. A number of families that participated in the Socials suggested that they organize

High Holiday services that used the same prayer tunes and melodies of the Bene Israel and Cochin Jews in a conservative Judaic format favored by the majority of the Indian Jewish families in Toronto at the time. Indian Jewish services were affordable, unlike the membership fees required at Ashkenazi synagogues, since the Indian Jewish community organizers were able to secure inexpensive rent. In September 1979, Indian Jews held their first High Holiday services and have done so every year since then. Congregation BINA (Bene Israel North America) obtained official charitable status as a religious organization in 1980.

One of the traditions that Congregation BINA brought with it from India is food. Some traditional foods for Passover include a spicy *glatt*-kosher lamb curry. Other Passover dishes include a charoset (a paste made from nuts and fruit eaten at the Seder) made from Medjool dates. As for many Sephardic Jews, rice is an acceptable part of Passover but must be checked carefully for grains of wheat.[3] These traditions are a good reminder that Passover and quintessentially "Jewish" recipes vary across the Americas. In Suriname, for example, the charoset includes local Surinam cherries, coconut, a variety of dried fruits, cinnamon, and ginger jam. Unleavened bread made from cassava, a local starchy root vegetable, often supplements hard-to-obtain wheat matzah.

Congregation BINA reflects Toronto's diverse Jewish community. The sources included here help us understand how inclusion and belonging impact settlement in a new country. The Indian Jewish community established the congregation to imbue its children with a sense of pride in their Indian Jewish identity, culture, and customs, as well as to create and reinforce a place of inclusion. Indian Jews continue to experience discrimination even today, revealing how Jewishness in the Canadian context continues to be associated with a white, Ashkenazi Jewish identity. Lastly, the sources remind us that the Indian Jewish community in Toronto organized its own congregation partly as a form of resistance to the discrimination it faced and partly to ensure the survival of Indian Jewish cultures and identities.

PRIMARY SOURCE

Ingredients

1 pound boneless chicken, cut into cubes
1–2 big onions (finely chopped)
1 tomato
4 garlic cloves
1/2 an inch of fresh ginger root
1 teaspoon salt (or according to taste)
1/2 teaspoon turmeric
1 teaspoon garam masala (optional)
1/2 cup fresh lemon juice
1 bunch coriander
1–2 green chilies (depending on how spicy you want it to be)
1 teaspoon sugar (white or brown)
2 tablespoons cooking oil

Classic Passover Indian chicken green curry, recipe by Neeli Moses. (Courtesy Congregation BINA)

Instructions

1. In a blender, add chopped coriander, garlic, ginger, green chilies, tomato, and 2 tablespoons of lemon juice and blend into a smooth consistency. Set aside. Add some water if the mixture is difficult to blend.
2. Wash the chicken and add the rest of the lemon juice to it. Let it rest until ready to cook.
3. In a saucepan, on medium heat, add cooking oil. Add in onion and sauté until slightly golden brown, about 4–6 minutes.
4. Add salt, turmeric, and garam masala at this stage and cook for 30 seconds more.
5. Now immediately add the blended green-herb mixture to the saucepan. Leave it to cook on low heat for 10 minutes or until the water evaporates and the curry becomes thick. You will see the mixture start separating from the oil. That is when it is ready for the next step.
6. Add sugar.
7. Add chicken and let it cook until ready and fully cooked, around 20 minutes.

8. **Before taking the curry off the stove, make sure that the chicken is tender and has cooked all the way through. If the chicken isn't tender yet, add a little more water and cook for 5 minutes more.**
9. **Once ready to serve, garnish it with chopped coriander leaves.**

Congregation BINA Canada, poster for thirtieth anniversary celebration, May 23, 2010. (Congregation BINA member listserv)

QUESTIONS

1. How does the poster balance the community's Indian, Jewish, and Canadian ties?
2. What does it mean to be a minority within a minority?
3. Do minority Jewish community institutions, such as Congregation BINA, create a sense of empowerment for their members? If so, how?
4. What, if anything, is Jewish about the chicken green curry recipe? If your family is Jewish, what recipes do you tend to serve on Passover?

NOTES

1. Pew Research Center, "Race, Ethnicity, Heritage and Immigration among U.S. Jews."
2. The Environics Institute's 2018 survey of Canadian Jews assumed that people of color and Jews were mutually exclusive categories (Environics Institute, "2018 Survey of Jews in Canada").
3. Henry, "Passover a Spicy Affair for Toronto's Indian Jews."

99

Tradition and Modernity among Iranian Jewish Women

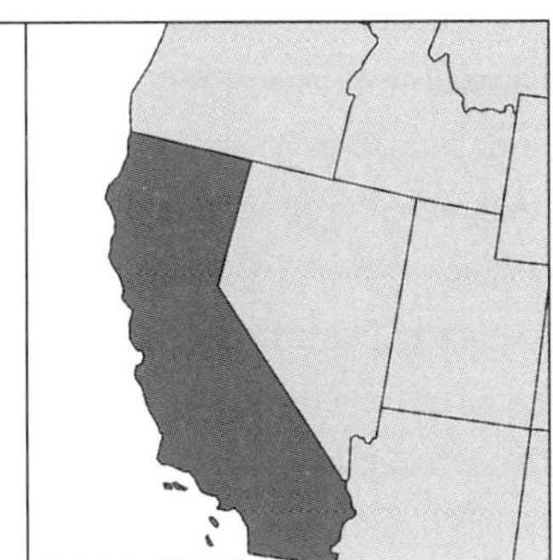

CALIFORNIA, 1979–2015

Laura Arnold Leibman

Iranian Jews are one of several groups of Mizrachi Jews that have settled in the Americas. Iranian Jews, like the Jews of Iraq and Yemen, have one of the oldest Mizrachi communities, which dates back to antiquity.[1] The story told in the book of Esther, for example, is about the Jews who lived in Persia (now Iran) in the fifth century BCE (see chapters 4 and 9). Iranian Jews brought distinctive experiences in the Middle East, as well as a unique culture, with them to the Americas, and women played a crucial role in both maintaining and updating these traditions.

One element that made Iranian Jewish culture unique was their experience of "modernization" under the shah of Iran. Modernization is the process by which countries move from primarily rural, traditional, and agrarian to urban, secular, and industrial societies. For Jews in western Europe and the Americas, modernization often brought about emancipation (see part 2). As we have seen in chapters 63 and 68 modernization of Mizrachi Jewish communities was often conflated with Europeanization. Iranian Jews' experience of modernization, however, was filtered through the policies of the shah of Iran, who reigned from 1941 to 1979. The shah not only continued to welcome Iranian Jews even after the establishment of Israel in 1948 but also maintained positive relations with the State of Israel. Because many Jews stayed in Iran during this key period, Iranian Jews experienced a local form of modernity that some scholars have referred to as "indigenous modernity" or "authoritarian modernity," as it emphasized technological and material change but not political participation.[2] Iran's open stance toward Jews changed abruptly, however, with the Islamic Revolution of 1979. Following the overthrow of the government, seventy thousand Iranian Jews relocated to the United States.[3] Early Iranian American synagogues such as the Chicago area's Persian Hebrew Congregation, which opened in the early 1900s, now were flooded with a new generation of immigrants.

One of the largest new communities, however, was in Los Angeles, where in 1980 Rabbi David Shofet founded the Nessah (eternal) Synagogue. Nessah became a place for Iranian Jews to preserve their distinctive history and *minhagim* (traditions). Like other Mizrahi Jews, Iranian Jews brought with them to the Americas a culture that emerged under Arab culture and Muslim rulers. As a result, their prayer rites and material culture differed dramatically from those of the Ashkenazi majority living in Los Angeles. As the congregation grew, it moved into larger quarters, with the last move in 2002 to its current synagogue, in a remodeled building formerly owned by the First Church of Christ, Scientist at 142 Rexford Drive in Beverly Hills. By 2007, Los Angeles was home to about thirty to forty thousand Iranian Jews, with many living in Beverly Hills. Over the years, Nessah has been joined by the Iranian Jewish Federation and numerous Iranian synagogues, schools, *kollels*, and outreach centers in Beverly Hills, Pico-Robertson, Tarzana, and West Hollywood.

Women's culture in particular carried distinctive elements from Iran to the United States. Prior to immigration, Jewish women played a crucial role in Iranian synagogues and in some regions women served the honorary role of the *shamash*, who cared for the synagogue in general and the Torah ark in particular.[4] The kitchen was likewise understood as a sacred space, where Sabbath and festival meals were prepared.[5] Women, in turn, carried recipes and food-preparation traditions with them as they migrated. One distinctive Persian Jewish dish is the *tachin-e badenjan* (eggplant and rice casserole).[6] Today, traditional rice recipes can be found alongside "American" dishes like turkey at Thanksgiving celebrations.[7]

Women likewise played an important role in creating the ceremonial and nonceremonial textiles that are central to Iranian Jewish life. Velvet, with gold and silver embroidery, was particularly valued, and *maghdeh-duzi* (tinsel made from flattened metal embroidered onto fabric) is one of the community's distinctive crafts. Bridal gowns were traditionally created using this technique on white tulle (a lightweight netting). A tulle scarf was also used to cover the bride's hair. In parts of Iran, this scarf only left the face visible, a practice that reflected the local Muslim practice of wearing a *khimar* or *chador*. Today, these embroidered veils are often heirlooms.[8] This distinctive dress was accompanied by a *hennah-bandhan* ritual, in which henna was placed in the bride's hair and on the women's hands. Adult women would also wear a white dress and veil to synagogue.[9]

During the reign of the shah of Iran and his father, Reza Shah, Jewish women—like other women in Iran—increasingly wore more Westernized clothing.[10] After the Revolution, when many people in the community moved to the Americas, the trend of wearing Western fashions continued. In the Beverly Hills community, designer clothing and handbags became an important part of showing one's status.[11] For some, Orthodox conventions around modesty became a way to escape from these pressures, with some feeling that "Orthodox Judaism provided a less superficial community that placed its importance on God rather than on materialistic objects."[12] At the same time, other women combined the desire for high fashion with traditions surrounding modesty. One example of this trend is the Los Angeles–based brand Ra | Ju, created by Rachelle Yadegar and Judith Illulian. As they explain, "Raju is inspired by and dedicated to the real women. Our purpose is to create modest garments that can allow a woman to celebrate her beauty as well as embrace her femininity."[13] As in Iran, this notion of modesty is influenced by local conventions, with European-hair *sheitels* (wigs) favored by ultra-Orthodox Ashkenazi women, having replaced the *chador*, which had signaled modesty in Shi'a Muslim culture.

The three photos included here provide very different windows into Iranian Jewish life before and after migration. The first was taken by Elkan Nathan Adler, who traveled to Tehran in 1896–1897. The son of Nathan Marcus Adler ("Chief Rabbi of the British Empire"), Adler gazes through a British imperial lens, which saw Iranian Jews as "backward" and in need of European help. In contrast, the photo of Sormeh Kimiabakhsh was taken for the family (presumably by a local photographer) for their personal use and pleasure and was passed down by the generations. The third photograph was taken in Los Angeles in 2015 by an American photographer.

PRIMARY SOURCES

Synagogue of Asher Rofé at Tehran, Iran, c. 1897. (Adler, *Jews in Many Lands*, 189)

Sormeh Kimiabakhsh (*middle row, left*) photographed at her marriage to Morvārīd Khānom (Naneh Morvārīd) in Hamadan, Iran, 1910. (Courtesy Saba Soomekh)

Nessah Synagogue, Beverly Hills, California, 2015. (© Glenn Francis, www.PacificProDigital.com)

QUESTIONS

1. In Adler's book *Jews of Many Lands* (1905), in which the first image included here appears, he argues that Iranian Jews are not only poor but "ignorant" (190, 193). Yet, Rabbi David Shofet of the Nessah Synagogue, who was born in Tehran, was the twelfth generation of rabbis in his family, and his father was the chief rabbi of Iran from 1922 to 1980. How does the way Adler photographed the synagogue help substantiate his particular understanding of Iranian Jewish life as backward?
2. Two of Reza Shah's main reforms were related to men's dress (1928) and the unveiling of women (1936). Following the reforms, men were required to wear Western suits and forbidden to wear turbans. Even the fez, which was itself a substitute for the turban, was replaced with a French, military-style "Pahlavi cap" and then in 1935 with Western-style hats. What clothing in these photographs would have been outlawed by the shah's father? What potentially was lost in this forced "modernization"?
3. Compare and contrast the synagogues in Tehran and Beverly Hills. How does each simultaneously reflect tradition and the values specific to the time and place when and where the photo was taken?
4. Who or what is the focal point of each photograph? How does this focus represent the story that the photographer wishes to convey about Iranian Jewish life?

NOTES

1. Soomekh, *Sephardi and Mizrahi Jews in America*, ix–x.
2. Talattof, *Modernity, Sexuality, and Ideology*, 23.
3. Soomekh, *From the Shahs to Los Angeles*, 1.
4. Grossman and Haut, introduction to *Daughters of the King*, 6; Grossman and Haut, "From Persia to New York," 224.
5. Sered, "Synagogue as a Sacred Space," 206.
6. Marks, *Encyclopedia of Jewish Food.*
7. Sternfeld, "Iranian Jewish Los Angeles."
8. Carmeli, "Material Culture and Ritual Objects," 146–150, 164–165; Soomekh, "To Be an Iranian Jewish Bride."
9. Soomekh, *From the Shahs to Los Angeles*, 200, 29.
10. Soomekh, 83–84.
11. Soomekh, 139.
12. Soomekh, 106.
13. Ra | Ju, "Who We Are."

100

Jewish Argentine Memory and Justice in the Aftermath of the 1994 AMIA Bombing

ARGENTINA, 1994–2022

Natasha Zaretsky

The 1994 AMIA (Argentine Jewish Mutual Aid Society) attack in Buenos Aires killed eighty-five people, wounded hundreds, and destroyed the main Jewish community center in Argentina. Although this was the worst terrorist attack in Argentina's history, it remains unsolved twenty-eight years later, as the case has been marred by judicial irregularities and corruption. In 2005, the Inter-American Commission for Human Rights (IACHR) officially deemed that Argentina had failed to provide justice, and in 2022, Argentina officially took responsibility before the IACHR for failing to prevent the attack and for the impunity that followed. In response, social movements and community groups formed to demand justice and to keep the memory of the victims alive. In addition, security measures were installed at almost every Jewish building and site. While the community struggled to respond to the violence and loss, an added challenge was that the state's response visibly reinforced Jewish difference.

Various memorial practices developed in response to the bombing, all in the hopes of advocating for the victims of the bombing, sustaining their memory, and fighting for justice. One of the practices was the creation of a wall with the names of the victims that was installed at the site of the AMIA bombing, after the building was destroyed in 1994 but before the new building was rebuilt. At this site, family members of the victims convened monthly commemorations that have been taking place at the location of the AMIA attack every month; one of the groups behind the organization of these monthly events is Familiares y Amigos de las Víctimas (Family Members and Friends of the Victims of the AMIA). Such practices reshaped public space by incorporating regular weekly protests into the flow of daily life. In this way, Plaza Lavalle, a public park relatively close by, became an important site for protests, as it faces the high courts. Between 1994 and 2004, the group Memoria Activa (Active Memory) staged weekly protests demanding justice and memory in this plaza. At the start of every weekly gathering, the shofar was blown to mark a call to listen to the testimonies of citizens and supporters who spoke about the victims of the bombing or other issues related to impunity in Argentina. From 2004 to 2018, an informal group, Citizens of the Plaza, moved its protests to the monument in the plaza, still blowing the shofar and remembering the victims every week, choosing to locate the protests at the monument to the victims installed in this plaza, designed by the Jewish Argentine artist Mirta Kupferminc. The continued significance of this space further reinforces how material sites along with protests reshape the public sphere, sustaining the memory of the victims in society.

Together, these sources represent how Jewish Argentines responded to the violence and loss from one of the worst terrorist attacks in their history. Their response reflects the power of memory as a cultural practice and specifically how this site of memory reveals the negotiations over Jewish belonging in Argentina, even years after the violence took place. Further, they reinforce the power of cultural practices based in memory as a response to the AMIA bombing. The monument, for instance, has taken on various social and political uses over time, becoming a powerful site for Jewish memory and belonging after violence. Engaging memory in public spaces marks these practices as distinctly Argentine, while the incorporation of Jewish ritual and prayer in the public sphere—such as the invocation of the Mourner's Kaddish during the monthly commemorations of the bombing at the site of the attack—also asserts the significance of claiming a Jewish identity. Indeed, the use of the shofar in particular during protests in a public square marks a significant shift in Jewish practices intersecting with political activism, as Jews negotiated belonging in Argentina after the AMIA bombing.

PRIMARY SOURCES

See following pages.

QUESTIONS

1. What does the response of Jewish Argentines in public spaces suggest about the Jewish experience in the Americas?
2. Are the memory-based political practices specific to the cultural politics of Argentina, or can they translate to other nations in the Americas?
3. What does the AMIA memorial tell us about the transformations in Jewish ritual practice across American history?

Wall of names after AMIA bombing, 2012. (WC)

Shofars at Memoria Activa protest, Plaza Lavalle, Argentina. (Photograph by Natasha Zaretsky, 2004)

Monument to the victims of the AMIA bombing, Plaza Lavalle. (Photograph by Juan Pablo Chillón)

101

Crypto-Jewish Poetry

NEW MEXICO, 1996

Rachel Kaufman

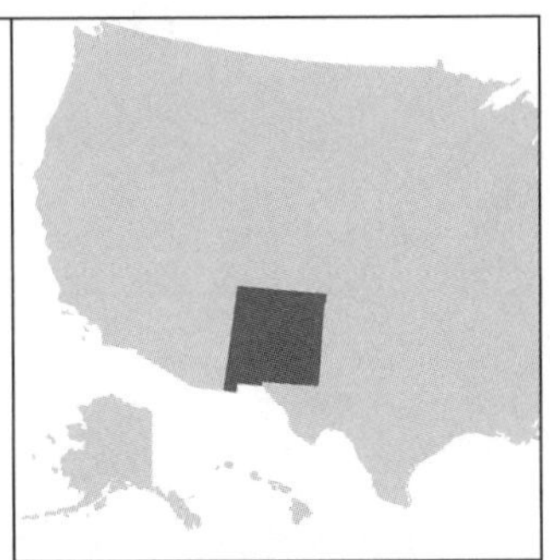

One branch of the Jewish American religious revivals that occurred following the Six-Day War was the return of descendants of crypto-Judaism to public Jewish worship, after centuries of worshiping in secret. One leader of this movement was Rabbi Yosef Garcia, president of the Association of Crypto-Jews of the Americas and founder of Avdey Torah Jayah. Originally founded in Portland, Oregon, Avdey Torah Jayah moved in 2019 to the southwestern United States, where there were larger communities of crypto-Jewish descendants. One of Rabbi Garcia's great contributions to the movement was cocreating a "Ceremony of Return" for crypto-Jews, which was recognized by the State of Israel and allowed congregants to make *aliyah*. The poetry of Isabelle Medina Sandoval, a New Mexican crypto-Jew, picks up on notions of return, transmission, and identity reclamation.

Sandoval traces her family history back to Juan de Oñate, the conquistador who invaded New Mexico in 1598. Sandoval has written extensively on her crypto-Jewish heritage, and one of her poems was included in the 1996 Sage Junior College museum exhibition titled *Llave: A Key to the Secret*. Curated by Andrea K. Nasrallah, *Llave* featured New Mexican poets, artists, and historians celebrating Sephardic Judaism's presence in the New World by means of the legend of *la llave* (the key). The legend claims that when the Spanish Inquisition demanded that Jews convert to Christianity or leave the Iberian Peninsula during the fourteenth and fifteenth centuries, some Jews took with them the keys to their homes in the hope of later return. The keys perhaps no longer contain the hope of actual return (though some physical keys continue to be passed down through generations). Instead, *la llave* serves as a symbol of a lost homeland and an emblem of renewed Sephardic identity for crypto-Jews in the Southwest. Crypto-Jewish traditions continue to be preserved and adapted among families in the region.

Sandoval's poetry situates distant memorial structures, the ancient ports, places, and customs of Sefarad, the ancient Iberian homeland of crypto-Jews, within her own family narrative through an object that is continually reinvested with present-day meaning: the key. The poem illustrates the importance of mythology and oral tradition in crypto-Jewish identity. Sandoval's perspective provides an intimate lens into her family's formation of cultural identity in New Mexico and the logics of crypto-Jewish tradition. Her poetry, alongside the poetry of other New Mexican crypto-Jewish writers, serves as an alternative entry point into crypto-Jewish history and stands apart from the scholarly and popular debates of the past few decades surrounding the authenticity or inauthenticity of crypto-Jewish identity in the Southwest, debates that rely on genealogical data and often flatten the complex ethnic and racial identities of New Mexican crypto-Jews.

Sandoval's poem and the crypto-Jewish identity it proclaims broaden notions of American Judaism by illustrating one voice from a community that is often dismissed as inauthentic or outside the bounds of normative Judaism by Jewish American scholars of the twentieth and twenty-first centuries. Crypto-Jews in New Mexico are often of Indigenous, Latinx, and Jewish descent and demand from Jewish scholars a cross-disciplinary approach to history and to American Jewish identity. "Opened Locks" exemplifies the abundant artistic production of New Mexican crypto-Jews, which asserts the long presence of Sephardim in the Americas and the multitude of practices, languages, and inheritances that make up the American Jewish landscape of past and present.

PRIMARY SOURCE

Opened Locks

Like a foreign country filled with adventures
we played on our Grandmother's high bed
knowing that the glass door knob on the door
is a way of traveling to other new worlds
A ray of light escapes from the lock

The keys of the doors are in the kitchen
to hide the profound secrets of the rooms
near the cupboard that Uncle Raquel bought for us
in a house where saints do not look through walls
Rays of light escape from the house

We separated and twenty years passed in
different states and we united for the first time
talking about the Jewish feeling we have
in the privateness of our understanding and being
Keys of thoughts open up our conversation

Piles of doors of pine and heavy paints
and ports of cities and ancient places of
customs foods and families shine like
the rock with the menorah on our uncle's land
Fires of light and keys illuminate our souls

The Sephardim of Spain escaped with a hidden key
and I know deep in my bones that this same key was
and that now we have found the key to the
sleeping *Neshama* [soul]

Isabelle Medina Sandoval, "*Trancas Abiertas* / Opened Locks." Translation by Isabelle Medina Sandoval.

QUESTIONS

1. Each stanza of the poem ends with a line about light and keys. What does the key (*la llave*) represent in Sandoval family history and heritage?
2. Are any Jewish traditions or symbols in the poem familiar to you? How does Sandoval use these symbols?
3. How does Sandoval remember the Sephardim of Spain? How has her family preserved Jewish tradition across generations, and how have traditions changed over time?
4. Review chapters 77 and 80, in which the past in Spain is mentioned. What is different, if anything, about this poem?

102

Kosher McDonald's Sign

ARGENTINA, 1998

Adriana M. Brodsky

The availability of kosher food has been a point of contention across the eras covered in this volume. In 1998, when the religious Jewish chairman of a real-estate company converted a major Buenos Aires landmark into a shopping mall, he decided to add a kosher McDonald's for the observant Jewish population in the area. Located in a Jewish neighborhood with more than three dozen synagogues around it, the Abasto Mall became the first place outside Israel to have a branch of the popular hamburger chain serving kosher food. The Abasto Mall has a *mezuzah* on the main entrance door and boasts two "regular" (nonkosher) McDonald's stands, where many customers are directed when they find out that they cannot buy a regular cheeseburger at the kosher counter. Following this trend, in 2018, a kosher hamburger and sausage stall made its appearance in Boca Juniors' soccer stadium, a space visited by thousands of people every Sunday.[1] While the kosher McDonald's stand could be seen as providing an existing Jewish market with a kosher alternative to the popular hamburger chain, that aim does not seem to apply to the soccer stadium, located in a neighborhood that is not (any longer) Jewish. Perhaps many people in the stands are, however.

The opening of the kosher McDonald's in Abasto Mall is indicative of the growth of an increasingly more observant Jewish population in Argentina and the religious revival across the Americas following the Six-Day War. While it is difficult to provide definite numbers given the lack of sociological studies of the Jewish community, Orthodoxy has been on the rise in Argentina since the 1940s but picked up steam in the 1970s. In 2005, a study suggested that between 8 and 10 percent of the population of Buenos Aires could be defined as Orthodox.[2] Orthodox Judaism is quite diverse, however, with Sephardic and Ashkenazi collectives and transnational groups, which started to grow with the arrival in the mid-1950s of Satmar Hasidism and emissaries from Chabad Lubavitch (see chapter 91). All these groups have been on the rise, in part because of the large number of children born of very observant families, because of the creation of Orthodox educational and religious institutions to sustain such growth in population, and as one of the responses to the decline of synagogues as central institutions of Jewish life, among non-Orthodox groups. These groups, however, were not large and not highly visible outside their communal institutions. (Chabad, with its outreach agenda, was perhaps the most visible in the streets of Jewish neighborhoods.) But, starting in the early 2000s, religious Jews have now challenged secular Jews for the leadership of the AMIA, the main Jewish community organization, reaching the presidency for the first time in 2008. Visible kosher food options, then, appear as another indication of important changes that the Jewish population in Argentina is undergoing.

While these Orthodox groups have responded to local contexts, created local institutions, and trained local leaders, many belong to larger transnational collectives. The Hasidic emissaries who arrived in the late 1950s, for example, were US-born rabbis. Members of these Orthodox groups truly inhabit and reproduce transnational spaces, linking North America, Israel, and Argentina, among other centers, both for study purposes and for familial and business connections.

PRIMARY SOURCE

Facing page: McDonald's kosher sign. (Photograph by Adriana Brodsky, 2004)

QUESTIONS

1. What is your reaction to learning that a famous shopping mall in Argentina hosts a kosher McDonald's? Including suburbs, Buenos Aires's Jewish population in 2005 was 244,000, and New York's was 1.4 million in 2002.[3] Why do you think the first kosher McDonald's outside Israel did not open in New York?
2. Do you think the kosher McDonald's contributes to making (Orthodox) Jews a visible group within Argentine society?
3. Like the Chabad emissaries following World War II, Rabbi Karigal (chapter 27) came to the Americas to promote Jewish education and observance. Today, Chabad emissaries typically travel as a husband-and-wife team, whereas Karigal's wife and son remained behind while he journeyed. Why do you think the Chabad Rebbe decided to send families rather than individuals into communities?

NOTES

1. Brodsky and Rein, "On Kosher Hamburgers," 345.
2. Jmelnizky and Erdei, *La población judía de Buenos Aires*, 80.
3. Jmelnizky and Erdei, 36; Singer and Grossman, "Jewish Population in the United States," 156.

McDonald's
Kosher

103

"They Left"

CUBA, 2002

Ruth Behar

While we have mostly focused on the arrival of Jews to American shores, this chapter reminds of the outward movement of Jews away from these lands. The stills presented in this chapter are from Ruth Behar's documentary *Adio Kerida / Goodbye Dear Love* (distributed by Women Make Movies, 2002). They depict a moment in the film when José Levy, then the president of Centro Hebreo Sefaradí in Havana, was showing the names of members of the congregation who had left the island in search of a better life in Israel and elsewhere. "Se fue, se fue" (this person left, this person left), he repeats, pointing to names crossed off the membership list.

The Sephardic community of Cuba was established in the early twentieth century with migrants largely from Turkey, who settled in Havana and in small towns all over the island. They spoke Ladino and quickly adapted to speaking Spanish while holding onto religious and cultural traditions. Both Sephardim and Ashkenazim prospered and expected to stay. But following the Cuban Revolution in 1959, the majority chose to leave. A Sephardic Cuban migration found its way to Miami and New York, and several of these immigrants, including family members of the filmmaker, are interviewed, as are Sephardic Cubans who stayed on the island.[1] The film offers a range of portraits of Sephardic Cuban Jews, exploring the diverse ways in which they have clung to their unique heritage while adjusting to displacements throughout history.

The source offers a fresh perspective on the Jewish Diaspora by looking at the settlement and migration of Sephardic Jews to Cuba at the turn of the twentieth century, their departure to Miami and New York in the 1960s, and the recent migration of community members to Israel. While exact numbers are difficult to find, the entire Jewish community before 1959 consisted of approximately twenty thousand Jews, but 90 percent left following the Revolution. Several hundred Cuban Jews who stayed on the island and became part of the revitalized community in the 1990s later left for Israel with the help of the Jewish Agency. The Cuban government does not stand in the way of these departures, as it considers that Jews have a right to choose to live in the Jewish homeland. As a result of the various migrations from Cuba to the United States and Israel, there are now only about one thousand Jews left on the island, most living in Havana, with small communities made up of handfuls of Jews in the provincial cities of Santa Clara, Cienfuegos, Camaguey, Santiago de Cuba, and Guantánamo.

PRIMARY SOURCES

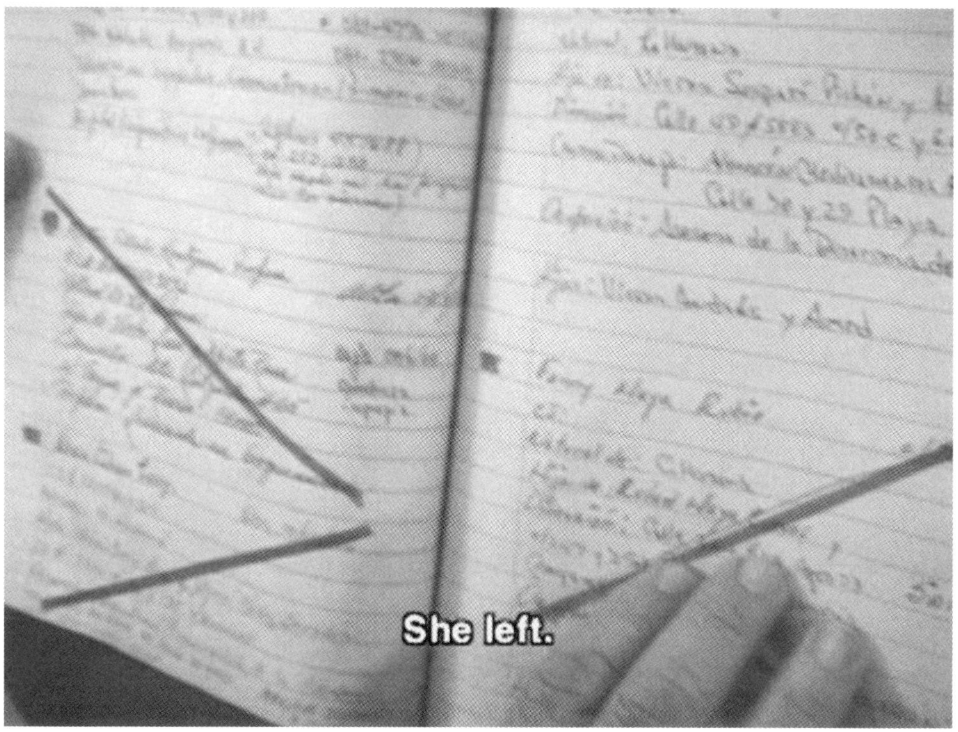

Ruth Behar, *Adio Kerida / Goodbye Dear Love*. (Documentary film, distributed by Women Make Movies, 2002)

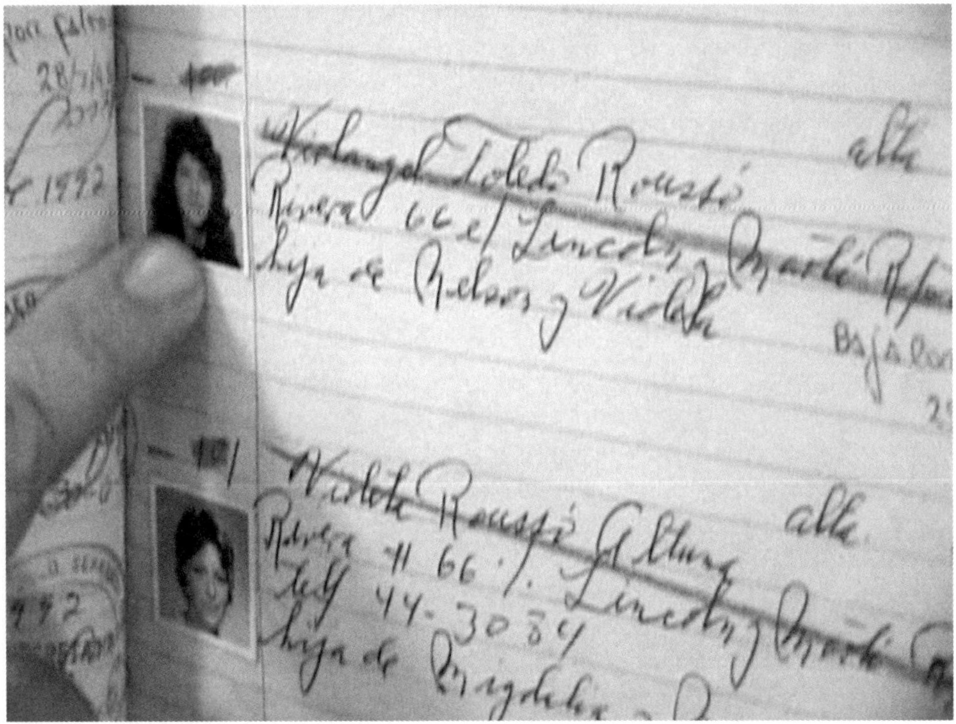

Ruth Behar, *Adio Kerida / Goodbye Dear Love*. (Documentary film, distributed by Women Make Movies, 2002)

QUESTIONS

1. How have the various Jewish Diasporas to and from Cuba created a unique sense of mixed Jewish Cuban, or "Juban," identity?
2. What features of Sephardic identity made it possible for Sephardic Jews to find a sense of home in Cuba?
3. In what ways do Sephardic Jews alter our received notions of what it means to be a Jew in the United States and in the Americas more broadly?

NOTE

1. Bettinger-López, *Cuban-Jewish Journeys*, 190.

104

Jewish Gender Transitions

NEW YORK, 2009, 2015

Laura Arnold Leibman

While transgender activism dates back to the Cooper Do-nuts Riot of Los Angeles (1959), Leslie Feinberg's groundbreaking pamphlet "Transgender Liberation: A Movement Whose Time Has Come" (1992) and novel *Stone Butch Blues* (1993) placed Jews at the center of the transgender-rights movement. Joy Ladin and Abby Stein are important Jewish transgender activists and artists who carry this mantle forward. Born in 1991, Stein was raised in a Hasidic community in Williamsburg, Brooklyn. After receiving her rabbinical ordination in 2011, she decided to transition and left the Hasidic community. The photos included here, taken by Melody Melamed, document Stein's process of becoming. Melamed often explores perceptions of gender and the female form in her work. Joy Ladin is a poet and held the David and Ruth Gottesman Chair in English at Stern College for Women at Yeshiva University. While Stein has become an atheist since transitioning, Ladin continues to explore religious themes in her work. Both women have been important voices in the transgender community.

As Noach Dzmura notes, "The transgender movement is a gathering place for expressions of gender that are outside of the traditional rubrics of 'male' and 'female.'"[1] Both inside and outside Judaism, the transgender movement has questioned that gender is—or ever was—a binary. Yet some transgender activists, such as Ladin, reject the popular notion, put forth by gender theorists such as Judith Butler, that gender is solely performative and that there is no "self that otherwise cannot be seen." As Ladin points out, "Though my female self is nothing if not a performance, for me, gender is more than performance. If it weren't, then someone like me, raised as a male, perceived as a male, and consciously performing as male, would simply *be* male; my lifelong sense that there was a true female self behind my male mask would be a delusion."[2] Ladin's understanding of Judaism and her insistence on her soul's gender—her true gender—helps explain why her essence is female and why bodily transformation was essential. Her prior male body was a façade, disconnected from her true soul self. As she explains, "A body is there, but it's not yours."[3] The disconnect between soul gender and the body's birthed gender causes a painful gender dysphoria; thus, to change physical genders so that her soul and body genders match is to become herself.[4] Stein similarly elucidates how Jewish mysticism helped her understand her early dysphoria. "Kabbalah helped me sort out so many questions," she explains. "I held right to the Kabbalistic idea that the gender of a soul and the gender of a body don't always align. . . . Many Kabbalistic prayers refer to God and to the Divine in feminine language. . . . If I couldn't express my physical femininity, relating to the divine feminine was the next best thing."[5] As artists and thinkers, Stein and Ladin invoke and transform the Jewish tradition.

The work of Stein and Ladin help us understand the ways in which Jewish American history has been filtered through a binary lens, that is, through a worldview that only recognizes two distinct, opposite forms of gender: masculine and feminine. Stein and Ladin's notion of the gender of a person whose soul and body can diverge sheds new light on other "gender-bending" Jewish figures featured in this volume.

PRIMARY SOURCES

Making Love

I reach for God
and brush your breast,

reach for you
and brush God

dangling and tipped,
gathered over years

of concealment and revelation
into this teardrop of flesh

spilling toward my lips.
I don't know

what is entering me.
I don't know what I've entered,

or when God became
a shudder of pleasure,

compressing the universe's exploding center
into this triangle of desire

so that touching you
is touching God

swaddled in arms and legs,
shy as a new-made planet

you and I, breath-filled clay,
were created to inhabit.

Joy Ladin, "Making Love," in *Impersonation* (Bronx, NY: Sheep Meadow, 2015), 62.

Melody Melamed, *Abby Stein, 1*, 2016, photograph.

Melody Melamed, *Abby Stein*, 2, 2016, photograph.

Melody Melamed, *Abby Stein, 3*, 2016, photograph.

QUESTIONS

1. How does Melody Melamed stage Abby Stein's Jewishness?
2. Abby Stein rarely looks at the camera in the photos taken of her by Melamed, but in the image taken in the bathroom, Stein looks at us indirectly. What does the use of the mirror add to the photo and the power dynamic of who looks at whom?
3. How does Joy Ladin take on questions of gender and binaries in her poem "Making Love"?
4. How does Ladin's poem call on and expand the Jewish tradition?
5. One description of Melamed's work notes that she is interested in "what the body cannot tell about the expression of gender and gender identity."[6] How does she convey that question in her photographs of Stein?

NOTES

1. Dzmura, *Balancing on the Mechitza*, xi.
2. Ladin, *Through the Door of Life*, 47.
3. Ladin, 42.
4. Ladin, 29.
5. Stein, *Becoming Eve*, 185.
6. Bjorn, "Artist Feature."

105

Moroccan-Amazonian Recipes

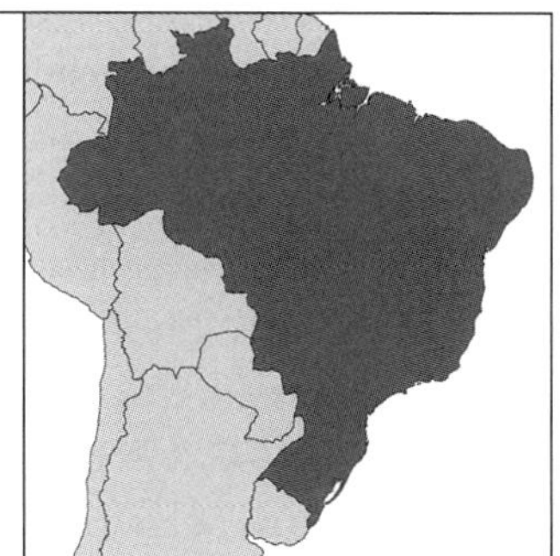

BRAZIL, 2014

Aron Sterk and Cecilia Sterk

Recipes are often embedded with stories from the past. While the recipes included here were written down in 2014, their history begins with the arrival of Moroccan Jews to northern Brazil after the start of the country's first liberal constitution in 1824 (see chapter 74). This constitution allowed for religious freedom for the first time since the brief Dutch occupation of Pernambuco in the seventeenth century. Moroccan Jewish émigrés were principally attracted by the opportunities of the rubber boom: latex had to be collected from the wild, but the massive demand for rubber meant that immense fortunes could be made. The immigration of Moroccan Jews to the Amazon increased significantly after the Spanish invasion of northern Morocco in the 1860s, and Moroccan Jews could be found all along the Amazon River, from the port of Belém at its mouth to Iquitos in the Peruvian Andes. Some of these Jewish men married local women and assimilated to the local population, and others (having made their fortune) returned to Morocco to try their fortunes in other parts of Latin America; but some brought family over from Morocco and settled in the cities of Belém and Manaus halfway up the Amazon River.

Two synagogues were founded in Belém—Shaar haShayim (Gate of Heaven) and Eshel Abraham (Tamarisk Tree of Abraham; Gen. 21:33) as early as the mid-1820s, and the cemetery dating from 1848 can still be seen in the city center. After 1910, immigration from Morocco practically ceased, and the two communities of the Amazon were isolated both from Morocco and from the larger Jewish communities of the South of Brazil. Over time, the community lost many of the Moroccan traditions of the early community, including its distinct form of Spanish, called Haquetía, and the community, to a greater extent, assimilated or integrated into the local communities of the states of Pará and Amazonas.

Today, Amazonian Jews number only some 2,000, out of a Brazilian Jewish population of about 120,000, and the community continues to be reduced by emigration to Israel and the cities of the South like Rio de Janeiro and São Paulo. Helena Obadia Benzecry's cookbook was compiled and published in 2014 in an effort to preserve the unique culinary traditions of her mother and grandmothers, including adaptations of Moroccan recipes and kosher versions of local recipes, before they, too, were forgotten.

The climate that the Jews found in the Amazonian rain forest was very different from that which they were used to in Morocco. Without trained *shochetim* (kosher slaughterers), it was hard to provide kosher meat, but there was a profusion of fish identified as kosher available from the coast and Amazon rivers, like the giant *pirarucu* and *pescada amarela* used in the recipes. The indigenous carbohydrate staple of North Brazil is manioc (cassava), and it is so prevalent that the Brazilian form of couscous (*cuzcuz* in Brazilian Portuguese) is made from manioc flour rather than wheat semolina. As the original ingredients for traditional Moroccan cooking were unavailable, the women of the community learned to adapt to these readily available local foodstuffs.

The recipe here illustrates these adaptations. *Almôndega* is a recipe that dates back to Sephardic Spain. Its name is derived from the Arabic *al-bunduqa* ("hazelnut"; a reference to the shape of the meat or fish balls), and among Spanish-speaking Jews, this traditional Sephardic dish is known as *albóndigas*. This version, however, uses the local fish *pescada amarela* and manioc flour to bind the fish balls together. Another recipe collected by Benzecry similarly shows a kosher adaptation of an indigenous Amerindian dish that is a ubiquitous street food throughout the Amazon, *tacacá*. The ingredients of *tacacá* are completely local: *tucupi*, a sauce extracted from manioc that has to be boiled for three to five days to remove the poison; *jambu*, a local plant whose leaves have a unique flavor—a grassy taste followed by a strong tingling or numbing sensation that leaves a cooling aftertaste in the throat; and small yellow peppers. The dish is served in a *cuia*: half of a dried gourd. However, *tacacá* is usually served with shrimps, which are not kosher for Jews. Benzecry's recipe substitutes dried, fried portions of *pirarucu*, a kosher fish of the Amazon River, for the shrimp.

Like many immigrants to the Americas, the Moroccan Jews had to adapt their own traditions and customs to very different conditions. The temptation to complete assimilation was particularly acute for such an isolated community—it is notable that none of the local Kohens in Belém are Jewish. These recipes illustrate how the community nevertheless endeavored to be local but remained observantly Jewish.

PRIMARY SOURCE

Almôndega (Fish balls in sauce)

Ingredients

1 kg filleted *pescada amarela* (cod or haddock may be used)
1 kg filleted (cod or haddock may be used)
Ginger marinade: grated root ginger steeped in 500 ml white rum (cachaça)
2 limes
3 tablespoons extra-virgin olive oil
1 diced onion

Almôndega. (Helena Obadia Benzecry, "Recipe for *Almôndega* (Fish balls in sauce)," in *Culinária tradicional Judaico-Marroquina* [Belém, Brazil: Editora Paka-Tatu, 2014], 64)

3 cloves of chopped garlic
4 leaves of chopped chicory of Pará (substitute more chopped cilantro)
4 tablespoons of chopped cilantro
1 chopped chili pepper (optional)
Salt to taste
1 teaspoon nutmeg
A large pinch of turmeric
Yolks of 3 eggs
2 tablespoons fine cassava meal or matza meal
A quarter cup of extra-virgin olive oil

Sauce
1 large chopped onion
3 tablespoons of oil
2 ltrs water
Half teaspoon urucum (substitute sweet red paprika)

2 leaves of chicory of Pará (use cilantro)
1 teaspoon salt
1 large diced tomato, skinned and deseeded
1 chopped leek

In a pan, brown the onion in the oil, add the 2 liters of water and the remaining ingredients. Put to one side.

Preparation
Wash the fish in the Ginger marinade. Cut the fish into small pieces, put them in a bowl of water with the juice of the 2 limes and soak for 3 minutes. Take the fish out of the bowl, squeezing off the excess water, and put to drain in a colander. In a frying-pan brown the onion and garlic in olive oil, allow it to cool, and then mix with the fish, cilantro, and the chili (if used) in the food processor. Season with salt, nutmeg, turmeric, add the egg yolks, meal, the juice of 1 lime and mix until smoothly well-mixed. Wet the hands and form into balls, drop into the boiling sauce, and simmer on a low heat until the sauce is reduced. Separately cook potatoes and add them to the pan of fish balls. Take off the heat and drizzle with oil.
Serve on Shabbat and Holidays.

Helena Obadia Benzecry, *Culinária tradicional Judaico-Marroquina, inclui receitas paraenses segundo preceitos judaicos* [Traditional Jewish Moroccan cuisine, including recipes of Pará according to Jewish precepts] (Belém: Editora Paka-Tatu, 2014), 65.

QUESTIONS

1. Food seems to be a powerful carrier of meaning for many Jews. Why is this aspect of Jewish culture so important for Jewish identity?
2. In the introduction to the book of recipes, Elias Dahan (cantor of the Israelite Association of the Amazon) talks about recipes as "narratives." What are the narratives that this dish tells?
3. Like songs (chapter 81), recipes form part of oral tradition that contain layers of both the past and the present. What are the temporal layers visible in this recipe? How does this recipe compare to the recipe for chicken green curry (chapter 98)?

106

Eichmann's Capture as a Graphic Novel

ARGENTINA, 2015

Darrell B. Lockhart

Eichmann's Capture is one of three graphic novels published in Spanish in a single volume under the title *Road to Auschwitz and Other Stories of Resistance* by the Argentine author Julián Gorodischer (b. 1973). The other titles are *Road to Auschwitz* and *Partisan, Hero of Warsaw*. All three texts are auto/biographical and written based on stories from his own family. In the novels, Gorodischer appears as a character who takes on the role of a journalist—his actual profession—to interview family members about their experience during and following the Holocaust. In *Eichmann's Capture*, excerpted here, he interviews his Aunt Luba about her participation in the capture of the Nazi war criminal Adolf Eichmann in 1960 in Buenos Aires, while he helps her to recuperate from an accident.

The kidnapping of Eichmann, which came to be known as "Operation Garibaldi" after the street on which Eichmann lived, was organized and carried out as a secret mission by the Israeli Mossad, with the assistance of a few local Argentine Jews. Eichmann, who lived under the assumed name of Ricardo Klement, had arrived in Argentina in 1950. He sent for his wife and four children to join him two years later. Argentina was commonly believed to be a safe haven for Nazi criminals looking to escape Europe. Another infamous war criminal, Josef Mengele, was known to have fled to Argentina. Mengele escaped capture while Germany and Argentina negotiated the terms of his extradition. This was the primary reason why Israel decided against following international legal procedures to secure the capture of Eichmann. He was captured on May 11, 1960, and held at a secure location in Buenos Aires for nine days until his removal from the country could be orchestrated. Once in Israel, he was tried on numerous counts that included crimes against humanity, war crimes, and crimes against the Jewish people. He was sentenced to death and died on June 1, 1962.

The Eichmann case brought to the fore the fact that Argentina, under the government of Juan Domingo Perón, had been willing to harbor Nazi criminals. Such refugees, like those who were accepted in the United States, were valued for their scientific expertise and for the potential contributions they could make toward the modernization of their host society. The Eichmann case drew attention to the complicity of the Catholic Church in aiding Nazi refugees with fabricated identities and falsifying documents to emigrate to Argentina and other countries. The Eichmann case is but one example that underscores the often complicated existence of Jewish Argentines throughout the twentieth century. *Eichmann's Capture* calls attention to the broad reach of the repercussions of the Holocaust, which extended into Latin America. It also signals the fact that the capture of Eichmann in Argentina was the starting point of diplomatic relations between Argentina and Israel (see chapter 95). In subsequent decades, Israel would come to play an important role in the lives of Argentine Jews.

Eichmann's Capture joins the body of creative work produced by authors and artists in Argentina who as first-, second-, or third-generation Holocaust survivors contribute their voices and their distinctive experiences to a broader understanding of post-Holocaust Jewish life throughout the Americas and the world. More specifically, as a graphic novel, *Road to Auschwitz and Other Stories of Resistance* is the first from Latin America to add to the growing number of texts that address the Holocaust through the unique lens of graphic narrative.

PRIMARY SOURCE

Following pages: Julián Gorodischer, *Camino a Auschwitz y otras historias de resistencia* [Road to Auschwitz and other stories of resistance], illustrated by Marcos Vergara (Buenos Aires: Emecé, 2015), 80, 81, 90, 91.

QUESTIONS

1. How can a graphic novel portray the story of the capture of Eichmann in ways that other texts (history, literature, biography) cannot? Who might be the audience?
2. The character of the author/narrator, Julián Gorodischer himself, states in the beginning that "this is a true story." How does this statement affect the way the text is read/interpreted?
3. As the team prepares to carry out Operation Garibaldi, the narration begins with a verse taken from Ezekiel 16:6, "And when I passed by you and saw you struggling in your own blood, I said to you, in your blood, live!" How does this scripture frame the capture of Eichmann, and what does it mean in this context?
4. What is Luba's reaction upon encountering Adolf Eichmann in person?
5. Compare the way that Gorodischer balances the tensions between Jewishness and Argentineness that arose during Eichmann's capture and those revealed in the sources in chapter 95.

Ever since I can remember, my Aunt Luba has presided over our family ceremonies. But this is a sad night: Mom let us know that Luba fractured her hip in the bathtub and will have to spend the night alone.

1942. Work will make us free. She was the strongest and most efficient girl in all of Auschwitz-Birkenau.

1944. She had a lot to live up to. Legend has it that her cousin Paie consoled the anguished right up to the last second, ignoring her own fate.

1945. She always told us that a star with the face of her cousin showed her how and when to escape.

In honor of those lives and out of respect for Paie's last words in Auschwitz, for the next month I am going to take care of Aunt Luba.

This is a true story.

Octubre de 2005. She asks me to scratch her leg with a rod under the cast that they put on her after her hip fracture.

We like chatting about the days in Auschwitz-Birkenau, with the TV making noise in the background to soften the impact of the story.

I take her out for a stroll in the park and the breeze transports us 45 years into the past, to a Monday in May the year that she joined the Garibaldi Operative that captured Adolf Eichmann in Argentina to be put on trial in Israel.

1960: 150° Aniversario de la Revolución de Mayo.

The newspapers were covering only the celebrations along the Avenida de Mayo. Argentina, under the government of Arturo Frondizi, received hundreds of delegations from all over the world, who were arriving to celebrate the birthday of the richest republic of Latin America.

Luba lands on what was the first and only charter flight that united the capitals of Israel and Argentina.

10 de mayo de 1960. She enters as just another member of the Jewish volunteers and functionaries who join the march along 9 de Julio Avenue. Supposedly, they are the flight crew of El-Al and Zionists from a secondary branch of government.

But later on, in an apartment in Belgrano, Luba swears allegiance to the leader of Operation Garibaldi. The objective: to kidnap the ex-Nazi leader Adolf Eichmann so that he stand trial in Israel.

2

10 de mayo / 11.55 pm.

"And when I passed by you and saw you struggling in your own blood, I said to you in your blood, live!"

12

That same night, Klement enjoys after dinner conversation with his wife and son in their humble chalet in San Fernando.

11 de mayo de 1960, 19:59 hs.

Peter Malkin, who touches him for the first time, uses latex gloves to attenuate the intensity of his disgust.

14 de mayo de 1960.

Luba feels the need to sneak into the room where he is being held captive when no one is looking and after introducing herself...

she feels the need to scream...

scream into the void, abstractly...

bringing to the present the disgusting odor of the laundry truck that took her out of Auschwitz...

15 de mayo de 1960. Malkin, the leader, and agent Abraham Shalom, silence her and place her in isolation for a few days.

5 days later they transport from Argentina the first executioner of Jews who would be brought to trial in Israel.

107

Soviet Jewish War Memory in New York

NEW YORK, 2015

Natasha Zaretsky

The post-Soviet Jewish community in New York emerged in the 1970s with the first significant wave of emigration from the former Soviet Union, resettling thousands of Jews from various Soviet republics primarily to the United States, Israel, and Germany. From 1970 to 1988, approximately 290,000 Soviet Jews left the Soviet Union, with 126,000 emigrating to the United States. As more Jews emigrated after 1989, the United States received 328,000 of those 1.1 million new Soviet Jewish immigrants. Over the past forty years, these migrations have reshaped the landscape of the global Jewish Diaspora and raised questions about Jewish belonging and practice. Being Jewish was considered a separate nationality under Soviet rule, and yet collective, public expressions of Jewishness were severely limited. It was only through migration, then, that Jews from various Soviet republics came to form a distinct community based on shared practices, as *Soviet* Jews, in ways that stood apart from the established secular and more religious American Jewish communities.

Den Pobedi (Victory Day)—celebrated on May 9—marks the end of World War II and remains one of the few Soviet holidays that Soviet Jewish migrants continued to celebrate in New York, both in public commemorations (like the Den Pobedi parade in Brighton Beach, Brooklyn) and in more private memories (like the memory shadow box that honors Leon Dubov's grandfather Iosif Chechik, a soldier in World War II). These new practices became important spaces for generating a sense of collective belonging in New York, but one that demonstrated Jewishness as a state of constitutive tension, generated through and against various forms of memory.

These commemorations help us understand the dynamics of diasporic Jewish memory in the US and, in particular, the specificities of post-Soviet Jewish memory. They offer an interesting expansion of the understanding of second- and third-generation memory, a concept akin to Marianne Hirsch's concept of "postmemory," which is defined as an event from the past having such a profound impact on future generations that they feel as if they experienced it themselves.[1] Post-Soviet Jews represent one of the largest Jewish communities in New York (an estimated seven hundred thousand Russian-speaking Jews live in the United States, with the largest community in New York, where post-Soviet Jews represent approximately 20 percent of the Jewish population of the city, numbering about two hundred thousand). In addition, Soviet Jews became part of an important political history for American Jews, as the subjects of the Saving Soviet Jewry movement. This movement, which started in the 1960s, led to protests and activism that helped Jewish Americans build a political voice as they advocated for Jews to be allowed to emigrate from the Soviet Union, because of the discrimination they experienced there. As Soviet Jews established communities in the US, their practices that incorporate their past Soviet experiences into their contemporary lives represent how they negotiate belonging and identity.

PRIMARY SOURCES

Veterans at Victory Day Parade, Brighton Beach, May 9, 2015. (Photograph by Konstantin Sergeyev, 2015)

World War II memory shadow box honoring Iosif Chechik. (Photograph by Leon Dubov)

QUESTIONS

1. How does this holiday's ongoing significance reveal the complexities of a diasporic Soviet Jewish identity?
2. What do these photos tell us about the importance of rituals and public, collective practices for the post-Soviet Jewish community? How do such rituals connect their Diaspora across time and space?
3. The photographs reveal two dimensions of Soviet Jewish memory: the public rituals (such as the commemoration of Den Pobedi) and the more private forms of remembrance (the shadow box). How do memory practices help us understand the relationship between individual and collective memories?

4. Where else in this volume have we seen examples of second- and third-generation memory, or "postmemory"—events from the past that have a profound impact on future generations such that they feel that they experienced the events themselves?

NOTE

1. Hirsch, *Generation of Postmemory*, 3–6.

108

Queer *Mikveh*

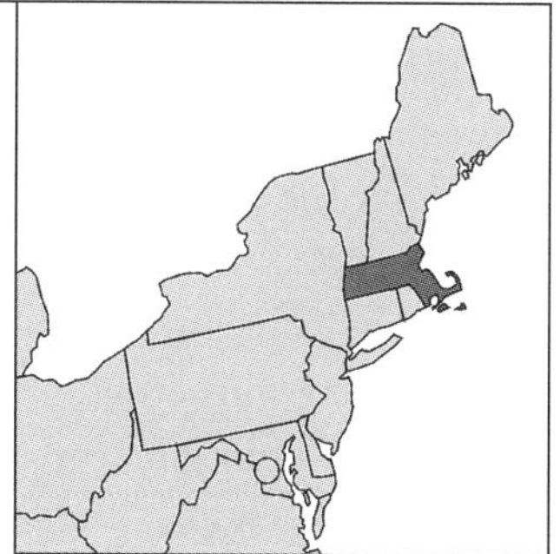

MASSACHUSETTS, 2016–2019

Cara Rock-Singer

According to the Jewish textual tradition, the *mikveh* has the power to transform whoever (or whatever) is immersed in it from a state of impurity (*tameh*) to purity (*tahor*). Traditional uses of *mikveh* are gendered: for women, Jewish law commands *mikveh* immersion for a bride before her wedding or for a married woman after a menstrual cycle and before resuming sexual contact; there are no parallel commandments on men today, though some men choose to immerse to prepare for sacred occasions like the High Holidays. The transformative powers of the *mikveh* are part of conversion ceremonies to Judaism.

Activists and community projects like Mayyim Hayyim, located in a suburb of Boston, are working to improvise on the traditional *mikveh* in order to create transformative rituals available for anyone, including queer bodies and sexualities. Mayyim Hayyim's expansive vision seeks to radically expand traditional uses of *mikveh* to meet spiritual needs, whether healing after an illness, celebrating an important birthday, or marking a gender transition or affirming a sexual identity. In addition to training *mikveh* guides to welcome, educate, and facilitate rituals in their own facility, Mayyim Hayyim's Ritual Creation Team has drawn on traditional liturgy and textual resources to author ceremonies that people can use to help shape meaningful ritual, from setting intentions for the immersion process to offering prayers and choreography to do while in the water.

Though immersions in the ritual bath are typically individual acts, often witnessed by one facilitator, *mikveh* projects like Mayyim Hayyim promote new forms of Jewish community. Mayyim Hayyim has supported efforts to queer the *mikveh*, including an initiative called the Watershed Project (2019), which sought to create "trans-informed, gender-inclusive ritual for people who are transgender, nonbinary, or gender-questioning and who self-identify as Jewish, to any extent."[1] Along with other queer *mikveh* projects across North America, Mayyim Hayyim seeks to create safe, welcoming Jewish spaces for people with marginalized identities, including Jews of color and those with disabilities. Many queer *mikveh* initiatives have also sought to extend their missions to use ritual as a spiritual and political tool for justice projects, from the climate crisis to Indigenous land rights.

The majority of American Jews ceased to use *mikveh* over the course of the twentieth century, and in the 1970s, prominent Jewish feminists began to criticize *mikveh* as misogynistic for associating menstruation with uncleanliness. Yet beginning with the opening of Mayyim Hayyim in Newton, Massachusetts, in 2004, there has been a "rising tide" of community *mikveh* projects across North America working to reclaim the ritual bath from orthodoxy. The *mikveh* movement has been reimagining *mikveh* as a fully embodied, transformative ritual capable of marking any life transition.

Twenty-first-century Jewish feminist reclamations of *mikveh* work to balance tradition with innovation, rooting new spiritual *mikveh* practices in the Jewish legal and textual tradition. In addition to attention to the rules governing how a *mikveh* should be built and how immersions should be performed, *mikveh* innovators have drawn on traditional associations of the *mikveh* with the womb of God and its waters as potent for healing. Queer *mikveh* activists have been inspired by the *mikveh* as a tool for facilitating bodily transitions and changes in identity and have stretched the ritual frame to make it accessible and welcoming to queer individuals and communities. Queer *mikveh* dismantles structures that assume cis-bodies, heterosexual marriages, and Jewish exclusivity in order to bring the Jewish tradition into the service of liberation movements.

Histories of American Judaism are often dominated by "official," elite laws and practices, but such narratives fail to recognize the messy realities of Jewish life as it is lived. Queer *mikveh* activists' innovative and improvisational practices reveal how queer Jews creatively engage with Jewish tradition. The use of *mikveh* within social justice movements for decolonization, environmentalism, and racial and sexual equality, in turn, problematizes the assumption of the separation of religion and politics within secular states. Furthermore, queer *mikveh* sheds light on and disrupts cis-gendered and heterosexual normativity, as well as Ashkenazi and white dominance, which are prevalent in North American Jewish life.

PRIMARY SOURCES

See following pages.

Pride at the *mikveh*. (Photograph courtesy Mayyim Hayyim)

Gender Transition Milestone

AN IMMERSION CEREMONY

Intention

כוונה KAVANAH

To be read while preparing for immersion:

מִן הַמֵּצַר קָרָאתִי יָּהּ, *Min hameitzar karati Yah,*
עָנָנִי בַמֶּרְחָב יָהּ. *anani vamerchav Yah.*

Out of a narrow place, I called to God. God heard me fully and answered.[1]

Immersion

טבילה T'VILAH

FIRST IMMERSION—LETTING GO

To be read at the mikveh's *edge before you enter the water:*

The Hebrews are called "*Ivrim*," the crossing-over people.
As we left *Mitzrayim*, the narrow places of Egypt, we transformed ourselves—
a painful, yet redemptive, spiritual transition.[2]
So, too, do I cross through a narrow place,
letting go of my own bondage,
and moving toward personal freedom.

בָּרוּךְ אַתָּה, יְיָ אֱלֹהֵינוּ, מֶלֶךְ הָעוֹלָם *Baruch atah, Adonai Eloheinu, Melech ha-olam*
הַמַּעֲבִיר אֶת הָעוֹבְרִים. *hama-avir et ha-ovrim.*

Blessed are You, Eternal One, our God, Ruler of Time and Space, the Transforming One,
for those who transition, transform, and cross over.[3]

Slowly descend the steps into the mikveh *waters and immerse so that every part of your body is covered by the warm water. When you emerge, recite the following blessing:*

בָּרוּךְ אַתָּה, יְיָ אֱלֹהֵינוּ, מֶלֶךְ הָעוֹלָם *Baruch atah, Adonai Eloheinu, Melech ha'olam*
אֲשֶׁר קִדְּשָׁנוּ בִּטְבִילָה בְּמַיִם חַיִּים. *asher kidshanu bi-t'vilah b'mayyim hayyim.*

Blessed are You, God, Majestic Spirit of the Universe
who makes us holy by embracing us in living waters.[4]

"Gender Transition Milestone," by Rachel Stock Spilker and adapted by Matia Rania Angelou and Judith D. Kummer. (Courtesy Mayyim Hayyim)

Honoring the Process of Coming Out

AN IMMERSION CEREMONY
FOR AN INDIVIDUAL

Intention

כוונה KAVANAH

To be read before preparing for immersion:

I know that I am created *b'tzelem elohim*, in the image of God,
and that a divine spark resides within me. *Hineini.*
Here I stand, no longer alone, on my way to becoming fully unafraid,
knowing that I can create safe space for myself,
knowing that I have a circle of loved and loving ones who will support and protect me,
knowing that I am sheltered beneath the wings of *Shechinah*,
knowing my own power.[1]

כָּל הָעוֹלָם כֻּלּוֹ גֶּשֶׁר צַר מְאֹד *Kol ha'olam kulo gesher tzar m'od*
וְהָעִקָּר לֹא לְפַחֵד כְּלָל. *v'ha-ikar lo l'facheid klal.*[2]

All the world is a narrow bridge
and the essence of living is not to be afraid.

Immersion

טבילה T'VILAH

To be read at the mikveh's *edge before you enter the water:*

As the Israelites walked through the sea, so I walk into this *mikveh*
as I choose to liberate myself from old restraints.[3]

נְבָרֵךְ אֶת עֵין הַחַיִּים, אֲשֶׁר נָתְנָה לִי *N'varech et Eyn HaChayyim, asher nat'na li*
הָעָצְמָה לָצֵאת מִן הַמְּצָרִים. *ha'otzma latzeyt min ham'tzarim.*

Let us bless the Source of Life for giving me the courage to come out.[4]

"Honoring the Process of Coming Out," by Matia Rania Angelou, Deborah Issokson, and Judith D. Kummer. (Courtesy Mayyim Hayyim)

QUESTIONS

1. What does it mean to "queer" a ritual? Can you think of other traditions that have been queered?
2. Queer uses of *mikveh* stretch the boundaries of *mikveh* traditions. Is there a point at which a practice no longer can be considered *mikveh*? Who gets to decide, and based on what criteria?
3. Jews are often thought of as "people of the book," though some scholars have suggested that Jews are "people of the body." How does *mikveh* help us negotiate within these two frameworks?
4. To prepare for *mikveh* immersion, people ready their body by making it as close as possible to the way they were born, so they can emerge from the water reborn. What might queer *mikveh* users find particularly powerful, and particularly problematic, about this framing?
5. Compare the Mayyim Hayyim *mikveh* (and its use) with the earlier chapters on ritual baths in this volume (chapters 15, 48, and 59). How do the look of the baths, where they are located, or the patterns of use differ?

NOTE

1. Mayyim Hayyim, "Watershed Project."

109

Protest and the End of Community Consensus

BRAZIL, 2017

Misha Klein and Michel Gherman

Today, most of Brazil's Jewish community is in three southeastern cities: São Paulo, Rio de Janeiro, and Porto Alegre. In spite of varied national origins, languages, cultural practices, and religious observances, the Jewish community created inclusive shared entities, including clubs that serve as community centers. The photos included in this chapter are from an April 2017 protest organized by (mostly) Jews in front of a Jewish club in Rio de Janeiro. Inside the club, a controversial career politician, Jair Bolsonaro, was giving a speech. Protestors gathered in front of the club to oppose him and the people entering to hear the speech. While both the audience inside and the protestors outside claimed that their positions were based on Jewish history and values, they drew on different understandings of the lessons of history.

The photos depict the first protest against Bolsonaro's newly announced presidential candidacy. Protestors rallied around the hashtag #NotinOurName (#NãoemNossoNome), in response to the club president's invitation "in the name of the community." "Dizemos não pelos nossos valores judaicos" (we say no because of our Jewish values) refers to the social justice ideals that many Jews associate with Jewishness. The protestors repudiated the audience members for not remembering the lessons of the Shoah and the threat of fascism. They also referenced Brazil's military dictatorship, with chants about Bolsonaro defending torturers, and carried signs featuring Jews and non-Jews who were "disappeared" during the dictatorship, such as Iara Iavelberg. Though the signs faced inward toward the invitees entering the club, the protest was in public and was interpreted by Jewish community leadership as exposing the community to external view and critique.

Understood to be at the "white" end of the color spectrum, Brazilian Jews attribute their success to the national ideology of "racial democracy," which claims that Brazil is a color-blind society (infamous inequalities notwithstanding), one with national laws against racism and without a history of organized antisemitism. The widely circulated racist, sexist, and homophobic quotes from Bolsonaro's speech and the invitation-only (mostly) Jewish audience's laughing support of them, connect the Jewish community with Bolsonaro's rise to the presidency. This protest marked a definitive moment in Brazilian Jewish history when the community ruptured along national political lines, as opposed to internal distinctions. Brazilian society is similarly divided and confrontational, abandoning the "cordiality" for which Brazil was previously famous. This incident and its aftermath illustrate the way that Jews reflect and participate in national culture. It reveals how local history intersects with larger historical moments, such that it is possible to speak of the Holocaust and Brazil's military dictatorship as emerging from similar ideologies.

PRIMARY SOURCES

See following pages.

QUESTIONS

1. What Jewish values do the protest signs refer to as the basis for the protest?
2. Why would Jews be specifically concerned with fascism, and why would this be a concern with respect to the club's speaker?
3. In protesting a speech by a contemporary politician, why would protestors bring signs commemorating individuals who were tortured and disappeared by the military dictatorship?
4. Bolsonaro has often been compared to former US president Donald Trump (see chapter 111). Why might either president have courted Jewish support?

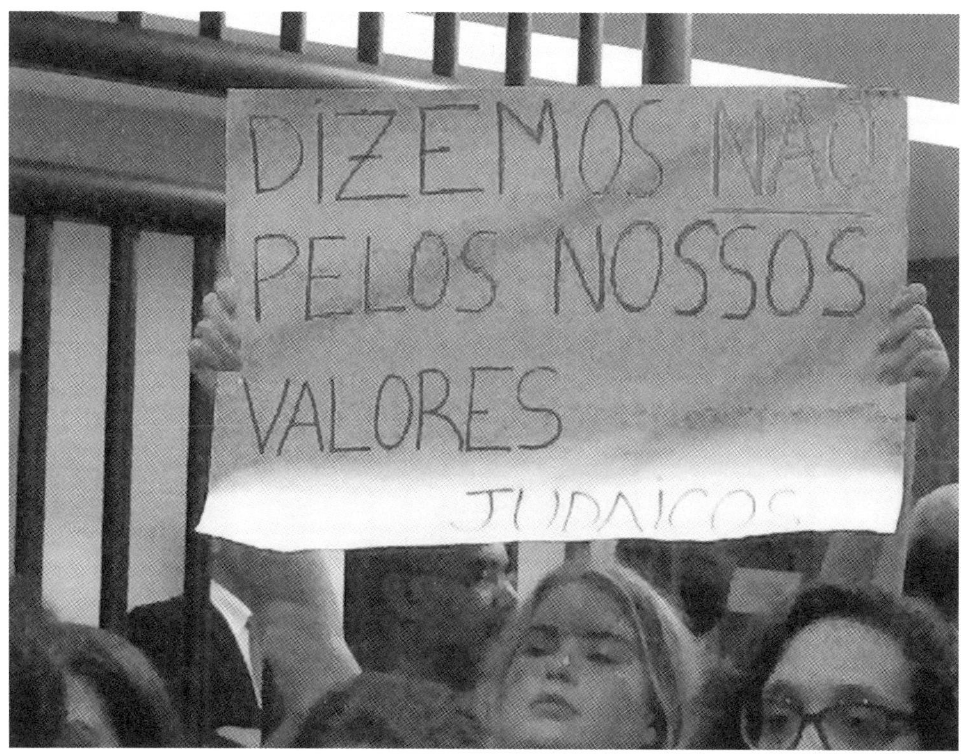

"Nossos valores judaicos" (Our Jewish values). (Photograph by Misha Klein, 2017)

"Fora fascista" (Out with fascists!). (Photograph by Misha Klein, 2017)

Iara Iavelberg. (Photograph by Misha Klein, 2017)

Facing inwards. (Photograph by Misha Klein, 2017)

110

How to Eat a Taco

ISRAEL, 2019

Paulette Schuster

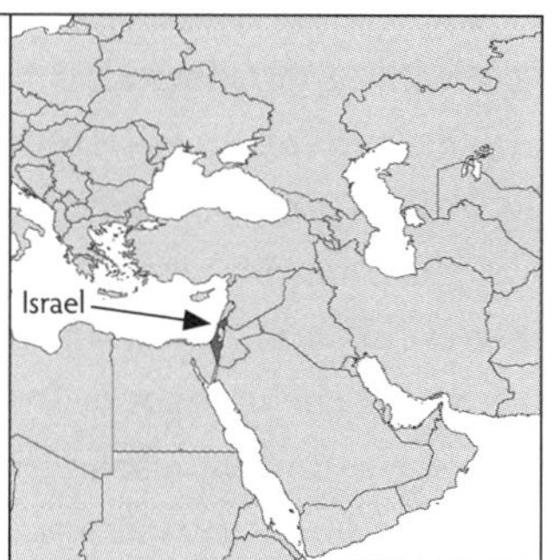

One response to the dictatorships in Latin America was the migration of Jews to Israel. As in chapter 103, the source in this chapter focuses on the presence of Latin American Jews in Israel and on the globalization of Latin American food. In particular, Mexican food in Israel has gained popularity in the past decade, and there are many Mexican restaurants in Tel Aviv. The disposable paper menu presented here is the individual diner's place mat for a small restaurant in the trendy Florentin neighborhood of Tel Aviv. The food on the menu is arranged around the illustration, which presents the "Complete Diner's Manual/Guide—How to Eat Tacos."

The language of the menu is modern Hebrew, with transliterated names of Spanish foodstuffs including tacos, tostadas, quesadillas, margaritas, beer, and tequila. The main courses consist of chili con carne, burritos, chimichangas, nachos, and shrimps (both pickled and "a la diabla"). In the bottom middle is the complete guide: a comic strip explaining the do's and don'ts of eating tacos. In addition to tacos, the menu serves tostadas, quesadillas, and other dishes, some of which are not Mexican but rather Tex-Mex. Notably, the menu includes dairy and nondairy dishes and shrimp in various styles and condiments, rendering this establishment nonkosher. There is no pork, as is common even in nonkosher Israeli restaurants.

The globalization experienced in Israel is a by-product of the high-tech explosion that made the country less parochial. Until the mid-1980s you could not leave the country without permission from the army. However, with the easing of travel restrictions, more accumulated wealth, and the elimination of currency controls, Israelis came into contact with others around the world. As a result, economic barriers that existed prior to the 1980s were greatly weakened. Israelis came to be open to other cultures and foodstuffs. Food variety in the supermarkets reflected this new openness, as well as the ability to accept hyphenated identities or dual identities. Tel Aviv is known as a cosmopolitan city with a multitude of culinary options and niches. For example, Tel Aviv houses more than four hundred vegan/vegan-friendly restaurants and has been declared the vegan capital of Israel.[1] The menu as a whole helps us to understand the culinary evolution of Israel in general and of Tel Aviv in particular.

Today, more than 40 percent of the Jewish population in Israel define themselves as secular, while approximately 20 percent identify as traditional; 12 percent are defined as traditional with religious leanings; 11 percent as religious; and 10 percent as ultra-Orthodox.[2] Tel Aviv is a microcosm of Israel's religious plurality and melting pot of cultures. Latin American music, novels, films, and food have enjoyed popularity in Israel for decades. Interest in Latin American culture has grown dramatically in recent years as a result of the increase in the number of Israeli youngsters who travel to South America after their military service and the rise in the popularity of the *telenovelas* (TV soap operas).[3] The menu presented here serves as a sample of the diversity of religious views and multiculturalism that exist in the country.

PRIMARY SOURCE

"Complete Diner's Manual/Guide—How to Eat Tacos," 2019. (Courtesy of Mezcal Restaurant)

The Complete Guide for Eating Tacos

× Do not rub your eyes after eating spicy food. That ends in tears.

✓ It is recommended to treat spice as a friend, without fear. Well . . . maybe just a little.

× Do not eat tacos with a knife and fork. That insults them (and us too, a bit).

✓ Hold the tacos with a hand underneath to grip both their sides.

× Do not lean back when eating tacos. It's a lifelong stain.

✓ When eating, approach the tacos leaning forward.

QUESTIONS

1. Why do you think a guide was included with the menu?
2. Comic strips are not popular in Israel. Why do you think the guide is presented in this format?
3. Describe the comic strip itself. What does it tell us about Israeli, Jewish, and/or Mexican culture?
4. What, if anything, is Jewish or American about this menu?

NOTES

1. Srivastava, "Going Green Tel Aviv Way."
2. Israel Central Bureau of Statistics, "Population Censuses."
3. Lesser and Rein, introduction to *Rethinking Jewish-Latin Americans*, 20.

111

Executive Order Combating Antisemitism

WASHINGTON, DC, 2019

Britt Tevis

On December 11, 2019, US President Donald Trump issued an executive order announcing a plan to combat antisemitism, particularly as it appeared on college campuses. The order declared that the United States would thwart anti-Jewish harassment by withholding funding from institutions that improperly discriminated against Jews in violation of Title VI of the Civil Rights Act of 1964, which forbids discrimination based on race, color, or national origin. Although that law did not pertain to discrimination based on religion, it did apply when discrimination against Jews was based on the perception of Jews as a race or nationality. In a shift from past precedent, the executive order expanded what the federal government would define as violating the 1964 law by employing a controversial definition of antisemitism, which included expression of certain criticisms of Israel. Because of its use of this definition, its stated focus on colleges, and its vague classification of Jewish and Jews, the order exacerbated existing divisions around the very nature of antisemitism in the United States and how best to address it.

While ostensibly challenging anti-Jewish violence, discrimination, and bias, the order most immediately reflected debates about expressions of anti-Israel sentiments on college campuses in the United States during the early twenty-first century, thereby further illuminating preexisting ideological and political divisions among US Jews. Many who welcomed Trump's order viewed organized critiques of Israel as wrongly targeting Jews. In contrast, many who condemned the order understood it as an attempt by the federal government to use the 1964 civil rights law as a means to silence criticisms of Israel and to improperly stymie political debate on college and university campuses generally.

US Jews held a range of attitudes about these matters and consequently expressed varying opinions about the order. Organizations including Union for Reform Judaism and the Central Conference of American Rabbis and many Jewish studies scholars expressed grave concern, because the order appeared to classify Jews as a "nationality." Historically, classifying Jews as sharing a national origin had resulted in the identification of Jews as foreigners, a supposition that Jews in the United States overwhelmingly rejected. Conversely, organizations such as the Anti-Defamation League, the American Jewish Committee, the Conference of Presidents of Major American organizations, and the Orthodox Union Advocacy Center endorsed the order, because they believed that it would protect Jewish university and college students who faced anti-Jewish discrimination because of their Jewish identities. To a large extent, Jews' stance on the executive order symbolized their range of opinions about the Trump administration and revealed the realignment of American Jews' political orientations in the early twenty-first century.

The Executive Order Combatting Antisemitism and the flood of responses to it reflect the perpetual shifts in how US Jews have defined themselves as a people and the broader historical relationship between US Jews and the federal government. Since the nation's founding, Jews in the United States have sought promises from federal officials assuring Jews' safety and rights; these petitions collectively reveal changing notions of what "being Jewish" has meant in US history. In August 1790, a member of the Hebrew Congregation of Newport, Rhode Island, wrote to George Washington asking for such a promise while claiming to represent "the children of the Stock of Abraham."[1] His characterization of Jews revealed a self-conceptualization of Jews as a religious and quasi-racial community, as did Washington's reply. Starting in the 1870s and through the 1950s, some Jews in the US adopted a racial definition of themselves, believing that such a conceptualization would protect them from external pressures to assimilate. At the same time, non-Jews adopted a racialized construction of Jews as a way to fit Jews into the prevailing Black-white racial dichotomy. Paradoxically, throughout this time, Jews challenged the government in instances when it tried to apply a racialized classification to Jews, especially in the context of immigration laws.

In the mid-twentieth century, armed with a new awareness of the dangers of deploying racial definitions of themselves, Jews assumed an understanding of themselves as a people and as an "ethnic group," definitions that allowed them to distinguish themselves from their non-Jewish neighbors while still permitting social integration. At this same moment, many Jews and non-Jews began to identify Jewish difference as merely one of religion, a reconceptualization that coexisted with the idea of Jewishness as an ethnicity through the start of the twenty-first century. Since 2000, while upholding the definition of Jewishness as an ethnic identity and/or religious designation, the federal government endeavored to squash antisemitism by asserting that discrimination based on the perception of Jews as a race or nationality amounted to the violation of the Civil Rights Act of 1964. The Executive Order Combatting Antisemitism marked another turn in that effort, reasserting Jewish difference in the language of race and nationality and including in its definition of antisemitism certain critiques of Israel.

PRIMARY SOURCE

Section 1. Policy. **My Administration is committed to combating the rise of anti-Semitism and anti-Semitic incidents in the United States and around the world. Anti-Semitic incidents**

have increased since 2013, and students, in particular, continue to face anti-Semitic harassment in schools and on university and college campuses.

Title VI of the Civil Rights Act of 1964 (Title VI), 42 U.S.C. 2000d et seq., prohibits discrimination on the basis of race, color, and national origin in programs and activities receiving Federal financial assistance. While Title VI does not cover discrimination based on religion, individuals who face discrimination on the basis of race, color, or national origin do not lose protection under Title VI for also being a member of a group that shares common religious practices. Discrimination against Jews may give rise to a Title VI violation when the discrimination is based on an individual's race, color, or national origin.

It shall be the policy of the executive branch to enforce Title VI against prohibited forms of discrimination rooted in anti-Semitism as vigorously as against all other forms of discrimination prohibited by Title VI.

Sec. 2. Ensuring Robust Enforcement of Title VI. (a) In enforcing Title VI, and identifying evidence of discrimination based on race, color, or national origin, all executive departments and agencies (agencies) charged with enforcing Title VI shall consider the following:

(i) the non-legally binding working definition of anti-Semitism adopted on May 26, 2016, by the International Holocaust Remembrance Alliance (IHRA), which states, "Antisemitism is a certain perception of Jews, which may be expressed as hatred toward Jews. Rhetorical and physical manifestations of antisemitism are directed toward Jewish or non-Jewish individuals and/or their property, toward Jewish community institutions and religious facilities"; and

(ii) the "Contemporary Examples of Anti-Semitism" identified by the IHRA, to the extent that any examples might be useful as evidence of discriminatory intent.

(b) In considering the materials described in subsections (a) (i) and (a) (ii) of this section, agencies shall not diminish or infringe upon any right protected under Federal law or under the First Amendment. As with all other Title VI complaints, the inquiry into whether a particular act constitutes discrimination prohibited by Title VI will require a detailed analysis of the allegations. . . .

Donald J. Trump
The White House,
December 11, 2019

Donald J. Trump, "Executive Order on Combating Anti-Semitism," December 11, 2019. (Trump White House Archives, https://trumpwhitehouse.archives.gov)

QUESTIONS

1. What is the purpose of issuing an executive order to protect a minority population?
2. What histories or historical events do people for and against this executive order draw on to support their claims?
3. Some US Jews were concerned that the Executive Order Combatting Antisemitism defined Jews as a nationality. What is at stake in the decision to define Jews as a nationality, race, or religion?

4. How has the definition of Jewishness changed over the course of this collection? What other moments does this order echo from within that history?
5. The International Holocaust Alliance rejects the spelling "anti-Semitism" because "the hyphenated spelling allows for the possibility of something called 'Semitism,' which not only legitimizes a form of pseudo-scientific racial classification that was thoroughly discredited by association with Nazi ideology, but also divides the term, stripping it from its meaning of opposition and hatred toward Jews."[2] Why do you think it was spelled "anti-Semitism" in Trump's order?

NOTES

1. Hertzberg, *Jews in America*, 69.
2. International Holocaust Remembrance Alliance, "Spelling of Antisemitism."

112

A Challenging Editorial

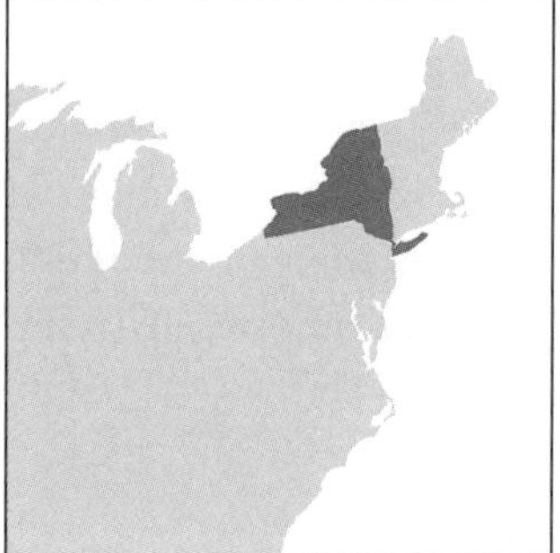

NEW YORK, 2019

Justin Jaron Lewis

In 2012, kaveshtiebel.com (the coffee house) was founded for freewheeling Yiddish-language discussions among Hasidic Jews, mostly young married men from Hasidic neighborhoods and towns in the New York area. In 2016, participants launched a quarterly Yiddish magazine, *Der Veker* (The alarm clock or The awakener). While committed to Orthodox Judaism, the magazine is intellectually open and has a reformist agenda regarding the rigidity and narrowness of Hasidic Jewish life. The text in this chapter is a translation, from the original Yiddish, of the editors' introduction to a recent issue.

In both the form and content of *Der Veker*, it grapples with Hasidic Jews' relationship to modernity. Hasidic Judaism arose concurrently with the *Haskalah*, but unlike the proponents of the Enlightenment, Hasidim emphasized mysticism (rather than rationalism) and were more (rather than less) stringent about following Jewish law. Because of their concern for the nuances of observance, today Hasidim are included in the larger category of *Haredi* (God-fearing) or "ultra-Orthodox" Jews. One example of this stringency is the trend of excluding women from (or editing women out of) pictures in Haredi publications. This practice, which has increased in recent decades, reflects both the rejection of secular culture and the emphasis on female modesty as a central Jewish value. Editing out women is often criticized by outsiders but is similarly a source of in-group controversy.

Increased stringencies following the Holocaust were one way Hasidim adapted to the changing world around them. Most European Hasidim were murdered in the Holocaust, but surviving spiritual leaders built thriving communities in America and Israel in the postwar era (see chapters 91 and 102). These groups, whose share of the Jewish population is increasing because of high birthrates, are often insular, with distinctive ways of life, maintained through separate institutions and internal self-policing. The use of Yiddish as a daily language provides a sense of continuity with the European past and separation from the non-Hasidic world. The internet, however, challenges this separateness. Though forbidden or denounced by many Hasidic leaders, it is widely used and has inspired and emboldened some people to leave the Hasidic fold in search of personal and intellectual freedom (see chapter 104). Less heard are the voices of those who remain within their communities and maintain Yiddish as their preferred language, while also exploring the world of ideas on the internet and questioning the orthodoxies of their community. *Der Veker* gives us a glimpse of the concerns and creativity of this dynamic minority within the growing Hasidic world.

The Yiddish language has played a significant role in Jewish life in the Americas since the great immigration of the late nineteenth and early twentieth centuries (see chapters 79, 80, 81, and 90). Fading away over the generations like most immigrant languages, it remained a touchstone for nostalgia. Yiddish is cultivated by some creatives and activists as an alternative to mainstream Jewish organizations' focus on Hebrew and Israel. In the twenty-first century, however, it is mainly among Hasidim that Yiddish is the mother tongue and daily language of tens of thousands of children and adults. In this largely gender-segregated society, Yiddish is used more commonly by and among men than women.

Compared to the Yiddish used a generation or two earlier by largely secular Yiddish American novelists and poets, Hasidic American Yiddish is sometimes seen as an impoverished, anglicized Yiddish that is put into writing only for didactic religious purposes. *Der Veker* challenges that stereotype. Written in literary Yiddish and addressing all kinds of topics, it is a glimpse of the possibilities of Yiddish as a living language in the Americas today.

PRIMARY SOURCE

The lead article in this issue is one of a kind, covering a subject that may seem trivial, but is actually fundamental in our lives as Haredi Jews. Tearing women out of Jewish publications [by excluding pictures of them in publications] is, on the one hand, an essential problem in our relationship with 50 percent of the Jewish People; on the other hand, it is an example of how things that have no relevance to Judaism or our tradition can be transformed, over a generation or two, into supposedly essential elements of faith.

In the dozens of pages of the research project "Women Forbidden!," you will read about this subject: its history; documentation from dozens of newspapers, magazines, and books published by Haredi and Hasidic Jews in the past hundred years; and the harmful consequences toward which ever more radical extremism is leading us.

In the column "Flashes," we report the news that the Hasidic institutions have collaborated with the City of New York to force parents to vaccinate their children, in keeping with the recommendations of over 90 percent of specialists. It surely is a general rule in life that we should accept the advice of experts in a subject, and not those of people with half-baked conspiracy theories. But we must also remember that even experts make mistakes. This is documented and portrayed in the wonderful article "When Academics Don't Know *Modeh Ani*" [a prayer said upon waking up, learned in childhood].

The terrible events last Heshvan [October] in a Pittsburgh synagogue are still tugging at every Jewish heart. Katle Kanye ["Reed-cutter," a Talmudic idiom for an ignoramus] shares his melancholic thoughts about reactions to that slaughter. And, "from the house of mourning to the house of feasting" [Ecclesiastes 7:2]: in honor of the month of Adar [which includes the festival of Purim], Katle Kanye bestows on us his humorous and sweet *haymish*

[homey, here Hasidic] adaptation of "Goldilocks and the Three Bears," accompanied by captivating original illustrations.

. . . "According to the effort is the reward" [Pirke Avot 6.26]. This issue is especially precious because of the difficulty we had with continuing to print the *Veker*. As some of our readers are certainly aware, the company that has been printing the *Veker*, CreateSpace, has closed. Its place has been taken by a new company that currently cannot print Yiddish or the Holy Language [religious Hebrew].

About two months ago, we asked our readers, through social media, to send letters to the company demanding the option of printing in Yiddish. Although the company has answered that it will consider the possibility of Yiddish printing in the future, we had to find another company to print the *Veker* in the meantime. But we are very proud of the many letters sent by our readers from all over the world to ask the company to change its mind, and the continuous encouragement we have been receiving.

Thank you to all the readers who have sent letters, encouraged us, and helped us with advice and counsel. . . . Likewise, we are pleased to see our work welcomed positively by writers and media specialists, as in . . . the assertion of Professor Justin Jaron Lewis, at the conference of the Association for Jewish Studies, that our publication is "the *New Yorker* of the Hasidic-Yiddish world."

The enthusiasm and expectation of our thousands of readers who thirst for each issue, the many letters of encouragement, and the articles that our readers send us give us the encouragement and strength to keep on going, knowing that this inspires such a countless multitude of Jews, leaving fingerprints for a better today and tomorrow.

At the same time, we wish to repeat that we are here to serve as your platform, to publish articles, opinions, and art. Don't be shy and don't be lazy! Take thought and take the *Veker* microphone in hand. The editors are here for you, to give feedback and constructive criticism, to help bring your writing talents to higher levels. . . .

Happiness always,
The Awakeners

"A Word from the Editors," *Der Veker*, no. 15 (Adar–Nisan 5779 / March–April 2019), 2–3.

QUESTIONS

1. The editorial mentions a Yiddish-language adaptation of "Goldilocks and the Three Bears." Letters in the following issue speak of children's delight at hearing this story in Yiddish—and adults' amusement at its use of satire. What does this incident tell you about the readers of *Der Veker*, including what else they read?
2. What do *Der Veker*'s printing troubles tell you about the contemporary situation of Yiddish in the Americas?
3. What impressions does this editorial give you of *Der Veker*'s attitude toward non-Hasidic academics and writers (such as Justin Jaron Lewis)?
4. How does the use of Yiddish by *Der Veker* transform the surrounding society into a *haymish* (homey) space?

113

Indigenous and Jewish: The Photography of Kali Spitzer

BRITISH COLUMBIA, 2016, 2019

Laura Arnold Leibman

The Indigenous femme queer photographer Kali Spitzer lives and works on the traditional unceded lands of the Tsleil-Waututh, Skxwú7mesh, and Musqueam peoples in the Canadian province of British Columbia. Her photography and ceramics weave together the traditions from both sides of her family: Kaska Dena from Daylu (Lower Post, British Columbia) on her father's side and Jewish from Transylvania (Romania) on her mother's side. The photographs included here represent her work in the tintype form of photography, a genre that she reclaims from the colonizers' lens.

Tintypes are an unusual form for a contemporary photographer. Invented in the 1850s, tintypes quickly followed on the heels of daguerreotypes (see chapter 45). They were less fragile than daguerreotypes and could be more easily sent through the mail to loved ones. They were incredibly cheap, selling for as little as two cents.[1] As settlers moved westward across Canada in the 1870s–1880s, they brought cameras with them (see chapter 56). As Jarod Hore explains, early photographs of landscapes, such as tintypes and daguerreotypes, "fed into settler belonging and produced new ways of thinking about territory and history. During this key period of settler revolution, a generation of photographers came to associate 'nature' with remoteness, antiquity, and emptiness, a perspective that disguised the realities of Indigenous presence and reinforced colonial fantasies of environmental abundance."[2] Even portraits of Indigenous Americans, such as Edward Curtis's *The Vanishing Race* (1904), often staged their subjects to suggest that American Indian cultures were disappearing, leaving their land vacant for settlement. Indigenous Americans have long countered this dangerous myth. During the 1980s, for example, the author Leslie Marmon Silko (Laguna Pueblo) used her father's photographs in her work to recenter "Indigenous voices through camera angle, perspective, and form" and to subvert ethnographic practices of photographic surveillance of Indigenous peoples by Edward Curtis and other early photographers.[3]

The artists Kali Spitzer, Will Wilson (Diné/Navajo), Greg Staats (Mohawk), Adrian Stimson (Blackfoot), and Krista Belle Stewart (Upper Nicola) have similarly all used wet-plate collodion photography to rethink and restore the archive of how Indigenous peoples are visualized. Some of these photographers deliberately juxtapose modern objects and clothing with the tintypes' irregular tones in order to disrupt history and Western notions of time.[4] This disruption is particularly powerful when used, for example, by Spitzer to call attention to the ongoing violence against and abduction of Indigenous women. In the United States alone, the rate of violent crime against Indigenous women is two and a half times that of women in general. In Canada, Indigenous women are five times more likely to suffer death due to violence.[5] By using a nineteenth-century form, Spitzer ties recent violence to the abduction of thousands of girls in state-run boarding schools in Canada between 1863 and 1998. As an Indigenous Jew, Spitzer creates work that asks Jews to rethink their own histories. By photographing her mother, Audrey Siegl, in a similar format to Indigenous women living on the same lands, Spitzer reinforces the authority of an Indigenous presence that has neither vanished nor ceded the rights to its land.

Spitzer's photography emphasizes the importance of remembering the diversity of cultures that Americans bring to the Jewish experience. While Jews of color typically make up between 8 and 15 percent of Jewish communities in the United States, most academic discussions of Jews of color typically highlight Jews who are Black, Hispanic, or Asian and ignore the category of Indigenous Jews. Similarly, discussions of Jews and Indigenous peoples often assume that these categories are mutually exclusive. Yet people who are both American Indian and Jewish are well represented across the arts and society, including the cartoonist Emily Bowen Cohen (Muscogee/Creek), the author of *An American Indian Guide to the Day of Atonement*; the critic and writer David Treuer (Ojibwe); the Washington State Supreme Court justice Raquel Montoya-Lewis (Pueblo of Isleta); and the novelist and scholar Greg Sarris (Pomo/Coast Miwok), who is chairman of the Federated Indians of Graton Rancheria. Their work is a reminder of the wide range of Jewish experiences across the Americas.

PRIMARY SOURCES

See following pages.

Eloise Spitzer, Jewish of Transylvania and Polish descent, West and North of Canada. Kali Spitzer, *Eloise Spitzer*, 2015, 8 × 10 wet plate collodion (tintype), made on aluminum, shot on Deardorff 8 × 10 Studio camera with century-old brass portrait lens.

kʷasəlwət, sχ̓ɬemtəna:t, St'agiid Jaad, Audrey. Kali Spitzer, *Audrey Siegl*, 2019, 8 × 10 wet plate collodion (tintype), made on aluminum, shot on Deardorff 8 × 10 Studio camera with century-old brass portrait lens.

"We created these images to honor Maria and all of our stolen women. We held space for Maria's spirit to be with us. Safe spaces for our women are non-existence . . . unless WE build them. By doing this work together we fostered a safe space for each other. We are both working in our communities to expand these spaces. With our work we are creating visibility and voice where there has only been silence and oppression, whether it is through photography, activism or being on the land gathering medicine, trapping or hunting. As indigenous women we are inseparable from the land and the water. As we rise to protect our women we inherently protect our water and land in which we all come from." Kali Spitzer, *Honoring Maria*, 2019, 8 × 10 wet plate collodion (tintype), made on aluminum, shot on Deardorff 8 × 10 Studio camera with century-old brass portrait lens.

QUESTIONS

1. What does the medium of tintypes add to Spitzer's portraits?
2. Compare the way the sitters in these portraits look at the camera to those in chapter 75. When does the sitter look directly at the photographer? Who smiles at whom?
3. Across the Americas in the nineteenth century, white photographers began to use photography to create portraits of types—typically exotic Others. What strategies does Spitzer use to circumvent the white, male gaze and allow her sitters to be more than types?
4. Ancestral trauma and its ability to shape lives today is an important part of Jewish ritual and liturgy. How does Spitzer's work challenge or augment the story of ancestral trauma told in Jewish ceremonies today?
5. Consider where this collection began. How does Spitzer's presentation of what it means to be Indigenous and Jewish compare to that in chapter 6?

NOTES

1. Maurice, "Snippets of History."
2. Hore, *Visions of Nature.*
3. Hernandez, "Disrupting White Settler Colonial Narratives," i, 7.
4. Racette, "Returning Fire," 82.
5. Agtuca, "Beloved Women," 3–4; Hargreaves, *Violence against Indigenous Women.*

ACKNOWLEDGMENTS

In February 2019, while at the Jews at the Americas conference organized by the University of Florida's Center for Latin American Studies, we sat down to think about the need for a new documentary reader that would better help students see the connections, similarities, and differences that existed in the experiences of Jews in the American continents since their arrival on these shores. Many of the conference presentations, on synagogues, movies, women, and daguerreotypes, among others, inspired us to imagine a volume that would engage students by providing them with a variety of sources with which to understand how Jews lived in the past. We got to work on this volume shortly after. The responses, many from participants we had met and heard at the University of Florida, were overwhelmingly positive. It became clear that the contributors were also excited to produce a volume that presented a fresh, inclusive, and complex picture of Jewish life in the Americas. COVID-19 came a year into the process, and as you can imagine, we all slowed down, facing multiple challenges and needing to use our energy on more pressing matters. Yet we did not give up.

More than four years after first envisioning this volume, we are happy to finally see the project through. We thank, first and foremost, the talented contributors, who work in nine countries and who represent a range of stages in their career and types of institutions where they work inside and outside the academy. They all understood the importance of showing today's students a new way of thinking about the Jewish experience in the Americas. They responded with patience and enthusiasm to our multiple requests, late-hour changes, translation queries, and editing suggestions. We are also grateful to the many archives, historical societies, individuals, and institutions across the American continents and the ocean that provided us with the necessary permissions to put these fascinating documents together, particularly the two flagships of our field, the American Jewish Historical Society and the American Jewish Archives. We thank, as well, our institutions, Reed College and St. Mary's College of Maryland, for helping us with the indexing of the project and a Ruby-Lankford Grant, for providing us the funding to hire Caitlin Berrol, Samuel Johnson, Meera Balan, and Blaise Hilde Albis-Burdige, outstanding student assistants whose help was invaluable at various points in the process. Last but far from least, we would like to thank our families for their patience and their understanding during these difficult past few years.

BIBLIOGRAPHY

Abdullah al-Ahari, Muhammed. "The Caribbean and Latin America." In *Islam Outside the Arab World*, edited by Ingvar Svenberg and David Westerlund, 443–461. London: Routledge, 1999.

Adichie, Chimamanda Ngozi. "The Danger of a Single Story." Filmed July 2009 in Oxford, England. TED video, 18:33. www.ted.com.

Adler, Elkan Nathan. *Jews in Many Lands*. Philadelphia: JPS, 1905.

Agtuca, Jacqueline. "Beloved Women: Life Givers, Caretakers, Teachers of Future Generations." *Sharing Our Stories of Survival: Native Women Surviving Violence*, edited by Sarah Deer, Bonnie Clairmont, and Carrie A. Martell, 3–27. Lanham, MD: AltaMira, 2008.

Aiken, Carol. "Conservation Reports, January and September 2001." Special Collections, Addlestone Library, College of Charleston, Charleston, SC.

Aizenberg, Edna. *On the Edge of the Holocaust: The Shoa in Latin American Literature and Culture*. Boston: Brandeis University Press, 2015.

Aizenberg, Isidoro. *La comunidad judía de Coro 1824–1900. Una historia*. Caracas: Asociación Israelita de Venezuela-Centro de Estudios Sefardíes de Caracas, 1995.

Andrews, George Reid. *Afro-Latin America, 1800–2000*. New York: Oxford University Press, 2004.

———. "Race and the State in Colonial Brazil." *Latin American Research Review* 19, no. 3 (1984): 203–216.

Andrien, Kenneth J. *The Human Tradition in Colonial Latin America*. Wilmington, DE: Scholarly Resources, 2002.

Angel, Marc D. "The Sephardim of the United States: An Exploratory Study." *American Jewish Year Book* 74 (1973): 77–138.

Arbell, Mordehay. *The Jewish Nation of the Caribbean: The Spanish-Portuguese Jewish Settlements in the Caribbean and the Guianas*. New York: Gefen, 2002.

———. *The Portuguese Jews of Jamaica*. Kingston, Jamaica: Canoe, 2000.

Bacon, Jacqueline. *Freedom's Journal: The First African-American Newspaper*. Lanham, MD: Lexington Books, 2007.

Behar, Ruth. "Sex and Sin, Witchcraft and the Devil in Late-Colonial Mexico." *American Ethnologist* 14, no. 1 (1987): 34–54.

Belisario, I. M. *Sketches of Character, in Illustration of the Habits, Occupation, and Costume of the Negro Population, in the Island of Jamaica. Drawn after Nature, and in Lithography*. Kingston: J. R. DeCordova, 1837–1838.

Bendjoya, Regina. "Los templos y la juventud." *Adama*, November 1958.

Ben-Jacob, Michael. "Nathan Simson: A Biographical Sketch of a Colonial Jewish Merchant." *American Jewish Archives* 51, no. 1 (1999): 11–37.

Ben-Ur, Aviva. *Jewish Autonomy in a Slave Society: Suriname in the Atlantic World, 1651–1825*. Philadelphia: University of Pennsylvania Press, 2020.

Ben-Ur, Aviva. "Jewish Savannah in Atlantic Perspective: A Reconsideration of North America's First Intentional Jewish Community." In *The Sephardic Atlantic: Colonial Histories and Postcolonial Perspectives*, edited by Jonathan Schorsch and Sina Rauschenbach, 183–214. Berlin: Springer, 2019.

———. "Peripheral Inclusion: Communal Belonging in Suriname's Sephardic Community." In *Religion, Gender, and Culture in the Pre-modern World*, edited by Alexandra Cuffel and Brian M Britt, 185–210. New York: Palgrave Macmillan, 2007.

Ben-Ur, Aviva, and Rachel Frankel. *Remnant Stones: The Jewish Cemeteries and Synagogues of Suriname: Essays*. Cincinnati: Hebrew Union College Press, 2012.

Ben-Ur, Aviva, and Jessica Vance Roitman. "Adultery Here and There: Crossing Sexual Boundaries in the Dutch Jewish Atlantic." In *Dutch Atlantic Connections, 1680–1800: Linking Empires, Bridging Borders*, edited by Gert Oostindie and Jessica V. Roitman, 183–223. Leiden: Brill, 2014.

Bettinger-López, Caroline. *Cuban-Jewish Journeys: Searching for Identity, Home, and History in Miami*. Knoxville: University of Tennessee Press, 2000.

Biale, David, David Assaf, Benjamin Brown, Uriel Gellman, Samuel C. Heilman, Moshe Rosman, Gadi Sagiv, and Marcin Wodziński. *Hasidism: A New History*. Princeton, NJ: Princeton University Press, 2018.

Bjorn, Amanda. "Artist Feature: Melody Melamed." *Feminist*. Accessed November 20, 2022. www.feminists.co.

Boom, Mattie. *The First Photograph from Suriname: A Portrait of the Nineteenth-Century Elite in the West Indies*. Amsterdam: Rijksmuseum, 2014.

Boyarin, Daniel. *Unheroic Conduct: The Rise of Heterosexuality and the Invention of the Jewish Man*. Berkeley: University of California Press, 1997.

Brackman, Harold D. *Ministry of Lies: The Truth behind the Nation of Islam's "The Secret Relationship between Blacks and Jews."* New York: Four Walls Eight Windows, 1994.

Brand, Itzhak. "On Suspicion: Justice, Ethics, and Society—between Rationalism and Pietism." *Jewish Law Annual* 21 (2015): 19–46.

Brodkin, Karen. *How Jews Became White Folks and What That Says about Race in America*. New Brunswick, NJ: Rutgers University Press, 2000.

Brodsky, Adriana. *Sephardi, Jewish, Argentine: Creating Community and National Identity, 1880–1960*. Bloomington: Indiana University Press, 2016.

Brodsky, Adriana, Beatrice Gurwitz, and Rachel Kranson. "Editors' Introduction: Jewish Youth in the Global 1960s." *Journal of Jewish Identities* 8, no. 2 (2015): 1–11.

Brodsky, Adriana, and Raanan Rein. "On Kosher Hamburgers, Yiddish Tangos and Non-affiliated Jews: Writing Jewish Latin America into the Americas." *American Jewish History* (2019): 345–363.

Bronski, Michael. *A Queer History of the United States*. Boston: Beacon, 2011.

Carmeli, Orit. "The Material Culture and Ritual Objects of the Jews of Iran." In *The Jews of Iran: The History, Religion and Culture of a Community in the Islamic World*, edited by Houman Sarshar, 144–172. London: I. B. Tauris, 2014.

Carment, David, and Ariane Sadjed. *Diaspora as Cultures of Cooperation: Global and Local Perspectives*. Basingstoke, UK: Palgrave Macmillan, 2018.

Carter, Sarah P., Laura J. Osborne, Keith D. Renshaw, Elizabeth S. Allen, Benjamin A. Loew, Howard J. Markman, and Scott M. Stanley. "Something to Talk About: Topics of Conversation between Romantic Partners during Military Deployments." *Journal of Family Psychology* 32, no. 1 (2018): 22–30.

Casteel, Sarah Phillips. "Making History Visible: Caribbean Artist Josef Nassy's Visual Diary of Nazi Internment." *Small Axe* 64 (2021): 28–46.

Chauncey, George. "Manhattan's Roaring Gay Days." *Advocate*, no. 1001 (January 29, 2008): S56+.

Chesnut, Mary. *Mary Chesnut's Civil War*. Edited by C. Vann Woodward. New Haven, CT: Yale University Press, 1981.

Chisholm, Clinton. "Religion and the 2011 Census." *Gleaner*, November 4, 2012. https://jamaica-gleaner.com.

Cohen, Judah M. *The Making of a Reform Jewish Cantor: Musical Authority, Cultural Investment*. Bloomington: Indiana University Press, 2019.

———. *Through the Sands of Time: A History of the Jewish Community of St. Thomas, U.S. Virgin Islands*. Hanover, NH: Brandeis University Press, 2012.

Cohen, Martin A., and Abraham J. Peck. *Sephardim in the Americas: Studies in Culture and History*. Tuscaloosa: University of Alabama Press, 2003.

Cohen, Yolande. "Sephardi Jews in Montreal." In *Canada's Jews: In Time, Space and Spirit*, edited by Ira Robinson, 168–180. Brighton, MA: Academic Studies, 2013.

CONADEP (Comisión Nacional sobre la Desaparición de Personas). *Nunca más: Informe de la Comisión Nacional sobre la Desaparición de Personas*. Buenos Aires: Eudeba, 1984. English version available at https://web.archive.org.

Cootz, Stephanie. *Marriage, a History: How Love Conquered Marriage*. New York: Penguin, 2005.

Cooperman, Jessica. *Making Judaism Safe for America: World War I and the Origins of Religious Pluralism*. New York: New York University Press, 2018.

Cristidou, Ellen. "The Representation of Suriname and Surinamese People in the Rijksmuseum and Voor Volkenkunde, Leiden." *Journal of Museum Ethnography*, no. 30 (2017): 148–163.

Cromley, Elizabeth C. *Alone Together: A History of New York's Early Apartments*. Ithaca, NY: Cornell University Press, 1990.

Cung Sulkin, Paloma. *Tierra para echar raíces: Cementerios Judíos en México*. Consejo Nacional para la Cultura y las Artes, Instituto Nacional de Antropología e Historia, México, 2006.

DAIA, Centro de Estudios Sociales. *Informe sobre la situación de los detenidos-desaparecidos judíos durante el genocidio perpetrado en Argentina 1976–1983*. Buenos Aires: DAIA, 2007.

Dean-Olmsted, Evelyn. "Arabic Words in the Spanish of Syrian Jewish Mexicans: A Case for 'Heritage Words.'" *Texas Linguistics Forum* 55 (2012): 20–32.

de Jonge, Annemarie. *Kotomisi: De kracht van klederdracht*. Netherlands: n.p., 2019.

Della Pergola, Sergio. "Demographic Trends of Latin American Jewry." In *The Jewish Presence in Latin America*, edited by Judith Laikin Elkin and Gilbert W. Merkx, 85–133. Boston: Allen and Unwin, 1987.

Della Pergola, Sergio, and Susana Lerner. *La población judía en México: Perfil demográfico, social y cultural*. México and Jerusalem: Centro de Estudios Demográficos y de Desarrollo Urbano, Colegio de México, Instituto Avraham Harman de Judaísmo Contemporáneo, and Asociación Mexicana de Amigos de la Universidad Hebrea de Jerusalén, 1995.

de Sola Pool, David, and Tamar Hirschensohn de Sola Pool. *An Old Faith in the New World*. New York: Columbia University Press, 1955.

Deutsch, Nathaniel, and Michael Casper. *A Fortress in Brooklyn: Race, Real Estate, and the Making of Hasidic Williamsburg*. New Haven, CT: Yale University Press, 2021.

Diner, Hasia. *We Remember with Reverence and Love: American Jews and the Myth of Silence after the Holocaust, 1945–1962*. New York: New York University Press, 2009.

Dinnerstein, Leonard. *Antisemitism in America*. New York: Oxford University Press, 1995.

Dorman, Jacob S. *Chosen People: The Rise of American Black Israelite Religions*. New York: Oxford University Press, 2013.

Dornan, Inge. "Masterful Women: Colonial Women Slaveholders in the Urban Low Country." *Journal of American Studies* 39, no. 3 (2005): 383–402.

Drinkwater, Gregg. "LGBTQ Jews on Their Own Terms." Paper presented at the AJS annual conference, December 21, 2021.

Duff, James, Earl of Fife. *Catalogue of the Portraits & Pictures in the Different Houses Belonging to James Earl of Fife*. London: T. Collins, 1807.

Dzmura, Noach. Introduction to *Balancing on the Mechitza: Transgender in Jewish Community*, edited by Noach Dzmura, xiii–xxix. Berkeley, CA: North Atlantic Books, 2014.

"Editors' Introduction." *American Jewish History* 105, nos. 1–2 (2021): xi–xiii.

Eleff, Zev. *Who Rules the Synagogue? Religious Authority and the Formation of American Judaism*. New York: Oxford University Press, 2016.

Elliott, Kamilla. *Portraiture and British Gothic Fiction: The Rise of Picture Identification, 1764–1835*. Baltimore: Johns Hopkins University Press, 2012.

Emmanuel, Isaac S. *Precious Stones of the Jews of Curaçao*. New York: Bloch, 1957.

Environics Institute. "2018 Survey of Jews in Canada." 2018. www.environicsinstitute.org.

Epstein, Lawrence J. *At the Edge of a Dream: The Story of Jewish Immigrants on New York's Lower East Side, 1880–1920*. San Francisco: Jossey-Bass, 2007.

Fatah-Black, Karwan. *White Lies and Black Markets: Evading Metropolitan Authority in Colonial Suriname, 1650–1800*. Leiden: Brill, 2015.

Feder, Shira. "During the AIDS Crisis, This Gay Jewish Cookbook Kept a Community Together." *Forward*, August 13, 2018.

Feingold, Henry L. *A Time for Searching: Entering the Mainstream, 1920–1945*. Baltimore: Johns Hopkins University Press, 1995.

Fertig, Mark. *Take That, Adolf! The Fighting Comic Books of the Second World War*. Seattle: Fantagraphics Books, 2017.

Feuer, Alan, "No One There, but This Place Is Far from Empty." *New York Times*, January 14, 2009. www.nytimes.com.

Fogel, Keith, and Marian E. Fogel. *Conversos of the Americas: Emergence and Descent of the Converted Jews of Spain*. New York: Xlibris US, 2004.

Ford, Emily, and Barry Stiefel. *The Jews of New Orleans and the Mississippi Delta: A History of Life and Community along the Bayou*. Charleston, SC: Arcadia, 2012.

Fortune, Stephen. *Merchants and Jews: The Struggle for British West Indian Commerce, 1650–1750*. Gainesville: University Press of Florida, 1984.

Fowler, Will. *Mexico in the Age of Proposals, 1821–1853*. Westport, CT: Greenwood, 1998.

Frank, Robin Jaffee. *Love and Loss: American Portrait and Mourning Miniatures*. New Haven, CT: Yale University Press, 2000.

Fried, Louis. "Jacob Riis and the Jews: The Ambivalent Quest for Community." *American Studies* 20, no. 1 (1979): 5–24.

Gendler, Carol. "Pioneer Jews of Omaha: The First Sixty Years." *Western States Jewish History* 49, no. 2 (2017): 175–240.

Gerchunoff, Alberto. *The Jewish Gauchos of the Pampas*. Translated by Prudencio de Pereda. Albuquerque: University of New Mexico Press, 1998.

Germani, Gino. *Política y sociedad en una época de transición: De la sociedad tradicional a la sociedad de masas*. Buenos Aires: Paidos, 1965.

Gilbert, Martin. *The Routledge Atlas of Jewish History*. London: Taylor and Francis, 2010.

Gitlitz, David M. *Living in Silverado: Secret Jews in the Silver Mining Towns of Colonial Mexico*. Albuquerque: University of New Mexico Press, 2019.

———. *Secrecy and Deceit: the Religion of the Crypto-Jews*. Albuquerque: University of New Mexico Press, 2002.

Gleizer, Daniela. *Unwelcome Exiles. Mexico and the Jewish Refugees from Nazism, 1933–1945*. Leiden: Brill, 2013.

Gold, Roberta S. "The Black Jews of Harlem: Representation, Identity, and Race, 1920–1939." *American Quarterly* 55, no. 2 (2003): 179–225.

Goldstein, Eric. "The Great Wave: Eastern European Jewish Immigration to the United States, 1880–1924." In *The Columbia History of Jews and Judaism in America*, edited by Marc Lee Raphael, 70–92. New York: Columbia University Press, 2008.

———. *The Price of Whiteness: Jews, Race, and American Identity*. Princeton, NJ: Princeton University Press, 2006.

Groeneveld, Anneke. *Fotografie in Suriname, 1839–1939 / Photography in Surinam, 1839–1939*. Amsterdam: Fragment, 1990.

Grossman, Susan, and Rivka Haut. "From Persia to New York: An Interview with Three Generations of Iranian Women." In *Daughters of the King: Women and the Synagogue—A Survey of History, Halakhah, and Contemporary Realities*, edited by Susan Grossman and Riva Haut, 217–226. Philadelphia: Jewish Publication Society, 1991.

———. Introduction to *Daughters of the King: Women and the Synagogue—A Survey of History, Halakhah, and Contemporary Realities*, edited by Susan Grossman and Riva Haut, 3–12. Philadelphia: Jewish Publication Society, 1991.

Gurock, Jeffrey S. *American Jewish History: The Colonial and Early National Periods, 1654–1840*. New York: Routledge, 1998.

Gurwitz, Beatrice. *Argentine Jews in the Age of Revolt: Between the New World and the Third World*. Leiden: Brill, 2016.

Halberstadt, Moshe Leib. "Mamzer in Jewish Cemetery." Kislev 1, 5770 [November 18, 2009]. *Yeshiva: The Torah World Gateway*. www.yeshiva.co.

Hamui Halabe, Liz. *Transformaciones en la religiosidad de los judíos en México: Tradición, ortodoxia y fundamentalismo en la modernidad tardía*. Mexico City: Noriega Editores, 2005.

Hargreaves, Allison. *Violence against Indigenous Women: Literature, Activism, Resistance*. Waterloo, ON: Wilfrid Laurier University Press, 2017.

Haynes, Bruce D. *The Soul of Judaism: Jews of African Descent in America*. New York: New York University Press, 2018.

Henry, Michele. "Passover a Spicy Affair for Toronto's Indian Jews." *Toronto Star*, April 2, 2015. www.thestar.com.

Hernandez, Chelsea Ann. "Disrupting White Settler Colonial Narratives: Leslie Marmon Silko's Use of Photography in Storyteller and Sacred Water." MFA thesis, University of Washington, 2019. http://hdl.handle.net/1773/43925.

Hertzberg, Arthur. *The Jews in America: Four Centuries of an Uneasy Encounter: A History*. New York: Columbia University Press, 1997.

Herzog, Dagmar. *Sexuality in Europe: A Twentieth Century History*. Cambridge: Cambridge University Press, 2011.

Higgins, Kathleen J. *Licentious Liberty in a Brazilian Gold-Mining Region: Slavery, Gender, and Social Control in Eighteenth-Century Sabará, Minas Gerais*. University Park: Pennsylvania State University Press, 2010.

Hirsch, Marianne. *The Generation of Postmemory: Writing and Visual Culture after the Holocaust*. New York: Columbia University Press, 2012.

Hore, Jarrod. *Visions of Nature: How Landscape Photography Shaped Settler Colonialism*. Berkeley: University of California Press, 2022.

Huussen, Alfred H. "The Legal Position of the Jews in the Dutch Republic c. 1590–1796." In *Dutch Jewry: Its History and Secular Culture (1500–2000)*, edited by Jonathan Irvine Israel, 25–41. Leiden: Brill, 2002.

Hyman, Paula E. "Immigrant Women and Consumer Protest: The New York City Kosher Meat Boycott of 1902." *American Jewish History* 70, no. 1 (1980): 91–105.

Inabinet, L. Glen. "'The July Fourth Incident' of 1816: An Insurrection Plotted by Slaves in Camden, South Carolina." In *South Carolina Legal History: Proceedings of the Reynolds Conference, University of South Carolina, December 2–3, 1977*, edited by Herbert A. Johnson, 209–221. Spartanburg: University of South Carolina, 1980.

International Holocaust Remembrance Alliance. "The Spelling of Antisemitism." Accessed December 2, 2022. www.holocaustremembrance.com.

Israel, Jonathan. *Diasporas within a Diaspora: Jews, Crypto-Jews, and the World of Maritime Empires (1540–1740)*. Leiden: Brill, 2002.

———. "Jews and Crypto-Jews in the Atlantic World Systems, 1500–1800." In *Atlantic Diasporas: Jews, Conversos, and Crypto-Jews in the Age of Mercantilism, 1500–1800*, edited by Richard L. Kagan, and Philip D. Morgan, 3–17. Baltimore: Johns Hopkins University Press, 2009.

Israel Central Bureau of Statistics. "Population Censuses." 2021. www.cbs.gov.il.

Janvier, Thomas Allibon. *The Mexican Guide*. New York: Scribner, 1898.

Jewish Virtual Library. "Total Jewish Immigration to Israel by Select Country by Year (1948–Present)." 2021. www.jewishvirtuallibrary.org.

———. "Total Jewish Population in the United States." 2021. www.jewishvirtuallibrary.org.

Jews of Color Initiative. "Counting Inconsistencies: An Analysis of American Jewish Population Studies, with a Focus on Jews of Color." 2019. https://jewsofcolorfieldbuilding.org.

Jmelnizky, Adrián, and Ezequiel Erdei. *La población judía de Buenos Aires: Estudio sociodemográfico*. Colección Investigaciones. Buenos Aires, Argentina: AMIA, JOINT, MEIDÁ, 2005.

Jones-Rogers, Stephanie E. *They Were Her Property: White Women as Slave Owners in the American South*. New Haven, CT: Yale University Press, 2019.

Julius, Anthony. *Trials of the Diaspora: A History of Anti-Semitism in England*. Oxford: Oxford University Press, 2010.

Kailbourn, Thomas R., and Peter E. Palmquist. *Pioneer Photographers from the Mississippi to the Continental Divide: A Biographical Dictionary, 1839–1865*. Stanford, CA: Stanford University Press, 2005.

Kalmar, Ivan D. "Moorish Style: Orientalism, the Jews, and Synagogue Architecture." *Jewish Social Studies* 7, no. 3 (2001): 68–100.

Kaplan, Dana Evan. *American Reform Judaism: An Introduction*. New Brunswick, NJ: Rutgers University Press, 2003.

Kaplan, Marion. *Dominican Haven: The Jewish Refugee Settlement in Sosúa, 1940–1945*. New York: Museum of Jewish Heritage, 2008.

Katz, Jonathan Ned. *The Daring Life and Dangerous Times of Eve Adams*. Chicago: Chicago Review Press, 2021.

Katz, Maya Balakirsky. *The Visual Culture of Chabad*. New York: Cambridge University Press, 2010.

Kaufman, David. *Shul with a Pool: The "Synagogue-Center" in American Jewish History*. Lebanon, NH: University Press of New England, 1999.

Klor, Sebastian. *Between Exile and Exodus: Argentinian Jewish Immigration to Israel, 1948–1967*. Detroit: Wayne State University Press, 2017.

Koffman, David S., and Pierre Anctil. "State of the Field: The Animating Tensions of Canadian Jewish Historiography." *American Jewish History* 105, no. 3 (2021): 403–429.

Kolektiv Goluboy Vagon. Home page. Accessed January 3, 2022. www.kolektivgoluboyvagon.com.

Kosek, Joseph Kip. *American Religion, American Politics: An Anthology*. New Haven, CT: Yale University Press, 2017.

Kraay, Hendrik. "Introduction: Afro-Bahia, 1790s–1990s." In *Afro-Brazilian Culture and Politics: Bahia, 1790s–1990s*, edited by Hendrik Kraay, 3–29. New York: Taylor and Francis, 2016.

Ladin, Joy. *Impersonation: Poems 2004–2014*. Rhinebeck, NY: Sheep Meadow, 2015.

———. *Through the Door of Life: A Jewish Journey Between Genders*. Madison: University of Wisconsin Press, 2012.

Lambert, Josh. *Unclean Lips: Obscenity, Jews, and American Culture*. New York: New York University Press, 2014.

Landing, James E. *Black Judaism: Story of an American Movement*. Durham, NC: Carolina Academic, 2001.

Laqueur, Thomas. *Making Sex: Body and Gender from the Greeks to Freud*. Cambridge, MA: Harvard University Press, 1992.

Leibman, Laura Arnold. *Art of the Jewish Family*. New York: Bard Graduate Center, 2020.

———. *Messianism, Secrecy and Mysticism: A New Interpretation of Early American Jewish Life*. London: Vallentine Mitchell, 2012.

———. "Poetics of the Apocalypse: Messianism in Early Jewish American Poetry." *Studies in American Jewish Literature* 33, no. 1 (2014): 35–62.

———. "Virus as Hyperobject: Jews of the Early Atlantic World and Yellow Fever Epidemics." In *Routledge Handbook of Material Religion*, edited by S. Brent Rodriguez Plate, Jennifer Hughes, and Pooyan Tamimi Arab. New York: Routledge, 2023.

Lesser, Jeffrey. *Welcoming the Undesirables: Brazil and the Jewish Question*. Berkeley: University of California, 1994.

Lesser, Jeffrey, and Raanan Rein. Introduction to *Rethinking Jewish-Latin Americans*, edited by Jeffrey Lesser and Raanan Rein, 1–21. Albuquerque: University of New Mexico Press, 2008.

Limonic, Laura. *Kugel and Frijoles: Latino Jews in the United States*. Detroit: Wayne State University Press, 2019.

Litvak, Olga. *Haskalah: The Romantic Movement in Judaism*. New Brunswick, NJ: Rutgers University Press, 2012.

Lombard, Anne S. *Making Manhood: Growing Up Male in Colonial New England*. Cambridge, MA: Harvard University Press, 2003.

Lowenberg, Mrs. I. "The Philomath Club." In *Western Jewry: An Account of the Achievements of Jews and Judaism in California*, 57–58. San Francisco: Temple Emanu-El, 1916.

Marks, Gil. *Encyclopedia of Jewish Food*. Hoboken, NJ: Wiley, 2010.

Masterson, Daniel. *The History of Peru*. Santa Barbara, CA: ABC-CLIO, 2009.

Maurice, Philippe. "Snippets of History: The Tintype and Prairie Canada." *Material Culture Review* 41, no. 1 (1995). https://journals.lib.unb.ca.

Mauss, Marcel. *The Gift: The Form and Reason for Exchange in Archaic Societies*. London: Taylor and Francis, 2002.

Mayyim Hayyim. "The Watershed Project." Accessed January 4, 2022. www.mayyimhayyim.org.

Mendoza de Arce, Daniel. *Music in Ibero-America to 1850: A Historical Survey*. Lanham, MD: Scarecrow, 2001.

Menkis, Richard. "Reform Judaism in Canada." In *Canada's Jews: In Time, Space and Spirit*, edited by Ira Robinson, 294–307. Boston: Academic Studies, 2013.

"Message from the President of the United States, transmitting the correspondence in relation to the proceedings and conduct of the Choctaw Commission, under the Treaty of Dancing Rabbit Creek." 1844. American Indian and Alaskan Native Documents in the Congressional Serial Set: 1817–1899. University of Oklahoma College of Law Digital Commons. https://digitalcommons.law.ou.edu.

Meyer, Michael A. *Response to Modernity: A History of the Reform Movement in Judaism*. Detroit: Wayne State University Press, 1995.

Mirelman, Victor A. "Jewish Life in Buenos Aires before the East European Immigration (1860–1890)." *American Jewish Historical Quarterly* 67, no. 3 (1978): 195–207.

———. "A Note on Jewish Settlement in Argentina (1881–1892)." *Jewish Social Studies* 33, no. 1 (1971): 3–12.

———. "The Semana Trágica of 1919 and the Jews in Argentina." *Jewish Social Studies* 37, no. 1 (1975): 61–73.

Morais, Henry S. *The Jews of Philadelphia: Their History from the Earliest Settlements to the Present Time*. Philadelphia: Levytype, 1894.

Moore, Deborah Dash. "Freedom's Fruits: the Americanization of an Old-time Religion." In *A Portion of the People: Three Hundred Years of Southern Jewish Life*, edited by Theodore Rosengarten and Dale Rosengarten, 10–21. Columbia: University of South Carolina Press, 2002.

———. "Signposts: Reflections on Articles from the Journal's Archive: How a Kosher Meat Boycott Brought Jewish Women's History into the Mainstream—A Historical Appreciation." *American Jewish History* 99, no. 1 (2015): 79–91.

———. "When Jews Were GIs: How World War II Changed a Generation and Remade American Jewry." In *American Jewish Identity Politics*, edited by Deborah Dash Moore, 23–44. Ann Arbor: University of Michigan Press, 2008.

Nadler, Steven. *Menasseh ben Israel: Rabbi of Amsterdam*. New Haven, CT: Yale University Press, 2018.

National Park Service. *Lower East Side Tenement National Historic Site: General Management Plan and Environmental Assessment*. Philadelphia: US Department of the Interior, 2006.

Nation of Islam. *The Secret Relationship between Blacks and Jews*. Chicago: Nation of Islam, 1991.

Nouwen, Mollie Lewis. *"Oy, My Buenos Aires": Jewish Immigrants and the Creation of Argentine National Identity, 1905–1930*. Albuquerque: University of New Mexico Press, 2013.

Olson, Christa. "Casta Painting and the Rhetorical Body." *Rhetoric Society Quarterly* 39, no. 4 (2009): 307–330.

Oppenheim, Samuel. "Will of Nathan Simson, a Jewish Merchant in New York Before 1722, and Genealogical Note Concerning Him and Joseph Simson." *Publications of the American Jewish Historical Society*, no. 25 (1917): 87–91.

Oren, Michael B. *Six Days of War: June 1967 and the Making of the Modern Middle East*. New York: Random House, 2017.

Parent, Anthony S. *Foul Means: The Formation of a Slave Society in Virginia, 1660–1740*. Chapel Hill: University of North Carolina Press, 2012.

Parker, Charles H., and Gretchen Starr-LeBeau, eds. *Judging Faith, Punishing Sin: Inquisitions and Consistories in the Early Modern World*. Cambridge: Cambridge University Press, 2017.

Penyak, Lee M., and Walter J. Petry, eds. *Religion in Latin America: A Documentary Reader*. Maryknoll, NY: Orbis Books, 2006.

Perelis, Ronnie. *Narratives from the Sephardic Atlantic: Blood and Faith*. Bloomington: Indiana University Press, 2016.

Pew Research Center. "A Portrait of Jewish Americans." Berman Jewish Databank, 2013. www.jewishdatabank.org.

———. "Race, Ethnicity, Heritage and Immigration among U.S. Jews." Religion & Public Life Project, November 15, 2021. www.pewforum.org.

———. "U.S. Jews' Connections with and Attitudes toward Israel." Religion & Public Life Project, November 15, 2021. www.pewforum.org/.

Polland, Annie, and Daniel Soyer. *Emerging Metropolis: New York Jews in the Age of Immigration, 1840–1920*. New York: New York University Press, 2012.

Prell, Riv-Ellen. *Fighting to Become Americans: Assimilation and the Trouble between Jewish Women and Jewish Men*. Boston: Beacon, 1999.

Price, Richard. *Alabi's World*. Baltimore: Johns Hopkins University Press, 1990.

Prinz, Deborah R. *On the Chocolate Trail: A Delicious Adventure Connecting Jews, Religions, History, Travel, Rituals and Recipes to the Magic of Cacao*. 2nd ed. Nashville, TN: Turner, 2017.

Raber, Ariel. "Beyond Borders. Argentina, the American Jewish Joint Distribution Committee and the Aid to the Victims of the Second World War." *Contemporary Sociological Global Review* 7, no. 7 (2017): 40–50.

Racette, Sherry Farrell. "Returning Fire, Pointing the Canon: Aboriginal Photography as Resistance." In *The Cultural Work of Photography in Canada*, edited by Carol Payne and Andrea Kunard, 70–92. Montreal: McGill-Queen's University Press, 2011.

Ra | Ju. "Who We Are." Accessed January 1, 2022. www.rajushoppe.com.

Rein, Raanan. "Argentine Jews and the Accusation of 'Dual Loyalty.'" In *Argentine Jews or Jewish Argentines? Essays on Ethnicity, Identity, and Diaspora*, 169–193. Leiden: Brill, 2010.

Ribak, Gil. "'The Jew Usually Left Those Crimes to Esau': The Jewish Responses to Accusations about Jewish Criminality in New York, 1908–1913." *AJS Review* 38, no. 1 (2014): 1–28.

Rock, Howard B. *Haven of Liberty: New York Jews in the New World, 1654–1865*. New York: New York University Press, 2015.

Roitman, Jessica Vance. "Portuguese Jews, Amerindians, and the Frontiers of Encounter in Colonial Suriname." *New West Indian Guide* 88, nos. 1–2 (2014): 18–52.

Rom, Michael. "Brazilian Belonging: Jewish Politics in Cold War Brazil, 1930–1985." PhD diss., Yale University, 2019.

Rome, David, and Jacques Langlais. *Jews and French Quebecers: Two Hundred Years of Shared History*. Waterloo, ON: Wilfrid Laurier University Press, 2010.

Rosenbaum, Fred. *Cosmopolitans: A Social and Cultural History of the Jews of the San Francisco Bay Area*. Berkeley: University of California Press, 2011.

Rosengarten, Theodore. Introduction to *A Portion of the People: Three Hundred Years of Southern Jewish Life*, edited by Theodore Rosengarten and Dale Rosengarten, 1–9. Columbia: University of South Carolina Press, 2002.

Rosengarten, Theodore, and Dale Rosengarten. "First Families." In *A Portion of the People: Three Hundred Years of Southern Jewish Life*, edited by Theodore Rosengarten and Dale Rosengarten, 59–89. Columbia: University of South Carolina Press, 2002.

———, eds. *A Portion of the People: Three Hundred Years of Southern Jewish Life*. Columbia: University of South Carolina Press, 2002.

Rosenstein, Eric Daniel. "A Symbol and Tool of Hybridity." BA honors thesis, Dickinson College, 2010.

Rosenwaike, Ira. *Population History in New York City*. Syracuse, NY: Syracuse University Press, 1972.

Roth, Laurence. "Coda: Punching Hitler." *Modern Language Studies* 47, no. 1 (Summer 2017): 78–92.

Rothenberg, Celia. *Serious Fun at a Jewish Community Summer Camp: Family, Judaism, and Israel*. Lanham, MD: Lexington Books, 2016.

Rupert, Linda M. "Trading Globally, Speaking Locally: Curaçao's Sephardim in the Making of a Caribbean Creole." In *Jews and Port Cities, 1590–1990: Commerce, Community and Cosmopolitanism*, edited by David Cesarani and Gemma Romain, 109–122. Portland, OR: Vallentine Mitchell, 2006.

Safran, William. "Diasporas in Modern Societies: Myths of Homeland and Return." *Diaspora: A Journal of Transnational Studies* 1, no. 1 (1991): 83–99.

Sarna, Jonathan D. *American Judaism: A History*. 2nd ed. New Haven, CT: Yale University Press, 2019.

Schnoor, Randall. "The Contours of Canadian Jewish Life." *Contemporary Jewry* 31, no. 3 (2011): 179–197.

———. "The Jews of Canada: A Demographic Profile." In *Canada's Jews: In Time, Space and Spirit*, edited by Ira Robinson, 121–132. Brighton, MA: Academic Studies, 2013.

Schorsch, Jonathan. "Transformations in the Manumission of Slaves by Jews from East to West: Pressures from the Atlantic Slave Trade." In *Paths to Freedom: Manumission in the Atlantic World*, edited by Rosemary Brana-Shute and Randy J. Sparks, 69–96. Columbia: University of South Carolina Press, 2009.

Schwartz, Matthew B. *Jews in America: The First 500 Years*. Eugene, OR: Wipf and Stock, 2019.

Seeligmann, Sigmund. "David Nassy of Surinam and His 'Lettre Politico-Theologico-Morale sur les Juifs.'" *Publications of the American Jewish Historical Society*, no. 22 (1914): 25–38.

Segev, Zohar. *The World Jewish Congress during the Holocaust: Between Activism and Restraint*. Berlin: De Gruyter, 2014.

Seider, Shari. "Looking Forward to the Past: The Ultra-Orthodox Community of Buenos Aires, Argentina." PhD diss., Stanford University, 1999.

Senkman, Leonardo. *Argentina, la Segunda Guerra Mundial y los refugiados indeseables, 1933–1945*. Buenos Aires, Argentina: Grupo Editor Latinoamericano, 1991.

Sered, Susan Starr. "The Synagogue as a Sacred Space for the Elderly Oriental Women of Jerusalem." In *Daughters of the King: Women and the Synagogue—A Survey of History, Halakhah, and Contemporary Realities*, edited by Susan Grossman and Riva Haut, 205–216. Philadelphia: Jewish Publication Society, 1991.

Shapiro, Leon. "World Jewish Population." *American Jewish Year Book* 52 (1951): 195–200.

Sherwin, Byron. "World Jewish Community." *Spertus*. Accessed November 20, 2022. www.spertus.edu.

Sheskin, Ira M., and Arnold Dashefsky. *American Jewish Year Book 2019: The Annual Record of the North American Jewish Communities since 1899*. Berlin: Springer, 2020.

Shneer, David. *Through Soviet Jewish Eyes: Photography, War, and the Holocaust*. New Brunswick, NJ: Rutgers University Press, 2011.

Silverblatt, Irene. "New Christians and New World Fears in Seventeenth-Century Peru." *Comparative Studies in Society and History* 42, no. 3 (2000): 524–546.

Simon, Joe, and Jim Simon. *The Comic Book Makers*. New York: Vanguard, 2003.

Singer, David, and Lawrence Grossman. "Jewish Population in the United States, 2002." In *American Jewish Yearbook 2003*, edited by David Singer and Lawrence Grossman, 155–182. Binghamton, NY: American Jewish Committee, 2003.

Smith, Ellen, and Jonathan D. Sarna. Introduction to *The Jews of Rhode Island*, edited by George M. Goodwin and Ellen Smith, 1–10. Waltham, MA: Brandeis University Press, 2004.

Smith, Shawn Michelle. *Photography on the Color Line: W. E. B. Du Bois, Race, and Visual Culture*. Durham, NC: Duke University Press, 2004.

Soomekh, Saba. *From the Shahs to Los Angeles: Three Generations of Iranian Jewish Women between Religion and Culture*. Albany: State University of New York Press, 2012.

———. Introduction to *Sephardi and Mizrahi Jews in America*, edited by Saba Soomekh, ix–xiv. West Lafayette, IN: Purdue University Press, 2015.

———. "To Be an Iranian Jewish Bride." In *100 Years of Sephardic Los Angeles*. Los Angeles: UCLA Alan D. Leve Center for Jewish Studies, 2021. https://sephardiclosangeles.org.

Srivastava, Priya. "Going Green Tel Aviv Way, the Recent Vegan Capital of the World!" *Times Travel*, November 26, 2016. https://timesofindia.indiatimes.com.

Stein, Abby. *Becoming Eve: My Journey from Ultra-Orthodox Rabbi to Transgender Woman*. New York: Basic Books, 2019.

Stern, Malcolm. *First American Jewish Families: 600 Genealogies, 1654–1988*. 3rd ed. Baltimore: Ottenheimer, 1991.

Sternfeld, Lior. "Iranian Jewish Los Angeles." In *100 Years of Sephardic Los Angeles*. Los Angeles: UCLA Alan D. Leve Center for Jewish Studies, 2021. https://sephardiclosangeles.org.

Stiefel, Barry L. *Jewish Sanctuary in the Atlantic World: A Social and Architectural History*. Columbia: University of South Carolina Press, 2014.

Stiles, Ezra. *The Literary Diary of Ezra Stiles*. Vol. 1. Edited by Franklin Bowditch Dexter. New York: Scribner, 1901.

Szurmuk, Mónica. *La vocación desmesurada: Una biografía de Alberto Gerchunoff*. Buenos Aires: Sudamericana, 2018.

Talattof, Kamran. *Modernity, Sexuality, and Ideology in Iran the Life and Legacy of a Popular Female Artist*. Syracuse, NY: Syracuse University Press, 2011.

Tarshish, Allan. "The Charleston Organ Case." *American Jewish Historical Quarterly* 54, no. 4 (1965): 411–449.

Thompson, John Herd, and Morton Weinfeld. "Entry and Exit: Canadian Immigration Policy in Context." *Annals of the American Academy of Political and Social Science* 538 (1995): 185–198.

Traub, James. *Judah Benjamin: Counselor to the Confederacy*. New Haven, CT: Yale University Press, 2021.

Tulchinsky, Gerald. *Canada's Jews: A People's Journey*. Toronto: University of Toronto Press, 2008.

Uchmany, Eva Alexandra. "The Participation of New Christians and Crypto-Jews in the Conquest, Colonization, and Trade of Spanish America, 1521–1660." In *The Jews and the Expansion of Europe to the West, 1450 to 1800*, edited by Paolo Bernardini and Norman Fiering, 186–202. New York: Berghahn Books, 2001.

United States Holocaust Memorial Museum. *Americans and the Holocaust*. Online exhibition. Washington, DC. https://exhibitions.ushmm.org.

van Russel-Henar, Christine. *Angisa tori: De geheimtaal van Suriname's hoofddoeken*. Suriname: Stichting Fu Memre Wi Afo, 2008.
Vasconcellos, Colleen A. *Slavery, Childhood, and Abolition in Jamaica, 1788–1838*. Athens: University of Georgia Press, 2015.
Vink, Wieke. *Creole Jews: Negotiating Community in Colonial Suriname*. Leiden: Brill, 2010.
Wald, Pinie. *Koshmar—Pesadilla*. Translated into Spanish by Simja Sneh. Buenos Aires: Astier Libros, 2019.
Weinstein, Rochelle. "Sepulchral Monuments of the Jews of Amsterdam in the Seventeenth and Eighteenth Centuries." PhD diss., New York University, 1979.
"Will of Abraham Minis." Written October 21, 1754; recorded May 5, 1757. Book AA, 20–21. Georgia Colonial Wills. Georgia Department of Archives and History.
Wilson, Kristina. *Mid-century Modernism and the American Body: Race, Gender, and the Politics of Power in Design*. Princeton, NJ: Princeton University Press, 2021.
Winsberg, Morton D. "Jewish Agricultural Colonization in Argentina." *Geographical Review* 54, no. 4 (1964): 487–501.
Wischnitzer, Mark. *Visas to Freedom: The History of HIAS*. Cleveland, OH: World, 1956.
Wolf, Edwin, and Maxwell Whiteman. *The History of the Jews of Philadelphia: From Colonial Times to the Age of Jackson*. Philadelphia: Jewish Publication Society of America, 1975.
Wolf, Simon. "The American Jew as Soldier and Patriot." In *The Colonial and Early National Period 1654–1840*, edited by Jeffrey S. Gurock, 1–20. London: Taylor and Francis, 2014.
Wolin, Penny Diane. *The Jews of Wyoming: Fringe of the Diaspora*. Buffalo, NY: Crazy Woman Creek, 2000.
World Jewish Congress. "Jamaica." 2008. www.worldjewishcongress.org.
Yarfitz, Mir. *Impure Migration: Jews and Sex Work in Golden Age Argentina*. New Brunswick, NJ: Rutgers University Press, 2019.
Zadoff, Efraim. "Muñoz Borrero and the Attempt to Rescue Jews with Ecuadorian Passports." *Israel Journal of Foreign Affairs* 4, no. 2 (2010): 115–132.
Zerin, Edward. *Jewish San Francisco*. Mount Pleasant, SC: Arcadia, 2006.
Zeveloff, Naomi. "First Generation of Transgender Rabbis Claims Place at Bima." *Forward*, July 15, 2013. www.forward.com.

ABOUT THE EDITORS

ADRIANA M. BRODSKY is Professor of History at St. Mary's College of Maryland. Her work focuses on the history of Sephardim in Argentina. She has coedited (with Raanan Rein) *The New Jewish Argentina: Facets of Jewish Experiences in the Southern Cone* (2013), which won the Best Book Award from the Latin American Jewish Studies Association in 2013, and is the author of *Sephardi, Jewish, Argentine: Community and National Identity, 1880–1960* (2016). She has also published articles on Sephardic food, schools, beauty contests, and Latin American Jewish history in general. A native Argentine with a degree in education and a PhD from Duke University, Adriana has been a Kluge Fellow at the Library of Congress and a Fulbright Senior Scholar at Tel Aviv University. She is currently finishing a manuscript on the role played by Jewish youth (1940–1976) both in Argentina, helping modernize and energize the local communities, and in Israel, as members of kibbutzim, keeping their Argentine and Latin American identities alive.

LAURA ARNOLD LEIBMAN is the William R. Kenan Jr. Professor of English and Humanities at Reed College in Portland, Oregon. Her work focuses on religion and the daily lives of women and children in early America and uses everyday objects to help bring their stories back to life. She is the winner of four National Jewish Book Awards and the author of *Once We Were Slaves* (2021), *The Art of the Jewish Family* (2020), *Messianism, Secrecy and Mysticism* (2012), and other books. She has been a visiting scholar at Oxford University, Utrecht University, and the University of Panama, as well as the Leon Levy Foundation Professor of Jewish Material Culture at Bard Graduate Center. She is currently Vice President of Program for the Association of Jewish Studies.

ABOUT THE CONTRIBUTORS

JEANNE ABRAMS is Professor at the University of Denver Center for Judaic Studies and University Libraries. She has published numerous books in American history, including *Jewish Women Pioneering the Frontier Trail: A History in the American West* and *A View from Abroad: The Story of John and Abigail Adams in Europe*.

DIANNE ASHTON was Professor Emerita, Director of American Studies, and Chair of the Department of Philosophy and Religion at Rowan University. She published extensively in the fields of US Jewish and women's history and served as editor of the journal *American Jewish History*.

ALAN ASTRO is Professor of Modern Languages at Trinity University San Antonio, author of *Autour du yiddish de Paris à Buenos Aires*, editor of *Yiddish South of the Border: An Anthology of Latin American Yiddish Writing*, and coeditor (with Malena Chinski) of *Splendor, Decline, and Rediscovery of Yiddish in Latin America*.

RUTH BEHAR is the James W. Fernandez Distinguished University Professor of Anthropology at the University of Michigan. Her scholarly books include *The Presence of the Past in a Spanish Village*, *Translated Woman*, *The Vulnerable Observer*, *An Island Called Home*, and *Traveling Heavy*. Other works include poetry, a documentary, and novels.

CELIA J. BERGOFFEN is Adjunct Associate Professor of Art History at the Fashion Institute of Technology, author of *The Bronze Age Cypriot Pottery from Sir Leonard Woolley's Excavations at Alalakh (Tell Atchana)*, articles on Mediterranean and New York City archaeology, and archaeological reports for the New York Landmarks Preservation Commission and New York State Office of Historic Preservation.

MERRIE BLOCKER is a retired foreign service officer, translator of *On a Clear April Morning*, a Brazilian Jewish immigrant story, and creator of TheBaronHirschCommunity.org.

EDITH BRUDER is Research Associate at the French National Center for Scientific Research and at the University of South Africa and President of the International Society for the Study of African Jewry. She has published numerous books and articles on African Judaism, including *The Black Jews of Africa*.

ARIEL PAIGE COHEN is an educator at Geffen Academy at the University of California, Los Angeles, where she teaches civics and American history. Ariel earned her PhD at the University of Virginia and her master's degrees at Columbia University and the Jewish Theological Seminary.

JUDAH M. COHEN is Lou and Sybil Mervis Professor of Jewish Cultural Arts, Professor of Musicology and Jewish Studies, and Associate Vice Provost for Faculty and Academic Affairs at Indiana University–Bloomington. He is coeditor of the journal *American Jewish History* and recently published *Jewish Religious Music in Nineteenth-Century America*.

JESSICA COOPERMAN is Associate Professor in the Department of Religion Studies at Muhlenberg College and the author of *Making Judaism Safe for America: World War I and the Origins of Religious Pluralism*. She is also coeditor of the journal *American Jewish History*.

PALOMA CUNG SULKIN is a Mexican author, Yiddish teacher, and translator. Her works include the books *Judíos por herencia, Mexicanos por florecer* and *Tierra para echar raíces: Cementerios judíos en México* and the documentary *Viaje alrededor de la casa*.

MAX MODIANO DANIEL is a teacher of Jewish History at Kehillah Jewish High School in Palo Alto, California. He earned a PhD at UCLA and has published several articles and chapters on Sephardic Jews in the United States.

JACOB S. DORMAN is Associate Professor at the University of Nevada, Reno. He has written *The Princess and the Prophet* and *Chosen People: The Rise of American Black Israelite Religions*, which won the Wesley-Logan Prize from the American Historical Association in 2014, among other awards.

INGE DORNAN is a historian who focuses on histories of race and gender in Britain and the Americas. She is Deputy Head of the Department of Social and Political Sciences and Division Lead of Politics and History at Brunel University London.

ZEV ELEFF is President of Gratz College and Professor of American Jewish History. Among his published books is *Who Rules the Synagogue: Religious Authority and the Formation of American Judaism*.

MARK FERTIG was Chair and Professor of Art and Design at Susquehanna University. He published *Hang 'Em High: 110 Years of Western Movie Posters, 1911–2020*; *Take That, Adolf! The Fighting Comic Books of the Second World War*; and *Film Noir 101: The 101 Best Film Noir Posters from the 1940s–1950s*.

TAMARA GLEASON FREIDBERG is a PhD candidate in the Hebrew and Jewish Studies Department at University College London and has published chapters on Jewish antifascism and Yiddish literature in Mexico.

MICHEL GHERMAN is a Research Fellow at Vidal Sassoon International Center for the Study of Antisemitism and Adjunct Professor in the Department of Sociology at the Federal University of Rio de Janeiro. He is also Academic Director of the Instituto Brasil-Israel.

MAXWELL GREENBERG is the Postdoctoral Fellow in Jewish Studies at Washington University in St. Louis.

BRIAN HAMM is Assistant Professor of History at Samford University.

LORI HARRISON-KAHAN is Full Professor of the Practice of English at Boston College. She is the author of *The White Negress: Literature, Minstrelsy, and the Black-Jewish Imaginary*, editor of *The Superwoman and Other Writings by Miriam Michelson*, and coeditor of *Heirs of Yesterday by Emma Wolf.*

SUSANNAH HESCHEL is Eli M. Black Distinguished Professor of Jewish Studies at Dartmouth College and chairs its Jewish Studies Program. She wrote *Abraham Geiger and the Jewish Jesus* and *The Aryan Jesus: Christian Theologians and the Bible in Nazi Germany*. She is a Guggenheim Fellow and has received numerous awards.

MICHAEL HOBERMAN is Professor of American Literature at Fitchburg State University. His books include *New Israel / New England* and *A Hundred Acres of America*. His forthcoming book, *Imagining Early American Jews*, explores contemporary representations of Jewish American history for popular audiences.

REGINA IGEL is Professor Emerita (2021) at the University of Maryland and the Portuguese Program's former director. Among her publications are the books *Osman Lins, uma biografia literária* and *Imigrantes judeus, escritores brasileiros*. She is also a former Contributing Editor for *Handbook of Latin American Studies*, Library of Congress.

STEVEN JACOBS is Professor of Religious Studies and Emeritus Aaron Aronov Endowed Chair of Judaic Studies at the University of Alabama, Tuscaloosa. His research foci are the Hebrew Bible, the Dead Sea Scrolls, the Holocaust and genocides, and Jewish-Christian-Muslim relations.

MARION KAPLAN is Professor of Modern Jewish History at New York University and a three-time National Jewish Book Award winner. Her publications include *Between Dignity and Despair*, *Dominican Haven*, *Hitler's Jewish Refugees*, and *Gender and Jewish History* (with Deborah Dash Moore).

RACHEL KAUFMAN is a PhD student in history at UCLA, working on Latin American and Jewish history. Her work centers on crypto-Jewish memory practices and cross-ethnic networks of female transmission and ritual in New Mexico and Mexico from the fifteenth to the twentieth centuries. She published *Many to Remember*, her first poetry collection, in 2021.

MISHA KLEIN is Associate Professor of Anthropology at the University of Oklahoma. Her book *Kosher Feijoada and Other Paradoxes of Jewish Life in São Paulo* explores the intersecting meanings of race, class, and belonging for the transnational and multicultural Jewish population in Brazil.

DAVID S. KOFFMAN, the J. Richard Shiff Chair for the Study of Canadian Jewry and an Associate Professor of History at York University, is the author of *The Jews' Indian: Colonialism, Pluralism, and Belonging in America* and Editor in Chief of the journal *Canadian Jewish Studies / Études juives canadiennes*.

SOPHIA LEVIN is the Pediatrics and Maternity Chaplain at Mount Sinai Hospital (New York City) and an independent scholar and researcher. She holds an MA from the Bard Graduate Center for Decorative Arts, Design History, and Material Culture and an M.Div. from Harvard Divinity School.

FRANCES LEVINE is a history museum consultant who served as President of the Missouri Historical Society in St. Louis. Previously, she was Director of the New Mexico History Museum. Her publications include works on the history of *conversos* and the presence of the Inquisition in colonial New Mexico.

JUSTIN JARON LEWIS is Associate Professor in the Department of Religion at the University of Manitoba, author of *Imagining Holiness: Classic Hasidic Tales in Modern Times*, and editor/translator of *Many Pious Women*, an early modern Yiddish text in praise of women.

JULIA R. LIEBERMAN is Professor of Spanish and Intercultural Studies at Saint Louis University. She is a contributor and editor of the following three books: *Los estudios sefardíes para estudiantes de español*, *Sephardi Family Life in the Early Modern Diaspora*, and *Charity in Jewish, Christian, and Islamic Traditions*.

BLANCA DE LIMA is a historian and social anthropologist who worked at the Francisco de Miranda University (Coro, Venezuela) until her retirement. She is a member of the Venezuelan National Academy of History and has published more than fifty books, chapters, journal articles, and museum catalogs.

DARRELL B. LOCKHART is Vice Provost for Faculty Affairs and Professor of Spanish at the University of Nevada, Reno. He is Editor in Chief of *Latin American Jewish Studies*, the journal of the Latin American Jewish Studies Association. His research focuses on Jewish literature and popular culture in Latin America.

GINA MALAGOLD is Assistant Teaching Professor of Spanish language, literature, and culture in the Department of Spanish and Portuguese at Georgetown University.

DEVI MAYS is Associate Professor of Judaic Studies at the University of Michigan. Her book *Forging Ties, Forging Passports* won the 2020 National Jewish Book Award, among other prizes. Her work focuses on transnational Jewish networks in the Mediterranean and global contexts, with a focus on Sephardic Jews.

STANLEY MIRVIS is Associate Professor of History and the Harold and Jean Grossman Chair of Jewish Studies at Arizona State University. He is the author of *The Jews of Eighteenth-Century Jamaica: A Testamentary History of a Diaspora in Transition* (2020).

VALERIA NAVARRO-ROSENBLATT is Professor of History at Universidad Diego Portales and Universidad Autónoma de Chile.

PATRICIA G. NURIEL is Associate Professor of Spanish in the Department of Modern Languages, Literatures, and Cultures at Wofford College and coeditor (with Luca Barattoni) of *Jewish Identities in Latin American Cinema* and (with Nora Glickman) of *Interviews with Latin American Women Filmmakers*, both in *Post Script: Essays in Film and the Humanities*.

JOSH PARSHALL is Director of History at the Goldring/Woldenberg Institute of Southern Jewish Life. He works on American Jewish culture and politics, Yiddish language and culture, and southern studies.

RONNIE PERELIS is Chief Rabbi Dr. Isaac Abraham and Jelena (Rachel) Alcalay Associate Professor of Sephardic Studies at Yeshiva University. His research explores the connections between Iberian and Jewish culture and history. His first book was *Narratives from the Sephardic Atlantic: Blood and Faith*.

REBECCA SANDLER PERTEN is Assistant Dean of Graduate and Undergraduate Studies at the Jewish Theological Seminary of America.

TONI PITOCK is Associate Teaching Professor in the Department of History and faculty in the Jewish Studies program at Drexel University.

RABBI DEBORAH PRINZ is an independent scholar and the author of *On the Chocolate Trail: A Delicious Adventure Connecting Jews, Religions, History, Travel, Rituals, and Recipes to the Magic of Cacao*. Forthcoming books include *The Boston Chocolate Party* and *On the Bread Trail: Jewish Celebratory Breads*.

DANA RABIN is Professor of History at the University of Illinois, Urbana-Champaign. She is the author of *Britain and Its Internal Others, 1750–1800: Under Rule of Law* and *Identity, Crime, and Legal Responsibility in Eighteenth-Century England.*

SHARI RABIN is Associate Professor of Religion and Jewish Studies at Oberlin College and the author of *Jews on the Frontier: Religion and Mobility in Nineteenth-Century America.*

JACKIE RANSTON, OD (Jamaica), is an Independent scholar. Among her Jewish publications are *Belisario: A Historical Biography of a Jamaican Artist, The Lindo Legacy, Masonic Jamaica and the Cayman Islands,* and *Behind the Scenes at King's House.* She is a contributor to *The Jews of the Caribbean* and *Freemasons in the Transatlantic World.*

JONATHAN RAY is Samuel Eig Professor of Jewish Studies at Georgetown University and has published several books on Sephardic History, including *The Sephardic Frontier: The Reconquista and the Jewish Community in Medieval Iberia, After Expulsion: 1492 and the Making of Sephardic Jewry,* and *Jewish Life in Medieval Spain: A New History.*

RAANAN REIN, Elías Sourasky Professor of Latin American and Spanish History at Tel Aviv University, has published numerous books, including *Fútbol, Jews, and the Making of Argentina, Populism and Ethnicity: Peronism and the Jews of Argentina,* and *Jewish Self-Defense in South America: Facing Anti-Semitism with a Club in Hand.*

JUDITH RIQUELME RÍOS is Professor in the Information Management Department of the Metropolitan Technological University, Chile. She is coauthor of *"And the archives kept their voices": Poles, Catholics, and Jews under Chilean Protection (Italy, 1941–1943).*

IRA ROBINSON is Distinguished Professor Emeritus, Department of Religions and Cultures, Concordia University. He has published extensively, most recently *A Kabbalist in Montreal: The Life and Times of Rabbi Yudel Rosenberg* and *"A Link in the Great American Chain": The Evolution of Jewish Orthodoxy in Cleveland to 1940.*

YOSEF DOV ROBINSON is an independent scholar living in Montreal, Quebec. His most recent complete scholarly project is translating Chaim Kruger's *Der Rambam: Zayn leben un shafn* from Yiddish to English, and he is interested in the history of early twentieth-century Jewish life in Montreal.

CARA ROCK-SINGER is Assistant Professor of Religious Studies in the Religious Studies Program at the University of Wisconsin–Madison.

JESSICA VANCE ROITMAN is Professor of Jewish Studies at Vrije Universiteit Amsterdam. She specializes in Atlantic and Caribbean Jewish history and colonialism. She wrote *The Same but Different? Inter-cultural Trade and the Sephardim* and coedited (with Gert

Oostindie) *Dutch Atlantic Connections, 1680–1800*. More recently, she published *Highlights of the Mongui Maduro Museum and Mongui Maduro Library*.

MICHAEL ROM is a Postdoctoral Research Fellow in the Department of History at the University of British Columbia in Vancouver, Canada.

ELI ROSENBLATT is Wallerstein Assistant Professor of Jewish Studies and Director of the Jewish Studies Program at Drew University.

DALE ROSENGARTEN is the founding curator of the Jewish Heritage Collection at the College of Charleston. Her publications include *A Portion of the People: Three Hundred Years of Southern Jewish Life*, *Row upon Row: Sea Grass Baskets of the South Carolina Lowcountry*, and *Grass Roots: African Origins of an American Art*.

LAURENCE ROTH is Charles B. Degenstein Professor of English at Susquehanna University and author of *Unpacking My Father's Bookstore* and *Inspecting Jews: American Jewish Detective Stories* and coeditor, with Nadia Valman, of *The Routledge Handbook to Contemporary Jewish Cultures*.

RACHEL RUBINSTEIN is Dean of the School of Arts and Sciences at Springfield College. She is the author of *Member of the Tribe: Native America in the Jewish Imagination* and coeditor, with Roberta Rosenberg, of *Teaching Jewish American Literature*.

SIMONE SALMON is a PhD student in the Ethnomusicology Department at UCLA, where she specializes in Sephardic Jewish music from the late Ottoman Empire to today. Salmon has several online and forthcoming publications in, among others, *Smithsonian Pathways* and *Musica Judaica*. She hosts a radio show, *Los Bilbilikos*, about music in Judeo-Spanish.

EDWARD SANDERS is an independent scholar focusing on life in the antebellum South. He works as a manager at the United Negro College Fund in Washington, DC.

JONATHAN D. SARNA is University Professor and the Joseph H. & Belle R. Braun Professor of American Jewish History at Brandeis University. His many books include *American Judaism: A History, Coming to Terms with America* and an edition of Cora Wilburn's *Cosella Wayne*.

ANA E. SCHAPOSCHNIK is Associate Professor in the Department of History at DePaul University and the author of *The Lima Inquisition: The Plight of Crypto-Jews in Seventeenth-Century Peru*.

PAULETTE SCHUSTER is Registration and Absorption Coordinator at Reichman University. She has published books on food and identity, and transnationalism, including *The Syrian Jewish Community in Mexico City in a Comparative Context: Between a Rock and a*

Hard Place, *Modelando el Transnacionalismo*, and *Trayectorias y jornadas: Transnacionalismo en acción*.

ZOHAR SEGEV is Professor of Jewish History at Haifa University in Israel and head of the Wolfson Chair in Jewish Religious Thought and Heritage. He is the author of *The World Jewish Congress during the Holocaust* and *From Ethnic Politicians to National Leaders*.

NOAM SIENNA is Visiting Assistant Professor in Religion at St. Olaf College (Northfield, Minnesota) and the editor of *A Rainbow Thread: An Anthology of Queer Jewish Texts from the First Century to 1969*.

STEPHEN SILVERSTEIN is Associate Professor in the Department of Modern Languages and Cultures at Baylor University and author of *The Merchant of Havana: The Jew in the Cuban Abolitionist Archive*.

PERLA SNEH is Associate Professor and Senior Researcher at the National University of Tres de Febrero and has published many essays and books, among them *Palabras para decirlo—Lenguaje y exterminio*, which won the National Award from the Ministry of Culture of the National Government of Argentina.

HOLLY SNYDER, now retired, was a research librarian at Brown University for two decades. Her ongoing scholarship focuses on Jews in the early modern British Atlantic and has been published in a wide array of academic journals and critical anthologies, most recently in the *Oxford Research Encyclopedia in American History*.

ARON STERK is Associate Lecturer in the School of History and Heritage at the University of Lincoln.

CECILIA STERK is an independent researcher.

BARRY L. STIEFEL is Associate Professor in the Historic Preservation and Community Planning Program at the College of Charleston and the author of several books and articles, including the forthcoming book *Monuments of Diverse Heritage: Early American Placemaking and Preservation by Black, Indigenous, and Jewish Peoples*.

HILIT SUROWITZ-ISRAEL is Assistant Professor in the Religion Department at Rutgers University. She coedited *Jews in the Americas, 1776–1826*.

HERNAN TESLER-MABÉ is Assistant Professor and Coordinator of the Jewish Studies Program at Huron at Western (London, Ontario); President of the Association for Canadian Jewish Studies; and author of *Mahler's Forgotten Conductor: Heinz Unger and His Search for Jewish Meaning, 1895–1965*.

BRITT TEVIS is a historian with special interests in law and Jewish studies. Her research examines the ways in which local, state, and federal authorities condoned and/or incited anti-Jewish discrimination. She recently published "The People's Judge" in the *American Journal of Legal History*, among other pieces.

KELLY AMANDA TRAIN is a Contract Lecturer in the Department of Sociology at Toronto Metropolitan University (formerly Ryerson University) in Toronto and the author of more than ten peer-reviewed articles and book chapters on North African and Indian Jews in Toronto.

MICHAEL WAAS is a genealogist and historian and cofounder of Hollander-Waas Jewish Heritage Services.

MATTHEW D. WARSHAWSKY is Professor of Spanish at the University of Portland and the author of *The Perils of Living the Good and True Law: Iberian Crypto-Jews in the Shadow of the Inquisition of Colonial Hispanic America*.

MIR YARFITZ is Associate Professor of History and Director of Jewish Studies at Wake Forest University and author of *Impure Migration: Jews and Sex Work in Golden Age Argentina*.

NATASHA ZARETSKY is Clinical Associate Professor at New York University and directs the Truth in the Americas Initiative at Rutgers University's Center for the Study of Genocide and Human Rights. She is the author of *Acts of Repair: Justice, Truth, and the Politics of Memory in Argentina*.

INDEX

Page numbers in italics indicate illustrations.